THE FINEST INSTRUMENTS EVER MADE

GEORGE TIEMANN & CO.'S SURGICAL INSTRUMENTS.   115

PHLEBOTOMY.

FIG. 1645.—Spear-pointed Thumb Lancet.

FIG. 1647. Tiemann & Co.'s Spring Lancet.

FIG. 1646.—Broad-pointed Thumb Lancet.

FIG. 1648. Button Trigger Spring Lancet.

CUPPING.

FIG. 1650.—Tiemann & Co.'s Patent Scarificator.

FIG. 1649. Plain Spring Lancet.

FIG. 1653. Tiemann & Co.'s Soft Rubber Cupping Cup.

FIG. 1651. Ten-Bladed Scarificator.

FIG. 1652. Twelve-Bladed Scarificator.

FIG. 1654. Glass and Rubber Cup.

FIG. 1655.—Cupping Pump, Stop-cock and Cup.

No. 1 Cupping Set.
$13.

Contains :
  1 Brass Cupping Pump.
  3 Stop-cocks.
  3 Glass Cups.
  1 Ten-bladed Scarificator.
  1 Mahogany or Black-walnut Case, lined with velvet.

No. 1. Without Scarificator.... $9.00

Also, Breast Pumps.

No. 2 Cupping Set.
$15.

Contains :
  1 Brass Cupping Pump.
  3 Stop-cocks.
  6 Glass Cups.
  1 Twelve-bladed Scarificator.
  1 Mahogany or Black-walnut Case, lined with velvet.

No. 2. Without Scarificator.... $10.50

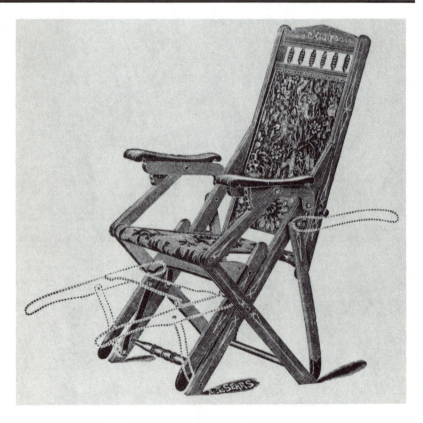

Audrey B. Davis and Mark S. Dreyfuss

THE FINEST INSTRUMENTS EVER MADE

A Bibliography of Medical, Dental, Optical, and Pharmaceutical Company Trade Literature; 1700–1939

Medical History Publishing Associates I
Arlington, Massachusetts

Library of Congress Catalog Card Number: 86-061666
ISBN: 0-9616748-0-6

Designed by Ben Birnbaum

86 87 88 / 5 4 3 2 1

TABLE OF CONTENTS

TRUAX & COMPANY

The Geyser Vaporizer and Inhaler.

(PATENTED.)

We desire to call the attention of the MEDICAL PROFESSION to this new instrument.

It is neat, simple and substantial, meeting all the requirements of a vaporizer for the treatment of disease by inhalation.

By means of a new mechanical device we are able to dispense with suction tubes, which are a source of much annoyance to those employing the old method.

The Air Jet being surrounded by the liquid to be vaporized, much less compressed air is required to produce a given amount of vapor than by any other instrument. This will be appreciated by those who use the hand pump.

It is adapted to the use of oils as well as ordinary liquids.

The annexed cut represents a sectional view.

Fig. 1, a glass globe six inches in diameter, furnished with a threaded neck.

Fig. 2, a metal ring encircling the glass neck, being beveled to neatly fit the globe. This ring terminates in a metal arm (Fig. 9). This metal arm is mounted upon a polished wooden standard (Fig. 10).

A hard rubber cap, (Fig. 3,) furnished with a beveled orifice, is secured on the glass neck, holding the metal ring tightly in place.

Fig. 4 is a hard rubber hollow stopper, through which passes a tube, (Fig. 12,) terminating with a valve, allowing the atmosphere to enter when required. The compressed air tube also passes through the stopper. Its outer end is supplied with a screw nipple, (Fig. 7,) for convenience in connecting with air receiver. The other end terminates with a small cup, (Fig. 6,) through the bottom of which the pressure tube passes, having a small orifice (Fig. 14) for the escape of the air jet. In the bottom of the cup are two apertures, (Figs. 15 and 16,) which allow liquid to *enter the cup as rapidly as the air jet vaporizes it*. By this method the *entire circumference* of the air jet is fed with fluid. On the top of the hollow stopper is placed a movable elbow (Fig. 8,) for the attachment of breathing tube. The breathing tube is provided with an improved saliva trap, as seen in the picture.

Price, complete, ready to connect with air receiver.............$12 00

Full directions for using, together with a few formulæ of approved remedies, will be sent with each instrument.

Manufactured by A. J. PALMER, M.D., Brooklyn, N. Y.
FOR SALE BY CHAS. TRUAX & CO.

LIST OF ILLUSTRATIONS

BULLET EXTRACTING.

DR. GIRDNER'S TELEPHONIC BULLET PROBE.

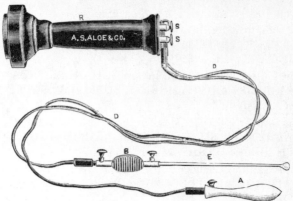

Girdner's Telephonic Bullet Probe—Instrument Complete.

Detach the receiver or hand piece, R, from any ordinary telephone by loosening the screws in its binding posts, marked SS.

To each of these binding posts attach one end of each of the conducting wires marked D, and to the free end of one of these conducting wires attach the aluminium bulb, A, by means of the binding screw at its end.

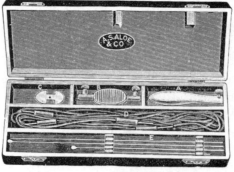

3974.

To the free end of the other wire attach the probe handle marked B, and in the other end of the probe handle insert one of the probes marked E.

Be certain to have all binding posts tight, to ensure perfect electrical contact, and the instrument is complete and ready for use as shown in first illustration.

It is well to experiment with the instrument to train the ear before employing it in actual practice. To do this have an assistant place the bulb, A, in his mouth between the teeth and the cheek, i. e. in the buccal cavity; then have him thoroughly wet one of his hands, and firmly grasp in it a bullet or small piece of lead. The operator now places the receiver R. to his ear with one hand, and with the other he takes the handle B of the probe and probes for the lead held in the assistant's hand, and each slightest touch of the probe against the lead produces a rasping, clicking sound in the receiver held to his ear. Contact with the flesh, the nails or with a piece of bone held in the hand will produce no sound in the receiver.

In actual practice the bulb is of course placed in the patient's mouth as in the experiment, but instead of probing for lead placed in the hand, the probe is made to pass into the wound made by the bullet.

THE FINEST
INSTRUMENTS
EVER MADE

THE LARGEST MANUFACTORY OF ARTIFICIAL LIMBS.

IN THE WORLD.

UNITED STATES GOVERNMENT MANUFACTURER.

TWENTY-FOUR CONSECUTIVE FIRST PREMIUMS.

ARTIFICIAL LIMBS

WITH PATENT

RUBBER HANDS & FEET

701 ✦ A. A. MARKS. ✦ 701

BROADWAY.

A. A. MARKS,
701 BROADWAY,
NEW YORK CITY.

LIST OF ABBREVIATIONS
FOR INSTITUTIONS
HOLDING TRADE LITERATURE

ABD	Audrey B. Davis
ACR/MAH	American College of Radiology Collection at the National Museum of American History, Smithsonian Institution
ACS	American College of Surgeons
ADA	American Dental Association
AFMM	Armed Forces Medical Museum
AO	American Optical Co.
APS	American Philosophical Society
BDA	British Dental Association
BLEL	Bakken Library of Electricity and Life
BRML	British Museum/Library
CDMC	Crescent Dental Manufacturing Co.
CHS	Connecticut Historical Society
CPP	College of Physicians of Philadelphia
CS	Codman & Shurtleff
CTY/B	Yale Medical History Library
CUHSL	Columbia University Health Science Library
FI	Franklin Institute
HDM	Howard Dittrick Museum
HML	Hagley Museum and Library
HUBL	Harvard University Baker Library

ISUM	Southern Illinois School of Medicine, Medical Library
JHIHM	Johns Hopkins Institute for the History of Medicine
LACMA	Los Angeles County Medical Association
LC	Library of Congress
LON	Library of Medicine, University of Nebraska
LLU	Loma Linda University
MAH	The National Museum of American History, Smithsonian Institution
MCFM	Maryland Medical and Chirurgical Faculty Library
MF/MAH	Microfilm/ The National Museum of American History, Smithsonian Institution
MRLB	Medical Research Library of Brooklyn
MSL	Mystic Seaport Museum, White Library
MUM	Mütter Museum, Philadelphia
NLM	National Library of Medicine
NWUCML	Northwestern University Church Medical Library
NYAM	New York Academy Medicine Library
RCSL	Royal College of Surgeons Library, England
SBMC	Saint Bartholomew's Medical Collection
SLSC	Saint Louis Science Center
TMHM	Museum of the History of Medicine, Toronto
UBML	University of Buffalo Health Sciences Library
UCLABM	University of California Biomedical Library
UCSF	University of California/San Francisco
UNSW/A	University of New South Wales, Australia
UPL	University of Pittsburgh Health Sciences Library
UPSDM	University of Pennsylvania School of Dental Medicine
UREGML	University of Rochester, Edward G. Miner Library
URRR	University of Rochester, Rush Rhees Library
UTP	University of Toronto, Faculty of Pharmacy

UVHSL	University of Virginia, Claude Moore Health Sciences Library
UWL	University of Wisconsin Middleton Health Sciences Library
VM	V. Mueller
WMScM	Wellcome Museum at the Science Museum, London
WOC	William O. Campbell
YB	Yale Beinicke Rare Book and Manuscript Library
YML	Yale Medical Library
ZUR	Zurich Medical Museum and Library

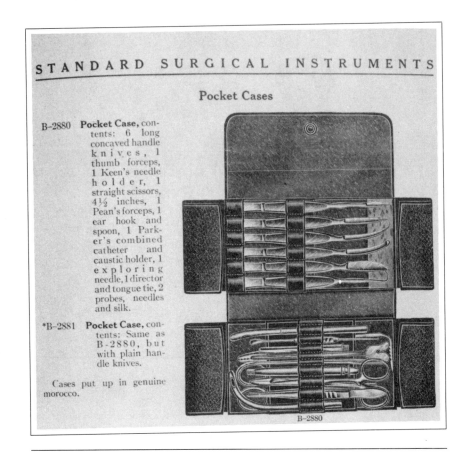

INSTRUMENTS FOR PHYSICAL DIAGNOSIS.

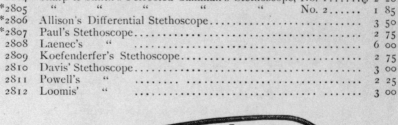

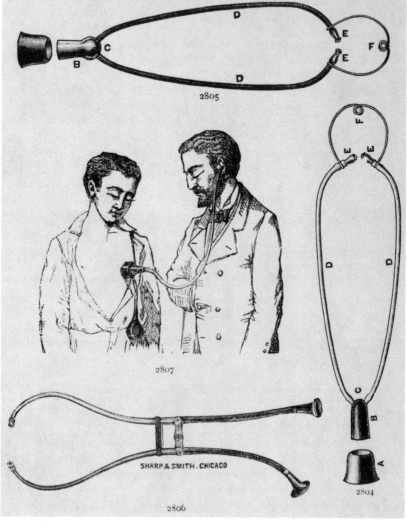

2805

2807

2806

2804

SHARP & SMITH. CHICAGO

INTRODUCTION

Medical Trade
Literature to 1939

A trade catalog is a dictionary of a manufacturer's products. In this bibliography, the products surveyed include medical, dental, and optical instruments, appliances, and assorted pharmaceutical products and aids to restore health and assist in the discovery and recovery from illness or disablement. The trade catalog is the major publication of the instrument manufacturer and distributor. It is organized, annotated, and illustrated to present a concise description of the instruments offered for sale. Pictures and drawings of the manufacturing plant and production processes may also appear. Directions are included for ordering and insuring the safe delivery of items. Items are singled out when a new type of equipment is introduced. Awards won by the company for its products are festooned on the cover and title page. Often these awards were bestowed at national and international trade fairs where manufactured pieces on display competed for quality of workmanship, function, design, etc. Major instrument dealers boasted of the useful technical information provided only in their trade catalog. A new and often enlarged edition of the catalog usually appeared each year or every two or three years. Sections of a comprehensive catalog were generally distributed separately to the specialist physicians who used the particular type of equipment advertised in that section. The brochure and pamphlet are smaller publications organized to promote a few special items. The brochures consisted of 2, 4, 8, 16 or 32 pages and may have been extracted from the general company catalog.

All trade catalogs share common characteristics. Of special note in medical instrument catalogs are the following:

1. The trade catalog is organized by type of instrument and illustrated with diagrams and pictures, some of which show the product in use and help to explain its function. Medical instrument catalogs published before 1850, and there were relatively few of them, were not illustrated. Until the post WW I period most illustrations in trade catalogs were line drawings, rather than photographs of instruments. Price lists were appended to the trade catalog or distributed as a separate list on a monthly, semi-monthly or annual basis.

2. The trade catalog may contain references to discussions of the instrument in the medical and scientific literature or, in some instances, an article or an extract from a medical journal, which is reprinted in the catalog.

3. In addition to the basic data on implements, the trade catalog contains testimonials from pleased customers, stating how they benefit from the product. In the medical trade catalog both physicians and patients testify to the benefits of using certain products and instruments. Brochures, such as one published by T. A. Willson in 1877, succinctly sum up the special features and advantages of a product and include the statement of a prominent user. Willson produced violet tinted spectacle lenses (Arundel Tint) to stop the orange-red rays of the visible spectrum, and thus, eliminate their heating effect on the eyes and face. The lens was of uniform density, and the tint was unobservable to the wearer of spectacles. Joseph Henry, Secretary of the Smithsonian Institution, wrote a letter which was quoted in a Willson brochure. He notes that, "The Arundel Tint I find agreeable and the form of the glass and frame of the Spectacles, for near and far vision, is a very convenient arrangement."

4. The trade catalog contains claims made on behalf of the inventor and, if appropriate, improvements and additions to the product, sometimes contrasting these changes with the features of a competing company's product.

5. Introductory remarks in the trade literature of the 19th century explicitly remind physicians of the additional income they could earn by equipping their offices with the latest medical instruments and furniture to make their patients comfortable. For instance, Charles Lentz and Sons of Philadelphia, Pennsylvania, which was established in 1866, state in the preface to their 1882 catalog:

"Within the past quarter century science and the art of surgery advanced rapidly, stimulating the trade in surgical instruments, by an increased consumption, to an unprecedented degree. This rapidly increased trade, the legitimate offspring of scientific investigation and wide dissemination of knowledge gained, has been greatly augmented by a growing disposition among the medical profession for larger and more complete surgical armamentariums, it having been fully demonstrated that those supplied with the best and most elaborate office outfits (other things being equal) are the most successful in building up a lucrative practice."

The increased use of medical instruments was a factor in lowering the cost to the medical instrument buyer. Lentz explained: "due to rapidly increasing demand we are enabled to manufacture all goods in large quantities and with improved facilities produce instruments that are not only of superior quality of finish, but with great saving of labor and material. This reduction in cost of manufacturing has enabled us to give a discount from nearly all the list prices."

F. Alfred Reichardt & Co. of New York stated the manufacturing conditions which influenced its pricing policies on imported medical instruments in a price list published in May 1885 (No. 36):

"All instruments are either imported by us from the best foreign makers, where cheaper labor permits more time to be used on finishing goods at a low price, or made for us by a number of smaller manufacturers here, who having worked for and been educated to the business by the older well known manufacturers, turn out now, in contrast with us, goods of the best quality and at much lower figures than the profession has ever been supplied with."

The range of medical and surgical instruments is extensive. Surgical tools were the earliest and most widely applied implements in the practice of medicine. Their style and function have remained standard for centuries. In addition, refined and specialized surgical tools were introduced as operations became more complex, after the use of anesthetics and antiseptics became routine. Catalogs of medical instruments are often called "Surgical," although a greater variety of instruments for diagnosing and treating illnesses by methods other than surgery were introduced in the nineteenth century and advertised in many trade catalogs. Medical trade catalogs feature specialized instruments including stethoscopes, urologic and ophthalmic equipment. Promotion of preventive medicine and public health fostered more frequent and more extensive physical examinations requiring many types of medical and diagnostic instruments. Thus by the end of the nineteenth century instruments applied to patients included not only the surgeon's arsenal of knives, scalpels, scissors, forceps, and other cutting implements, but also anesthetic devices, diagnostic devices, resuscitative and rehabilitative apparatus and a burgeoning assortment of hospital equipment. In addition remedies and devices to be used in the home, often with little or no professional assistance, were advertised in the medical trade literature. Some of this trade literature was skillfully presented to promote interest in the product and convince the doctor and patient of the value of special equipment to maintain and restore good health.

Enterprising distributors and manufacturers provided some of the newer non-surgical equipment, however major surgical instrument manufacturers and distributors also enlarged their inventory to include diagnostic devices and post-operative and convalescent care appliances. Diagnostic medical devices include those with the capacity to measure and record bodily processes manifested by sounds, colors and quantity of fluids, and temperature changes, as well as by muscle function and nervous conduction. Among the implements designed to ameliorate illness are those which heat, cool, exercise, relax, desensitize, correct nerve and muscle malfunctions, and substitute for missing organs and appendages.

When the need for certain devices expanded, suppliers began to specialize in the production of a few popular instruments or appliances. Among the specialized suppliers of medical equipment were the American Sterilizer Company which produced sterilizers of all sizes for physician's offices, biological laboratories and hospitals; S. S. White and Company which produced dental equipment and furniture; and N. D. Whitney and Company of Boston, Massachusetts, which supplied Holmgren standard colored wool, to use in color blindness testing of employees whose color sense was crucial to the performance of their jobs.

Widely used medical equipment sometimes possessed components or contained materials and methods of application which were adapted to other uses. In the 19th century, which was the first period of intensive and extensive use of devices to aid medical care, the most common ways of affecting the body provided by medical implements were heating, cooling and stimulating the body with electricity. Machines which could deliver electricity and hot or cold air and water were in demand by physicians and patients. For example, the Terry Heater Company of Cleveland, Ohio, advertised its heaters for delivering dry heat at temperatures of 400 to 500 degrees Fahrenheit, which it called a form of thermo-therapy, that had been the "sheet anchor in medicine" since antiquity. The improvement introduced in the Terry heater consisted of directing compressed air to a specific place on the body requiring dry heat. In 1904 compressed air heaters were operated by gas or electricity. The special insulated coil designed by the Terry Heater Company for physician's heaters was soon applied to electric heaters for other purposes, especially those used to provide heat in rooms and automobiles. The Terry Heater is an example of improving technology to meet therapeutic goals, and then, adapting the improved device to more general uses.

The Buffalo Dental Manufacturing Company founded in 1867, profited enormously by selling instruments to the lay person as well as the professional. The company developed blowpipes, stoves, vulcanizers and laboratory glassware, primarily for dentists, who made artificial teeth for their patients, and also sold many stoves and heating units to the public. The Buffalo Dental Manufacturing Company also developed pumping units to inflate rubber mattresses used by campers, and gasolene generators and blowers used in schools to teach crafts.

One of the purposes of this bibliography is to inspire readers to look at trade literature to understand those aspects of the practice of medicine which involved apparatuses, tools, aids, etc. Trade literature provides another source for the historian to investigate the type of information physicians relied on throughout their careers and, in many instances, to which they contributed and responded. Manufacturers who advertised over several decades demonstrated the techniques which were effective in getting physicians to buy and prescribe their products. The descriptions and explanations found in the medical trade literature provide examples of the type of language and arguments that were successful in selling specific medical aids to physicians. For physicians, especially those in practice in small towns not located near teaching centers, medical trade literature was a primary source of information about changes in treatment developed after they graduated from medical school.

One of the largest manufacturers of medical instruments, Down Brothers of London, illustrates the evolution of trade literature. Down Brothers issued eighteen successively enlarged catalogs between 1880 and 1930, in addition to a number of pamphlets, circulars and other publications to present new, advanced and improved equipment to the medical profession and medical institutions. Eight of these catalogs are known to us. The Down catalog of July, 1929, contains 3028 pages and seventy-seven pages of index to the instruments. All of these catalogs delineate the physical characteristics of the medical tools used during these fifty years of the company's existence. The instruments represent the most popular implements in western medicine as well as showing the introduction of new devices and, by their omission, the discontinuance of other instruments.

Down company catalogs in combination with those published by other respected and successful medical distributors and manufacturers including Truax and Greene, George Tiemann, Arnold and Sons, Codman and Shurtleff, S. S. White and Jetter and Scherer document the acceptable and readily available medical technology during the nascent period of its development (late 19th and early 20th centuries). These trade catalogs and others of a more local interest provide data, including changes in the cost of instruments, changes in materials used to make implements, and less directly, the effects of medical theories on the design and production of medical tools.

Medical trade literature links the medical instrument manufacturer and the medical care professional. Trade catalogs affirm through illustrations and commentary the increasing reliance on technology to prevent, diagnose and cure illness or to carry out any of these functions with generally greater ease and safety and, sometimes, with special knowledge and increased difficulty. For instance, in 1916, Mayer of London began to sell stainless steel surgical instruments which could be sterilized in hot water without rusting. This innovation, however, could not be applied to all surgical instruments. Some implements such as ophthalmic knives, lithotrites and guillotines for removing tonsils were not sufficiently flexible unless made from a type of steel composed of carbon and crucible carbon, which, however, was not rust proof when steam sterilized. To preserve the instrument's qualities as a good surgical tool, it had to be made from a type of steel (carbon) which required more effort to sterilize and maintain.

The physician's daily practice included examination of a variety of individuals for many types of illnesses. Medical instruments were constructed of varying sizes and shapes to meet individual differences in color, sex, size, etc.. Instruments applied to patients especially when inserted into the body had to be carefully crafted. Instruments such as bougies and catheters when inserted into the patient's orifices required a definite size. Therefore catheters and bougies, designed to enter the urethral, vaginal, aural, rectal, nasal, bronchial and esophageal channels were manufactured in sets of a dozen or so graduated in size from small to large.

By the end of the 19th century there were three major systems, English, French and American, for measuring the sizes of these instruments, based on their diameters. The English system was based on measurement in inches and feet. The French system, based on metric measurements, was straightforward. Each catheter was assigned in succession a number beginning with one and each number was equivalent to the diameter of the instrument in millimeters. The American system, also based on the metric system, increased in size by half millimeters so that a catheter designated number two was one and a half millimeters in diameter and the next size, numbered three, was two millimeters in diameter. In 1879, Charles H. Thomas, a Philadelphia physician, suggested that a general scale be assigned to all instruments to be inserted into body cavities. He recommended that the metric system be applied so that the number of millimeters be used to designate the sizes of the smaller instruments and the number of centimeters be assigned to the larger devices and the orifices into which they were inserted. Each number was to represent the actual diameter of the instrument in either millimeters or centimeters. To measure the diameter of those instruments already in use, Thomas fashioned the Adaptable Metric Gauge which could be slipped around the instrument. J. H. Gemrig and Sons, instrument manufacturer of Philadelphia, produced Thomas' gauge, applied the scale to the instruments it manufactured, and offered to supply a gauge to any physician free of charge. ("A General System of Measurement for Urethral, Uterine, Rectal and other Instruments and an Adaptable Metric Gauge", *Philadelphia Medical Times*, 1897).

The busy professional was foremost in the minds of the writers and designers of medical trade literature. Advertisements and catalogs were marked "for the physician only". To insure that a request for an implement came from a medical doctor, the practitioner was asked to include a business card or state his request on letterhead stationary. Some forms of medical trade literature were designed to be readily accessible. They were published in 8, 16, or 32 page pocket sized booklets which could be carried in the physician's bag and readily consulted in the sickroom and office when necessary. The prose used to explain the product and its therapeutic uses is appealing and must have encouraged the baffled physician to try the proffered drug, antiseptic or device on his patients who suffered from such difficult to treat diseases as cancer, tuberculosis, constipation, syphilis and "female diseases". Antiseptic, cathartic and nutritional ingredients were the mainstay of drugs advertised to treat severe and chronic diseases. Case histories of the successful use of medicinals and the devices used to administer them were often embellished with a description and history of the discovery of the item for sale.

The best example of the finest American medical trade literature is a well organized, superbly descriptive text published in 1899 by Charles Truax. Located in Chicago, Truax noted the paucity of information and descriptions in medical trade catalogs. He rectified this by producing a thick (1024 pages), informative volume entitled *The Mechanics of Surgery: comprising detailed Descriptions, Illustrations and Lists of the Instruments, Appliances and Furniture Necessary in Modern Surgical Art.* His goal was to provide practical information about surgical instruments and to suggest "a standard nomenclature for surgical instruments." Truax criticized the practice of naming surgical instruments after physicians and surgeons instead of calling them by the terms known to mechanics, but alas, Truax's attempt to standardize the surgical instrument nomenclature was not effective. (pp. 7-8). His discussions and illustrations of surgical and medical instruments include descriptions of the materials from which they were made, and the bearing of these materials on the use and care of the instruments. In addition he provided basic designs and relevant information to assist the physician and surgeon in selecting and using these items. Truax's catalog served as a text book on medical instruments at the turn of the century and continues to give historians and technicians a wealth of details about the mechanical aspects of medical and surgical instruments.

The pharmaceutical and chemical company trade literature offers special insights into the practices of the physician. The rich collection of medical trade literature of the College of Physicians of Philadelphia Library reveals, through the names of physicians stamped on the catalog covers and correspondence inserted in the catalogs, that physicians including the Philadelphia based practitioners J. Solis Cohen, L. F. Flick, Barton Chance, and Oscar V. Batson were offered, requested and received a variety of trade literature and sample products throughout their careers. It was in the interest of manufacturers to sell their products to prominent medical practitioners and to solicit testimonials about the value and efficacy of the therapy. Testimonials from physicians and patients constitute a significant part of the drug and personal device trade literature. Artificial limbs and a variety of drugs with antiseptic, germicidal and nutritional properties were among the leading items sold through advertising pamphlets supplemented with correspondence describing personal satisfaction with the product. A letter to J. Solis Cohen indicates how some of these testimonials were obtained. Cohen was sent a sample of Hydroleum (water soluble petroleum) with menthol and camphor on May 24, 1907, by the B. G. Pratt Company of New York. He was encouraged to use it and indicate other substances he would combine with it and prescribe to his patients. Another letter of April 11, 1911, offered Dr. Cohen a quantity of Vanadiol, a non-toxic germicide for use in the oral cavity and respiratory tract. He was asked to observe its effect on his patients. Equipment was offered gratis if the physician agreed to use it and note the effects it produced on his patients. One of these devices, the Germicidal Lung Cabinet was offered to Dr. Cohen in 1902.

There are few instances of humor in medical literature of any type— one source is trade literature designed to attract the busy practitioner by the use of colored cartoons emphasizing and exaggerating the effect of, or lack of a specific treatment. The Miller Rubber Company provides one of the few illustrations of this type of advertising.

Manufacturers in conducting their business through their catalogs and other advertising literature reminded physicians of their obligations to their patients as well as establishing and preserving the reputations of the physician and manufacturer. Many medical instrument catalogs include a preface which states that the manufacturer will provide the best equipment at a reasonable cost with quality being the foremost consideration. The emphasis on quality was based on the premise that good medicine was linked to the best instruments which could be produced at any cost. Saving money at the expense of quality in purchasing a medical instrument was an unethical and immoral action that no respectable manufacturer or physician would sanction.

An effective method of providing value to an instrument was to name an instrument after its inventor or the medical practitioner who promoted its use through endorsements and publications. Instruments such as forceps that are used to clamp arteries were produced in a multitude of shapes and sizes and many of these bear the surnames of distinguished surgeons including Jones, Liston, Mayo, Dieffenbach, Dalziel, etc. Many other types of surgical and diagnostic instruments bear the names of obscure but respected surgeons and physicians. These names are meaningful to those who know the history of medicine, but appear arbitrary to the medical novice and medical instrument classifier.

During the period covered by this bibliography, medical treatments requiring expensive and/or large medical devices were provided by Medical Institutes. These specialized institutions responded to the need to provide a place to use medical equipment which was too large and/or expensive for the private physician to purchase and install. The institutes purchased or rented this unique medical equipment which usually delivered one form of therapy. The instruments and devices were installed and operated by technicians who followed the prescription of the patient's physician. In the major Eastern cities, institutes were established in the nineteenth century to deliver mechanico-electro therapy such as the Philadelphia Orthopedic Institute and School of Mechano-Therapy founded in 1898. To gain the cooperation and approval of the medical profession, the Institute only treated patients who were referred by a physician and presented a written prescription authorizing treatment. The Institute provided electrical stimulation, hot air, water and massage therapy, and various gymnastic exercises through a range of apparatuses and devices. Another Philadelphia institute established by Dr. A. Graham Reed in 1896 advertised the Sprague Method for the treatment of gout and rheumatism. Dry hot air confined within a covered container called a body apparatus was applied and followed up with a massage.

The most popular devices prescribed for therapy or rehabilitation were the Zander exercise machines, which could be used by the patient without assistance. Zander machines were manufactured in Germany and installed in spas in Europe and America in the nineteenth and twentieth centuries. These machines were used by patients, suffering from muscular, nervous and bone disorders, who were instructed by their physicians and who could afford to go to the resort spa. The exercise was passive, in that the device was powered mechanically or electrically and caused the part of the body attached to it to move in a prescribed way. The treatment usually consisted of performing a specified number of definite movements daily.

GENERAL SUPPLIERS:

Frank S. Betz and Company of Chicago was the premier supplier of low cost medical equipment in the U.S. beginning in 1895 and continuing throughout the twentieth century. The company published monthly catalogs and repeatedly offered discounts for a variety of instruments. Betz recognized the economic gain of expanding his business to include the sale of all types of instruments and supplies for the physician and hospital. Those instruments that he could not manufacture he imported. The company served 100,000 physicians and maintained $200,000 worth of stock by the mid 1920's. As a distributor of large quantities of many instruments, Betzco offered reduced prices for each item purchased by the physician. Betzco catalogs, bulletins and booklets were available for the following items: bath supplies, bed and bedding, blood pressure instruments, dental supplies, dental furniture, elastic stockings, hot air devices, hospital supplies, invalid chairs, kitchen supplies, laboratory outfits, light therapy and radiant heat devices, medical cabinets, orthopedic devices, radiator covers, surgical instruments, urinalysis equipment, anesthesia and analgesia equipment, beauty parlor supplies, drugs and pharmaceuticals, eye, ear, nose and throat instruments, hospital clothing, office furniture, and veterinary equipment.

Among the incentives used to urge physicians to buy Betzco products were articles published by the company such as, "History and Evolution of the Intubation Apparatus," which explained how changes in the design and application of this basic tool for admitting air into the lungs enabled the cost of the intubation set to be reduced from fifty dollars to twelve dollars and fifty cents. The article presents a brief review in text and illustrations of the intubation set and shows how the "Rational Intubation Set" is an improvement over all preceding intubation devices. Three handles of different sizes were provided to grasp the tube to be inserted and removed from the throat. Betzco also included instructions for assembling a simple device upon which to practice using the intubation set. The substitute mannikin consisted of a quart wine bottle half-filled with shot for support. The mouth of the bottle was to be covered with thick leather or buckskin into which a slit was made for practicing how to insert the tube.

SURGICAL INSTRUMENT MANUFACTURERS:

Codman & Shurtleff, Inc.

Brief "histories" of companies may sometimes be obtained from the files of those companies which are still in business, such as Codman and Shurtleff, Inc., of Randolph, Massachusetts. In 1838, Thomas P. Codman, a mechanic of Roxbury, Massachusetts, manufactured and offered for sale to the medical profession of Boston his "Pocket Cupping Instrument." It was so well received that Codman decided to make cupping sets and other surgical instruments which he distributed through local druggists. (Nathaniel Simkin II, Vice-President, C&S, Randolph, M.A., 1983). A company file explains that:

"During 1855, Benjamin S. Codman, Asahel M. Shurtleff, and Franklin O. Whitney entered into partnership, establishing the firm of Codman & Shurtleff. Moving to more spacious quarters at 13-15 Tremont Street, the company offered a full line of medical, surgical, dental, and veterinary instruments and supplies. From his Tremont Street office Dr. Codman continued to practice medicine while employed as head of the firm. In 1860 Codman and Shurtleff issued its first catalog of thirty-two pages."

In the 1860's atomization of liquids to treat respiratory ailments became fashionable. A variety of atomizers were produced. In 1862 Codman and Shurtleff marketed a "Patented Steam Atomizer" designed by Shurtleff. It was advertised widely and became popular worldwide. The atomizer was shipped in a wooden container and packed with instructions printed in five languages. The profits from the sale of atomizers provided for major growth of the company which also produced amputation sets required by army surgeons during the Civil War. Amputation sets continued to be sold for many years after the war, especially to frontier doctors, many of whom were ex-army surgeons. The atomizer and amputation set were the most celebrated products of the company during this formative period of its history.

The company was incorporated in May, 1904, as Codman and Shurtleff, Inc. During the Depression of the 1930's the company lost many customers and assets. By 1936, Codman & Shurtleff, Inc. was on the verge of bankruptcy. The company maintained a small cadre of highly skilled, German-trained instrument-makers for manufacturing high quality surgical instruments, who also trained younger skilled craftsmen. Frank G. Ruggles, company sales manager in 1938, purchased the company and shepherded it to solvency by developing its repair department. Diverted during World War II into manufacturing parts for torpedo fuses and diver's knives, Codman and Shurtleff's surgical business declined. After reorganization the company once again concentrated on surgical instruments and in 1950 produced a catalog of sixty pages, the first it had published in over thirty years. In 1954 a major catalog appeared with over four hundred pages. After residing in a few intermediate locations the company moved in 1967 to its present location in Randolph, Massachusetts.

George P. Pilling Company.

Through correspondence we learn historical details about the operation of some instrument manufacturers such as the esteemed George P. Pilling Company of Philadelphia. Oscar V. Batson explained in a letter to the librarian of the College of Physicians Library in Philadelphia in April, 1972, that C. J. Pilling, son of George P. Pilling, had been apprenticed to the instrument maker Gemrig. Gemrig was especially noted for his surgical sets beginning in the mid-nineteenth century. During the depression of the thirties, however, Gemrig had gone out of business. These two outstanding medical instrument craftsman's families were then able to share a wealth of techniques. Pilling continued the tradition into the modern period by keeping a complete shop including facilities for making wood and leather cases to hold the surgical instruments.

DENTAL MANUFACTURERS:

Samuel Stockton White.

The foremost dental manufacturing firm in the U.S. was the S.S. White Dental Company founded in 1844 by the dentist Samuel Stockton White (1822–1879), and incorporated as the S.S. White Dental Manufacturing Company in 1881. White noted the lack of durable, high-quality artificial teeth in the marketplace and began to manufacture porcelain teeth. His business grew rapidly so that he soon abandoned his dental practice. S.S. White porcelain teeth won the highest awards at the Crystal Palace Exhibition in London in 1851 and at the Centennial Exhibition in Philadelphia in 1876. At the time of its incorporation, S.S. White acquired the plant of Johnston Brothers of New York located on Staten Island where a major portion of the products were manufactured. Branch sales offices opened in New York, Boston, Brooklyn, Chicago, Atlanta, St. Paul and Peoria, and abroad in Berlin, St. Petersburg, Toronto, London, Paris, South America, Japan and Australia. The logo of the SSW Company was introduced in its second catalog of 1867, the first catalog having appeared in 1862. The logo consisted of two S's superimposed on a W and was stamped on all instruments made and sold by the company.

Among the innovations S. S. White introduced were the first all metal dental chair, the flexible shaft engine, precision steel instruments, revelation burs and tooth powder. The flexible shaft, for driving the spindle of a tool chuck, was used primarily with dental tools until post World War I when it was applied to a variety of industrial tools including the speedometer, a valve control, an engine governor and a massage apparatus. Records of the S. S. White Company are well preserved and organized in the Hagley Historical Library. These include original patent specifications and drawings, correspondence related to all phases of the business, and all types of trade literature including a rich collection of catalogs. The Smithsonian Institution, National Museum of American History holds a number of trade catalogs and a rich variety of patent models and manufactured specimens of S. S. White products dating to the mid-nineteenth century. The University of Pennsylvania Dental Library also holds S. S. White literature. These three sources provide the primary documents and materials which could be used to produce an historical volume on this premier dental instrument and appliance manufacturer.

An important service provided by S. S. White to the dental industry was to evaluate and reduce the multiplicity of dental instruments and sets manufactured in the last decade of the nineteenth century. The company organized an "Instrument Congress" in 1889 to which six dentists were invited. Their assignment was to compare all forms of each type of instrument, to suggest alterations and to cull out the most efficient and essential items. Among the most arduous tasks for this group was evaluating the pluggers (used to fill teeth) of which existed thousands of models. Instruments were numbered and divided into two major categories: long (fixed) handle and cone socket types. Most instruments were nickel plated, rather than made out of bronze or brass as in previous years. Among those instruments which remained were Varney's, Chappel's, Watling's, Butler's and Webb's pluggers, Palmer's, Butler's and Brown's "Heroic" chisels and Abbott's scalers. Perhaps the most appealing result of the reorganization was a reduction in cost of the instruments to the dentist. With the elimination of duplicate items and those of lesser value to the consumer, manufacturing costs were reduced and passed on to the dentist who bought these items.

The excellence of the S. S. White dental hand tools also was recognized by surgeons who used dental engines and assorted tools to perform minor surgery. The S. S. White Company engine became so popular among surgeons that the company, fearing the instruments would not be adequate, warned their surgeon customers not to use these implements for major surgical operations, not even those equipped with extra heavy sleeves, cables and hand pieces.

Buffalo Dental Manufacturing Company

The dentists George B. Snow, Theodore G. Lewis, B. G. Whitney and George E. Hayes on May 1, 1867, founded the Buffalo Dental Manufacturing Company. The company was formed to produce and sell a plugger patented by Snow and Lewis on October 30 and November 20, 1866. The automatic plugger was conceived by Snow, who discussed the instrument with dentists at a meeting of the American Dental Association in Chicago in 1865. He brought back suggestions for improving the plugger to T. G. Lewis who further modified the instrument. Snow and Lewis began to manufacture the plugger in October, 1865, using the lathe and tools in Lewis' dental office, and within a few months, Snow gave up his dental practice to spend full time in the business. The Snow and Lewis partnership was marred by dissension and disagreements over patent rights and royalties. By the end of the century Lewis, alone or with a co-inventor, had obtained fourteen patents for a variety of dental instruments and appliances. His ingenuity guided the Buffalo Dental Manufacturing Company, the third oldest successful dental instrument maker in the U.S., into the twentieth century with his son and grandson succeeding him. In 1956, the manufacturing plant was sold to Novocal and moved to Brooklyn, New York, where it bears the original name of the company. A retail business continues in Buffalo under the leadership of the founder's grandson, Theodore M. Lewis.

R. I. Pearson Co.

An innovator in catalog design was the R. I. Pearson Company of Kansas City, Missouri and Memphis, Tennessee. In 1891, the company produced an unusually fine catalog of dental instruments containing a detailed index and footnotes to document information on each page. These notes provided additional information based on the published literature concerning the use of the instruments sold by the company.

An excellent source for information about dental manufacturers, especially in Europe, is a list in an appendix to J. Menzies Campbell's book on historic dental instruments in the Royal College of Surgeons of Edinburgh.

DRUG COMPANIES:

The history of drug and pharmaceutical companies is more accessible than the history of medical instrument manufacturers. Among the oldest American pharmacies are Tilden Co., established in 1824 at New Lebanon, New York; William S. Merrill Co., established in 1828 at Cincinnati; and Strong, Cobb and Co., Inc., of Cleveland, founded in 1833. Powers and Weightman began in 1847, and merged with Rosengarten in 1905, and later in 1927, was bought by Merck.

The history of the more successful drug companies is provided in Tom Mahoney's *The Merchants of Life: An Account of the American Pharmaceutical Industry* (Harper and Bros., New York, 1959). Among the companies discussed are: Smith, Kline and French, Wyeth, E. R. Squibb and Sons, Parke Davis and Co., Eli Lilly and Co., Burroughs Wellcome & Co., The Upjohn Co., Abbott Laboratories, G. D. Searle and Co., Lederle Laboratories, S. B. Pernick and Co., Merck and Co., Sterling Drug, Inc., Charles Pfizer and Co., and the Schering Corp. These companies were selected for the special drugs they produced and represent a small fraction of the more than 1100 firms existing in the 1930's and 1300 firms which existed by the 1950's. A series of articles on the founders of drug companies began to appear in the journal *Medical Times* beginning in 1958. A more recent source of company histories is *Pharmaceutical Company Histories*, edited by Gary L. Nelson. Volume I, containing thirteen company histories, was published by Woodbine Publishing Co., Bismarck, N.D., in 1980.

A few companies, primarily drug companies, may be studied in greater depth through published monographs. These histories were often sanctioned and paid for by the company and, therefore, bear the earmarks of the company sponsored chronological compendium. These books contain basic information from which the reader may derive useful data for further research. Among these histories are: *The Long White Line: The Story of Abbott Laboratories* by Herman Kogan, New York: Random House, 1963; *Medicine Makers of Kalamazoo: The Story of the Upjohn Company* by Leonard Engel, New York: McGraw Hill Inc., 1961; *The Road to Market: The Story of McKesson and Robbins* published by McKesson and Robbins Inc., 1958; *All in a Century: the First One Hundred Years of the Eli Lilly Company* by E. J. Kahn, Jr., privately published by Eli Lilly Co. 1975; *Threescore Years and Ten* by Roscoe Clark, Chicago: the Lakeside Press, 1946; *Dr. Squibb, The Life and Times of a Rugged Idealist* by Lawrence G. Blockman, New York: Simon and Schuster, 1958; *Through a City Archway: The Story of Allen and Hanburys (1715–1954)* by Desmond Chapman-Huston and Ernest C. Cripps, London: John Murray, 1954; and *Geschichte des Geigy-Unternehmens von 1758 bis 1939* and *Geigy heute* by Alfred Burgin, Basel: J. R. Geigy; Kommissionsverigg Birkhauser, 1958.

OPTICAL MANUFACTURERS:

The most complete collection of optical related trade literature is found in the rare book department of the University of Rochester's Rush Rhees Library. It was assembled by the Bausch and Lomb company at the end of the nineteenth and early twentieth centuries for use by the company's patent research and design departments. A listing of these catalogs is included in this bibliography.

Kryptok Sales Co.

From trade catalog introductions are gleaned the details of a company's history. For instance, the Kryptok Company began manufacturing lenses in 1908, and took in its first retail orders on 20 February 1908, although it made sales in 1907. Photographs of the company and an explanation of the process of manufacturing appears in the August, 1914, issue of Kryptok Sales Co. Bulletin, Vol. V. A few details about expansion of the business and selling arrangements are mentioned in the March 1917 issue of the Company Bulletin, Vol. VIII. In 1918, because of the effects that WW I had on sales and supplies, there was a reorganization of the General Optical Company, Inc., and its affiliated corporation, Krptok Sales Co., Inc., with a subsequent takeover of the management by the Board of Directors.

McAllister Co.

A leading optical manufacturer in the U.S. was the McAllister Company originally located in Philadelphia and subsequently opening a branch in New York. A chronology of the McAllister Company was published in 1971 by N.M. and M.A. Graver of Rochester, New York, in a reprint of T. H. McAllister's, "Condensed List of Optical Goods," catalog ca. 1880. The chronology begins with the birth in February, 1753, of John McAllister in Glasgow, Scotland, and ends with the last listing for McAllister-Keller Co., Inc., 20 Vesey Street, New York, in the city directory for 1938–42. Seven successive McAllister catalogs are listed by the Gravers.

John McAllister in 1783, bought a stock of spectacles to sell while pursuing his business as a manufacturer of cartouche boxes, whips and walking sticks. The quick sale of these spectacles and encouragement from Benjamin Franklin persuaded McAllister to continue to market spectacles. George Washington is reputed to have been one of McAllister's customers. By 1796, when located on 48 Chestnut Street, McAllister sold " a large assortment of spectacles, reading glasses, concave glasses, magnifiers, goggles, and put new glasses in old spectacle frames." McAllister's son, John Jr., graduated from the University of Pennsylvania and became a partner with his father in 1811, when the firm became "McAllister and Son." McAllister fitted spectacles for many well known American clients and John Jr. is believed to have been the first to diagnose and correct ocular astigmatism in a patient—Chauncey E. Goodrich. After his father's death in 1830 the company became known as John McAllister and Co., "Opticians and Dealers in Philosophical Apparatus." In 1855 the firm was called McAllister and Brother, "Opticians and Dealers in Mathematical Instruments" and in 1860, McAllister and Brother, "Opticians and C." The sons of John Jr. were Thomas Hamilton, William Young and John Allister McAllister. In 1865, Thomas Hamilton moved to New York to establish his own business (See also: Deborah J. Warner, "Optics in Philadelphia during the Nineteenth Century," *Proc. Amer. Phil. Soc.* (1985) 129: 291-299).

E. B. Meyrowitz

The most successful American manufacturer and distributor of spectacles and ophthalmological equipment was the Meyrowitz family. E. B. Meyrowitz of New York specialized in selling optical equipment to diagnose eye, ear, nose and throat diseases. By 1892 Meyrowitz was the leading manufacturer in the world of ophthalmologically related equipment. In 1906 Meyrowitz opened a branch in London and published a fifth edition of the company's catalog.

Voigtlaender and Son Optical Co.

One of the earliest companies to use the highest quality optical glass was Voigtlaender and Son Optical Co., the American branch of Voigtlaender & Sohn of Braunschweig, Germany. Christopher Voigtlaender founded the firm in 1756, in Vienna with the manufacture of reading glasses, microscopes and terrestrial telescopes. Freidrich Voigtlaender, another owner of the firm, inspected all the available types of optical glass and improved upon them by constructing lenses on a scientific basis. In 1886, the technical laboratory at Jena brought out the "New Jena Glass" which Voigtlaender & Sohn were the first to apply in all of their lenses. One variety of these lenses, in 1894, was used in the production of the Collinear series of lenses used in photographic instruments.

Treatment of rare diseases and reclamation of the functions of a diseased organ mark the advance of twentieth century American medicine. Use of a greater range of diagnostic and therapeutic procedures came in response to the availability of specialized equipment. A few examples of this type of equipment are antiseptic bandages, lamps of various types and respiratory apparatus.

ANTISEPSIS:

Approval by the medical community of the concept of antisepsis in the 1870's led Johnson and Johnson, in 1886, to manufacture medicinal plasters, absorbent cotton, surgical dressings and appliances. Johnson and Johnson, as the first American manufacturer to produce sterilized dressings, provided the essential materials for American physicians to practice antiseptic medicine. Improvements in these materials including changes in design of the bandages followed. From the beginning distinctive forms of containers and packages were employed to distribute and advertise Johnson and Johnson sterile products. A red cross on blue paper was the symbol used to identify their medical products. Competing firms who wished to trade on the world wide recognition and reputation of Johnson and Johnson applied similar designs in their packaging materials until they were restrained by court order from using the red cross and blue paper to wrap up their products. Johnson and Johnson continues to manufacture sterilized bandages and related materials.

LIGHTING:

Lighting in physician's offices and hospitals was poor until manufacturers such as Hanovia of Newark, N. J., offered special lamps to the medical profession. Hanovia, one of the earliest and largest suppliers of mercury vapor lamps, introduced the quartz lamp to the medical profession in 1905. More than 100,000 lamps were distributed by 1929. As the need for greater intensity and light of varying wavelengths arose, Hanovia introduced special lamps to keep up with the demand of clinical practice.

RESPIRATORY APPARATUS:

Warren E. Collins, designer of one of the early iron lungs in the 1930's, began as an instrument maker at Carnegie Nutrition Laboratory in Boston where he was employed between 1908 and 1920. An advertisement in the *Journal of Nutrition*, 1931, vol. 4, explains that Warren E. Collins, Inc., of 555 Huntington Ave., Boston, Massachusetts, had been a specialist in respiration apparatus since 1908. Among the types of apparatus constructed by Collins were respiration chambers for infants, children and adults, portable metabolism apparatus, the Benedict-Roth device, spirometers of all sizes from one half-liter to six hundred liters capacity, Benedict oxy-calorimeter and numerous metabolism accessories which include the Benedict Gas Sampling pump. The designer of the Benedict apparatus was Dr. Francis G. Benedict, Director of the Carnegie Nutrition Laboratory.

AIDS FOR THE HANDICAPPED:

Trade catalogs and special issues of trade literature sometimes summarize the history of an instrument or device manufacturer. One example of this type of historical bulletin is *The Gloved Hand: The Story of the Hanger Arm* by J.E. Hanger, Inc. (est. 1861), ca. 1940. The American limb making industry began to flourish around the period of the Civil War. Patents were taken out for improved limbs by Freas, A.A. Marks, Condell, Engelbrecht, Boeklin, Hanger, Rowley, Bly, Potts and Palmer. By 1930, there were 257 limb makers and assembly plants in the U.S. making approximately 21,000 limbs each year. ("That They May Walk: A History of Artificial Limb Making," C. H. Davies, *A.S.T.A. Journal*, Oct., 1931.)

Invacare, a leading American manufacturer of innovative wheelchairs and hospital beds, traces its roots to 1885, when the Worthington Company in Elyria, Ohio, began producing wheelchairs for the physically handicapped. In the early twentieth century, the company's name was changed to the Colson Company as a result of a merger with a leading manufacturer of rubber wheels and casters. In 1957, the wheelchair division of Colson was bought out by three employees who named the company Mobilaid, Inc. This company expanded and became Invacare in 1971. ("Invacare: A Brief History," 1983).

SCIENTIFIC INSTRUMENT COMPANIES:

Companies occasionally were organized at the suggestion of scientists who required special equipment for their experiments. In 1861, the Société Genevoise was founded with the assistance of the prominent scientists, Professor August de la Rive and M. Thury, of Geneva. The preface to Circular 104, distributed by Queen and Co. of Philadelphia, relates that "the idea which inspired the organization of our factory (Société Genevoise) was the desire to offer to physicians and all scientists instruments which are simple and at the same time accurate, and we made it a guiding principle never to sacrifice really essential points in order to reduce cost of construction." Many universities used equipment manufactured by this company. Of special interest to readers of this bibliography are their microscopes and electromagnetic equipment, used in physiology and medicine.

Queen and Co., one of the major American manufacturers and suppliers of scientific equipment, was founded in 1853 by James W. Queen. He had been a member of the optical firm of McAllister and Co. Queen brought over many instruments manufactured in Europe. He eventually sold his business to S.L. Fox in 1893. After passing through a financial crisis in 1893–94, the firm was bought by J. G. Gray, who increased the manufacture of scientific apparatus. By 1903, Queen and Co. had eight sales departments and four factories with laboratories. An office was established in New York with agencies in principal cities throughout the country. The oldest department furnished optical equipment and spectacles. Queen was the first company to make spectacles from oculists' prescriptions and by 1903, had over 125,000 prescriptions on file. Queen and Co. also made the first oculist's trial test lenses in the United States. Queen supplied eye testing apparatus and color tests to railroad personnel and the Navy Department.

The Search
for Sources

This bibliography grew out of an obvious need and a desire to place the history of the technology of medicine on a firmer foundation. Trade literature casts a significant light on the production, advertisement, sale and function of medical instruments and other equipment. This literature, in combination with instruments and other original and secondary accounts, is yet to be satisfactorily utilized in scholarly works. We hope this bibliography will encourage and inspire readers to contribute to the historiography of medicine and medical innovation and development.

Source materials, such as trade catalogs, can rarely be found in card catalogs (and only at the more conscientious libraries). Most libraries classify medical trade catalogs as ephemera, often out of lack of experience with their use. Until the last few years, trade catalogs were not available through book dealers. Those that were advertised, were generally sold to the few researchers and medical instrument collectors who needed them.

Manufacturer and distributor company literature is housed in many places. In addition to university and major libraries, this material is found in history of medicine collections, archives, rare book rooms, medical libraries and storage areas where access is sometimes very difficult. Catalogs may also be found in professors' offices, museum curators' offices and museum work areas where the huge task of documenting artifacts occurs. Also a direct line between book dealers and collectors keeps trade catalogs which do turn up out of wider circulation.

Care for this literature is determined not only by where but by how long catalogs are kept. The better libraries lock their older and rarer materials in environmentally controlled cabinets while others punch holes in the catalogs and place them in three ring binders. If all libraries employed uniform handling methods of trade catalogs, assembling this bibliography would have been easier.

Up to now, the researcher used Lawrence B. Romaine's *A Guide to American Trade Catalogs: 1744–1900* (New York: Arno Press, 1960), which lists approximately 150 medical and 100 dental catalogs in chapters 35 and 17, respectively. Our bibliography includes almost 10,000 citations for nearly 2,000 companies. This list is compiled from catalogs, brochures, fliers, leaflets, bulletins, advertisements, company stationery, referrals from other companies, and labeled or engraved objects. The wealth of information found in these sources includes, under ideal circumstances, not only the company name and address, but its date of establishment, incorporation date, products, including those not previously mentioned anywhere else, and technical product information. Much of this information was confirmed through secondary sources, e.g., Etna M. Kelley's, *The Business Founding Date Directory* (Scarsdale, N.Y.: Morgan & Morgan Publishers, 1954) and Keane and Emmerich's, *Marvyn Scudder Manual of Extinct and Obsolete Companies* (Vol. 1, New York City: Marvyn Scudder Manual of Extinct and Obsolete Companies, Inc., 1926).

To contact or visit every health science library or collection demands more support and time than the authors possessed. Thus, the libraries, museums and collections presented here represent major and typical holders of American and Western European manufacturers' literature. The listings reflect the holdings that were found by the researchers of this book and the library staffs. For this reason, not every small or duplicate piece of trade literature is listed.

Changes in library holdings occur on a regular basis. Literature found years ago may not remain at the same location today. Catalogs, especially the cheaply made ones of wood pulp based paper, deteriorate due to acidity within the pages. To conserve shelf space, libraries give or sell their collections to other libraries known for quality care. Some libraries simply throw the catalogs away. On the other hand, some libraries add new material to their collections so often that even a recent listing is out of date. We will be grateful for corrections for those citations that are not correctly cited or are not printed here which libraries and owners wish to share with us. If enough additional trade literature information is received another edition of this bibliography will appear.

The names of some instrument makers who did not produce catalogs or other literature have been obtained from the notes made by Raymond Russell. The original list is filed in the Royal College of Surgeons Library in England. Russell gathered these names from instruments he had observed in various museums and collections in the British Isles. All of these makers are listed alphabetically along with the names of the instrument manufactured and bear the code letters **RCSL**. Elisabeth Bennion also consulted the Russell list and added other European instrument makers in an appendix to her book, *Antique Medical Instruments* (Sotheby Parke Bernet and University of California Press, 1979). A few other instruments which bore names not found among catalogs are included in this bibliography. Another rich source of other instrument makers, who are also recorded in this bibliography, are those mentioned by John Read, early 19th century English instrument maker. (see listing in this book for source).

Other sources of medical instrument makers include city directories and city, state and regional histories. Larger city directories contain the names and locations of craftsmen and companies often not represented by existing trade literature. The Albany, New York directory was searched for medical instrument makers by Patricia Wells, volunteer in the Division of Medical Sciences at the National Museum of American History, Smithsonian Institution. Her findings are included in this bibliography.

The best test of accuracy in any bibliography is to compare it with the sources. In all the collections represented here, only rarely was it not possible to go back and check the original document. Variations will occur, especially within titles, pages, and dates. There are also variations depending on where a manufacturer or distributor was located. Regional copies may have variations built in which were designed for the local market. The wholesale or distribution company, typified by Standard Surgical Instruments, added its own changes to the catalogs it distributed.

In using this finder's index, remember that there are companies or editions of catalogs not listed here. Most, if not all, libraries and museums hold more catalogs than could be listed, and time would be well spent digging and searching for other sources.

We thank the staffs of the museums and libraries and holders of private collections who took the time to check our compilations and confirm the exact holdings in each location. Our gratitude is extended further to those who donated their catalogs and company literature to libraries and museums and made this material available for research. We also thank those instrument and book dealers who have responded to our requests to find trade literature. There is a need for even more catalogs especially to fill the lacuma among the company literature not represented in this listing.

This project began over fifteen years ago as a result of searching for material to identify medical, dental, optical and pharmaceutical museum objects. At that time, Miss Doris Leckie set up the basic files upon which the data was collected. Her work was invaluable to us. We also benefitted from the support of our colleagues, Ray Kondratas and Michael Harris, who realized the importance of this project and pointed out appropriate literature. Other keen collectors who shared their collecting acumen and even donated some splendid examples are Richard Glenner, William Helfand, Eric P. Muth, J. William Rosenthal, and the American College of Radiology.

EXAMPLE OF CITATION

1   2

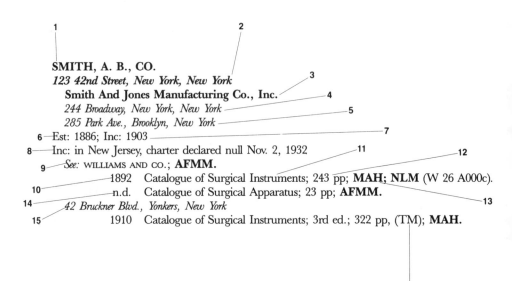

SMITH, A. B., CO.
123 42nd Street, New York, New York
Smith And Jones Manufacturing Co., Inc.
244 Broadway, New York, New York
285 Park Ave., Brooklyn, New York
Est: 1886; Inc: 1903
Inc: in New Jersey, charter declared null Nov. 2, 1932
See: WILLIAMS AND CO.; **AFMM.**
1892   Catalogue of Surgical Instruments; 243 pp; **MAH; NLM** (W 26 A000c).
n.d.   Catalogue of Surgical Apparatus; 23 pp; **AFMM.**
42 Bruckner Blvd., Yonkers, New York
1910   Catalogue of Surgical Instruments; 3rd ed.; 322 pp, (TM); **MAH.**

KEY

1 Title of company.

2 Earliest address.

3 Later title of company.

4 Address for later title of company.

5 Later address, no known date of move.

6 Establishment date.

7 Incorporation date.

8 Information about company.

9 Reference to other company.

10 Date of catalog.

11 Bibliographic citation.

12 Number of pages, not listed if unknown.

13 Abbreviation for institution holding catalog, call numbers given when available.

14 No date for catalog available, or no date can be confirmed.

15 Address associated with next citation following.

16 Trademark given in catalog.

NOTES REGARDING
THE ENTRIES

John Read references were listed in the Royal College of Surgeons (RCS) List of Instrument Makers compiled by Raymond Russell. The actual references used by Russell were not located by the authors.

Pagé (the veterinary instrument maker) references were listed in the Royal College of Surgeons (RCS) List of Instrument Makers compiled by Raymond Russell. The Actual references used by Russell were not located by the authors.

In cases where the only reference to a maker was a name stamped on an instrument or instrument case the reference notes the instrument, its location and call number if available, exactly as listed by the institution.

BIBLIOGRAPHY OF TRADE LITERATURE BY MANUFACTURER

ABBOTT ALKALOIDAL COMPANY, THE
    Aug. 1899   Price List, Therapeutic, Cost of $1.00 to Physicians; 64 pp, index; **MAH.**

ABBOTT LABORATORIES
4739-57 Ravenswood Avenue, Chicago, Illinois.
  4753 Ravenswood Avenue, Ravenswood Station, Chicago, Illinois.
  31 E. 17th Street, New York, New York.
  634 I. W. Hellman Building, Los Angeles, California.
  227 Central Building, Seattle, Washington.
  559 Mission Street, San Francisco.
  57 Colborne St., Toronto, Canada.
Est: 1888

1901	Alkaloidal Suggestions; 49 pp; **CPP.**
1903	Abbott Laboratories (assorted ads); 64 pp; **CPP.**
1904	Abbott's Alkaloidal Digest, A Brief Therapeutic with Clinical Applications, Calcidin Abbott; 8 pp; **CPP.**
Sep. 1, 1905	Alkaloidal Laboratory Products; 64 pp; **CPP.**
1913–14	Pharmaceutical and Biologic Products; **MRLB.**
1914	Prices Current 1913–14; 106 pp; **CPP.**
1921	Subcutaneous Intramuscular and Intravenous Medication; 33 pp; **CPP.**
1922	Butyn, A New Synthetic Local Anesthetic: Report Concerning Clinical Use by Albert E. Bulson, Jr. (JAMA 1922) with Price List; 8 pp; **CPP.**
ca 1923	Pepto-Iodine; 4 pp; **CPP.**
ca 1923	Sodium Thiosulphate, A Remedy for the Treatment of Reactions following Employment of Arsphenanine and its Derivatives; 4 pp; **CPP.**
ca 1923	Butyn, A New Local Anesthetic Having Important Advantages Over Cocaine; 14 pp; **CPP.**
1924	Potassium Bismuth Tartrate with Butyn; 4 pp; **CPP.**
1924	Sulpharsphenamine for Use Where Veins are Hard to Reach, The Drug of Choice in Neuro-Syphilis; 4 pp; **CPP.**
ca 1924	Thiosinamine; 4 pp; **CPP.**
1924	Superior Neo-Arsphenamine; 4 pp; **CPP.**
1925	Metaphen, a Further Advance in Mercurial Germicides; 31 pp; **CPP.**
1925	Sodium Thiosulphate; 4 pp; **CPP.**
1925	Price List of Pharmaceutical and Biologic Products and Fine Medicinal Chemicals with Therapeutic Notes and Clinical Suggestions; 209 pp, index; **NYAM; MF/MAH.**
n.d.	An Approved Surgical Technic for the Application of Dakin's Dichloramine; 9 pp; **CPP.**

North Chicago, Illinois.
May 1928   Price List of Pharmaceutical and Biologic Products and Fine Medicinal
Chemicals with Therapeutic Notes and Clinical Suggestions; 166 pp,
index; **NYAM; MF/MAH.**
Nov. 1929   Price List; 32 pp; **NYAM; MF/MAH.**
1931   Catalog, Pharmaceutical and Biological Specialties of the Abbott Swan
Meyers and Dermatological Research Laboratories; **LACMA** (149
AB2c).
1933   Contribution to Medicine Developed by 45 years of Specialization and
Research; 10 pp; **CPP.**
ca 1930   Answering Your Questions About Some of the New and Scientific
Abbott-Swan-Myers and D.R.L. Products; 9 pp; **CPP.**
ca 1933   A Pictorial Pilgrimage—Giving New Facts on the Origin, Production and
Uses of the Richest Available Natural Sources of Vitamins A & D; 7
pp; **CPP.**
n.d.   From Deep North Pacific Waters, The Secret of an Improved Vitamin
and Mineral Preparation; 7 pp; **CPP.**

ABBOTTS ALDERNAY DAIRIES, INC.
31st and Chestnut Streets, Philadelphia, Pennsylvania.
3043 Chestnut Street, Philadelphia, Pennsylvania.
Est: 1876
n.d.   What Does Certified Mean?; 6 pp; **CPP.**

ACHILLI, ACHILLE
Via Delle Cave N. 8, Roma, Italy.
E. 20 c   Catalog N. 31, Mobili per ospedali, arredi chirurgici; 47 pp; **AFMM;
MAH.**
E. 20 c   Catalog, Mobili per ospedali, arredi chirurgici; 72 pp; **AFMM.**
via Appia Nuova No 67. (Rome, Italy).
E. 20 c   Impianti completi moderni di sterilizzazione e Disinfezione
autoclavi-sterilizzatrici-potabilizzatori; **MAH.**

ACME X-RAY COMPANY
341-351 West Chicago Avenue, Chicago, Illinois.
Dec. 1921   Pamphlet, no. 6200 Acme Stereoscope, Bulletin no. 5.; 4 pp; **MAH.**
Apr. 1922   Pamphlet, Roentgen Accessories. Acme Coronaless Overhead System,
Bulletin no. 4; 15 pp; **MAH.**

ACME-INTERNATIONAL X-RAY COMPANY
See: AMERICAN X-RAY CORPORATION and ACME INTERNATIONAL SALES COMPANY
Oct. 1922   Pamphlet, Bulletin no. 10, Vertical Fluoroscope and Fluoroscopic Unit; 4
pp; **MAH.**
Jan. 1923   Pamphlet, Bulletin no. 12, Combination Roentgen Tables; 7 pp; **MAH.**
Feb. 1, 1923   Pamphlet, Bulletin no. 13, Horizontal Roentgen Tables; 3 pp; **MAH.**
Feb. 15, 1923   Leaflet, 210 K.V. Roentgen Generator; 1 pp; **MAH.**
Apr. 1, 1923   Pamphlet, Bulletin 21, 120 K.V. Roentgen Generator; 7 pp; **MAH.**
Apr. 15, 1923   Pamphlet, Bulletin no. 18, 150 K.V. Roentgen Generator; 7 pp; **MAH.**
Apr. 15, 1923   Pamphlet, Bulletin no. 11, Stereoscope and Viewing Box; 3 pp; **MAH.**
May 1, 1923   Pamphlet, Bulletin no. 16, 210 K.V. Roentgen Generator; 11 pp; **MAH.**
1923   Pamphlet, Bulletin no. 20, Deep Therapy Tube Stand with Protective
Cylinder and Table; 7 pp; **MAH.**
Jun. 15, 1923   Pamphlet, Bulletin no. 23, Coronaless Overhead Systems; 7 pp; **MAH.**
Sep. 1, 1923   Pamphlet, Bulletin no. 24, Small Accessories and Supplies; 7 pp; **MAH.**

Dec. 1, 1923   Pamphlet, Bulletin no. 26, X.R.V. Plate Changer; 3 pp; **MAH.**
711 West Lake Street, Chicago, Ill.
    1928   Catalog, no. 9-C, Precision Mobile X-Ray Apparatus; 7 pp; **MAH.**
    1920's   Catalog, no. 40-A, Precision Coronaless Roentgen Generators for Fast Radiography and Therapy; 15 pp; **MAH.**
    1930's?   Catalog, no. 45, Precision Coronaless Deep Therapy Apparatus; 30 pp; **MAH.**

ADAMS
See: CLAY-ADAMS.

ADAMS X-RAY COMPANY, THE
Maple and Rinard Streets, Detroit, Michigan.
    ca 1915   Stereographs of Adams Dental X-Ray Unit-Type B; 10 pp photocopy; **MAH.**

ADAMS, GEORGE
    1777   A Catalogue of Mathematical, Philosophical and Optical Instruments Made Under the Inspection and Direction of George Adams; 14 pp; **MAH.**

ADAMS-MORGAN CO.
Upper Montclair, New Jersey.
    ca 1911   Electrical Apparatus and Supplies, Dynamos, Motors, Chemicals, Wireless Telegraph and Telephone Instruments, Books and Tools . . .; 48 pp; **BLEL.**

ADERER BROTHERS
1308 Broadway, New York, New York.
See: JULIUS ADERER, INC.
    1901   Catalog, Refiners and Manufacturers, Gold, Gold Solder, Gold Foil, Amalgams, etc. for Dentist's Use, Laboratory Gold Crowns, Badges and Plates, Dental Specialties; 30 pp; **MAH.**
729 Sixth Ave., New York, New York.
    ca 1901   Condensed Price List; 8 pp; **MAH; NYAM.**
    ca 1910   Pamphlet, Ideal Gold Lines Vulcanite Plates . . .; 4 pp; **MAH; NYAM.**
    ca 1910   Pamphlet, Dental Laboratory Tool Specialties; 4 pp; **MAH; NYAM.**
    ca 1910   Pamphlet, Plastic Fibrous Gold; 4 pp; **MAH; NYAM.**

ADERER, JULIUS, INC.
47 West 42nd Street, New York, New York.
See: ADERER BROTHERS.
    1922   Pamphlet, Of Special Interest to Orthodontists; 32 pp; **MAH; NYAM.**

ADLANCO INDUSTRIAL PRODUCTS CORPORATION
54 Lafayette Street, New York, New York.
See: SIEMENS-REINIGER-VEIFA COMPANY.
    ca 1910   Katalog 410/451/445/446/470. Heliodore. Roentgenapparate für Diagnostik, Oberflachen und Tiefentherapie; 21 pp; **NYAM, MF/MAH.**

ADNET, E. et FILS
26, rue Vauquelin, Paris, France.
See: CARL ZEISS; 1902; **AFMM.**
    1896   Catalogue, Générale illustre des instruments de chimie, de bactériologie et utensiles de laboratoire; 260 pp; **NYAM, MAH.**
    1900   Matèriel de laboratories, chemie-bactériologie, no. 19; 895 pp; **AFMM.**

1900   Catalogue illustre des appareils de bactériologie et de micrographie; 298 pp, previous ed. 1895; **AFMM.**

1900   Catalogue illustre des appareils de bactériologie et de micrographie; 302 pp; **AFMM.**

ca 1900   Catalogue illustre spéciale de verreries porcelaines, terre, grès et utensiles de laboratoires de chimie, sucreries, distilleries, lacteries, analyses agricoles, métallurgie, etc.; 201 pp; **MAH; NYAM.**

ca 1905   Catalogue, no. 11, Verrerie, Porcelaine, Terre et Grès; 201 pp; **NYAM.**

ca 1910   Catalogue, no. 19, Matériel de Laboratories Chimie-Bactériologie; 895 pp; **NYAM; MAH; AFMM.**

n.d.   Depositaire des Microscopes et Appareils Zeiss; 865 pp; 3 pp, biblio., index; **AFMM.**

AESCULAP
Luisenstrasse 41, Berlin, Germany.

E. 20 c   Instrumente Chirurgie, Dental, Veterinair-Instrumente, Injektions-spritzen, Sterilisatoren; pp: Section A: 1-193, B: 301-750, C: 901-1230, D: 1401-1675, E: 1801-1931, F: 2001-2256, J: 2501-2545, K: 2701-2848, No Section G, nor H, index each section; **NLM** (W26qA315e).

E. 20 c   Instrumente Chirurgie, Dental, Veterinair-Instrumente, Injektions-spritzen, Sterilisatoren; pp: Section A: 1-111, B: 301-626, C: 901-1317, E: 1801-1926, F: 2001-2249, No Section D, each section bound separately with own index; **NLM** (W26 qA315e).

AESCULAPIUS
Aesculap Werke 181, Tuttlingen, Germany.
See: JETTER and SCHEERER.

ca 1900   Aesculap-Kolbenloser, Nr. 5011-Cn; 1 pp; **WMScM.**

ca 1900   Folder, no. 189-Cn, Syringe containers, injection outfit; 2 pp; **WMScM.**

ca 1900   Leaflet, no. 167-C, Aesculapius 15 Laboratory Centrifuge; 6 pp foldout; **WMScM.**

ca 1900   Prospetat, Nr. 58-Cn, Aesculap Electro-Sanger; 6 pp foldout; **WMScM.**

ca 1900   Pamphlet, Record Syringes, Stamped 5% price increase; 4 pp; **WMScM.**

ca 1900   A-Prospectus, 161-C, Electric Aspirator B15070; 4 pp; **WMScM.**

ca 1900   Prospekt, Nr. 131-C, Lumbalpunktions-Besteck; 4 pp; **WMScM.**

ca 1900   Prospectus, no. 168-C, Laboratory Centrifuge, Aesculapius 100; 4 pp; **WMScM.**

ca 1900   Prospectus, no. 174–Cn, Pocket Instrument Set, Aseptic; 4 pp; **WMScM.**

AHL, DAVID, DR.
Newville, Cumberland Co., Pennsylvania.

1875   Ahl's Adaptable Porous Splints: With Directions for Their Employment in Fractures and Other Surgical Lesions; 17 pp; **YML.**

36 South Fifth St., Philadelphia, Pennsylvania.

ca 1877   Ahl's Adaptable Porous Splints With Directions for Their Employment in Fractures and Other Surgical Lesions; 26 pp; **CPP** (Bolenius Coll).

AKERS
See: SUPPLEE & CO.

1926   Brochure, Akers Technique of Partial Denture Restorations . . .; **NYAM.**

AKOUPHONE MFG. CO.
36 East 20th Street, New York, New York.
See: E. B. MEYROWITZ; **CPP.**

1902   Catalogue, Akouphone Sound Waves, Akouphone Mfg. Co., Owners of Instruments to Enable the Deaf to Hear, Patented by Mr. M.R. Hutchinson, descriptions of use of instruments, listing of parts, price list & photos & illustrations; 19 pp; **MAH.**

n.d.   Sold by Meyrowitz Brothers; 6 pp; **CPP.**

ALBATROSS STEEL EQUIPMENT CO.
Gen. Offices & Plant, Los Angeles, California.
Distributors: ALSTOCK FAY & CO., Portland, Oregon.

Oct. 15, 1927   Price List of Metal Furniture for Physicians, Dentists, Hospitals; 10 pp; **MAH.**

THE ALBEE METHOD OF BONE TRANSPLATION
See: KNY-SCHEERER CO. THE, 1916; **MF/MAH.**

ALBRECHT, EUGEN
Universitätsmechaniker in Tubingen, Germany.

1892   Anleitung zum Gebrauche des Hufnerschen Spectro-photometers in seiner neuesten, verbesserten Form 1 plate; 20 pp; **NYAM; MF/MAH** (date 1892, handwritten: current to Oct. 1897).

ca 1892   Preis-Verzeichnis botanisch-physiologischer Apparate nach Angabe von Herrn Prof. Pfeffer angefertigt von Eugen Albrecht; 4 pp; **NYAM; MF/MAH** (date 1897, in handwritten note).

1892   E. Albrecht's absolute Vorlesungselektrometer nach Prof. F. Braun; 3 pp, prices; (date 1892, handwritten note says current 1897); **NYAM; MF/MAH.**

L. 19 c?   Preis-Verzeichnis botanisch-physiologischer Apparate, and E. Albrecht's absolute Vorlesungselektrometer, Brochures; 2 pp each, filed together; **NYAM.**

ALDEN, JAMES B.
P.O. Box 5, 844, New York, New York.

1866   Brochure, The Crosby Invalid ed., Invented and Patented by Dr. Josiah Crosby, Manchester, NY; 4 pp; **NYAM.**

ALEXANDER, DR. H. M., & CO., INC.
Biologic Laboratories, Marietta, Pennsylvania.

1901   For Protection Be Sure of the Source of Your Vaccine Virus; 4 pp; **CPP.**

ca 1907   The Diagnosis of Tuberculosis by the Ophthalmo-Tuberculin Test; 6 pp; **CPP.**

Jan. 1910   The Pasteur Treatment for the Prevention of Rabies; 16 pp; **CPP**

n.d.   Tuberculins for the Diagnosis and Treatment of Human Tuberculosis; 4 pp; **CPP.**

n.d.   Directions for the Application of the Ophthalmic Tuberculin Diagnostic Test; 4 pp; **CPP.**

10th Street & 3rd Avenue, New York, New York.
5609 Indiana Avenue, Chicago, Illinois.
Omaha, Nebraska.

post 1904   A Convenient Aseptic Vaccine Point Container; **CPP.**

n.d.   Directions for the Application of the von Pirquet Cutaneous Tuberculin Diagnostic Test; 4 pp; **CPP.**

n.d.   Directions for Application of the Petre Differential Tuberculosis Diagnostic Test; 4 pp; **CPP.**

n.d.   Directions for the Application of the Conjunctival-Ophthalmo-Tuberculin

Diagnostic Test; 4 pp; **CPP.**

n.d.   Directions for the Application of the Moro Percutaneous Tuberculin Ointment Diagnostic Test; 4 pp; **CPP.**

ALEXANDRE, J.
10 rue de Saintonge, 10, Paris (3me), France.

1920's   Constructeur, brevetée France et étranger brochure, instrumentation du Dr. Th. de Martel pour la trepanation, appareil de chirurgie-osseuse, craneotomie, laminectomie, atticotomie, osteomyelite, etc., moteurs à ressort et électrique; 12 pp; **NYAM.**

n.d.   Description des appareils de chirurgie du docteur Th. de Martel pour la trepanation; 14 pp; **NYAM; MF/MAH.**

ALKALOL CO., THE
Taunton, Massachusetts.

n.d.   Alkalol, A Scientific Therapeutic Agent Based Upon Correct Physiologic Principles Adapted for Practical Use; 16 pp; **CPP.**

n.d.   Nature and Action; 4 pp; **CPP.**

n.d.   Facts About Alkalol; 7 pp; **CPP.**

n.d.   Helping the Cell to Help Itself; 32 pp; **CPP.**

n.d.   Alkalol; 16 pp; **CPP.**

ALLEN & HANBURYS, LTD.
Plough Court, Lombard Street, London, E.2. England.
(Surgical Engineering)
Est: 1715

1900   The "Allenburys" Foods; 16 pp; **CPP.**

1904   Catalogue of Aseptic Operating Theatre and Ward Requisites, etc., etc., Manufactured and Sold by Allen & Hanburys; viii, 112 pp; **WMScM** (VA.AU(2). 23123).

1905   Supplement to Catalogue of Surgical Instruments and Appliances; xii, 119 pp; **TMHM.**

ca 1910   Catalogue of Surgical Instruments and Appliances, Ward Requisites, Aseptic Hospital Furniture, etc., Manufactured and Sold by Allen & Hanburys; lxxii, 1464 pp; **WMScM** (77516 Va.AU(2)); **TMHM.**

n.d.   The "Allenburys" Series of Infants' Foods: On the Principle of a Progressive Dietary; 8 pp; **CPP.**

n.d.   "The Allenburys" Series of Infants Foods; 16 pp; **CPP.**

n.d.   Sect. 3; Orthopaedic Instruments and Equipment; 122 pp, index; **WMScM.**

48 Wigmore Street, Cavendish Square, London, England.

1911   General List of Drugs, Pharmaceuticals, and the Allenbury Specialties; 431 pp; **WMScM** (60570 11C(2)).

1912   Supplementary Catalogue no. 2 to A & H's Reference List of Surgical Instruments and Aseptic Hospital Furniture; 47 pp, index; **NLM** (W26 A425c).

ca 1914   Supplementary Catalogue to A & H's Reference List of Surgical Instruments and Aseptic Hospital Furniture; pp 3-109, index. **NLM** (W26 A425c).

1925   Abridged Catalogue of Surgical Instruments and Appliances, Aseptic Hospital Furniture and Electro-Medical Apparatus Manufactured by Allen & Hanburys, Ltd. (Price list inside cover); **WMScM.**

1930   A Reference List of Surgical Instruments and Medical Appliances, Orthopaedic and Deformity Apparatus, Hospital Furniture and Equipment,
Electro-Medical and Surgical Apparatus, etc.; 1056 pp, pp 1201-1848,
1848 A-D, 1849–1974; **BLEL.**

1930   A Reference List of Surgical Instruments and Medical Appliances, Orthopaedic and Deformity Apparatus, Hospital Furniture and Equipment,
Electro-Medical and Surgical Apparatus, etc.; (811 illustrations); lxxxix,
1974 pp, index; **WMScM** (VA.AU(2) 954100); **SBMC; BDA.**

1938   Catalogue of Surgical Instruments and Medical Appliances, Operation
Tables, Sterilizers, Hospital Equipment, etc.; 1064 pp, index; **NLM.**

n.d.   Catalog of Surgical Instruments and Appliances, **BDA.**

n.d.   Catalogue of Surgical Instruments and Appliances, Ward Requisites,
Aseptic Hospital Furniture, etc., Manufactured and sold by Allen &
Hanburys, Ltd.; **ACS** (U 6 A/A 432c).

37 Lombard Street, London, E. C. 3, England.

n.d.   Organotherapeutic Products; 36 pp; **CPP.**

U.S. Branch Office, 80 Warren Street, New York, New York.

n.d.   Bynal, the "Perfected" Malt and Oil, Mfg. by Allen and Hanburys; 8 pp;
CPP.

Clive Buildings, Calcutta, India.

n.d.   "Torch" Brand Glucose D with Orange and Calcium; 4 pp; **CPP.**

ALLWIN
England.

See: RICHARDS, SON & ALLWIN, LTD.

ALOE & HERNSTEIN
300 N. Fourth Street, St. Louis, Missouri.

"Western and Southern Agents for Geo. Tiemann & Co.'s Celebrated Instruments."

1879   Illustrated Catalogue and Price List of Surgical Instruments and
Appliances, Orthopaedical Apparatus, Trusses, etc., includes section on
"Veterinary Instruments of Every Description;" (pp 234-37); 256 pp;
AFMM.

ALOE, A. S., CO.
513 Olive Street, St. Louis, Missouri.

Est: 1860

1890   Catalogue of Superior Surgical Instruments and Physicians and Surgeons
Supplies; 1071 pp; **HDM.**

Corner Fourth & Olive Streets, St. Louis, Missouri.

pre–1891   Catalogue of Surgical Instruments and Physician's Supplies, 4th ed.; i-iv,
378 pp, index, **RCSL.**

1891   Illustrated and Priced Catalogue of Superior Surgical Instruments,
Physician's Supplies & Hospital Furnishings no. 6; 1946 pp; **MAH.**

415 North Broadway, St. Louis, Missouri.

ca 1894   Catalogue; 1071 pp; **WOC.**

1895   Aloes Illustrated and Priced Catalogue of Superior Surgical Instruments,
Physician's Supplies and Hospital Furnishings; 6th ed.; 1071 pp;
NYAM; MF/MAH; MAH (C610.78055); **SLSC; CS.**

1912   Catalog of Superior Surgical Instruments and Physicians' and Surgeons'
Supplies; 16th ed.; **SLSC.**

1918   What Electro Therapy Means to the Physician; 10 pp; **CPP.**

1819-23 Olive Street, St. Louis, Missouri.
    ca 1920   Surgical Instruments, Equipment and Supplies; 448 pp; **WOC; LLU** (W
              26 A453).
      1926   Bulletin no. 123, Surgical Instruments, Hospital Equipment and
              Supplies . . . .; 132 pp; fragile, back cover missing; **NLM.**
    1927–8?   Catalogue no. 120, Surgical Instruments, Equipment and Supplies for
              Physicians and Hospitals; **SLSC.**
      1928   Opportunity Bulletin, Surgical Instruments, Equipment, and Supplies for
              Physicians and Hospitals; no. 133; 100 pp, (Mail-order catalogue);
              NYAM, MF/MAH; HML.
      1929   Opportunity Bulletin no. 135, Surgical Instruments, Equipment for
              Physicians and Hospitals; 116 pp; **NYAM; MF/MAH; CPP** (Ed/75).
    ca 1935   Catalog no. 159, Surgical Instruments, Equipment and Supplies; 486 pp,
              index; **NLM** (W26 A425c); **CS.**
1819-21-23 Olive Street, St. Louis, Missouri.
      1929   Bulletin no. 137, Surgical Instruments, Equipment and Supplies; 116 pp;
              NYAM; MF/MAH.
      1929   Catalogues and Price Lists of Instruments, Medical and Surgical
              Instruments, Equipment and Supplies for Physicians and Hospitals;
              CPP; NYAM.
      1939   Surgical Equipment, Instruments and Supplies; no. 169 pp; 520 pp;
              WOC.
      n.d.   Treatment Book for Use in Connection with Violet Ray High Frequency
              Currents; 46 pp; **CPP.**
      n.d.   Catalogue no. 124, Surgical Instruments, Equipment and Supplies for
              Physcians and Hospitals; **SLSC.**
      19?   Aloe's Illustrated and Priced Catalogue of Superior Surgical Instruments,
              Physican's Supplies and Hospital Furnishings; **LC** (RD 76-A5).
    1900s?   Catalogue, Surgical Instruments, Equipment and Supplies; **JHIHM** (RD
              76A 453).
1831 Olive Street, St. Louis 3, Mo.
      1949   Hospital Catalogue 185; 810 pp; **WOC.**

ALPHA AND OMEGA
See: PARKER, STEARNS & SUTTON.

ALVERGNIAT FRÈRES
20 Passage de la Sorbonne, Paris, France.
      1873?   Catalogue et prix des instruments de chimie et de physiologie; 96 pp; **YB**
              (Uai Ae87).

AMERICAN AGEMA CORPORATION
263 Fifth Ave., New York, New York.
    ca 1926   Cystoscopic Instruments; 28 pp, (possibly 3 issues bound together);
              NYAM; MF/MAH.
      1927   Brochure, Cystoscopic Instruments, group of about 20 single page ads in
              paper binder, some ads headed "Cystoscope Monitor, Issued
              Occasionally by American Agema Corporation, Compiled by Letitia
              Harrison;" (TM: AGEMA); **NYAM.**

AMERICAN AND CONTINENTAL "SANITAS" CO. LTD., THE
636, 38, 40, 42 West 55th Street, New York, New York.
Bethnal Green, London, England.
    ca 1889   A Report on Certain Experiments Undertaken to Ascertain the

Disinfection and Germicidal Power of "Sanitas" Preparations and Appliances by A. B. Griffiths; 16 pp; **CPP.**

Jan. 1891 Reports on "Sanitas" together with the History, Description and Directions for Use of the Several Sanitas Antiseptics, Disinfectants, and Oxidants; 3rd ed.; 37 pp; **CPP.**

1895 How to Disinfect: A Guide by C. T. Kingzett; 96 pp; **CPPP.**

AMERICAN APOTHECARIES CO.
Astoria, 272 Flushing Avenue, New York, New York.

n.d. Of Ambrozvin; Renal, Vesical & Cutaneous Disorders; 16 pp; **CPP.**

n.d. Depurative Therapy; 16 pp; **CPP.**

n.d. The "Ins" and the "Outs" in Pathology; 16 pp; **CPP.**

n.d. Acidosis as a Causative Factor in Disease; 16 pp; **CPP.**

299 Ely Avenue, Long Island City, New York.

1905 The Balance Wheel of Life Metabolism; 26 pp; **CPP.**

n.d. The Therapy of Acid States; 12 p. **CPP.**

n.d. Ads for Salvitae, Ambrozoin, **CPP.**

AMERICAN ARTIFICIAL LIMB CO.
1609 Chestnut St., Philadelphia, Pennsylvania.
Astor Place, Broadway, New York, New York.
19 Green St., Boston, Massachusetts.

ca 1867 Pamphlet on Formation of Company; 48 pp; **CPP** (Bolenius Coll).

AMERICAN ASKANIA CORP.
Houston, Texas.
Chicago, IL.

1931 Askania Optical and Industrial Instruments; 8 pp; **URRR** (A-113).

Bambergwerk, Berlin-Friedenau.

n.d. Pruefinstrumente fuer die Untersuchung loser und gefasster Optik; 28 pp; **URRR** (A-116).

AMERICAN ATOMOS CORP.

1931? Catalogue, Cecil Plummer Oxygen Therapy Apparatus, description, use and photo; 10 pp; **MAH.**

AMERICAN CABINET COMPANY, THE
Two Rivers, Wisconsin.
Rahway, New Jersey.
Est: 1880

1920's Catalogue Number 12, Dental Office Furniture in Wood of Various Finishes; 95 pp, index pp 95; (TM) **NYAM.**

1920's Catalogue Number 13, Various Types of Dental Cabinets in Wood and Steel of Various Finishes . . .; 91 pp, index pp 91; (TM); **NYAM.**

1920's Brochure, New Articles of Furniture (Dental Cabinets); 7 pp foldout; (TM); **NYAM.**

ca 1920 Leaflet, New Articles of Furniture; 8 pp; **NYAM.**

ca 1920 American Dental Office Furniture; 95 pp, index pp 95, plus various loose advertisements; **NYAM.**

1921 Price List, Dental Office Furniture, identified in upper righthand corner as "Eastern"; 11 pp; **NYAM.**

AMERICAN CYSTOSCOPE MAKERS, INC.
450 Whitlock Avenue, New York, N.Y.

1929 Catalogue of Diagnostic Instruments, Eye, Ear, Nose, and Throat Section;

Back of title page is statement, "to facilitate the introduction of additional sheets, the pages of this section are numbered beginning with page 201," Unbound, section paper clipped together; pp 201-212, pages missing; (TM); **NYAM.**

n.d. Catalogue, Diagnostic Instruments, Vol. 1; Various pp; **JHIHM.**

AMERICAN DENTAL MANUFACTURING COMPANY
Broadway, Corner 37th Street, New York, New York.

1886 Catalogue of Dental Instruments and Materials; 80 pp, index pp 79-80; (TM); **MAH.**

1888 Appendix to Catalogue of Instruments and Materials; 25 pp; (TM); **MAH.**

AMERICAN DENTAL TRADE ASSOCIATION

1931 Fifty Years of the A.D.T.A., listing all its members, addresses, branches, establishment dates and membership entry dates; pp 124-136; **MAH** (photocopy).

AMERICAN DENTAPHONE CO.
Cincinnati, Ohio.

1879 Brochure, The Dentaphone, a New Scientific Innovation, which Enables the Deaf to Hear by the Sound Vibrations Conveyed Through the Medium of the Teeth, and the Deaf and the Dumb to Hear and Speak; 24 pp; **MAH.**

AMERICAN FERMENT CO., INC.
Caroid & Pharmaceutical Preparations, Lab: 81 Steuben Street, Jersey City, New Jersey.
1450 Broadway, New York, 18, NY.
Subsid. of Sterling Drug, Inc.

Dec. 16, '98 Four page letter and ad to Dr. Flick Extolling Virtues of Caroid; **CPP.**

1898 The Present Status of the Digestive Ferments; 16 pp; **CPP.**

ca 1898 Caroid; 16 pp; **CPP.**

ca 1899 Digestion, A Function of Plants as Well as of Animals; 4 pp; **CPP.**

ca 1900 Caroid in the Removal of Tattoo Marks; 32 pp; **CPP.**

Buffalo, New York.

ca 1923 Fifty Infants Treated with Caroid by Russell Pemberton, M.D.; 15 pp; **CPP.**

n.d. Essence of Caroid; 10 pp; **CPP.**

n.d. Caroid; 4 pp; **CPP.**

AMERICAN HOSPITAL APPLIANCE CO.
63 South Robert Street, Saint Paul, Minnesota.

ca 1928 Pamphlet foldout, The Foley Cysto-Urography Table, A Mechanically and Technically Perfect Table Designed Exclusively for Cystoscopy and X-Ray Examination of the Urinary Tract; 5 pp; **MAH.**

AMERICAN OPTICAL COMPANY
14 Mechanics Street, Southbridge, Massachusetts.
Est: 1833; Inc: 1869
See: SPENCER LENS CO.; **MAH.**
First published catalog in 1894; Company started by William Beecher, company names and dates are as follows: William Beecher, 1833–40; Ammidown & Putney, 1840–2; Ammidown & Son, 1842–9; Ammidown & Co., 1850–9; Beecher & Cole, 1860–2; Robert H. Cole & Co., 1862–9; American Optical Co. 1869–.

1894 Illustrated Catalogue of Spectacles and Eyeglasses . . .; 15 pp; **AO.**

Also: New York, Chicago, San Francisco, & no. 39 Hatton Garden, London.

1912   Catalogue, Spectacles, Eyeglasses, Lenses . . .; Contains history of the company, 1833–1912, pp 10-20 (illustrations) plus half tone photos of George W., Channing M., Albert B., and J. Cheney Wells, Pres., V. P., Treas. and Secretary, respectively; 347 pp, index pp 345-347; (TM); **NYAM, AO.**

1912?   Catalogue, American Optical Company, Spectacles, Eyeglasses, Lenses; 348 pp; (TM); **AO; YB** (UAI Am 347).

Factories at Southbridge, Worcester, Cambridge, Mass and Camden, N.J. Nicolet, P.Q., and Belleville, Ont. Sales: Hdq: 70 West 40th Street, N.Y., Branches in principal cities.

1925   Wellsworth-DeZeng Diagnostic Instruments, Ophthalmic Equipment and Trial Sets; 116 pp; **AO.**

Oct. 1928   Brochure, Tillyer Prescription Price List, TM: "Wellsworth" plus American Optical TM. "Tillyer lenses . . . are fully covered by trade marks and by patents until 1943;" 6 pp; **NYAM.**

1929   Catalogue, Solid White Gold Spectacleware; 14 pp; (TM); **NYAM.**

n.d.   Cruxite Lenses; 14 pp; **YB** (UAI Am 347).

n.d.   Catalogue of Spectacles and Eyeglasses in 8-K, 10-K and 14-K Gold, Platinum, Alumnico, Roman Alloy, German Silver, Filled Gold, Steel, Frameless, etc., etc., Lenses, Trial Sets and Material; 96 pp; **URRR.**

70 W. 40th St., New York, New York.

pre–1926   Wellsworth Souter's Tonometer, Gives Direct Readings of the Intraocular Tension; 4 pp; **YB** (UAI Am 347).

AMERICAN OXYGEN ASSOCIATION
119 East 28th Street, New York, New York.

1888   Illustrated Catalog and Price List of the American Oxygen Association of New York; 56 pp; **CPP.**

AMERICAN PEROXIDE AND CHEMICAL CO.
88 Maiden Lane, New York, New York.
Inc: in N.J., dissolved Aug. 27, 1906

Aug. 1902   Special Preparations of the American Peroxide and Chemical Co.; 37 pp; **CPP.**

n.d.   The Am. P. & C. Co.'s Peroxide of Hydrogen; 4 pp; **CPP.**

n.d.   Liquor Alkalinis cum Lithia "The Great Eliminant"; 4 pp; **CPP.**

n.d.   Liquor San; 4 pp; **CPP.**

n.d.   Peruvian Ointment; 4 pp; **CPP.**

n.d.   Parolum Liquid & Solid; 4 pp; **CPP.**

n.d.   Misteria Catecha Compound for the Treatment of Diarrhea and Dysentery; 4 pp; **CPP.**

n.d.   Stearate of Zinc Compound and Its Combinations; 4 pp; **CPP.**

AMERICAN PLASMON SYNDICATE LTD.
39-41 Astor Court Buildings, 18-20 West 34th Street, New York, New York.

Jun. 1900   Plasmon in a Case of Prolonged Enteric-Fever; 4 pp, reprint; **CPP.**

n.d.   Virchow's Report on Plasmon; 12 pp; **CPP.**

n.d.   Plasmon Nature's Nutrient; 32 pp; **CPP.**

n.d.   Plasmon Recipes; 4 pp; **CPP.**

n.d.   Plasmon Biscuits vs Ordinary Biscuits; 1 pp; **CPP.**

Plasmon Co. of America
116 Broad Street, New York, New York.

n.d.   A Few Hints for Using Plasmon; 13 pp; **CPP.**

n.d.   One Hundred Ways to Use Lasmon; 32 pp; **CPP.**

n.d.   Plasmon Nature's Nutrient Powder, Biscuits, Coca, Chocolate; 7 pp; **CPP.**

AMERICAN PHARMACOLOGIC SOCIETY, THE
New York.

1906   Bulletin no. 1, Working Bulletin for the Collective Investigation of the Somnos Brand of Trichlorethadene Propenyl Ether Recommended by H. K. Mulford Co.; 46 pp; **CPP.**

AMERICAN SPECTACLE CO.

1941   Absorb-O-Ray Planotoric Lenses, Sunglasses and Goggles Designed Especially for Sportsmen; 4 pp, date stamped; **URRR** (A-90).

AMERICAN STERILIZER COMPANY
Erie, Pennsylvania.

1927   Catalogue, Illustrated Sterilizers, Disinfectors; 60 pp, index; **MAH.**

AMERICAN SURGICAL CO.
Bridgeport, Montgomery County, Pennsylvania.
Inc: 1894

1895   Catalog and Price List of the ASC, Mfrs. and Exporters of Antiseptic Dressings, Surgical and Hospital Supplies, Druggists' Sundries, etc; 25 pp; **CPP.**

1899   Illustrated Catalog and Price List; 58 pp; **CPP.**

AMERICAN SURGICAL INSTRUMENT CO.
112-114 East 19th Street, New York, New York.

Jan. 1929   Illustrated Catalogue of Standard Surgical Instruments and Allied Lines; 458 pp, 34 pp index; **MAH** (27626).

AMERICAN VACUUM COMPANY
1001 Chesnut Street, Philadelphia, PA.

1930   Brochure, Original Muller X-Ray Tubes, Radiographic and Therapeutic, Imported by American Vacuum Co; 6 pp foldout; **ACR/MAH.**

n.d.   Leaflet, X-Ray Tubes, Plates, Films, etc., "Largest Stock of X-ray Plates and New Tubes in Philadelphia," "Immediate attention given Coolidge tube repairs;" 8 pp foldout; **ACR/MAH.**

AMERICAN X-RAY EQUIPMENT COMPANY
401-405 East 31st Street, New York, New York.
29 E. Madison Street, Chicago, Illinois.
See: ACME INTERNATIONAL X-RAY CO. and ENGELN ELECTRIC COMPANY.

1915   Catalogue A Dental X-Ray Apparatus and Accessories; 42 pp, index; **NYAM; MF/MAH.**

1916   Catalogue, Dental Electro-Therapeutic Appartus for High Frequency Treatment and Ionic Medication; 32 pp; **NYAM; MF/MAH.**

Mt. Vernon, New York.
50 E. 42nd Street, New York.
29 E. Madison Street, Chicago.
140 Geary Street, San Francisco.

1917   Catalogue Dental X-Ray Apparatus and Accessories; 55 pp, index pp 53-55; **NYAM; MF/MAH.**

AMMOND CHEMICAL CO.
36 East 14th Street Corner University Place, New York, New York.

1895   Ammonal Excerpta; 48 pp; **CPP.**

ca 1895　Ammonal is an Effective Malarial Germicide, Relieves Pain and Induces Sleep; 6 pp; **CPP.**

n.d.　Ammonal: The Stimulant, Antipyretic and Analgesic; 4 pp; **CPP.**

n.d.　Ammonal (Ammoniated-Phenylacetimade) Stimulant, Antipyretic and Analgesic; 4 pp; **CPP.**

AMSTERDAM BROTHERS
274 South 20th Street, Philadelphia, Pennsylvania.

n.d.　Foot Supports: Surgical and Orthopedic Appliances; 4 pp; **CPP.**

ANDERSON, NORDEN & COMPANY
Chicago, Illinois.

1907　Catalogue no. 10, Nelson Static Machines, and X-Ray Tubes and Apparatus; pp 3, 4, 5, 7, 8, 10, & 15 only; **ACR/MAH.**

1907　Catalogue no. 10, Filed under Nelson address: 18-30 W. Randolph Street, Chicago; 16 pp; **MAH.**

ANDREWS, WILLIAM, ARTIFICIAL SPECIALTIES, THE
30 East Bleachery St., Lowell, Massachusetts.

1913　Illustrated and Exemplified Catalogue of Artificial Specialties, "Manufacturer for U.S. Government"; 99 pp, price list; (TM); **MAH.**

ANGIER CHEMICAL CO.
Boston 34 Massachusetts.
32 & 33 Snow Hill, London E C, England.

1912　Danger Signals in Medical and Surgical Practice; 64 pp; **CPP.**

1915　A Study of the Therapeutics of Petroleum Oil; 32 pp; **CPP.**

1927　The Rational Treatment of Coughs; 16 pp; **CPP.**

1928　Intestinal Absorption and its Relation to Malnutrition; 16 pp; **CPP.**

1930　Angier's Emulsion; 4 pp; **CPP.**

n.d.　Phthisis, Bronchitis: Why Does Cod Liver Oil Fail?; 12 pp; **CPP.**

n.d.　The Efficiency of Angier's Emulsion in the Treatment of Influenza, Bronchitis, Coughs and Grippe; 11 pp; **CPP.**

n.d.　Why Angier's Emulsion Gives Superior Results to Clear Petroleum Oil in the Treatment of Constipation; 11 pp; **CPP.**

n.d.　Angier's Petroleum Emulsion; 4 pp; **CPP.**

n.d.　Constipation, A Practical Consideration of its Treatment by Mechanical Measures; 30 pp; **CPP.**

ANGLO-AMERICAN PHARMACEUTICAL CORP.
39a Tunworth Road, Croydon, London, England.
U.S. Agents: 30 North William Street, New York, New York.

n.d.　The Acid-Glycero-Phosphates by Edmund L. Gros; 14 pp; **CPP.**

n.d.　The Patent Medicine Question Versus Simple Remedies of Known Composition; name on cover: C. G. Dodson, 127 South 4th Street, Philadelphia, Pennsylvania; 12 pp; **CPP.**

n.d.　Calcium Therapy Excerpts from Current Medical Opinion; 12 pp; **CPP.**

n.d.　Why Does Betul-ol Relieve Pain?; 6 pp foldout; **CPP.**

n.d.　Huxley's Menthol & Wintergreen Cream Wintogen; 1 pp; **CPP.**

ANGLE, EDWARD H.
n.d.　E.H. Angles Patents; **UPSDM.**

ANON, GILLIS & GEOGHEGAN
New York.
Est: 1866

1896   Contains Photographs of Buildings that Use Steam Heaters, Offices,
         Hospitals, and Hotels; 40 pp; **NYAM; MF/MAH.**

ANTAOS-WERKE, G.M.B.H.
Dental-Fabrik, Brieffach, München 2, Germany.

1925   Catalogue of Operative and Technical Instruments for Cat. 3, Dentistry
         (Eng., Germ., Fr., Span.) 298 pp, index pp 272-299 (589 stamped on
         cover); **WMScM.**

1925   Price List, 1925/2 for Catalogue 1925 of Operative and Technical
         Instruments for Dentistry; 7 pp; **WMScM.**

ANTIKAMNIA CHEMICAL CO., THE
1723 Olive Street, St. Louis, Missouri.
British Office: 46 Holborn Viaduct, London E C.
French Office: 5 rue de la Paix, Paris, France.

Sep. 3, 1900   Superficial Palmas Arch Deep Palmer Arch Dorsal Blood Supply
                 Illustrated, "Possibly 9/10ths of the Contents of This Little Book Will
                 Be of No Value to You Today But What About That One Tenth?"; 12
                 pp; **CPP.**

Jan. 5, 1903   Diseases of the Nervous System and Muscles, Reference Chart (Hill's); 8
                 pp foldout; **CPP.**

n.d.   Antikamnia Tablets; 16 pp; **CPP.**

n.d.   The Coal-Tar Remedies; 1 pp; **CPP.**

n.d.   Antikamnia Preparations Distribution Centers; 1 pp; **CPP.**

n.d.   Regarding the Composition and Dosage of Antikamnia and Heroin
         Tablets; 2 pp; **CPP.**

n.d.   A Selection of Practical Prescriptions Alphabetically Arranged for Ready
         Reference; 32 pp; **CPP.**

n.d.   Antikamnia Action, History, Indications, Administration; 32 pp; **CPP.**

n.d.   "Good" AK Combinations; 4 pp foldout; **CPP.**

ANTON, H. M.
Berlin, Germany.

19–20 c   Illustrated Catalogue, Medical Devices, Syrups, Trusses, Atomizers, etc.;
            40 pp; **MAH.**

ARCHER MANUFACTURING COMPANY
5,7,9 N. Water Street, Rochester, New York.
Branch Office: 153 Centre St., New York.

1900?   Illustrated Price List of Archer's Patent Gynecological Chair, etc; 16 pp;
          NYAM; MF/MAH.

19–20 c   Brochure, Archer's Patent Gynecological Chair, etc.; 16 pp; (TM);
            NYAM.

ARCHER, GEORGE W.
Rochester, New York.

n.d.   Price List of Archer's Gynecological Chairs; **CPP.**

ARGOL CO., CHEMISTS, THE
Danbury, Connecticut.
Agents for Great Britain, Thomas Christy & Co., 25 Lime Street, London E C, England.

n.d.   Feralboid, A Peptonized Albuminate of Iron: Its History & Clinical Uses;
         14 pp; **CPP.**

n.d.   Lyptol, A Perfect Antiseptic Ointment for Surgical Uses; 2 pp; **CPP.**

n.d.   Lyptol, A Surgical Preparation; 6 pp; **CPP.**

ARLINGTON CHEMICAL CO., THE

Yonkers, New York.

See: PALISADES MANUFACTURING CO.

May 15, 1892   Decius Repetita Placebit (Phospho-Caffeine), Comic Book pamphlet; 30 pp; **CPP.**

1892   The Office Boy's Essay on Heads; Phospho-Caffein and Beef Peptonoids; 8 pp; **CPP.**

1894   Yankie Fie; 12 pp; **CPP.**

1899   Phosphorus & the Organic Phosphorized Compounds Phosphagon; 13 pp; **CPP.**

Oct. 27, 1914   A Clinical Report on Cultol; 2 pp; **CPP.**

1915   Intestinal Toxemia & its Effective Treatment with Cultol; 24 pp; **CPP.**

n.d.   Beef Peptonoids Phospho-Caffein Compound Series no. 2; **CPP.**

n.d.   Cultol, A Pharmaceutical Achievement; 22 pp, foldout; **CPP.**

n.d.   Arlco-Pollen Extracts; 4 pp; **CPP.**

n.d.   The Doctor in Fiction being Brief Outlines of the Characteristics of Doctors as Presented by Authors of International Fame; Ad for Peptonoids; **CPP.**

n.d.   Pathogonomy of Pain—Some Suggestions Relative to the Diagnostic Significance of Pain as a Symptom and Its Interpretation; 28 pp; **CPP.**

n.d.   Liquid Peptonoids in Cholera Infantum; 5 pp; **CPP.**

n.d.   List of Preparations Mfg. by New York Pharmacal Association; **CPP.**

n.d.   Aseptic Nutrition in Intestinal Toxemia; 2 pp; **CPP.**

n.d.   Milk Mishaps in Typhoid; 2 pp; **CPP.**

n.d.   Seasonable Suggestions; 3 pp; **CPP.**

n.d.   In the Diet Lurks the Germ; 2 pp foldout; **CPP.**

n.d.   Follow the Rule; 8 pp foldout; **CPP.**

n.d.   Instruction Leaflets for Tuberculin Patients to be torn out and left with patient (perforated); **CPP.**

ARMOUR & CO.

The Armour Laboratory, Chicago, Illinois.
59 & 60 Tooley Street, London, England.

Est: 1885

Apr. 1892   Armour's Essence of Pepsin; 2 pp; **CPP.**

1893   Products of the Armour Laboratory: The Digestive Ferments and Their Uses in Medicine and Surgery; 71 pp; **CPP.**

Nov. 1, 1895   Price List Brochure; 6 pp foldout, **CPP.**

1895   Influence of the thyroid gland on Nutrition; **CPP.**

1898   Organotherapy no. 2; **CPP.**

Jan. 14, 1899   Organotherapy no. 3; **CPP.**

n.d.   Organotherapy no. 4; **CPP.**

n.d.   Organotherapy no. 5; **CPP.**

July 1899   Organotherapy no. 6; **CPP.**

Aug. 18, 1900   Organotherapy no. 9; **CPP.**

post 1914   Pituitary Liquid; 16 pp; **CPP.**

July 28, 1922   Suprarenalin (Epinephrin); 4 pp; **CPP.**

1425 W. 42nd St., Chicago 9, Illinois.

n.d.   Suprarenalin & the Suprarenal Preparations; 59 pp; **CPP.**

n.d.   Pancreatin & Soda Tablets; 4 pp; **CPP.**

n.d.   Nutrient Wine of Beef Peptone; 3 pp; **CPP.**

n.d.   Parotid Gland Extract in the Treatment of Disease; 4 pp; **CPP.**

n.d. Suprarenalin Inhalant; 1 pp; **CPP.**

n.d. Suprarenalin Solution 1-1000, Ideal Astringent, Hemostatic and Heart Stimulant; 4 pp, foldout; **CPP.**

n.d. Suprarenal Therapy in Hay Fever; 2 pp; **CPP.**

n.d. Foods for the Invalid; 4 pp; **CPP.**

n.d. Culinary Wrinkles by Helen Louise Johnson: Recipes and Directions for the Use of Armour's Extract of Beef; 47 pp; **CPP.**

n.d. Extract of the Mammary Gland; 2 pp; **CPP.**

n.d. Extract of the Red Bone Marrow; 2 pp; **CPP.**

n.d. Eucapren Astringent and Anesthetic; 3 pp; **CPP.**

n.d. Aqueous Extract of Suprarenal Capsules; 2 pp; **CPP.**

n.d. Bone Marrow in Tuberculosis; 3 pp; **CPP.**

n.d. Parotid Gland Extract in the Treatment of Disease; 2 pp; **CPP.**

n.d. Thyroid Therapy; 15 pp; **CPP.**

ARMSTRONG, WILLIAM H., & CO.
Indianapolis, Indiana.

1894 Catalogue, Illustrated and Prices of Surgical Instruments, Orthopaedic Appliances, and Hospital Supplies; 3rd ed.; xv, 604 pp; **UTP; WOC; AFMM; LACMA; HDM.**

1901 Catalogue of Surgical Instruments, Deformity Apparatus, Aseptic Furniture, and Hospital Supplies; 4th ed.; 800 pp; **UWL** (QGX.AR5); on cover: N. W. Mallery, San Francisco, California, **BLEL.**

ARNOLD, JAMES
See: ARNOLD & SONS, London.

1852 A Catalogue of Goods; 36 pp; **WMScM.**

1854? With manuscript corrections, Date on cover altered to 1854; **WMScM.**

n.d. Illustrated Catalogue of Medical Instruments, prices in English pounds, Instrument Maker of Royal Veterinary College; **MAH.**

ARNOLD & SONS
London, England.
Est: 1819
See: JAMES ARNOLD and BELL & CROYDEN.

ca 1865 A List of Veterinary Instruments; 20 pp; **WMScM** (X.AU[2]).

1870? A List of Veterinary Instruments; 27 pp; **WMScM** (X.AU[2]).

1873 A Catalogue of Surgical Instruments; iii-iv, v-xx index, 256 pp; **WMScM;** 192 pp; **TMHM.**

1873 A Catalogue of Surgical Instruments; xx, 224 pp; **WMScM** (320642).

1874 A Catalogue of Veterinary Instruments; 56 pp; **WMScM** (X.AU[2]).

1876 A Catalogue of Surgical Instruments; xxiv, 368 pp; **WMScM;** 403 pp; **TMHM.**

1880 Catalogue of Surgical Instruments; 390 pp; **WMScM.**

1882 A List of Veterinary Instruments; viii, 125 pp; **WMScM** (X.AU[2]).

1885 A List of Veterinary Instruments; xi, 153 pp; **WMScM** (X.au[2]).

1885 A Catalogue of Surgical Instruments; xxvi, 660 pp; **WMScM** (V.AU.).

1886 A List of Veterinary Instruments; xi, 153 pp; **WMScM.**

1893 Catalogue, Veterinary Instruments Manufactured by Arnold & Sons; 667 pp; **WMScM.**

31, West Smithfield & 1, 2, & 3 Gittspur St., London, England.

1893 List of Field Equipments Manufactured by Arnold & Sons; 34 pp; **WMScM.**

1893 List of Veterinary Instruments; viii, 216 pp; **WMScM.**

1895	Catalogue of Surgical Instruments and Appliances; 818 pp; **WMScM.**
Mar. 1895	Catalogue of Surgical Instruments and Appliances; ix-xlvii index, 848 pp; **WMScM; BLEL.**
1895	List of Veterinary Specialties; 22 pp; **WMScM.**
1897	Catalogue of Aseptic Hospital Requisites; 70 pp; **WMScM.**

26, 30 & 31 West Smithfield, 1, 2, & 3 Gittspur St., London.

1898	Catalogue of Aesptic Hospital Requisites, Surgical Instruments, Manufacturers; 138 pp, index; **RCSL.**
n.d.	Insert: Extra Section on Hearing Trumpets, Conversation Tubes; 4 pp; **RCSL.**
1899	Catalogue of Nurses' Requisites; 94 pp; (front illustrated); **WMScM.**
1899	List of Surgical Appliances Manufactured by Arnold & Sons; 52 pp; **WMScM.**
1895	List of Surgical Appliances Manufactured by Arnold & Sons; New display pictured; **WMScM.**
1902	Catalogue of Veterinary Appliances, etc.; 88 pp; **WMScM** (X.AU[2]).
1902	Catalogue of Specialties; 80 pp; **WMScM.**
1902	List of Surgical Appliances; cover torn; 75 pp; **RCSL.**
1902?	Catalogue of Veterinary Instruments and Appliances; viii, 303 pp; **WMScm** (X.AU).
1904	Catalogue of Surgical Instruments and Appliances; pref, index iii-lxvi, 1864 pp, 22 pictures, 37 gold medals; **WMScM; BLEL.**
n.d.	Supplementary Catalogue of Surgical Instruments, etc.; 180 pp; 1904 first supplement; **RCSL.**
1904	Supplementary Catalogue of Surgical Instruments, etc.; Second supplement; 122 pp; **RCSL.**
1906	Catalogue of Opthalmic Instruments; xvi, 79 pp; **WMScM.**
ca 1915	Catalogue of Surgical Appliances; 100 pp; **NLM.**
ca 1919	Catalogue of Surgical Instruments and Appliances; pref iii-iv, index v-lxvi, 1864 pp; (2 pictures foldout); **WMScM.**
1933	Catalogue of Syringes, Aspirators, and Enemas; 76 pp; **NLM.**
n.d.	No title page, Therapeutic and Gynecological Instruments, Women's Disease Treatment; 20 pp; **WMScM.**
n.d.	Catalogue of Asesptic Hospital Requirements; 138 pp; **WMScM.**
n.d.	No title page; 40 pp; **WMScM.**
n.d.	No title page; 20 pp; **WMScM.**
n.d.	No title page, Splints; 40 pp; **WMScM.**
n.d.	No title page, Surgical and Obstetric Instruments; 32 pp; **WMScM.**
n.d.	No title page, Aseptic Instruments; 16 pp; **WMScM.**
n.d.	No title page, Operating Instruments; 24 pp; **WMScM** (H XV19/a).
n.d.	Catalogue of Nurses Requisites; 94 pp; (pages have graph sheets below); **RCSL.**

26, 30 & 31 West Smithfield, 1, 2 & 3 Gittspurt St., London.

| n.d. | Improved High Pressure Steam Sterilizer for Dressings, Instruments, Clothing, and Bedding; 16 pp; Suggested by W. Bruce Clark, F.R.C.S. Also at 42, Beaumont St. Weymouth St. W., Factory 14, 15, & 16 Bishops Court, Old Bailey Warehouse: Little Britain, E.C.; **RCSL.** |

ARROW SUPPLY AND IMPORTING COMPANY
New York, New York.

| 1930 | Catalogue, Tools and Supplies for Dentists and Dental Laboratories, 138 pp; **UPSDM.** |

ART-CRAFT OPTICAL CO.
Rochester, New York.
>1935 Artcraft Frames and Mountings; 40 pp; **URRR** (A-110).
>1937 Artcraft Frames and Mountings; 48 pp; **URRR** (A-111).

ARTIFICIAL LIMB MFG. CO.
909 Penn Ave., Pittsburgh, Pennsylvania.
>1893 Catalogue of Trusses, Limbs, Elastic Stockings, Supporters, Surgical Instruments; 328 pp, 8 pp appendix, index, **UVHSL** (RD 76.A77); **MAH.** (photocopy).

ASH, CLAUDIUS & SONS
7, 8, & 9 Broad Street, Golden Square, London, England.
Amalgamated Dental Co., Ltd., after 1930.
Est: 1886 in U.S.
See: ARTHUR S. UNDERWOOD.
>1858 Catalogue; **BDA.**
>1871 Catalogue of Artificial Teeth, Dental Materials, Instruments, Tools, and Furniture; **BDA.**
>1871 Catalogue, Artificial Teeth, Dental Materials, Instruments, Tools, Furniture, etc . . .; 201 pp; **UPSDM; MAH.**
>1871 A Catalogue of Artificial Teeth, Dental Materials, Instruments, Tools, Furniture, etc., Manufactured, Imported, and Sold by . . .; 302 pp, contents 6-8; **RCSL.**
>1873 Appendix to C. Ash & Sons Catalogue of 1871; pp 207-261, index pp 240-261; **RCSL; MAH.**
>1875 A Catalogue of Artificial Teeth, Dental Materials, Instruments, Tools, Furniture, etc.; 3rd ed.; 302 pp, index pp 279-302; **NYAM; MF/MAH; HDM.**
>1878 Catalogue, dents artificielles, matériaux dentaires, instruments, outils, meubles, etc.; 299 pp; **UPSDM.**
>1880 A Catalogue of Artificial Teeth, Dental Materials, Instruments, Tools, Furniture, etc., Manufactured, Imported, and Sold by . . .; 2nd ed.; 302 pp; **UBML; BDA; RCSL.**
>July 1882 Appendix to 1875 Catalogue; 3rd ed.; 48 pp, bound together; **MAH.**
>1899 Catalogue of Dental Materials . . .; various pp; **MAH; BLEL.**
>1901 Forceps, Elevators, Lancets, Mouth Mirrors, Tweezers, Syringes, Instrument Cases, etc.; **CS.**
>1912 Illustrated Catalogue of Ash's Mineral Teeth; 178 pp; **HDM.**
>1921 A Century of Dental Art, A Centenary Memoir 1820-1921; 64 pp; **ABD.**

ASHMEAD, JAMES H., & SONS
Hartford, CT.
Est: Gold Foil Dept by J. H. Ashmead, 1839.
Est: Dental Depot by James Ashmead and Sons, 1867.
>1868 Dental Catalogue; 103 pp; **MAH** (C 617.6085).

AUBREY, A.
6 Boulevard Saint-Michel, Paris, France.
Est: 1832
>1900 Fabricant d'instruments de chirurgie, orthopédie, bandages, ceintures sciences, hygiène, histoire naturelle, chirurgie vétérinaire, coutellerie fine; 324 pp; **UCSF.**

AULDE, JOHN DR.
Edgand Farm, Kennett Square, Pennsylvania.
The Aulde Chemical Co.
1305 Arch Street, Philadelphia, Pennsylvania.

    1898   Dyspepsin, Its Causation & Systemic Effects, A Study in Reconstruction Metamorphosis, Physical and Physiological Cellular Therapeutics; 72 pp; **CPP.**

    1901   Nuclein Solution, An Epitome of Its Clinical Application Alphabetically Arranged; 24 pp; **CPP.**

    1903   Therapeutic Guide in Physiological Medication; 15 pp; **CPP.**

    1903   Manual of Physiological Cell Medication; 72 pp; **CPP.**

    1906   The Blue Book for Students and Practitioners; 128 pp; **CPP.**

    n.d.   Hepatin; 4 pp; **CPP.**

B. B. W. MANUFACTURING CO., INC.
251 W. 19th Street, New York.

    1924   The House with a Purpose; 23 pp; **AO.**

BABCOCK, L. A.

    n.d.   Silver Uterine Supporter; **CPP** (Bolenius Col).

BACHELET, ÉMILE
134 South Clifton Street, Kretschmer, New York.
The Bachelet General Magnet Co.
1107 Flat Iron Building, New York, New York.

    1906   The Bachelet Magnetic Wave Generators and Their Use in the Cure of Diseases; 15 pp; **CPP.**

    1908   Bachelet Therapuetic Co-Acting Magnetic Wave Generators and Their Use in the Treatment of Disease; revised ed.; 11 pp; **CPP.**

BAILEY, W. H., & SON, LTD.
38 Oxford Street, 2 Rathbone Place, London, England.
Est: 1833

    E. 20 c   A Catalog of Surgical Instruments and Appliances for Sick Nursing; 161 pp, index; **WMScM.**

    n.d.   Hospital Furniture; 162 pp; **MAH** (0666).

BAIRD & TATLOCK
14 Cross St., Hatton Garden, Holborn, London, E.C.
Factory: Walthamston.

    1898   Price List of Physical Apparatus manufactured by . . .; 226 pp, index, pp 72-88 on sound; **WMScM.**

    1903   Trenner's Formaldehyde Disinfector; 27 pp, ads for other apparatus; **NYAM; MF/MAH.**

    1903   Brochure, Trenner's Formaldehyde Disenfector, Patented and Patent Pend.; 27 pp; **NYAM.**

    1912   Catalogue, Price List of Apparatus for Experiments in Practical Physics; 650 pp, illustrated, index pp 625-650; (TM); **NYAM.**

    1922   Standard Catalogue Vol. II of Physiological, Histological, and Biochemical Apparatus, and Instruments; 482 pp, index pp 469-482; (TM); **NYAM.**

    1924   Pure Chemicals, Reagents and Stains, includes enormous chart of all the catalogs they published; 63 pp; (TM); **NYAM; MF/MAH.**

    Oct. 1924   Catalogue no.3, Pure Chemicals, Reagents and Stains; 63 pp; (TM); **NYAM.**

BAKER & ADAMSON LABORATORY REAGENTS
See: ALLIED CHEMICAL, GENERAL CHEMICAL DIVISION; **MAH.**

BAKER AND CO. (OR BAKER PLATINUM WORKS)
408, 410, 412, 414 N.J. Railroad Ave., Newark, New Jersey.
120 Liberty St., New York, New York.
> 1900   Gold, Silver and Platinum Refiners, Assayers and Sweep Smelters, for use by dentists; 7th ed.; 56 pp; **NYAM; MF/MAH.**

54 Austin St., Newark, N.J.
> 1935   Baker Orthodontic Appliances and Materials; 19 pp, 4 pp price list; **NYAM; MF/MAH.**

BAKER, C.
243 and 244 High Holborn, London, England.
Est: 1765
See: AMERICAN OPTICAL COMPANY; **AFMM.**
> ca 1884   A Catalogue of Achromatic Microscopes, Object Glasses, and Apparatus, Materials, and Instruments for Collecting, Preparing, Mounting, etc.; 16 pp; **MUM** (AA60 pam 9c).
> 1890   Catalogue of Surgical Instruments, Apparatus and Appliances; 64 pp; **NLM** (W26 q B168).
> ca 1900   Optical and Surgical Instrument Warehouse; **WMScM.**
> 1932   Microscopes and Accessories; 112 pp; **URRR** (B-432).

BAKER ELECTRICAL CO., THE
Hartford, Conn.
> ca 1905   Electro Therapeutical Apparatus, including X-Ray Tubes; 31 pp; **ACR/MAH.**

BAKER X-RAY CO.
438 Asylum Street, Hartford, Conn.
> ca 1905   Leaflet, pocket, Baker Water Cooled Tungsten Target Tube, patented and pat. applied for, and Baker Heavy Anode Tungsten Target Tube; 4 pp; **ACR/MAH.**

BALTIMORE BIOLOGICAL LABORATORY
See: BECTON, DICKENSON AND CO., BIOQUEST, Div. of; **MAH.**

BANNING, EDMUND P(RIOR), M.D.
New York.
> 1868   A Rational Treatise on the Trunkal Muscles, Elucidating the Mechanical Cause of Spinal Pelvic, Abdominal, and Thoracic Affections . . . With the Rationale of Their Cure by Mechanical Support (trusses); xvi, 352 pp; **LC** (RD71.B2); **LLU** (WBJ B219r 1868).

BANTAM, JOHN
3 Fox–Home 7 Fox, (1837) Home 35 North Pearl, (1841) 2 Canal–home 64 Pearl, Albany, New York.
> 1833–41   Cutler and Whitesmith listed in Albany City Directory.

BARKER, JAMES
99 Regent St. W., London
> 1906   Barker Vibrator, Rec'd 1906 in ink; 24 pp, 7 pp photocopied; **MAH; WMScM.**

BARKER VIBRATOR
See: JAMES BARKER; **WMScM.**

BARNES, A. C., CO.
24 North 40th Street, Philadelphia, Pennsylvania.
  BARNES & HILLE
32 Snow Hill, London E C, England.
ca 1903	About Silver; 16 pp; **CPP.**
ca 1903	An Important Advance Argyrol; 16 pp; **CPP.**
Dec. 17, '04	An Important Advance in Iron Therapy Ovoferrin; 6 pp; **CPP.**
Dec. 1905	A Fifteen Months' Study of Ovoferrin in the Clinics of Dr. M. Litten of Berlin and Dr. F. Klemperer; 16 pp; **CPP.**
ca 1905	What is the Practice of the Leading Surgeons as Stated in the Latest Textbooks, the Published Proceedings of Scientific Societies, the High Class Medical Journals, in Treating Gonorrhea, Purulent Ophthalmia and Other Inflammations of the Genito-Urinary Organs, the Eye, Ear, Nose and Throat?; 16 pp; **CPP.**
1908	An Unique Record Argyrol; 16 pp; **CPP.**
ca 1925	Why Ovoferrin Has Been in Constant Daily Use in Large Hospitals and Dispensaries for Over 25 Years as the Perfect General Tonic in Nervous Exhaustion, Convalescence, Loss of Appetite, Anaemia, Malnutrition; **CPP.**
n.d.	To Determine the Clinical Value of Argyrol as a Germicide; 4 pp; **CPP.**
n.d.	The Safety of Argyrol; 4 pp; **CPP.**
n.d.	The Unique Clinical Value of Argyrol; 4 pp; **CPP.**
n.d.	Argyrol Eight Years' World-wide Experience; 13 pp; **CPP.**

BARTON MANUFACTURING CO.
338 Broadway, New York, New York.
ca 1900	Medical Outline Stamps for Recording Cases; 8 pp, **NYAM; MF/MAH.**

BATH & CO.
No. 399 Oxford St. (corner of Dean St.), Soho, London, England.
n.d.	Folio of medical advertisements; **BRML,** in Miss Banks Collection (LR 301 h3).

BATTLE & CO.
4026-28 Olive St., St Louis, Missouri.
2001 Locust St., Philadelphia, Pennsylvania.
76 New Bond Street, London W, England.
9 & 10 Dalhousie Square, Calcutta, India.
80 Montague-de-la-tour, Brussels, Belgium.
28 Nieuwe Haagstraat, Amsterdam.
1885	Professional Opinions of Bromidia; 31 pp; **CPP.**
ca 1886	Relief: Papine the Anodyne; 40 pp; **CPP.**
Aug. 1896	The Blood and Its Diseases, by D. S. Maddox; 8 pp; **CPP.**
ca 1890	Sommeil Bromide the Hypnotic; 40 pp; **CPP.**
ca 1893	Papine in America; 32 pp; **CPP.**
ca 1893	The Standard Anodyne Papiner; 32 pp; **CPP.**
Nov. 1894	Anodyne—Papine; 18 pp; **CPP.**
Nov. 1895	Scrofula; 18 pp; **CPP.**
1895	Iodia as a Remedy in Syphilis; 8 pp; **CPP.**
Aug. 1896	Pain, Its Importance and Therapeutics; 8 pp; **CPP.**
Nov. 1896	The Value of Certain Drugs in Combination: Curran Pope; 8 pp; **CPP.**
Aug. 1897	Opium; 8 pp; **CPP.**
Nov. 1897	Traumatic Tetanus; 16 pp; **CPP.**
Feb. 1899	On Ecthol; 16 pp; **CPP.**

Feb. 1899	Trigeminal Neuralgia; 16 pp; **CPP.**
May 1899	Anodyne, Pain, and its Remedy by J. D. Albright; 8 pp; **CPP.**
May 1899	Hypnotic: The Study of the Perfect Hypnotic by Wm H. Morse; 8 pp; **CPP.**
May 1899	Antipurulent (Scrofula) by S.C. Martin; 8 pp; **CPP.**
May 1899	Alteratives; 8 pp; **CPP.**
Aug. 1899	Tuberculosis and Carbuncles, no. 3; 8 pp; **CPP.**
Nov. 1899	Blood Dyscrasia, no. 6; 16 pp; **CPP.**
Nov. 1899	Malarial, Neuralgia, and Puerperal Eclampsia, no. 5; 8 pp; **CPP.**
Feb. 1900	Erysipelas: Treatment; 8 pp; **CPP.**
Feb. 1900	Alterative Treatment; 8 pp; **CPP.**
n.d.	Diet Chart for Chronic Dilatation of the Stomach; 14 pp; **CPP.**
n.d.	Functional Diagnosis with a Word as to Treatment; 16 pp; **CPP.**
n.d.	Intestinal Infections of Children; 14 pp; **NYAM; MF/MAH.**
n.d.	The Tools of the Craft; 14 pp; **CPP.**
n.d.	Verdicts from Clinical Evidence, Nerve Sedation, Satisfactory Analgesia; 15 pp; **CPP.**
n.d.	Clinical Experiences vs Test Tube Experiments; 16 pp; **CPP.**
n.d.	Modern Therapy in Surgical Practice; 14 pp; **CPP.**
n.d.	The Growing Scope of the General Practitioner in Special Therapy; 14 pp; **CPP.**
n.d.	Surgical Therapeutics: The Application of Drug Therapy to Surgical Cases; 16 pp; **CPP.**
n.d.	Forcep Deliveries and Versions; 23 pp; **CPP.**
n.d.	The Child in Medicine; 21 pp; **CPP.**
n.d.	The Modern States of Goitre; 20 pp; **CPP.**
n.d.	Recent Advances in Dietetics; 20 pp; **CPP.**
n.d.	Pain as a Symptom in the Chest, Abdomen & Pelvis; 16 pp; **CPP.**
n.d.	Modern Aspects of Syphilis; 16 pp; **CPP.**
n.d.	Blood Pressure its Measurement, Interpretation and Management; 18 pp; **CPP.**
n.d.	Some of the More Common Ailments Encountered in General Practice; 13 pp; **CPP.**
n.d.	Sleep; 64 pp; **CPP.**
n.d.	All of Above Advertise Papine, Bromidia, Ecthol, Iodia; **CPP.**
1924	Some of the More Common Ailments Encountered in General Practice; stamped with this date; 14 pp; **CPP.**

BATTLE CREEK HEALTH BUILDER
See: SANITARIUM EQUIPMENT COMPANY; **NYAM.**

BATTLE CREEK SANITARIUM FOOD CO., THE
Battle Creek, Michigan.
Est: 1876

1903	Do You Want to Know?; 8 pp; **CPP.**
1905	The Battle Creek Diet List; 45 pp; **CPP.**
n.d.	Toasted Wheat Flakes; 4 pp; **CPP.**
n.d.	Diet in Diabetes; 32 pp; **CPP.**
n.d.	The Photophone; 4 pp; **CPP.**
n.d.	Prepared Foods; 4 pp; **CPP.**
n.d.	A Brochure on the Battle Creek Sanitarium Food Idea; 32 pp; **CPP.**
n.d.	Diabetes; 31 pp; **CPP.**
n.d.	Undigested Cereals the Cause of American Dyspepsia; 16 pp; **CPP.**

1924   Healthful Living, Fundamental Facts About Food and Feeding, name on
cover: E. Bradford Clarke Co., 1520 Chestnut Street, Philadelphia, Pa.;
47 pp; **CPP.**

BAUDIN
Paris, France.

n.d.   Prix courant des instruments de physique et de metéorologie construits et
graduée, par Baudin . . .; 7 pp; **CPP** (Pam/F 87).

BAUER & BLACK
Chicago, Illinois.
Bauer & Black, Div. Kendall Co.
2500 S. Dearborn St., Chicago 16, Illinois.
Est: 1893

1905   Catalog Medicinal Plasters, Surgical Plasters, Absorbent Cottons, Surgical
Dressing Ligatures, Suspensories, Chamois Vests and Chest Protectors;
39 pp; **CPP.**

BAUSCH & LOMB OPTICAL CO.
37 Maiden Lane, New York, New York.
130 Fulton Street. P. O. Box 432, New York, New York.
179 & 181 N. St Paul St. and 515-543 North St. Paul St.; P.O. Box 354. Rochester,
New York (factory).
Branch and Warerooms: Fulton Bldg., 130 Fulton, corner Nassau St., N.Y.C.
Est: 1853
John Jacob Bausch opens store at 20 Arcade, Rochester in 1853 after immigrating to U.S.,
develops first power lens grinding machine in 1861. In 1867, moves to Waters & Andrews Street.
In 1872 makes first B & L microscope.
See: CHAS. LENTZ & SON; **AFMM.**

1877   Catalogue, Price List of Microscopes, 16 pp; **CTY/B** (Uai B329).

1879   Microscopes, Objectives & Accessories; 36 pp; **CTY/B** (Uai B329).

1880   Catalogue, Condensed Price List of Microscopes, Objectives and
Accessories; 5th ed.; **CTY/B** (Uai B329); **YB.**

1883   Catalogue of Microscopes, Objectives, and Accessories and Other Optical
Instruments; 7th ed.; 46 pp; **MAH;** (C681.4085 B187 pri).

1884   Catalogue of Microscopes, Objectives and Accessories, and Other Optical
Instruments; 9th ed.; 64 pp; **MAH.**

1887   Illustrated Catalogue of Microscopes, Objectives, and Accessories; 11 ed.;
98 pp, Name "H. Bausch" stamped in gold on cover; **AFMM; CTY/B**
(Uai B329).

Jan. 1889   B & L Optical Co. Rapid Universal and Wide Angle Photographic
Objectives and Diaphram Shutter; 7 pp; **MUM** (AA 60 pan 20).

Mar. 1889   Supplementary Catalogue of Microscopes, Objects and Eyepieces
Manufacturered by B & L Optical Co.,; 40 pp; **MUM** (AA 60 pam
21).

1889   Illustrated Catalogue of Microscopes, Objectives and Accessories; 12th ed.;
110 pp, index, **AFMM; MUM** (AA 60 pam 19).

1892   Illustrated Catalogue of Microscopes, Objectives and Accessories. 13th ed.;
117 pp, biblio., index; **AFMM.**

1893   Catalogue of Microscopes, Objectives and Accessories, Microtomes,
Apparatus for Columbian Photo-Micrography and Bacteriology,
"Columbian Edition"; 14th ed.; 133 pp, index; **AFMM; HDM.**

Sep. 1894   Second Supplement to Catalogue of Microscopes. Columbian ed.; 14th
ed.; 22 pp; **CTY/B** (Uai B329).

1895 Eyeglasses, Lenses, Magnifiers, Readers and Other Optical Instruments, 9th ed.; 79 pp; **AO.**

1895 "An Explanation." 4 pp; Explaining why B&L was late with deliveries to schools of the BB Continental microscope; lists universities and colleges using B & L microscopes (explanation photocopied); **NYAM; MF/MAH.**

1895 Appendix to 1893 Columbian ed., Embodying 1st and 2nd Supplements to Microscope Catalogue; 48 pp; **AFMM; CPP.**

1896 Microscopes, Microtomes, Apparatus for Photo-Micrography and Bacteriology, Laboratory Supplies; 15th ed.; 256 pp, index, **AFMM; MAH** (C681.4085 B187m); **CTY/B** (Sh15 228d).

1898 Supplement to 1896, 15th ed., Microscope Catalogue; 40 pp, **AFMM; CPP.**

1899 Catalogue B, Microtomes and Accessories; 16th ed.; 24 pp; **CTY/B** (Uai B 329).

1900 Catalogue A, Microscopes and Accessories; 16th ed.; 186 pp; **AFMM; MAH** (C 681.4085 B187m); **CTY/B** (Sh 15 228e).

Aug. 1900 Catalogue E, Bacteriological Apparatus; 163 pp; **HDM; CTY/B** (Uai B 329).

1904 Catalogue F, Apparatus and Supplies for Chemical and Biological Laboratories; 438 pp; **CTY/B** (UAI B 329); **HDM.**

1904 Catalogue A, Microscopes and Accessory Apparatus; 17th ed.; 79 pp, index; Revised Price List 1905; 4 pp; **AFMM, MAH** (C681.4085 B187 mid).

1905 Revised Price List Microscopes & Accessories, Supplement to Catatlogue A; 4 pp; **CTY/B** (UAI B 329).

n.d. Microscopes and Accessories; 48 pp; **AFMM.**

Branches: Broadway & 25th St., New York.

120 Boylston St., Boston.

156 Wabash Ave., Chicago.

1629 Geary St., San Francisco.

606 13th St., N.W., Washington, D.C.

1906 Lenses, Their History, Theory and Manufacture; 47 pp; **AO.**

1906 Catalog A, Microscopes and Accessory Apparatus; 80 pp; **AFMM.**

1907 Catalog A, Microscopes and Accessory Apparatus; 19th ed.; 79 pp, index; **MAH** (C681.4085 B); **AFMM.**

1908 A Triple Alliance in Optics, Being the Association of Bausch and Lomb Optical Co., Carl Zeiss, Optical Works, Jena, and George N. Saegmulller, Under the Name of Bausch and Lomb Optical Co., Rochester, N.Y.; 31 pp; **AO.**

1908 Microscopes and Accessories; 19th ed.; 71 pp, index; **MAH** (C681.4085 B); **AFMM.**

1908 Microtomes and Accessories; 18th ed.; 22 pp; **NYAM; MF/MAH.**

1908 Apparatus for Photo-Micrography; 24 pp; **AFMM.**

1909 *PRISM*, A Little Magazine concerning that World of Wonder and Beauty Revealed by the Lens, April, Vol. LL; no. 11; 14 pp; **AO.**

1909 Catalogue A; 186 pp; **MUM.**

1909 Catalogue of Photo-Engravers' Optical Accessories; 19 pp; **AFMM.**

1910 Brochure, Project Lenses; 24 pp; **AFMM.**

1910 Catalogue of Microscopes and Accessories; (Same intro as 1910 reaffiliation with Zeiss); 69 pp, index; **AFMM.**

1910 Balopticons For All Kinds of Projection; 23 pp; **AFMM.**

1910	Brochure, Balopticon (A high grade lantern) Model C for General Projection Work; 16 pp; **AFMM; NYAM.**
ca 1910	Has B & L, Zeiss, Sagemuller Combination TM; Taken from code on brochure "D-g-2 XII-10."; **NYAM.**
1911	Microscopes and Accessories; 22nd ed.; 75 pp, index, 10 pp; **AFMM.**
1911	Catalogue of Balopticons and Accessories; 66 pp, index; **AFMM.**
1911	Catalog of Microscopes and Accessories; 19th ed.; 75 pp, index; **MAH** (C681.4085 B).
1911?	Catalogue, Ungraduated Laboratory Glassware, Jena-Bohemian-German; (TM); **CTY/B** (Uai B329).
1912	Brochure, New B & L Microscopes, Model F and Model FF; 5 pp; Arthur H. Thomas Co. distributor; **AFMM.**
1913	Brochure, A New Fine Focusing Adjustment and a New Microscope (Model FFS8); 3 pp; **AFMM.**
1913	The Balopticon in Church Work; 13 pp; **AO.**
1913	Brochure, B&L Microscopes. 6 pp; **AFMM.**
1913	Brochure, B&L Convertible Balopticon (New Model); 15 pp; **AFMM.**
1913	Catalog of Microtomes; 36 pp, index; **AFMM.**
1914	Microscopes and Accessories, 23rd ed.; 117 pp, index; **AFMM; MAH** (C681.4085B).
ca 1914	Catalogue of Bacteriological Apparatus; Section A, 29 pp; Section B, 34 pp; **AFMM.**
1914	Catalog of Microscopes and Accessories; 19th ed.; 117 pp, index; **MAH** (C681.4085 B).
1914	Revised Price Schedule (for Balopticon); various pamphlets bound together; **AO.**
1915	Location of the Opthalmic Lens Before the Eye and Its Correcting Power; **NYAM; MF/MAH.**
1915	Ophthalmic Lenses and Accessories, Lenses, Frame Magnifiers and Readers; 148 pp; **UREGML; AO.**
1915	Catalog of Optical Instruments for Inspection and Testing of Materials; 35 pp, with separate revised prices effective 1 January 1918; **MAH** (C681.4085 B187ai).
1916	Ophthalmic Lenses and Accessories; Lenses, Frames, Magnifiers and Readers . . .; **UCLABM** (W26 B329o).
1916	Ophthalmic Lenses and Accessories; 148 pp; (TM); **MAH** (C617.75085 B187).
1916	Microscopes and Accessories; 25th ed.; 129 pp, index; **AFMM.**
1916?	Ultex Onepiece Bifocal Lenses, Description, Charts, Tables and Directions; 16 pp; **AO.**
1917	Microscopes and Accessories; 26th ed.; 130 pp, index; **AFMM.**
1917	Brochure, Ophthalmic Test Frame and Lenses, 12 pp; **NYAM.**
1918	Catalogue of Microscopes and Accessories; 27th ed.; 45 pp, index; **AFMM.**
1919	Microscopes and Accessories; 28th ed.; 109 pp, index; **MAH** (C681.4085); **AFMM.**
1919	Optical Glass, A Manual and Catalog; 20 pp; **AO.**
1919	Bausch & Lomb Surface Grinding Machines; 11 pp; **AO.**
1919–20	Microscopes and Accessories, B & L introduction says 28th ed. but coded by them as V-20, note different number of pages 1919 and 1920; 109 pp, index; **AFMM.**
1920	Projection Apparatus, cover title; Balopticons and Accessories, title pg; 96

pp, index; **NYAM; MF/MAH.**

E. 20 c   Catalogue of Photomicrographic Equipment and Micro-Projectors; 54 pp, index; **AFMM.**

1921   Bausch and Lomb Bifocal Lenses, Kryptok, Ultex, Bitex, A Manual of Information; 20 pp; **AO.**

1921   Supplement no. 1 to Price List, Ophthalmic Products; 51 pp; **AO.**

Branches: 200 Fifth Ave., New York.
122 S. Michigan Blvd., Chicago.
613 Fifteenth St., N.W., Washington, D.C.
154 Sutter St., San Francisco.
37 & 38 Hatton Garden, E. C., London.

1922   Microscopes, Microtomes and Accessories; 164 pp, index; **MAH** (C681.4085 B187); with Price List July 5, 1923; **AFMM; AO.**

1922   The *REFLECTOR*, Vol. III, no. 7; **AO.**

1923   Microscopes, Microtomes and Accessories; 30th ed.; 166 pp, index; **AFMM.**

1923   Price List of Balopticons and Accessories; 16 pp; Not illustrated; **AFMM.**

1923   Catalogue of Microscopes, Large Models for Research and Photomicrographic Work; 28 pp; **MAH** (C681.4085 B187).

1923   Catalogue of Microscopes, Microtomes and Accessories for Educational Institutions; 24 pp; **MAH** (C681.4085 B187).

1924   Nuway Reading Glass, Magni no. 4; 4 pp foldout; **MAH.**

1924   Magnifiers and Readers; 8 pp; **MAH.**

1924   Catalogue of Microscopes, Microtomes and Accessories for Educational Instituions; 24 pp, with separate slip showing new and reduced microscope prices as of 1 May 1925; **MAH** (C681.4085).

Apr. 1, 1924   Price List of Bausch & Lomb Spectacle and Eyeglass Frames, and Mountings, Gold Filled and Zylonite; 35 pp; **AO.**

1925   Bausch & Lomb Magazine, Vol. II, no. 5, **AO.**

Sep. 1, 1925   Price List of Bausch & Lomb Spectacle and Eyeglass Frames, Mountings, and Materials, Solid Gold-10K and 14K; 38 pp; **AO.**

1926   Microscopes, Microtomes, Colorimeters, Optical Measuring Instruments and Accessories; 31st ed.; 218 pp, index; **MAH** (C681.4085 B187); **AFMM.**

1926   Catalogue of Microscopes, Microtomes, Colorimeters, Spectometers, Refractometers; 211 pp, biblio., index; **AFMM.**

1926   Ophthalmic Instruments; 72 pp; **MUM.**

Mar. 1, 1926   Price List of Bausch & Lomb Spectacle and Eyeglass Frames, Mountings, and Materials, Solid Gold-10K and 14K; 35 pp; **AO.**

Mar. 1, 1926   Price List of Bausch & Lomb Spectacle and Eyeglass Frames and Mountings, Gold Filled and Zylonite; 35 pp; **AO.**

Mar. 1, 1926   Price List of Bausch & Lomb Spectacle and Eyeglass Cases, Leather and Arolyn; 8 pp; **AO.**

1927   Price List of Bausch & Lomb Magnifiers and Readers; 10 pp; **MAH.**

1927   Brochure, Physicians' Microscope FFS = 8; 5 pp fold out; **MAH** (C681.4085 B187).

1927   Catalogue, Microscopes and Accessories for Educational Institutions; 31 pp; **MAH** (C681.4085 B187).

1927   Catalogue, Projection Apparatus, Balopticons, Micro-Projectors, Photomicrographic Equipment, Photographic Lenses; 118 pp; (TM); **NYAM; MF/MAH.**

1927   B & L Projection Apparatus; 116 pp, prices; **MAH.**

Feb. 18, 1927	Price List of Bausch & Lomb Spectacle and Eyeglass Frames and Mountings, Gold Filled and Aylonite; 33 pp; **AO.**
Dec. 15, 1927	Price List of Bausch & Lomb Ophthalmic Equipment; 36 pp; **AO.**
Jun. 15, 1928	Price List of Bausch & Lomb Ophthalmic Equipment; 19 pp; **AO.**
1928	Catalog of Optical Equipment for Hospitals, Medical Institutions and Physicians; 79 pp; **MAH** (C681.4084).
May 15, 1929	Prescription Price List; 18 pp; **MAH.**
1929?	The Chamot Chemical Microscope; 15 pp, prices; **MAH.**
1929	Catalogue, Microscopes and Accessories, Photo-Micrographic and Micro-Projection Apparatus, Microtomes, Colorimeters, Optical Measuring Instruments and Refractometers; Vol. 3; 318 pp, index pp 315-18; (TM) "To Help You Select Your Microscope" pp x-xiii," brief history, pp ix; **NYAM; UPSDM** (617.604 B328); **LACMA** (149 B 32M); **CTY/B** (Sh15 228g); **MAH** (C 681.4085 B 187 mic).
1929	Bausch & Lomb Magnifiers and Readers; 15 pp; **AO.**
1920's	B & L Ophthalmic Test Frame and Lenses; 12 pp; (TM); **NYAM; MF/ MAH.**
1930	Ophthalmic Instruments; 79 pp; **HDM.**
1930	Catalog of Microscopes and Balopticons for Educational Institutions; 114 pp, index; **MAH** (C681.4085).
Jun. 15, 1930	Price List of Bausch & Lomb Ophthalmic Equipment; 19 pp; **AO.**
1931	Design Magic; 4 pp, foldout; **MAH.**
May 11, 1931	Orthogon Prescription Price List; 4 pp; Orthogon lenses introduction 1928; **MAH.**
Jun. 1, 1931	Price List Orthogon Uncut Lenses and Semi-Finished Blanks; 4 pp, foldout; **MAH.**
Aug. 15, 1931	Orthogon "D" Prescription Price List; 4 pp. foldout; **MAH.**
1932	Catalog D-20, Instruments for Spectographic Analysis; 28 pp; **AFMM.**
1932	Catalogue D-20, Lenses, Prisms and Mirrors; 18 pp, index; **AFMM.**
Dec. 27, 1933	Revised Price List of Optical Instruments and Accessories; 34 pp; **AFMM.**
Oct. 1935	Bausch & Lomb Prescription Price List of Ophthalmic Lenses; 24 pp; **AO.**
1935	Ophthalmic Lenses, Their History, Theory and Application; 88 pp; **AO.**
1935	Panoptik Primer; 24 pp; **MAH.**
1935	Catalog of Laboratory Microscopes and Accessories; 22 pp, index; **MAH** (C681.4085).
1937	The 1937 Minute Man Appointment Book, 4 pp foldout; **MAH.**
1937	Catalogue, Microscope Accessories; D-185; 20 pp; **CTY/B** (Uai B329).
n.d.	B&L Balopticon (high grade lantern) Model C for General Projection Work; 16 pp, plus Query Sheet for Selection of Balopticon Equipment; 4 pp; **NYAM; MF/MAH.**
n.d.	Catalog nos. 31-33-75, 76, 77, 78, Spherical Illuminator, List of Part Numbers, Specifications and Directions for Use; 8 pp; **MAH.**
n.d.	Illustrated Price List of Microscopes, Objectives and Accessories; **CTY/B** (Uai B 329).
n.d.	Microscopes and Accessories; **CTY/B** (Uai B 329).
n.d.	Spherical Illuminator; 8 pp; **MAH.**
n.d.	The New Improved KW wide Field Binocular Microscope; **CTY/B** (Uai B 329).
n.d.	Why Bausch & Lomb's Instruments are Preferred; 32 pp; **CPP.**
n.d.	Euphos-Glass Protection Against Invisible U-V Rays of Light; 4 pp; **CPP.**
n.d.	B & L Exophthalmometer; 4 pp; **CPP.**

n.d.   B & L Lens Comparator; 4 pp; **CPP.**

n.d.   B & L Optical Co. Bacteriological Apparatus; Section A; 29 pp; **AFMM.**

n.d.   Photomicrographic Equipment Micro Projectors; 54 pp; **AFMM.**

n.d.   Balances and Weights; 60 pp; **AFMM.**

n.d.   Laboratory Microscopes and Accessories, Catalog D-185; **CTY/B** (Uai B 329).

1935   Microscope Accessories Catalog D-184; 18 pp; **CTY/B** (Uai B 329); **HDM.**

Branch: 388 Yonge St., Toronto, Ontario, Canada.

Apr. 1940   Bausch & Lomb Frames and Mountings; 40 pp; **AO.**

ca 1940   Scientific Instruments; Catalog D-111; 287 pp; **CPP.**

BAYER CO.
Farbenfabriken of Elberfeld Co.
Agents U.S.: P.O. Box 2162, 117 Hudson Street, New York, New York.
Bayer Co., Div. Sterling Drugs, Inc.
1450 Broadway, New York, 18, NY.
Est: 1899

post 1911   Taunnigen Intestinal Astringent; 16 pp; **CPP.**

1912   Sophol in Ophthalmology; 12 pp; **CPP.**

post 1913   Veronal Sodium Hypnotics and Sedatives; 32 pp; **CPP.**

1914   Adalin Sedative and Hypnotic; 20 pp; **CPP.**

1914   Elarson The New Organic Arsenic; 12 pp; **CPP.**

1914   Sajodin Agreeable Iodin Medication; 20 pp; **CPP.**

n.d.   Asurol by Prof. Alb. Neisser of Breslau; 8 pp; **CPP.**

n.d.   Bayer Pharmaceutical and Technical Products; 47 pp; **CPP.**

n.d.   Bayer Pharmaceutical and Technical Products; 32 pp; **CPP.**

n.d.   Bayer Pharmaceutical and Technical Products; 36 pp; **CPP.**

n.d.   Bayer Pharmaceutical and Technical Products; 28 pp; **CPP.**

n.d.   Iothion Oil-Bayer, Local Iodin Preparations; 12 pp; **CPP.**

n.d.   Material Medica Bayer; 114 pp; **CPP.**

n.d.   Novaspirin AntiRheumatic-Analgesic; 16 pp; **CPP.**

BAYHA, C. BRUNO
Tuttlingen, Germany.

n.d.   Fabrik chir. Instrumente, Spezial-Katalog über Instrumente fur Harnröhre und Blase, Fernsprecher No. 155; 24 pp, Preis-liste, attachments; **MAH** (12690).

BAY STATE OPTICAL CO.
Attleboro, Massachusetts.

May 10, 1898   Illustrated Catalogue of Gold Filled and Silverine Spectacles and Eyeglasses; 63 pp; **AO.**

1900   Illustrated Catalogue; 69 pp; **AO.**

Branches: 14 John Street, New York.
Heyworth Building, Chicago.
42 Gray's Inn Road, London.

Jan. 1912   Price List, Gold and Gold Filled Eye-Glass Chain, Hooks and Hair Pins; 4 pp; **AO.**

May 15, 1915   Price List, Gold and Gold Filled Eye-Glass Chain, Hooks and Hair Pins; 4 pp; **AO.**

July 1, 1916   Price List, Gold and Gold Filled Material, Eye-Glass Chain and Findings; 12 pp; **AO.**

BBL
See: BECTOM. DICKENSON and CO., BIOQUEST, Div. of; **MAH.**

BEAL AND TUCKER
Baltimore.
See: EDWARD TUCKER, L. 18 c.

BECK, G., Dr.
Nov. 1, 1878 Illustrirte Vierteljahrsschrift der aerztlichen Polytechnik; I. Jahrgang 1879; 240 pp; **ZUR.**
Jan. 1, 1879 Illustrirte Vierteljahrsschrift der aerztlichen Polytechnik; I. Jahrgang 1879; 187 pp; **ZUR.**
Jan. 1, 1880 Illustrirte Vierteljahrsschrift der aerztlichen Polytechnik; II. Jahrgang 1880; 196 pp; **ZUR.**
Jan. 1, 1881 Illustrirte Vierteljahrsschrift der aerztlichen Polytechnik; III. Jahrgang 1881; 40 pp; **ZUR.**
Jan. 1, 1882 Illustrirte Vierteljahrsschrift der aerztlichen Polytechnik; IV. Jahrgang; 296 pp; **ZUR.**

BECK, R. & J.
31 Cornhill, No. 1016 Chestnut St., Philadelphia, PA. (W.H. Walmsley-manager).
London.
See: SMITH, BECK & BECK; **AFMM.** QUEEN, JAMES & CO.; **MAH.** WALMSLEY, W.H. & CO., **MAH.** WILLIAMS, BROWN & EARLE, **MAH.**
1865 Illustrated Catalogue of Scientific Instruments, Part 1; 45 pp; **AFMM.**
Aug. 1866 Catalogue of Scientific Instruments, Test Types, Ophthalmic Instruments, Trial Sights, Spectacles, Folders, etc., Part IV; 27 pp; **NLM** (W26 S643).
Apr. 1867 Catalogue of Scientific Instruments, Opera and Race Glasses, Telescopes, Astronomical Surveying and Nautical Instruments, Pocket Compasses, Drawing Instruments, Part IV; 36 pp; **NLM** (W26 S643).
1868 Catalogue of Microscopes, Dissecting Instruments, Mounting-Materials, Cabinets, Tables, etc., Part I; 42 pp; **NLM** (W26 S643).
1868 Meterological Instruments, First 5 pp; in this section headed R & J Beck, remainder, Smith, Beck and Beck, Part II; Indexed by catalogue number; **NLM** (W26 S643).
Mar. 1869 Catalogue, An Illustrated Catalogue of Scientific Instruments; Medals; **CTY/B** (Uai B388).
ca 1870 Catalogue of Achromatic Microscopes and Accessories, James W. Queen & Co. Sole Agents for the United States; 103 pp, index; Bound with *The Lens,* Vol. I, 1872; **MAH** (578.0573).
Jan. 1870 Illustrated Catalog of Scientific Instruments and Accessories, Part I; 42 pp; **AFMM; CTY/B** (UAI B 388).
Feb. 1873 Illustrated Catalogue of Scientific Instruments; 2nd ed.; 38 pp; **AFMM; CTY/B** (UAI B 388).
Feb. 1876 Catalogue of Scientific Instruments and Accessories; 4th ed.; 31 pp, (some pages may be missing); **AFMM.**
ca 1878 Illustrated Price List of Microscopes, Microscopic Apparatus and other Scientific Instruments; 70 pp, biblio,; **AFMM.**
ca 1878 Illustrated Catalogue of Microscopes, and Other Scientific Instruments; 72 pp; **MUM.**
1880 Illustrated Catalogue of Microscopes, Microscopic Apparatus, and Other Optical Instruments; 166 pp, illustrations, 2 pp biblio., index; **AFMM.**

1880	Catalogue, Illustrated Price List of Microscopes, Microscopic Apparatus, and Other Optical Instruments; 8th ed.; Part 1; 156 pp; **CTY/B** (Uai B388).
July 1880	Catalogue of Surgical Instruments, Enlarged ed.; 45 pp; **RCSL.**
1881	An Illustrated Catalogue of Microscopes and Other Optical Instruments; 10th ed.; 176 pp; **CPP** (Bolenius Coll); **MUM** (pam 6 1881).
1882	Catalogue of Microscopes and Other Optical Instruments; 170 pp, illustrations, 2 pp biblio, index; **AFMM.**
May 1, '83	An Illustrated Catalogue of Microscopes and Other Optical Instruments; 13th ed., Part I; 176 pp; **CPP; CTY/B** (Uai B 388).
1886	Catalogue of Microscopes and Accessories; 19th ed.; 136 pp; **MUM** (pam 7 post 1885).
Apr. 1887	Catalogue of Scientific Instruments, Opera and Race Glasses, Telescopes, Astronomical Surveying and Nautical Instruments, Pocket Compasses, Drawing Instruments, etc.; Part III; 26 pp; **NLM** (W26 S643).
1888	An Illustrated Description of the "National" Microscope in its Various Forms; pp 1-18, **MAH.**
1900	The London Microscope, A New Microscope on the Continental Model, Decidedly Lower in Price; 19 pp; **NYAM, MF/MAH.**
ca 1900	A New Microscope, The Handle Model, London Microscope; 4 pp; **NYAM; MF/MAH.**
1901	The London Microscope, Five Models; 20 pp; **NYAM; MF/MAH.**
ca 1902	The London Microscope, Iris Model; 4 pp; **NYAM; MF/MAH.**
1902	The London Microscope, Six Models; 24 pp; **NYAM; MF/MAH.**
ca 1905	Brochure, The London Microscrope, Iris Model, Five Ordinary Models, London Microscope, illustrated on back page; 4 pp; **NYAM.**
ca 1910	Brochure, The London Microscope, The Handle Model, A New Microscope; 4 pp; **NYAM.**
ca 1920	Brochure, Beck Research Microscopes; 12 pp; **NYAM.**
ca 1923	Microscopes and Apparatus; 80 pp; **URRR** (B-469-4).
1930	Brochure Presenting Their Angular Model and Combined Binocular and Moacular Model; 11 pp; **AFMM.**
1939	Beck Microscopes; 123 pp; **URRR** (B-469).
n.d.	A Condensed List of a Few of the Most Desirable Microscopes of Moderate Cost and Accessories, Mounting Implements . . .; **CPP** (Bolenius Coll); **CTY/B** (Uai B 388); **MUM** (pam 5).

68 Cornhill, London
| n.d. | Microscopical Appliances; 22 pp; **AFMM.** |

69 Mortimer St. (London).
| n.d. | Beck London Model no. 29 Microscopes; 12 pp; **URRR** (B-442). |

BECK-LEE CORP.
Chicago, Illinois.
| n.d. | Beck-Lee Model E, Electrocardiagraph; 32 pp; **MAH** (C616.12078B). |
| n.d. | B-L Model E, Electrocardiograph Handbook; 31 pp; **MAH** (C616.12078B). |

BECKEN, A. C.
156 Wabash Avenue, Chicago.
Est: 1892
| 1907 | Optical Goods Wholesale Manufacturing and Importing Optician; 48 pp; **AO.** |

BECKER, JULIAN H.
Delft, Holland.
    1929   Catalogue, Makers of Balances and Weights; Price List; **MAH.**

BECTON, DICKINSON & CO.
Rutherford, N.J.
45 Vesey St., New York, New York.
160-162 Duane; 24-28 Hudson St., New York, New York.
Sole Agent: Charles F. Thackray, Leeds & London.
Est: 1897
  See: CLAY ADAMS, after 1869
    Sep. 1902   Catalogue, 60 pp, index pp 3-5; **MAH** (C610.78085 B227).
    1904   Catalogue of Surgeons and Veterinary Instruments and Supplies; 158 pp, index pp 132-158; (TM); **MAH.**
    1904   Trade Catalogue, Gold, Silver and Plated Instruments for Surgeons and Veterinarians; 131 pp, index pp 132-158; (TM); **MAH** (C610.78085 B227).
    1911–12   Catalogue, Clinical Thermometers, Hypodermic and Other Syringes, Atomizers, Physicians' Leather Goods, Wrought and Tubular Surgical Instruments; 160 pp, index pp 157-160; (TM); **MAH** (C610.78085 B227).
    1914   Catalogue, Foreign Dept; pp 1-20 only; **MAH.**
    1917   General Catalogue of Druggists, Surgical, Dental and Veterinary Specialities; 191 pp, index pp 188-191; (TM); **MAH** (610.78085 B 227).
    1918   Physician's Catalogue of B-D Fever Thermometers, Genuine Luer Syringes, Yale Quality Needles, Asepto Plungerless Syringes, Bender's Ideal Bandages and B-D Physicians's Leather Goods; 95 pp; **CPP.**
    1922   General Catalogue of Physicians', Druggists', and Veterinary Specialties; 160 pp; **WOC; AO.**

BEDFORD, LEEDS
    ca 1825   Instrument maker mentioned by John Read.

BEIERSDORF, P., & CO.
Apotheker, Altona, Oelkersallee no. 82.
    ca 1891   Verzeichniss dermato-therapeutischer Praeparate und Apparate nach Dr. P.G. Unna . . .; 54 pp; **NYAM; MF/MAH.**
    ca 1895   Verzeichniss dermato-therapeutischer Praeparate und Apparate nach Dr. P.G. Unna . . .; 54 pp, no index, no illustrations; (TM); pamphlet paper clipped together; **NYAM.**

BELGARD SPERO, INC.
Mallers Bldg., 5 South Wabash Avenue, Chicago, Ill.
Branch Office: Sheridan Trust Bldg., Cor. Broadway and Lawrence, Chicago.
    1924–5   Designers and Makers of Fine Spectacles; 54 pp; **AO.**

BELL, JOHN & CROYDEN
  See: ARNOLD AND SONS; **NLM.**

BELL, JOHN & CROYDEN, In Assoc. With SAVORY & MOORE LTD., CHEMISTS
Armond and Sons, 50-52 Wigmore St., London W 1, England.
Acoustic Dept.: 8 Welbeck St., London, W.1.
Est: 1798
"Chemists to the King"

1930s   Illustrated List of Acoustic Instruments, Electrical and Non-Electrical; 5th ed.; 48 pp; **WMScM.**

BENAS
Boulevard du Palais, Paris, France.
"Brévète s.g.d.g."
1876   Catalogue, Instruments de Chirurgie en Gomme; 15 pp; **NYAM.**
1876   Fabrique Spéciale d'Instruments de Chirurgie en Gomme; 15 pp; **NYAM; MF/MAH.**

BENAS' SON
1293 Broadway, New York, New York.
No. 5 Boulevard du Palais, Paris, France.
"Sole Manufacturer in America"
1881   Catalogue, Bougies, Catheters and Other Gum Instruments; 12 pp; **NYAM; MF/MAH.**
n.d.   Brochure, Paquelin-Cautery (Thermo-Cautery); 10 pp; **NYAM; MF/MAH.**

BENNINGHOVEN, PROF. DR. WIHL
Turnstrasse 19, Berlin N.W. 21.
Factory: Neuses near Coburg.
Germany.
Jun. 1911   Illustrated Catalog of Anatomical Models; 72 pp; **CPP.**
1913   Catalogue, Anatomische Lehrmittel-Anstalt.; 134 pp, index, some color photographs; **NYAM.**
Aug. 1913   Anatomische Lehrmittel, no real title. Anatomic models, also see X-Ray Positive; 134 pp, index; **NYAM; MF/MAH.**

BENSON, CHARLES PETERS, AND ROBERT LEE BENSON
Chicago, Illinois.
Est: Jan. 1, 1901
1904   The Bensonizer System of Pneumotherapy for the Treatment of Diseases of the Air Passages; 55 pp; **CPP.**

BENSON, N. P., OPTICAL CO.
205-210 Syndicate Bldg., 519 Nicollet Ave., Minneapolis, MN.
1915   The X-L-R House, exclusively wholesale; Price List of Lenses, Mountings, Frames, Oculists' and Opticians' Supplies, Ophthalmological Instruments and Accessories; Catalog A; 1st ed.; 112 pp; **URRR** (B-70 N.P.); **AO.**
1928   Prescription Catalog; 10th ed.; 36 pp; **URRR** (B-488 N.P.).

BERBECKER, JULIUS AND SONS, INC.
15 E. 26th St., New York, New York.
Importers
n.d.   Catalogue of Surgeons' Needles; no. 2; 44 pp, index pp 3-7; **MAH.**

BERGE, (J.& H.)
New York.
See: AMBROSE L. RANNEY, M.D.
1881   The Latest Improved Holtz Electrical Machines, Instruments Medical and Surgical, Catalogues and Price Lists; **NYAM** (135698).
1885   Practical Suggestions Respecting the Varieties of Electrical Currents and the Uses of Electricity in Medicine; **MAH.**

1889   Illustrated and Descriptive Catalogue of Chemical and Physical Apparatus, Assayers' Supplies, Chemicals and Reagents, etc.; 194 pp; **BLEL.**

BERGER, C. L., AND SONS
37 Williams St., Boston, MA.
1912   Standard Instruments of Precision; **URRR** (B-76).

BERGUERAND, FELIX, BRÉVÈTE
1865   Catalogue des Instruments de Chirurgie; 2nd ed.; Illustrated binder's title: Exposition Universelle 1867; 18 pp; **YML** (RD 76 867p); **CTY/B** (60-3557x).

BERNSTEIN, ALBERT L.
New York.
1870   Illustrated Catalogue of Surgical Instruments and Appliances: in Fact Everything Used by Surgeons and Physicians; 184 pp; **UBML** (HSL W26 H557i).

BERRY, W. T., SURGICAL INSTRUMENT CO.
Louisville, KY.
1908   Catalogue; 515 pp; **WOC.**

BERSTEIN MFG. CO.
917 Richmond St., Philadelphia, Pennsylvania.
"Makers of High Grade Aseptic Hospital Furniture, Sterilizing Apparatus, Metallic Bedsteads."
L. 19 c   Brochure, Facts About Sterilizing Apparatus for the Hospital and Surgeon; 8 pp; (no TM); **NYAM.**
1910   Improvement is the Order of the Age, Facts About Sterilizing Apparatus for the Hospital and Surgeon; 8 pp, unpaginated; **NYAM, MF/MAH.**

BESELER, CHARLES
218 Centre Street, New York, New York.
1888   Illustrated Price List of Compressed Air Atomizers; 24 pp; **CPP.**
1895   Illustrated Catalogue of High Grade Laryngoscopes, Compressed Air Atomizers, Air and Gas Compressors, Globe Inhalers, Gas Receivers, etc., also Pure Oxygen Gas and Oxygen Compounds for Inhaling Purposes and the Most Improved Outfits for Preparing Oxygen; **NYAM.**

BETTS, ARLINGTON U., & CO.
Toledo, Ohio.
1895-6   Red Cross, Rubber Sundries, Catalog no. 10; 33 pp, index; **MAH** (29519).

BETZ, FRANK S., & CO.
35 & 37 Randolph St., Chicago.
Hammond, Indiana.
348-352 W. 34th St., New York; 6 & 8 W. 48th St, New York.
Santa Fe Building, Dallas.
634 S. Wabash, Chicago.
30 E. Randolph St., Chicago.
88-90 Wabash Ave., Chicago.
105 N. Wabash Ave., Chicago.
Sante Fe Building, Dallas, Texas.
Est: 1895

1900	Manual of Physiological Therapeutics; 96 pp, illustrated; **MAH** (C615.8085B).
ca 1900	Invalid Chairs; 16 pp; **MAH** (29514).
ca 1901	Manual of Physiological Therapeutics with Special Reference to the Treatment of Acute and Chronic Diseases by: Thermo-Therapy, Electro-Therapy, Massage Hydro-Therapy With Appendix on Orthopedic Appliances, Trusses and Supporters, by over 50 authors; Containing prices, illustrations, photos, and description of use; 96 pp; **MAH** (C615.8085B).
Apr. 1902	Betz' Bargain Bulletin, Sale-Surgical Supplies and Equipment; 16 pp; **MAH**.
Sep. 1902	Betz' Bargain Bulletin, Sale-Surgical Supplies and Equipment; 16 pp; **MAH**.
1903	Catalogue, Galvanism vs. Hysterectomy, Betz Galvanic and Roller Cabinet Battery, Other Betz products giving descriptions, photos, uses, price list and advertisements; 32 pp; **MAH** (C615.84085B).
1907	Catalog 50, Drug section, Betz Money Saver Book Medicinal Tablets, Pharmaceuticals, Drugs & Chemicals, Sundries, etc.; no. 59; 48 pp, index on back of front cover; **MAH** (C615.1373B).
1907	Catalogue no. 103, Dental Furniture, Instruments, and Material, Drugs, and Pharmaceuticals; 126 pp, index pp 123-26; **NYAM**.
1907	Catalogue no. 514, Surgical Instruments, Hospital Furniture and Supplies, Drugs and Pharmaceuticals, Dental Equipment Veterinary Instruments and Apparatus; 270 pp; **NLM** (W26 B565c); **NYAM; WOC**.
1910	Catalogue no. 44, Surgical Instruments, Hospital Furniture, and Supplies, Drugs, and Pharmaceuticals; 254 pp, index pp 251-254; **NYAM; WOC**.
1910	Additional sheets, picture of plant on cover, X-Ray Pharmaceutical; **NYAM; MF/MAH**.
ca 1910	Betz Bulletin of Dental Supplies; 16 pp; **HML**.
ca 1910	Untitled, assorted dental supplies; 6 pp; **NYAM; MF/MAH**.
ca 1910	Sale of Crown Surgical Instruments Co. of N.Y. Stock, including furniture and pharmaceuticals; 82 pp; **NYAM; MF/MAH**.
ca 1910	Catalogue, Sale, Surgical Supplies and Equipment; "Announcing the Purchase of the Crown Surgical Instrument Co. of New York."; 80 pp; **NYAM; CPP**.
1912	Selections from large 1912 Betz Catalogue, no. 46; 212 pp, drugs from pp 254; **CPP**.
1912	Catalogue no. 47, Electro-, Radio-, Thermo-, Hydro-, and Mechano-Therapeutic Apparatus; 69 pp; **ACR/MAH**.
ca 1913	Catalogue no. 48; 290 pp; **CPP**.
ca 1913	Surgical Instruments, Hospital Furniture, and Supplies, Drugs, and Pharmaceuticals, also X-Ray; Catalogue no. 14; 272 pp, index, additional sheets; picture of Hammond Plant on Cover; **NYAM; MF/MAH**.
1913	Surgical Instruments, Hospital Furniture, and Supplies, Drugs, and Pharmaceuticals, Catalogue no. 48; 292 pp, index; **NYAM; MF/MAH**.
1915	Betz Direct Service, Catalogue no. N-15, Surgical Instruments, Hospital Furniture, Physicians' and Hospital Supplies, Electro Therapeutic Appliances, Drugs and Pharmaceuticals; 326 pp, 16 pp addendum, index; cover has many views of plant; **NYAM; MF/MAH; LLU; CPP; MCFM; TMHM**.

1916 Catalogue, Dental Office Furniture, Apparatus and Equipment, Surgical Instruments, Materials, Supplies, Drugs, and Pharmaceuticals; 204 pp; index pp 201-204; **NYAM.**

1916 Progressive Equipment Dental Office Furniture, Apparatus, and Equipment, Instruments, Material Supplies, Drugs, and Pharmaceuticals; 205 pp, index; additional sheets (unusually reserved cover for Betz); pictures of plant workshop; **NYAM; MF/MAH.**

1916 Price list for R-16 Surgical Catalogue; 16 pp; **NYAM; MF/MAH.**

1916 Harvard Surgical Bulletin; Physician Furniture, Equipment, Instruments, and Supplies, price list for R-16 Surgical Catalogue; 66 pp; **NYAM; MF/MAH.**

1916–32 A group of approximately 35 Betz clearance/sale catalogues of approximately 34-78 pp each; Annual Fall Bulletin, Annual Fall Sales, Christmas Bulletin, Pre-Inventory Sales, Post Inventory Sale, etc.; **NYAM.**

Jan. 1917 Surgical Bulletin, Furniture, Equipment, Supplies and Instruments, includes X-Ray, etc.; Picture of Frank Betz, Louis Curtis, and factory on inside cover; 66 pp; **NYAM; MF/MAH.**

1917 Bi-Monthly Special of Surgical Instruments and Supplies, Hospital Furniture, Electro-Therapeutic Apparatus; 81 pp; **CPP.**

1917 Price list for R-16 Surgical Catalogue; 16 pp; **NYAM; MF/MAH.**

Mar. 1917 Surgical Instruments and Supplies, Hospital Furniture, Electro Therapeutic Appliances, and price list for R-16 Surgical Catalog; picture of factory on cover; 68 pp; **NYAM; MF/MAH.**

ca 1917 Surgical Supplies, Equipment, Furniture, and Instruments; 80 pp; **NYAM; MF/MAH.**

1918 Catalogue, Surgical Instruments and Supplies; 167 pp, index pp 167; **NYAM; MF/MAH; CPP.**

Jan. 1918 Bulletin, Physicians and Surgeon's Supplies; 80 pp; **CPP.**

Jun. 1918 Betz Surgical Bulletin, Instruments, Supplies, Furniture and Equipment; 34 pp; **NYAM; MF/MAH.**

ca 1918 Catalogue no. 20, "The Betzco Line," Physicians and Hospital Supplies and Equipment; 256 pp, index pp 253-256; **NYAM; CPP.**

ca 1919 Betz Reconstruction Bulletin; (Surgical Supplies); picture of physician returning from war on cover; 84 pp; **NYAM; MF/MAH.**

1919 Surgical Supplies for Summer 1919; Equipment, Supplies, Instruments, and Furniture; 82 pp; **NYAM; MF/MAH.**

1920 Physicians and Hospital Supplies and Equipment; no. 20; 256 pp, index; **NYAM; MF/MAH.**

1920 Catalog no. 50; Dental Equipment, Instruments and Supplies; 158 pp, index pp, 155-158, separate price list; (TM); **NYAM.**

1920's Catalog, Equipment and Supplies for the Dentist; 64 pp; **NYAM.**

1920's The Betzco Electric, a Superior Electro-Therapeutic Cabinet, Advertisements; 4 pp; **AO.**

1920's The Modern White Office, Yours-On Easy Terms; 4 pp; **AO.**

ca 1920 Special Spring Sale; 36 pp; **NYAM; MF/MAH.**

ca 1920 Catalogue, The Betzco Line; Supplies and Equipment for Physicians and Hospitals; 212 pp, index 209-212; **AO; NYAM.**

1922 A Complete Catalog of Equipment for Hospitals, including Steel Hospital Furniture, High Pressure Sterilizers, Therapeutic Bath Equipment; **CS.**

Aug. 1, 1922? No. 205; 40 pp, index; separate price; **MAH.**

1923	The Betzco Line, Supplies and Equipment for Physicians and Surgeons; 220 pp; **UCSF.**
1925	The Betzco Line, Supplies and Equipment for Physicians and Surgeons; 256 pp; **CPP; HML; WOC.**
Apr. 1, 1925	The Betzco Line, Supplies and Equipment for the Dentist; **CDMC.**
ca 1925	Betzco Post Inventory Sale Bulletin of Dental Equipment, and Supplies, "Check These Prices," picture of New York office on cover; 36 pp; **NYAM; MF/MAH.**
ca 1925	Hospital Equipment, untitled, on cover: "The Capacity of this great plant . . .," picture of factory and N.Y. Store on cover; 29 pp; **NYAM; MF/MAH.**
ca 1925	Surgical Supplies, Instruments and Equipment, on cover: This Book Offers A Thousand Inducements to Order By Mail . . .; **NYAM; MF/MAH.**
ca 1925	Dental Equipment and Supplies; Heading on cover: This Book Offers A Thousand Inducements to Order By Mail From Betz, Save Time and Money; 83 pp; **NYAM; MF/MAH.**
ca 1925	Betzco Annual Fall Sale Dental Bulletin: Boiled Down Prices Dental Supplies; **NYAM; MF/MAH.**
ca 1925	Catalog of Instruments, Supplies, Furniture, and Equipment for Physicians, Surgeons, Dentists and Hospitals; 252 pp, index; **NLM** (W26 B565c).
1925	The Betzco Hospital Book; a Complete Catalog of Superior Equipment for Hospitals; 400 pp; **HML; MAH** (C610.78085 B).
1926	The Betzco Hospital Book; 396 pp, index; **MAH.**
1926	Betzco Line for Physicians and Surgeons; 298 pp; **CPP.**
ca 1926	Betzco Post Inventory Sale Bulletin; 65 pp; **NYAM; MF/MAH.**
1926	Betzco Annual Fall Sale Surgical Bulletin; 34 pp, prices; **MAH.**
ca 1926	Flyer promoting Electro-Therapy Apparatus; flyer promoting Therapeutic Lamp; "Post Inventory Sale Bulletin;" 65 pp; **AFMM.**
1926	Complete Illustrated Catalogue of Superior Equipment for Hospitals including White Kraft Steel Furniture, TruTest Pressure Sterilizer, Therapeutic Bath Equipment with special sections on Surgical Instruments and Dressing Rubber Goods, Hospital Specialties; 395 pp, 5 pp index; **MAH** (C610.78085B).
1927	The Betzco Line for 1927, Everything the Physician Needs From a Single Source; 284 pp, index pp 281-284; **NYAM; MF/MAH; MAH.**
1927	Catalogue, Physicians' Hospital Furniture, Instruments and Supplies; 284 pp, Index pp 281-284; (TM); **NYAM.**
1927	Betzco Annual Fall Sale Physicians and Surgeons Supplies; 56 pp; **NYAM; MF/MAH; MAH.**
1927	"Success Brings Expansion," Betzco 32nd annual Post Inventory Sale Surgical Supplies and Equipment; Had just expanded NY office from old 48th St. ones (??); 72 pp; **NYAM; MF/MAH.**
1927	Betzco Dental Supplies and Equipment; 80 pp, index pp 81; **NYAM; MF/MAH.**
1927	Annual Dental Catalogue, Supplies and Equipment; 80 pp, index; **NYAM.**
1928	Betzco Line for 1928; 256 pp; **CPP** (Ed/66).
1928	Betzco Annual Pre-Inventory Clearance Sale of Surgical Instruments Supplies and Equipment; 108 pp; **NYAM; MF/MAH.**

1928	Betzco 33rd Yearly Pre-Inventory Sale, Physicians' Supplies and Equipment; 108 pp; **NYAM; MF/MAH.**
1928	34th Annual Spring Sale Physicians' and Surgeons' Supplies; 56 pp; **NYAM; MF/MAH.**
1928	Betz's Annual Mid-Summer Sale Surgical Supplies and Equipment; **NYAM; MF/MAH.**
1928	Surgical Supplies and Equipment, Betzco 34th Annual Fall Sale; 107 pp; **MAH.**
1929	Catalog, Physicians and Hospital Supplies and Equipment; 284 pp, index pp 278-280; **NYAM.**
1929	Betzco Line for 1929, Everything a Physician Needs From a Single Source; 252 pp; **LACMA (149B46B).**
1929	Betzco Line for 1929, Everything a Physician Needs From a Single Source; 284 pp, index pp 278-280; **NYAM; MF/MAH; UCSF.**
ca 1929	Betzco Annual Clearance Sale of Dental Furniture, Equipment, Instruments and Supplies; 66 pp; **NYAM; MF/MAH.**
1929	Betzco Annual Spring Bulletin: Physicians Supplies and Equipment; 80 pp; Cover: physician visiting scarlet fever house; **NYAM; MF/MAH.**
1929	Catalog, Betzco Mid-Summer Bulletin of Surgical Instruments, Supplies, and Equipment; 78 pp, index pp 78; **MAH.**
1929	Betzco Annual Fall Bulletin: Physicians' Equipment and Supplies; 80 pp; **NYAM; MF/MAH; MAH; CPP.**
1929	Betzco 34th Annual Fall Sale: Surgical Supplies and Equipment; 108 pp; **NYAM; MF/MAH.**
1929	Betzco 35th Annual Fall Sale: Dental Furniture, Equipment, Instruments and Supplies; 48 pp; **NYAM; MF/MAH.**
1929	Christmas Bulletin and Pre-Inventory Sale: Surgical and Hospital Instruments and Supplies; 80 pp, index; **NYAM, MF/MAH.**
1930	Pre-Inventory Sale: Surgical Equipment, Instruments and and Supplies; General Price Reductions; 48 pp; **NYAM; MF/MAH; MAH.**
1930	Betzco Post Inventory Bulletin: Physicians' Instruments, Equipment Furniture and Supplies; 79 pp, index; **NYAM; MF/MAH; CPP.**
1930	35th Annual Clearance Sale: Surgical Instruments, Supplies and Equipment; 102 pp; **NYAM; MF/MAH; CPP.**
1930	Betzco 36th Annual Fall Sale: Surgical Supplies and Equipment; 62 pp, index pp 62, prices; **MAH.**
1930	Catalogue; 288 pp; **WOC.**
ca 1930	A Complete Laboratory Outfit for General Practice with Latest Model Microscope; Supplement to Catalog M25; pp 158; 3 pp; **NYAM; MF/MAH.**
ca 1930	The Perfected Therapeutic Lamp; 4 pp; **NYAM; MF/MAH.**
ca 1930	Betzco 32nd Annual Mid-Summer Sale: Surgical Equipment and Supplies; 36 pp; **NYAM; MF/MAH.**
1931	Betz Dental Book: Dental Furniture, Equipment, Instruments, and Supplies; 113 pp, index; **NYAM; MF/MAH.**
1931	Post Inventory Bulletin; 78 pp; **CPP.**
1932	Betz Physicians' and Hospitals' Book 1932, Physicians' & Hospitals Furniture, Instruments and Supplies; 404 pp, index, prices; **NYAM; MF/MAH.**
n.d.	Physician and Hospital Supplies 4 pp; **NYAM; MF/MAH; CPP.**
n.d.	The Perfected Therapeutic Lamp; 4 pp, foldout; **MAH.**

1936 Betz Fall and Winter Book for Physicians, vol. 36, no. 16; 48 pp, prices; **MAH.**

n.d. Announcement and Price List of German Imported Tubes Used by X-Ray Specialists; shows photos of Cramer X-Ray plates with tubes, description, in English and German; prices in both languages; 2 pp; **MAH** (C616.0757 B).

n.d. Circular Announcement, Extraordinary, Best Imported German Tubes, None Better to Be Had At Any Price; 1 pp, prices; **MAH** (C616.0757 B).

n.d. We Better Serve as We Progress; 34 pp; **CPP.**

n.d. A Bulletin of Surgical Supplies, Instruments and Equipment from the Betzco Line; 34 pp; **CPP.**

n.d. A Bulletin of Surgical Supplies; 34 pp; **CPP.**

n.d. Special Spring Sale; 34 pp; **CPP.**

n.d. Surgical Supplies; 80 pp; **CPP.**

n.d. Surgical Supplies, Drugs and Pharmaceuticals Direct by Mail; 80 pp; **CPP.**

n.d. Great Reduction Sale Surgical Supplies 25 to 50% off Regular Prices; **CPP.**

n.d. The New Betzco Surgical Bulletin; 34 pp; **CPP.**

n.d. No cover; 106 pp; **CPP** (Ed/66).

n.d. Manual of Physiological Therapeutics; 96 pp; **CPP.**

n.d. Invalid Rolling Chairs; 36 pp; **CPP.**

n.d. History and Evolution of the Intubation Apparatus; 16 pp; **CPP.**

n.d. Eye-Ear-Nose & Throat Instruments, Equipment and Supplies; 80 pp; **CPP.**

n.d. Invalid Rolling Chairs, Catalog no. 715; 33 pp; **CPP.**

n.d. The Betzco Line; 212 pp; **CPP.**

n.d. Retail Store Service at Mail Order Prices Post Inventory Sale Bulletin; 35 pp; **CPP.**

BICKENBACH FABRIKATE & CO.
Berlin-Steglitz.

n.d. Pocket Microscopes; 1 pp, other 1 pp ads for microscopes and binoculars; **URRR** (B-382).

BIDDLE, JAMES G.
910 Drexel Building, Philadelphia, Pennsylvania.

1897 Catalog no. 240, "Concerning X-Ray Apparatus," Catalog issued in connection with exhibit of up-to-date X-ray apparatus; 32 pp; **NYAM.**

1897 Concerning X-Ray Apparatus; 33 pp; also has good list of those already using their apparatus (Biddle announces he has in his office a working exhibit of X-ray apparatus); **NYAM; MF/MAH.**

1903 Roentgen Induction Coils and Other X-Ray Apparatus; Catalog 480; 33 pp; **NYAM; MF/MAH; ACR/MAH; CPP.**

1112-1114 Chestnut Street, Philadelphia, Pennsylvania.

1904 Catalog 500, Some "Roentgen" Specialities; 8 pp; **ACR/MAH; CPP.**

1904? Brochure 505, Variable Inductance, Roentgen Coils with Primaries Having Variable Inductance; 4 pp, badly faded unidentified photo; **ACR/MAH.**

1904 Catalog 525, "Roentgen" Induction Coils and Other X-Ray Apparatus; 52 pp; **ACR/MAH; CPP.**

Jan. 1905 "Roentgen" Ammeter for X-Ray Tubes, Catalog 540; 6 pp; **CPP; ACR/MAH.**

Apr. 1905   X-Ray Tubes, no. 555; 4 pp; **CPP.**

1905   Catalog 585, Typical Roentgen Equipments; 20 pp, some prices pencilled in; **ACR/MAH; CPP.**

BIENAIME, L.
Paris.

1841   Orthopédie examen pratiques des difformités osseuses; 40 pp; **ABD.**

BIOGEN CO., INC., THE
90 William Street, New York, New York.

1903   Biogen is Prompt and Powerful Oxidizer Therapy of Perfect Blood Oxidation Biogen, Magnesium Dioxide; 13 pp; **CPP.**

ca 1904   Biogen and Dermogen Portable Oxygen Products; 16 pp; **CPP.**

n.d.   Magnesium Dioxide, A Capillary Assimilable Oxygen: A New Therapy of Perfect Blood Oxidation; 13 pp; **CPP.**

n.d.   Practical Views on Chlorosis; 7 pp; **CPP.**

BISCHOFF, C., & CO., INC.
451-53 Washington Street, New York, New York.
87-89 Park Place, New York, New York.

1897   Peroxoles no. 1; 8 pp; **CPP.**

1899   The Efficacy of Hydragogin by Dr. K. Goldberg; 8 pp; **CPP.**

1899   Bisol (Bismuthium phosphoric soluble); 6 pp; **CPP.**

n.d.   Modern Medical Products; 48 pp; **CPP.**

n.d.   Kryofine Analgesic, Hypnotic, Sedative, Antipyretic; 6 pp; **CPP.**

n.d.   Pharmaceutical of Established Merit; 18 pp; **CPP.**

BISCHOFF
135 Hudson Street, New York, New York.

n.d.   Styptysate in Hemorrhage Control; 6 pp; **CPP.**

BISHOP COMPANY, THE
North Attleboro, Massachusetts.

1920's   Master Optical Products; 24 pp; **AO.**

BLACKISTON, SON & CO.
1012 Walnut Street, Philadelphia, Pa.
Successors to Lindsay & Blackiston

Jan. 2, 1882   Catalogue no. 1, Catalogue of Medical, Dental, Pharmaceutical and Scientific Publications; 46 pp, index; **MAH** (8610).

BLEES-MOORE INSTRUMENT CO.
906 Pine St., St. Louis, Missouri.
Factory: 1103 Chestnut Street, St. Louis.
Absorbed by A. S. Aloe Co. in 1910

1901   Catalogue of Surgical Instruments, Hospital and Physician's Supplies; 645 pp, index; **SLSC.**

BLUE ISLAND SPECIALTY CO.
Blue Island, Illinois.

1916   Orthodontic Appliances, Materials and Supplies . . .; General Catalog no. 14; 175 pp; **UPSDM** (D617.604 B625).

ca 1920   Bisco Brand Line, Dental Specialities; 84 pp, index, price list; **NYAM; MF/MAH.**

1930?   Catalogue, Dental Impression Trays; 27 pp; **NYAM.**

n.d.   Specialties for the General Practitioner, Vol. 1; **UPSDM** (D617.604 B625.2).

BLY, DOUGLAS
Rochester, New York.

ca 1860 A New, Curious and Important Invention; 18 pp; **CPP.**

1862 A New and Important Invention by Douglas Bly: The Principles of the Natural Leg in an Artificial One; 30 pp; **CPP.**

n.d. Anatomical Leg and Arms with New Shoulder Motion; **CPP** (Bolenius Coll).

BOEKEL, WM., AND CO.
518 Vine St., Philadelphia, Pa.

1913 Supplement no. 2 to Catalogue F of Surgical Goods; 44 pp; **HML.**

n.d. Catalogue E, Surgical Goods, Bacteriological, Chemical Apparatus; 114 pp, index pp 113-114; **RCSL; AFMM.**

n.d. Surgical Goods, Chemical Apparatus Bacteriological Apparatus, Illustrated Supplement no. 3 to Catalog E; 38 pp; **AFMM.**

BOERICKE & BUNYON CO.
242&244 W. 41st St., New York, New York.
319 Madison Ave., New York, New York.
Branches in: L.A.; Phila; San Fran; Oakland, CA; Portland, Oregon.
"Importers and Manufacturers of Homeopathic Medicines and Publishers of Medical Literature"

ca 1900 Physicians' Price Current of Homeopathic Medicines, Medicine Cases, Medical Books, Surgical Goods and General Supplies for Physicians' Use; 187 pp, index pp 181-187; **NYAM; MF/MAH.**

BOERICKE AND TAFEL
Manufactory, 1011 Arch Street, Philadelphia, Pennsylvania.
1409 Chestnut Street, Philadelphia, Pennsylvania.
145 Grant Street, New York, New York.
7 West 42nd Street, New York, New York.
36 E. Madison Street, Chicago, Illinois.
228 North Howard Street, Baltimore, Maryland.
627 Smithfield Street, Pittsburgh, Pennsylvania.
170 W. Fourth Street, Cincinnati, Ohio.
Est: 1835
"Homeopathic Pharmaceutists, Importers and Publishers"

1887 Physician's Catalogue and Price Current of Homeopathic Medicine and Books and All Articles Pertaining to a Physician's Outfit; 136 pp; **CPP.**

1890 Physician's Catalogue and Price Current of Homeopathic Medicines and Books . . .; 160 pp; **BLEL.**

ca 1890 Homeopathic Catalogue; 163 pp; **WOC.**

post 1893 Price List of Tablet Triturates; 32 pp; **CPP.**

1894 Physicians' Catalog and Price Current of Homeopathic Medicines and Books and All Articles Required by Physicians; good example of homeopathic publication; 184 pp, index v-viii; **NYAM; MF/MAH.**

1897-8 Physician's Catalogue and Price Current; 110 pp; **CPP; UREGML.**

1900 Homeopathic Medical Index; 32 pp; **CPP.**

ca 1920 Standard Prescriptions in Tablet Form; 48 pp; **MAH.**

n.d. A Treatise on Loeflund's Dietetic Preparations for Infants and Invalids, Translated from German; 8 pp; **CPP.**

n.d. Phytolacca-Berry Tablets in the Treatment of Obesity; 4 pp; **CPP.**

n.d. Therapeutic Specialties: Tablets, Antiseptics, Cathartics, Cerates, Elixirs,

Decoctions, Powders, Syrups, Tonics, Sprays, Suppositories; 131 pp; **MAH.**

n.d.   Excelsior Medicine Cases and Leather Bags; 24 pp; **MAH.**

n.d.   Boericke & Tafel Export Biochemic Remedies; **MAH.**

n.d.   Catalog and Price List—Pharmaceutical Products; 164 pp; **MAH.**

n.d.   Tinctures and Dilutions Catalog; **MAH.**

n.d.   Physicians' Leather Bags & Medicine Cases; **MAH.**

n.d.   Boericke & Tafel Sundry Catalog; **MAH.**

n.d.   List of Swan's High Potencies (Morbific Products, Nosodes and other Remedies); 30 pp; **MAH.**

ca 1950   Alpha Remedies Homeopathic: Tables Especially Compounded to be Used in the Home for the Alleviation of Discomforts Due to Simple Ailments; 24 pp; **MAH.**

BOERICKE, R., & CO.
495-503 Wells St., Chicago, Illinois.

post 1856   Manufacturers of the DePew Convertable (sic) Operating Chair; Physicians Cabinets, Dentists Cabinets, Rolling Chairs, New Patent Crutches, Commodes, Nursery Chairs, Folding Bed Trays, Invalid Self-Propelling Chairs . . .; Medals; 4 pp, foldout; **CTY/B** (Uai B633).

1885   Catalog, Patent Self Propelling Invalid Chairs, De Pew's Convertible Operating Chairs, Parlor Reclining Chairs, Rolling Chairs, Nursery Chairs, etc.; 16 pp; **CTY/B** (Uai B633).

BOERICKE & RUNYON
518 Sixth Avenue, New York.
11 West 42nd Street, New York, New York.

1905   Special Prescription Tablets, Giving their Uses, Dosages, etc.; 28 pp; **MAH.**

1906   Physicians' Catalogue; 112 pp; **MAH.**

1922   Special Preparation Tables Giving their Uses, Dosage, etc.; 40 pp; **MAH.**

1923   Special Prescription Tablets Giving their Uses, Dosage, etc.; 40 pp; **MAH.**

1930   Patillas Homeopaticas De Recetas Especiales Sus Diversas Aplicaciones, Dosis, etc.; 40 pp; **MAH.**

n.d.   Physicians' Catalogue and Price List; 104 pp; **MAH.**

n.d.   Catalog and Price List—Pharmaceutical Products; 164 pp; **MAH.**

BOGNER
Strasburg.

n.d.   Case of Trephines in Old Ashmolean include brace signed "Bogner Strasburg", **WHM** (R 3672/1936) bleeding lancets, one by Bogner; **RCSL.**

BOLTE, C. W., NACHF.
Hamburg, Germany.

ca 1878   No title page; Catalog of Medical, Surgical, Electro-Therapeutic, Orthopedic Apparatus, includes section on veterinary instruments; 2,280 illustrations, 189 pp, index.; Fragile; bound in three ring binder; **AFMM.**

BONNEELS, MAISON
See: GEORGE CLASEN; **NYAM.**

BONSCHUR & HOLMES
1527 Chestnut Street, Philadelphia, Pennsylvania.

1894   Catalogue and Price List of Optical Instruments; 106 pp; **MUM** (ZZ Ky 2).

1533 Chestnut St., (Philadelphia, PA.).

1898   Catalogue Part A, Test Cases, Ophthalmoscopes, Phorometers, Ophthalmometers, Perimeters, Ophthalmic Surgical Instruments; 74 pp; **MUM.**

E. 20 c   Catalog, Part Z, Test Cases, Ophthalmoscopes, Phorometers, Ophthalmometers, Perimeters, and the Varied Instruments used by the Ophthalmic Surgeon; 71 pp, index pp 2; **NYAM.**

ca 1905   Optical Goods Part A; 74 pp, index, no real title pg; **NYAM; MF/MAH; CPP.**

1916   Part A, Test Cases, Ophthalmoscopes, Photometers, Perimeters and Varied Instruments used by Ophthalmic Surgeons; 74 pp; **URRR** (B-107).

n.d.   Part C, General Optical Goods, including Glasses . . .; 50 pp; **CPP; MUM.**

BONWILL, DR.

See: PATRICK AND CARTER; **UPSDM.**

BOOK, LOUIS

312 Broadway, New York, New York.

n.d.   Reynal's Porte Remede or Medicated Bougies for the Treatment of Blennoirhea; 6 pp; **CPP.**

BORSCH, JOHN L., & CO.

1324 Walnut Street, Philadelphia, Pennsylvania.

1903   The Use of Kryptoks; 10 pp, 2 inserts; **URRR** (B-109).

n.d.   Price List & Illustrated Catalogue of Ophthalmological & Optical Instruments; 76 pp; **CPP.**

BOSCH, J. & A.

Muensterstrasse 15, Strassburg.

ca 1905   Price list no. 18; Precision Balances and Weights; 36 pp, price list; **NYAM; MF/MAH.**

BOSCH & SPEIDEL

Fabrick Medizinischer Apparate, Jungingen/Hohnzollern, Germany.

1920s   Mecurette and Miniature Sphygmomanometers; 4 pp; **WMScM.**

BOSTON DENTAL MFG. CO.

174 Tremont Street, Boston, Massachusetts.

Originated as part of Codman and Shurtleff, dental division, until 1880s.

1893   Catalog, Confidential Trade List, binder's title: Boston Dental Mfg. Co. Catalog; 217 pp; **UPSDM** (D 617.604 B657).

1893   Catalog, Dental Instruments and Materials; (TM); **UPAL.**

BOSTON OPTICAL WORKS

75 Kilby St., Boston, Massachusetts.

(R. Tolles, Supt.), (Charles Stodder, Agent and Treas.)

"Importer and Agent for W. Wales' and Jos. Zentmayer's Microscopes"

See: CHARLES STODDER

ca 1870   (This is bound with Smith, Beck and Beck's 1866 "An Illustrated Description of the Popular Microscope) Description of TOLLES' Student Microscope, and "The Pocket Microscope." 12 pp, no covers;

includes "Report of the Judges, on Philosophical Apparatus, eleventh exhibition of the Massachusetts Charitable Mechanic; Assoc. held in Boston, Sept. 1869; **NLM** (W26 qS643).

131 Devonshire corner of Milk Street, (Boston, MA.).
1879   Catalog of Tolles Microscopes, 15th ed.; 23 pp, **NLM** (W 26B747).
1910   Lorgnettes; 4 pp, non-med 4 pp; **URRR** (B-112).

BOSWORTH, HARRY J.
1106-7-8 Tower Bldg., Madison and Michigan Ave., Chicago, Illinois.
Est: 1914
"Exclusive Dental Office Equipment"
ca 1915   Five single page ads paper clipped together advertising various pieces of dental office equipment; **NYAM.**
ca 1915   A Few Bosworthy Ideas . . .; Dental Catalog; 15 pp; **NYAM; MF/MAH.**

BOULANGER-DAUSSE ET CIE
(Laboratories Pharmaceutiques Dausse), 4 rue Aubriot, Paris, France.
1921   Les remèdes galeniques; 23 pp; **CPP.**

BOULITTE, G.
7 rue Linné, Paris.
342 Madison Ave., New York.
15 a 21, rue Bobillot, Paris XIII, France.
Est: 1875
"Ancien Maison Ch. Verdin" "Ingénieur-Constructeur" A. Gaudin—agent and Managing Director, Tainturier, Pirard et Coeurderuche
7 rue Blainville, Paris V, France.
ca 1912   Viscosimètre de Hess; 3 pp; **NYAM; MF/MAH.**
1875   Catalog, Scientific Instruments for Medicine and Physiology; 14 pp; **MAH.**
1913   Catalog D, appareils pour la méthode graphique et accessoires, appareils de physiologies, appareils de clinique médicale et de diagnostic, appareils de psychologie et neurologie; (opposite title pg 3-color illustration of medals won) Albert C. Gaudin, NYC, Stamped on cover; 380 pp, index pp 189-194; (TM); **NYAM; MF/MAH; CPP; NLM** (W26 B763c).
ca 1913   Brochure describing Viscosimètre de Hess; 4 pp; **NLM.**
1920   Électrocardiographe (Nouveau modèle); 13 pp; **NYAM; MF/MAH.**
ca 1920   Nouveaux instruments scientifiques mesure du métabolisme basal; 10 pp; **NYAM; MF/MAH.**
ca 1920   Scientific Instruments for Medicine and Physiology; 18 pp; **NYAM; MF/MAH.**
ca 1920   Portable Electrocardiograph; 1 pp; **NYAM; MF/MAH.**
ca 1920   Enregistreur électrique universal; 3 pp; **NYAM; MF/MAH.**
ca 1920   Centrifugeuse électrique; 3 pp; **NYAM; MF/MAH.**
ca 1920   Spirometre de Ch. Verdin; 2 pp; **NYAM; MF/MAH.**
ca 1920   Mesure de la pression du liquide cephalo-rachidien; 3 pp; **NYAM; MF/MAH.**
ca 1920   Installation de cylindres enregistreurs pour travaux pratiques de physiologie; 3 pp; **NYAM; MF/MAH.**
1920?   Phonendoscope de MM Bazzi et Bianche; 3 pp; **MF/MAH; NYAM.**
ca 1920   Compresseur simple des Docteurs Legrand and Chuffart pour la mesure réflexe oculo-cardiaque; 3 pp; **NYAM; MF/MAH.**

ca 1920   Polygraphe portatif; 4 pp; **NYAM; MF/MAH.**
ca 1920   Nouveaux instruments scientifique pour la clinique ou la physiologie; 2 pp; **NYAM; MF/MAH.**
ca 1920   Capsule oscillographique; 2 pp; **NYAM; MF/MAH.**
ca 1920   The Measure of Arterial Pressure Pachon's Sphygometric Oscillometer; 11 pp; **NYAM; MF/MAH.**
ca 1920   Gastronometre clinique du Doctor Réné Gaultier; 3 pp; **NYAM; MF/MAH.**
ca 1920   Appareil du Prof Henri Claude pour la mesure de la pression du liquide cephalo-rachidien; 4 pp; **NYAM; MF/MAH.**
ca 1920   Enregistreur électrique universal; 4 pp; **NYAM; MF/MAH.**
ca 1920   Mesure du débit respiratoire maximum par la masque manomètrique; 4 pp; **NYAM; MF/MAH.**
ca 1920   Polygraph portatif; 3 pp; **MF/MAH; NYAM.**
ca 1920   Centrifuge électrique; 2 pp; **NYAM; MF/MAH.**
ca 1920   Appareillage pour la mesure des réactions psycho-motrices chez homme; 3 pp; **MF/MAH; NYAM.**
    1922   Brochure, Electrocardiographic Set, New Improved Model (Patent, but no patent no. appears in text); 17 pp; **NYAM; MF/MAH.**
    1922   Electrocardiographic Set, New Improved Model, Stamped on cover: Albert C Gaudin, General Agent, 342 Madison Ave; 18 pp; **NYAM; MF/MAH.**
ca 1922   Nouveau sphygmanomètre pour la mesure des pressions arterielles maxima et minima par la méthode ausculatoire de Korotkow; 3 pp; **NYAM; MF/MAH.**
ca 1922   Insufflateur des Docteurs Leuret and Delmas pour pneumothorax artificiel, injection; d'oxygène, pneumo péritoine, etc . . .; 8 pp; **NYAM; MF/MAH.**
1920's   Brochure, Nouveaux instruments scientifiques; 7 pp; **NYAM.**
    1923   Catalog F, Appareils de diagnostic, sphygmographes et polygraph sphygmomanomètres, appareils pour la percussion et l'auscultation, thermomètres, appareils pour l'étude et la mesure des organs de la respiration, appareils pour l'étude des muscles et des réflexes, esthesiomètres, etc.; 34 pp, index pp 34; (TM); **NYAM; MF/MAH.**
    1924   Catalog G. Phonétique, stamped on cover: Albert C. Gaudin, NY City; 11 pp; (TM); **NYAM; MF/MAH; CPP.**
Aug. 1924   Price List no. 1, "Taken from General Calalogue," Scientific Instruments for Medicine and Physiology, has price list dated September 1924; 14 pp; (TM); **NYAM; CPP.**
Aug. 1924   Scientific Instruments for Medicine and Physiology; 14 pp; **NYAM; MF/MAH; MAH.**
ca 1925   Pamphlets describing various physiological and measuring instruments; 114 pp; **NLM.**
ca 1925   Brochure, Portable Electrocardiograph, New Improved Model, patented, on front cover: Albert C. Gaudin, 342 Madison Ave., New York City; 17 pp; (TM); **NYAM.**
    1928   Électrocardiographe, nouveau modèle perfectionné; 27 pp, 4 color photos, Separate sheets, letter 1938; **WMScM** (File no. 1-1972); **CPP.**
    1928   Catalogue A, Cylindres enregistreurs, inscripteurs à air et électromagnetiques, appareils pour la mesure et l'enregistrement du temps; 43 pp; **BLEL; CPP.**
    1928   Catalogue M, Appareils pour la mesure du métabolisme basal et des

échanges respiratoires; 32 pp, inserts; **BLEL; CPP.**

1929   Catalogue B, Appareils de physiologie humaine psychologie et psychotechnique orientation professionnelle anthropometrie; 17 pp; **CPP.**

1929   Catalogue D, Appareils pour physiologie expérimentale; 61 pp; **CPP.**

Oct. 1930   Électrodes, thermophores, cables, minutories, petits accessoires pour diathermie, matériel complet du Dr. P. E. Roncayol; 18 pp; **CPP.**

1930   Appareils pour le diagnostic sphygmographes et polygraphes, sphygmomanomètres, appareils pour l'auscultation, appareils pour l'étude et la mesure des organes respiratoires; 37 pp, inserts; **CPP.**

1931   Électrocardiographe portatif; 18 pp; **CPP.**

E. 20 c   La mesure de la pression arterielle maxima and minima par l'oscillomètre sphygometrique du Professeur V. Pachon, illustrated pamphlet; 11 pp French, 12 pp English; **AFMM.**

n.d.   Capsule oscillographique, pamphlet; 3 pp; **MF/MAH; NYAM.**

n.d.   Brochure, Appareil du Dr. Henri Claude pour la mesure de la pression du liquide cephalo-rachidien; 4 pp; **MF/MAH; NYAM.**

BOURQUE OPTICAL CO., THE
1033, 1035 Canal Street, New Orleans, LA.

1910s   Illustrated Catalogue of Optical Goods, cover only; **AO.**

BOVININE CO., THE
Laboratory: Chicago, Illinois.
Main Office: 65 South 5th Avenue, New York, New York.
32 Snow Hill, London E C.
75 West Houston Street, New York, New York.
2 Barclay Street, New York, New York.

n.d.   A Practical Treatise on How to Preserve Perfect Nutrition Bovinine; 110 pp; **CPP.**

n.d.   Bovinine Food Tonic Cell Stimulant; 32 pp; **CPP.**

n.d.   Bovinine Molecular Renovation of Living Protoplasm; 32 pp; **CPP.**

BOWEN, C. W. & R. M., CO.
86 Weybosset St., Providence, Rhode Island.

Apr. 1903   Illustrated Price List of Latest Improved High Grade X-Ray Tubes; 2 pp; **MAH** (C616.0750 B).

1903   Price List of Latest Improved High Grade X-Ray Tubes; **MAH** (C616.0757 B).

ca 1920   Catalog, Photo-Therapy: The Surgery of Light, Mfgs, Importers and Dealers in High Grade Electro-Therapeutic and X-Ray apparatus, Contains detailed information on the Finsen's Light, photo, use and price; 4 pp; **MAH** (C615.831085).

BOYVEAU, PELLETIER et CIE, SUCCESSEURS
Rue des Francs-Bourgeois-Saint-Michel, 8, Paris.

L. 19 c   Prix courant des produits chimiques, instruments, utensiles de laboratoire, etc., de la fabrique de robiquet, Membre de l'Institut Boyveau et Pelletier; 20 pp; **CTY/B** (Uai B714).

BOZE, A., FIRM
St. Petersburg, Russia.

1894   Atlas Khirurgicheskikh instrumentov; 58 pp, index; **NLM.**

1894   Atlas Meditsinskikh, Khirurgicheskikh. Instrumenton, Bandazhei,

Ortopedicheskikh, Snariadov, Presented in German, Russian, and English; **NLM** (W26 B793a).

BRADBURY, WILKINSON & CO. LTD.
U.S. Agents, J. Movins & Son, 79 Murray Street, New York, New York.
1890   Antipyrin, Dr. Knorr; 77 pp; **CPP.**

BRADLEY-COLLINS CO.
Chicago, Illinois.
13 & 15 W. 29th St. (Revillon Building), New York, New York.
(B.J. Kershaw, agent)
ca 1900   The Bradley Antiseptic Cabinet, Dental, and Sterilizer; 16 pp; **MF/MAH; NYAM.**
ca 1901   Dental Catalog, Antiseptic Dental Cabinet; 16 pp; **NYAM.**
1901   Physicians' Catalog, Antiseptic Physicians, and Sterilizer, C. A. Bradley, M.D., inventor, good picture of unit; Testimonials thru 1900; 16 pp; **NYAM.**

BRADY, GEO. W., & CO.
809-11 S. Western Ave., Chicago, Illinois.
1930's   Sign, X-Ray Tubes, "Symptoms of Tubes and How to Treat Them," to be Hung in X-Ray Lab for Reference; 1 pp; **ACR/MAH.**
1930's   Signs, X-Ray Tubes, "Symptoms of Tubes and How to Treat Them," to be Hung in X-Ray Lab for Reference; 2 pp; **ACR/MAH.**
1930's   Leaflet, Paragon X-Ray Plates; **ACR/MAH.**

BRADY & MARTIN (CO.)
29 Mosley St. Northumberland Rd., Newcastle-upon-Tyre(?), England.
1882   Catalog of Surgical & Physiological Instruments, Microscopes, Appliances and Sundries; 144 pp; **UVHSL** (RD71.C3).
1897   Catalog of the Instruments, Appliances and Fittings Used in Surgery and Medicine to Which is Added an Appendix; vii-xvi, 548 pp, index pp 529-548; **SBMC; RCSL.**

BRAMHALL, DEANE CO.
261-263-265 W. 36th St., New York, New York.
1903   Sterilizing Apparatus, Catalog no. 3; 62 pp; **CPP.** Hospital Edition Illustrated Catalog B D Co. Mfg of Sterilizing Apparatus; 23 pp; **CPP.**
1920s–30s   Catalog no. 23, Sterilizing Apparatus, list of institutions which have instruments; pp 29-31; Mfg for 1/2 ct. spec. sheet metal work; 32 pp, index pp 32; (TM); **NYAM.**
post 1930s   Sterilizing Apparatus, Catalog no. 23; 23 pp, index; **NYAM; MF/MAH.**

BRAUN, B.
Luisenstrasse 63, Berlin.
Gartenstrasse 69-71, Breslau.
Kettenhosweg 123, Frankfurt am Main.
Schwanthalerstrasse 73, Melsungen, München.
E. 20 c   Brochure, Syringes, Thermometers, Laboratory Equipment, Hospital Beds, Splints; fragile, front page half missing; 18 pp; (TM); **NYAM.**
ca 1920s   no title page; Surgical Supplies, including hospital and general needs; 17 pp, additional pp; **NYAM; MF/MAH.**
n.d.   Melsungen; 148 pp; (TM); contents 4 pp; **ZUR.**
n.d.   Sterile Catgut Kuhn, Medical Supplies of Every Description; **WMScM.**

BREEDING AND LABORATORY INSTITUTE
619 Kent Avenue, Brooklyn, New York.
    post 1930   Brochure, Science, Medicine, and Health, stocks of lab animals; 4 pp;
        NYAM; MF/MAH.

BREGUET
Brequet, Maison
59, Quai de L'Horloge, Paris, France.
    1884   Extrait du catalogue général illustre: instruments de physiologie de M. J.
        Marey, appareils pour l'électricité médicale; 31 pp; **BLEL.**
    n.d.   Appareils et instruments de physiologie du Dr. Marey; 4 pp; **MUM.**

BREITENBACH, M. J., CO.
53, 56 & 58 Warren Street, New York, New York.
Laboratory: Leipzig, Germany.
    July 21, 1892   Chlorosis and Rhachitis by ed. Hoenigshmied; 8 pp; **CPP.** Notes on the
        Treatment of Anaemia; 8 pp; **CPP.**
    ca 1896–97   Report from Dr. Mackewrodt's Gynaecological Clinic by Dr. Gellhorn
        (Berlin); 8 pp; **CPP.**
    1897   Irregular Menstruation in Young Women Due to Anaemic Conditions by
        H. Edwin Lewis (Burlington, Vermont); 8 pp; **CPP.**
    1897   After Gynecological Operations by C. A. von Randohr; 4 pp; **CPP.**
    n.d.   How to Assist Young Girls to Womanhood by Edward C. Hill; 9 pp;
        CPP.
    n.d.   The Influence of Pepto-Mangan upon the Blood and Nervous System by
        L. Braun, M.D. and B. Licht, M.D. translated from German; 12 pp;
        CPP.
    n.d.   The Treatment of Chlorosis and of Rhachitis with Gude's Pepto-Mangan;
        8 pp; **CPP.**

BRESETTE, M. H., X-RAY & RADIO CO.
See: ACME-INTERNATIONAL Bulletin, 16 Oct 1922; **ACR/MAH.**

BRETON FRÈRES
23 rue Dauphine, Paris, France.
See: DRAPIER et FILS; **NLM.**
    1863   Catalogue des instruments de physique, de chimie, d'optique, de
        mathématiques, et d'astronomie qui se trouvant et s'executent dans les
        magasins et ateliers de M. Breton . . .; 104 pp, index pp 97-104;
        NYAM.
    186?   Notice et descriptions du nouvel appareil électrodynamique complet,
        construit par M. Breton Frères; 12 pp; **BLEL.**

BREXTON
    n.d.   Medical and Surgical Bags and Cases, with trade price list no. 21; 1 pp,
        foldout; **WMScM.**

BRICKERHOFF & PENTON
    1904   Information from Catalog, PETER VAN SCHAACK & SONS, **NYAM.**
Successors to: Peter Van Schaak & Sons, 1885, Van Schaak & Stevenson & Co., 1877, Van
Schaak, Stevenson & Reid, 1870, E.P. Dwyer & Co., 1865, Smith & Dwyer, 1860, Penton,
Robinson & Smith, 1859, Penton & Robinson, 1857, Brickerhoff & Penton, 1844.

BRINGHURST, F.
620 Arch Street, Philadelphia, Pennsylvania.

1866   Patent Artificial Limbs: Their Adjustment & Construction; **CPP.**
1887   Surgical Appliances; 24 pp; **CPP.**

BRIN'S OXYGEN COMPANY, LTD.
Connaught Mansions, Victoria Street, Westminster S. W.
    n.d.   Oxygen and Its Medical Applications; 20 pp; **CPP.**

BRITESUN
See: WAPPLER ELECTRIC CO.; **NYAM**

BRITISH CYSTOSCOPE CO., THE
44-48 Clerkenwell Rd., London EC 1.
Oct. 15, 1935   Wynsbury White's Cystoscope for Applying Diathermy to Bladder
             Growths; 3 pp; **WMScM.**
    n.d.   E. Canny Ryall's Universal Operating Cysto-Urethroscope; 4 pp;
            WMScM.
    n.d.   Catalog of Electrically Lighted Instruments and Accessories; 53 pp;
            WMScM.

BRITISH THOMSON-HOUSTON CO., LTD.
See: WATSON & SONS LTD., 1925?; **MAH.**

BROUGHTON, W. R.
    n.d.   Description and Use of the Phorometer; 8 pp; **MAH** (C617.75085 B).

BROWN, D. V.
736, 738, 740 Sansom St., Philadelphia, PA.
    1911   *Our Own Idea*, Devoted to the Interest of the Optical Business, Vol. XVIII,
            no. 2, February; **AO.**
    n.d.   Catalog of Optical Goods, Optical Instruments Trial Cases and Accessories,
            Opticians' Machinery, etc.; 173 pp; **URRR** (B-132).

BROWN, FREDERICK W., CO.
591 The Bourse, Philadelphia, Pennsylvania.
Laboratory and Office: Wynette, Pennsylvania.
Feb. 8, 1896   Aseptolin by Cyrus Edson; 15 pp; **CPP.**
    n.d.   A Formulated Treatment for Tuberculosis, Septicaemia, Malaria and La
            Grippe with reports of cases; **CPP.**
NE Corner Fifth Street and Chestnut Street, (Phila., PA.).
Mar. 1, 1888   Antiseptic Pastilles; 2 pp; **CPP.**
600 Broad Street, (Phila., PA.).
    n.d.   Price Catalog; 82 pp; **CPP.**

BROWN, WILLIAM AND EARLE
918 Chestnut Street, Philadelphia, Pennsylvania.
    n.d.   Radium for the Treatment of Cancer, Lupus, etc., and For Experimental
            Work; 4 pp; **CPP.**
    n.d.   The American Hemoglobinometer; 4 pp; **CPP.**

BROWNING, JOHN
63, Stone, W.C. 111, Minorities E, London, England.
Factory: 6 Vine St. E.C. London.
Apr. 1894   Optical and Physicial Instrument Maker; Spectroscopes and Spectrum
           Apparatus; 54 pp; prize medal, 1862; **RCSL.**

BROWNING MFG. CO., THE
Milwaukee, Wisconsin.

ca 1910   Direction Book of the Browning Mfg. Co.; Dental Machine, Instructions for Use; not a Catalog, but instruction manual for use and installation; 16 pp; **NYAM; MF/MAH.**

E. 20 c   Directions for Using and Caring for Various Apparatus using Electricity, Dental Materials; Cautery; **NYAM.**

BRUCK, L.
Belmont Building, Sydney, Australia.

1911   Catalog, Surgical Instruments; 17th ed. with 1912 supplement; pp 1001-1117, 2001-2175, 3001-3267, 4001-4110, 5001-5190. Bound with this Catalog is Kny-Scheerer Co. New York Catalog entitled Modern Aseptible Surgical Furniture; 112 pp; Appears that Bruck Catalog was essentially an American one, published over the name of the Sydney Firm; TM is a cadusis surmounted by crown; **UNSW/A.**

BRUENINGS INSTRUMENTS
See: F. L. FISCHER; ca 1907.

BRUNSWICK PHARMACAL CO., THE
92 William Street, New York, New York.

1899   A Thousand Dyspeptics; 23 pp; **CPP.**
1899   A Study in Dyspepsia (same text as above); 23 pp; **CPP.**
1900   On Dyspepsia; 24 pp; **CPP.**
1900   Papoid in Surgery; 23 pp; **CPP.**
1901   The Story of the Papan, by Fred. B. Kilmer; 32 pp; **CPP.**
n.d.   Vino-Kolafra; 16 pp; **CPP.**
n.d.   Dyspepsia: Diagnosis and Treatment; 24 pp; **CPP.**
n.d.   Papoid in External Therapeutics; 30 pp; **CPP.**
n.d.   Power in a Nutshell; 33 pp; **CPP.**

BUCK X-OGRAPH CO.
St. Louis, Missouri.

1927   Catalog and Technic, Radiography; 31 pp; (TM); **ACR/MAH.**
1937   Catalog, X-Ray Supplies and Accessories; 22 pp; (TM); **ACR/MAH.**
1937   Bulletin no. 2500, The Buckite Line of Developing Tanks; 13 pp; **ACR/MAH.**

BUCKEYE STATE OPTICAL CO., INC. THE
Columbus, Ohio.

Feb. 1, 1930   Buckeye Regular Toric and Correct Curve Pair and Prescription Price List; 4 pp; **AO.**

BUFFALO DENTAL MANUFACTURING CO.
Court St., Corner of Pearl and (factory & wholesale dept) 13 & 15 Pearl St. (Cor. Terrace), Buffalo, New York.
307 & 309 Main St., Buffalo, New York.
587 and 589 Main Street, corner of Chipewa, Buffalo, New York.
Est: 1867

See: FLETCHER, THOMAS, of Warrington, England; **YML.** Codes to Catalogue A, Dentists' Specialties; Catalogue B, Chemical Laboratory Appliances; Catalogue C, Vulcanizers and Appurtenances; Catalogue D, Dental Laboratory Implements; Catalogue E, Automatic Pluggers and Points; Catalogue F, Nitrous Oxide Gas and Apparatus; Catalogue G, Workshops and Tool-Room.

Feb. 1878   List no. 2, Laboratory Apparatus; 8 pp; **CTY/B** (Uai B 862).

May 1878	Supplementary List no. 3; New Laboratory Apparatus; 1 pp; **CTY/B** (Uai B 862).
Aug. 1879	Fletcher's Laboratory Apparatus. List no. 5; 14 pp; **CTY/B** (Uai B862).
Sep. 1882	Catalog of Fletcher's Laboratory and Special Heating Apparatus; 31 pp; **CTY/B** (Uai B862).
May 1887	Catalog, Gas Cooking Apparatus for Household Purposes, Designed and Patented by Thos. Fletcher, F.C.S., Warrington, Eng.; List no. 19; 30 pp; **CTY/B** (Uai B862).
1888	Price List of Vulcanizers and Dentists' Specialities; 80 pp, index pp 70-80; **MAH** (C617.6085B).
1890	Chemists Lab Apparatus; 44 pp; **UPSDM** (617.604 B 863).
1890	Price List of Vulcanizers and Dentists' Specialities; 92 pp, index pp 82-92; **MAH** (C617.6085B).
1891	Laboratory Appliances, Catalog B, no. 28; 48 pp, index pp 47-48; **MAH** (C617.60853).
1893	Catalog D, Implements, Appliances and Tools for the Dental Laboratory; **CTY/B** (Uai B 862).
1893	Lewis Combined Soldering and Ladle Furnace; 6 pp; **MAH** (C617.6085).
1893	The Lewis Nitrous Oxide Gasometer and Appurtenances; 12 pp; **MAH** (C617.6085).
1893	Lab Appliances, Catalog B, no. 29; 49 pp, index pp 48-49; **MAH** (C617.6085).
1893	Catalog A, List of Dentists' Specialities; 24 pp; **MAH** (C617.6085).
1894	Catalog C, Price list of Vulcanizers and Their Appurtenances for the Dental Lab; 28 pp; **MAH** (C617.6085).
Feb. 1895	Catalog B, Lab Appliances; 53 pp; index, pp 49-52; **MAH** (C617.6085 B).
1895	Catalog C, Price List of Vulcanizers and their Appurtenances for the Dental Lab; 28 pp; **MAH** (C617.6085).
1895	Catalog E, Automatic Pluggers and The Snow & Lewis Pluggers; 10 pp; **MAH** (C617.6085).
1896	Catalog D, Implements, Appliance, and Tools for the Dental Lab; 32 pp, index pp 32; **MAH** (C617.6085).
1897–1915	Catalogs, General Instructions for Operating Dental Vulcanizers; **MAH**.
1897	Price List of Vulcanizers and their Appurtenances for the Dental Lab, "Original Mfgrs. of Dntl. Vulcanizers;" 28 pp; **NYAM; MF/MAH; MAH** (C617.6085).
1897	Catalog E, Automatic Pluggers; 10 pp; **MAH** (C617.6085).
1898	Catalog A, List of Dentists' Specialties, lists present catalogs on inside cover; 24 pp; (TM); **NYAM; MF/MAH.**
1898	Catalog F, The Lewis Nitrous Oxide Gasometer and Appurtenances; 12 pp; **MAH** (C617.6085).
1899	Catalog D, Implements, Appliances and Tools for the Dental Lab, Especially Adapted for Melting, Soldering and Working Metals for Bridge-Work, Crown-Work and All Dental Metal Work; 39 pp, index pp 39; **NYAM; MF/MAH.**
1900	Catalog E, Automatic Pluggers; 8. pp; **MAH** (C617.6085).
1901	Catalog and Price List of Dentists' Supplies; 675 pp, index; **MAH** (C617.6085); **UBML** (WU 26B929d).
Jan. 1901	Catalog, Price List of Dentists' Supplies; 675 pp, index pp 652-675; (TM); **MAH** (C 617.6085 B).

1901	Catalog A, List of Dentists' Specialties; 24 pp; **MAH** (C617.6085).
Oct. 1901	Catalog B, Laboratory Appliances; 54 pp, index pp 51-54; **MAH** (C617.6085).
1901	Catalog E, Automatic Pluggers; 13 pp; **MAH** (C617.6085 B).
1902	Catalog C, Vulcanizers and Their Appurtenances; 24 pp; (TM); **MAH** (C617.6085 B).
1902	Catalog D, Implements for Melting, Working and Soldering Metals, and Bridge and Crown Work; 36 pp; **MAH** (C617.6085 B).
1902	Catalog G, Brazing Stands, Blowpipes, Tool-Forges, Foot-Blowers, Gas Burners; 16 pp; (TM); **MAH** (C617.6085 B).
1903	Catalog A, Dentists' Specialties; 32 pp; (TM); **MAH** (C617.6085 B); **SLSC.**
1903	Catalog C, Vulcanizers and Their Appurtenances for the Dental Laboratory; 28 pp; (TM); **MAH** (C617.6085).
1903	Catalog D, Dental Laboratory Implements; 36 pp; (TM); **MAH;** (C617.6085 B).
1904	Catalog C, Vulcanizers and Their Appurtenances for the Dental Lab; 28 pp; **MAH** (C617.6085 B).
1904	Catalog E, Automatic Pluggers; 14 pp; **MAH** (C617.6085).
Feb. 1910	Catalog B, List no. 35, Laboratory and Workshop Appliances for Colleges, Schools, Chemists, Assayers, Manufacturing Jewelers, Experimental Laboratories, Workshops, and Tool-Rooms; 71 pp; **CTY/B** (Uai B862).
Sep. 1913	Catalog B, List no. 36, Laboratory and Workshop Appliances for Colleges, Schools, Chemists, Assayers, Manufacturing Jewelers, Experimental Laboratories, Workshops, and Tool-Rooms; 80 pp; **CTY/B** (Uai B862).
1915	Catalog C, Vulcanizers and Their Appurtenances for the Dental Lab and Dental College; 34 pp; **MAH** (C617.6085).
1915	Catalog D, Working, Heating, Melting and Soldering Metals in the Dental Laboratory Employing Illuminating Gas, Natural Gas or Gasoline as Fuel; 61 pp; **NYAM; MF/MAH.**
1916	Catalog E, Automatic Pluggers; 12 pp; (TM); **MAH** (C617.6085).
1917	Catalog A, List of Dentists' Appliances; 48 pp; (TM); **MAH** (C617.6085).
1917	Catalog C, Vulcanizers and Their Appurtenances for the Dental College; 34 pp; **MAH** (C617.6085 B).
1918	Catalog D, Appliances and Implements for Working, Heating, Melting and Soldering Metals; Crown and Bridge Work; 60 pp; (TM); **MAH** (C617.6085 B).
1919	Catalog A, Dentists' Appliances for Operating Room and Laboratory; 45 pp; **NYAM; MF/MAH.**
1919	Catalog A, Dentists' Appliances; 43 pp; **MAH** (C617.6085 B).
1920	Catalog E, Automatic Pluggers; 13 pp; **MAH** (C617.6085 B).
1920	Catalog E, The Lewis and S & L Automatic Pluggers; 15 pp, index; **MF/MAH; NYAM.**
1920	Booklet no. 4, Soldering by Means of Gasoline Gas; 5 pp; **NYAM.**
ca 1920	Booklet no. 9, Electric Heating Oven; 11 pp, 1 pp Price List; Advertizes Booklets 1-9; **NYAM.**
1921	Catalog A, Dentists' Appliances for Laboratory and Operating Room; 43 pp, separate price list under back cover; **MAH** (C617.6085 B).
1921	Catalog C, Vulcanizers and Their Appurtenances for the Dental Lab and College; 33 pp, **MAH** (C617.6085 B).
1923	Catalog D, Appliances and Implements for Working, Heating, Melting

and Soldering Metals; Inlay, Cast Denture, Crown and Bridge Work; 50 pp, separate price list under back cover; **MAH** (C617.6085 B).

1924   Catalog A, Dentists' Appliances for Lab and Operating Room; 44 pp; **MAH** (C617.6085 B).

1924   Catalog E, List of Automatic Pluggers; 12 pp, 1 pp price list; (TM); **MAH** (C617.6085 B).

1925   Catalog A; Dentists' Appliances for Operating Room and Laboratory; 48 pp, price list, additional sheets; **MF/MAH; NYAM.**

775 Main Street, (Buffalo, N.Y.).

1925   Catalogue E, Automatic Pluggers; 14 pp; loose Price List Jan 1927; **NYAM; MF/MAH.**

ca 1925   General Catalog, Dentists' Appliances for Lab and Operating Room; 92 pp, Price List pp 76-92; (TM); **NYAM.**

1926   Catalog C, Vulcanizers and Flasks; 36 pp, price list; **MF/MAH; NYAM.**

1927   Catalog D, List of Heating Appliances and Implements for Working and Heating, Melting and Soldering Metals; Inlay, Cast Denture, Crown and Bridge Work; 47 pp, 4 pp Price List; (TM); **MF/MAH; NYAM.**

ca 1929   Vulcanizers and Vulcanizing: The Evolution of the Dental Vulcanizer and How to Obtain Best Results; Booklet no. 3; 20 pp; **NYAM; MF/MAH.**

ca 1929   Soldering by Means of Gasoline Gas, Booklet no. 4; 7 pp; **NYAM; MF/MAH.**

ca 1930   General Catalog, Dentists' Appliances for Laboratory and Operating Room; 92 pp; **NYAM; MF/MAH.**

ca 1930   Electric Heating Ovens; Booklet no. 9; 12 pp; **NYAM; MF/MAH.**

n.d.   lists names of other booklets on inside cover; **NYAM; MF/MAH.**

Kehr Street corner Urban, (Buffalo, N.Y.).

n.d.   Vulcanizers and Their Appurtenances; Incomplete, only pp 27-30; **NYAM; MF/MAH.**

n.d.   Dental Appliances; Incomplete, only pp 35-38; **NYAM; MF/MAH.**

BULL, LEWES

ca 1825   Instrument maker mentioned by John Read.

BULL & METCALFE

Hartford, Connecticut.

1833   Catalog of Drugs, Patent Medicines, Wines, Teas, etc. for Sale By . . . Druggists and Apothecaries; Sign of the Good Samaritan, . . . Hartford: Printed by Goodwin and Co.; 18 pp; **CHS** (1833B935c).

BULLOCK & CRENSHAW

528 Arch Street, running through to 531 North Street, Philadelphia, Pennsylvania.
Successors to Smith and Hodgson

May 1, 1854   Catalogue of Drugs, Pharmaceutical Preparations and Medicinal Wares; 39 pp; **MUM** (2r-56 pam36).

103 & 105 Sixth St., (Phila., PA.).

1858   Catalog of Chemicals, Chemical and Pharmaceutical Apparatus. 96 pp; Fragile; **NLM** (W 26qB938).

6th St. & Arch, (Phila., PA.).

1860   Catalog of Drugs, Pharmaceutical Preparations, Utensils, Apparatus, Surgical Instruments, Anatomical Preparations, etc.; 111 pp, 9 pp of ads; **NLM.**

May 1860   Catalog of Drugs, Pharmaceutical Preparations, Utensils, Apparatus, Surgical Instruments, Anatomical Preparations, etc.; Price List for

Sugar Coated Pills and Granules Dated March 1867 attached; 5th ed.; 112 pp; **NLM** (W 26qB938); **HML; ABD.**

1881   Catalog of Chemicals, Chemical and Pharmaceutical Apparatus; **CPP** (Bolenius Coll).

BULLOCH, W. H.
Nos. 99 and 101 W. Monroe St., Chicago, Illinois.
Est: 1866
"Sole Agents for New York and Vicinity: Meyrowitz Brothers"

1890   Catalog, Optical Instruments, Microscopes . . . Accessories; 40 pp; covers missing, Filed in envelope; **MAH.**

BURDICK RESEARCH LABORATORIES
Burdick Corporation, The
Burdick Cabinet Company,
Milton, Wisconsin.
Est: 1914

1923   Pamphlet, Manual of Infra-Red Technique, A Practical Manual of Invisible Light Therapy Embracing Technique for Burdick Infra-Red Compresses and Pads and for Burdick Infra-Red Orificial Appliances, included in sales notebook cover: The Englin Electrical Co.: X-Ray Apparatus; 24 pp; **ACR/MAH, MAH.**

1923   Catalog, Infra-Red Therapy, A Practical Manual of Invisible Therapy, by F. F. Burdick; 47 pp; **ACR/MAH, MAH.**

n.d.   Catalogs of physical therapy and electro-surgical equipment; **NLM** (W26 B951c).

BURGE, WARREN & RIDGLEY
11 Clerkenwell Green, London, E.C., England.
Surgical Instrument Manufacturers.

n.d.   Catalog, Surgical Instruments, Drugs, Sundries; Index viii, 150 pp; **RCSL.**

BURGOYNE, BURBRIDGES, & CO.
Coleman Street, London, England.

post 1890   Catalog, Surgical Instruments, Appliances, Electrical Apparatus and Aseptic Furniture, Revised and enlarged; index v-xxxi, 736 pp; **RCSL.**

BURKHARDT CO., INC., THE
Burkhardt Bldgs., Larned at 2nd Ave., Detroit, Michigan.

ca 1915   Catalog no. 10, Hospital Record and Accounting Books Loose Record Forms; 12 pp, sample of forms, forms carry preprinted date 19 . . .; **NYAM.**

n.d.   Hospital and Account Books, Case Record Form; Catalog no. 10; 44 pp; **NYAM; MF/MAH.**

BURNHAM SOLUBLE IODINE CO.
Boston, Massachusetts.
Auburndale, Massachusetts.
Inc: Maine, but dissolved in 1916

ca 1903   Iodine Without Iodinine; 19 pp; **CPP.**
1911   The Modern Treatment of Septic Processes; 15 pp; **CPP.**
1912   Auto-Intoxication; 20 pp; **CPP.**
1918   Iodine its Effective Use, Dosage and Administration; 16 pp; **CPP.**
1919   Iodine vs Toxins; 8 pp; **CPP.**

1920	The Intensive Use of Iodine; 13 pp; **CPP.**
1921	The Iodine Age; 16 pp; **CPP.**
n.d.	The Arrest of Tuberculosis; 16 pp; **CPP.**
n.d.	Burns Soluble Iodine; 15 pp; **CPP.**
n.d.	Analysis of Burnham's Soluble Iodine by the Council on Pharmacy and Chemistry of the American Medical Association; 3 pp; **CPP.**

BURNS DENTAL CASTING MACHINE CO.
88 State St., Flushing, New York.

1918?	Hints on Dental Casting; 17 pp; by John E. Burns; **NYAM; MF/MAH.** Demonstrated at Jas. L. Carter Laboratory, 105 West 40th Street, New York, New York.
1920	Burns Dental Casting Machine; 16 pp; **NYAM; MF/MAH.**
ca 1920	Burns Dental Casting Machine; 16 pp; (TM); **NYAM;** (these machines sold by all dental supply dealers) Patents: 18 July 1916, no. 1191659; 10 July 1917, no. 1233182; 16 July 1918, no. 1272912.

BURROUGHS WELLCOME AND CO.
London, England.
35, 37, & 39 West 33rd St., New York, New York.
45 Lafayette St., New York, New York.
Montreal, Canada.
Est: 1901 in U.S.

Oct. 1900	Price List of Fine Products; 90 pp; **MAH** (12239).
1903	Ancient Cymric Medicine; 52 pp; **CPP.**
1904	Iron; 6 pp; **CPP.**
1904	Hemisine; 12 pp; **CPP.**
1905	Iron in Blood Formation; 12 pp; **CPP.**
Jan. 1906	Constipation, A Summary of its Causes and Treatment; 24 pp; **CPP.**
1906–7	Price List of Fine Products; xi, 157 pp; **TMHM.**
1908	Descriptive Notes on the Exhibits of Burroughs, Wellcome and Co., at the Franco-British Exhibition; London; 100 pp; **CPP.**
post 1908	Soamin; 23 pp; **CPP.**
1910	Price List of Fine Products; 175 pp; **UCSF.**
1911	Formulary of Fine Products, bound with The Evolution of Urine Analysis . . .; Formulary begins pp 93 through 247; (general and specific TM's); **MAH** (C616.B 972).
post 1911	How Medicinal Substances are Synthesized; 24 pp; **CPP.**
post 1911	New Light on Old Problems; 24 pp; **CPP.**
1913	Animal Substances in Medicine; 36 pp; **CPP.**
1913	Malt Extract as a Vehicle; 15 pp; **CPP.**
1913	Price List of Fine Products; 249 pp; **TMHM.**
n.d.	From Ergot to Ernutin; 16 pp; **CPP.**
n.d.	Hypoloid Ideal Hypodermic Doses; 8 pp; **CPP.**
n.d.	Serum Therapy with Notes on Vaccines and Tuberculosis; 116 pp; **CPP.**

9 & 11 E. 42st Street, New York, New York.

1907–8	Excepta Therapeutica; ixviii, 286 pp; (General and specific TM's); **MAH** (C615.1373 B 866).
1908	*From Ergot to Ernutin'*. London; 232 pp, illustrated; **MAH.**
1926	Price List of Fine Products, Illustrated, some in color; index pp 3-5; (TM); **NYAM.**

BUSCH, EMIL, A.-G., RATHENOW
 1937 Busch Metaphot; 4 pp; **URRR** (B-449).

BUSH, J. P., MFRN. CO., THE
42 & 44 Third Avenue, Chicago, Illinois.
 ca 1888 Bush's Fluid Foods and Original Preparations, Bovinine the Vital
 Principles of Beef Concentrated; 32 pp; **CPP.**

BUSH, W. J., & CO.
11 East 38 Street, New York, New York.
Est: 1851
 Mar.–Apr. 1933 Manufacturing Chemists, Essential Oil and Essence Distillers; 32 pp;
 NYAM.

BUTLER ELECTRO-MASSAGE CO.
New York.
 ca 1888 A Curious and Remarkable Invention, Dr. John Butler's Electro-Massage
 Machine, or Electric Manipulator, for Curing Disease at Home; 48 pp;
 BLEL.

BUTLER, ST. PAUL'S CHURCH YARD
 ca 1825 Instrument maker mentioned by John Read.

CAMBRIDGE BOTANICAL SUPPLY CO.
Cambridge, MA.
 1907–08 Catalogue of Scientific Instruments and Laboratory Apparatus for Use in
 Universities, Normal Schools and High Schools; 79 pp; **URRR** (C-7).
 1925 Cambridge Scientific Instruments for Special Applications; Booklet no. VI;
 64 pp; **URRR** (C-9).

CAMBRIDGE SCIENTIFIC INSTRUMENT CO.
Saint Tibbs Row, Cambridge, England.
 July 1883 Price List of Scientific Instruments; no. 4; 4 pp; **CTY/B** (Uai C143).
 Dec. 1883 Price-list of Scientific Instruments; no. 5; 8 pp; **CTY/B** (Uai C143).
 Aug. 1884 Price List of Scientific Instruments; no. 6; 8 pp; **CTY/B** (Uai C143).
 Feb. 1885 Price List of Scientific Instruments; no. 7; 8 pp; **CTY/B** (Uai C143).
 July 1885 Price List of Scientific Equipment; 8 pp; **CTY/B** (Uai C143).
 Aug. 1888 Price List of Scientific Instruments; no. 8; 8 pp; **CTY/B** (Uai C143).
 Feb. 1889 No. 3, A Descriptive List of Anthropometric Apparatus Consisting of
 Instruments for Measuring and Testing the Chief Characteristics of the
 Human Body; 3rd ed.; no pictures; 12 pp; **NYAM; MF/MAH.**
 1900 Catalog, Mechanical Laboratory Apparatus, designed by Prof. Ewing,
 F.R.S., Cambridge; 15 pp; **CTY/B** (Uai C143).
 1901 Microtomes, Microscopes and Accessories; 32 pp; **URRR** (C-10).
 1902 Mikrotome and Nebenapparate; Berlin; 18 pp; **ZUR.**
 1904 General Instruments, Supports for Apparatus, Recording and
 Time-Marking Apparatus Mechanics, Sound, Light, Heat, Magnetism,
 Electricity, Seismographs; 99 pp, illus., index; **AFMM.**
 1906 General Laboratory Equipment, Spatial and Angular Measurement,
 Recording and Time-marking Apparartus, Mechanics, Ballances and
 Weights, Sound, Light, Heat, Magnetism, Seismographs, Examples of
 Special Apparatus; 67 pp, index; **AFMM.**
 1906 Technical Thermometry for Dental Project; **CTY/B** (Uai C 143).

1920   Microtomes Embedding Baths, etc., List No 57a; 16 pp; **URRR** (C-237).

n.d.   Advertisement for apparatus called the Rocking Microtome; 1 pp; **CTY/B** (Uai C143).

CAMERON-MILLER
329 S. Novil St., Chicago, IL. 60612.

20 c   Catalog; **MAH.**

CAMERON SURGICAL SPECIALTY CO.
666 W. Division St., Chicago 10, IL.

20 c   Trade Catalog; **MAH.**

n.d.   Cameron High Visibility; 32 pp; **URRR** (C-260).

CAMP, S. H., & CO.
19 Hanover Sq., London, W. 1, England.
Windsor, Ontario.
109 W. Washington Ave., Jackson, Michigan.
Est: 1908

1927   A Manual of Camp Physiological Supports for Physicians and Surgeons, Men's Section; 6th ed.; no. 114; 43 pp, illus.; **NLM** (W26 qC 186).

n.d.   The Camp System of Physiological Supports: Women's and Children's Section; 6th ed.; 64 pp; (TM); **NYAM.**

n.d.   The Camp System of Supports for Women, Children, Men; 10th ed.; 55 pp, index pp v-vi; **MAH.**

1930s   A Manual of Camp Physiological Belts for Doctors and Surgeons, The Analysis of Applied Science in a System of Abdominal Supports; 32 pp, illus.; **WMScM.**

CAMPBELL BROS.
"Manufacturers, Electrical Apparatus"
   See: CAMPBELL ELECTRIC CO.; **ACR/MAH.**

July 1905   No. 24a; X-Ray and High Frequency Apparatus; 14 pp; **ACR/MAH.**

CAMPBELL ELECTRIC CO.
Lynn, Massachusetts.
   See: CAMPBELL BROS.

July 1, 1908   Catalog no. 29, X-Ray and High Frequency Apparatus; 28 pp, index pp 3; (TM); **ACR/MAH.**

1908   Practical Electro-Therapeutics; 31 pp, 2 illus.; (TM); **ACR/MAH.**

1918   Catalog, Campbell X-Ray Transformer and Accessories. **ACR/MAH.**

Sep. 1, 1918   Campbell X-Ray Apparatus; Medal of Honor; 39 pp; Prices in Effect; 4 pp; (TM for "Surex"); **ACR/MAH; MAH.**

ca 1920   Dental Bracket Tube Holder, Catalog no. 2006; 1 pp; **ACR/MAH.**

Sep. 1, 1920   Catalog, X-Ray and High Frequency Apparatus for Physicians, Hospitals, Dentists, Industrial Purposes, Group of Brochures bound together in Campbell binder; Approx 50 pp, separate price list; (TM's: Campbell SUREX Transformers, CLINEX X-Ray Plants); **ACR/MAH.**

1920   Campbell-Coolidge Clinical X-Ray Unit, Catalog no. 2084, U.S. Patents: 19 December 1911, 22 April 1913, 07 August 1917. 4 pp; **ACR/MAH.**

Apr. 1, 1920   Prices in Effect; 12 pp; Photo of plant is the only illustration; (TM); **ACR/MAH.**

ca 1925   Model E Coil X-Ray and High Frequency Apparatus; 6 pp; **ACR/MAH.**

n.d.   Pamphlet, Campbell Surex no. 1; 5 pp, unpaginated; (TM); **ACR/MAH; MAH.**

n.d.   Pamphlet, foldout, Clinix Campbell Clinix X-Ray Plant, Catalog no. 2087; (TM); **ACR/MAH; MAH.**

CANADA OPTICAL CO.
207 St. James St., Montreal.
ca 1912   Catalogue and Price List of Eye Glasses, Spectacles, Lenses; 137 pp; **URRR** (C-12).

CANALI
Pisa, Italy.
n.d.   Exhibition Paris 1887; **RCSL.**

CANTON SURGICAL AND DENTAL CHAIR CO.
Canton, Ohio.
1891?   Yale Surgeon's Chair; 14 pp; **HML.**

CANZIUS, J.
1804   Catalogus van mathematische, physische, anatomische, chirurgische en andere instrumenten, te bekomen in de fabricq van Mr. J.H. Onderdewyngaart Canzius to Delft; 35 pp; **YML; CTY/B** (62-2722x); **LC; BRML.**

CAPRON, A.
Paris.
n.d.   On fleam, WHM lancet case; also in R 3713/1936, R 4094/1936; **RCSL.**

CARMAN PROJECTOR
See: A. T. THOMPSON & CO.; **MF/MAH.**

CARNES ARTIFICIAL LIMB CO.
904-906 E. 12th Street, Kansas City, Missouri.
ca 1915   The Carnes Arm Puts You on the Payroll; 8 pp; **NYAM; MF/MAH.**
ca 1920   Brochure: The Carnes Arm Puts You on the Payroll; 6 pp, testimonials thru 1915; **NYAM** (photocopy).

CARNRICK, G. W., CO.
417-421 Canal Street, New York, New York.
25 Sullivan Street, New York, New York.
Hornsey, London, England.
ca 1907   Enzyme Therapy in Tuberculosis no. 6, Metabolism Monographs; 16 pp; **CPP.**
1910   Salivary and Pancreatic Ferments Not Destroyed in the Stomach; 16 pp; **CPP.**
1914   Successful Treatment of Diabetes Mellitus; 16 pp; **CPP.**
1914   Secretogen the Hormone Treatment of Digestive Insufficiencies and Constipation; 32 pp; **CPP.**
Oct. 17, 1922   Physicians' Price List; 4 pp; **CPP.**
ca 1922   Organotherapy in General Practice; 32 pp; **CPP.**
ca 1923   General Principles of Organotherapy; 31 pp; **CPP.**
ca 1923   General Principles of Organotherapy (Larger size catalog); 31 pp; **CPP.**
post 1928   The Clinical Problem of Increasing the Patient's Strength; 15 pp; **CPP.**
ca 1930   Trypsogen for Diabetes; 7 pp; **CPP.**
n.d.   Liver Extract Erythogen Brand; 4 pp; **CPP.**
n.d.   Organotherapy in Tuberculosis; 8 pp; **CPP.**
n.d.   The Successful Treatment of Asthenic Conditions; 15 pp; **CPP.**

n.d.   Pentenzyme in *Cholera infantum* and Summer Diarrhea of Children; 8 pp; **CPP.**

n.d.   Pluri Glandular Therapy in Menstrual Disorders; 15 pp; **CPP.**

n.d.   The Ritual Treatment of High Blood Pressure; 8 pp; **CPP.**

CARPENTIER, A. LE
See: J. de la CROIX; **AFMM.**

CARPOCAPSA LABORATORY
375 Lehigh Ave., East Liberty Station, Pittsburgh, Pennsylvania.

n.d.   Catalog of Collection and Mountings Supplied Carpocapsa Biological Laboratory Supplies & Inserts, etc.; 11 pp; **NYAM.**

n.d.   Carpocapsa, Butterflies, and Equipment; 12 pp; **NYAM; MF/MAH.**

CARSTENS MANUFACTURING CO.
565-571 W. Lake St., Chicago, Ill.

1927   Illustrated Catalog, Surgical, Dental, Veterinary and Electrical Instruments; 12th ed.; **CS.**

CARTER, ALFRED, LTD.
47 Holborn Viaduct, London, E.C. England.
New Showrooms: 31 & 32 Shoelance, (London, Eng.).

1897   Manufacturers of Invalid's Furniture and Appliances, Bath Chairs, Ambulances, etc.; large 1 pp foldout, illustrated; **WMScM.**

CASE, CALVIN S., CO.
92 State St., Chicago, Ill.

1899   Based on book by Dr. Calvin S. Case: Technics and Principles of Dental Orthopedia; **NYAM.**

ca 1905   Catalog and Price list Manufacturers of Orthodontia Supplies; 67 pp, price list, index 8 pp; **NYAM; UPSDM** (D 617.604. C 267).

post 1930?   Catalog and Price List for the C. S. Case Co., Mfg. of Orthodontia Supplies; 67 pp; **NYAM; MF/MAH.**

CASELLA, L. P.
23, Hatton Garden, E.C., London, Eng.
Regent House, Fitzroy Sq. W.1.
147 Holborn, London, E.C., England.

1860   An Illustrated and Descriptive Catalog of Philosophical, Meterological, Mathematical, Surveying, Optical and Photographic Instruments; title page and 56-57 pp dealing with microscopes in reference file; **AFMM.**

1860   Catalog, copy lent to WMScM by C. F. Caseda Co., Ltd.; **WMScM.**

1871   An Illustrated and Descriptive Catalog of Mathematical, Surveying, Philosophical, Optical, and Photographic Instruments; 242 pp, index; **NLM** (W26 C337); 260 pp; **BLEL.**

1883   List with Notes on Thermometers; Standard Meteorological and Other Instruments; 72 pp; **NYAM.**

CASSEL, B. B.
Frankfurt am Main, Germany.

19-20 c   from Catalog of surgical instruments and appliances; pages missing up to 48; **NYAM.**

n.d.   Physicians' and Surgeons' Instruments and Equipment; missing first few pages; 50 pp, poor; **NYAM; MF/MAH.**

CASTAGNA, LUDWIG
Scharzspanierstrasse 17, Wien, Austria IX/3.
1899? Physiologische, physikalische und pflanzenphysiologische Instrumente; 31 pp; **NYAM; MF/MAH.**
ca 1900 Catalog, physiologische, physikalische und pflanzenphysiologische Instrumente; 31 pp; **NYAM.**
1909 Physiologische und medizinische Apparate; 36 pp; **NYAM; MF/MAH.**

CASTLE
Mar. 1935 Castle Lights; 8 pp; **URRR** (C-228).

CASTLE, WILMOT CO.
Est: 1883
See: WILMOT, CASTLE CO.
n.d. Castle Hospital Sterilizers, Dressing Sterilizers; 16 pp; **NYAM.**
n.d. Catalogue of Sterilizers, Water Stills, Food Warmers; 16 pp; **NYAM.**

CASWELL, HAZARD & CO.
Broadway, Corner 24th St., New York, New York.
Manufacturers, Importers and Dealers
Combined with W. F. Ford, "Manufacturers, Instrument Maker to Bellevue, Charity and all Other New York City Hospitals; also St. Luke's Mount Sinai and New York State Woman's Hospital."
1874 Catalog of Surgical, Dental, Orthopedic Instruments, Trusses, Appliances etc.; **AFMM.**
1874 Illustrated Catalog of Surgical Instruments and Appliances; 3 parts; 129 pp, index; **NYAM; MF/MAH; NLM** (W26 F711).
1880 Illustrated Catalog of Surgical Instruments and Appliances; 227 pp, index pp xxii; TM has 1780 date; **NYAM; MF/MAH; NLM** (W26 qC356).

CAULK, L. D., CO., THE
Broad & Chestnut Sts., Philadelphia, Toronto, London, Zurich.
Labs: Milford, Delaware.
Est: 1877
ca 1910 Catalogue Book Two, De Trey's Synthetic Porcelain; 39 pp; **NYAM; MF/MAH.**
1911 Illustrated Catalogue of L.D. Caulk Dental Supplies; 775 pp; **MAH.**
1913 DeTrey's Synthetic Porcelain; 36 pp; **AFMM.**
1920 Mercitan Catalogue, Treatment for Pyorrhea and All Diseases of the Oral Tissues; 32 pp; **NYAM; MF/MAH.**
1923 Synthetic Porcelain Restorations; 35 pp; **UPSDM** (D 617. 604.C311).
1924 Synthetic Porcelain Restorations; 63 pp; **HML.**
1924 Materials and Instruments for Oxogenation; 22 pp; **NYAM; MF/MAH.**
ca 1930 Retail Price List of Materials and Products of the L. D. Caulk Co., Dental Appliances, etc.; 44 pp, index; interesting logos; **NYAM; MF/MAH.**
M. 20 c Catalog advertising DeTrey's Synthetic Porcelain, Includes manual, illustrations of instruments to be used and price list; filed with Columbia 1913 Catalog; **AFMM.**
n.d. Catalogo, Materials Dentales Para Obturar Especialidades Dentales; 48 pp; **UPSDM** (D 617.604.C311).

CEGIELSKI, C.
Poznan-Selacz, Pololska 16/17, Oddzial W, Warszawie.
See: HELLIGE; **AFMM.**

CELLASIN COMPANY, THE
Buffalo, New York.
      n.d.   Cellasin Sugar Splitting Ferment; 16 pp; **CPP.**

CELLULOID MFRN. CO.
      1878   Celluloid as a Base for Artificial Teeth; 32 pp; **MAH.**
Jan. 1881   Brochure Artificial Teeth; 24 pp; **MAH** (C617.6085C).

CENTRAL OPTICAL CO., INC.
Cincinnati, OH.
      1935   Frames Mountings, Style Selections; 25 pp; **URRR** (C-220A).

CENTRAL SCIENTIFIC CO.
345-359 W. Michigan Street, Chicago, Illinois.
Est: 1889; Inc: 1900
L.E. Knott Apparatus Co. of Boston merged with CSC April 1, 1930.
    Jun. 1910   Lantern Slides for Educational Institutions . . ., Catalog Q, actually a
                  compendium of various Catalogs on an assortment of slide topics-few
                  medical; 93 pp; **NYAM; MF/MAH.**
         1912   Physical Apparatus for Universities and Colleges, Catalog K, contains
                  microscopes, and biological apparatus; 179 pp, index; **NYAM;**
                  MF/MAH.
    May 1912   Physical and Chemical Apparatus, Catalog M; 486 pp; insert Spezial-Liste
                  26 ueber Praezisions-Apparate fuer experimentelle Psychologie und
                  Paedagogik of E. Zimmermann; 40 pp; **MAH.**
  Mar. 2, 1931   Laboratory Apparatus for Chemical, Industrial, Metallurgical,
                  Bacteriological, Biological, Board of Health, Clinical, Hospital and
                  Commercial Testing Laboratories; Catalog C, no. 227-3; 776 pp;
                  CTY/B (Uai C 3362).
         1931   Laboratory Apparatus and Chemicals for Chemical, Industrial,
                  Metallurgical, Bacteriological, Biological, Board of Health, Clinical,
                  Hospital and Commercial Testing Laboratories; various pp 780; **BLEL.**
460 E. Ohio Street, Chicago, Illinois.
      n.d.   Spencer Microtomes, Rotary & Sliding Accessories; 16 pp; **NYAM.**

CEZERAC & SOUX
64 rue de Rome, Marseille, France.
      1899   Bandages, orthopédie, instruments de chirurgie, fournisseurs des hôpitaux
                  civils, militaires de la marine, de la compagnie, du chemin de fer
                  P.-L.-M. des grands chantiers, usines et des mines; 112 pp, index pp
                  111-112; **ZUR.**

CHAMBERLAIN, N. B., & SONS
300 Washington St., Boston, Massachusetts.
      186?   Price and Description of Philosophical Apparatus, with illustrations;
                  CTY/B (Uai C3539).

CHAMBERS, INSKEEP & CO.
88-90 Wabash Avenue, Chicago, Illinois.
      1900   Illustrated Catalog; v. 10; **CPP** (Ed/49).
      1902   Illustrated Catalog of Eye, Ear, Nose and Throat: Surgical Instruments
                  and Ophthalmological Apparatus; insert-cover formerly with E.B.
                  Meyrowitz, now with Oelschleager Bros., Opticians, 42 E. 23rd St.;
                  112 pp, index pp 111-112; (TM); **NYAM; MF/MAH.**
      n.d.   Illustrated Catalogue of Spectacles, Eyeglasses, Reading Glasses,

Microscopes . . . Ophthalmoscopes, Artificial Eyes, Lorgnettes, Trial Cases, Lenses; 8th ed.; 151 pp; **URRR** (C-45).

1910   Frank Betz at this address.

CHANDLER

RCS Dressing and General Catalog, no. 2A, Large abcess knife in a surgical pocket case which belonged to George Buckstin Browne (1756-1911), great grandfather of Sir George Buckstin Brown, FRCS, the donor; (spelling of "Buckstin" may be in error); **RCSL**.

CHAPPEL FORMULA

See: MCKESSON & ROBBINS; **MF/MAH**.

CHARDIN, CHARLES
Paris.

1886?   Électricité médicale et industrielle, sonneries électriques, acoustique, téléphonie, catalogue général; théorique partie; 167 pp; **BLEL**.

1886   Supplement au catalogue général de 1886; 63 pp; **BLEL**.

1922   Électricité médicale . . . catalogue général XXI; 63 pp; **BLEL**.

CHARRIERE
rue de l'École-de-Médecine, 6 entre la rue Hautefeuille et Le Boulevard Sebastopol, Paris, France.
Depot Chez Mr. F. Liese, 102 John Street, à New York.

1862   Notice des instruments de chirurgie humaine et vétérinaire, appareils et coutellerie de la Maison Charriere . . .; 218 pp; **MUM** (Ed 51 pam 14 1862).

1865–66 Catalog, Général des instruments et appareils de chirurgie, bound in hardcover with Mathieu, L., 1867, and undated Leplanquais; Incomplete, pp 1-64 only; covers missing; **AFMM**.

CHARRIERE, JOSEPH FRANCOIS BERNARD
Successeur de son père.
Rue de l'École-de-Médecine, 6, Paris, France.
Depot chez Mr. F. Liese, 102 John St., New York.
Est: pre–1836

1840   Nouvelles drogues de sauvetage et nouveaux instruments pour donner des . . . secours aux asphyxies; 32 pp; **APS** (610 Pam. no. 89).

1856   Notices sûr les instruments et appareils de chirurgie; 120 pp; **AFMM**.

1859–65 Nouveaux étuis à dissection, trousses nouveau modèle, avec instruments nouveaux; **CPP** (Ed/2, Pamp 1-2).

1860   Trousses nouveau modèle, avec instruments nouveaux; 31 pp, 4 illus. plates; **NYAM; MF/MAH**.
        Note: Accompagnée de planches représentant les instruments nouveaux et particulièrement les instruments de dissection et deux qui, d'un usage de chaque jour, peuvent être places dans des trousses. (Introduction worth noting, particularly modifications "apportées au monde d'articulation des instruments à deux branchs").

1862   Notice des instruments de chirurgie humaine et vétérinaire; **CPP**.

1865–66 Catalog, Général des instruments et appareils de chirurgie, bound with Mathieu, L. 1867; incomplete, 64 pp; **AFMM**.

CHEVALIER, ARTHUR
(Fils et successeur de Charles Chevalier)
(Petit-fils de Vincent Chevalier)
Palais-Royal, 158, Paris, France, and N.Y.
Est: 1760

Nov. 1863 Instruments et appareils de micrographie; 32 pp; **MAH** (C 681.4085c4).
n.d. Exhibited dental instruments, Paris 1867; **RCSL**.

CHEVALIER, CHARLES
See: ARTHUR CHEVALIER; **MAH.**
See: LE DOCTEUR ADOLPHE HANNOVER, De la construction et de l'emploi du microscope, Paris, 1855.

CHEVALIER, VINCENT
See: ARTHUR CHEVALIER; **MAH.**

CHICAGO APPARATUS CO.
40-42 Quincy Street, Chicago, Illinois.
701 W. Washington Blvd., Chicago, Illinois.
Est: 1908
1909 Catalogue of Laboratory Apparatus and Supplies for Educational Institutions; 142 pp; **URRR.**
1922 Catalogue of Scientific Instruments, Lab Supplies, Chemicals; illustrated; no. 29; 239 pp, index; **AFMM.**
1924 Scientific Instruments, Laboratory Supplies, Chemicals; 326 pp; **URRR** (C-181).

CHICAGO DENTAL MFG. CO.
144 Dearborn Street, Chicago, Illinois.
Est: 1882
1882 Catalog, Dental Materials, Instruments, Furniture, etc . . .; 158 pp; **UPSDM** (D617.604. C 432); **UPL.**
1886 Catalog, Dental Materials, Instruments, Furniture, etc., Manufactured and for Sale by the Chicago Dental Mfg. Co.; 168 pp; **UPSDM** (D617.604. C 432).
1890 Catalogue; **CDMC.**

CHICAGO DIETETIC SUPPLY HOUSE, INC.
1750 W. Van Buren Street, New York.
retail store: 152 N. Wabash Ave., Chicago, Illinois.
New York Branch: 5 E. 40th Street.
1929 Foods and Equipment for Use in the Control of Sugar and Starch Restricted Diets; A Catalog of Special Diet Foods and Equipment, 3rd ed.; 32 pp; **NYAM; MF/MAH.**
1930 Foods and Equipment for Use in the Control of Sugar and Starch Restricted Diets; 4th ed.; 32 pp; **NYAM; MF/MAH.**
Nov. 1, 1930 Foods and Equipment for Use in the Control of Sugar and Starch Restricted Diets, another copy of previous Catalog; 32 pp, revised prices; **NYAM; MF/MAH.**

CHICAGO FLEXIBLE SHAFT CO.
5600 Roosevelt Road, Chicago, Illinois.
Est: 1890
ca 1930 Sunbeam Ultra-Violite, Certified Sunshine For Better Health and Stronger Bodies; 32 pp; **NYAM; MF/MAH**; (includes testimonials to date 1927).

CHICAGO LABORATORY SUPPLY AND SCALE CO.
31-45 W. Randolph Street, Chicago, Illinois.
Successors to W. A. Olmsted Scientific Co., Chicago, Illinois.
Est: 1878

1901   Catalog of Physical, Chemical, and Biological Apparatus for Use in
        Laboratories of Universities, Normal Schools, and High Schools, Cat.
        A; 317 pp, index 16 pp; **CTY/B** (Uai C4326).

CHICAGO PHARMACAL CO.
141 Kinzie Street, Chicago, Illinois.
645 St. Clair Street, Chicago, Illinois.
Est: 1900
"Manufacturing Pharmacists"
        1904   Catalog, Pharmaceuticals; 152 pp; (TM); **NYAM.**
        1905   Catalog, Pharmaceuticals; 152 pp; (TM); **NYAM.**
        1906   Catalog, Pharmaceuticals; 152 pp; (TM); **NYAM.**
    Sept. 1, 1922   Catalog, Chicago Pharmacal Co. Mfg. Chemists; 192 pp; **CPP.**

CHICAGO REFINING CO.
156 5th Avenue, Chicago, Illinois.
Thomas & Sewell, Proprietors
        1880   Catalog of Dental Materials; 164 pp, illustrations; **ADA** (D881 C43).
314-324 West Superior Street, Chicago, Illinois.
        1921   Catalog of Sectional Lab Furniture; 11 pp, illustrated; **AFMM.**

CHIRURGIE-INDUSTRIE G.M.B.H.
Cleverstrasse, Düsseldorf.
L'Industrie-Chirurgicale, 49 rue Jourdan, Bruxelles.
        ca 1910   Normalstuhl nach Depage-Maurice Schaerer mit Normalgelenken; 4 pp;
                NYAM; MF/MAH.
        E. 20 c   Brochure, "Neu," Normalstuhl nach Depage-Maurice Schaerer mit
                Normalgelenken; **NYAM.**

CHIRON-WERKE G.M.B.H.
Tuttlingen, Germany.
        1920s   Catalog, gives instructions on how to keep rustproof instruments; 7th ed.;
                48 pp; **WMScM.**

CHLORIDE OF SILVER DRY CELL BATTERY CO., THE
Baltimore, Maryland.
London: Saracen Chambers, Snow Hill E C, England.
        1898   Catalog no. 8, Medical Batteries; 72 pp; **BLEL.**
        189?   Descriptive Catalogue of Medical Batteries; 4th ed.; 31 pp; **BLEL.**
        1900   Supplemental Issue to Catalog no. 8; 20 pp; **CPP.**
        ca 1902   Chloride of Silver Dry Cell Batteries, Electrodes and Accessories, General
                Catalog; 63 pp; TM on back cover; **MAH;** (C615.84085 C); **BLEL.**

CHRYSTAL, ANDREW
Marshall, Michigan.
        ca 1899   Catalogue of Professor Chrystal's Electric Belts and Appliances, Consisting
                of Electric Belts and Bands, and Electric Belts with Electric Suspensory
                Appliances; 48 pp; **BLEL.**

CIBA CO., INC.
Pharmaceutical Branch:
Cedar and Washington Streets, 91 Barclay Street, New York, New York.
    Mar. 8, 1918   Lipoidine "Ciba", by Dr. J. Laboraderie; 16 pp; **CPP.**
        n.d.   Lipoidine "Ciba"; 16 pp; **CPP.**
        n.d.   Cibalgine for Relief of Pain, "Ciba"; 4 pp; **CPP.**

n.d.   The Intravenous Injection of Coagulin "Ciba" by E. Vogt; 12 pp; **CPP.**

n.d.   Gigifoline "Ciba"; 4 pp; **CPP.**

n.d.   Dial "Ciba" Hypnotic and Dedative Non-Narcotic and Cibalgine "Ciba" Analgesic, Antipyretic, and Sedative; 5 pp foldout; **CPP.**

post–1930   Nupercaine "Ciba" Local Anesthetic Widely Applicable Prolonged Action; 15 pp; **CPP.**

CLAFIN, GEORGE, CO.
Providence, Rhode Island.

1934   Standard Surgical Instruments and Hospital Supplies; 447 pp; **WOC.**

CLAPP & EASTHAM CO.
120 Boylston Street, Boston, Massachusetts.

ca 1905   Bulletin Q, The Quality Coil for The Production of High Frequency Currents, "For Sale by Keystone Electric Co., 135 S. 10th St., Philadelphia, PA.; 6 pp; **ACR/MAH.**

729 Boylston Street, Boston MA.

1906–07   The Ceco Coil, Portable for X-Ray and High Frequency Uses; 7 pp; **ACR/MAH.**

CLAPP, OTIS, AND SON
10 Park Square, Boston, Massachusetts.
417 Westminster Street, Providence, Rhode Island.
439 Boylston St., Boston 16, Mass.
Est: 1840; Inc: 1901

1903   X-Ray Catalog; 15 pp; **ACR/MAH.**

n.d.   Roentgen Apparatus, Description of X-Ray Equipment and Apparatus, with photos; **MAH** (C 616.0757c).

n.d.   Roentgen Apparatus; 27 pp, illus.; **MAH** (C616.0757 C).

CLARK, A. C., AND CO.
Masonic Temple, Grand Crossing, 102 & 104 Michigan Avenue, Chicago, Illinois.
Est: 1895, Inc: 1907

ca 1905   Clark Fountain Spittoons; 20 pp; **NYAM; MF/MAH.**

1920   Clark Fountain Spittoons, for dental use; could be earlier, the additional sheets which are dated may be added on; 18 pp; **MF/MAH; NYAM.**

1920   Clark Fountain Spittoons, Pioneers in Fountain Spittoon Building; 15 pp, price list; **NYAM.**

19–20 c   Brochure, Clark Fountain Spittoon; 19 pp; **NYAM.**

n.d.   Clark Fountain Spittoons; 30 pp; **CPP.**

CLARK AND ROBERTS
127 E. 23rd Street, New York, New York.
313-315 Holton Place, Indianapolis, Indiana.
1321 Arch Street, Philadelphia, Pennsylvania.

1902   Surgical Furniture; 64 pp; **WOC.**

ca 1910   For Physicians, Furniture for Operating Rooms, Hospitals, etc.; 7 pp; **NYAM; MF/MAH.**

L. 19 c   Brochure, All Kinds of Aseptic Surgical Furniture for Operating Rooms, Hospitals, etc.; 4 pp; **NYAM; CPP.**

E. 20 c   Brochure with Price List High Grade Aseptic Hospital Furniture; 7 pp; **NYAM.**

20 c   Surgical Furniture, High Grade Aseptic Furniture for Physicians and Hospitals; 8 pp; **CPP.**

n.d.   Manufacturers of Surgical Furniture: Physicians Operating Chairs, Surgical Tables, Instrument Cabinets and Aseptic Hospital Furniture of All Kinds; 89 pp; **CPP.**

n.d.   Manufacturers of Surgical Furniture . . .; 86 pp; **CPP.**

214 North Delaware Street, Indianapolis, Indiana.

n.d.   Manufacturers of Surgical Furniture; 60 pp; **CPP.**

CLASEN, GEORGES
34, rue de l'Hôpital, Bruxelles, Belgium.
Est: 1783

post 1883   Catalogue illustre; gynécologie et obstétrique; probably attached to previous Catalog; an alphabetical index paginated 193-214; doesn't match previous Catalog, pages labeled H. Galante et Fils; **NYAM; MF/MAH.**

1895   Apparatus and Instruments used by Dr. C. Jacobs for Vaginal and Abdomino-Vaginal Hysterectomy; 28 pp; **RCSL.**

L. 19 c   Catalogue illustre d'instruments et d'appareils de gynécologie et d'obstétrique; 70 pp, index 69-70; very fragile; **NYAM; MF/MAH.**

L. 19 c   Ancienne Maison Bonneels, successor to J. Staf, gynécologie et obstétrique (only table remains); pp 193-218; Exposition de Gand, 1820; **NYAM.**

CLAUDE, HENRI, M. D.
See: BOULITTE; **MF/MAH.**

CLAY-ADAMS
117-119 East 24th Street, New York, New York.
See: DR. PROF. SPALTEHOLZ, Human and Zoological Specimens

Jan. 1928   Surgical, Dental, Laboratory Instruments and Specialties, Anatomical Models and Preparations; In binder form; **MAH.**

1929   Adams Surgical Instruments Chrome and Nickel Plated; 14 pp, price list for Catalog no. 30; **MAH.**

CLEMENT CLARKE LTD.
16 Wigmore St., London, England.
n.d.   The Fincham Coincidence Optometer; 10 pp; **URRR** (C-259A).

CLERMONT-FERRAND
1893   Lactucarium (the milky juice of the lettuce), Its Production Composition and Therapeutic Uses; 16 pp; **CPP.**

CLEV-DENT CO. OF NEW YORK CITY, THE
300 East 35th Street, New York, New York.
1924   Section one of the Clev/Dent Catalog; 16 pp; **MF/MAH; NYAM.**

1949   Catalog of Dental Operating Instruments, Furniture-Engines, Engine Equipment, Filling Materials, Operating Appliances; 96 pp, index, price list; **NLM** (W26 C635c).

n.d.   Woodbury-Crendall, Instruments for Cavity Preparation; 4 pp; prices given; **NYAM; MF/MAH.**

CLEVELAND DENTAL MANUFACTURING CO.
236 & 238 the Arcade, Cleveland, Ohio.
Est: 1896

1899   Catalog; 154 pp, index pp 151-154; **UPSDM** (C617.6085c).

1915–16   Standardizing the Amalgam Filling, by Walter G. Crendell, D. D. S.; 2nd ed.; Crendell article is followed by Clev-Dent instruments for use with amalgam; 72 pp; **NYAM; MF/MAH.**

1917   Catalog of Dental Laboratory Appliances; 53 pp, index pp 54-56, price list 4 pp; **NYAM; MF/MAH.**

Jan. 1918   Price List; **NYAM; MF/MAH.**

Sep. 1918   Catalog, Forceps, Elevators and Extracting Accessories; 80 pp, index pp 79-80, separate price list; (TM); **NYAM; MF/MAH.**

1919   Catalog of Dental Operating Instruments, Furniture-Engines, Engine Equipment, Filling Materials, Operating Appliances; 96 pp, index, price lists for Jul 1 1919; Mar 1 1920; **NYAM; MF/MAH; NLM** (W26 C637c).

1921   Instruments for Exodontia and Oral Surgery, Prosthetic Appliances and Materials; pp 101-159, index, Terms 7 pp (a price list) with discounts; Price List no. 10, Jan 1920; **NYAM; MF/MAH.**

n.d.   Standard Exolevers and Ossisectors, from Designs by Dr. George B. Winter of St. Louis, Mo.; **CDMC.**

CLEVELAND ELECTRIC CO. LTD.
130 Great Portland Street, London W, England.

1912   Catalogue of X-Ray Apparatus, Electro-Medical Apparatus and Allied Apparatus of Every Description; 245 pp; **NLM** (W26 C381).

CLIFTON, CHARLES
13 Beaver, Albany, (NY).

1845   Cutler in Albany City Directory.

CLINIX
ca 1920   Trademark of Campbell Electric Co., Lynn, Mass., for X-Ray plants.

CLIN'S LABORATORIES
Paris: F. Comar & Fils & Cie, 20 rue des Freres-Saint-Jacques, France.

n.d.   Enesol Specific Arsenico-Mercurial Treatment of Syphilis; 32 pp; **CPP.**

1907   Therapeutische und Klinische Notigen Elektrische Kolloid-Metalle no. 4; 39 pp; **CPP.**

CLOW, JAMES B., & SONS
534-536 S. Franklin St., Chicago, Illinois.
sales office: NY, SF, St. Louis, Detroit, etc.
201 N. Talman Ave., Chicago 8, Illinois.
Est: 1878

1917   R.U.V.(radii Ultra Violacei); Ultra Violet Ray Water Sterilization for Drinking Water, Swimming Pools and All Commercial Domestic Purposes; 16 pp; **NYAM; MF/MAH.**

1918   Catalog, Ultra Violet Ray Water Sterilization for Drinking Water, Swimming Pool and all Commercial and Domestic Purposes; 16 pp; (TM): **NYAM.**

COCKER
On a curved hernia bistory in WHM Minor operating instrument set no. 12345; set under Savigny; **RCSL.**

CODMAN & SHURTLEFF
13-15 Tremont Street and 139 Columbus Ave., Boston, Massachusetts.
Est: 1838; Inc: 1906
Codman and Shurtleff since 1853

See: BOSTON DENTAL MANUFACTURING CO.; 1893 Catalog; **MAH** (C617.6085).

1853   Surgical and Dental Instruments and Kindred Articles; **CPP** (Bolenius Coll).

1866   On the Inhalation of Atomized Fluids, by H. Beigel, M.D., M.R.C.P.;
        On the Treatment of Chronic Diseases of the Lung by Morell
        Mackenzie, M.D.; A New Mode of Treating Diseases of the Cavity of
        the Nose by J. L. W. Thudichum, M.D., M.R.C.P.; 24 pp; **MUM**
        (Ed 51 pam 37 1866).

1868   Description of Apparatus for Treatment of Diseases of the Throat & Lungs
        by Means of Atomized Medicated Liquids, . . . by the Method of J. L.
        W. Thudicum, M.D., M.R.C.P. and of Other Instances of Recent
        Inventions Made by Codman & Shurtleff; 16 pp; **MUM** (pam 38
        1868).

ca 1870 Catalog of Surgical Instruments and Druggists Articles; 128 pp; (Bound
        with Tiemann & Co.) **NLM** (W 26q 562c).

ca 1874 Catalog of Surgical Instruments and Druggists Articles; 32 pp, illus.; Items
        presented in alphabetical order; **AFMM.**

Jan. 1874 Supplementary Dental Catalogue; 36 pp; fragile; **AFMM.**

Jun. 1875 Illustrated Catalog of Surgical and Dental Instruments and Kindred
        Articles; 88 pp; **AFMM; HDM.**

1875   Catalog of Surgical Instruments and Appliances; Catalog includes reprints
        of: Beigel, H.M.D.L.R.C.P, "On the Inhalation of Atomized Fluids,"
        From the London *Lancet* (date and page not given); 90 pp, illus.;
        AFMM.

1875   Surgical and Dental Instruments and Kindred Articles; **AFMM.**

1875   Illustrated Catalog of Surgical Instruments and Appliances; 88 pp; **MAH**
        (C610.6085 C6); **CPP** (Bolenius Coll, Ed/116); **AFMM; CPP.**

1877   Illustrated Catalog of Surgical Instruments and Appliances; 128 pp;
        AFMM.

ca 1877 Illustrated Catalogue Dental Instrument and Appliances; **CS.**

1878   Catalog of Surgical Instruments and Appliances; 132 pp; **AFMM.**

1879   Surgical and Dental Instruments and Kindred Articles; 134 pp; **NYAM.**

1879   Illustrated Catalogue of Surgical Instruments and Appliances; 136 pp;
        MAH (C610.78085); **NYAM.**

1882   Catalog of Dental Instruments and Materials; 227 pp, index pp 209–227;
        MAH (C 617.6085c); **CS; UPSDM** (D 617.604 c645); **ADA** (D 881 C
        64).

1886   Surgical and Dental Instruments, and Kindred Articles; vi, 140 pp;
        NYAM.

1898   Illustrated Catalogue Surgical Instruments and Appliances; **CS**; also:
        Catalog of Surgical and Dental Instruments, and Kindred Articles; 142
        pp; brochures bound together; **NLM** (W26 C671 c).

1890   Surgical and Dental Instruments and Kindred Articles; 143 pp; **NYAM.**

1899   Poluboskos (Greek), A Vegetable Albumen; 24 pp; **CPP.**

18??   Catalog of Invalid Rolling Chairs; 32 pp; **CTY/B** (Uai C 648).

1915–20 Illustrated Catalogue of a Complete Line of Standard Surgical Instruments;
        367 pp, index; **HDM.**

n.d.   Illustrated Catalog of Surgical Instruments and Appliances. **CPP** (Bolenius
        Coll).

n.d.   Anaemia and Chlorosis, by George M. Norton; 14 pp; **CPP.**

n.d.   Description of Apparatus for Treatment of Diseases of the Throat and
        Lungs, also of Apparatus for Treating Diseases of the Nasal Passages,
        and of Other Instruments of Recent Invention; **CPP** (Bolenius Coll).

COGIT ÉTABLISSEMENTS
36, Boulevard Saint-Michel, Paris, France.
Est: 1876
> July 1923   Catalogue général, spécialité de fournitures pour la micrographie, la bactériologie et la biologie, Agents généraux pour la France des microscopes Koristka, de Milan, Leitz, de Wetzlar, Spencer lens de Buffalo, S.F.I.O. de Française des instruments d'optique, Le Havre; 254 pp, index pp 231-254; **NYAM.**
> July 1923   Catalogue générale; 53 pp; Table of instruments by names of authors; 254 pp, general index; **NYAM; MF/MAH.**
> n.d.   Colorants pour micrographie fascicule I; 8 pp; **NYAM; MF/MAH.**

COLD ELECTRIC LIGHT CO., THE
43 & 45 Park Street, New York, New York.
> n.d.   Dental and Surgical Lamps; 12 pp; **CPP.**

COLE, ARTHUR C., AND SON
244 High Holborn, London.
> post 1867   List of Microscopical Specimens and of Pathological, Physiological, and Educational Preparations For the Microscope in Series; 8 pp; **MUM** (AA60 pam 22).

COLEMAN & BELL CO. INC., THE
> *See:* EDWARD P. DOLBEY & CO.; 1923 price list; **NYAM; MF/MAH.**

COLLIN
Rue de l'École-de-Médecine, 6, Paris, France.
> *See:* ROBERT & COLLIN; **AFMM.**

COLLIN, CHEZ, & CIE
Rue de l'École-de-Médecine 7, Paris.
Madrid and Naples.
> 1876   Mfg. d'instruments du l'orthopédie, hygiène, sciences, bandages, herniaires, chirûrgie vétérinaire; Illustre catalog d'instruments de chirurgie; 141 pp; **MAH** (C610.78085 c7).

COLLIN & CIE
Rue de l'École-de-Médecine, 6, Paris 7, France.
Successeurs de Charriere
> 1876   Catalog, d'instruments de chirurgie; medals; 146 pp, index pp 143-146; **MAH** (C 616.78085c7).
> 1879   Catalogue général d'instruments de chirurgie; 158 pp; fragile; bound w/ 1885, 1890, 1895; **NYAM.**
> 1879   Catalogue général d'instruments de chirgurie; 160 pp, index; **AFMM.**
> 1882   Catalogue général d'instruments de chirurgie; 214 pp, index; Name on spine is CHARRIERE. Title page reads as above; **NLM** (W26 C699).
> Jan. 1932   Price List; Dated Janvier 1932 and identified as Catalogue 1925 Tarif; **AFMM.**

COLLIN, MAISON CHARRIERE
Rue de l'École-de-Médecine, 6, Paris 7, France.
> 1885   Fabricant d'instruments de chirurgie; 214 pp; medals 217; **ZUR.**
> 1885   Catalogue général illustre d'instruments de chirurgie; 218 pp, index; **AFMM.**

1890 Catalogue général illustre d'instruments de chirurgie; 234 pp, index;
      NYAM; WOC; AFMM; MUM.
1890 Catalogue général d'instruments de chirurgie; 229 pp, index; **AFMM.**
1894 Catalogue général d'instruments de chirurgie; 251 pp, index; **AFMM;
      NYAM.**
1894 Catalogue général illustre d'instruments de chirurgie; 96 pp; **NYAM;
      MF/MAH.**
1898 Catalogue, Fabrique d'instruments de chirurgie; 268 pp; **UCSF.**

(CHARRIERE, MAISON)
Rue de l'École-de-Médecine, 6, Paris, France.
      1925 Catalogue général d'instruments de chirurgie; 326 pp, index; **AFMM.**

COLLINS, WARREN E., INC.
555 Huntington Ave., Boston, Massachusetts.
Est: Since 1908 as specialists in respiration apparatus
1934-Sixteen years Experience stands back of each Collins product.
      1928 Advertisement, A Standard Size Drinker-Collins Respirator that Tilts and
            Rotates; 1 pp; **CTY/B** (Uai C696).
      n.d. Advertisement, The New Tilting Rotating Orthopedic Drinker-Collins
            Respirator; 1 pp; **CTY/B** (Uai C696).
      n.d. Advertisement, The New Improved Collins Oxyflo Tent; 4 pp; **CTY/B**
            (Uai C696).
      n.d. Advertisement, The New Collins Vasculex; 1 pp; **CTY/B**(Uai C696).
      n.d. The Value of the Incubator Feature of the Infant Respirator; 1 pp; **CTY/B**
            (Uai C696).
      n.d. Fight Polio and Asphixia Cases with the New Improved, Inexpensive
            Drinker-Collins Respirator; 4 pp; **CTY/B** (Uai C 696).
      n.d. Don't Gamble When Selecting Your Metabolism Apparatus; 4 pp foldout;
            CTY/B (Uai C 696).
      n.d. Collins Contracts; 4 pp; **CTY/B** (Uai C 696).
      1935? The New Collins Vasculator & Vasculex; 4 pp; **CTY/B** (Uai C 696).
      1936? The Collins Oxygen Tent; 1 pp; **CTY/B** (Uai C 696).

COLONIAL OPTICAL CO.
Boston, Rochester, New York.
      Fall 1932 Prescription Catalog; 48 pp; **URRR** (C-232).

COLSEN CO., THE
7 East 19th Street, New York, New York.
Est: 1885
      post 1910 Catalog no. 62, Catalog of a Very High Grade of Specially Vehicles and
                 Equipment Made for All Conditions of Invalidism and Disability; 78
                 pp, index pp 78; (TM); **MAH.**

COLUMBIA DENTAL CHAIRS
      See: RITTER DENTAL MFG. CO.; **AFMM.** 1915; Oct. 1905; Jun. 1898; Sep. 1909; **MF/MAH.**

COLUMBIA DENTAL & X-RAY CORP.
131 E. 23rd Street, New York, New York.
      1924 The Endo-Form, A Necessary Wherewithal in Dental Practice; 24 pp,
            price list; **NYAM; MF/MAH.**

1930   Brochure, Ivorine dentoforms, dental models; 6 pp, foldout; (Ivorine is reg. TM); **NYAM.**

n.d.   Ivorine Dentoforms; 6 pp, price list; **NYAM; MF/MAH.**

COLUMBUS ASEPTIC FURNITURE CO.
Columbus, Ohio.
See: THE COLUMBUS DENTAL MFG. Co.; The Art of Crown and Bridgework . . .; 1916; **NYAM.**

ca 1925   Catalogue of Office and Hospital Furniture; 111 pp, index; **NLM** (W26 c726).

COLUMBUS DENTAL MFG. CO., THE
634 Wager Street, Columbus, Ohio.
18 & 20 East 41st Street, New York, New York.
634 Wager Street, Columbus 6, Ohio.
Est: 1903

1903   Booklet, Steele's Interchangable Tooth for Crown and Bridge Work; 24 pp; (TM); **MAH.**

ca 1916   The Art of Crown and Bridgework, Technic in Words and Pictures for Achieving Success in Crown and Bridgework, Using—Steele's Interchanging Teeth; 44 pp; **NYAM; MF/MAH.**

Dec. 1, 1933   Quantity Rates . . . Steele's Interchangeable Teeth & Backings & General Price List; **MAH.**

COMMERCIAL OPTICAL CO.
963 Bleury St., Montreal, Canada.

May 2, 1928   Price List, Frames, Lenses, Cases and Material, An Independent House; 32 pp; **URRR** (C-220E).

CONDELL, J., & SON
645 Broadway, New York, New York.

Oct. 1878   Condell's Life-Like Artificial Legs and Arms; **ABD.**

852 Broadway, New York, New York.

Sep. 1897   Condell's Improved Life-Like Artificial Legs and Arms; 128 pp; **MAH.**

CONSOLIDATED DENTAL MANUFACTURING CO.
115 W. 42nd Street, New York, New York.

1890?   Illustrated and Descriptive Catalogue, Classified into Departments and Numbers; 462 pp; **UBML** (WU 26 C755i); **ADA** (D881 C76i).

1897?   Catalog, Instruments, Appliances, Furniture . . .; 472 pp, index pp 1-xxii; (TM); **MAH** (C 617.6085C).

1897   Illustrated and Descriptive Catalog of Dental Supplies; **ADA** (D881 C 76).

pre–1900   Ads, pamphlets and brochure mounted in scrapbook, some loose dated 1 Sep 1893, 15 Feb 1898; **MAH** (C 617.6085 c).

130, 132, 134 Washington Place, New York, New York.

1904   Catalog for Selecting our Porcelain Teeth and Davis Crowns; 100 pp; (TM); **MAH** (C 617.6085c).

ca 1904   Catalog, Selecting our Porcelain Teeth and Davis Crowns; 103 pp; **UPSDM** (D 617.604 C 765.2).

1904   Condensed Catalog, Porcelain Teeth and Davis Crowns; 100 pp; **SLSC.**

Jan. 1904   Catalog and Price List of Dental Supplies; 485 pp, index pp i-xvii; (TM); **MAH.**

1908   Catalog of Dental Supplies Comprising Office Furniture Engines and Equipment, Operating Instruments and Appliances, Gold and Other

Filling Materials, Lab Appliances, Tools and Materials, and Other Dental Goods; 485 pp, index pp i-xvii; (TM); **NYAM.**

1913   The Application of the Davis Crown in Prosthetic Dentistry; 20 pp; **AFMM.**

1914   Catalog of Dental Supplies Comprising Office Furniture, Engines and Equipment and Appliances, Gold and Other Filling Materials, Lab Appliances, Tools and Materials and Other Dental Goods; 492 pp, index pp i-xiv; (TM); **MAH; UPSDM** (D 617.604 C765); **SLSC.**

n.d.   Illustrated and Descriptive Catalog and Price List of Dental Supplies; **HML.**

CONTINENTAL LABORATORY SPECIALTIES CO.
Formerly Continental Specialties Co.
5300 N. Spaulding Ave., Chicago, Ill.

Jan. 1924   Wholesale Buyer's Guide, Chemicals and Apparatus for Chemistry, Biology, Physics, and Geology; 24 pp; **MAH.**

814 N. Franklin St., Chicago, Illinois.

1930   Catalog, Wholesale Buyer's Guide, Chemicals and Apparatus for Chemistry, Biology, Physics, and Geology; 16 pp; **CTY/B** (Uai C7683).

CONTINENTAL OPTICAL CORP.
2 to 8 West 46th St., New York, New York.

1927   Price Lists hooked together: Feb 26, 1927, 23 pp; Frames, Mountings and Materials, Feb 26, 1927, 18 pp; Ophthalmic Lenses, Feb 26 1927, 15 pp; Spectacle and Eyeglass Cases, Oct 1 1927, 19 pp; Frames, Mountings and Materials; **URRR** (C-78).

Aug. 1929   Price List, Frames, Mountings and Materials; 26 pp; **URRR** (C-78C).

Aug. 15, 1925   Price Lists, 25 pp; Spectacle and Eyeglass Cases, 10 pp; Lenses and Lens Grinding Materials, 17 pp; Eyeglass Chains and Eyeglass Holders, 7 pp; **URRR** (C-78A).

Apr. 1, 1926   Price Lists, 37 pp; Gold, Gold-filled and Xylonite Spectacle and Eye-Glass Frames, Mountings and Materials, 18 pp; Spectacle and Eyeglass Cases, Chains and Holders, 21 pp; Single Vision, Bifocal, Trifocal and Multifocal Lenses; **URRR** (C-78-B).

Oct. 1, 1930   Frames and Mountings; 26 pp; **URRR** (C-78D).

Aug. 1, 1932   Frames and Mountings; 18 pp; **URRR** (C-78E).

Aug. 1, 1932   Continental High Hat Frames and Mountings; 7 pp; **URRR** (C-787).

Nov. 1, 1934   Frames Mountings Lenses; 32 pp, price list 16 pp; **URRR** (C-230).

Apr. 1935   Introducing Lectro No-Scru Solder Straps for Continental Mountings; 8 pp; **URRR** (C-233).

n.d.   Continental Frames and Mountings; 32 pp, price list 16 pp; **URRR** (C-238).

COOKE, TROUGHTON & SIEMENS LTD.
York, London, Cape Town, Johannesburg.

n.d.   Abridged Brochure; 8 pp foldout; **AFMM.**

n.d.   Cooke Polarizing Microscopes; Sales agents: The R. Y. Ferrier Co., 110 Pleasant St., Boston 48, MA; 30 pp; **AFMM.**

1934   Vickers Projection Microscope; 12 pp, b & w photos inserted; **URRR** (C-234).

COOLIDGE DENTAL X-RAY UNIT (CDX)
See: VICTOR, X-RAY COMPANY; **MF/MAH.**

COOPER HEWITT

1930 Better than Daylight for Industrial Lighting, Catalog no. 500; 3rd ed.;
  URRR (C-205).

CORBIN, C. M.
Agent
702 Girard Building, Broad and Chestnut Streets, Philadelphia, Pennsylvania.
  n.d. Chloro-Naptholeum; 16 pp; **CPP.**

CORNELSON, G. H.
16, rue St. Marc, Paris, France.
  1895 Catalogue dentaire; 338 pp, index pp 325-38; **NYAM.**

COSBY & McGOVERN
Richmond, Virginia.
  n.d. Cosby's Invalid Bedstead; **CPP** (Bolenius Coll).

COXETER, JAMES, & SON
23 and 24, Grafton Street East, Tottenham Court Road, W.C., London, England.
  1863 Catalog of Surgical Instruments and Apparatus; 112 pp, index; **AFMM;**
    MAH (photocopy).
  1870 A Catalog of Surgical Instruments and Apparatus; 139 pp, index 11 pp;
    AFMM; NYAM; MF/MAH; YML (RD76870C).

CRANE CO.
23 W. 44th Street, New York, New York.
22 W. 45th Street, New York, NY.
Est: 1855 by R. T. Crane
  July 1910 Circular 532 B. Surgical and Dental Labatories; 24 pp; **NYAM;**
    MF/MAH.

CRANZ, CHARLES
Akron, Ohio.
  1859 Cutler listed in Akron City Directory.

CRESENT DENTAL MFG. CO.
2214-18 So. Sawyer Avenue, Chicago, Illinois.
  ca 1920 Brochure, Dental Impression Trays; 1 1/2 pp foldout; (TM); **MAH.**
  n.d. Price List no. 20 of Our Products; **CDMC.**

CRITTENTON, CHARLES N., CO., THE
115-117 Fulton Street, New York, New York.
  1900–01 Catalogue of Propietary Medicines and Druggists' Sundries; **MAH**
    (27370-27371).
  1902–03 Catalogue of Proprietary Medicines and Druggists' Sundries;
    MAH (000132).
  1904–05 Catalogue of Proprietary Medicines and Druggists' Sundries; **MAH.**
  n.d. Scrofula and Its Constitutional Treatment, by Henry Y. Ostrander; 5 pp;
    CPP.
  n.d. Emulsions: The Rationale of their Preparation, by N. B. Kerr; 7 pp;
    CPP.
  n.d. Representative Cases Illustrating the Clinical Value of Cod Liver Oil in
    Tubercular Inflammation, by H. Y. Ostrander; 6 pp; **CPP.**
  n.d. Fat: A Dietetic Specific in Phthisis Pulmonalis; 6 pp; **CPP.**
  n.d. Cod-Liver Oil & How to Give It, by A. N. Bell; 6 pp; **CPP.**

n.d. General Debility and the Medicinal Agents We Can Usually Depend on for Its Relief; 3 pp; **CPP.**

n.d. Rebuilding the System in Typhoid Fever; 6 pp; **CPP.**

n.d. Creating Hunger When the Appetite Fails; 6 pp; **CPP.**

n.d. Consumption and Wasting Diseases Successfully Treated by Hydrated Oil, Now Known as Hydrolene, by G. Overend Drewry; 5th ed.; 47 pp; **CPP.**

n.d. Hydrolene by William F. Waugh; 8 pp; **CPP.**

n.d. The Pancreas in its Relation to Emaciation and Decline; 7 pp; **CPP.**

CROCKER, SAMUEL A., & CO.
117, 119 and 121 W. 5th Street, Conrad Bldg., Cincinnati, Ohio.
18-20 W. 7th Street, Cincinnati, Ohio.
Est: 1872; Inc: 1911
"Successors to Spencer & Crocker, Ohio Dental and Surgical Depot"

1886 Catalog of Surgical Instruments and Appliances; 216 pp, index; **AFMM.**

1915 Catalogue of Dental Specialties; 96 pp; **NYAM; MF/MAH.**

n.d. Illustrated Catalog and Price List of Surgical Instruments, Orthopedic Apparatus and Physicians' Supplies; 3rd ed.; 560 pp; **BLEL.**

n.d. Crocker's Bulletin; 4 pp; varied dental products w/prices; **MF/MAH; NYAM.**

CROCKER-FELS CO., THE
Cincinnati, Ohio.

1929 Illustrated Catalogue of Domestic and Imported Surgical Instruments; 6th ed.; **CS.**

CRODON
See: T.M. EDWARD WECK & CO., INC., Catalog no. 41; **MAH.**

de la CROIX, J.
Paris.

1931 Instruments de chirurgie; 240 pp; **AFMM.**

CROSBY INVALID FURNITURE CO.
11¹/₂ Water Street, Nashua, New Hampshire.
See: JAMES B. ALDEN

1866 Brochure; **NYAM.**

post 1890 The Crosby Invalid Bed, catalogue with testimonials; 24 pp; **MAH** (16128).

CROSBY, JOSIAH
Manchester, New Hampshire.

ca 1865 Brochure, The Crosby Invalid Bed; 4 pp, mostly testimonials, not a trade Catalog; **NYAM; MF/MAH.**

CROSS TRIFOCAL LENSES

1924 Monocentric; 8 pp, insert; **URRR** C-245).

CROUCH, HENRY
See: JAMES W. QUEEN; Agent for Crouch, late 19th c.

ca 1866 Catalog of Achromatic Microscopes, Telescopes, Race and Marine Glasses, etc.; 24 pp; **NLM** (W 26 c 952).

CROUCH'S MICROSCOPE & ACCESSORIES
See: MAW'S SON & SONS

CROWN SURGICAL INSTRUMENT CO. OF N. Y.
See: FRANK S. BETZ
ca 1910   Sale Catalog; **NYAM.**

CUXSON, GERRARD, & CO.
Birmingham and Oldbury, England.
ca 1910   Price List of Aseptic and Antiseptic Surgical Dressings, Instruments, Appliances and Hospital Furniture; 417 pp; **BLEL.**

C. V. LENS CO., INC.
Rochester, N.Y.
1925   Bifocal Sales Manual; 16 pp; **URRR** (C-104).

CYSTOGEN CHEMICAL CO.
St Louis, Missouri.
Mar. 1, 1902   Essential Facts about Cystogen; 24 pp; **CPP.**
n.d.   Cystogen-Lithium; 12 pp; **CPP.**
n.d.   Cystogen; 4 pp; **CPP.**
n.d.   Cystogen and the Surgeon; 4 pp; **CPP.**
230 23rd Street, Brooklyn, New York.
1927   Internal Antisepsis and Reinfection Prevention; 15 pp; **CPP.**

DAD CHEMICAL CO.
105 Chambers Street, New York, New York.
ca 1900   Menopause; 24 pp; **CPP.**
ca 1916   Neurilla, the Ideal Nerve Calmant; 4 pp; **CPP.**
n.d.   Respiton; 16 pp; **CPP.**
n.d.   In Growing Favor; 16 pp; **CPP.**
n.d.   Practical Experience; 16 pp; **CPP.**
n.d.   Plain Facts About a Sedative; 12 pp; **CPP.**
n.d.   Anticepaton for Pregnancy, Menstruation; 24 pp; **CPP.**
n.d.   Roll Call of Neurille by States; 24 pp; **CPP.**

DAKIN BROTHERS
n.d.   2 curved bistories in tortoise shell clasp handles, made and given by Skidmore are stamped: Dakin Bros. Leadenhall St. E.C. & Dakin Brothers; **RCSL.**

DANIEL, JOHN B.
34 Wall Street, Atlanta, Georgia.
pre–1900   Pineapple Phosphates and Concentrated Passiflora Incarnata; 16 pp; **CPP.**
n.d.   A Safe Sedative; 12 pp; **CPP.**
n.d.   Daniel's Concentrated Tincture Passiflora Incarnata; 32 pp; **CPP.**
ca 1915   The Passing of Chloral and the Bromides; 16 pp; **CPP.**

DANIELS, DR. A. C., INC.
172 & 174 Milk & Central Streets, Boston, Massachusetts.
1925   Catalog, Veterinary Medicines and How to Use Them, provides home treatment for dogs and puppies, list of Dr. Daniels' horse & cattle medicine and prices; 65 pp, index; **MAH** (C636.70896D).
1925   Home Treatment for Dogs and Puppies; 70 pp, index; **MAH.**

DARRACH, S. A.
Newark, New Jersey.
1877   Description of New and Improved Orthopedic Apparatus Invented and

Manufactured by S. A. Darrach; 24 pp, illus.; **NLM** (W26 P624); **CPP.**

DARTON & CO.
142 St. John St., Clerkenwell, E.C., London.
n.d.   Illustrated Catalog of Spectacles and Folders, Microscopes, Medical Batteries, and Appliances, and Various Physical Science and Engineering Instruments; 119 pp; **URRR** (D-5F).

DATE
Deichstrasse 36, Hamburg 11, Germany.
May 1924   Catalog 23, Chirurgie-Sterilisation-Desinfektion; 75 pp, index pp 73-75; (TM); **ZUR.**

DAVIDSON & CO.
29 Great Portland St., London, W 1.
Est: 1890
1914?   The "Davon" Micro-Telescope and Super Microscope, Cornell and Davidson's Patents, Instrument for Anything Too Small for the Telescope or Too Large for the Microscope; 32 pp; **URRR** (D-116).
1923   The "Davon" Patent Super-Microscope for Metallography, Brochure C; 24 pp; **URRR** (D:127).

DAVIDSON RUBBER CO.
30 Franklin Street, Boston, Massachusetts.
1876   Catalog of Rubber Goods, supplement which includes 17 pp listing of mfrs. who keep Davidson goods in stock; 76 pp, index; **NLM** (W26 D 253).

DAVIS B. LEVY STERLING
Surgical Products, 118-120 East 25 Street, New York, New York.
Sep. 1927   Catalog, 27 yr. since started Sterling products; 32 pp, 1 pp index, all pages loose; **NYAM.**

DAVIS, DANIEL, JR.
Boston, Massachusetts.
1848   Catalogue of Apparatus, to Illustrate Magnetism, Galvinism, Electro-Dynamics, Electro-Magnetism, Magneto-Electricity, and Thermo-Electricity; 46 pp; **BLEL.**

DAVIS AND GECK, INC.
57 Welloughby Street, Brooklyn, New York.
Laboratories: 217-221 Duffield St., Brooklyn, New York.
585 Mission Street, San Francisco.
1303 Fourth Ave., Seattle, Washington.
147 Farringham Road, London E C, England.
Est: 1909?
Surgical Ligatures and Sutures Exclusively
1898   Illustrated Price List, Information, Exporters of Proprietary Medicinals, Pharmacy Preparations, Druggists, Sundries, etc.; 54 pp, index, ads; **RCSL.**
1916   Chromatized Chart Prepared to Resist Absorption for Definite Periods; 5 pp; **CPP.**
1916   Kalmerid, An Improved Catgut to Supercede Iodized Sutures, grew out of

experimentation explained in *JAMA* article by Douglas MacFarlane, 3 Jan 1914; 4 pp; **CPP.**

n.d. General assortment of materials dealing with suture materials some date 1914, 1935, 1940, etc.; **MAH.**

DAVIS AND LAWRENCE CO., LTD.
Providence, Rhode Island.
Successor to Perry Davis and Son
Est: 1839; Inc: 1883

1898 Illustrated Price List, Proprietary Medicine, Pharmacy Preparations, Druggist's Sundries, etc.; 54 pp; **RCSL.**

DAVIS AND LEYDEN
Surgical Depot, 91-93 State Street, Rochester, New York.

n.d. Gynecological Chair and Desk and Varieties of Surgical Instruments; **CPP** (Bolenius Coll).

n.d. Price List of Ritter's Gynecological Chair; **MUM** (Ed119 v.2 p. 402).

DEAN, ALFRED E.
Leigh Place, Brooke Street, Holborn, London.
"Maker of Electro Medical Apparatus"

ca 1913 Catalog of Electro Medical Apparatus, group of about 50 brochures bound together in Dean binder; **ACR/MAH.**

DEANE
(Sterilizers etc.)

See: BRAMHALL DEANE CO.; **NYAM.**

DELAMOTTE, MAISON
Rondeau Frères (successeurs)
68, rue J.J. Rousseau, Paris, France.
Est: 1789

n.d. Album des instruments de chirurgie et bandages en gomme polie sans vernis; 35 pp; **MF/MAH; NYAM.**

DEMAS, BARNES & CO.
21 Park Row, New York.

See: JOHN F. HENRY; **MAH.**

DENIS
Bruxelles, Belgium.

n.d. Van Huevels Peloimeter; Loan collection no. 150; **RCSL.**

DENOYER-GEPPERT CO.
5235-5257 Ravenswood Ave., Chicago, Il.

1925–26 Biology Catalog no. 5B, Models, Skeletons, Charts, Specimens and Slides; 96 pp; **URRR** (D-64).

DENTAL MANUFACTURING CO., INC.
917-919 Chandler Bldg., 220 West 42 Street, New York, New York.
71a Grosvenor Street, Manchester, England.
8 Westbrook Row, Dublin, Ireland.
6, 8, 10 Lexington Streets, London, England.
See: THE DENTISTS' SUPPLY CO.

1887 Lists of Specialties manufactured . . .; **BDA.**

1899 Catalog, 618 pp, 4 pp pictures of factory, alphabetical price list, index pp

477-618; (beautiful catalog); **RCSL.**

1899 Catalog of Mineral Teeth, Dental Rubbers, Furniture, Instruments, Precious Metals, Stoppings, Electrical Apparatus, Apparatus for the Production of Anaesthesia, Drugs and Chemicals, Workroom Apparatus, Tools, and Sundries, Manufactured, Imported, and Sold by the Dental Mfg. Co., Ltd., London; 618 pp, illus.; **UCLABM** (W 26 D433c).

1912 Catalog; **BDA.**

1912 Catalog, Dental Furniture; 110 pp, index pp 1-14; (TM); **MAH** (C 617.6085d).

Alston House, Newman Street, London W, England.

1914 Catalog; **BDA.**

ca 1915 Catalogue with separate sections, various pages; **BLEL.**

Jan. 1916 The D. M. Co.'s Pneumatic Pressure Metal Casting Outfit for Interesting Facts Concerning Porcelain Teeth of British Manufacture; 16 pp, price list; metal casting outfit, 1 pp brochure; **NYAM; MF/MAH.**

1917 Catalog, Interesting Facts Concerning Porcelain Teeth of British Manufacture; 16 pp; (TM); **NYAM.**

Apr. 1918 Catalog, Dental Goods; 40 pp, separate price list; (TM); **NYAM; MF/ MAH.**

July 1919 Supplementary Catalogue of Dental Goods Needed by the Progressive Dentist; 19 pp, 1 pp cards and brochures; **NYAM; MF/MAH.**

Dec. 1919 Supplementary Catalog of Dental Goods Needed by the Progressive Dentist, no. 2; pp 21-36, index pp 22; **NYAM; MF/MAH.**

July 1919 Supplementary Catalog of Dental Goods; 18 pp; **NYAM.**

ca 1920 Complete Dentures, Bridges and Inlays; How to Cast-Uppers or Lower Plates, Bridges, Inlays, General Hints as to Casting; 16 pp; **NYAM; MF/MAH.**

May 1920 Catalogue, Supplementary, no. 3; Dental goods pp 39-56; (TM); **NYAM.**

Dec. 1920 Supplementary Catalog of Dental Goods, Needed by the Progressive Dentist; no. 3; **NYAM; MF/MAH.**

1920 Catalog no. 4, Dental Goods; pp 59-100; (TM); **NYAM; MF/MAH.**

July 1921 Catalog no. 5, Dental Goods; 144 pp; Special Reduced Prices; (TM); **NYAM; MF/MAH.**

E. 20 c The D. M. Co.'s Pneumatic Pressure Metal Casting Outfit for Complete Dentures, Bridges and Inlays, How to Cast Upper or Lower Plates, Bridges, Inlays, General hints as to Casting; i-xvi pp; (TM); **NYAM.**

n.d. Alston Improved Metal Casting Outfit; 8 pp; (TM); **MAH** (C 617.6085).

n.d. Metal Casting Outfit; 18 pp; (TM); **MAH** (C617.60850).

n.d. Anesthetic apparatus; S.19.22; **RCSL.**

n.d. Alston Cement; 8 pp; foldout; **NYAM.**

DENTAL PRODUCTS CO.
5 S. Wabash Avenue, Chicago, Illinois.
7512 Greenwood Ave. (1931), Chicago, Illinois.
Est: 1916
New Jersey charter cancelled Jan. 28, 1918.

n.d. Armamentarium for Conduction Anesthesia; 23 pp; (TM); **MAH** (C 610.78085D).

DENTAL PROTECTIVE SUPPLY CO., THE
1101-3 Champlain Bldg., Chicago, Ill.

Jan. 1, 1897 Condensed Price List of Dental Specialties; 33 pp; (TM); **MAH** (C 617.6085D).

DENTAL SPECIALTY CO., THE
1638 California Street, Denver, Colorado.
Est: 1897
      ca 1900   Canning's Cable Spring Arch Regulating Appliance and Other Specialties;
                12 pp; **HML.**
       1917?   Catalog of Dental Specialties; 32 pp; **MAH** (C 617.6085 D 257).
       1927   Catalog of Dental Specialties; 32 pp; **UPSDM** (D 617.604. D 434).
232 Republic Building, Denver, Colorado.
       1928   Visual Education in Dentistry; 39 pp, price list with color plates; **NYAM.**
      ca 1928   Visual Education in Dentistry, Models to Convince Patients to Have
                Dental Work Done; 39 pp, price list; **NYAM; MF/MAH.**
       n.d.   Catalog, Dental Specialties; **UPL; MAH.**

DENTISTS' SUPPLY CO. OF NEW YORK, THE
Candler Bldg., Times Square & 220 West 42nd Street & 109 W. 42nd St., New York,
New York.
47-65 W. 42nd St., New York, New York.
Est: 1899
Los Angeles, CA charter cancelled Nov. 30, 1906.
See: DENTAL MANUFACTURING CO., INC.
      ca 1900   Whitley's High-Fusing Porcelain Inlay Material, directions for use; 20 pp,
                unpaginated, prices given; **NYAM; MF/MAH.**
       1901?   Catalog, Whiteley's High-Fusing Porcelain Inlay Material; 16 pp; **NYAM.**
      ca 1905   Catalog, "Twentieth Century" Teeth . . . and Crowns, "Dentsply"
                Facings, Whiteley's Porcelain Inlay Materials, Introduced by articles on
                A Twentieth Century Tooth Factory and A Brief Chronology of Ceramic
                Art; 96 pp; (TM); **NYAM; MF/MAH.**
      ca 1910   The Gysi Simplex Articulator; 35 pp; **NYAM; MF/MAH.**
  Mar. 30, 1911   Price List of Teeth in Effect; 34 pp; **NYAM; MF/MAH.**
       1911   Dental Catalog; 775 pp, index pp 755-775; **MAH** (C 617.60851);
                UPSDM.
       1913   Twentieth Century Dentsply and Solila Crowns, The Science and
                Economics of Their Selection; 77 pp; **NYAM; MF/MAH.**
      ca 1913   Meeting Price Competition; 33 pp; **NYAM; MF/MAH.**
       1913   The Gysi Adaptable Articulator, directions for use; 29 pp; **NYAM;**
                MF/MAH.
       1914   Twentieth Century Mould Book; 3rd ed.; 395 pp; **UPSDM** (D 617.604
                D438); **SLSC.**
       1915   The Twentieth Century Mould Book, Containing Illustrations and
                Measurements of Twentieth Century Dentsply, Solila Teeth, 1920
                Trubyte Crowns Preliminary Announcement; 39 pp; **NYAM;**
                MF/MAH.
       1920   Catalog, Trubyte Crowns; 39 pp; (TM); **NYAM; MF/MAH.**
       1920   Trubyte Facings are Now Ready in the Same Upper Anterior Moulds and
                Shades as Trubyte Vulcanite Teeth; 40 pp; **HML.**
      1920s   Solila Teeth; 15 pp, prices; **NYAM; MF/MAH.**
       1922   The Twentieth Century Solila Mould Book; Twentieth Century Solila
                Teeth Discussion of the Product Dimensions of the Various Moulds; 63
                pp; **NYAM; MF/MAH.**
      ca 1928   Brochure, The New Trubridge (Tube) Anteriors for Cast Gold Bridges and
                Partial Dentures; 18 pp; **NYAM; MF/MAH.**

1928	Catalog, Trubridge (Tube) Anteriors, Fine Tube Teeth for Fine Cast Work; 17 pp; **NYAM**.
E. 20 c	Brochure, 20th Century Solila Teeth, Gold Clad Pins; 4 pp; **NYAM**.
E. 20 c	The Gysi Simplex Articulator; 35 pp; **NYAM**.
1930	Color in Teeth; **MAH**.
1931	The New Trubyte Teeth; 75 pp; **NYAM**.
1935	New Trubyte Posteriors Funetanal 20 degree Shallow Bites; **MAH**.
n.d.	Brochure, 20th Century Solila Teeth, Gold Clad Pins; 8 pp; **NYAM; MF/MAH**.
n.d.	Price List of Dentists' Supplies; 16 pp; **MAH** (C 617.6085D).
n.d.	Twentieth Century Teeth; 96 pp; **NYAM**.
n.d.	Whiteley's High Fusing Procelain Inlay Material; 14 pp; **NYAM**.
n.d.	Alston Cement; 8 pp foldout; **NYAM**.

DENVER CHEMICAL MANUFACTURING CO.
163-167 Varick Street, New York, New York.
Inc: 1893

| 1899 | For Inflammation and Congestion Antiphlogistine is Best; 11 pp; **CPP**. |

451-53 Washington Street, 396-98 Broadway, (New York, N.Y.).

1903	A Decade of Antiphlogistine; 15 pp; **CPP**.
1903	A Study of the Scientific Action and Therapeutic Value of Antiphlogistine; 15 pp; **CPP**.
1904	Antiphlogistine depletes Inflamed Areas; 16 pp; **CPP**.
ca 1926	Infected Hand Therapy; 32 pp; **CPP**.
1930	Gynaecological Hints; How to Make a Tampon; 16 pp; **CPP**.
n.d.	Antiphlogistine; 4 pp; **CPP**.
n.d.	Antiphlogistine An External Application for Inflammation and Congestion; 32 pp; **CPP**.
n.d.	Antiphlogistine; 29 pp; **CPP**.

DEPUY MFG., CO.
Warsaw, Indiana.

ca 1920s	DePuy Fracture Appliances and Their Application; 48 pp, index; **MAH** (22535).
ca 1928	DePuy Fracture Appliances and Their Application, pictures of extension appliances, attached to hospital beds; 7th ed.; 67 pp, index; **MF/MAH; NYAM**.
n.d.	Catalogs of fracture appliances; **NLM** (W26 D425).

DERAISME, AD & ED, Successeurs
167 rue St., Maur., Paris.
Mons Moreau-Teigne Balland Gavet Reunies

| ca 1893 | Fabrique d'instruments d'optique; 22 pp; **URRR** (D-18). |

DERMATOLOGICAL RESEARCH LABORATORIES OF PHILADELPHIA
See: ABBOTT LABORATORIES, foreward to 1928; Catalog; **NYAM**. Purchased by Abbott, 1 November 1922.

DERMODY, THOMAS
58 Arch, Albany, N.Y.

| 1842,45 | Cutler listed in Albany City Directories. |

DERR, LOUIS
Boston, Massachusetts.

ca 1918   Portraits of Eminent Men in Science, lists a series of lantern slides;
          NYAM; MF/MAH.

DESAGA, P.
Universitäts-Mechanikus in Heidelberg.
Mar. 1859   Preis Verzeichniss Nr. 4 der Bunsenschen Apparate; 6 pp;
            CTY/B (Uai D451).
1863   Catalog, Preisverzeichniss Nr. 5 der Bunsenschen Apparate nebst Anhang:
       Apparate fuer Aerzte und andere specielle Zwecke; 24 pp; **CTY/B** (Uai
       D451).
1867   Catalog, Preisverzeichniss Nr. 5 der Bunsenschen Apparate und der
       gebräuchlichsten chemischen und pharmaceutischen Instrumenten und
       Geraethschaften; 30 pp; **CTY/B** (Uai D451).

DETERT, RUDOLF
9 Karlstrasse & Französische Strasse No. 53, Berlin, V W 6, Germany.
1874   Fabrik chirurgischer Instrumente, Apparate, Bandagen, orthopaedischer
       Maschinen und kuenstlicher Gliedmassen; 103 pp, index; **AFMM.**
1909   Katalog-Auszug und Aenderungen so wie Neuheitean aus Gruppe Nase
       und Kehlkopf; 16 pp; **ZUR.**
ca 1911   Katalog; 23 pp. **ZUR.**
1913   Instrumente fuer Ohr, Nase, Hals, Schlund und die Nebengebiete; 235
       pp, illus.; **YML** (RF 87 913D).
1914   Nachtrags-Katalogs D zum Hauptkatalog D ueber Instrumente fuer
       Ohr-Nase-Hals, Schlund und die Nebengebiete; 27 pp; **ZUR.**

deTREY, E., & SONS
See: TREY, E. DE, & SONS.

DETROIT DENTAL MFG. CO.
20-22 Milwaukee Ave. W., Detroit, Michigan.
91-97 Shelby Street, Detroit, Michigan.
No. 93 Shelby Street, Detroit, Michigan.
Est: 1891
ca 1895   Catalog no. 9, Dental Specialties; 20 pp; (TM); **MAH** (C 617.6085D).
ca 1900   Brochure no. 6, Mfg. of Dental Specialties, J.H. Downie, D.D.S., John
          Kerr; 15 pp; **NYAM; MF/MAH.**
1912   Detroit Dental Mfg. Co. Patentees and Mfg. of Nerve Canal Instruments
       Impression Compounds, Mouth Mirrors, Inlay Casting Materials,
       Waxes and Dental Specialties; 48 pp; **NYAM; MF/MAH.**
1915   Illustrating and Describing the Instruments and Equipment used in Dr.
       Edouard M. Hall's Course on Pulp Canal Operations; 10 pp; **NYAM.**
ca 1915   Detroit Dental Mfg. Co. Patents and Mfg. of Kerr Pulp Canal
          Instruments; 11 pp; **NYAM; MF/MAH.**
Mar. 15, 1917   Home of "Kerr" Specialties; Pat. and Mfrs. of Gilmore Adjustable attach;
                32 pp, index back cover; (TM); **NYAM; MF/MAH.**
Mar. 1, 1919   Patentees and Mfrs. of Gilmore Adjustable Attachments, Nerve Canal
               Instruments, Impression Compounds, Inlay Casting Materials, Mouth
               Mirrors, Waxes, and Dental Specialties; 32 pp, index; Special no. 6;
               NYAM; MF/MAH.
Jun. 1920   Detroit Dental Manufacturing Co . . .; 36 pp, index; **MF/MAH; NYAM.**
ca 1920   Brochure, Home of "Kerr" Specialties Patentees and Mfrs. of Kerr Pulp
          Canal Instruments; 11 pp; (TM); **NYAM.**

ca 1920   Catalog, Dental Specialties; 32 pp, index back cover; (TM); **NYAM; MF/MAH.**

6081-6095 Twelfth St., (Detroit, MI).
post 1930   Illustrating and Describing the Instruments and Equipment used in Dr. Eduard M. Hall's Course on Pulp Canal Operation; 10 pp; **NYAM; MF/MAH.**
    n.d.   Dental Specialties, no. 8; **CDMC.**

DEUTSCHE ORTHOPÄDISCHE WERKE, G.M.B.H.
General-Pape-Strasse, Berlin-Schöneberg.
    Aug. 1931   Preis-Liste für Kunstglieder, orthopädische Apparate, Bandagen und deren Instandsetzungen; 44 pp; **NLM** (W26 D486c).

DEVILBISS MFG. CO.
300 Phillips Ave., Toledo, Ohio.
Est: 1888
Commercial Spray Paint Equipment
    1919   Brochure, Dental Atomizers for Professional and Home Use; 7 pp, separate price list; **MAH.**

DEWITT & HERZ
Georgenkirch-Strasse 24, Berlin N.O.24.
    1891   Catalog, Illustrirtes Preis-Verzeichniss der Fabrik Chirurgischer Instrumente Engos Export; Stamped: Watson, Hartman and Co., 13, Barnhill Row, E.C. Inhalts-Verzeichnung; 106 pp, Nachtrag, 8 pp index; **RCSL.**
    1893   Catalog, (Weltausstellung Chi.; Hoechste Auszeichnung) separates in instrument size; 188 pp, 185-188 inhalts and large foldout; **RCSL.**

DEYROLLE, LES FILES D'ÉMILE
46, rue du Bac, Paris 7e, France.
    1890s   Anatomie humaine organes; 112 pp; **AFMM.**
    Apr. 1901   Catalogue des cabinets d'histoire naturelle et des collections diverses d'histoire naturelle; 96 pp, index; **NYAM; MF/MAH.**
    Oct. 1901   Catalogue des instruments pour la recherche des objects d'histoire naturelle et leur classement en collection; many anatomy models; 94 pp; **NYAM; MF/MAH.**
    1901   Catalogue des instruments pour la recherche des objects d'histoire naturelle et leur classement en collections; 78 pp, index pp 76-78; pp 33-128 of another catalog tied with it; **NYAM.**
    ca 1902   fragment, picture of factory; first pp is 33, paginated, index pp 128; appears to be attatched to no. 4 in this series; **MF/MAH; NYAM.**
    Apr. 1904   Projections, photographies et photomicrographies sur verre pour projections lumineuses: histoire naturelle géographie; 78 pp; **NYAM; MF/MAH.**
    Feb. 1905   Catalogue des pièces d'anatomie humaine, d'anatomie compares et d'anatomie botanique; title page only, section is confused; **MF/MAH.**
    July 1905   Catalogue de micrographie; 48 pp; **CTY/B** (Uai D533).
    Dec. 1905   Projections, photographies et photomicrographies sur verre pour projections lumineuses: histoire naturelle, géographie; 80 pp; **NYAM; MF/MAH.**
    Feb. 1906   Catalogue des instruments pour la recherche des objects d'histoire naturelle et leur classement en collection; 78 pp, index; **NYAM;MF/MAH.**
    Mar. 1906   Enseignement technique collections et matériel; 64 pp, pp 61 microscope panoramique; **NYAM; MF/MAH.**
    Aug. 1908   Projections, photographies et photomicrographies sur verre pour projections

lumineuses concernant sciences naturelles geographie; 112 pp, index; **NYAM; MF/MAH.**

Aug. 1908   Photographies sur verre pour projections lumineuses zoologie anatomies humaine; 112 pp; **NYAM.**

1908   Cabinets d'histoire naturelle et collections diverses d'histoire naturelle; 208 pp, index; **NYAM; MF/MAH.**

1908   Catalogue des meubles; 80 pp; Instruments de'histoire naturelle; 74 pp; **NYAM.**

Jan. 1908   Catalogue des meubles-science physiques et naturelles; 38 pp; **NYAM; MF/MAH.**

Sep. 1910   Catalogue raisonné des appareil pour les expériences et les études de physiologie végétale; 32 pp; **CTY/B** (Uai D 533).

Feb. 1910   Catalogue raisonné des collections et du matériel pour l'enseignement technique; 160 pp; **CTY/B** (Uai D533).

Aug. 1910   Catalogue descriptif des pièces d'anatomie humaine, d'anatomie compares, d'anatomie végétale; 112 pp; **NYAM; MF/MAH.**

Apr. 1912   Catalogue des instruments d'histoire naturelle (recherches, classement, préparation, travaux de laboratoire); 88 pp, index; **NYAM; MF/MAH.**

July 1912   Diapositifs sur verre pour projections photographies et microphotographies; 144 pp; **NYAM; MF/MAH.**

July 1912   Diapositifs sur verre pour projections photographies et microphotographies; 144 pp; **NYAM.**

Mar. 1922   Les Fils d'Émile Deyrolles; extrait de la catalogue des cabinets d'histoire naturelle; 32 pp; **CTY/B** (Uai D 533).

E. 20 c   Catalogue d'animaux invertébrés et vertébrés; **NYAM.**

E. 20 c   Instruments pour l'étude pratique des sciences naturelles et le rengement des collections; 74 pp; **NYAM; MF/MAH.**

n.d.   Catalogue d'animaux invértébres and vertébrés prépares en liquides conservateurs; 16 pp, prices; **NYAM; MF/MAH.**

n.d.   No title page, part of another Catalog, cabinets for natural history; 128 pp, index; **MF/MAH.**

n.d.   Section of a Deyrolle catalog on models; similar if not same as previous; pp 17-94; **MF/MAH.**

n.d.   Deyrolle catalog missing cover page on human anatomy; 176 pp, index; **MF/MAH.**

n.d.   Title page missing; Catalogue des instruments des objects d'histoire naturelle et leur classement en collection; 56 pp; **CTY/B** (Uai D 533).

DEZENG
Camden, New Jersey.

1921   DeZeng's Eye, Ear, Nose and Throat Diagnostic Equipment in Miniature; 5th ed.; 32 pp; **URRR** (D-25).

DE ZENG-STANDARD CO., THE
313-315 Vine St., Philadelphia, Pennsylvania.
12 Henrietta St., London, England.
Camden, New Jersey.
Est: 1888

1908   Ophthalmoscopes, Retinoscopes, Perimenters, Optometers, Rotary Prisms, Rotary Cylinders, Light Screens, Electric Ophthalmoscopes, Retinoscopes, Transilluminators, Pupil Testers, Batteries, Controllers, etc.; **NYAM.**

1908   Optometrical Instuments and Ophthalmologic Apparatus; 20 pp; **NYAM; MF/MAH.**

Jan. 1, 1910   Ophthalmological Equipment; 28 pp; **URRR** (D-24).

1923   A Third of Century of DeZeng Instrumentation, by Charles Sheard, editor and author; 47 pp; **NYAM; MF/MAH; CPP.**

DIALOY
See: J.M. NEY CO.; **MF/MAH.**

DIAMOND BRAND
See: LIPSHAW MANUFACTURING CO.; **AFMM.**

DICK X-RAY CO., THE
3974 Olive Street, St. Louis, Missouri.
St. Louis Street, St. Louis, Missouri.

Mar. 1, 1923   A Complete List of Prices Effective for X-Ray Equipment and Accessories; 21 pp; (TM); **ACR/MAH.**

ca 1930   Catalog of X-Ray Accessories and Supplies; 76 pp, index pp 73-76; **ACR/MAH.**

ca 1930   Dick Bi-Plane Custom Built, Shock Proof, Fluoroscope and Bronchoscopic Table; 1 pp, B&W photo pasted on; **ACR/MAH.**

DICKSON, ADAM
See: JOHN DICKSON.

DICKSON, JAMES
1828–30   Cutler and Surgical Instruments maker listed in Albany City Directory.

DICKSON, JOHN
1823–1898   Cutler and Surgical Instrument maker listed in Albany City Directory 1823-1929, James Dickson appears in 1829, related? Listed as cutler with Adam Dickson in Colonie 1819.

1827   Advertisement in front of Albany City Directory.

DILLON AND GUYER
88 Broadway, Albany, New York.

1844   Instrument Makers, listed in the Albany City Directory.

DIMOND, HENRY C., & CO.
22 Milk Street, Boston, Massachusetts.

E. 20 c   Catalog, Rubber Medical Diagrams and Charts for Recording and Pathological Work; 12 pp; **NYAM.**

n.d.   Rubber Medical Diagrams and Charts for Recording and Pathological Work, rubber stamps for charts and histories; **NYAM; MF/MAH.**

DIRECT SALES CO.
Buffalo, New York.

Oct. 1, 1916   Pharmaceutical Products; Sell by Mail only; 6th ed.; 72 pp; **CPP.**

DITMAN, A. J.
2 Barclay Street, New York, N.Y.

E. 20 c   Catalog of Surgical Appliances, Trusses, Abdominal Supporters, Elastic Hosiery, Artificial Limbs, and Instruments to Aid the Hearing; 48 pp, index 2 pp; **NYAM.**

ca 1900   Illustrated Catalogue of Surgical Appliances, Trusses, Abdominal Supporters, Elastic Hosiery, Artificial Limbs and Instruments to Aid the Hearing; 48 pp, index; **NYAM; MF/MAH.**

DITTMAR, EMIL & VIERTH
148 Spaldingstrasse, Hamburg 15, Germany.
Jan. 1907   Catalog, Spezial-Preisliste ueber Apparate zur vereinfachten
Elementaranalyse nach Prof. Dr. Dennstedt . . .; 100 pp; **CTY/B** (Uai
D638).

DIXON, WILLIAM, INC.
32-36 East Kinney Street, Newark, New Jersey.
Est: 1868
1930   Catalog of Dental Equipment and Supplies; **NLM** (W26 D621c).
n.d.   Dixon Dental Catalog; 150 pp; **UPSDM** (D617.604 D647).

DOCKSON CORP.
3839 Wabash, Detroit 8, MI.
n.d.   Dockson Head and Eye Protection, Catalog No S-49; 48 pp; **URRR**
(E-54).

DOLIBER-GOODALE CO.
291 Atlantic Avenue, Boston, Massachusetts.
n.d.   Mellin's Food for Infants and Invalids; 16 pp; **CPP**.

DOLBEY, EDWARD P., & CO.
3613 Woodland Avenue, Philadelphia, Pennsylvania.
1923   Price list, Biological Stains, Chemical Indicators, Organic Chemicals, and
Laboratory Reagents, this name and address appear on front cover as
Distributor, on title page appears the name: The Coleman & Bell
Company Inc., Norwood, Ohio; 42 pp; **NYAM; MF/MAH.**
ca 1923   Electrical Laboratory Equipment; 32 pp; **NYAM; MF/MAH.**
ca 1923   Cabinets for Microscopical Slides; 2 pp; **NYAM; MF/MAH.**
3621 Woodland Ave, Philadelphia, Pennsylvania.
n.d.   Apparatus, Reagents and Chemicals as Used in the Newer Methods of
Blood Chemistry, mostly chemicals; 11 pp, unpaginated; **NYAM;
MF/MAH.**
1925   Illustrated Catalog of Standard Surgical Instruments and Supplies; 416 pp;
HML.

DONIGER & CO.
New York, New York.
1918   Catalogue of Surgical Instruments and Appliances, Lab Supplies and
Hospital Equipment; 327 pp, index; **NLM** (W26qD683).

DORRANCE, D. W.
Elm Street, San Jose, California.
ca 1930   Catalog of Dorrance Hooks, artificial hands, over 30 photographs, BW, of
Dorrance using his hooks for eating, driving, carrying, operating a drill,
etc.; 35 pp, index pp 3; **MAH.**

DOUGHERTY, H. D., & CO., INC.
17th & Indiana Avenue, Philadelphia, Pennsylvania.
1922   Faultless Aseptic Hospital Furniture; 20 pp; **WOC.**
n.d.   Faultless Aseptic Hospital Equipment; 225 pp; **CPP.**

DOUGHERTY, JAMES T.
409-411 W. 59th Street, New York, New York.
Est: 1888
1902   Illustrated Catalogue of Microscopes and Accessories, Bacteriological and

Chemical Apparatus, Stains and Reagents, Catalogue C; 181 pp, index; **AFMM.**

E. 20 c   Catalog, Microscopes and Accessories, Bacteriological and Chemical Apparatus, Stains and Reagents, Sole U.S. Agency for Carl Reichert, Vienna, Austria . . . Microscopes; vi pp index, 175 pp; **NYAM.**

n.d.   Inserts: 1. C. Reichert's microscopes (2)
2. C. Reichert's microscopes (4)
3. mechanical stage (2); **NYAM.**

n.d.   Catalog, Illustrated Catalog of Microscopes and Chemical Apparatus; vi, 175 pp, index; **NYAM; MF/MAH.**

DOW PORTABLE ELECTRIC CO.
Factory: Braintree, Massachusetts.
218 Tremont Street, Boston, Massachusetts.
1135 Broadway Street, New York, New York.
1213 Filbert Street, Philadelphia, Pennsylvania.
21 La Salle Street, Chicago, Illinois.
Inc: 1896

ca 1898   Catalogue of the Dow Portable Electric Assistant (Pat. 1895, 97, 98), introduced 9 years ago and was first portable electric light manufactured for medical use; 50 pp; **CPP.**

DOWN BROS.
3 St. Thomas' Street, London, England.

1885   A Catalogue of Surgical Instruments and Appliances; v-xix, 177 pp, index; **MAH** (Q185.7 D74); **RCSL; LLU** (WO D748c 1885).

3 & R St. Thomas, (London).

1890   Catalog of Surgical Instruments and Appliances; 526 pp, index; **AFMM; TMHM.**

1891   Appendix to 1890 Catalog; pp 527-678, indexed; **AFMM.**

21 St. Thomas Street, London S E, England.

1900   A Catalog of Surgical Instruments and Appliances, Also of Aseptic Hospital Furniture and Sterilizers, shown at the Paris Exhibition; 96 pp; **ZUR.**

1900   Catalog, Surgical Instruments and Appliances, Also of Aseptic Hospital Furniture . . .; 1210 pp; **JHIHM** (RD 76.D74); 1345 pp; **TMHM.**

Jan. 1904   A Further Appendix to Down Bros.' Catalog of Surgical Instruments and Appliances, Twentieth Century ed.; 156 pp; **NLM** (W26 D748C).

1906   A Catalogue of Surgical Instruments and Appliances, Also of Aseptic Hospital Furniture Including a Large Number of Original Designs Manufactured and Sold by Down Bros., Ltd.; 1407 pp, 200-2247 pp; **BLEL; TMHM.**

Oct. 1910   Appendix to Down Bros.' Catalog of Surgical Instruments and Appliances; 239 pp, index; **NLM** (W 26 D748c).

21 & 23 St. Thomas Street, (London).

1910   Appendix to Down Bros. Catalog of Surgical Instruments and Appliances; Grand Prix, Paris 1900, Brussels 1910; 239 pp, index pp 241-250; **RCSL.**

1914   Catalog; 16th ed.; **BDA.**

1929   Part of Catalog; pp 1387-1456; **AFMM.**

July 1929   Catalog of Surgical Instruments and Appliances, Laboratory Equipment and Supplies, Hospital Furniture and Equipment; 3028 pp, index; **NLM** (W26 qD748).

n.d.   Catalog of Surgical Instruments and Appliances; 19th ed.; Canadian ed.;
        SBMC.

n.d.   Surgical Instruments Manufacturers, A Catalog of Surgical Instruments
        and Appliances, Also of Aseptic Hospital Furniture and Sterilizers; 96
        pp; **ZUR.**

DRAPIER ET FILS
41, rue de Rivoli et Boulevard de Sebastopol, 7, Paris, France.
Est: 1829
Successeurs Van Steenbrugghe & Breton
        1924   Catalogue des instruments de chirurgie, mobilier chirurgical, appareil de
                sterilisation, électricité médicale; 186 pp, index, separate price list; **NLM**
                (W 26 6766c).

DRESCHER, LUIS
New York.
        ca 1873   Drescher's Illustrated Catalogue and Price List of Electro-Therapeutic
                   Apparatus; 20 pp; **BLEL.**

DRESSLER, CHARLES E., & BRO.
17 Lexington Ave., 140-148 E. 23rd St. (College Building), 1 Madison Ave. (Metropolitan Building), New York.
Est: 1884
        1901   Illustrated Catalogue of Scientific Apparatus and Instruments for
                Educational and Other Purposes, Mfr. of Models of All Types Including
                Cross Sections of Microscopes, Acoustic Apparatus, Feedback
                Mechanisms; 24 pp; **URRR** (D-37).

DRIVER-HARRIS WIRE CO.
201 Middlesex St., Harrison, New Jersey.
Est: 1899
        May 1915   Resistance Materials, Catalogue M, various cords and wires; 62 pp;
                    NYAM; MF/MAH.
        ca 1915   Concerning Specialties of the Alloy Nichrome, Pamphlet, Dipping Baskets
                   and Wire Cloth; **NYAM; MF/MAH.**

DROLL, L.
        1910   Instrument Katalogs; **CPP** (Bolenius Coll, Ed/65).

DRUCE, H.
England.
        n.d.   Hey's saw in Trephine Case, stamped H. Druce; **RCSL.**

DRUG PRODUCTS CO., THE
Pharmaceutical Chemists, 48-52 West 4th Street, New York, New York.
        1918   A Successful Treatment for High Blood Pressure; 24 pp; **CPP.**

DRUGGISTS APPLIANCE CO.
P.O. Box 395, Port Richmond, New York.
        n.d.   Suppository Machines; 1 pp; in Acc. file, no. 113,800; **MAH.**

DUBOIS, CH.
rue Monsieur le Prince, 21, pres l'École de Médecine, Paris, France.
Est: 1872
        1884   Catalogue des instruments de chirurgie, sciences, hygiène, orthopédie,
                bandages, herniaires, chirurgie vétérinaire, histoire naturelle, coutellerie
                fine; 113 pp, index pp 111-113; **NYAM; MF/MAH.**

DUBOSCQ, J.
Ateliers: rue Monsieur-Le-Prince, 30, Paris, France.
- 1862   Catalogue des appareil employés pour la photographie sur plaque, sur verre, sur papier, construits dans les atelieres; 40 pp; **CPP** (Bolenius Coll); **MUM** (pam 22 1862).
- 1863   Catalogue, Raisonné des spectroscopes; 12 pp; **CPP** (Bolenius Coll); **MUM** (pam 21 1862).
- 1864   Catalogue, systématique de appareil d'optique; 35 pp; **CPP** (Bolenius Coll); **MUM** (Ed51 pam 20 1864).
- 1876   Catalogue, systématique des appareil d'optique; 36 pp; **CPP.**

DUCK, J. J., CO.
Toledo, Ohio.
- 1912   Anything Electrical . . .; **BLEL.**

DUCRETET, E.
75 rue Claude-Bernard, Paris, France.
- Oct. 1877   Notice général sur les payons X du Professeur Docteur Roentgen applications générales; 24 pp out of order; **NYAM; MF/MAH.**
- 1879   Catalogue des instruments de précision, première partie, deuxième partie; 3rd ed.; 176 pp; **NYAM; MF/MAH.**
- Mar. 1892   Catalog, Électricité statique, machines Wimshurst et accessories pour les, expériences des cours de physique et les applications médicales . . .; 16 pp; **CTY/B** (Uai D859).
- 1893   Catalogue des instruments de précision de E. Ducretet et L. Lejeune; 236 pp; **CTY/B** (Uai D 859).

DUCRETET, E., ET CIE
89 rue des Feuillantines, Paris, France.
- 1879   Catalogue des instruments de précision, troisième partie, magnétisme, électricité statique et dynamique; 124 pp, index pp 121-124; fragile; **NYAM; MF/MAH.**
- Oct. 1897   Brochure, Rayons X du professeur Docteur Rontgen; A group of approx. 42 loose pp; **NYAM.**
- 1900   Catalogue des instruments de précision de E. Ducretet, troisième partie; 271 pp; **BLEL.**

DUMAURIER CO.
Elmira, New York.
- n.d.   Constructions and Descriptions German Pocket Microscopes; 1 pp; **URRR** (D-133).

DUMOTIEZ
See: PIXII, PERE et FILS; successors to Dumotiez.

DUNGSWORTH, JOHN
Cornhill, Sheffield, England.
- n.d.   Lancet and Phleme maker (p 1818); **RCSL.**

DUNHAM-REIFEL CO.
408 Pittsburg Life Bldg., Pittsburgh, Pennsylvania.
- n.d.   Brochure, Lennox Nitrous Oxide and Oxygen for Anesthesia; 12 pp; (TM); **MAH** (C 617.780850).

DUNKLEY, J. L., CO.
Chicago(?)
- 1905?   Condensed Price List; 40 pp; **HML.**

DUPONT de NEMOURS, E. I., & CO.
Wilmington, Delaware.
Est: 1802
    1938   Cold Light Surgical Instruments Developed with "Lucite" Plastic; 2 pp; **HML.**

DURBIN, J., SURGICAL SUPPLY CO.
1632 Welton Street, Denver, Colorado.
Est: 1874
    1929   Catalog of Surgical Instruments and Apparatus, Supplies and Equipment for Physicians and Hospitals, Microscopes and Accessories, Artificial Limbs and Orthopedic Apparatus, etc.; 458 pp, index pp 433-458, price list missing from envelope inside front cover; **MAH** (C 610.780850).

EASTERN LABORATORIES, INC.
New York.
    1920s   How to Treat with Violet Rays; 23 pp; **BLEL.**

EASTMAN KODAK
343 State Street, Rochester, New York.
Est: 1880
    ca 1920   Pamphlet, X-Ray Films, Seed X-Ray Plates; 8 pp; **ACR/MAH.**
    1922   Catalog, X-Rays; 52 pp; (TM); **MAH.**
    Apr. 1926   Pamphlet, an announcement, Eastman Safety Dupli-Sized X-Ray Films; 2 pp; **ACR/MAH.**
    1926   Catalog, X-Ray Materials and Accessories; 20 pp; (TM); **ACR/MAH.**

EDELMANN, M. TH., DR. & SOHN
Muenchen, Germany.
    Dec. 1878   Katalog nr. VI der physicalischen, meteorologischen, physiologischen und medizin. etc., Instrumente und Apparate für electrisches Licht; 19 pp; **CTY/B** (Uai Ed 27).
    Sep. 1882   Illustrirter Katalog, Nr. IX: der erdmagnetischen, physicalischen, meteorologischen, physiologischen und medicinischen Instrumente und der Apparate fuer electrisches Licht; 34 pp; **CTY/B** (Uai Ed 27).
    1888   Katalog Nr. XI, der erdmagnetischen, physikalischen, meteorologischen, physiologischen, medicinischen und elektrotechnischen Instrumente; 39 pp; **NYAM; MF/MAH.**
    1890   Illustrirtes Verzeichniss Nr. II, der elektro-medizinischen Praecisionsapparate; 13 pp; **NYAM.**
    1890   Illustrirtes Verzeichniss Nr. XII, von stets fertig in Vorrath gehaltenen physikalischen, electrotechnischen, physiologischen und erdmagnetischen Apparaten; 38 pp; **NYAM; MF/MAH.**
    1890   Illustrirtes Verzeichniss Nr. II, der elektro-medizinischer Praecisions Apparate construirt und verfertigt in dem Physikalisch-mechanischen Institut; 13 pp; **NYAM; MF/MAH.**
    Sep. 1891   Illustrirtes Preis-Verzeichniss ueber Widerstands-Apparate aus Manganin (Nickel-Mangin-Kupfer der physikaltechn. Reichsanstalt); 4 pp; **NYAM; MF/MAH.**
    Jun. 1892   Preis-Verzeichniss Nr. 14, der physikalischen, elektro-technischen, physiologischen und erdmagnetischen Apparate; 16 pp, tabloid size, no covers, folded, in extremely fragile condition; **NYAM; MF/MAH.**

July 1895   Illustrirtes Preis-Verzeichniss Nr. 16, Speciell über Scalenfernrohre;
Apparate zur Spiegelablesung vermittels Projection (Lampenablesung);
neue Apparate zur Spiegelablesung vermittels Collimator; Apparate für
Objective-Projection; 6 pp; **NYAM; MF/MAH.**
Sep. 1895   Illustriertes Preis-Verzeichnis Nr. 17, speciell über Galvanometer; 10 pp;
NYAM; MF/MAH.
Physikalisch-mechanisches Institut von Dr. M. Th. Edelmann.
Oct. 1895   Illustriertes Preis-Verzeichniss Nr. 18, speciell über Rheostate,
Messbruecken und Condensatoren; 8 pp; **NYAM; MF/MAH.**
1895   Illustriertes Verzeichniss Nr. III, der medizinischen Präcisions-apparate
construirt und verfertigt in dem Physikalisch-mechanischen Institut; 17
pp; **NYAM; MF/MAH.**
1899   Illustrirtes Preis-Verzeichniss Nr. 22, speziell über Praecisions-Messapparate
für elektrotechnische, physikalische, physiologische etc., Laboratorien; 32
pp; **NYAM; MF/MAH.**
1907   Illustrirtes Preis-Verzeichniss Nr. 27; 93 pp, not medical; 2 pp, insert dated
1906; **NYAM; MF/MAH.**
n.d.   Transportabler, absolut geaichter Apparat fuer Erzeugung Faradischer
Stroeme (Edelmann's transportable Faradimeter); 1 pp; **NYAM;
MF/MAH.**
Nov. 1933   Stamped: Neuer transportabler Elektrokardiograph fuer Herzspezialisten
und Kuranstalten; 4 pp; **CTY/B** (Uai Ed 28).

EDISON MANUFACTURING CO.
(under the authority of Thomas A. Edison)
No. 110 E. 23 St., New York, N.Y.
New Jersey charter cancelled Jan. 18, 1916
1896   Edison X-Ray Apparatus; 15 pp, price lists; **NYAM; MF/MAH.**
post 1896   Edison X-Ray Apparatus, Edison Cautery Transformers, . . . Edison
Electro Medical Appliances; 36 pp; **NYAM; MF/MAH.**
n.d.   Catalog of Edison/Lalande Batteries, Edison Motors & Fan Outfits, Edison
Projecting Kinetoscopes, Edison X-Ray Apparatus, Edison
Electro-Medical Appliances; 68 pp; **NYAM; MF/MAH.**
n.d.   Catalog of Edison-Lalande Batteries, Battery Motors, Measuring
Instruments, Medical Apparatus, etc.; 28 pp; **CPP.**
Broadway & 26th St. (St. James Building), New York, New York.
E. 20 c   Catalog, Edison X-Ray Apparatus, Cautery Transformers, Electromedical
Appliances; 36 pp; (TM); **NYAM.**

EDUCATIONAL SUPPLY CO., THE
6 Hamilton Place, Boston, Massachusetts.
ca 1885   Part I, Microscopical Apparatus, Catalog of Scientific and Educational
Apparatus . . .; 44 pp, covers missing, fragile cond., filed in envelope;
MAH.
19 c   Illustrated Catalogue of Scientific and Educational Apparatus, Comprising
Standard Apparatus in the Departments of Physics, Chemistry, and
Microscopy, Part I: Microscopical Department; 44 pp; **CTY/B** (Uai Ed
83).

EDWARDS, JAS. W., & CO.
825 Market St., San Francisco, California.
323 Geary St., San Francisco, California.

Est: 1882 as Edwards & Co. Manufacturing Electricians,
4th Ave. & 14th St., N.Y.

> 1915 General Catalog of Dental Furniture Instruments and Supplies; 982 pp, index pp 967-982; **MAH** (C 617.6085E).
>
> n.d. S. S. White Condensed Catalog of Dental Supplies; 288 pp; **UCSF.**
>
> n.d. Electric Bells, Burglar Alarms, Annunciators, Fire Alarms, Door Openers, Apparatus for Gas Lighting by Electrictity . . .; 32 pp; **NYAM; MF/MAH.**

EHRLICH, J., & SONS
223 6th Ave. at 15th Street, New York, New York and four other locations in N.Y. and one in Brooklyn.
Est: 1862

> 1919 Catalog, Eyesight Efficiency, Facts of Vital Importance About the Care and Value of Eyesight . . .; 32 pp; **NYAM.**

EIMER & AMEND
205, 207, 209, 211 Third Avenue, New York, New York.
633 Greenwich St., New York.
Est: 1851; Inc: 1897

> Oct. 1877 Price List of Chemicals, Minerals, Chemical Apparatus, Glassware and Porcelain-Ware; 107 pp; **CTY/B** (Uai Ei 59).
>
> n.d. Price List of Chemical Apparatus and Assay Goods; 175 pp, 10 pp index; **CTY/B** (Uai Ei 59).
>
> 1880 Price List of Chemicals, Chemical Apparatus and All Assay Goods; 216 pp, 11 pp index; **CTY/B** (Uai Ei 59).
>
> Apr. 1886 Prices Current of Chemicals; 46 pp; **CPP.**
>
> n.d. The Riva Rocci Sphygmomanometer Modified by Dr. H. W. Cook; 4 pp; **CPP.**
>
> n.d. Phosphorin Compound Manufactured by Laboratories Wetzler of Germany, Greenwich, Connecticut; 8 pp; **CPP.**
>
> 1887? Catalog, wholesale, Chemical and Assay Apparatus; 281 pp, pp i-x index; **NYAM.**
>
> 1896 Prices Current of Chemicals, Minerals, etc.; 80 pp; **CTY/B** (Uai Ei 59).
>
> Sep. 1897 Catalog, The Tintometer, An Instrument for the Analysis, Accurate Measuring, and Recording of all Colors, and a New Haemoglobinometer, and a New Haemocytometer; 31 pp; **CTY/B** (Uai Ei59).
>
> 1897 Catalog, Chemical and Physical Apparatus and Assay Goods; 418 pp, index pp 411-418; **NYAM.**
>
> 1898 Prices Current of Chemicals, Minerals, etc.; 72 pp; **CTY/B** (Uai Ei 59).
>
> 1900 Prices Current of Chemicals, Minerals, etc.; 80 pp; **CTY/B** (Uai Ei 59).
>
> 1903 Catalog, Filter Papers in Sheets, Rolls, Circles and Folded-Filters, Carl Schleicher and Schuell, Filter Paper Mfg. Dueren; **CTY/B** (Uai Sch 37).
>
> 1904 Chemicals, Chemical Apparatus, and Assay Materials; 96 pp; **CTY/B** (Uai Ei 59).
>
> n.d. Price list no. 10 of Physical Apparatus as Manufactured by Max Kohl, Chemnitz, Germany; **LACMA** (149 Ei 5p).

205, 207, 209 & 211 East 18th Street, New York, New York.

> Jan. 1905 Catalog, Wholesale Prices Current Drugs, Chemicals and Pharmaceutical Preparations; **CTY/B** (Uai Ei 59).
>
> 1909 No title page, Sections; 143 pp; **CTY/B** (Uai Ei 59).

1915	Catalog B, Sections I and II, Bacteriological and Biological Lab Apparatus; 143 pp, index pp 139-143; (TM); **NYAM; MF/MAH.**
ca 1916	Balances and Weights; 39 pp; **NYAM; MF/MAH.**
1923	Microscopes and Other Apparatus for Biological Laboratories, Catalog B; **HDM.**
1927	Catalog BCM, Biological, Chemical and Metallurgical Laboratory Apparatus; 871 pp, index pp 785-871; **NYAM.**
E. 20 c	Brochure, Lab Apparatus; 11 pp random no. ed., pp 160-546 bound in paper E & A cover; (TM on Cover); **NYAM.**
n.d.	Catalog, Charles Schleicher and Schull, Dueren, Filtering Papers, . . . Filtering Paper no. 597; **CTY/B** (Uai Sch37).
n.d.	Catalog, Charles Schleicher and Schull's of Prussian's Filter Papers; **CTY/B** (Uai Sch 37).
n.d.	Catalog, Complete Set of Standard Apparatus for Qualitatve and Quantitative Urinary Analysis; 18 pp; **CTY/B** (Uai Ei 59).
n.d.	Pamphlet, Fermentation Saccharometer, and Apparatus for the Rapid Estimation of Urea; 4 pp; **MAH** (C 616.07566E).
n.d.	Complete Set of Standard Apparatus for Qualitative and Quantitative Urinary Analysis; 4 pp, illus., prices; **MAH** (C 616.07566E).
n.d.	Catalog, Clamps, Rubber Goods, "Supports", ie. lab stands, etc., lab goods; pp 160-164, 488-93, 522-29, 545-546; **NYAM; MF/MAH.**
n.d.	Varsity Electric Ovens; 1 pp; **NYAM.**

EISEN, WILLIAM M.
413 Eighth Avenue, New York, New York.
Est: 1888
Mfg. for the Leading Hospitals of N. Y. City, Successor to Ph. H. Schmidt & Son, formerly at Broadway & 34th St.

| 1908? | Illustrated Catalogue Trusses, Orthopedic Appliances, Artificial Limbs, Abdominal Supporters, Shoulder Braces, Elastic Stockings, Crutches, Splints, Suspensory Bandages, etc.; 114 pp; **AFMM; NYAM; MF/MAH.** |

EISLER ENGINEERING CO., INC.
750-762 South 13th Street, Newark, New Jersey.

| n.d. | Catalog R-G, Radio Tube Machinery and Its Application; 64 pp; **NYAM; MF/MAH.** |

EISNER & MENDELSON CO.
156 Franklin Street, New York, New York.

post 1890	Complements of Johann Hoff (Berlin) Malt Preparations; 32 pp; **CPP.**
1899	Poluboskos (Greek), A Vegetable Albumen; 24 pp; **CPP.**
n.d.	Anaemia and Chlorosis by George M. Norton; 14 pp; **CPP.**

EISSNER, F., & CO.
19 Bible House, New York, New York.
9th St. & 3rd Ave., New York, New York.
Est: 1878; Inc: 1910s

ca 1918	Catalogue Surgical Instruments, Hospital Supplies and Equipment, Trusses, Supports, and Surgical Appliances; 416 pp; **HML.**
1920's	Catalog, Surgical Instruments, Hospital Supplies and Equipment, Trusses, Supporters, and Surgical Appliances; 447 pp, index pp 427; **NYAM.**
1922	Catalog, Surgical Instruments, Hospital Supplies and Equipment, Trusses,

Supporters, and Surgical Appliances, Distributor for Standard Surgical Instruments; 416 pp, index; **MAH** (23518).

ELBERFELD CO.
P.O. Box 2162, 66 Lafayette Street, New York, New York.
40 Stone Street, New York, New York.
 1895 Clinical Reports on Panopepton; 13 pp; **CPP.**
 Jun. 1898 Price List of Bayer's Pharmaceutical Products and Technical Preparations; 24 pp; **CPP.**
 Jun. 1899 Price List of Bayer's Pharmaceutical Products and Technical Preparations; 30 pp; **CPP.**
 1899 Tacsnopine; 4 pp; **CPP.**
 1913 The Behavior of Sajodin in the Organism, by A. Europhen; 14 pp; **CPP.**
 n.d. Protargol (Protein silver salt); 4 pp; **CPP.**

ELCONAP
See: ELECTRIC HEAT CONTROL APPARATUS CO.; **NYAM.**

ELECTRIC HEAT CONTROL APPARATUS CO.
245-247 New Jersey R.R. Ave., Newark, N.J.
141 Fifth Avenue, New York, New York.
 E. 20 c Catalog, Patented Bacteriological Electric Incubators, Paraffin Embedding Ovens, Wasserman Baths, Inactivation Baths; 12 pp, index pp 12; (TM: ELCONAP); **NYAM.**

ELECTRIC OZONE CO.
149 South Broad Street, Philadelphia, Pennsylvania.
 1906 Letter asking physicians to visit company and see uses of ozone in treating diseases; **CPP.**

ELECTRIC SOLAR CO., INC.
1115-17 No. Franklin Rd., Chicago, Illinois.
 1927 Catalog, "Solar Britesun" Radiant Therapy, Ultra Violet, Infrared, Radiation in the Treatment of Disease; 23 pp; **CTY/B** (Uai E1242).

ELECTRIC STORAGE BATTERY CO.
Drexel Building, Philadelphia, Pennsylvania.
Est: 1888
 Sep. 11, 1897 Chloride Accumulator, Catalog A; 10th ed.; 36 pp; **CPP.**

ELECTRO-DENTAL MFG. CO.
122-124 So. 8th Street, Philadelphia, Pennsylvania.
Inc: 1897
Incorporated in N.J., but dissolved Jan 6 1902.
 1895 The Register, All Cord Electric Engine; 4 pp; **NYAM; MF/MAH.**
 ca 1900 Brochure, The Electric Lathe; 4 pp; **NYAM.**
 ca 1900 Brochure, The Register, All Cord Electric Engine; 4 pp; **NYAM.**
1220-1228 Cherry St., Philadelphia, Pennsylvania.
 1905 Catalog, Electro-Dental Mfg. Co. New Appliances Alternating Current Lathe, Atomizer Heater, and Dynamotor for 500 volts; 40 pp; **NYAM; MF/MAH; CDMC.**
 Sep. 1907 No. 37 Automatic Air Compressor Unit; 6 pp foldout; **CPP.**
 Jun. 1908 Catalog, Dental Engines, Laboratory Lathes, Compressed Air Apparatus, Switchboards, Illuminators, Heating Appliances; 61 pp, index pp 3; **NYAM; MF/MAH.**

Jun. 1908   Electrical Appliances Compressed Air Apparatus; Stamped: Perry Russell, 10 & 12 23rd Street, New York; 62 pp; **NYAM; MF/MAH.**

1913   Catalog, Dental Engines, Lab Lathes, Compressed Air Apparatus, Switchboards, . . .; 6 pp, mutilated; **MAH** (C617.6085E).

33rd & Ash Streets, Philadelphia, Pennsylvania.

1925   The Electro Dental Unit; 54 pp, index pp 55-59; (TM); **MAH.**

n.d.   Electric Lathe . . .; 2 pp; Electric Water Heater; 1 pp; **MF/MAH; NYAM.**

ELECTRO MEDICAL MANUFACTURING CO.
740 W. 60th Street, Chicago, Illinois.

post 1890   Illustrated Catalog and Price List of Physcians and Surgeons' Electrical Supplies; 46 pp; **NYAM; MF/MAH.**

350 Dearborn Street, Chicago, Illinois.

1898   Illustrated Catalogue of High Grade Electro-Therapeutic Appliances for Physicians', Surgeons', and Hospitals' Electrical Supplies, no. 8; 61 pp, prices; **MAH** (C 615.84085E).

1900   Illustrated Catalog of High Grade Electro-Therapeutical Appliances; 2nd ed., no. 9; 133 pp, index; **NYAM; MF/MAH.**

Distributor: **Western Surgical Instrument House,** *647-653 W 59th St., Moved to S.E. Corner 59th Street and Wallace St., (Chicago, IL).*

1900   Catalog of High Grade Electro-Therapeutical Appliances, Physicians', Surgeons', and Hospitals' Electrical Supplies; 133 pp, index pp 133; **NYAM.**

740 W. 60th Street, Chicago, Illinois.

L. 19 c   Catalog, Physicians' and Surgeons' Electrical Supplies; 46 pp; **NYAM.**

ELECTRO-RADIATION CO.
532 Columbus Avenue, Boston, Massachusetts.

1905   Catalog of High Frequency and X-Ray Apparatus, Dr. Strong's Hercules H-F Apparatus, the Ajax, and the Ajax Jr.; 20 pp; **ACR/MAH.**

ELECTRO SURGICAL INSTRUMENT CO.
Beckley Building, Rochester, New York.
Est: 1896; Inc: 1901

1908   Catalog, Electrically Lighted Surgical Instruments and Electro-Therapeutic Apparatus; 5th ed.; 81 pp; **YML.**

1909   Catalog, Electrically Lighted Surgical Instruments and Electro-Therapuetic Apparatus; 6th ed.; 81 pp; **AFMM.**

1912   Catalog, Electrically Lighted Surgical Instruments & Electro-Therapeutic Apparatus; 7th ed.; 81 pp; **MAH** (C 610.78085 E).

ca 1914   Manufacturers of Electrically Lighted Surgical Instruments, Storage Batteries, Cauteries, etc.; 6 pp; **CPP.**

n.d.   A New Oesophagoscope; 4 pp; **CPP.**

n.d.   Dr. Chevalier Jackson's Instruments with Direct Illumination for Tracheo-Bronchoscopy Oesophagoscopy and Gastroscopy; 4 pp; **CPP.**

1918   Catalogue, Electrically Lighted Diagnostic and Surgical Instruments; 8th ed.; 69 pp; **NLM** (W26 E39); **MAH.**

1923   Catalogue, Electrically Lighted Diagnostic and Surgical Instruments; 9th ed.; 79 pp; **MAH; BLEL.**

1927   Catalogue, Electrically Lighted Diagnostic and Surgical Instruments; 10th ed.; 76 pp; **MAH.**

1930's   Price List Eye, Ear, Nose and Throat Instruments; 8 pp; **CTY/B** (Uai El 257).

ELECTRO-THERAPEUTIC CO.
32 E. 23rd Street, New York, New York.
> 1897-98   Brochure, Synthesis on Cataphoresis or Electro-Medicamental Diffusion, includes descriptive catalog of products of company; 40 pp; **NYAM.**
> ca 1896   Synthesis on Cataphoresis, or Electro-Medicamental Diffusion; 40 pp, price list; **NYAM; MF/MAH.**

ELECTRO THERAPY PRODUCTS CORP.
New York, Los Angeles, St. Louis, San Francisco, Chicago, Minneapolis, Portland, Detroit, Milwaukee, Seattle.
> 1932   Cold Quartz, lamps; 15 pp; **CPP.**

ELEKTROTECHNISCHES INSTITUT FRANKFURT (am Main)
Kirchnerstrasse 6, Frankfurt am Main, Germany.
Fabrik elektromedizinischer Apparate und elektrischer Messinstrumente.
> post 1894   Apparate und Instrumente zur Anwendung der Elektrizitaet in der Medizin; 44 pp, index; **NYAM; MF/MAH.**
> ca 1900   Catalog elektromedizinischer Apparate und elektrischer Messinstrumente; 44 pp; **NYAM.**

ELLIOTT, ASHFORD
Clitheroe, Lanes.
> ca 1825   Instrument maker mentioned by John Read.
> n.d.   RCS Q 7 Case of Dissecting Instruments label printed; Elliott, Surgical Instrument Maker; **RCSL.**

ELLIOTT OPTICAL CO., LTD.
104 and 105 Great Saffron Hill, London E.C. 1.
> n.d.   List No 8A, The Synoptophore, The Training Stereoscope, the Variable Prism Stereoscope and the Coloured Light Phoria Test; 11 pp; **URRR** (E-371).

ELLIOTTS AND AUSTRALIAN DRUG PTY. LTD.
Sydney, Australia.
> 1938   Illustrated Catalogue of Surgical Instruments and Appliances; 318 pp; **AFMM.**

ELLIS OPTICAL CO.
Croydon, England.
> Dec. 1911   Catalog of Ophthalmological and Surgical Instruments; 94 pp, price list 11 pp; **URRR** (E-1).
> 1932   The Eldridge-Green Colour Perception Lantern with diagram of instrument used by British and American navies; Two 2 pp brochures; **URRR** (E-43).

EMPIRE ELECTRIC CO.
Los Angeles, California.
> ca 1915   Pamphlet, Useful Information and Suggestions on the X-Ray and High Frequency Currents for Physicians and Surgeons, Photograph of Rose Portable X-Ray and High Frequency Apparatus; 21 pp; **ACR/MAH.**

ENDO-FORM
> *See:* COLUMBIA DENTAL AND X-RAY CORP.; 1924; **NYAM.**

ENERGEN WORKS
Therapeutic Foods Co., Willesden, N. W., London, England.
> n.d.   Insulin, New Treatment of Diabetes; 12 pp; **CPP.**

ENGELHARD, CHARLES

41 Cortlandt St., New York, New York.

stamped in address: Engelhard, Hudson Terminal Bldg., 30 Church St., N.Y.

    1911   The Medicinal Quartz Lamp; 20 pp; **URRR** (E-54).

ENGELN ELECTRIC CO.

Euclid Ave. at 46th Street, Cleveland, Ohio.

    See: AMERICAN X-RAY CORP., Circular no. 241; **ACR/MAH.**

    See: STANDARD ENGELN CORP.; **ACR/MAH.**

    ca 1919   The Engeln Dental X-Ray Unit with Dental Radiator Coolidge Tube; 2 pp; (TM); **ACR/MAH.**

Superior Ave at E. 39th Street, Cleveland, Ohio.

Display Offices: 178 E. 85th Street, New York, New York.

    1920's   Brochure, A Complete Line of Physiotherapy Equipment; 6 pp foldout; (TM); **NYAM.**

    ca 1920   K-K Standard Interrupterless Transformer Eight Fifteen, Catalog no. 23; 40 pp; **ACR/MAH; MAH.**

1904 Euclid Ave., Cleveland, Ohio.

4601-4611 Euclid Ave., Cleveland, Ohio.

    ca 1920   Pamphlet, The Engeln Bucky-Potter Diaphram, included in sales notebook of Engeln pamphlets, c/ cover: The Engeln Co. X-Ray Apparatus; 3 pp, unpaginated; (TM); **ACR/MAH; MAH.**

    ca 1920   Pamphlet, The DupleX-Ray with Motor Drive Table, included in sales notebook of Engeln Pamphlets, c/ cover: The Engeln Co. X-Ray Apparatus; 5 pp; **ACR/MAH; MAH.**

    ca 1920   Pamphlet, The Engeln Mobile X-Ray Unit for Bedside X-Ray Efficiency, included in sales notebook of Engeln Pamphlets, c/ cover: The Engeln Co. X-Ray Apparatus; 3 pp; (TM); **ACR/MAH; MAH.**

July 10, 1921   Catalog of X-Ray Accessories and Supplies, has a number of Keleket accessories illus.; 76 pp, index pp 73-76, with separate price list; (TM); **ACR/MAH.**

    ca 1921   Pamphlet, no title, cardboard-bound booklet of 6 unidentified photographs of X-Ray apparatus; 6 pp, no text; (TM); **ACR/MAH; MAH.**

    ca 1922   Pamphlet, The Engeln Grier Head Rest, The Engeln Sinus Board, The Engeln Cassette Changing Tunnel, Engeln Fluoroscopic Grids; 3 pp; (TM); **MAH; ACR/MAH.**

    ca 1922   Pamphlet, The Engeln 105,000 V X-Ray Apparatus with Tube Rectification; 11 pp; (TM); **ACR/MAH; MAH.**

Mar. 1, 1923   Price list, X-Ray Equipment and Accessories, A Complete List of Prices, included in sales notebook c/cover: The Engeln Electric Company X-Ray Apparatus; 21 pp; TM blue paper; **ACR/MAH.**

    ca 1923   Catalog of X-Ray Accessories and Supplies, included in sales notebook c/ cover: The Engeln Electric Company X-Ray Apparatus; 76 pp, index pp 73-76; (TM); **ACR/MAH; MAH.**

    Apr. 1923   Pamphlet, X-Ray Protective Materials, Prices Subject to Change without Notice, included in sales notebook of Elgeln Pamphlets, c/ cover: The Engeln Electric Company X-Ray Apparatus; 3 pp; (TM); **ACR/MAH; MAH.**

    Apr. 1923   Pamphlet, Dark Room, Developing Tanks, included in sales notebook of Engeln Pamphlets, c/ cover: The Engeln Electric Company X-Ray Apparatus; 3 pp; (TM); **ACR/MAH; MAH.**

    Apr. 1923   Pamphlet, The Engeln DupleX-Ray and Kelley-Koett Motor Drive Fluoroscopic Table, included in sales notebook of Engeln Pamphlets, c/

cover: The Engeln Electric Company X-Ray Apparatus; 12 pp; (TM); **ACR/MAH; MAH.**

Apr. 1923 Pamphlet, X-Ray Protective Materials; 3 pp; (TM); **ACR/MAH; MAH.**

ca 1923 Pamphlet, The Engeln Protective X-Ray Combination, Bucky-Potter Diaphragm, Table and Tube Stand, Designed for A Definite Purpose; included in sales notebook of Engeln Pamphlets, c/ cover: The Engeln Electric Company X-Ray Apparatus; 3 pp (TM); poor condition; **ACR/MAH; MAH.**

ca 1925 Illuminators for X-Ray Plates and Films; 2 pp; (TM); **ACR/MAH.**

ca 1925 Bucky Table Combination; 2 pp; (TM); **ACR/MAH.**

ca 1925 Bucky-Potter Diaphragm X-Ray Unit; 2 pp; **ACR/MAH.**

ca 1925 Pamphlet, The Engeln Flat Grid Bucky Diaphragm, Engeln Bucky Tables; 3 pp; **ACR/MAH; MAH.**

ca 1925 Pamphlet, The Engeln Number Three X-Ray Plant, Complete for Diagnostic Radiography and Fluoroscopy; 3 pp; (TM); **ACR/MAH; MAH.**

ca 1925 Pamphlet, The New Engeln Bucky-Potter Diaphragm; 3 pp; **ACR/MAH; MAH.**

ca 1925 Pamphlet, The Engeln Triple X, A Self Contained X-Ray Equipment Incorporating New Combined Advantages in Bucky Radiography and Vertical Fluoroscopy; 6 pp; **ACR/MAH; MAH.**

ca 1925 Pamphlet, The Engeln .15MV X-Ray Apparatus; 11 pp; (TM); **ACR/MAH; MAH.**

ca 1925 Pamphlet, The Engeln Bucky Table Combination; 3 pp, 2 copies, one with 1921 pencilled in, one with 1925; **ACR/MAH; MAH.**

n.d. Pamphlet, The Engeln Bucky Table Combination, included in sales notebook of Engeln Pamphlets, c/ cover: The Engeln Electric Company X-Ray Apparatus; 3 pp; (TM); **ACR/MAH; MAH.**

16 S. 17th Street, Philadelphia, Pennsylvania.
617 Fulton Building, Pittsburgh, Pennsylvania.
David-Whitney Building, Detroit.

ca 1925 Pamphlet, Illuminators and Stereoscopes for X-Ray Films; 3 pp; **ACR/MAH; MAH.**

ca 1926 Pamphlet, The New Engeln Simplex, A Practical X-Ray Equipment for Your Office Radiographic Work; 5 pp foldout; **ACR/MAH; MAH.**

1926 Pamphlet, The Engeln Stabilizer Filament Transformer, Remote Filament Controls; 5 pp foldout; (TM); **ACR/MAH; MAH.**

ca 1930 Pamphlet, The Engeln .12MV X-Ray Apparatus; 7 pp; (TM); **ACR/MAH; MAH.**

n.d. Pamphlet, Illuminators for X-Ray Plates and Films, includes in sales notebook c/ cover: The Engeln Electric Co. X-Ray Apparatus; 3 pp; (TM); **ACR/MAH; MAH.**

n.d. Pamphlet, The New Engeln Bucky-Potter Diaphram, includes in sales notebook c/ cover: The Engeln Electric Co. X-Ray Apparatus; 3 pp, unpaginated; **ACR/MAH; MAH.**

n.d. Pamphlet, Gelobakin Sulphate Cream, A Preparation for Radiologic Examination, prices typed in, PWR, founded 1818; includes in sales notebook c/ cover: The Engeln Electric Co. X-Ray Apparatus; 3 pp; TM on back, not Engeln; **ACR/MAH; MAH.**

n.d. Engeln Deluxe Physiotherapy Equipment; 2 pp; 1 pp announcement, Physiotherapy and X-Ray Display; **NYAM; MF/MAH.**

n.d. A Complete Line of Physiotherapy Equipment; 4 pp foldout; **CPP.**

2920 Superior Avenue at 13th Street, Cleveland, Ohio.
     n.d.   The Engeln Special Descriptive Bulletin, Quartz Light Therapy; 15 pp;
          CPP.

EPPENDORF
Hamburg, Germany.
     n.d.   RCS S. 19. 33 Anaesthetic apparatus; **RCSL.**

ERBE, C.
Tuebingen (Wuerttemberg), Germany.
Est: 1847
     1896   Preis-Verzeichnis von C. Erbe Mechanische und Optische Werkstaette
          Mikrotomen, Perimeter nach Forster; 17 pp; **NYAM; MF/MAH.**

ERIKSON, E. H., CO.
12 Washington Avenue, North, Minneapolis, Minnesota.
Est: 1892
     1926   Illustrated Catalog, The Erikson Artificial Limbs: Description of and Use
          of Limbs; 111 pp, index; **MAH.**

ERNECKE, FERDINAND
Koeniggratzer-Strasse Nr. 112, Berlin S.W.
  post 1899 Roentgen-Rohr fuer Inductoren mit electrolytischem Unterbrecher nach
          Wehrnalt; 8 pp, but some appear missing; 2 pp leaflet; **MF/MAH;**
          NYAM.
   ca 1900 Brochure, Roentgen-Rohr für inductoren mit electrolytischen unterbrecher
          nach Wehnelt; 4 pp; (TM); **NYAM.**

ERNST, F. G.
     1921   Orthopaedic Apparatus; 106 pp, indexed, 198 illustrations; **RCSL.**

ESOCARDIO
   ca 1892 Apparecchio per cura meccanica in varie malattie; Refers to Dr. S. S.
          Salaghi, 1888; 3 pp, 3 pp in French; **CPP.**

ESTERLUS, M.
Mariannengasse 2, Wien, IX, Austria.
Est: 1854
     n.d.   Undated catalogs and pricelists of 20 pp each, Preisliste ueber aerztliche
          Instrumente aus nichtrostendem Stahl. Preisliste Instrumente und
          Apparate fuer die allgemeine Praxzis, Spezialliste Nr. 35,
          Verbandschienen, Lagerungs-und Extensions-Apparate sowie Hilfsmittel
          zum Anlegen von Verbaenden; price list; **AFMM; MAH.**
     n.d.   Nr. 36, Tragbahren, Krankentransportwagen Schnellverbaende,
          Rettungskasten; 15 pp; **MAH.**
     n.d.   Spezial Prospekt Nr. 110 Der Neue Universal-Operations-Tisch; **AFMM.**
     n.d.   Spezialliste Nr. 45, Einrichtungsgegenstaende fuer aerztliche
          Ordinationszimmer; 15 pp; **AFMM; MAH.**
     n.d.   Katalog Nr. 104, Kranken-Fahrstuehle, Selbstfahrer, Rollstuehle,
          Tragstuehle, Gehschule; **AFMM; MAH.**
     n.d.   Spezialprospekt Nr. 203 M, Spezialinstrumente zur Chirurgie der Niere,
          Harnblase, Prostata, etc.; **AFMM.**
     1938   Katalog Nr. 50, Operations und Krankenhaus Moebel; 44 pp; **MAH.**
     1938   Sterilisierapparate fuer Instrumente, Verbandstoffe, etc., Katalog Nr. 51;
          MAH.

n.d.   Spezial-Liste Nr. 202, Instrumente und Apparate fuer die allgemeine
         Praxis; 8 pp; **MAH.**

n.d.   Spezial-Liste Nr. 205, Preisliste ueber aerztliche Instrumente; 10 pp;
         MAH.

ETNA CHEMICAL CO.
313 West Street, New York, New York.
E. J. Reid, 11 Dunedin House, Basinfield Street, London, England.

1898   Phenalgin, An American Coal-Tar Product, The Only Synthetic,
         Stimulant Non-Toxic, Antipyretic Analgesic & Hypnotic; 24 pp; **CPP.**

1898   Notes on Phenalgin; 24 pp; **CPP.**

1899   Clinical Conditions for Hospital Experience; 6 pp foldout; **CPP.**

1902   Nerves and Their Disturbances; 29 pp; **CPP.**

pre–1913 The Nerve System; 32 pp; **CPP.**

n.d.   Phenalgin in Painful Disturbances of the Teeth, Phenalgin is most
         Excellent; 6 pp; **CPP.**

EUREKA RHEOSTAT
P.O. Box 4020, Philadelphia, Pennsylvania.

n.d.   Eureka Rheostat and Electric Current Controller; 2 pp; **CPP.**

EVANS, GEORGE B.
1106 Chestnut Street, Philadelphia, Pennsylvania.
8th & Arch, Philadelphia, Pennsylvania.
2330 North Front, Philadelphia, Pennsylvania.

Nov. 1899 Evan's Catalog of Drugs, Chemicals, Medicinals, Proprietary Articles,
         Sick-Room Supplies, Tools for the Toilet; 96 pp; **CPP.**

EVANS CO.
New York.

ca 1900 The Evans Am. Crown; 14 pp; **HML.**

EVANS, OLD CHANGE

1825   Instrument maker mentioned by John Read.

EVANS & WORMULL
81 Stamford Street, London, S.E., England.

1876   Illustrated Catalogue of Surgical Instruments, Appliances, Apparatus, and
         Utensils, Veterinary Instruments, Cutlery, etc.; 80 pp; **TMHM.**

1889   Illustrated Catalog of Surgical Instruments, Apparatus and Appliances;
         CPP (Ed/84).

1893   Catalog of Surgical Instruments, Apparatus and Appliances; Army
         Medical Suppliers; 720 pp, index, includes 2 pp of microscopes with
         Crouch stands; **AFMM; LACMA** (149 Ev 11).

EVERILL
See: SAVIGNEY, 1810; **NLM.**

EYNARD FRANCE
See: C. R. BARD, INC.

EYNARD, J.
12 rue de l'Eperon, Paris, France.

1908   Catalog, Fabrique d'instruments de chirurgie en gomme et en caoutchouc,
         spécialté de sondes bougies et drains chirurgicaux; 48 pp, index;
         NYAM; MF/MAH.

n.d.   Illustrations of a Few Catheters and Drains Manufactured by J. Eynard,

Paris; 4 pp; **NYAM; MF/MAH.**

EXPRESS EQUIPMENT
See: SURGICAL APPLIANCES CO.; **WMScM.**
    n.d.   Anaesthetic Dressing and Instrument Tables; price lists; **WMScM.**

FABRIQUE DE TÉLÉGRAPHES ET APPAREILS ÉLECTRIQUES
Directeur: Dr. M. Hipp
Neuchatel, Suisse.
    1877   Prix-courant illustre; 7 pp, 1 plate with 36 engravings; **NLM** (W26 F127c).

FAIRCHILD BROTHERS & FOSTER
82 and 84 Fulton Street, New York, New York.
60 Fulton Street, (New York).
    See: JOHN B. FOSTER AND BRO. CO.; **CPP.**
    1873   The Fairchild Preparations of the Gastric and Pancreatic Ferments; 117 pp; **CPP.**
  Apr. 1883   Extraction Pancreatis; 44 pp; **CPP.**
  1901–02   Clinical Reports on Enzymol; 16 pp; **CPP.**
    n.d.   The Fairchild Preparations; 15 pp; **CPP.**

FAIRCHILD CHEMICAL LABORATORY, THE
St. Louis, Missouri.
    1884   Peptogenic Milk Powder Yields a Food for Infants; 16 pp; **CPP.**
  Apr. 1886   The Fairchild Preparations of the Pure Digestive Ferments and Kindred Products; 15 pp; **CPP.**
    1892   Fairchild Handbook of the Digestive Ferments; 127 pp; Same for 1893, 1894, 1901 and 1902; **CPP.**
    1910   The Fairchild Preparations Descriptive Notes; 117 pp; **CPP.**
    1918   The Fairchild Preparations Descriptive Notes; 33 pp; **CPP.**
    1919   The Fairchild Preparations Descriptive Notes; 33 pp; **CPP.**

FANNIN & CO.'S, LTD.
41 Gosften Street, Dublin, Ireland.
    1887   Catalogue of Medical and Surgical Appliances; 170 pp, index v-ix; orthopaedic pp 128-156; **RCSL.**
    1908   Wholesale Illustrated Catalogue and Price List of Surgical Instruments and Medical Apparatus; **TMHM.**
    1936?   Illustrated Catalogue; Surgical Instruments, Surgical Appliances, Hospital Theatre Furniture; 3rd ed.; 575 pp; **BLEL.**

FARBENFABRIKEN OF ELBERFELD CO.
P.O. Box 2162, New York.
Patterson, New Jersey.
Name changed to AMERICAN PHARMACEUTICAL CO., Oct. 22 1917
    1904   Dioxogen; 32 pp; **CPP.**
    1909   Sophol in Ophthalmology; 8 pp; **CPP.**

FARBEWERKE-HOECHST CO.
34 Beach Street, New York, New York.
Successors to Victor Koechl & Co.
  ca 1905   Comments on Novocaine and L-Suprarenin Combination; 48 pp; **CPP.**
  ca 1913   Melubrin Remedia Hoechst; 29 pp; **CPP.**
    1914   Comments on Melubrin Phenyl-Dimethyl-Pyrazolan Amidomethan-Sulphonate of Sodium; 8 pp; **CPP.**

FARRINGTON EYE GLASS CASES
Green and Amory Sts., Boston, MA.
   May 1933   Catalog no. 12; 16 pp; **URRR** (F-190).

FARRINGTON MANUFACTURE COMPANY
Plant and Executive Offices, Jamaica Plains Station, Boston 30, Mass.
Est: 1902, Introduced first spring back case in 1902
   Sales Offices: 116 Nassau Street, New York.
            160 Broadway, New York City.
            5 So. Wabash Ave., Chicago.
      1917   Eyeglass and Spectacle Cases, Catalog no. 11; 24 pp; inserts, **AO.**
   Sales Offices: 53 Park Place, New York.
            37 So. Wabash, Chicago.
            Canadian Factory: Toronto.
   Oct. 1, 1925   Farrington, Eyeglass & Spectacles Cases, Price List; 7 pp; **AO.**

FAULTLESS RUBBER CO., THE
Ashland, Ohio.
      1929   Faultless Druggists, Surgical and Household Rubber Goods, Catalogue
           no. 30; 32 pp; (TM: Wearever); **AO.**

FEICK BROTHERS
215 6th Street, Pittsburgh, Pennsylvania.
Est: 1881
      1896   Illustrated Catalog of Surgical Instruments, Orthopaedical Apparatus,
           Artificial Limbs, Trusses, etc., Medical Batteries, Fine Microscopes,
           Physicians and Hospital Supplies, Aseptic Hospital Furniture; 3rd ed.;
           584 pp, index pp 577-584; **MAH** (C610.78085F).
  ca 1890   Illustrated Catalog and Price List of Surgical Instruments, Artificial Limbs,
           Deformity Apparatus, etc.; **HDM.**
      1903   Catalog of Surgical Instruments, Artificial Limbs and Deformity
           Apparatus; 322 pp, 10 pp of advertisements, index, fragile condition,
           bound in 3 ring binder; **AFMM.**
      1925   Surgical Instruments, Office Equipment, Artificial Limbs, Orthopedic
           Service; 416 pp, index; **UVHSL** (RD76 F44).
      n.d.   Catalog, Price List of Surgical Instruments, Artificial Limbs, Deformity
           Apparatus, etc.; 328 pp; **LACMA.**

FELLOWS MEDICAL MANUFACTURING CO., INC.
26 Christopher Street, New York, New York.
Est: 1866
      1883   Some Affections of the Nervous System, Part III; 63 pp; **CPP.**
      1883   Some Affections of the Organs of Respiration, Part II; 63 pp; **CPP.**
      1884   Some Conditions of Infancy and Childhood in Which the Syrup of
           Hypophosphates . . . is Beneficial; 32 pp; **CPP.**
      1886   Phthisis, Lungenswalt, Part VI, The Various Forms of Phthisis in Which
           the Syrup of Hypophosphites (Fellows) is Beneficial; 94 pp; **CPP.**
      1888   Some of the Affections of the Condition of Muscular Debility . . ., Part
           VIII; 96 pp; **CPP.**
      1890   Some Remarks on the Uses of Phosphorus and Its Compounds in the
           Human Economy, Part X; 96 pp; **CPP.**
      1891   Zymosis and Pathogenesis, Part XI; 126 pp; **CPP.**
      1893   A Bacteriological Sketch Metabolism, Part XII; 96 pp; **CPP.**
      1909   The Support of Authority; 16 pp; **CPP.**

1910	Some Posological Hints and Other Useful Information; 24 pp; **CPP.**
1911	Some Rough Notes on Modern Diagnostic Methods; 34 pp; **CPP.**
1913	Some Remarks Mostly Diagnostic; 16 pp; **CPP.**
1914	Some Important Memoranda for the Busy Physicians, Fellows Compound Syrup of Hypophosphites; 28 pp; **CPP.**
1916	A Few Ophthalmic Reminders for the Busy Practitioner; 14 pp; **CPP.**
1918	The Therapeutic Value of Chemical Foods; 16 pp; **CPP.**
1919	More Data on the Therapeutic Value of Chemical Foods; 20 pp; **CPP.**
1921	Pulmonary Tuberculosis, Its Diagnosis and Treatment; 32 pp; **CPP.**
1923?	Cancer; 31 pp; **CPP.**
1924	The Heart and its Disorders; 36 pp; **CPP.**
1926	A Few Notes Regarding Psychoanalysis; 32 pp; **CPP.**
1927	A Survey of Focal Infection; 32 pp; **CPP.**
1928	A Few Award Notes Diagnosis and Therapeutics; 16 pp; **CPP.**
n.d.	Consideration Concerning Convalescence; 16 pp; **CPP.**
n.d.	The Test of Time and Experience; 16 pp; **CPP.**
n.d.	Help for all Forms of Pulmonary Tuberculosis; 16 pp; **CPP.**
n.d.	The Illustration of Therapeutic Conservatism; 16 pp; **CPP.**
n.d.	The Logic of Nervous Ailment Therapy; 16 pp; **CPP.**
n.d.	The Oncome of Age; 15 pp; **CPP.**
n.d.	The Needed Element; 16 pp; **CPP.**
n.d.	The Philosophy of Waste and Repair; 16 pp; **CPP.**
n.d.	Fellows Syrup of Hypophosphates; 12 pp; **CPP.**
1935	The Therapeutic Value of Mineral Foods; 32 pp; **CPP.**

FERGUSON, JOSEPH C., JR.
8 & 10 South 15th Street, Harrison Building, Philadelphia, Pennsylvania.

Nov. 1903	Electro Medical Equipment Circular no. 8; 20 pp; **CPP.**
May 1909	Bulletin no. 13, Eye, Ear, Nose and Throat Instruments; 32 pp; **URRR** (F-116).

FERMENT CO., THE
124-26 West 31st Street, New York, New York.
American Licensee La Société de Ferment, Paris, France.

1909	Tablets of Lactobacilline, Seul fournisseur du Professeur Metchnikoff; 7 pp; **CPP.**
1909	Lactobacilline-S; 8 pp; **CPP.**
1911	Products of Lactobacilline; 4 pp; **CPP.**

FERRIS & CO.
Bristol, England.

n.d.	Stamped on 3 instruments: 1. sharp aneurism needle, 2. blunt & sharp (trachistomy) hooks in Dr. Peeton's box of Evans instruments, maker, Nepenthe; **RCSL.**

FERRIS, J. & E.
48 Great Russell St., London, W.C.
Est: pre-1876

ca 1905	Brochure, Artificial Limbs; 48 pp; medals; **NYAM; MF/MAH.**

FETTKE & CO.
Doebern, L.N., Germany.

July 1925	Catalog, Glashuettenwerke Hedwigshuette; 14 pp; **MF/MAH; NYAM.**
n.d.	Catalog, Glaeser für medizinischen Bedarf; 16 pp; **MF/MAH; NYAM.**

FETTKE & ZEIGLER
1896   Dobelt; Catalog; **RCSL.**

FIBRE-METAL PRODUCTS CO., THE
Chester, Pennsylvania.
Est: 1905
> pre–1936   Booklet no. 16, Arc Welding Helmets, Hand Shields, Electrode Holders, Industrial Face Protection, Fibre Specialties; 32 pp; **AO.**

FINZELBERG'S, N., NACHFOLGER CHEMISCHE WERKE
Andernach.
Est: 1870
> n.d.   Ueber Cornutinum Ergoticum Bombelon; 16 pp; **CPP.**

FISCHER, F. L.
Kaiserstrasse 113/115, Freiburg im Breisgau.
> Jan. 1906   Gynaekologische Instrumente und Apparate; 16 pp; **NYAM; MF/MAH.**

> ca 1907   Brochure, Bruenings Instruments for Direct Laryngo-Tracheo-Bronchoscopy and Oesophagoscopy; 16 pp; **NYAM; MF/MAH.**

> Jun. 1908   Catalog, Instrumentarium zur direkten Laryngoskopie, Tracheoskopie Bronchoskopie und Oesophagoskopie nach Bruenings; 12 pp; medals; (TM); **NYAM; MF/MAH; CPP.**

> Oct. 1909   Catalog, Chirurgische Instrumente; 23 pp; medals; (TM); **NYAM; MF/MAH.**

> 1910?   Gesamtes Instrumentarium zur Laryngo-Tracheo-Broncho- und Oesophagoskopie sowie Schwebelaryngoskopie und Rektoskopie; **CPP** (Ed 187).

> Aug. 1912   Spezialkatalog 1908 über die technischen Hilfsmittel des Spezialartes für Ohren-Nasen- und Halskrankheiten; 138 pp; **ZUR.**

> Feb. 1914   Catalog, Schwebelaryngoskopie und chirurgische Instrumente; 44 pp; (TM); **NYAM; MF/MAH.**

> n.d.   Catalog, Fabrik fuer chirurgische Instrumente und Krankenhaus Bedarf; 14 pp; (TM); **NYAM; MF/MAH.**

FISCHER, H. G., & CO.
2334-5 Wabansia Ave., Chicago, Illinois.
> Feb. 1920   Price List for Catalog no. 6; 4 pp; **ACR/MAH; MAH.**

> ca 1920   Pamphlet; Fischer Portable Diathermy and Electro-Coagulation Apparatus, included in sales notebook with cover: the Engeln Electric Co. X-Ray Apparatus; 12 pp; (TM); **ACR/MAH; MAH.**

2333-2343 Wabansia Ave., Chicago, IL.
> Jan. 1926   Catalog no. 16, Physiotherapeutic and X-Ray Supplies and Accessories; 115 pp, index pp 113-115; (TM); **MF/MAH; NYAM.**

> Jan. 1929   Catalog no. 22, Physical Therapy Supplies and Accessories; 88 pp, index pp 86-88, pp 84-85 missing; (TM) **NYAM; MF/MAH.**

> n.d.   Catalog, Instruments, Appliances and Accessories for Anaesthesia, Oral Surgery, and Exodontia; 27 pp, no index; **NYAM; MF/MAH.**

> n.d.   Catalog, Instruments, Appliances and Accessories for Anaesthesia, Oral Surgery, and Exodontia; 23 pp, no index; **NYAM; MF/MAH.**

> n.d.   Catalog, Instruments, Appliances and Accessories for Anaesthesia, Oral Surgery, and Exodontia; 74 pp; **NYAM; MF/MAH.**

2323-2337 Wabansia Ave., Chicago, IL.

n.d.   Instructions for Assembling the Fischer Twin Carbon Arc Lamp Model M; **MCFM**.

FISHER, ISABELLA
185 Ratcliffe Highway.
   1821 A Cutler, referred by Page, the veterinary instrument maker, in catalog at **RCSL**.

FISHER, JOHN
34 Wapping Street, London?
Est: 1805
   n.d. Seton needle in tortoiseshell handle in large Evans box stamped Fisher; **RCSL**.

FISHER, JOHN C., MFG. CO.
Long Island, New York.
   1930 Dental Supply Catalog; 158 pp; **UPSDM** (D 617.604 F 534).

FLATTERS & GARNET LTD.
32 Dover St., 16 & 18 Church Rd., Longsight, Manchester, England.
   1906 Catalogue of Microscopical Slides, Microscopes and Accessories; 75 pp; **URRR** (F-114).
   1910 Microscopes and Accessories, Catalogue B; 68 pp; **URRR** (F-3).
   1936 Scientific Apparatus; **MAH**.

FLAVELL, G. W., & BRO., INC.
1011 Spring Garden Street, Philadelphia, Pennsylvania.
Est: 1876
   n.d. Elastic Stockings; 12 pp foldout; **CPP**.
   n.d. Elastic Trusses, Abdominal Supporters, Elastic Stockings; 18 pp; **CPP**.
   n.d. Elastic Stockings, Abdominal Supporters . . .; 26 pp; **CPP**.
1005 Spring Garden Street, Philadelphia, Pa.
   n.d. Elastic Stockings, Knee Caps, Anklets, etc.; 4 pp foldout; **CPP**.
248 North Eighth Street, Philadelphia.
   n.d. New Price List to Physicians; 16 pp; **CPP**.
   n.d. Illustrated Catalog of Orthopaedic Apparatus; 26 pp; **CPP**.
  pre-1914 Illustrated Catalog of Reliable Goods Abdominal Supporters; 48 pp; **CPP**.
   1915 Illustrated Catalog of Reliable Goods, . . .; 48 pp; **CPP**.

FLEISCHMANN CO., THE
701 Washington Street, New York, New York.
595 Madison Ave., New York 22, New York.
The Fleishmann Distilling Co., subsidiary of Standard Brands, Inc
Est: 1869
Yeast originally produced in 1868
  ca 1921 A Symposium on Yeast: The Food Value, Therapeutic Value, Manufacture, Physiology, and Chemistry of Yeast; 23 pp; **CPP**.

FLEMING, J. & R.
146 Clerkenwell Rd., London E.C.
  July 1931 Revised Price List no. 286 of Prescription Service Including Bifocals and Repairs; 19 pp; **URRR** (F-184A).
   1933 Industrial Goggles Helmets and Respirators, List no. 302; 12 pp; **URRR** (184).

FLEMMING, OTTO

729 Arch Street, Philadelphia, Pennsylvania.

Successors to Fleming & Talbot

post 1877   Flemming Electro-Medical Instrument Manufactory, Cabinet Battery, Permanent Office Table, Combination Battery, Portable Constant Galvanic Current Battery, no. 0 Faradic Battery, Keyboard for Galvanic Battery, Nos. 1, 2, 3 Faradic Batteries, Faradic Apparatus for Office Table, Drescher's Patent Electromagnetic Pocket Batteries, Imported French Gaiffe Battery, Water Rheostat, and Cell; 24 pp; **CPP** (Bolenius Coll); **MUM** (Ed.119 v.2 p.590ff).

1886   Flemming Electro-Medical Instrument Manufactory, Illustrated Catalogue of Flemming's Electro-therapeutic Apparatus, Electro-Surgical Apparatus, Electrodes, etc.; 42 pp; **BLEL.**

n.d.   Faradic Battery, Queen's New Toepler-holtz Electrical Machines, Automatic Rheotome, Grenet Cell, Dental Helix, Electrolytic Needles, Electrodes; **CPP** (Bolenius Coll).

FLETCHER, THOMAS, F.C.S.

Warrington, England.

Feb. 1878   List no. 2, Laboratory Apparatus . . . Designed and Patented by Thomas Fletcher; 8 pp; **YML.**

Sep. 1885   List no. 17, Laboratory Apparatus, Designed and Patented by . . . Fletcher . . . Manufactured in the United States by Buffalo Dental Manufacturing Co.; 32 pp; **YML.**

FLICOTEAUX & CO.

Bureaux et Ateliers, 83 rue du Bac, Paris, France.

1895   Catalog, Appareil spécieux pour hôpitaux; 59 pp; **NYAM; MF/MAH; CPP.**

1897   Catalog, Appareil spécieux pour hôpitaux; 99 pp, 1 pp index; medals; **NYAM; MF/MAH; NLM** (W26 F 621 c).

Jun. 1900   Catalog, Appareil pour salles d'opérations et hôpitaux; 144 pp, 1 pp index; **NYAM; MF/MAH.**

E. 20 c   Catalog, without title; 301 pp, index pp 300-301; metals; **NYAM; MF/MAH.**

FOLKERS, J. H. A., AND BROTHERS

118 Montgomery Street, San Francisco, California.

Sole agent for George Tiemann & Co., dealers in S. S. White, Phliadelphia Dental Goods.

1873   Catalogue of Surgical Instruments, Appliances, Bandages, Apparatus for Deformities, Dislocations, Fractures, Trusses, etc.; 166 pp; **UCSF.**

1883   Catalog of Dental Goods; 270 pp; **MAH** (C 617.6085F).

FOLMER & SCHWING MANUFACTURING CO., THE

No. 407 Broome Street, New York, New York.

Inc: in New Jersey, dissolved Jul 12 1907

1904   Catalog and Price List of Photographic Apparatus and Specialties Manufactured by . . . and pp 56 from Catalog Illustrating Folmer's X-Ray Reflecting Stereoscope; **ACR/MAH.**

FORD, W. F.

315 5th Ave. at 32nd Street, New York, New York.

Est: 1851

See: CASWELL, HAZARD & CO. **NYAM; AFMM; NLM.**

85 Fulton St., 150 William St., 5th Ave. Hotel for 17 yrs., (New York).
>   1851   Illustrated Catalog of Surgical Instruments and Appliances; 216 pp;
>   **RCSL.**
>   ca 1868 Catalog, Surgical Instruments and Appliances; 216 pp; **NYAM;**
>   **MF/MAH.**
>   1873   Catalog of Surgical Instruments and Appliances; 216 pp, index; **NLM** (W
>   26qF 711); **MAH** (C 610.78085F).

Broadway, Corner 24th St., New York, New York.
>   1874   Illustrated Catalogue of Surgical Instruments and Appliances, Caswell
>   Hazard & Co. Mfrs., Importers and Dealers in Every Description of
>   Surgical Instruments; 129 pp, index; **NYAM; MF/MAH; RCSL.**
>   1893   Catalog of Surgical Instruments and Appliances; 216 pp; **MAH** (C
>   610.78085F).
>   18??   Catalog of Surgical Instruments and Appliances; 216 pp; **CUHSL** (RD76
>   F 75).
>   1900   Illustrated Catalog of Surgical Instruments and Appliances; **CPP** (Ed/40).

FORT DODGE LABORATORIES INC.
300 1st Ave., Fort Dodge, Iowa.
Subsidiary of American Home Products Corp.
Est: 1912
>   n.d.   Catalog, Biological, Pharmaceutical, Veterinary Supplies; 241 pp, index pp
>   228-239; **NYAM; MF/MAH.**

FOSTER, JOHN B., AND BRO. CO., THE
138 Roseville Avenue, Newark, New Jersey.
Inc: in N.J., dissolved Feb. 27, 1902
>   *See:* FAIRCHILD BROTHERS AND FOSTER; **CPP.**
>   n.d.   Recipes for the Preparation of Peptonized Foods for the Sick by the
>   Fairchild Process, Booklet of Instructions to Tear Out; **CPP.**
>   n.d.   Panopepton, The Ideal Food for the Sick; 1 card; **CPP.**
>   n.d.   The Fairchild Products; 4 pp; **CPP.**
>   n.d.   Clinical Reports on Enzymol, A Physiological Solvent Deodorizer and
>   Healing Agent; 16 pp; **CPP.**
>   n.d.   Holadin and Bile Salts; 3 pp; **CPP.**
>   n.d.   Clinical Reports on Panopepton, 2nd Ser.; 12 pp; **CPP.**
>   n.d.   The Fairchild Preparations of the Pure Digestive Ferments and Kindred
>   Products; 16 pp; **CPP.**
>   n.d.   Pepsencia, Essence of Pepsine, Fairchild; 9 pp; **CPP.**
>   n.d.   The Fairchild Culture of the *Bacillus bulgaricus*; 4 pp; **CPP.**
>   n.d.   Practical Recipes for the Preparation of Peptonized Foods for the Sick; 12
>   pp; **CPP.**

FOUGERA, E., & CO., INC.
90-92 Beckman Street, New York, New York.
6 rue de la Tacherie, Paris, France.
>   1876   Notice on the Therapeutic Use and Special Manner of Admitting the
>   Iodous-deuto-Iodine Dragees and Depuratory Syrup of Dr. Gibert; 12
>   pp; **CPP.**
>   1888   Notes on Pure Peptine, by P. Chapoteant, Paris; 32 pp; **CPP.**
>   1888   Lactucarin Syrup and Paste, by H. Ambergier; 16 pp; **CPP.**
>   1893   The Therapeutic Uses of Iodo-Tannated Wine or Vin Noury Iodotane; 23
>   pp; **CPP.**

1893 A Clinical Report on Vin Nourry Iodotane, by Dr. Madeleine Bres; 15 pp; **CPP.**

1899 The Treatment of Arthritism; 16 pp; **CPP.**

27 rue de la Procesion, Paris XVe.

Wholesale: 45 rue du Docteur-Blanche, Paris.

1901 The Therapeutical Use of Cypridol, A Specific in Iodized Oil in Syphilis, by Dr. Ph. Chapelle; 16 pp; **CPP.**

1901 Grippe and Other Contagious Diseases; 15 pp; **CPP.**

1902 Notes on Some New Remedies Introduced by Chapoteant of Paris; 16 pp; **CPP.**

1902 Cerevisine, Pure Desicated Yeast *Saccharomyces cerevisiae*; 8 pp; **CPP.**

1904 Glycogen in Typhoid and Infectious Diseases Illustrated with Charts; 32 pp; **CPP.**

1906 Enesal Notes on a New Mercurial Compound Suitable for Injections; 20 pp; **CPP.**

ca 1906 Ampoules Fraisse pour injections hypodermiques; 15 pp; **CPP.**

1910 Enesol, The Present Position of Antisyphilitic Treatment, Arsenic and Mercury; 27 pp; **CPP.**

1916 Pharmacology of (10 drugs) from Labs of Dr. Ph. Chapelle, Paris; 32 pp; **CPP.**

1921 Pain Articular, Muscular, Neuralgic; 15 pp; **CPP.**

pre–1928 Adsorption; 2nd ed.; 9 pp; **CPP.**

1928 Adsorption; 3rd ed.; The Kaylene Treatment for Toxaemias of Intestinal Origin; 12 pp; Kaylene Ltd., 7 Mandeville Place, London, England; **CPP.**

1931 Pharmaco-Therapeutics of Delbiase, A Compound of the Halogen Salts of Magnesium; 24 pp; **CPP.**

1931 A Primer of Practical Dermatology, by Dr. Francois Debat; 13 pp; **CPP.**

n.d. Glycogen as a Therapeutic Aid by Jacques de Nittis; 10 pp; **CPP.**

n.d. Arheol Gonorrhea *Cystitus pyelitis*; 15 pp; **CPP.**

n.d. New Therapeutic Agents; 24 pp; **CPP.**

n.d. Cervisine, Colchifior, Hydrargyne, Apicoline, Morrhuol, Morrheol Creosote, Phosphoglycerate of Lime, Sental Midy, On Pancreatine and Pancreatic Preparations, Their Application in the Treatment of Disease; 20 pp; **CPP.**

n.d. For the Soda Fountain Department, Use the Pure Lactic Ferment Fermentactyl; 4 pp; **CPP.**

n.d. Price List of Preparations Manufactured in the Laboratories of Riganol and Chapoteant, 8 Rue Vivienne, Paris; 4 pp; **CPP.**

FOWLER'S PESSARIES
order from: **A. FILSON DALZELL**
104 2nd Avenue, Pittsburgh, Pennsylvania.

n.d. Fowler's Pessaries; 6 pp; **CPP** (Bolenius Coll).

FOX, H. C., & SONS
Sutherland Avenue, del Bainbridge Street, Philadelphia, Pennsylvania.

n.d. Price List Glass Manufacturers, Drug Bottles; 38 pp; **CPP.**

FOX, PETER
5 Beaver, Albany, N.Y.

1826–30 Surgical Instrument Maker listed in Albany City Directory.

6 Beaver, Albany, N.Y.

1827 Ad in front of Albany City Directory.

FOX, THOMAS
Halbert and Hart, Lombard St., London, England.
    1705   Stamped on bleeding lancet of RR in a small leather case for 2 fleams;
            RCSL.

FRAAS, (AUG. E.), CO.
15 West 50th Street, New York, New York.
    1922   Fraasstruments, Instrument Makers to the American Osteopathic
            Association and American Society of Ophthalmology and
            Oto-Laryngology; 1 pp in Acc. no. 93430; **MAH.**
    n.d.   Complete Hospital Appliances . . ., no. 1230; 250 pp, illus.; **NYAM** (S
            125).

FRANK, ARTHUR, & CO., INC.
71-73 Nassau St., New York.
    . . Apr 1924   *AFCO News*, Vol. 2, no. 4., Wholesale Opticians; also 1925, 1926 issues;
            AO.

FRANK, C. L., DENTAL SUPPLY CO.
Chicago Illinois.
    1911   Illustrated Catalogue of Dental Materials, Instruments, Teeth and
            Furniture; 1st ed.; 774 pp, price list, index; **ISUM** (W 26 C583i).

FRANKLIN EDUCATIONAL CO.
Boston and Chicago.
"Importers, Manufacturers, and Publishers."
    1895   Catalogue of Microscopes, Accessories and Microscope Material;
            Distributor: Natchet, Zeiss, Leitz; 78 pp, index; **AFMM; URRR**
            (F-129).
    1895   Catalogue of Microscopes, Accessories and Microscope Material for Use in
            Biological Laboratories; 75 pp, index; **MAH** (C681.4085 F831).

FRANKLIN X-RAY CORPORATION
Philadelphia, Pennsylvania.
    ca 1930?   Brochure, Model A Radiographic Headstead; 2 pp; **ACR/MAH.**

FRASER TABLET, TRITURATE MFG. CO., THE
262 Fifth Avenue, Chicago, Illinois.
28 Washington Street, Chicago, Illinois.
    Mar. 1896   Tablet Triturates, Hypodermic and Compressed Tablets, Chocolate Coated
            Tablets, Physicians' Private Formulas, and Vial Cases; 112 pp; **CPP.**
    Mar. 1897   Tablet Triturates . . .; 120 pp; **CPP.**
    1903   Fraser's Tablets Current Price List, Formula Description Indication Dose;
            Fluid Extracts, Elixirs, Special Remedies, Syrups, Wines, Medicine
            Cases; 356 pp; **CPP.**
    1905   Fraser's Tablets Current Price List . . .; 112 pp; **CPP.**

FRAZIER, CHARLES M.
See: GEORGE PILLING & SON, 1926; **MF/MAH.**

FRIEDLANDER, R., & CO., INC.
1130-32 Masonic Temple, Chicago, Illinois.
"Manufacturers & Importers"
    1902   Catalog of X-Ray Tubes and Barium-Platinum-Cyanide Screens; 40 pp;
            (TM); **ACR/MAH.**

1903 Catalog, Manufacturers and Importers of X-Ray Tubes and Barium, Platinum, and Cyanide Screens; Contains photos, description, facts concerning use of tubes & prices, Terms of payment, etc., Copyright 1902 by R. Friedlander & Co., Patented 23 Dec 1902; 40 pp; **MAH** (C616.0757F).

ca 1909? Catalog no. 3; Electro-Therapeutic Apparatus, X-Ray Tubes, Shields, Fluoroscopes, etc., chair patented 19 July 1904, illus pp 108; 192 pp, index pp 190-191; (TM); **MAH** (C615.84085F); **ACR/MAH.**

1921 Catalog, Medical Supplies; 32 pp; (TM); **NYAM; MF/MAH.**

FRIEDMAN, HUGO, MANUFACTURING CO.
3654 Milwaukee Avenue, Chicago, Illinois.

n.d. Catalog Dental Instruments; 39 pp, insert for Dr. E. A. Bock's adapted needle; **NYAM; MF/MAH.**

FRIEDMAN SPECIALTY CO.
Marshall Field Bldg., Chicago, Illinois.

1929 Scientific Instruments for the Scientific Man; 56 pp, index pp 56; (TM); **NYAM; MF/MAH.**

FRIES BROS. MANUFACTURING CHEMISTS
92 Reade Street, New York, New York.

1899 Rheumacelate, Its Therapy in Rheumatism, Neuraligia, Myalgia, Sciatica . . . & All Forms of Pain; 16 pp; **CPP.**

1899 Clinical Reports and Other Data on Graduated Kelene, a General Anesthetic, Creosote Phosphate-Phosphate-Phosphotal Guaiacol, Phosphite-Gaiacophosphal; 31 pp; **CPP.**

1901 Kelene, The Purest Ethyl Chloride as a Local & General Anaesthetic, Kelene, Medicinal Autosprays; 16 pp; **CPP.**

n.d. Formaldehyde Trillat System of Disinfection by the Vapors of Formochloral; 19 pp; **CPP.**

n.d. Clinical Reports . . .; 31 pp; **CPP.**

FRITZ, C. P., & CO.
123 & 125 So. 11th St., Philadelphia, Pennsylvania.

pre–1900 Catalog of Dental Instruments 16 pp; **MAH** (C617.6085F).

FRITZ AND HAWLEY CO., THE
816 Chapel Street, New Haven, Connecticut.
1030 Main Street, Bridgeport, Connecticut.

1929 Leaflet, Wide-Angle Tillyer Lenses, Accurate to the Very Edge; 4 pp; **CTY/B** (Uai T468).

FROBER-FAYBOR CO.
4612 Prospect Ave., Cleveland, OH.

n.d. Visual Photometer Bio-Photometer Aptometer; 32 pp on use of instrument to measure vitamin A deficiency; **URRR** (F-181).

FROSCO
Trademark of F. C. Schoedinger; **NLM.**

FRY, TUNBRIDGE WELLS
ca 1825 Instrument maker mentioned by John Read.

FRYE, GEORGE C.
320 & 322 Congress Street, Portland, Maine.

1881 Catalog of Surgical Instruments, Electric Batteries, Orthopedic Appliances, etc.; approx. 175 pp, 20 pp of ads for other companies; **NLM** (W26 F948).

ca 1900   Bulletin of Surgical Instruments; 4 pp, double newspaper size; **NLM** (W26 F948).

Franklin & Congress Sts., Portland, Maine.

n.d.   Illustrated Catalogue of Surgical Instruments and Appliances. Georg C. Frye, Druggist and Apothecary; **NLM** (W26 C356).

FUERSTENAU

Aug. 1921   Pamphlet, Fuerstenau X-Ray Tubes, Intensimeter and Accessories, Eppens Intensifying Screens; 24 pp; **MAH; ACR/MAH.**

ca 1921   Pamphlet, Fuerstenau Intensimeter; 8 pp; **ACR/MAH; MAH.**

FUESS, R.

Vorm. J.G. Greiner Jr. and Greissler, 18 Heizschnitten, Berlin-Steiglitz.

1891   Katalog, Mikroskope fuer krystallographische und physikalische Untersuchungen; 42 pp; **NYAM; MF/MAH.**

1894   Erganzungen zum Preisverzeichnisse, Katalog Mikroskope; 11 pp; **NYAM; MF/MAH.**

1894   Brochure, Demonstrations-Mikroskope fuer den mineralogisch petrographischen Unterricht; 4 pp, no index; **NYAM; MF/MAH.**

1895   Mess-Okulare fuer Mikroskope, 4 pp segments linked together on microscopes and physical science equipment; **URRR** (F 171A).

1895   Ergaenzungen zu den Preis-Verzeichnissen; 28 pp; Mikroskopen; **NYAM; MF/MAH.**

1895   Mikroskope und deren wichtigste Nebenapparate fuer krystallographische und petrographische Untersuchungen; 36 pp; **URRR** (F-146).

1924   The Fuess Shop Microscope sold by American Krueger and Toll Corp., 522 Fifth Ave, N.Y.; 4 pp; **URRR** (F-104).

n.d.   Katalog Nr. 100, Projections-Apparate und Optische Banke; 32 pp; **NYAM; MF/MAH.**

FULLER, GEORGE R., CO.

111 Arcade, Rochester, New York.
Successor to Dr. Douglas Bly

1866   An Anatomical Leg; 6 pp; **CPP** (Bolenius Coll).

FULLER & FULLER CO.

Chicago, Illinois.

ca 1906   Price Current, Druggists' Sundries, Surgical Instruments, Medicine Cases, Glassware, Furniture and Fixtures, Part 3; **CS.**

FUNK, C.

Lancaster Avenue & 41st Street, Philadelphia, Pennsylvania.

n.d.   Funk's Vaporizers for the Use of Balsams; **CPP.**

FUNKE, RUDOLF

Duesseldorf and Berlin, Germany.

1927   Studie ueber Zahnbohrer unter besonderer Beruecksichtigung des Solila-Bohrers; 42 pp; **UPSDM** (D617.604.F963).

1928   A Study on Dental Burs with Particular Reference to Jota Burs; 23 pp; **UPSDM** (D 617.604.F963).

GAERTNER, WILLIAM, AND CO.

5347-5349 Lake Avenue, Chicago, Illinois.

1899   Clinical Reports on Hypo-Quinedol; 24 pp; **CPP.**

1890   Gardner's Syrup of Hydriotic Acid; 8th ed.; 39 pp; **CPP.**

1893   Syrup of Hydriotic Acid, The Facts Report; 15 pp; **CPP.**

1904   Circular M-L-A, Instruments of Precision Laboratory Apparatus, Astronomical Instruments; 70 pp, index pp 70; **NYAM; MF/MAH.**

n.d.   Chemically Pure Hypophosphites; 18 pp; **CPP.**

n.d.   Swing of the Pendulum; 8 pp; **CPP.**

n.d.   List of Garden's Special Pharmaceutical Preparations; **CPP.**

n.d.   Laboratory Apparatus; 28 pp; Inserts: The De. K (R.?)hotinsky Laboratory Cements, 1 pp; D'arsonval Galvanometer 4 pp; Circular S, Universal Laboratory supports 16 pp; 1900; **NYAM; MF/MAH.**

GAIFFE, A.
40, rue Saint-Andre-Des-Arts, Paris.

1874   Notice sur les appareil électro-médicaux construits par. A. Gaiffe; 208 pp; **BLEL.**

1892   Catalogue descriptif du matériel électrotherapique complement au catalogue en 1889; 46 pp, index pp 45-46, loose pages and cover; **NYAM; MF/MAH.**

Aug. 1907   Électricité médicale notice des appareil exposés au Congress de Reims; 28 pp, last page factory illustration; **NYAM; MF/MAH.**

Sep. 1910   X-Ray Tubes no. 6; 4 pp foldout, **NYAM; MF/MAH.**

Oct. 1910   Conseils pour praticiens pour la manipulation des ampoules Roentgen; 18 pp; **NYAM; MF/MAH.**

Nov. 1910   Revue mensuelle mesureur d'induction, Brochure no. 7; 4 pp; **NYAM; MF/MAH.**

Oct. 1911   Brochure, Commutateur tournant Gaiffe; 8 pp; **NYAM; MF/MAH.**

n.d.   Pocket Electro-Medical Apparatus, imported by F. G. Otto & Sons; **CPP** (Bolenius Coll).

n.d.   Électricité médicale notice; 1 vol., various pp; **JHIHM** (R 856 G137).

GALANTE, HENRI, ET FILS
2, rue de l'École-de-Médicine, Paris.
London: J. Cohen, 13, Noble St., (London).
Naples: Galeante & Pivetta, 2, Strada San Giacome.
Est: 1851

1853   Catalogue of Instruments Used in the Practice of Medicine and Surgery; **CPP.**

1855   Catalogue of Instruments Used in the Practice of Medicine and Surgery in Vulcanized Caoutchouc; **CPP; MUM** (ED 51 pam 3).

1855   Catalogue illustre des instruments de chirurgie, appareils de prothèse, orthopédie-bandages, etc.; 218 pp; **MUM** (Ed 52 pam 14 1855); **CPP.**

1863   Notice sur un nouveau matelas hydrostatique pour prévinir la gangrène par compression dans les maladies chroniques; **CPP.**

1863   Manufacture d'instruments de chirurgie; **CPP; MUM** (Ed 51 pam 24 1864).

1864   Note sur l'emploi de l'oxygène en thérapeutique et sur son administration; 8 pp; **CPP; MUM** (Ed 51 pam 24 1864).

1866   Notice sur quelques nouveaux instruments et appareil de chirurgie; 46 pp; **YML** (RD 76.867P); **CTY/B** (60-3560F).

1867   Notice aux quelques nouveaux instruments et appareil de chirurgie, Fabriques par H. Galante, Binder's title: Exposition universelle; 46 pp, illus.; **YML.**

1885   Catalogue illustre des instruments de chirurgie appareil de prothèse orthopédic-bandages, etc.; 191 pp, loose no cover; **NYAM; MF/MAH; CPP.**

n.d.   Fabricants d'instrument de chirurgie; **CPP.**

n.d.   Nelaton's Bullet-probe, Firm Exhibited Paris 1867; **RCSL** (N3A).

GALESKI, S., OPTICAL CO., THE
915 East Main Street, Richmond, Virginia (Office).
Factory: 8 South Tenth St., Richmond.
23 Granby Street, Norfolk, Virginia.
Washington, D.C.

1884   Illustrated and Descriptive Catalogue of Spectacles and Eyeglasses for the Improvement and Preservation of the Eyesight, . . .; 39 pp; **AO.**

1899   Wholesale Price List and Catalogue of Optical Goods, 3rd Revised ed.; 47 pp; **AO.**

Apr. 1920   Wholesale Prices of Spectacles, Eyeglasses, Their Parts and Accessories for Prescription Work; 23 pp; **AO.**

GALL & LEMBKE
21 Union Square, New York, New York.
7 E. 48th St., New York 17, NY.
Est: 1842

ca 1915   Booklet by W. R. Broughton, M.D., *Description and Use of the Phorometer,* Instrument devised for testing ocular muscles and determining the amount of heterophoria, contains directions, photos, and prices; 6 pp; **MAH** (C 617.75085 B).

GALVANO-FARADIC MANUFACTURING CO.
New York.

ca 1871   Portable Electro-Magnetic Machines, and Portable Galvanic Batteries; 27 pp; **BLEL.**

1890   The Standard Electrical Instruments for Physicians, Surgeons and Family Use; 22 pp; **BLEL.**

1891   Galvano-Faradic Manufacturing Co.'s Illustrated Catalogue, Description, and Price List of their Standard Electrical Apparatus for Medical Use; 26th ed.; 48 pp; **BLEL.**

n.d.   The Standard Electrical Instruments for Physicians, Surgeons and Family Use; 22 pp; **BLEL.**

GAMBS, J.
4 rue President-Carnot, Lyon, France.

Apr. 1932   Matériel d'examen oculaire des Docteurs Lemoinc and Valois; 4 pp; **URRR** (G-401).

GA NUN & PARSONS
5 West 42nd Street, New York, New York.
"Mfrs, Importers and Dealers in Optical Goods of Every Description"

n.d.   Foldout leather binder of printed text for testing vision, proceeding from no. 1, smallest print to no. 13, largest print, fragile; **NYAM.**

GARDNER, J., AND SON
32 Forrest Road, Edinburgh, Scotland.
Est: 1866

ca 1890   Catalog of Surgical Instruments and Appliances; xxxii, 600 pp; **UWL** (W26 G227c).

Aug. 1913   Catalog of Surgical Instruments and Appliances, Aseptic Furniture,

Surgical Bandages, Artificial Limbs; 5th ed.; 776 pp, index pp ix-xxxix, pref pp vii-viii; **ABD.**

GARDNER, R. W.
158 William Street, New York, New York.
Orange, New Jersey.
Est: 1878

1879	Further Details of Dr. Churchill's Method of Using the Hypophosphites in Phthisis; 2nd ed.; 40 pp; **CPP.**
Nov. 1884	Hydriotic Acid; 3rd ed.; 64 pp; **CPP.**
Jan. 1887	Hydriotic Acid, Hypophosphites in Phthisis; 5th ed.; 16 pp; **CPP.**
Aug. 1888	Hydriotic Acid, Hypophosphites in Phthisis, Gardner's Syrup of Hydriotic Acid; 6th ed.; 47 pp; **CPP.**

P. O. Box 1525, City Hall Station, New York, New York.

Oct. 1900	Internal Administration of Iodine (Gardner); 24 pp; **CPP.**
1900	Why Hydriotic Acid is Superior to All Other Forms of Iodine for Internal Use; 16 pp; **CPP.**
ca 1900	Gardner's Syrup of Hydriotic Acid and its Imitators; 7 pp; **CPP.**
1901	Hydrogen Iodide Syrup; 24 pp; **CPP.**
1902	Iodine Phosphorus; 150 pp; **CPP.**
1904	New Clinical Reports; 110 pp; **CPP.**
1907	The Applications of Iodine Ammonium Hypophosphite; 111 pp; **CPP.**
1923	Gardner's Syrup of Hydriotic Acid, Fourty-Five Years of Faithful Service to the Medical Profession; **CPP.**
n.d.	Therapeutic Suggestions, by R. W. Gardner; 22 pp; **CPP.**
n.d.	Brief Notes on Physiochemistry, Pharmacology, Therapeutics; 10 pp; **CPP.**
n.d.	The Influenza Pandemic and its Recurrent Waves; 6 pp; foldout; **CPP.**
n.d.	Gardner's Perfected Pharmaceutical Products; 12 pp; **CPP.**
n.d.	Seven Things; 11 pp; **CPP.**

GARRETSON, JAMES EDMUND
Philadelphia, Pennsylvania.

1877	A Surgical Engine; 8 pp, reprinted from the *Philadelphia Medical Times*; **UPSDM.**

GASPARI, J., & CO.
136 West 52nd St., New York, New York.
55 East Washington St., Chicago, IL.

1938	Frames, Mountings and Oxfords; 24 pp; **URRR** (G-399).

GAUDIN, ALBERT C.
342 Madison Avenue, New York, New York.
See: B. BOULITTE; **NYAM;** Gaudin was New York distributor for Boulitte.

GEMBLOUX, MANUFACTURE BELGE DE, S. A.

1931	Ophthamologie ORL; 371 pp; **AFMM.**
1931	Mobilier; 242 pp; **AFMM.**
1933	Chirurgie; 427 pp; **AFMM.**
n.d.	Catalog; **CUHSL.**
n.d.	Exhibit Dental Instruments in Paris, 1867; **RCSL.**

GEMRIG, J. H., & SON
109 South 8th Street, Philadelphia, Pennsylvania.
Est: 1839
Became Gemrig & Son in 1879

ca 1840	Catalog of Surgical Instruments, Appliances, Apparatus for Deformities, Dislocations and Fractures; may be 1st ed.; 128 pp; **AFMM.**
ca 1865	Catalog of Surgical Instruments, Apparatus for Deformities, Trusses, etc.; 139 pp; **AFMM.**
1867	Exhibit of Dental Instruments in Paris; **RCSL.**
ca 1870	Catalogue of Surgical Instruments, Appliances, Bandages, Apparatus for Deformities, Dislocations and Fractures . . .; 128 pp; **NLM** (W26 G323c).
ca 1876	Catalogue of Surgical Instruments, Orthopedical Apparatus, Trusses, etc.; 3rd ed.; 188 pp, index, fragile, in 3-ring binder; **AFMM; MUM.**
1879	Illustrated Catalogue of Surgical Instruments, Orthopedical Apparatus, Trusses, etc.; 4th ed.; **MUM.**
1882	Illustrated Catalogue of Surgical Instruments and Orthopedical Apparatus, Trusses, etc.; 5th ed.; **MUM.**
1887	Catalogue of Surgical and Veterinary Instruments, Orthopedical Apparatus, Trusses, etc.; 6th ed.; 219 pp, index; **AFMM; MUM.**
L. 19 c	Catalogue of Surgical Instruments, Appliances, Bandages, Apparatus for Deformities, Dislocations and Fractures, etc.; 128 pp, back cover missing; **NLM** (W 26 H 136).
n.d.	Illustrated Catalog of Surgical Instruments, Appliances, Bandages, Apparatus for Deformities, Dislocations and Fractures, Trusses, etc.; **CPP.**
n.d.	Illustrated Catalog of the Apparatus Required for the Treatment of Deformities, Contraction, Debilities, and Paralysis of the Human Frame, and Diseases of the Joints; **CPP** (Bolenius Coll).
n.d.	Catalog of Surgical Instruments; 128 pp, index, photocopy; **MAH.**

GENERAL ELECTRIC CO.
Harrison, New Jersey.
570 Lexington Ave., New York 22, NY.
Est: 1878

See: WATSON & SON, England **MAH.** WATSON & SONS LTD., 1925; **MAH.** VICTOR X-RAY CORP., late 1920's.

Jun. 28, 1897	Roentgen Ray Apparatus no. 9050, illustrated with photographs of radiographs and equipment, and some drawings, All the apparatus here described was designed by Prof. Elihu Thomson . . ., its manufacture is subject to his personal direction . . . apparatus is made at . . . Schenectady, N.Y., vacuum tubes . . . at Harrison, N.J.; 50 pp; **ACR/MAH.**
Dec. 6, 1897	General Catalogue and Price List of Lighting Supplies, no. 7514; **BLEL.**
April 1919	Instruction Book 89136A, supersedes 89136, Coolidge X-Ray Tube; 23 pp, 14 figures; (has Coolidge/GE TM); **ACR/MAH.**

Schenectady, New York.

| July 1907 | Electrically Heated Appliances and Utensils for Physicians, Dentists and Hospitals, no. 3573; 8 pp; **CPP.** |

GENERAL ELECTRIC X-RAY CORPORATION
2012 Jackson Blvd., Chicago, Illinois.
Est: 1892

| 1930's | Publication 7A-156A, CDX-Model E Dental X-Ray Unit, Completely Oil Immersed; 19 pp; (TM); **ACR/MAH.** |
| ca 1928 | Bulletin no. 206, X-Ray Tables, Roentgenoscopes, Stereo Units, Tube |

Stands, Fluorographic Units, Accessories; 67 pp; (has Victor and GE TM's); **ACR/MAH.**

1929   Bulletin no. 212, Snook X-Ray Apparatus, 140 KV.P., Formerly Victor X-Ray Corp Diagnostic and Light Therapy, 200 KV.P., Combination Deep Therapy and Diagnostic; 31 pp; (GE & Victor TM's), *See*: Freed in Victor folder; **ACR/MAH.**

ca 1930   Booklet, Victor Lantern Slide Service, Lantern Slides from many sources for illustrating lectures and talks on X-Ray and Physical Therapy; 23 pp; (Victor & GE TM's), *See*: Victor folder; **ACR/MAH.**

ca 1930   Supplement to Bulletin no. 212, Snook Jr. X-Ray Apparatus for Diagnostic Service; 8 pp; (GE & Victor TM's); **ACR/MAH.**

ca 1930   Brochure, Victorean X-Ray Measuring Instruments; 8 pp; (Victorean TM); **ACR/MAH.**

1930's   Publication 7A-5B, New D Series Shockproof Oil-Immersed X-Ray Units; 22 pp; (TM); **ACR/MAH.**

1930's   Publication 7A-5C, The Model D-2 Series Shockproof Oil-Immersed X-Ray Units; 22 pp, prices inked in; (TM); **ACR/MAH.**

1935   Muscle Stimulating Apparatus, Bulletin no. 294; 6 pp; **BLEL.**

GENERAL OPTICAL CO.
Mount Vernon, New York.

1920   Genothalmic Refracting Room Equipment; 23 pp; **URRR** (G-309).

Jan. 1, 1923   Price List Genothalmic Instruments and Equipment; 19 pp; **URRR** (G-301).

GENEVA OPTICAL CO.
63 & 65, 67, & 69 Washington Street, Chicago, Illinois.
St. Louis, Missouri.
Des Moines, Iowa.
Minneapolis, Minnesota.
Est: 1875

Feb. 1, 1889   Catalog of Optical Goods, The Prisoptometer; 10 pp, insert; **CPP.**

1891–92   Wholesale Priced and Illustrated Catalog of Optical Goods, includes microscopes,compasses, thermometers, hygrometers, telescopes; 136 pp, index; **ACR/MAH; AFMM; CPP.**

1898   Catalog, Stock and Prescription Work, Trial Cases, Cameras and Optical Appliances; 196 pp, index pp 196; **MAH** (C617.75085G).

1903   21st Annual Wholesale Priced and Illustrated Catalogue of Stock and Prescription Work; Trial Cases, Lens Measures and Optical Appliances used by the Oculist and Optician; 195 pp; **URRR** (G-7).

1903   Revised Price List of Geneva Optical Equipment, contains terms, discounts, catalog nos., item and cost per dozen; 59 pp, Few photos, no index; **MAH** (C 617.75085G).

1904–5   Price List, contains terms, discounts, Catalog nos. item and cost per dozen, price list of prescription work, etc.; 59 pp, no index; **MAH** (C 617.75085 G); **URRR** (G-9).

1907   Price List; 28 pp; **CPP.**

1926   28th ed., issued on 51st Anniversary; 80 pp; **URRR** (G-8).

n.d.   The Geneva Ophthalmoscope; 7 pp; **URRR** (G-10).

n.d.   The Knu-Automatic Eyeglass; 20 pp; **URRR** (G-208).

n.d.   Geneva Optical Co.; each section indexed on right side; 148 pp; **URRR** (G-261).

GENEVOISE, SOCIÉTÉ
5, Chemin Gourges, Geneva, Switzerland.

    1907   Illustrated Price List of Physicians and Medical Instruments made by the Société; 260 pp, index of names pp 251; **RCSL.**

GENNARI
    n.d.   D. & G. no 76/7G Bleeding lancet in pocket use with instruments made mostly by Mathieu; **RCSL.**

GENTILE
Paris.

    n.d.   G 342, Luy's urine separator; **RCSL.**

GERBER
St. Petersburg, Russia.

    n.d.   RCS Loan Collection. no. 53 Lazarewitch's Straight Long Forceps, with crossed handles; **RCSL.**

GERHARDT, C.
Bornheimstr. 100-96, Bonn am Rhein, Deutschland.

    1925   Preisverzeichnis uber Bakteriologische Apparate Sonderliste Nr. 95; 40 pp, indexes pp 36-40; **NYAM; MF/MAH.**

GERMAN ELECTRIC BELT AGENCY
313 and 315 Fulton Street, Brooklyn, New York.

    ca 1890   The German Electric Belts and Appliances; 24 pp; **BLEL; NLM** (W26 G373c).
    ca 1891   The German Electric Belts and Appliances; 24 pp; **BLEL.**
    ca 1901   The German Electric Belts and Appliances; 32 pp; **BLEL.**

GIRARD CO.
1308 Sansom Street, Philadelphia, Pennsylvania.

    1903   The Girard Co. Pharmaceutical Chemical Catalog of Preparations; 24 pp; **CPP.**
    n.d.   Colbrylith; 6 pp; **CPP.**
    n.d.   Catalog of Special Pharmaceuticals Manufactured by Girard Co.; 24 pp; **CPP.**
    n.d.   Report of Tests of the Antiseptic Power of Lignol by J. B. Nichols; 12 pp; **CPP.**
    n.d.   Special Pharmaceuticals; 36 pp; **CPP.**

GIROUX, L.
114 rue du Temple, 19 rue de l'Odeon, Paris, France.

    n.d.   A New Tonometer by Dr. P. Bailliart; 12 pp; **CPP.**

GLAENZER, J., AND CO.
35, Boulevard de Strasbourg, Paris.
27 Chambers Street, New York.
Agents for Tramond, Paris.

    post 1878   Catalog of Anatomical Osteology, Human Anatomy and of Natural and Artificial Preparations; 56 pp, index pp 56; **NYAM; MF/MAH.**

GLAROMETER CO.
Chicago, IL.

    1935   New Instrument that Measures the Effect of Glare; 6 pp foldout; **URRR** (G-357).

GLAZIER AND KEMP
Brighton, England.
        1825   Instrument makers mentioned by John Read.

GLITSCHKA, A.
Ghent, Brussels.
        n.d.   RCS Loan Collection; no. 66; Boddearts's lever; **RCSL.**

GLOBE MANUFACTURING CO.
Battle Creek, Michigan.
301-03 Odd Fellow's Temple, Temple Building, Broad Street, Philadelphia, Pennsylvania.
    Oct. 1897   Eucaine Hydrochlorite A to B; 16 pp; **CPP.**
        1904   Catalog and Formulary Nebulizers, Vibrators, Electric Air Pumps, Preparations; 4th ed.; 48 pp; **CPP.**
        1904   Nebulization and Allied Methods; 24 pp; **CPP.**
        1908   Catalog and Formulary; 5th ed.; 48 pp; **CPP.**
        1909   Catalog, Nebulizers, Vibrators, Electric Air Pumps, Preparations, Compressed Air for Medical Purposes; 7th ed.; 24 pp; **CPP.**
        1920   *The Globe News*; Vol. XV; no. III; 59 pp; **NYAM.**
        1920   *The Globe News*; Vol. XV; no. V; 99 pp; **NYAM.**
        n.d.   Physicians's Air Compressors; Physicians' Hydraulic Outfit no. 201; 8 pp; **CPP.**
        n.d.   The Globe Nubulizer; 8 pp; **CPP.**
        n.d.   A Catalog & Price List of Air Compressors, Receivers and Accessories; 8 pp; **CPP.**
        n.d.   Physicians Air Compressors; 9 pp; **CPP.**
        n.d.   Globe Compressed Air Vibrator; 7 pp foldout; **CPP.**
        n.d.   Globe Formulary; 22 pp; **CPP.**
        n.d.   Globe Equipments spell R-E-S-U-L-T-S; 8 pp foldout; **CPP.**
        n.d.   Superheated Air in Medicine; 12 pp; **CPP.**
        n.d.   Globe Nebulizers; 16 pp foldout; **CPP.**
        n.d.   The Shaw Air Compressors; 4 pp; **CPP.**

GLOBE OPTICAL CO.
Marlboro Bldg., 403 Washington St., Boston, 2, Massachusetts.
California charter suspended Mar 3 1923 for failure to pay taxes.
Est: 1889
        1904   Manufacturers, Importers, Jobbers, Headquarters for Optical Goods in the Eastern States; 175 pp; **AO.**
        1908   General Catalogue of Optical Goods, Instruments, Machinery and Accessories; 324 pp, price list of May 1904 inserted; 15 pp; **URRR** (G-17); **AO.**
    Branches: Augusta, Lewiston, Bangor, New Haven, Bridgeport, Providence, Burlington, Springfield, Hartford, Worcester.
  Aug. 15, 1922   Globe Optical Machinery and Shop Specialties, Catalogue F; 23 pp; **AO.**
    pre–1930s   Illustrated Price List, Prescription Work, Trial Cases, Instruments; 39 pp; **AO.**
        n.d.   Price List of Frames, Lenses, Cases, etc.; 8 pp; **AO.**
        n.d.   Electrotypes for Advertising; 4 pp; **AO.**

GLYCENE DENTURES
  See: GEORGE WEICHERT.

GOEBELER, H., & CO.
14 Bond Street, New York, New York.

1877   Descriptive Catalog of Chemico-Technical Apparatus, Requisites, Chemical, etc . . . Agents for Fr. Schmidt & Haensch, Improved Saccharometer; **CTY/B** (Uai Sch 53).

GOLDBACHER, ERNEST
98 Fulton Street, New York, New York.
1885   Catalog, Useful Holiday Presents, Spectacles and Eyeglasses, . . . Thermometers . . . the Polyopticon or Wonder Camera; 8 pp; **CTY/B** (Uai G565).

GOLDENBERG
n.d.   WHM R2895/1936, This is a large ornate frame saw possibly 16th or early 17th Century with detachable blade stamped GOLDENBERG (not old lettering) **RCSL.**

GOLDSCHMIDT, S.
Wilhelm Strasse 84, Berlin, Germany.
Est: 1834
n.d.   Systematische Zusammenstellung der Instrumente und Apparate für Medicin, Chirurgie, Geburtskunde, Kriegsheilkunde Hospitaldienst und Krankenpflege; 224 pp; 4 pp Inhalt Orthopaedie pp 108-154 Anthroplastik; **RCSL.**
Dorotheen Strasse 28, Berlin, Germany.
1868   Katalog und Preisverzeichniss der Königl. Preuss. patentirten Bruchbänder, Bandagen, orthopadischen, maschinen, künstlichen Glieder Apparate zur Pflege und Erleichterung für Kranke und chirurgischen Instrumente welche von den berühmtesten ärztlichen Autoritaten bei Operationen, bei den Deformitäten des Rückgrats und der Extremitäten angewendet werden; 124 pp; **NLM** (W26 G624c).

GOLDSMITH BROTHERS SMELTING & REFINING CO.
29 E. Madison St., Chicago, Illinois.
111 N. Wabash Ave., Chicago, Illinois.
Est: 1867
ca 1910   Catalogue of Dental Supplies; 232 pp; **HML; CDMC.**

GOOD HEALTH PUBLISHING CO.
Battle Creek, Michigan.
ca 1909   Twentieth Century Therapeutic Appliances, for Use in Sanitariums, Hospitals, Medical Institutions, Physicians' Offices and Residences; 94 pp; **BLEL.**

GOODRICH, B. F., CO., THE
500 S. Main Street, Akron, 18 Ohio.
Est: 1867
n.d.   A Catalog of Newer Surgical Rubber Specialties; 47 pp; **CPP.**

GOODRICH, STEPHAN & CO.
See: J. JUNGMANN; **NLM.**

GOODWIN, GEORGE C., & CO.
38 Hanover St., Boston, MA.
1874–5   Catalogue of Patent Medicines, Druggists' Sundries, Perfumery, Toilet Articles, etc.; 73 pp; **HUBL.**
1876–7   Catalogue; 128 pp; **HUBL.**
1885   Catalogue; 384 pp; **HUBL.**

GOODYEAR RUBBER CURLER CO.
309 9th St., N.W., Washington, D.C.
729 Broadway, New York, New York.
  ca 1885 Catalog; 96 pp, index pp 1-2; **MAH.**
  ca 1886 Trade Journal; 119 pp, index; **NLM** (W 26 G658c).

GORDON AND MORRISON WHOLESALE OPTICIANS
199-201 E. Madison St., Chicago; IL.
 210-212 W. Madison St., Chicago, IL.
Est: 1892
   1910 Catalogue no. 201; 231 pp; **URRR** (G-28).
   1912 Catalogue no. 226; **AO.**
   1916 Catalogue no. 231; pp 159-214; **URRR** (G-29); **AO.**

GORDON MANUFACTURING CO.
Toledo, OH.
  ca 1900–10 Gordon Invalids' Chairs; 90 pp; **MAH** (8433).

GORMAN, SAM J., CO.
Chicago, Illinois.
   191? Electro Therapeutic Apparatus; 10th ed.; 61 pp; **BLEL.**
   n.d. The Physician's Vibragenitant; 23 pp; **BLEL.**

GORSE, FRANK W., CO.
Highlandville, Massachusetts.
   n.d. Catalog of Elastic Hosiery Supporters etc.; 12 pp; **CPP** (4/Ed).

GOSLEE CROWN & BRIDGE TOOTH
 See: CONSOLIDATED DENTAL CO.

GOTHOM OPTICAL INSTRUMENT & MACHINERY CORPORATION
39-41 Eldrige, New York, NY.
Est: 1905
   1930s Gothom Achievements in Modern Optical Machinery; 16 pp; **AO.**

GOUBEAUX, A.
216 Boulevard St. Germain, Paris, France.
   1891 Optique médicale instruments d'ophtalmologie; 12 pp; **CPP.**

GOWLLAND, WILLIAM, LTD.
Moreland Rd., Croydon, England.
   1913 Illustrated Catalogue and Price List of Ophthalmoscopes, Retinoscopes,
     Trial Frames, Laryngoscopes, Sight Testing and Ophthalmological
     Apparatus; 150 pp; **URRR** (G-261).

GRADY, W. R.
Chicago, Illinois.
   1900 Illustrated and Descriptive Price List of Surgical Appliances, Sect. VIII;
     192 pp; **VM.**

GRAF, R., & CO.
16 Gleihbuehlstrahe, Nuernberg, Germany.
   1928 Tebeprotin nach Prof. Dr. Toenniessen zur spezifischen Diagnostik und
     Therapie der Tuberkulose; 6 pp; **CPP.**

GRAF-APSCO CO., THE
109 West Austin Avenue, Chicago, Illinois.

Successor to American Profession Supply Co.

  Aug. 1938 Rebuilt Microscopes; 23 pp; **AFMM.**

5868 Broadway, Chicago, IL.

  Apr. 28, 1958 Medical Microscopes; 4 pp; **URRR** (G-402).

GRAFATH, CHARLES
New York, New York.

  1915 Dental Instruments Catalog; 20 pp; **UPSDM.**

GRAIFF, A.
Paris.

  n.d. Stamped on Apostoli's needle; Aberdeen University collection; **RCSL.**

GRAY, JOSEPH, & SON
Sheffield.
London, England.
Est: 1849

  189? The Improved Magneto-Electric Machine, for Nervous Diseases, with Improved Indicator, Invented and Manufacturered by J. Gray & Son, Makers of Surgical, Dental and Veterinary Instruments; 24 pp; **BLEL.**

  1930s Illustrated Catalog of Dental Instruments, Section D; 119 pp; **WMScM.**

GRAY, PETER, AND SONS, INC.
86-88 Union Street, Boston, Massachusetts.

  1909 Catalog, Milk Inspectors' Outfits also Special Laboatory Equipments, Culture Tube Incubators, Microscope Slides Cabinets, Animal Cages; 10 pp; **CTY/B** (Uai G793).

GRAYBAR ELECTRIC CO.
 GEC, Inc.
 420 Lexington Ave., New York 17, New York.
Est: 1869

  n.d. Appears as distributor on several Machlett Laboratories, Inc. brochures during the 1940's and '50's; (TM); **ACR/MAH.**

GREEN & BAUER INC.
30 East Randolf Street, Chicago, Illinois.
243 Pearl Street, Hartford, Connecticut.

  May 28, 1917 Brochure, 4 pp, illus., price list; **NYAM; MF/MAH.**

GREEN, WILLIAM P.
Philiadelphia, Pennsylvania.

  1885 West Philadelphia Dental Depot Price list; 20 pp; **UPSDM** (D 617.604 G827).

GREINER, EMIL
78 John Street, New York, New York.

  1902 Catalog, Chemical, Physical and Bacteriological Apparatus and General Laboratory Supplies; 256 pp; (medals); **CTY/B** (Uai G863); **CPP.**

GREINER & FRIEDRICHS
Stuetzerbach.
Est: 1862

  1880 Preisverzeichniss Utensilien und Apparate; 2 pp price list, 3 pp catalog, 1 pp additional price list, 1 pp leaflet; **NYAM; MF/MAH.**

  May 1881 Verzeichniss Apparate, Instrumente und Geraethschaften; 39 pp; separate

price list; 48 pp; **NYAM; MF/MAH.**
1886 Brochure, Quecksilberluftpumpe; 2 pp; **NYAM; MF/MAH.**
1886 Verzeichniss; no title page (may not be a G&F); 17 pp, illus., prices; **NYAM; MF/MAH.**
Feb. 1886 Catalog, Apparate und Utensilien; 11 pp; Separate price list; 8 pp; **NYAM; MF/MAH.**
1902 Price List of Chemical Physical and Bacteriological Apparatus; 5th ed.; 172 pp; **HDM.**
1912 Katalog von Greiner & Friedrichs, Fabrik und Lager von Apparaten und Geraetschaften fuer Chemie, Physik, Bacteriologie, Mikroskopie und verwandelte Zweige; 383 pp; **CTY/B** (Uai G8633).

GREINER, J. G., & GREISSLER
See: R. FUESS.

GREISHABER, ERNST
Schaffhausen (Suisse).
n.d. Augeninstrumente; Instruments for Micro-Surgery; 3 pp; **WMScM.**

GRESSLER, EDUARD
1167 Johannisstrasse, Erfurt, Germany.
post 1853 Preis-Courant . . . über chemische, pharmaceutische, physikalische, etc., Apparate, Instrumente, & Utensilien . . .; I theil; 80 pp; **CTY/B** (Uai G867).
n.d. Catalog, Verzeichniss chemischer, pharmaceutischer, physikalischer, etc., Apparate, Instrumente und Utensilien, pharmaceutischer und chemischer Standgefaesse . . .; 77 pp; **CTY/B** (Uai G867).
1854 Preis Courant von Edward Gressler; II theil; 32 pp; **CTY/B** (Uai G 867).

GRIBLE
Germany.
n.d. RCS Loan Coll. no. 15, Mursinna's Forceps; **RCSL.**

GRIFFEN, JOHN JOSEPH, AND SONS
22 Garrick Street, Covent Garden, W C, London, England.
1877 Chemical Handicraft: A Classified And Descriptive Catalog of Chemical Apparatus; xvi, 479, iv pp index; **UTP.**
1896 Ad on back of: *Archives of Clinical Skiagraphy;* **WMScM.**
1900 Illustrated Price-list of Bacteriological Apparatus; **CPP** (Cgg/457).
1905 Scientific Apparatus including Laboratory Fittings, Balance and Weights, List no. 50; 735 pp; **WMScM.**
ca 1910 Griffin's Scientific Handbook; 14th ed.; **UTP.**

GRIFFITH, E. H.
Fairport, Monroe Co., New York.
ca 1882 Catalog, Griffith Club Microscopes; 7 pp; **CTY/B** (Uai G877).

GRISWOLD SYSTEM
See: RITTER DENTAL DEPOT; **MF/MAH.**

GRISWOLD, W. E., D.D.S.
Denver, Colorado.
n.d. A System of Removable Bridge Work, synopsis of papers read and clinics given between 1900 and 1901 by Griswold; 24 pp, separate price list on letter; **NYAM; MF/MAH.**

GROSHALY, CHARLES F.
634 Arch Street, Philadelphia, Pennsylvania.
     n.d.   Miller Molded Water Bottles; 4 pp; **CPP.**

GROSSMANN, JULIUS
8 Catharinenstrasse, Hamburg, Germany.
     1895   Monthly Price List of J. G., Chemical Manufacturing Refinery of Borax
            and Camphor; 22 pp; **CPP.**

GROSSMITH, W. R., LTD.
12 Burlegh Street, London, W.C. 2.
54 Dyke Road, Brighton.
Leeds.
Roehamton.
Glasgow.
Est: 1760 on Fleet Street
     1924   Artificial Limbs, Eyes, Crutches; 68 pp; **ABD.**
     1928   Artificial Limbs, Eyes, Crutches, Foot Supports, Belts and Other
            Appliances; 56 pp, price lists; **WMScM.**

GROSVENOR AND RICHARDS
49 Federal Street, Boston, Massachusetts.
100 Fulton Street, New York.
Inc: 1889
In New Jersey, franchise surrendered Nov. 11, 1897; in Maine, dissolved Feb. 1897; in Nashua,
New Hampshire, 1889, repealed 1925
     1886   A Physicians' Catalogue of Surgical Plasters, Antiseptics and Absorbants;
            54 pp, index; **MAH** (16127).
     1887   Physician's Catalog of Medicinal and Surgical Plasters, Absorbent and
            Antiseptic Dressings; 64 pp; **CPP** (Bolenius Coll).

GROUT MANUFACTURING COMPANY, B. T. ROBERTS
3514 Vincennes Ave., Chicago.
Est: 1890s
     1923   Grout Optical Equipment; 32 pp; **AO.**
     1925   Grout Optical Equipment, Catalog K; 32 pp; **AO.**
   3518 Ellis Avenue, Chicago.
     1930   Grout Optical Equipment, Catalog R; 32 pp; **AO.**

GROVES, T. W.
15 South Pearl Street, Home: 39 Van Zandt, Albany.
     1843   Sawmaker listed in Albany City Directory, his office is located in the area
            where the doctors have clustered.

GRUBER-HOLLBORN & GIEMSA STAINS
   See: PFALTZ & BAUER INC.; (1935); **MF/MAH.**

GRUEBLER, GEORG, DR.
Bayersche Strasse 12, Leipzig, Germany.
     post 1884   Leaflet, Preis-Liste der Farbstoffe und chemischen Praeparate fuer
            Mikroskopie; 16 pp; **CTY/B** (Uai G922).

GRUNBLATT, A.
Charkaw.
     n.d.   RLS Loan Coll.: no. 109; Lozurewitch's cephalotrite; **RCSL.**

GRUNOW, J. & W., & CO.
New Haven, Connecticut.
    1857   Catalog of Achromatic Microscopes, arranged as text and presented by chapters; 104 pp, fragile; **MAH** (578.08).
    1857   Illustrated Scientific & Descriptive Catalogue of Achromatic Microscopes; 104 pp; **CHS** (578.1 G891c).

GUERIDE, H.
    1867   Fabrique d'instruments de chirurgie et appareil d'orthopédie, binder's title: Exposition universelle 1867; 15 pp, illus.; **YML** (RD 76 867P).
  1844–1855 Instruments de chirurgie, instruments de physiologie, instruments de chirurgie vétérinaire, spécialité pour dentistes, appareil d'orthopédie and bandages; 40 pp; **CPP; MUM** (Ed 51 pam23).

GUILLOT, FERNAND
Paris.
    1932   Fernand Guillot Fabricant; 54 pp; **AFMM.**

GUNDLACH'S
Sold by L. R. Sexton.
Rochester, New York.
    n.d.   Microscopes and Objectives; 16 pp; **CTY/B** (Uai G 956).

GUSTAV, ERNST F.
80 & 82 Charlotte Street, Fitsroy Square, W., London, England.
    1905   Illustrated Catalog of Artificial Limbs for Use After Amputation and Congenital Deficiencies; 47 pp, index, 117 illustrations; **MAH.**

GUYOT, E.
  1914–15 Catalogue général illustré d'instruments de chirurgie; 446 pp, illus.; **NWUCML** (617.91 G99 in shelf list).

GYSI ARTICULATORS
  See: THE DENTISTS' SUPPLY CO., E. 20 c.; **NYAM.**

GYSI
  See: THE DENTIST'S SUPPLY CO.

HAERTEL, GEORG
Breslau.
    1896   Chirurgische Instrumente, Nr. 150; **CPP** (33Ed/5).

HAERTEL, HERMANN
33 Weidenstrasse, Breslau, Germany.
Est: 1819
Inhaber: Hermann Haertel und Georg Haertel
    1887   Verzeichniss von chirurgischen Instrumenten, Bandagen und Artikeln zur Krankenpflege; 221 pp, index; **NLM** (W26 H136).
    1887   Verzeichniss von chirurgischen Instrumenten Bandagen; 229 pp, index pp 223-229, separate price list; (TM); **NYAM; MF/MAH.**
  1880's–1890's Katalog anatomischer, chirurgischer, orthopaedischer und thieraerztlicher Instrumente, Inductions-und Rotations-Apparate . . .; 67 pp, index; **NLM** (W 26 H 136).
    1890   Preis Liste Manufacture von chirurgischen Instrumenten, Bandagen; 77 pp; Medals; (TM); **NYAM, MF/MAH.**

HAGAR & MEISINGER, G.M.B.H.
Düsseldorf, Germany.
Est: 1887
    1920's   Catalogue of Tooth Burrs, Polishers, etc., Catalog no. 15; 40 pp; **AFMM.**

HAGERTY, B. B. & J.
8 & 10 Platt Street, New York, New York.
    1862   Catalog, Glassware, Rubbergoods, Porcelain Ware and Sundries, Chemical and Philosophical Ware; viii, 76 pp; **YML.**

HAGERTY BROS.
New York, N.Y.
    n.d.   Catalog of Every Variety of Druggists, Chemists, Perfumers, etc.; 359 pp; **MSL** (RS356 H2.8).

HAHN, CHRISTIAN
16 North William St., New York.
Practical Glassblower and Mfr. of Artificial Eyes
    n.d.   Bound with Queen Catalogs in Box beyond alphabetically arranged collection of trade catalogs; **URRR.**

HAHN'S TRUSSES
No. 1515 Arch Street, Philadelphia, Pennsylvania.
Est: 1812
    n.d.   Hernia or Rupture and Other Displacements Successfully Treated and Cured; 96 pp; **CPP.**

HAJEK, F.
Vienna, Austria.
    ca 1880   Appears on Ohlhansen's Obstetrical Forceps; in Acc. file no. 316,358; **MAH.**

HALL, FRANK A., & SONS
118-120-122 Baxter St., New York, N.Y.
Est: 1828
    pre–1914   Aseptic Hospital Furniture and Bedding; 32 pp; **MAH** (16118).
    n.d.   Catalog, Hospital Furniture; 33 pp, separate price list; **NYAM; MF/MAH.**

HALL, G. W.
Buffalo, New York.
    n.d.   G.W. Hall's Patent Artificial Leg; **CPP** (Bolenius Coll).

HALL, THOMAS
Boston, Massachusetts.
    1869   Illustrated Catalog of Electro-Medical Instruments; 10th ed.; 48 pp, index; **MAH.**

HALL, WILFORD LABORATORIES
Port Chester, New York.
    1917?   Price List Medicinal Plasters, Surgical Plasters, Surgical Dressings and Suspensories, no. 17; 48 pp; **CTY/B** (Uai H 147).
    July 8, 1918   Revised Price List no. 17; 6 pp; **CTY/B** (Uai H 147).

HALSEY, W. D., & CO.
27 Washington Street, Chicago, Illinois.

1875   Shannon's Uterine Supporter and Self Adjusting Pessary; **CPP** (Bolenius
Coll. KY/1); **MUM** (Ed.119 v.2 p.401).

HAMBLIN, THEODORE, LTD.
15 Wigmore Street, London W.1.
1928   The Mayou Slit-Lamp no. 621; 7 pp; **URRR** (H-4).
1929   Ophthalmic Instruments and Apparatus, Detailed Descriptive Catalog;
CPP.
1931   Hamblin's Sporting Spectacles for All Kinds of Sports; 2 pp foldout;
URRR (H-319).
1933   Hamblin's Ophthalmic Instruments and Apparatus, Detailed Descriptive
Catalog; 139 pp; **URRR** (H-285).
1930s   Hamblin's Ophthalmoscope; 11 pp, back cover; **WMScM** (T.H. 501
1.k.1D 67).
1933   Hamblin's Ophthalmic Instruments and Apparatus, a Detailed Descriptive
Catalog; 140 pp; **WMScM.**

HAMMOND, JOHN F.
25 East 125th Street, New York, New York.
n.d.   Catalog, Electric Dental Engine; 15 pp, separate price list; **NYAM;**
MF/MAH.

HANFORD, E.
1819   A Catalogue of the Names of the Various Medicinal Articles Treated in
the London, Edinburgh, & Dublin Pharmocopoeias Alphabetically
arranged, intended to assist the memory of the Compounder of
medicines and to answer the purpose of A Druggist's Price Book,
London printed R. A. Taylor, Shoe Lane; Microfilm; **WMScM.**

HANGER, J. E., & CO. LTD.
531 Bluefield Avenue, Bluefield, West Virginia.
126 Wellington Street W, Toronto, Canada.
200 Sixth Aveue, Pittsburgh, Pennsylvania.
Jewelers' Building, 214-18 South 12th Street, Philadelphia, Pennsylvania.
Alabama & Pryor Streets, 16 South Pryor St., Atlanta, Georgia.
1914 Olive Street, St. Louis, Missouri.
221-223 G Street, N. W., Washington, D.C.
2218 North Fifth Avenue, Birmingham, Alabama.
1529 Tulane Avenue, New Orleans, Louisiana.
Bordeaux, Lyons, France.
Glasgow, Scotland.
Est: 1861
"Solviter Ambulando"
1926   Hanger Science Aids Nature; 24 pp; **CPP.**
1936?   Solvitur ambulando, A Symposium on Prosthetic Achievement; 72 pp;
TMHM.

HANHART & ZEIGLER
5 Bahnhofplatz, Zurich.
1910   Illustriertes Musterbuch chirurgischer Instrumente; 308 pp, index; **ZUR.**
n.d.   Illustrierter Katalog chirurgischer Instrumente; 468 pp, 19 extra pp; **ZUR.**

HANHART & CO.
Bahnhofstrasse 110, Ecke Bahnhofplatz, Zurich.

n.d.   Fabrikation und Konstruktion chirurgischer Instrumente; 784 pp; contents pp vii-xxi, index pp xxiii-xxxviii; (TM); **ZUR.**

HANNOVER, LE DOCTEUR ADOLPHE
Paris.

1855   De la construction et de l'emploi du microscope, Publiée par Charles-Chevalier, premier constructeur, en france, des microscopes achromatiques . . .; **MAH.**

HANOVIA CHEMICAL & MFG. CO.
Chestnut Street & New Jersey RR Avenue, Newark, New Jersey.
30 Church Street, N.Y.; Chicago; San Francisco.
Est: 1905

July 1920   Heliotherapy and the Quartz Light, Booklet no. 50; 32 pp; **CPP.**

Jun. 1921   Hanovia Therapeutic Quartz Lamps, The Alpine Sun Lamp, the Kromayer Lamp, Price List no. 60, included in sales note book c/cover: The Engeln Electric Company X-Ray Apparatus; 3 pp, 1 pp illustration; **ACR/MAH; MAH.**

Jan. 1923   The Kromayer Lamp and Alpine Sun Lamp, Catalog no. 60, The Engeln Electric Company X-Ray Apparatus; 23 pp; **ACR/MAH; MAH.**

1923   Catalog, Handbook on Quartz Light Therapy for Users of the Kromayer Lamps, The Engeln Electric Company X-Ray Apparatus; **ACR/MAH; MAH.**

1925?   The Hanovia Quartz Mercury Arc Lamp for Scientific Purposes; 6 pp, also Bulletin 20 (1927); **URRR** (H-367A).

Sep. 1, 1927   Catalog, Quartz Lamps; 23 pp; **NYAM; MF/MAH.**

1927   Hanovia Ultraviolet Lamps and Other Equipment for Laboratory Use; 13 pp; **URRR** (H-367).

1929   Hanovia Quartz Lamps; 39 pp; **URRR** (H-366).

1929   Catalog, Presenting Hanovia Quartz Lamps; 39 pp; **CTY/B** (Uai H196).

1940   Hanovia Examalite Model Quartz Lamp; bound with other single page ads for lamps; **URRR** (H-354).

1940   The Basis of UV Therapy for Users of the Alpine and Kromayer Lamps; 23 pp; **CPP.**

HANSCOM, P. L., & CO.
Union Bldg., 102-110 LaSalle Street, Chicago, Illinois.
114-150 Washington Street, Chicago, Illinois.
Est: 1865

1870   Catalog of Gummed and Cut Labels and prices 64 pp; **MAH.**

HANSEN, J. P.
Copenhagen (Kjobenhavn), Denmark.

n.d.   RCS G 233 Jacobson's crusher for small calculi; **RCSL.**

HANWAY, H. D.
12 E. 23rd Street, New York, New York.
Successors to New York Branch of Wilmington Dental Mfg Co.

1897   Catalog, Dental Furniture, Instruments, and Material; 594 pp, index pp 580-594; **MAH** (C617.6085).

HARAN, E.
12 rue Lacepede, Paris.
Est: 1879

1903   Fabricant, d'instruments de chirurgie, d'appareils orthopédiques, membres artificiels, bandages, béquilles, ceintures, gouttières, bas électriques, instruments en caoutchouc souple et durci et tous articles d'hygiène; 3rd ed.; 78 pp, iii pp index; **MAH** (26819).

HARDING, R. A.
1 Manvers St., Bath.
Works: James St., W., Bath.
273-274 High Holborn, London, W.C. 1.
56 Oxford Road, Manchester.
London, England.

1927   All at **WMScM:** 1. Invalid Carriages no. 216; 2. 19 Lower Bristol Rd., Bath, The Puttney, 4 pp; 3. Invalid Carriages & Motors—1930 period; Cat. XXVII, 34 pp and order blank; 4. 1927—Maners address Cat. (no other title) 59 pp plus back; last 3-1 foldout; 5. 28 pp also at 43 Aschcombe Rd; 6. 8 pp—R. A. Haring West—Super-Mare; 7. Pages form 1935 catalog showing improved models; 49 pp; **WMScM.**

1928?   Mfrs. of Invalid Carriages & Appliances; Illustrated Catalog, Description and Sizes; 35 pp; **MAH.**

1928   Press & Public Opinions of Harding's Invalid Cars; **MAH.**

n.d.   Invalid Carriages & Motors, The Pultney series motors flyer; **WMScM.**

1920s   Invalid Carriages & Appliances Press & Public Opinions of Harding—Invalid Cars, Sectional Catalog no. 2; 16 pp; **WMScM.**

HARDY, F. A., CO.
46 & 48 Madison Street, Chicago.
131-137 Wabash Avenue, Chicago, Illinois.
Est: pre–1896

1896   Price List of Oculists' and Opticians' Supplies, 9th ed.; 160 pp; **AO.**

1903   Price List of Spectacles, Eyeglasses and Lenses; 176 pp; **URRR** H-7F).

Nov. 1, 1906   Catalog of Eye, Ear, Nose, & Throat Surgical Instruments; 238 pp, index pp 236-238; (TM); **NYAM; MF/MAH; CPP.**

1906   The Hardy Peerless Mounting Catalog and Price List; 15 pp; **URRR** (H-216).

1907   Price List of Optical Prescription Work; 19th ed.; 64 pp; **AO.**

1908   Catalog & Price List of Eye, Ear, Nose and Throat Instruments; **CPP** (Ed/39).

1909   The C-I Ophthalmometer; 16 pp; **URRR** (H-212).

1909   The Hardy Ophthalmometer, Its Utility, Construction, and Manipulation; 16 pp; **URRR** (H-215).

Branches: 29 East 22nd Street, New York.
Grant Bldg, Atlanta, (GA).
Gas and Electric Bldg., Denver, (CO).
Praetorian Bldg., Dallas, (TX).
Phelan Bldg., San Francisco, (CA).
6th and Cedar St., St. Paul, (MN).

ca 1910   Catalog, The Improved Punctumeter, Contains description of instruments, illustrations, use and care as well as prices; 34 pp, no index; **MAH** (617.75085H).

1911   Catalogue of Eye, Ear, Nose, and Throat Instruments, Hand Forged; 2nd ed.; 192 pp; **VM; CPP.**

1915   The One Position Ophthalmometer (C.-I.); 19 pp; **URRR** (H-250).

Jun. 1, 1916   Catalog of Safety Glasses and Eye Protectors; 25 pp; **CTY/B** (Uai H221).
10 South Wabash Ave., Chicago.
      1917   Price List of Optical Prescription Work; 19th ed.; 64 pp; **AO.**
Aug. 15, 1918   Catalog of Safety Glasses and Eye Protectors; 34 pp; **CTY/B** (Uai H221).
      1918   Ophthalmological Catalog; 107 pp; **URRR** (H-5).
Jan. 1, 1920   Catalog, Eye, Ear, Nose, and Throat Instruments and Equipment; 4th
         ed.; 168 pp, index pp 165-168; (TM); **NYAM; MF/MAH; MAH.**
      1920   The Improved Punctometer; 6th ed.; 34 pp, illus.; **MAH** (C617.75085H).
Oct. 1920   Pamphlet, Catalog of Optical Goods, no. 6, Vol. XVI; 16 pp; **NYAM;
         MF/MAH.**
Apr. 1921   Brochure, Catalog of Optical Goods, no. 2, Vol. XVII; 15 pp, no index;
         NYAM; MF/MAH.
      n.d.   The Eye Muscle Testing Dynamometer, The Hardy Van Slyke Instruction
         Booklet; 20 pp; **URRR** (H-209).
      n.d.   The Punctometer; 3rd ed.; 16 pp; **URRR** (H-210).
      n.d.   The Worth-Black Deviometer; 1 pp; **URRR** (H-213).
      n.d.   The Stigmatometer; 4 pp; **URRR** (H-214).

HAROLD SURGICAL CORP.
115 Fulton Street, New York, New York.
204-6-8 E. 23rd Street, 83 Pine Street, New York, New York.
      1920's   Catalogs of Surgical Instruments, Hospital Equipment and Supplies, etc.,
         all paper bound, All vol. II; Catalog no. 3, 48 pp; "May Number", 46
         pp; no. 4, 48 pp; no. 7, 48 pp; no. 8, 64 pp; no. 9, 64 pp; **NLM**
         (W26 H 292c).
      n.d.   We are continuing our Half Million Dollar Sale of Army Surplus Medical
         and Hospital Supplies; 32 pp; **CPP; NLM** (W26 H292c).
Apr. 1920's   Catalog no. 4, Surgical Supplies, vol. II; 48 pp, no index; **NYAM;
         MF/MAH.**
      1926   Catalog no. 29, Equipment for the Physician and Surgeon, Vol. 3; 64 pp;
         MAH.
      1926   Catalog, Equipment for the Physician and Surgeon; 49 pp; (TM); **NYAM;
         MF/MAH.**
      1926   Catalog no. 2, Equipment for the Physician and Surgeon, Vol. III; 50 pp;
         (TM); **NYAM; MF/MAH.**
      1927   Catalog no. 34, Equipment for the Physician and Surgeon; 64 pp; **CPP**
         (Ed/64).
      1928   Catalog no. 41, Issue For Physiotherapy Apparatus, etc., Vol V.; 63 pp;
         (TM); **CTY/B** (Uai H23).
Mar. 1928   Catalog, Equipment for the Physician and Surgeon; 68 pp; (TM); **NYAM;
         MF/MAH.**
      1928   Catalog no. 40, Post Inventory Cash Clearences Sale, Vol. V; 64 pp;
         (TM); **CTY/B** (Uai H23).
      1930   Catalog no. 62, Surgical Instruments and Supplies; Vol. VII; 64 pp;
         (TM); **NYAM; MF/MAH.**
      192?   Catalog; Pages unnumbered covers missing; 71 pp, 3 loose; **NYAM;
         MF/MAH.**
      192?   No title page, Catalog Surgical Supplies; 61 pp; **NYAM; MF/MAH.**
      192?   Catalog, Equipment for the Physician and Surgeon; 64 pp; (TM); **NYAM;
         MF/MAH.**
      192?   Bulletin, Medical and Hospital Supplies; 69 pp; **NYAM; MF/MAH.**

192? Bulletin, Medical and Hospital Supplies; 82 pp; **NYAM; MF/MAH.**
Nov. 192? Bulletin, Medical and Hospital Supplies; 48 pp; **NYAM; MF/MAH.**
192? Bulletin, Surgical Supplies; 50 pp; **NYAM; MF/MAH.**
192? Bulletin no. 55, Surgical Instruments and Supplies; 32 pp; **NYAM; MF/MAH.**
192? Bulletin no. 55, Surgical Instruments and Supplies; 64 pp; **NYAM; MF/MAH.**
n.d. Catalog no. 1, Medical Instruments, Vol. II; 48 pp, no index; **NYAM; MF/MAH.**
n.d. Catalog no. 1, Our New Year "Special", Vol. III; 48 pp; **CPP.**
1926 Catalog no. 2, Vol. III; 48 pp; **CPP.**
n.d. Catalog no. 3, Medical Supplies; 17 pp; **NYAM; MF/MAH.**
n.d. Catalog no. 4, Medical Supplies, Vol. II; 47 pp; **NYAM; MF/MAH; CPP.**
n.d. Bulletin no. 4; 44 pp; **CPP.**
n.d. Bulletin no. 5, Comprising specially priced imported instruments and U.S. Government Army Surplus Medical and Hospital Supplies; 64 pp; **CPP.**
n.d. Bulletin no. 6; 64 pp; **CPP.**
July 192? Bulletin no. 7; 48 pp; **CPP.**
Aug. 192? Catalog no. 8, Physicians' Supplies, Vol. II; 64 pp; (TM); **NYAM; MF/MAH; CPP.**
Aug. 192? Bulletin no. 8; 48 pp; **CPP.**
Sep. 192? Bulletin no. 9; 48 pp; **CPP.**
Oct. 192? Bulletin no. 10; 48 pp; **CPP.**
n.d. Bulletin no. 12; 48 pp; **CPP.**
n.d. Catalog, no title page; 132 pp, starting pp 7, 1 pp index, pp missing; **NYAM; MF/MAH.**
n.d. Electro Physiotherapeutic Treatment of Diseases, Light Therapy; 4 pp foldout; **CPP.**

HARRIS, PHILLIP, & CO.
144 and 146 Edmond St., Birmingham, England.
Dublin, Ireland.
1929 Catalog of Surgical Instruments & Appliances, Revised Jul 1904 ed.; Manufactory Gt. Chas St. Cornwell St.; 3 pp, index pp 1-x; **RCSL.**

HARTFORD DENTAL DEPOT
96 Trumbull Street, Hartford, Connecticut.
1897 Dental Furniture, Instruments and Materials . . ., by W. C. Messinger; 594 pp; **CHS** (974.62H328hd).
1905 Illustrated Catalog of Dental Furniture, Dental Instruments and Dental Material; 3rd ed.; 808 pp, index pp 781-808; **UPSDM** (D617.604 H253); **MAH** (C617.6085H); **UPAL.**

HARLECO
See: HARTMAN-LEDDON CO., INC.; **MAH.**

HARTFORD WOVEN WIRE MATTRESS CO.
Hartford, Connecticut.
ca 1901 Catalog of Aseptic Furniture for Hospitals and Institutions, Apparatus for the Sterilization of Dressings, Instruments and Water, Operating Room Furniture, Ward and Private Room Tables; 129 pp, index; **NLM** (W26 H328).

HARTMANN UND BRAUN, A.-G.
Frankfurt am Main, Germany.

    1908   Instruments de mesure électriques pour l'usage industrial, extrait
            sommaire; 73 pp; **BLEL.**

HARTNACK, E.
39 Waisenstrasse no. 39, Potsdam, Germany & rue Bonaparte 1, Paris (before 1892).

   Mar. 1892   Preis verzeichniss der Mikroskope und mikroskopischen Neben-Apparate;
            24 pp; **URRR** (H-147).

   Dec. 1903   Katalog, Mikroskope und Mikroskopische Apparate; 38 pp; **AFMM.**

      1903   Preisverzeichniss Mikroskope und mikroskopische Apparate; 38 pp; **URRR**
            (H-146).

      1927   The Haemacytometer Blood Corpuscles-Counting Apparatus; 12 pp;
            URRR (H-8E).

HARTNESS, THOMAS L.
Beaver-Home 16 Orchard (1831-30), 5 Beaver (1832-3), North Market-Home Port Schuyler,
Troy Road, Albany, N.Y. (1833-36).

   1831-33   Instrument maker and cutler listed in Albany City Directory, 1831 Ad in
            front of directory.

HARTZ, J. F., CO., LTD.
No. 2 Richmond Street, East, Toronto, Ontario.

   ca 1900   Advertisement for Spencer Stand no. 1, filed with Spencer Catalogs; 1 pp;
            AFMM.

   E. 20 c   Catalogue of Sundries, hospital and sick room; 144 pp; **TMHM.**

      1928   Catalog, Sundries for the Physician, Nurse and Hospital; 146 pp, 14 pp
            index, price list inside front cover; **UTP.**

HARVARD FEVER THERMOMETERS
Ranfac, Boston.

      1917   12 pp; **CPP.**

HARVEY, G. F., CO.
Saratoga Springs, New York.

   1907-8   Catalog; **CS.**

   ca 1910   The Townsend Aseptic Surgical Sheet; 16 pp; **HML.**

HASLAM, FRED, & CO.
83 Pulaski Street, Brooklyn, New York.
Est: 1848; Inc: 1938

      1886   George A. Evans' Vaporizer and Inhaler for the Local Treatment of
            Pulmonary, Bronchial and Nasal Affections, stamped: Charles Lentz &
            Sons, Surgical Instruments, 18 N 11th St, Philadelphia; 30 pp; **CPP.**

      1908   Catalog of Surgeon's Instruments, Microscopes (Spencer's) and Accessories,
            Laboratory Apparatus, Hospital and Office Furniture, Electrical and
            X-Ray Apparatus, Orthopedic Apparatus, etc.; 502 pp, index; **AFMM.**

      1922   Illustrated Catalog, Standard Surgical Instruments; 4th ed.; 416 pp, index
            pp 393-416; **MAH.**

Jun. 10, 1930   Catalog of Rustless (Stainless) Steel Instruments; 36 pp, separate retail
            price list; **NLM** (W26 H352).

    1930?   Catalog of Standard Surgical Instruments, Microscopes and Accessories,
            Lab Apparatus, etc.; 432 pp, index; **AFMM.**

HASTINGS AND McINTOSH TRUSS CO., THE
912 Walnut St., Philadelphia 7, PA.
Est: 1870
 Oct. 1, 1963 Price List no. 122; **MAH.**

HATRICK, JAMES L., & CO., LTD.
58, Red Lion Street, London, E.C. 1.
 1930s Tiegel-Henle-Sauerbruch, Positive Pressure Anaesthetic Apparatus, patent
  applied for 4119/33; 4 pp; **WMScM.**

HATTEROTH, WILLIAM
San Francisco, California.
 1895 Surgical Instruments, Orthopedic Appliances, Trusses, etc., Hospital
  Supplies; 381 pp; **LACMA** (149 H 285).

HAUSMANN, A. G.
St. Gallen, Basl, Davos, Genf, Zurich.
 n.d. Illustrirter Katalog, Artikel fuer Kranken und Gesundheits Pflege; 163 pp,
  index; **ZUR.**
 n.d. Spezialhaus fuer alle Bedarfsartikel der Chirurgie, Medizin und Pharmacie.
  Komplette Einrichtungen fuer Aerzte, Kliniken und Spitale, Aseptisches
  Operations-mobiliar und Sterilisations-Anlagen; 52 pp; (TM); medals;
  ZUR.
 ca 1908 Spezial-Katalog ueber Einrichtungen für Aerzte und Krankenhäuser; vi,
  154 pp; medals, (TM); **ZUR.**

HAUSMANN, J., SR.
43, rue Greneta, Paris.
 1905 Instruments de chirurgie, accessoires pharmacie caoutchouc manufacture,
  Supplement no. 1; 52 pp, some color illustrations of measures;
  WMScM.

HAUSMANN, C. FRIEDRICH, SANITÄTSGESCHÄFT-HECHTAPOTHEKE
St. Gallen, Switzerland.
Est: 1873
 1894 Illustrirtes Preisbuch ueber Instrumente, Apparate, Utensilien Glas und
  Gummie Waaren usw. fuer Chirurgie, Medicin, Pharmacie,
  Krankenflege und Hygiene; no. 5; 538 pp; (TM); medals; **ZUR;**
  HDM.

HAUSSMANN & DUNN CO.
392 So. Clark Street, Chicago, Illinois.
 ca 1904 Catalog of Veterinary Instruments and Supplies; Turf Goods; 783 pp, 10
  pp index; **MAH; ABD.**

HAWKSLEY, T.
357, Oxford Street, London, W.
17 New Cavendish Street, London, W.1, England.
Est: 1869
 1909 Catalog of Otacoustical Instruments to Aid the Deaf; 6th ed.; 80 pp;
  WMScM.
 Hawksley, & Sons
 n.d. Hawksley Haemocytometers, and Haemoglobinometers; 1 pp foldout;
  WMScM.

HAYEM-SAHLI HAEMACYTOMETER
See: LEITZ; **NYAM; MF/MAH.**

HAYNES STELLITE CO.
New York.
S. Lindsey, Kokomo, Indiana.
Division of Union Carbide & Carbon, Corp.
Est: 1912
    ca 1925   A Ten Minute Story of Stellite; 12 pp; **HML.**

HAZARD, HAZARD & CO.
Broadway, corner 24th Street, New York.
    See: W. F. FORD
        1880   Illustrated Catalog of Surgical Instruments and Appliances . . .; xxix, 279 pp; **NYAM** (S125).
        ca 1887   Illustrated Catalog of Surgical Instruments and Appliances; pp xxix index, 260 pp; Supplement to Surgical Instrument Catalog, paginated 262-279; **NYAM; MF/MAH; CPP.**

HEARSON, CHARLES, & CO., LTD.
Hope Works, 68 Willow Walk, 235 Regent Street, W 1, London, S.E. 1, England.
    ca 1917   Catalog of Biological Incubators, Autoclaves and Centrifuges, Laboratory Apparatus and Specialties; 266 pp, index; **NLM** (W26 H436).
27 Mortimer St., London W, England.
    May 1926   The Hearson Capsule in the Service of the Scientist, A Record of 40 Years of Practical Accomplishment; 276 pp, 8 pp price list; **WMScM.**
        1932   The Hearson Microscope; 11 pp. 4 pp insert; **URRR** (H-356).

HEBBAR BROTHERS, LTD.
246 Thombu Chetty Street, Armenian Street G. T., Madras, India.
        1936   Aseptic Hospital Furniture; 2nd ed.; 7 pp; **MAH.**
        n.d.   Brochure "Coral" Aseptic Hospital Equipment; 7 pp; **MAH.**

HEBERT
        1802   Pamphlet, Hebert's Air Pump Vapour Bath; 8 pp; **APS** (610 Pam no. 175).

HEDER, HUGO
Liebigstrasse no. 10, Leipzig, Germany.
        n.d.*   Leaflet, Werkstatt fuer Electrotechnik und Feinmechanik nach Dr. W. Strauss; (elec. Kymograph); 4 pp foldout, *see year of *Archiv f d ges. Physiologie*, Band 81; **NYAM; MF/MAH.**

HEELE, HANS
No. 104 Grüner Weg, Berlin 0.27, Germany.
Est: 1875
        1903   Catalog, Werkstätten fuer Praecisions-Optik und Mechanik, distributor: Arthur H. Thomas Co., sole agents in U.S., 1200 Walnut St., Phila., PA; 64 pp; medals; **NYAM; MF/MAH.**
        1905   Leaflet, Heele's New Comparison Spectroscope and New Universal Spectroscope; Grand Prix Paris 1900; 4 pp unbound, 1 pp letterhead and enclosure; **NYAM; MF/MAH.**

HEIDBRINK CO., THE
2633 4th Avenue South, Minneapolis, Minnesota.
Est: 1911

1916–17   The Heidbrink Automatic Anesthetizer, A Comprehensive Treatise on Its
           Operation and Use for the Administration of Nitrous Oxide and
           Oxygen for Anesthesia and Analgesia; 28 pp, 1 pp price list; (TM);
           NYAM.
1922   The Heidbrink Anesthetizer; 32 pp, 4 pp price list; **MAH.**
1928   The Heidbrink Anesthetizer; 40 pp; (TM); **MAH** (C 617.96085H).
pre 1937   Catalog, The Heidbrink Resuscitator and Inhaler, Kreiselman Models; 7
           pp; **CTY/B** (Uai H362).
pre 1938   Catalog, The Kinet-O-Meter, A Scientifically Designed Gas-Oxygen
           Anesthesia Apparatus; **CTY/B** (Uai H362).
n.d.   Heidbrink Nasal Catheter Outfit for Oxygen Therapy; 4 pp; **CTY/B** (Uai
           H 362).
n.d.   Catalog, The Model C Heidbrink Junior, A Small, Efficient, Portable
           Gas-Oxygen-Ether Apparatus for Office and Hospital Use; 8 pp;
           (HI-CO, TM); **CTY/B** (Uai H362).
n.d.   Aero-Tent no. 52, Motorized Portable Oxygen Tent; 4 pp; **CTY/B** (Uai
           H 363).
n.d.   Aero-Tent no. 57, Motorized Portable Oxygen Tent; 4 pp; **CTY/B** (Uai
           H 362).
n.d.   The Heidbrink Oxygen Tent Deluxe Hospital Model no. 32; 4 pp;
           CTY/B (Uai H 363).

HEIL, HENRY
St. Louis, Missouri.
1904   (Chemical Company) Catalog; **SLSC.**

HEIMSTADT, OSKAR
1921   Ein stereoskopischer Aufsatz fuer Mikroskope. Sonderabruck, Zeitschrift
           fuer wissenschaftliche Mikroskopie und fuer mikroskopische Technik,
           Band 38, S. 321-333, reprint, fragile; **AFMM.**

HEINE, JOHANN GEORG
1807   Systematisches Verzeichniss chirurgischer Instrumente, Bandagen und
           Maschinen nach Anleitung der besten Wundaerzte aelterer und neuerer
           Zeit, welch nach beygesetzten Preissen verfertigt werden und zu haben
           sind, Wuerzburg, Stahel; viii, 96 pp; **CPP** (Pam 6250).
1811   Neues Verzeichniss chirurgischer Instrumente, Bandagen und Maschinen,
           welch um beygesetzte Preise verfertigt werden und zu haben sind bey J.
           G. Heine, chirurgischer Instrumentenmacher am Hospital, der
           Universitat und dem Juliuspital in Wuerzburg, Herausgeber;
           Nuernberg, J. E. Zehe; viii, 64 pp; **CPP** (Pam 6257).

HEINECKE, H.
Invalidenstr. 91, Berlin N.W. 40, Germany.
"Chirurgie-Mechanic"
Apr. 12, 1908 Mitteilung von Neuheiten auf dem Gesamtgebiete der Medizin: Chirurgie,
           Orthopaedie, Prothesen, Verbandstoffe, Bandagen, Operation und
           Lagerung, Elektro-medizin Heilgymnastik, Massage, und
           Vibration-therapie; Bakteriologie, Mikroscope, Sterilisierung,
           Desinfektion, Krankenpflege, Nr. 77; 50 pp; **ZUR.**

HEINZ-WANDNER X-RAY TUBE CO.
100 East Lake Street, Chicago, Illinois.
See: WANDNER & SON . . .; **ACR/MAH.**

ca 1900   Catalog, X-Ray Tubes and Electrodes, Chemical, Physical, Glass Apparatus; 15 pp; **ACR/MAH.**

HEILLIGE
Wylaczne przedstawicielstwo:
C. Cegielski, Poznan-selacz, Podolska 16/17, Oddzial w Warszawie.
Est: 1883

E. 20 c   Apparate fuer Medizin, Elektromedizin, Chemie-Physik-Industrie in weltbekannter Qualitaet; 10 pp, illus.; **AFMM.**

HELLIGE & CO.
Freiburg im Breisgau, Germany.

1925   Scientific Apparatus; no. R 3066; 4 pp; **URRR** (H-13F).

Aug. 1929   Booklet of Directions for the Various Tests as Carried Out with the Hellige Universal-Colorimeter Comprising the Use of "Normal Wedges," Filled with Permanent Standard Solutions; 47 pp; **URRR** (H-290).

Sep. 1929   Haemacytometer, Haemoglobinometer, Nonfade Colorimeter; 15 pp; **URRR** (H-?).

Nov. 1930   Hellige Wedge Type Colorimeters, List no. 400; 11 pp; **URRR** (H-259).

1931   Hellige for Better Haemoglobin Tests; 6 pp; foldout; **URRR** (H-285).

Jan. 1932   Hellige-Duboscq Rapid Kolorimeter; 6 pp; **URRR** (H-275 F).

Feb. 1932   Das Hellige Neoplan-Haemometer; 1 pp; **URRR** (H-280).

Mar. 1932   Hellige Reflexspiegel in neuer Ringfassung; 1 pp; **URRR** (H-281).

Mar. 1932   Hellige Diabetometer Pro 95 D; 2 pp; **URRR** (H-279).

May 1932   The Hellige-Wintrobe Haemometer List no. 370; 1 pp; **URRR** (H-299).

HENKE, GEORGE A.
Bergstrasse 27-29, Süd-Deutschland, Tuttlingen

n.d.   Fabrik chirurgischer, zahn und tieraerztlicher, Injektions-Instrumente, diagnostische Spezialitaeten, Kaniuber; extra Preis-lista zum Katalog Nr. 14, 25 yrs. experience mfrs. syringes, etc., surgical, dental and veterinary injection instruments needles, diagnostic specialties; 56 pp; **WMScM.**

HENRY
Coutelier de la Chambre des Paris,
Fabricant d'instrument de chirurgie, Paris, France.

1825   Précis descriptif sur les instruments de chirurgie anciens et modernes, contenant la description de chaque instrument, le nom de ceux qui y ont apporté des modifications, ceux préféres aujourd'hui . . . et l'indication des qualités que l'on doit rechercher dans chaque instrument, . . .; viii, 260 pp; **CTY/B** (51-2009) (RD 71 825h); **MAH** (RD 71 H 52); **LLU** (WO H521p 1825).

HENRY, JOHN F.
8 College Place, New York, New York.
21 Park Row, New York.
Successor to Demas Barnes & Co.

n.d.   Catalogue of Medicines, Perfumes and Fancy Goods inserted in 1874 Van Schaack, Stevenson and Reid Catalogue; **MAH.**

HENSHAW, DAVID & JOHN
33 India Street, Boston, Massachusetts.

Feb. 1828–9   Ad for a very extensive assortment of Surgical instruments in *Boston Medical and Surgical Journal*; **APS** (610 Pam Bo. 90).

HERMANN, P.
Zurich IV, Switzerland.
Est: 1867

        1911   Wissenschaftliche Messinstrumente, Anthropologie, Orthopaedie Verzeichniss C 11; 16 pp; **CPP.**

HERNSTEIN, A. L.
52 Maiden Lane, New York.
Atlanta, Georgia.
Est: 1825

     Jan. 1881   Illustrated Catalog of Surgical Instruments & Orthopedic Appliances; 339 pp; **CPP** (Bolenius Coll).

        1870   Illustrated Catalog of Surgical Instruments & Appliances; 134 pp; **CTY/B** (54-893); **NWUCML** (617.91H43); **MRLB; YML; NLM** (W 26 H 558); **RCSL; TMHM.**

HERRICK'S, DR. L. R.

        n.d.   Perforated Capsicum Plasters; 4 pp leaflet; **MAH** (C 615.8085H).

HERZHAUSE
Germany.

        n.d.   Scalpel by Herzhause; **RCSL.**

HESSLER, H. H., CO.

        n.d.   Bulletin of Blood Transfusion and Other Special Instruments; 15 pp, illus.; **CPP** (Pam 6822).

HETTINGER BROS. MFG. CO.
1009-11 Grand Avenue, Kansas City, Missouri.

        1911   Catalog of Dental Supplies; 4th ed.; 775 pp, index pp 755-775; (TM); **MAH** (C 617.6085H).

        1917   Catalog of Surgical Instruments and of Allied Lines; 672 pp, index; **LON** (617.91 H47).

        1922   Catalog, Standard Surgical Instruments; 416 pp; **SLSC.**

        1923   Hettinger Brothers, Dental Brothers; 184 pp; **SLSC.**

        1924   Catalog, Standard Surgical Instruments; **SLSC.**

HEWITT, A.
Chicago(?)

       1905?   Amberoid Cement for Permanent and Temporary Dental Fillings, Crowns, Bridges and Inlays; 1 pp; **HML.**

HEYNEMANN, C. G.
Elsterstrasse No. 13, Leipzig, Germany.

     ca 1901   Liste A, Ausgabe XI, Instrumente zur Behandlung von Harn und Blasen Krankheiten; 52 pp, contents pp 52; TM; **NYAM; MF/MAH.**

HIGBEE, E. W., M.D.
Springfield, Northampton, Massachusetts.

     Sep. 1875   The Harding and Higbee Thumb and Finger Speculum; 2 pp; **CPP** (Bolenius Coll); **MUM** (Ed.119 v.2 p.386).

     Sep. 1875   The Thumb and Finger Speculum; 3 pp; **CPP** (Bolenius Coll); **MUM** (Ed.119 v.2 p.386).

     May 1877   Patentee of the Higbee Speculum; 2 pp; **CPP** (Bolenius Coll); **MUM** (Ed 119 v.2 p.380).

        n.d.   Modified Hodge Pessary; 1 pp; **CPP** (Bolenius Coll).

HIGDEN
See: BORG; **RCSL.**

HIGH TENSION CO.
114-124 Columbia Street, Union City, New Jersey.
See: HIGH TENSION TRANSFORMER AND EQUIPMENT CORP.; **ACR/MAH.**
    1920's   Brochure, The Intermediate Mobile 9" X-Ray Unit, Model T-102; 5 pp;
        ACR/MAH.

HIGH TENSION TRANSFORMER AND EQUIPMENT CORP.
Hoboken, New Jersey.
See: HIGH TENSION CO.; **ACR/MAH.**
    1930's?   Brochure, Radiography with the Intermediate Unit; 2 pp; **ACR/MAH.**

HIGHLEY, SAMUEL
18, Green Street, Lexington Square, 32 Fleet Street, London W.C.
    Jun. 30, 1854   Descriptive Catalogue of Highley's Educational Collections of Specimens,
        Apparatus, Models, etc. Selected for Facilitating the Study of the
        Natural and Medical Sciences and Art; 22 pp; (TM); **CTY/B** (Uai,
        H538).
        1864   Mfrs. of Students' Microscopes, Objectives and Accessories, Photographs
        for the Magic Lantern, Oxy-Hydrogen & Electric Light apparatus
        Spectacles, Rare Glasses, Telescopes, Barometers. Ad in *Brit. Optical
        Journal*; **WMScM.**

HILGER, ADAM, LTD.
24 Rochester Place, 75A Camden Road, London, N.W. 1.
    Oct. 1, 1918   Abbe Refractometers With Water Jacketed Prisms; 13 pp; **NLM** (W26
        C6975).
    n.d.   Flyer, The Hilger Measuring Micrometer, postmarked 1929; Constant
        Deviation Wavelength Spectrometer; **MAH.**
    Jan. 1930   A General Catalog of the Manufactures of A. Hilger, LTD.; This concerns
        the instruments contained in Sect. D,E,F,H,K,L,M, and N apparatus
        appearing for the first time is marked New; no. of pages: D = 29,
        K = 03, E = 49, L = 09, F = 44, M = 30, H = 44, N = 16, index = i-x.
        NYAM; MF/MAH.

HILLIARD & CO.
53 South Bridge Street, (opp. the college), (Glasgow).
Manufactory: 65 Nicolson St., (Glasgow).
House: 12 Nicolson St., (Glasgow).
    n.d.   Full Page Ads, pp 279 Edin Div.; **RCSL.**
Hilliard, W. B., & Sons
65 Renfield Street, Glasgow, Scotland.
Est: 1834
    Sep. 29, 1892   Illustrated Catalog of Surgical Instruments, etc.; iii-viii pp index, 147 pp;
        date stamped; **RCSL.**

HIPP, DR. M.
See: FABRIQUE de TÉLÉGRAPHES et APPAREIL ÉLECTRIQUES; **NLM.**

HIRSCHMANN, W. A.
    1890   Apparate zur Anwendung der Elektricitaet in der Medicin; 53 pp; **BLEL.**
    1896   Elektro-medizinische Apparate; **CPP** (33Ed/1).

HODGMAN & CO.
459 and 461 Broadway, New York, New York.
Est: 1838
> 1884 Catalog of India Rubber Goods Manufactured and Sold by . . .; 104 pp, 4 pp index; **MAH.**

HOFFMAN-LA ROCHE CHEMICAL WORKS
51-53 Maiden Lane, New York, New York.
65 Fulton Street, New York, New York.
Nutley, New Jersey (post–1923).
The Roche Laboratories
51 Bowes Rd., London, N.13.
> 1910 Pantopon in Internal Medicine; 5 pp; **CPP.**
> 1914 Two New Roche Preparations: Larosan Sedobsol and the Well-Known Triad Digalen Pantopan Thiocol; 16 pp; **CPP.**
> 1915 Pantopen "Roche"; 12 pp; **CPP.**
> 1923 When Chemists Turned from Gold to Drugs, Pantopen; 12 pp; **CPP.**
> n.d. Medical Opinions of Digalen the Trustworthy Exponent of Digitalis Therapy; 60 pp; **CPP.**
> n.d. A Cup of Sedobrol "Roche"; 4 pp; **CPP.**
> n.d. Making the Action of Digitalis More Certain; 7 pp; **CPP.**
> n.d. The Doctor Visits "Roche"; 24 pp; **CPP.**
> n.d. Larodon the New Synthetic Analgesic; 13 pp; **CPP.**
> n.d. Roche Uncommon Organic Chemicals for Therapeutic Use; 14 pp; **CPP.**
> n.d. Roche Medical Specialties Fine Chemicals and Alkaloids; 24 pp; **CPP.**
> n.d. Whooping Cough; 4 pp; **CPP.**
> 1930s Roche Tubunic Ampoule Syringe; 8 pp, inside cover; **WMScM.**

HOLBORN SURGICAL INSTRUMENT CO., LTD., THE
26 Thavies Inn, Holborn Circus, London, E.C. 1.
> ca 1915 Brochure, untitled; 18 pp; 1 pp loose; **NYAM; MF/MAH.**
> ca 1920 Foldout, A few Novelties for the General Practitioner; 1 pp; **WMScM.**
> 1926 Catalog of Surgical Instruments and Appliances Invalid and Hospital Furniture; 125 pp, index 119-124; size chart last page; prize medals on cover; **NYAM; MF/MAH.**

HOLBORN RUBBER, GUTTA PERCHA, AND MacINTOSH WATERPROOF CO., THE
No. 2, High Holborn, London, W.C.
> 1869 Maw's Catalogue Distribution for S. Maw & Co.; **RCSL.**

HOLEKAMP-MOORE
St. Louis, Missouri.
> 1896 Illustrated Catalogue and Price Current; 2nd ed.; **CS.**

HOLLBORN, DR. CHARLES
71 Kronprinzstrasse, (late 63 Bayersche Strasse), Leipzig 53, Germany.
Est: 1897
> July 1, 1925 Brochure, Proprietor of Dr. G. Gruebbers, Dry and Fluid Stains, Coloring Reagents and Chemicals for Microscopy and Bacteriology; 1 pp, index; **NYAM; MF/MAH.**
> E. 20 c Preisliste, Farben für Mikroscopie und Bakteriologie; 32 pp, insert; 1 1/4 pp price list; (TM); **NYAM.**

HOLLISTER, B. K.
HOLLISTER-WILSON LABORATORIES, THE
6620 Kimbark Avenue, Chicago, Illinois.
      1917   Hollister's Sterile Ligatures and Surgical Specialties; Tubes of
              Distinction; 22 pp; (TM); **NYAM; MF/MAH; CPP.**

HOLMES, JAMES
Akron, Ohio.
      1859   Instrument maker listed in the Akron City Directory.

HOLOPHANE CO., INC.
342 Madison Avenue, New York, New York.
Est: 1898
      1930   Hospital Lighting Specifics; 18 pp; **CTY/B** (Uai H74).
  pre-1938   Catalog, Holophane Planned Lighting; (TM); **CTY/B** (Uai, H74).
      n.d.   Holophone Planned Lighting; 3 pp; **CTY/B** (Uai H74).
      n.d.   Catalog, Hospital Lighting Specifics; **CTY/B** (Uai H74).

HOMAN, F., SCIENTIFIC APPARATUS
   See: JOHN BELL & CROYDEN.

HOME VAPOR BATH, THE
12 East 23rd Street Near Broadway, Madison Square, New York.
      ca 1884   Disinfector, Inhaler & Needle Bath; 48 pp; **CPP.**

HOOD, JOHN, CO.
178 Tremont Street, Boston, Massachusetts.
Est: pre-1882
      1911   Catalog, Dental Supplies; 4th ed.; 775 pp; **UPSDM** (D 617.604 H
              761.2).
    E. 20 c   The Towle Veneer System, dental filling materials; 16 pp, ads in
              cover; **NYAM; MF/MAH.**

HOOD AND REYNOLDS
178 Tremont Street, 74 Tremont Street, Boston, Massachusetts.
      1881   Catalog of Dental Materials, Instruments, Furniture, Tools; 302 pp;
              UPSDM (D 617.604 H 759).
      1883   Catalog, Dental Forceps; 21 pp; **UPSDM** (D 617.604 H 761).
  ca 1885   Catalog, Dental Forceps and Specialties; 2nd ed.; 52 pp; (TM pp
              48); **MAH** (C 617.6085H).
   1889?   Catalog, Dental Forceps and Specialties; 3rd ed.; (TM p 80); **MAH**
              (C 617.6085H).
      1890   Catalog, Dental Forceps and Specialties; 4th ed.; 88 pp; (TM pp.
              86); **MAH** (C 617.6085 H).

HOOS ALBUMIN MILK
5232 Kenmore Avenue, Chicago, Illinois.
Sold by George B. Evans, 1106 Chestnut Street.
      n.d.   The Nutrition Disorders of Infants in the Light of Modern
              Research; 3rd ed.; 48 pp; **CPP.**

HOOSE, EDWARD H.
Room 321, Mint Arcade, Philadelphia.
      1906   Your Patients Notice the Appearance of Your Office; 8 pp; addressed
              to Dr. Flick; **CPP.**

HOOVER MFG. CO.
64-74 W. 23rd Street, New York, New York.
July 1, 1928   Customer's Catalog; Genuine Hoovercraft Apparel; 30 pp; (TM); **NYAM.**

HOPKINS-WELLER DRUG CO.
Main & Washington Streets, St. Louis, Missouri.
Jun. 1892   Prices Current; 58 pp; **CPP.**

HORLICK'S MALTED MILK
Horlicks Corp.
2120 Northwestern Ave., Racine, Wisconsin.
Est: 1873
    1907   Calorie Value of Foods; 12 pp; **CPP.**
    1910   How Shall We Improve the Physical Condition of Our School Children?; 16 pp; **CPP.**
    n.d.   Delicacies Prepared from Horlick's Malted Milk; 16 pp; **CPP.**
    n.d.   How to Prepare Cold at the Fountain; 4 pp; **CPP.**

HORN, WM. H., & BRO.
455 N. 3rd Street; 451-455 N. Third Street; 444 & 448 Belrose Street, Philadelphia, Pennsylvania.
Office, Factory & Shipping Dept.: 451-457 N. 3rd St., (Phila., PA).
Fitting Rooms: 25 S. 16th Street, (Phila., PA).
Est: 1842
    1876   Catalog of Trusses, Abdominal Supporters, Belts, Shoulder Braces, Suspensories, Elastic Hosiery, etc.; 96 pp, covers missing, probably incomplete; **AFMM.**
    1892   Illustrated and Descriptive Catalogue of Horn's Standard Hard Rubber, Leather Covered & Elastic Trusses; 96 pp; **AFMM.**
    1892   Price List of Horn's Standard Hard Rubber, Leather Covered & Elastic Trusses; 11 pp; **AFMM.**
    1896   Catalog no. 54, Horn's Standard Antler Brand Surgical Elastic Hosiery, Belts, Suspensories, etc., Trusses; 113 pp; **CPP.**
    1897   Catalog no. 255, Hernia or Rupture Mechanical Appliances; 49 pp; **CPP.**
    1900   Catalog no. 58, Horn's Standard Trusses; 144 pp; **CPP.**
1515 Arch St.
    1907   The Mechanical Treatment of Hernia or Rupture, With Trusses; 112 pp; **CPP.**
Jun. 1, 1924   Catalog no. 82, Horn's Standard Trusses; Abdominal Belts and Surgical Appliances; 93 pp; **WMScM.**

HORNE & THORNTHWAITE
121, 122, 123 Newgate Street, London, E.C. England.
Aug. 1860   Descriptive Catalog of Scientific Instruments . . . Part 2; Philosophical & Photographic Apparatus and Chemicals; 12th ed.; Medals; **CTY/B** (Uai H784).

HOSPITAL AND GENERAL CONTRACTS CO., LTD.
33 and 35 Martimer Street, London, W.
L. 19-E. 20 c   Mfrs. Catalog; 418 pp, 8 pp index; **WMScM.**

HOSPITAL PUBLISHING CO., INC., THE MODERN
Chicago, Illinois.

1919   The Modern Hospital Year Book, A Buyer' Reference Book of
        Supplies and Equipment for Hospitals and Allied Institutions;
        MAH (1986.3005).

HOSPITAL SUPPLY CO., THE
No. 36 Dey Street, New York, New York.
W. 14th Street, New York, New York.
33-45 W. 13th Street, New York, N.Y.
Main Office: 35-37 E. 20th Street.
        n.d.   Hamilton E. Smith's Late Patented System of Operating the
                Metalic (sic) Washing Machine; 24 pp; **CTY/B** (Uai H794).
290 Fifth Ave., Chicago, IL.
     ca 1910   Catalog Aseptic Furniture for Operating Rooms, Sect. 0; 158 pp,
                few pp loose; (TM); **NYAM; MF/MAH.**
        1913   Catalgue of Sterilizers Also a Treatise on Sterilizers and
                Sterilization, Sect. S; 63 pp, index pp 63; **NYAM; MF/MAH;**
                CPP.
        1916   Sections O and W of General Catalog, Catalog of Aseptic Steel
                Furniture and Hospital Equipment; 250 pp, index; **NLM** (W26
                H828c); **CS.**

Hospital Supply Co. and The Watters Laboratories, Consolidated
155-59 E. 23rd Street, New York.
        1922   Catalog of Hospital and Surgical Equipment and Supplies; 448 pp,
                index pp 436-48; (TM); **NYAM; MF/MAH; HML; UCSF.**
        1923   Catalog of Hospital and Surgical Equipment and Supplies; 435 pp;
                NYAM; MF/MAH.
       1920s   Catalog of Hospital and Surgical Equipment and Supplies; **NLM**
                (W26 H832c).
     ea 20 c   Catalog of Hospital Furniture and Sterilizers; 166 pp, index pp
                165-6; **NYAM; MF/MAH.**
        n.d.   Illustrated Catalog no. 2, Aseptic Hospital Furniture, Operating
                Room Furniture, Sterilizing Apparatus, Ward Furniture,
                Disinfecting Apparatus, published shortly after Mt. Sinai Hosp.
                was founded; 199 pp, index pp 164-166; (TM); **MAH; MRLB.**

HOSTELLEY, W. H., & CO.,
233 North 2nd Street, Philadelphia, Pennsylvania.
Laboratory: Collingdale Del Co., Pennsylvania.
        1890   Unalterable Syrup of Hydriodic Acid; 3rd ed.; **CPP.**
        1893   A Filtering and Distilling Cabinet; 20 pp; **CPP.**
        1901   The Brief Story of Prescription and How It Was Filled; 8 pp; **CPP.**
        1916   A Study of Drug Action, the Alleged Passing of the
                Hypophosphates, by Thomas J. Mays; 11 pp; **CPP.**

HOWARD, HERBERT B., & WASHBURN, FREDERIC A.
        n.d.   Home-Made Hospital Furniture, Massachusetts General Hospital;
                21 pp; **NYAM; MF/MAH.**

HUCLIN, G., & CIE
43 & 60 rue du Roi-de-Sicile, Paris, France.
Est: 1869
        1900   Catalogue illustré des instruments de médecine et accessoires de
                pharmacie; 172 pp, index, price list; **MAH** (26820).
        1905   La Prothèse et l'orthopédie, catalogue général avec description

iconographie; 108 pp, price list; **MAH** (26822).

1906   Catalogue illustré des instruments de chirurgie; 104 pp; **MAH** (26821).

HUDSON

1850–60s   Hudson's Artificial Limbs, Mechanical Surgery, A Specialty; 43 pp; **CPP** (Bolenius Coll.).

HUDSON PHARMACAL CO.
510 Liberty Street, Union Hill, New Jersey.

1922   Where Gland Therapy Fails; 16 pp; **CPP.**

1923   Formulary Price List of Hudson Pharmacal Company, Endocrine Gland Products; 10 pp; **CPP.**

n.d.   Clinically Demonstrated Facts; 3 pp folder; **CPP.**

HUDSON SURGICAL CO., INC.
10 Bergenline Ave., Union Hill, New Jersey.

Feb. 1924   Illustrated Catalogue of Standard Surgical Instruments and Allied Lines; 4th ed.; 416 pp, index, price list; **MAH** (12237).

HUERTL, DR.
Budapest, Hungary.
apply to: Dr. Alfred Muller, 2 Rector Street, New York City, New York.

1911   No title page; Surgical Stitching Instrument for the Suture of the Stomach and Intestines according to Dr. Huertl; 15 pp; **MAH.**

HU-FRIEDY PRODUCTS
See: FRIEDMAN, HUGO MFG. CO.

HUNZINGER
Germany.

n.d.   Fleam in case of bleeding lancets; WHM R3672/1936; **RCSL.**

HUSTON BROS. CO.
30 E. Randolph Street, Chicago, Illinois.

1917   Catalog of Surgical and Electrical Instruments, Hospital Supplies, Surgical Elastic Goods, Artificial Limbs, Artificial Eyes, Trusses, Crutches, Orthopaedic Appliances, Invalids' Requirements, etc.; 672 pp, index; **NLM** (W26 H972c).

HUTCHINSON, A., AND CO.
70, Basinghall Street, London, E.C.

Jun. 1892   Price List; 28 pp; (TM on cover); **RCSL.**

HUTCHINSON, W. & H.
Sheffield, England.

1904   Veterinary Surgeon's Instruments; 22 pp, price list pp 20-22; **RCSL.**

HYDE, R., CO., THE
Cor. 3rd and Prairie Streets, Milwaukee, Wisconsin.

E. 20 c   Brochure, no title; 12 pp; **NYAM; MF/MAH.**

HYFREX COILS
See: SYNCHRONOUS MANUFACTURING CO.; **ACR/MAH.**

HYNSON WESTCOTT & CO.
421-423 N. Charles Street, Charles and Franklin Streets, Baltimore, Maryland.

ca 1890   Catalog of Surgical Instruments, Medical Appliances, Office Fittings, Furniture, etc. for Physicians and Surgeons; 372 pp, index, pages 62 and 63 missing, Bound in two binders; **MAH; UVHSL** (R856. H9).

L. 19 c   Catalog of Surgical Instruments, Medical Appliances, Diagnostic Apparatus, etc.; 1001-5180 pp, pages not consecutive, some may be missing; **NLM** (W26 H997c); **MCFM.**

n.d.   Catalog; Surgical Instruments . . . etc.; **JHIHM** (RD 76. H95).

n.d.   3 Post card size ads: Ovarian Lutein Functionatin, Glycotauro Secretion of Bile; Amelioration of Typhoid symptoms Bulgara; **CPP.**

ILLINOIS SURGICAL APPLIANCE CO.
10, 12, 14 S. Wells St., Chicago, Illinois.
212 West Madison St., Chicago Illinois.

E. 19 c   Catalog of Surgical Instruments, Orthopedic Apparatus, Laboratory Equipment and Supplies; 96 pp; **NLM.**

1929   Catalog; **CPP.**

1929   1929 Specials; 128 pp; **MAH.**

1930?   No title; 104 pp; **MAH.**

IMMUNITY STEEL
See: FRIEDMAN, HUGO MFG. CO.

INDIANA BOTANIC GARDENS AND HERBS
See: JOSEPH T. MEYER.

INGRAM AND BELL, LTD.
Toronto, Canada.

ca 1910   Sundry Catalog; 192 pp; **TMHM.**

INGRAM, J. G., & SON, LTD.
Hackney Wick, London E.C.
Est: 1847

n.d.   The London India Rubber Works, Catalog of Surgical India Rubber Goods; 72 pp, 19 pp price list; received May 1934; **WMScM.**

INJECTA LTD.
Audrey House, Ely Place, London E.C. 1, England.

1927   Catalog Surgical and Dental Instruments, Hypodermic Needles, Catalog no. H/1927; 40 pp; **WMScM.**

INTERNATIONAL DISTRIBUTING CO. FOR THE DANISH "LEO" LTD.
8 Reventlowsgade, Copenhagen, Denmark.

ca 1925   Pamphlet, Danish Insulin "Leo," dealer: Ed. Wheeler, 477 W. 144th St., New York; 14 pp; **MAH.**

INTERNATIONAL EQUIPMENT CO.
352 Western Avenue, Brighton, Massachusetts.

1917   Centrifugal Separators and Other Laboratory Apparatus, Catalog C; 61 pp; **AFMM.**

INTERNATIONAL NICKEL CO., THE
67 Wall Street, New York, New York.

ca 1930   Directory, Users of Monel Metal for Hospital Equipment; 47 pp, 32 pp insert; **NYAM; MF/MAH.**

INTERNATIONAL X-RAY CORPORATION
326 Broadway, New York, New York.
    ca 1920   Brochure 2, Filament Current Register; 2 pp; **ACR/MAH.**
    ca 1920   Brochure 3, Self Rectifying X-Ray Tube Unit; **ACR/MAH.**
    ca 1920   Brochure 4, Interrupterless X-Ray Machine, Precision Type; 6 pp; **ACR/MAH.**
    ca 1920   Brochure 5, Interrupterless X-Ray Machine, Deep Therapy Type; 10 pp; **ACR/MAH.**
    ca 1920   Self Rectifying X-Ray Tube Unit, Universal Type; 2 pp; **ACR/MAH.**

INVERNIZZE, ERNESTO
Corso Umberto 1, 46-49, Rome, Italy.
    1879–1940   Catalogo generale, surgical instruments and apparatus; **ACS** (U 6 A/I 62 C).
    1937   Listino Di Prizzi, da usare con la via Edizione del catalogo generale illustrato 1933; 96 pp; **MAH.**

IVORY, J. W.
Philadelphia, Pennsylvania.
    n.d.   Catalog, Dental Specialties; 53 pp; **NYAM; MF/MAH.**

JACKSON
Baltimore, Maryland.
    n.d.   Buchamount & Klein's Safety Staff; **RCSL.**

JACKSON, CHEVALIER, INSTRUMENTS
See: GEORGE P. PILLING AND SON, CO., 1939; **MF/MAH.**

JACKSON, M., & CO.
See: J. ORME & CO., successor.

JAEGER'S SANITARY WOOLEN SYSTEM CO., DR.
827-829 Broadway, New York, New York.
366 Fulton Street, Brooklyn, New York.
97 Franklin Street, New York, New York.
    1886   Illustrated Catalog of the Dr. Jaeger's Sanitary Woolen System; **CTY/B** (Uai J175).
    1888–9   Illustrated Catalog and Price List of the Dr. Jaeger's Sanitary Woolen System Co.; 7th ed.; 90 pp; **CTY/B** (UaiJ175).
    1890–1   Illustrated Catalog & Price List; 10th ed.; 64 pp; **MAH.**
    1891–2   Illustrated Price List Selected from the 11th Regular ed. of our Complete Catalog; 46 pp; **CTY/B** (Uai J175).
    1892–3   Illustrated Catalog and Price List; 12th ed.; 68 pp; **CTY/B** (Uai J175).
    1903   Illustrated Catalog and Price List, Dr. Jaeger's Sanitary Woolen System Co.; 20th ed.; 40 pp; **CTY/B** (Uai J175).
    July 1913   Jaeger Puree Wool Wear; 36 pp; **CTY/B** (Uai J175).

JAPAN MEDICAL INSTRUMENT CATALOG
See: NIPPON IYAKUHIN NADO YUSHUTSU KUMIAI; **NLM.**

JEFFREY-FELL COMPANY
318-320 Pearl Street, Buffalo, New York.
    1908   Illustrated Catalog; 515 pp; **NYAM; MF/MAH; UBML** (W26J46).
    1928   Illustrated Catalog of Standard Surgical Instruments; 5th ed.; **UREGML.**
    1935   Catalog, Physician's, Hospital's, and Nurse's Supplies, no. 35; 511 pp;

LLU (W 26 J46c 1935).
  n.d. Surgical Dressings; 14 pp; **BLEL.**

JELCO
See: J. ELLWOOD LEE CO., 1907; **MAH.**

JELENKO, J. F., & CO., INC.
136 West 52nd Street, New York, New York.
  ca 1925 Brochure, Manual of Operation and Control for the Woodbury-Jelenko
            Heat Treating and Electric Furnace; 10 pp; **NYAM.**
  1934 Burlew Disc-Cleaning and Polishing Discs; **MAH.**
  1934 Denture Cast Gold; **MAH.**

JENKENS PORCELAIN ENAMEL
See: KLEWE & CO., INC.

JENSON-SALSBERY LABORATORIES
  1927 Jen-Sal Instrument Catalog; **CPP** (Ed/63).

JEPSON BROTHERS
See: WINKLEY ARTIFICIAL CO.; **MAH; NLM.**

JETTER & SCHEERER
Tuttlingen, Johanisstrasse 20-21, Berlin North, Germany.
63 High Holborn, London, W.C., England.
Sole Agent: Metzger, 84 & 85, Bloomsbury Sq., London, W.C. 1, England.
See: AESCULAP INSTRUMENTS.
  n.d. Aktiengesellschaft fuer Feinmechanik Vormals Jetter & Scheerer,
            Aesculap-Musterbuch; 2848 pp; **VM.**
  n.d. General Catalog; 2848 pp; **VM.**
  1902 Veterinary Instruments, Utensils and Appliances; 341 pp; index xvii-xxvi;
            RCSL.
  1905 Illustrated Catalogue of Surgical Instruments and Appliances; 6th ed.; 784
            pp; **BLEL.**
  1927 Sonder-Katalog ueber Instrumente zur Tierzucht und Tierpflege fuer den
            Landwirt; 25 pp; **WMScM.**

JEWELL MODELS
Carlinville, Illinois.
  n.d. Catalog of Jewell Models for Biology; **CTY/B** (Uai J549).

JOHNS-MANVILLE CO., H. W.
21-25 North Second Street, Philadelphia, Pennsylvania.
  n.d. The Electrotherm, an Electrical Heating Pad, A Substitute for the Hot
            Water Bottle; 8 pp; **CPP.**

JOHNSON BROTHERS
Brooklyn, New York.
Inc: in Maine, dissolved Sep. 1913
Inc. in Tennessee, charter cancelled Dec. 30, 1922
  1872 New System Cone Socket Instruments; 32 pp; **UPSDM.**
812 Broadway, New York, New York.
  Apr. 1874 Catalog, A Quarterly Advertiser of Dental Supplies; **UPL.**
  1876 Catalog of Instruments for Dental Engines; 34 pp; **MAH.**
1260 Broadway, New York, New York.

1880　Johnson Brothers New System Cone-Socket Instruments, Patented 26 Nov 1872; 32 pp; **MAH.**

188　Preliminary Catalog of Dental Materials; 219 pp; **UPSDM.**

JOHNSON & CO.
London, England.
See: ORME & CO., London; **RCSL.**

JOHNSON, HOLLOWAY & CO.
602 Arch Street, Philadelphia, Pennsylvania.

n.d.　Pure Japanese Ame; 4 pp; **CPP.**

1907　Physicians' Descriptive List Aseptic and Antiseptic; 63 pp; **CPP.**

1919　Cotton and Gauze Book; 40 pp; **CPP.**

n.d.　The J & H Methods of Preparing Sterile Surgical Dressing From Cotton Fibre; **CPP.**

n.d.　Vino-Kolafra in the Treatment of Anaemic Conditions, Cardiac Affections and Alcoholism; 8 pp; **CPP.**

n.d.　Papoid-Digestion by R. H. Chittenden; 46 pp; **CPP.**

JOHNSON & JOHNSON
New Brunswick, New Jersey.
Est: 1886

1886　On the Treatment of Diphtheria and Dyspepsia with Papoid; 82 pp; **CPP.**

1889　Recent Therapeutical Notes on the Use of Papoid in the Treatment of Dyspepsia and Diphtheria; 32 pp; **CPP.**

1891　The Recent Practical Improvements in Generating Ozone with Consideration of Its Place in Nature and Medicine; 32 pp; **CPP.**

1892　Papoid (Vegetable Pepsin), Formulae, and Methods of Use; 30 pp; **CPP.**

1894　Belladonna Illustrated; 72 pp; **CPP.**

1895　Gauze Dressings in Surgery; 24 pp; **CPP.**

1895　Koln Illustrated; 24 pp; **CPP.**

1897　Asepsis Secundum Art; 24 pp; **CPP.**

JOHNSON & LUND
27 North 7th Street, Philadelphia, Pennsylvania.
620 Race Street, Philadelphia, Pennsylvania.
Est: 1853

1871　Catalog of Dentists' Materials; 253 pp; **MAH** (C 617.6085J); **UPSDM.**

1876　Purchaser's Guide for the Selection of Dentists' Materials; 176 pp; **MAH.**

1881　Catalog, Dental Materials, Instruments, Furniture, Tools, etc.; 322 pp; **HDM; MAH.**

1888　Catalog of Dental Materials of All Descriptions; xx, 313 pp, index; **MAH** (C 617.6085J).

1888　Catalogo de efectos dentales de toda descripcion, fabricados y para la venta par Johnson & Lund; 312 pp; **HML.**

514 Wabash Avenue, Chicago, Illinois.

1896　Catalog Preliminary, Artificial Teeth; 3rd ed.; **UPL.**

1900　Catalog Dental Materials; 250 pp; **MAH** (C 617.6085J); **HML.**

1903　Catalog and Price List of Dental Materials; 328 pp, index pp 309-328; **MAH** (C 617.6085J).

n.d.　Tooth Catalog; 4th ed.; 146 pp, index pp 143-146; **MAH** (C617.6085J).

JOHNSTON, GEORGE S., CO.
90 Wabash Ave., Chicago, IL.

1909   Illustrated Catalogue and Price List; 152 pp; **URRR** (J-2).

1920   Prescription Catalog and Abridged Stock Price List; 49 pp; **URRR** (J-26).

JOHNSTON, J. M. & A. C., CO.
84 Wabash Avenue, Chicago, IL.

1911   Illustrated Catalogue and Price List, Manufacturing Opticians; 176 pp; **AO.**

JOHNSTON OPTICAL CO.
66 and 68 State Street, Detroit.
Est: 1876

1898   System.(?). Dimensions of Frames; 20 pp; **AO.**

1903   Illustrated Catalogue of Johnston Optical Co.; 234 pp; **AO.**

State Street and Washington Blvd., Detroit.

1907   Illustrated Catalogue, The World's Optical Center; 246 pp; **AO.**

JONES, W. & S.
Lower Holbrook, London.

1815   A Catalogue of Optical, Mathematical & Philosophical Instruments (spectacles), no. 30; 16 pp; **AFMM** (photocopy).

JOYANT
Paris, France.

n.d.   Bistouries at WHM no. 15677; **RCSL.**

n.d.   Scalpel at WHM no. 8849; **RCSL.**

JUDD, CHESTER
58 Union, Albany, New York.
1831-51 Green, Albany, New York.

1830–31   Listed as instrument maker in Albany City Directory; listed as a brass founder in 1831; Blacksmith and Whitesmith in 1832, and Locksmith and Laborer in 1829.

JUNG, RUDOLF
Heidelberg, Germany.

1883   Preis-Verzeichniss ueber Instrumente und Apparate aus der mechanischen Werkstaette von R. Jung; Heidelberg Universitäts-Buchdruckerei von J. Hoerning, Mikrotom, Apparate zur Untersuchung des Blutkreislaufes am lebenden Thiere, Apparate zum Harten in Alcohol-daempfen, Apparat zur Injection der Blutgefaesse bei constantem Drucke, Revolver für Mikroskop-Objective, Vivisectionstisch, Kopfhalter fuer Hunde; 15 pp; **CPP.**

1886   Preis-Verzeichniss ueber Instrumente und Apparate aus der mechanischen Werkstaette; 47 pp; **AFMM.**

Aug. 1890   Preis-Verzeichniss; PV ueber Instrumente und Apparatus der mechanischen Werkstaette; 58 pp; **URRR** (J-7).

1893   Price List of Instruments and Apparatus; 16 pp; **URRR** (J-8).

1895   Preis-Verzeichniss I Abteilung: Instrumente und Apparate fuer Mikrotomie und Mikroskopie; 62 pp; **URRR** (J-9).

1903   Preis-Verzeichniss I enthaltend Mikrotome; 75 pp (some missing); **URRR** (J-10).

1910   Katalog I Mikrotome; 43 pp; **URRR** (J-11).

JUNGMANN, J.
3rd Avenue and 61st Street, New York, New York.

Jungmann & Co., Inc.
Inc: New York., dissolved Oct. 21, 1921
 1893 Catalog of Surgical Instruments, Appliances and Physician's Supplies, Jungmann's name and address are scratched out on the cover and Stephan Goodrich & Co., 605 Main Street, Hartford, Connecticut is written in by hand in ink; 41 pp, 100 plates, index with description of each figure and price; **NLM.**

JUSTI, H. D.
1301 & 1303 Arch Street, Philadelphia, Pennsylvania.
Est: 1864
 1888 Catalog Dental Materials; 238 pp; **UPSDM.**
 1889 Catalog Dental Materials, etc.; 239 pp, index pp 223-239; **MAH.**
 1901 Catalog and Price List of Dental Supplies; **MAH; UPAL.**
 H. D. Justi & Son
  1916 Porcelain Teeth; 24 pp; **SLSC.**
  n.d. Illustrated Catalog of Forceps; 87 pp; **FI.**
  n.d. Justi Porcelain Products . . .; 47 pp; **UPSDM.**
  n.d. Keeler Ophthalmoscope; 8 pp; **URRR** (K-249).
 1920-30 Short ads linked together; **URRR** (K-249).

KAEHLER, MAX, & MARTINI
Wilhelm Strasse 50, Berlin, Germany.
Est: 1878
 See: The KNY-SCHEERER CO.
 Mar. 1894 Nachtrag zum Preisverzeichniss ueber chemische Apparate und Geraethschaften; 58 pp; **CTY/B9** (Uai K117).
 1897 Fabrik chemischer, electrochemischer und bacteriologischer Apparate, II Nachtrag; 20 pp; **CTY/B** (Uai K117).
 1898 Fabrik chemischer, electrochemischer und bacteriologischer Apparate, III Nachtrag; **CTY/B9** (Uai K117).
 Oct. 1899 Brochure chemischer, electrochemischer und bacteriologischer Apparate; 3 pp; **NYAM; MF/MAH.**
 1900 Special Liste Apparate zum Gebrauche in Vorlesungen; 2nd ed.; 80 pp; **NYAM; MF/MAH.**
 1900 Fabrik Chemischer . . . Preis-Verzeichniss chemische Apparate und Geraethschaften; 48 pp; **NYAM; MF/MAH.**
 Jan. 1900 Leaflet; 1 pp; **NYAM; MF/MAH.**
 1903 Preis-Verzeichniss ueber chemische Apparate und Geraethschaften fuer allgemeine Zwecke und chemische Praeparate; 498 pp; **CTY/B** (Uai).

KAHN, B., & CO.
No. 42 Maiden Lane, New York, New York.
No. 112 Kearney Street, San Francisco, California.
 1873 Illustrated Price List of Optical Instruments with Hard Rubber Frames; 28 pp; **MAH.**
 1875 Supplement to the Catalogue of the Vulcanite Optical Instrument Co.; 6 pp; **MAH.**

KALLMEYER, RICHARD, & CO.
Berlin, Germany.
 189? Preis-Buch ueber chirurgische, medicinische . . . Apparate und Geraethschaften. . . .; 175 pp; **NYAM** (S. 125).

KAROLEWSKI, FELIKS
Ulcia Senatorska Nr. 32, Warsaw, Poland.
    1939   Cennik Skladu Szkla Aptecznego, wszelkish przyborow Laboratoryjnysch i
            Kosmetycznych; 16 pp; **MAH.**

KATSCH, HERMANN
Bayerstrasse 25, Muenchen, Germany.
Est: 1865
        L. 19 c   Preis-Verzeichniss der Mikrotome; 16 pp; **URRR** (K-1).
        1906   Fabrik Haupt-Preisliste Chirurgischer Instrumente; 353 pp, index pp
                342-353; **NYAM; MF/MAH.**

KAYLE CO., INC.
220 West 42 Street, New York, New York.
        Feb. 1924   Brochure, The Kayle Attachment for Clasps; 18 pp; **NYAM; MF/MAH.**

K & B ELECTRIC EQUIPMENT CO., INC.
347 Second Avenue, New York, New York.
        See: KELLEY-KOETT MFG. CO., Oct 1919; **ACR/MAH.**

KEELER
21-27 Marylebone Lane, London, England.
47 Wigmore Street, London, WI, England.
        n.d.   Instruments for the Physicians and Hospital Catalog Supplement, Medical
                and Diagnostic Instruments for General Practice and Hospital
                Department, Allen Diagnostic Instruments, 7 pp foldout; **WMScM.**
        n.d.   Advanced Method L.V.A.; 4 pp; **WMScM.**
        n.d.   L.V.A. for the Partially Sighted; 4 pp; **WMScM.**
        n.d.   Keeler Advanced L.V.A. Method, Dispensary Notes; 4 pp; **WMScM.**
        n.d.   The Keeler Ophthalmoscope, by C. Davis Keeler; 10 pp; **WMScM.**
        n.d.   Keeler Ophthalmoscope; 8 pp; **URRR** (K-249).
        1920–30 Short ads linked together; **URRR** (K-249).
39 Wigmore Street, London, England.
5536 Baltimore Avenue, Philadelphia 43, Pennsylvania.
        n.d.   M.R.C. Photometer Detection for the Accurate Clinical Detection of
                Hemoglobin and other Blood Constituents, Instructions for Use; 8 pp;
                WMScM.

KELEKET
        See: KELLEY-KOETT MFG. CO., ENGELN 1921 Catalog; **ACR/MAH.**

KELLER DENTAL CO.
Chicago, IL.
        1903?   Fine Amalgam Science; Original Researches; 15 pp; **HML.**
        1904?   Keller's Patent Coin-Silver Amalgams; 4 pp; **HML.**

KELLEY, EDWARD G.
116 John Street, New York, New York.
Successor to John L. Fyfe
        1860   Descriptive Catalogue of Chemical and Philosophical Apparatus,
                Chemicals, and Pure Reagents; 8th ed.; 84 pp; **CTY/B** (Uai K 287).

KELLEY & HUEBER
Philadelphia, PA.
Successors to William Birmingham and Co.
Est: 1849

1926   Catalog and Price List of the Improved Birmingham Spectacle and Eye
        Glass Cases; 8 pp; **URRR** (K-253).

KELLEY-KOETT

See: ENGLEN ELECTRIC CO., ca 1920.

KELLEY-KOETT MFG. CO., INC.

Keleket Bldg., Covington, Kentucky.

ca 1912   Catalog, Improved Stereoscopic Tube Stand, no. 6; 18 pp; **CTY/B** (Uai,
           K 288).

4th and Russell Streets, Covington, Kentucky.

1913   A Simplified Universal X-Ray Apparatus; 1 pp; **CTY/B** (Uai K 288).

ca 1913   Universal X-Ray Apparatus, Interrupterless, The Keleket Transformer; 4
           pp; **CTY/B** (Uai, K 288).

1913   Form H 27, Improved Automatic Plate Changing Table Type G, and
        Stereoscopic Tube Stand no. 6; 20 pp; **ACR/MAH.**

ca 1914   X-Ray Tubes Vacuum Electrodes and Specialties, Catalog B; 11 pp; **CPP.**

1914   Catalog, Keleket X-Ray Apparatus, no. 21; 31 pp; **CTY/B** (Uai K 288).

1915   Catalog no. 22, Keleket X-Ray Apparatus; 18 A, B, C pp, devided into
        thirds; **CTY/B** (Uai, K 288).

1915   Catalog no. 23, Keleket X-Ray Apparatus; 40 pp; **ACR/MAH.**

ca 1915   Catalog C, X-Ray Tubes and Accessories; 18 pp, 1 pp index; **ACR/MAH.**

Nov. 1916   Catalog no. 24, Keleket X-Ray Apparatus; 40 pp; **ACR/MAH.**

Oct. 1919   Catalog no. 25, Keleket X-Ray Apparatus; 27 pp; **ACR/MAH.**

Oct. 1920   Catalog no. 25, Keleket X-Ray Apparatus; 3rd ed.; 28 pp; **ACR/MAH.**

ca 1920   Pamphlet, K-K Quality; 12 pp; **ACR/MAH; MAH.**

1924   Developments of the X-Ray, Contents: History of Progress of Company,
        photographs of J. Robt. Kelley, Pres, Albert B. Koett, Vice-President,
        G. ed. Geise, Secy-Treas, W.S. Werner, Elect Engineer, photo of plant
        and general views through plant, catalog of x-ray apparatus, pencilled in
        back that certain pages are missing; 80 pp; **ACR/MAH.**

Mar. 1, 1926   Bulletin no. 3, 140,000 Volt X-Ray Apparatus, Radiography and Therapy;
                8 pp; **ACR/MAH.**

Mar. 1, 1926   Leaflet no. 31, The Keleket Enclosed Tube Shield; 1 pp; **ACR/MAH.**

Apr. 1926   Bulletin no. 12, Portable Diathermy Unit; 8 pp; **ACR/MAH.**

May 1, 1926   Leaflet no. 11, Water Cooling System; 1 pp; **ACR/MAH.**

Jun. 1, 1926   Leaflet no. 10, Improved Stereoscope; 1 pp; **ACR/MAH.**

July 1926   Leaflet no. 34, Operator's Protective Screen; 1 pp; **ACR/MAH.**

July 1, 1926   Leaflet no. 25, Automatic Circuit Breaker; 1 pp; **ACR/MAH.**

Oct. 1, 1926   Leaflet no. 19, Equi-Contact Cassettes; 1 pp; **ACR/MAH.**

Oct. 1, 1926   Leaflet no. 30, Head Table; 1 pp; **ACR/MAH.**

Oct. 1, 1926   Leaflet no. 17, Fluorographic Unit; 1 pp; **ACR/MAH.**

Oct. 1, 1926   Bulletin no. 7, 230,000 Peak Volt X-Ray Apparatus, Deep Therapy,
                Radiography, Fluoroscopy; 12 pp; **ACR/MAH.**

Oct. 1, 1926   Leaflet no. 14, no. 6 Raid-Mounted Tube Stand, Universal Tube Model;
                1 pp; **ACR/MAH.**

Oct. 1, 1926   Leaflet no. 13, Combination Dark Room Lamp; 1 pp; **ACR/MAH.**

Nov. 1, 1926   Leaflet no. 9, The Mobile Unit; 1 pp; **ACR/MAH.**

Nov. 1926   Leaflet no. 26, Revolving Bucky Table; 1 pp; **ACR/MAH.**

Nov. 1, 1926   Leaflet no. 16, Potter Bucky Diaphragm; 1 pp; **ACR/MAH.**

Nov. 1, 1926   Leaflet no. 23, no. 8 Treatment Tube Stand; 1 pp; **ACR/MAH.**

Nov. 1, 1926   Leaflet no. 35, Quadruple Stereoscope; 1 pp; **ACR/MAH.**

Dec. 15 1926   Leaflet no. 27, Type G Fluoroscopic Unit; **ACR/MAH.**

Jan. 1, 1927	Bulletin no. 10, Automatic Tilt Table, Motor Driven; 7 pp; **ACR/MAH.**
Jan. 1, 1927	Bulletin no. 6, Power-Plus Generator; 165 Peak Kilovolts; 12 pp; **ACR/MAH.**
Feb. 1, 1927	Leaflet no. 38, The New Vertical Fluoroscope, 14" Horizontal Range Shift; 4 pp; **ACR/MAH.**
Mar. 1, 1927	Leaflet no. 18, Film Drying Rack; 1 pp; **ACR/MAH.**
Mar. 1, 1927	Leaflet no. 39, Fluoroscopic Fracture Table; 1 pp; **ACR/MAH.**
Mar. 1, 1927	Leaflet no. 40, Diagnostic Table; 4 pp; **ACR/MAH.**
Mar. 1, 1927	Leaflet no. 15, Eye Localizer, Dr. Sweet's Model; 1 pp, with 4 pp directions for use attached; **ACR/MAH.**
Mar. 1, 1927	Bulletin no. 11, 140,000 Peak Volt X-Ray Apparatus, Medium Therapy, Radiography, Fluoroscopy, 8 pp; **ACR/MAH.**
Mar. 1, 1927	Bulletin no. 2, 165,000 Volt X-Ray Apparatus, Therapy and Radiography; 7 pp; **ACR/MAH.**
Mar. 1, 1927	Bulletin no. 4, 107,000 Volt X-Ray Apparatus, 8 pp; **ACR/MAH.**
Mar. 1, 1927	Leaflet no. 26, Revolving Bucky Table; 1 pp; **ACR/MAH.**
Mar. 1, 1927	Leaflet no. 29, The Flat Bucky with Attachments; 1 pp; **ACR/MAH.**
May 1, 1927	Bulletin no. 8, 120,000 Peak Volt X-Ray Apparatus, Skin Therapy, Radiography, Fluoroscopy; 8 pp; **ACR/MAH.**
Jun. 1, 1927	Leaflet no. 21, no. 7 Stereoscopic Tube Stand, Radiator Tube only; 1 pp; **ACR/MAH.**
Jun. 1, 1927	Leaflet no. 36, Film and Cassette Changing Tunnels; 1 pp; **ACR/MAH.**
Jun. 1, 1927	Leaflet no. 20, Cones for the no. 7 and no. 9 Tube Stands or the Bedside Unit and for the nos. 4, 5, or 6 Tube Stands; 4 pp; **ACR/MAH.**
Jun. 1, 1927	Leaflet no. 39, Fluoroscopic Fracture Table; 1 pp, prices inked in; **ACR/MAH.**
Dec. 1, 1927	Leaflet no. 43, Vertical Fluoroscopic Combination; 1 pp; **ACR/MAH.**
May 1, 1928	Leaflet no. 46, Improved Stabilizing Unit; 1 pp; **ACR/MAH.**
Jun. 1, 1928	Leaflet no. 41, Portable X-Ray Unit; 4 pp; **ACR/MAH.**
Jun. 1, 1928	Leaflet no. 16, Potter Bucky Diaphragm; 1 pp; **ACR/MAH.**
July 1, 1928	Leaflet no. 48, Angulating Head Tunnel with Granger Attachments; 1 pp; **ACR/MAH.**
Nov. 1, 1928	Leaflet no. 49, Steel Enameled Developing Table; 4 pp; **ACR/MAH.**
Dec. 1, 1928	Leaflet no. 2, Vertical Stereoscopic Cassette Changer; 1 pp; **ACR/MAH.**
Feb. 1, 1929	Bulletin no. 10, Automatic Tilt Table, Motor Drive; 7 pp; **ACR/MAH.**
Mar. 1, 1929	Bulletin no. 15, Built-In X-Ray Control Panels; 4 pp; **ACR/MAH.**
Mar. 1, 1929	Leaflet no. 42, Film Viewing Cabinet; 2 pp; **ACR/MAH.**
Jun. 1, 1929	Leaflet no. 22, no. 6 Stereoscopic Tube Stand; 1 pp; **ACR/MAH.**
Sep. 1, 1929	Leaflet no. 33, Single Illuminator; 1 pp; **ACR/MAH.**
Sep. 1, 1929	Leaflet no. 44, Combination Tube and Cassette Changer; 2 pp; **ACR/MAH.**
Nov. 1, 1929	Leaflet no. 1, New Radiographic Genito-Urinary Table; 1 pp; **ACR/MAH.**
Nov. 1, 1929	Leaflet no. 40, Diagnostic Table; 4 pp; **ACR/MAH.**
Nov. 1, 1929	Bulletin no. 18, 150,000 Peak Volt X-Ray Apparatus; 10 pp; **ACR/MAH.**
Dec. 1, 1929	Leaflet no. 45, 17 x 17 flat Potter Bucky Diaphragm; 1 pp; **ACR/MAH.**
Dec. 1, 1929	Leaflet no. 47, Synchronous Impulse Timer; 1 pp; **ACR/MAH.**
Jun. 15 1930	Bulletin no. 10, New Automatic Tilt Table, Motor Driven; 11 pp; **ACR/MAH.**
July 1, 1930	Bulletin no. 41, Portable X-Ray Unit; 6 pp; **ACR/MAH.**
Jan. 1931	Leaflet no. 50, Angulating, Counterbalanced Head Stand, Tripod Mounted Model; 2 pp; **ACR/MAH.**

May 1, 1931   Bulletin no. 22, Type T Tilting Table, Manually Operated; 10 pp; **ACR/MAH.**

n.d.   Price List, Keleket Metal Photo Holders; 1 pp; Vertical Fluoroscope; 4 loose pp; **CTY/B** (Uai K 288).

n.d.   Pamphlet, 165,000 Volt X-Ray Apparatus Therapy and Radiography, included in sales notebook of Engeln pamphlets with cover The Engeln Electric Co. X-Ray Apparatus; 6 pp; **ACR/MAH; MAH.**

n.d.   Pamphlet, 200,000 Volt X-Ray Apparatus Deep Therapy and Radiography, included in sales notebook of Engeln pamphlets with cover The Engeln Electric Co. X-Ray Apparatus; 7 pp; **ACR/MAH; MAH.**

193?   Keleket X-Ray Accessories and Supplies; 1, vol looseleaf; **BLEL.**

KELLOGG
Chicago, Illinois.

n.d.   Dr. Kellogg's Catalogue of Dental Specialties; Vol. 6; 33 pp; **NYAM; MF/MAH.**

KENISTON AND ROOT
Los Angeles, (CA).

1922   Catalog, Standard Surgical Instruments; **LACMA** (149K325).

KENNEDY, J. E., & CO.
201 E. 23rd Street, New York, New York.

1917   Illustrated Catalog of Surgical Instruments and Allied Lines; 672 pp, index pp i-xix; **MAH** (C 610.78085 K3).

1920   Illustrated Catalog; 2nd ed.; 576 pp; **YML** (RD 76.960K); **CTY/B** (60-3945x).

KENT, EDWARD N.
116 John Street, New York, New York.

1848   Descriptive Catalogue of Chemical Apparatus, Chemicals, and Pure Reagents; 2nd ed.; 62 pp; **CTY/B** (Uai K414).

1852   Descriptive Catalogue of Chemical Apparatus, Chemicals, and Pure Reagents; 4th ed.; 57 pp; **CTY/B** (Uai K414).

1854   Descriptive Catalogue of Chemical Apparatus, Chemicals, and Pure Reagents; 5th ed.; 62 pp; **CTY/B** (Uai K414).

1855   Descriptive Catalogue of Chemical Apparatus, Chemicals, and Pure Reagents; 6th ed.; 62 pp; **CTY/B** (Uai K414).

KERN, HORATIO G., CO.
25 North Sixth Street, Philadelphia, Pennsylvania.
Est: 1837

1860   Catalog: Surgical and Dental Instruments, Elastic Trusses, Syringes, etc.; 58 pp; **UPSDM** (D 617.604.K459).

1868   Catalogue of Dental Instruments; 69 pp; **MAH** (C 617. 6085 K).

1883   Illustrated Catalogue of Surgical and Dental Instruments, Orthopedical Appliances, Trusses; 142 pp; **CPP** (Bolenius Coll).

21 North Sixth Street, (Phila., PA.).

1886   Catalogue of Surgical and Dental Instruments, Orthopedical Appliances, Trusses, etc.; iv, 110 pp; **MAH** (C 617.6085K).

KESSELRING X-RAY TUBE CO.
136 West Lake Street, Chicago, Illinois.

ca 1910   Catalog B, X-Ray Tubes, Vacuum Electrodes, and Specialties; 11 pp;
           ACR/MAH; CPP.

ca 1915   Catalog C, X-Ray Tubes and Accessories; 18 pp, 1 pp index; **ACR/MAH.**

KETCHAM & MCDOUGALL
n.d.   Automatic Eye-Glass & Pencil Holder, Trade Price List; 15 pp;
           URRR (K-2).

KETTNER, A(UGUST)
Neuenburgestrasse 29, Berlin S. W. 68.

1861   Fabrik Chirurgischer Instrumente; 50 Jubilee; 50th ed.; **WMScM.**

1911   Many Types of Instruments; 433 pp, index; **WMScM.**

1936   Catalog; 127 pp; **WOC.**

KEYSTONE BEDDING MANUFACTORY
William F. Bernstein, N. W. Corner Fourth & Vine Streets, Philadelphia, Pennsylvania.

n.d.   Illustrated Catalogue of the Keystone Bedding Manufactory; 34 pp; **CPP.**

KEYSTONE ELECTRIC CO., INC.
135 Tenth Street, Philadelphia, Pennsylvania.
Keystone Electric Appliance Co.
Inc: Delaware, charter repealed Jan 23 1922

ca 1903   Illustrated Catalogue and Price List of Electro-therapeutic Appliances,
           Cabinets, Storage Batteries, Static Machines, X-Ray Outfits,
           Physiological Laboratory Equipments . . .; 100 pp; **BLEL.**

ca 1905   Illustrated Catalog and Price List of Electro-Therapeutic Appliances,
           Cabinets, Storage Batteries, Static Machines, X-Ray Outfits,
           Physiological Laboratory Equipments; 100 pp; **ACR/MAH.**

n.d.   Illustrated Catalog and Price List of Electro-Therapeutic Appliances,
           Cabinets, Storage-Batteries, Static Machines, X-Ray Outfits,
           Physiological Laboratory Equipments; 29 pp; **CPP.**

KEYSTONE SURGICAL INSTRUMENT CO.
Philadelphia, Pennsylvania.

1929   Illustrated Catalog of Hand Forged and High Grade Imported Surgical
           Instruments; no. 4; **CPP** (Ed/113).

KIDDER, JEROME, M.D.
Dr. Jerome Kidder's Electrical Depot, 820 Broadway, New York.

1867   Highest Premium, Vitalizing, Genuine Six and Nine Current
           Electro-Medical Apparatuses; **CPP** (Bolenius Coll).

1871   Dr. Jerome Kidder's Highest Premium, Vitalizing, Genuine Six and Nine
           Current Electro-Medical Apparatuses; 9 pp; **BLEL; MUM** (Ed 119 p.
           616).

1874   Electro-Allotropo-Physiology, Uses of Different Qualities of Electricity to
           Cure Disease; 22 pp; **BLEL.**

1877   Researches in Electro-Allotropic Physiology, Uses of Different Qualities of
           Electricity to Cure Disease; **CPP** (Bolenius Coll); **MUM** (Ed 119
           p.636); **BLEL.**

ca 1887   Researches in Electro-Allotropic Physiology, Uses of Different Qualities of
           Electricity to Cure Disease; 115 pp; **BLEL.**

ca 1888   Researches in Electro-Allotropic Physiology, Uses of Different Qualities of
           Electricity to Cure Disease; 111 pp; **BLEL.**

ca 1895 Illustrated and Descriptive Catalogue of Their Superior Electro-Medical Apparatus; **CS.**

KIMAX
See: OWENS-ILLINOIS; **MAH.**

KIMBLE
See: OWENS-ILLINOIS; **MAH.**

KING, A. CHARLES, LTD.
34 Devonshire Street, Harley Street, London W I, England.

Dec. 1930 Apparatus for the Carbon-Dioxide Treatment of Hay Fever Vasomoter Rhinitis Asthmas; 4 pp foldout, **WMScM.**

1930 McKesson Nargraf for General Anaesthesia, interim list; 4 pp; **WMScM.**

n.d. Dental Anesthesia; 8 pp; **WMScM.**

n.d. Addenda to List of Anaesthetic Apparatus; 6 pp foldout; **WMScM.**

n.d. Anaesthetic Sundries; 16 pp; **WMScM.**

n.d. Devonshire Anaesthetic Table, Interim Sheet; 4 pp; **WMScM.**

n.d. Addendum Eight, Nasal Gas Apparatus; 8 pp foldout; **WMScM.**

n.d. Addendum Nine to List of Anaesthetic Apparatus; 4 pp foldout; **WMScM.**

1931? Addendum Ten to List of Anaesthesia Apparatus; 4 pp foldout; **WMScM** (3m.4.31).

n.d. Addendum Eleven of Anaesthetic Apparatus; 6 pp foldout; **WMScM** (3m.6.31).

n.d. Addendum Twelve, Reprint of Addendum on the Guy's Hospital Patterns of the Walton Patent, Gas and Oxygen Apparatus; 4 pp foldout; **WMScM** (3m10.31).

n.d. Addendum Fourteen, An Apparatus for the Administration of Nitrous Oxide Oxygen, Ether, Chloroform, Carbon-Dioxide suggested by Dr. Ivor Lewin; 4 pp foldout, **WMScM.**

n.d. An Abridged Temporary List of McKesson Apparatus; 7 pp; **WMScM** (E1M530).

n.d. Addendum Sixteen; 8 pp foldout; **WMScM.**

n.d. Addendum Seventeen, A New Nasal Inhaler; 4 pp; **WMScM** (3m6.33B).

n.d. Dr. Merrell's Modified Junker Bottle for Maternity Analgesia; 4 pp; **WMScM** (2m.6/33).

n.d. The Adam's Reducing Valve; 1 pp; **WMScM** (3m 1032).

n.d. Interim Sheet Two, The London Anaesthetic Table; 1 pp; **WMScM.**

n.d. Interim sheet Three, The 'Atoms" Suction Pump; 1 pp; **WMScM.**

May 4, 1934 R. J. Minnitt, M.D. Self-Administered Analgesia for the Midwifery of General Practice, The Minnitt Gas-Air Analgesia Apparatus; 19 pp; **WMScM.**

KING, JULIUS, M. D., OPTICAL CO.
10-12 Maiden Lane, New York, New York.
21 rue De L'Echiquier, Paris, France.
Est: 1866

n.d. Catalogue L, Restricted Trade Catalogue no. 2467, photograph Dr. King; 253 pp; **MAH.**

ca 1904 Catalogue K; 223 pp; **MAH.**

1910? Optical Co. Catalog; 48 pp; **URRR** (K-4).

1920 Gold Medal Safety Service; 24 pp; **URRR** (K-256).

KING, WILLIAM, JR.
Buffalo, New York.
1855   Catalogue, Drugs and Chemicals, Surgical and Dental Instruments, Perfumery and Fancy Articles Offered to Physicians and Dealers; 56 pp; **UPSDM** (D 617.604 K 589).

KINGMAN AND HASSAM
128 Washington Street, Boston, Massachusetts.
1855   Catalog of Surgical and Veterinary Instruments; 16 pp; pocket size; **NLM** (W 26 K54).

KINGSTONE, C. F.
72 University, New York, New York.
n.d.   Catalog Gum Surgical Instruments; 8 pp, pp 8-131 missing, ads pp 131-136; **NYAM; MF/MAH.**

KIPP, P. J., & ZONEN
J. W. Giltay, Oprolger, Delft, Holland.
Est: 1830
Dec. 1903   Prof. Julius' Antivibration Apparatus for Supporting Galvanometers; 11 pp; **CPP.**
1929   Review 29, Scientific Instruments; not consecutive pages; **MAH.**

KIRCH & WILHELM
Stuttgart, Germany.
Est: 1899
1925   Surgical Instrument Manufacturers D.R.G.M. 777654, Mfrs. of Every Kind of Surgical Instrument Made of Brass, Nickelplated, Silverplated and Celluloid, Especially, Price List bound with Diagnostic Instrument Catalog; 18 pp; Ear Trumpets; 5th ed.; 7 pp; Record Syringes; 24 pp; **WMScM.**

KIRCHEN, OTTO
Salzgässchen 7, Leipzig, Germany.
1922   Metallwarenfabrik sanitaerer Artikel, Schneedberg-Neustaedtel; 30 pp; **WMScM.**

KIRSTEIN'S, E., SONS CO.
39 State Street, Rochester, New York.
202, 204, 206 Court St., Rochester, New York.
Est: 1864
1896   Descriptive Price List of Spectacles, Eyeglasses, Lenses, 1907 Price List, Prescription Catalogue; 36 pp; **URRR** (K-244).
1907   Shur-on; 112 pp; **URRR** (K-245).
1908   Shur-on; 32 pp, insert on How To Order; **URRR** (K-161); **AO.**
1908   Modern Optical Goods and Appliances; 143 pp; **AO.**
242, 244, 246 Andrews St., Rochester, New York.
1909   Illustrated Catalog and Price List, Eye Glass and Spectacle Cases; 16 pp; **URRR** (K-157).
1912   Improvements in Shur-on Eyeglass and Spectacle Mountings; 10 pp foldout; **URRR** (K-160E).
1912   Eye Glass and Spectacle Cases; 20 pp; **URRR** (K-158).
1914   Illustrated Price List, Shur-on Goods; 16 pp; **URRR** (K-159).
n.d.   Kirsco Eyeglass and Spectacle Cases; 24 pp; **URRR** (K-?).

n.d.   Optical Specialties; 80 pp; **CPP.**

n.d.   Kirsco Eyeglass and Spectacle Cases; 3 pp; **URRR** (K-156).

n.d.   Catalog and Price List of Eye Glass and Spectacle Cases; 20 pp; **URRR** (K-156A).

n.d.   Modern Optical Goods and Appliances; 142 pp; **URRR** (K-162).

KISSNER, F., & CO.
New York, New York.

ca 192?   Catalog Surgical Instruments, Hospital Supplies . . .; 448 pp; **NYAM** (S.125).

KLEINE, CHARLES B.
274 Eighth Avenue, New York, New York.

n.d.   Catalog Illustrated Price List of Microscopes and Other Scientific Instruments; **CTY/B** (Uai K 673).

n.d.   Manufacturers and Dealers; Price List Microscopes and Other Scientific Instruments; 40 pp; **NYAM; MF/MAH.**

KLETT MFG. CO.
202 E. 46th St., New York, New York.
See: WILL CORP., Rochester, N.Y.

1918   Bock-Benedict Colorimeter; 2 pp; **URRR** (K-27).

1929   Klett Colorimeters, Nepholometers; 24 pp; **URRR** (K-231).

1930?   The New Klett Bio Colorimeter; 6 pp foldout; **URRR** (K-229).

n.d.   The New Klett Top Reader Colorimeter; 6 pp foldout; **URRR** (K-230).

KLEWE & CO., INC.
Dresden, Germany.
New Haven, Connecticut.
Est: 1896

1906   Catalog Prosthetic Porcelain and the Roach Automatic Pyrometer Furnace and the Entire Equipment for the Modern Porcelain Worker, Dr. Jenkins Porcelain Enamel; 24 pp; **NYAM; MF/MAH; SLSC.**

KLIEGL BROS.
New York.

1903   The Actinolite, for the Treatment of Disease by Actinic Light; 2nd ed.; 60 pp; **BLEL.**

KLINGELFUSS & CO., FR.
Basel, Switzerland.

1909   Innenpol Magnet, for Oculists; 4 pp; **CPP.**

n.d.   Therapeutic Cabinet; 4 pp; **CPP.**

KLOMAN INSTRUMENT CO., INC.
1114 14th St., N.W., Washington, D.C.
Charleston, West Virginia.

1924   Catalog of Standard Surgeons' Instruments and Apparatus; 1st ed.; **MCFM.**

1926   Standard Surgeon's Instruments and Apparatus; 416 pp; **WOC.**

1934   Catalog of Standard Surgeons Instruments and Apparatus; 4th ed.; 447 pp; **CPP.**

KLOSS, E. L.
Berlin, Germany.

1864   Preis-Verzeichniss galvanischer Apparate und Einrichtungen zu medicinischen und physiologischen Zwecken; 3 pp; **CPP; MUM** (Ed 51 pam27).

KNAUR, THOMAS
Viennae, Alberti.
> 1796 Selectus instrumentorum chirurgicorum in use discentium ex practicorum; in Latin and German; 48 pp; **LLU** (WZ 260 K67s 1796).

KNAUTH BROTHERS
3,5,7 West 29th Street, New York, New York.
> 1891 Catalog of Surgical Instruments and Physicians' Supplies, Electric and Orthopedic Apparatus; 7th ed.; 10 pp; **NYAM** (S.125).
> 1892 Catalog Surgical Instruments and Physicians' Supplies Electric and Orthopedic Apparatus; 115 pp, price list 41 pp; **NYAM; MF/MAH; WOC.**

295 Fourth Avenue, New York, New York.
> n.d. Catalog Physicians and Surgeon's Supplies; 103 pp; index 41 pp; 4 pp ads; **NYAM; MF/MAH.**

KNAPP
See: S. S. WHITE, Regulating Devices; **MF/MAH.**

KNOTT, L. E., APPARATUS CO.
16 Ashburton Place, Boston, Massachusetts.
> ca 1896 Leaflet; Crookes Tubes for "Radiograph" Work; 4 pp; **CTY/B** (Uai K759).
> 1901 Catalog List Containing the Apparatus for . . . The National Physics Course adopted by the National Educational Association at Los Angeles in July 1899; 87 pp; **CTY/B** (Uai K759).
> 1912 A Catalog of Physical Instruments, no. 17; 524 pp; **CTY/B** (Uai K759).

Ames and Amherst Streets, (Boston, MA.).
> 1916? A Catalog of Scientific Instruments: General Science, Physics, Chemistry, Biology, no. 21; 507 pp; **CTY/B** (Uai K759).
> Aug. 1921 Catalog of Scientific Instruments, no. 26; 326 pp; **CTY/B** (Uai K 759); **BLEL.**

14 Ashburton Place, (Boston, MA.).
> n.d. Brochure, Influence Machine; 4th ed.; 14 pp; **NYAM; MF/MAH.**

KNY, RICHARD, AND CO.
KNY-SCHEERER CO.
New York, New York.
Est: 1890
> 1894 Illustrations of Surgical Instruments and Physician's Supplies; 348 pp; **CPP** (ZEd/5).

48 Ritterstrasse, Berlin, Germany.
> n.d. Catalog Naturalist's Supplies, no. 1; 40 pp, index pp i-ix; **NYAM; MF/MAH.**

17 Park Place, New York, New York.
> ca 1908 Catalog Binder for Kny-Scheerer Co.'s Bulletins on Electromedical Apparatus (30) in German; **NYAM.**
> ca 1908 X-Ray Apparatus: Complete Outfits and Accessories for X-Ray Laboratories; 5th ed.; 80 pp; **BLEL.**
> 1908 Electrically Illuminated Instruments: Cystoscopes, Endoscopes . . .; 22 pp; **BLEL.**

1908 Catalog 10, Surgical Instruments; 402 pp; **WOC.**

1909 Illustrations of Surgical Instruments; 15th ed.; pp 1001-5184; **YML** (RD 76 909K); **CS.**

1910 Illustrated Catalog of Surgical Instruments, Illustrations of Eye, Ear, Nose and Throat Instruments . . .; 16th ed., Special ed.; 286 pp; **YML** (RD 76910K); **NYAM; CPP; HDM.**

1911 Illustrated Catalogue of Surgical Instruments; 17th ed.; **CS.**

1915 Catalog no. 15; X-Ray Equipment and High Frequency Apparatus and Accessories; 140 pp; **ACR/MAH.**

n.d. Catalog Aseptic Furniture for Hospitals and Physician's Offices, (In German with English title page); pp 49-155; **NYAM; MF/MAH.**

n.d. Catalog of Surgical Instruments, five sections in separate pages; 13th ed.; **NYAM.**

404-410 W 27th St., New York, New York.

1899 Illustrated Catalog of Surgical Instruments, Ophthalmic, Aural, Nasal, Dermal and Uranoplastic, Oral and Laryngeal, Oesophageal and Gastric Instruments, Atomizers, Inhalers and Repirators, Section Three; 3001-3192 pp, index pp v-viii; **MAH** (C 610.78085K).

1899 Catalog of Surgical Instruments, Section Four; 85 pp, index pp v-vii; **NYAM; MF/MAH.**

1899 Illustrated Catalog of Surgical Instruments, Urethral, Urocystic and Cysto-Lithic Instruments, Hernial and Intestinal Instruments, Anal and Rectal Instruments; Section Four; pp Di-D84; **MAH** (C 610.78085K).

1899 Gynecological Instruments, Obstetrical Instruments, Uterine-Diagnostic and Dressing Instruments, Vesico-Vaginal Fistula, Hysterectomy and Ovariotomy Instruments; Section Five; pp 5001-5180, index pp vii-viii; **MAH** (C 610.78085K).

ca 1899 Scientific Methods of Sterilization & Disinfection; pp 501-618; **CPP.**

ca 1890s Price List of Anatomical Models of Papier Mache, Osteological Preparations, etc.; 16 pp; **CPP.**

pre–1900 Sanatorium Supplies, Pneumatic Cabinet; 16 pp; **CPP.**

post 1900 Catalog, Chemical Apparatus and Laboratory Supplies; No 60; **CTY/B** (Uai K788).

post 1900 Catalog of Anatomical and Biological Models, and Osteological, Anatomical and Biological Preparations; 228 pp; **AFMM.**

ca 1900 Gynaecological Instruments, Obstetrical Instruments, Uterine-Diagnostic and Dressing Instruments; Vesico-vaginal Fistula, Hysterectomy and Ovariotomy Instruments; **CPP** (ZEd/12).

Jan. 1, 1900 Catalog, Modern Aseptic Hospital Supplies; 232 pp; **NYAM; MF/MAH.**

Mar. 1, 1902 Catalog, no title page, Surgical Supplies and Furniture; 311 pp; **NYAM; MF/MAH.**

1902 Illustrations of Surgical Instruments mfd. by the Kny-Scheerer Co . . .; **MCFM; MRLB; NYAM** (S125); **CS.**

1904 Illustrations of Surgical Instruments; 13th ed.; **HDM.**

ca 1909 Illustrations of Surgical Instruments; 15th ed.; **UREGML.**

ca 1910 Catalog of Surgical Instruments; 16th ed.; Sect. I, pp 1001-1117; II, pp 2001-2175; III, pp 3001-3267; IV, pp 4001-4110; V, pp 5001-5190; **AFMM; MAH** (C610.78085 K); **YML.**

ca 1910 Thermo-Electric Apparatus Devised by Dr. D. Tyrnauer, Karlsbad, Austria; 16 pp; **CPP.**

1910 Descriptive Catalogue no. III, Anatomical Models, Osteological, Anatomical & Biological Preps.; 230 pp; **MUM.**

1914   Surgical Instruments, 20th ed.; 1160 pp; **WOC.**

1914   Surgical Instruments; Section 2; 400 pp; **WOC.**

1914   The Improved Huntley-Kenyon Electric Operation Motor and Dr. Albee's Instruments for Bone Transplantation; 4 pp; **CPP.**

225-233 Fourth Avenue, New York, New York.

1904   Catalog, Roentgen X-Ray Apparatus and Accessories; 156 pp; **NYAM; MF/MAH.**

ca 1904   Bulling's Inhalation Apparatus: Guttager and Thermo Variator; 18 pp; **CPP.**

1905   Catalog, Roentgen X-Ray Apparatus and Accessories; 155 pp; **MAH** (C 616.0757 K).

1906   Surgical Instruments; 13th ed.; 613 pp; **WOC.**

ca 1906   Ariston Ampullae Injection Syringes, etc., Sterilized Sutures and Ligatures; 36 pp; **CPP.**

1906   Illustrated and Descriptive Catalog of Aseptic Surgical Supplies; **YML** (RD 76 906K).

1906   Illustrated and Descriptive Catalog of Aseptic Surgical Supplies for the Equipment of Operating Rooms, Sterilizing Rooms, Hospital Wards, Physicians' Offices, Sanataria and Sick Rooms; **NWUCML** (617.91 K 78); **LC** (RD 76K37).

1906   Catalog no. 9, Modern Hospital Supplies; 622 pp, index; **SLSC.**

Nov. 1906   A Direct Medium of Communication between the Physicians and Surgeons of America, no. 3, Vol. 1; pp 54-83; **CPP.**

May 1907   New Instruments, no. 4, Vol. 1; pp 85-115; **CPP.**

ca 1907   Dr. A. Bier's Vacuum Apparatus for the Induction of Artificial Hyperemia in the Treatment of Inflammatory Disease; 32 pp; **CPP.**

404-410 W. 27th St., New York, New York.

1914   The Improved Huntley-Kenyon Electric Motor and Dr. Albee's Instruments for Bone Transplantation; 4 pp; **CPP.**

1914   Electrically Heated Hot-Air Apparatus for Hyperacmic Treatment, Devised by Dr. D. Tyrnauer, Karlsbad, illustrating Dr. Tyrnauer's Apparatus and Its Use; 30 pp; **MAH.**

1914   Kinesotherapy, Medico-Mecahnical Treatment Illustrating the Zander Apparatus and Treatment; 142 pp, bound with above; **MAH.**

1914   Bone, Cranium, Fracture, Intestine, Rectum, Suture, Dressing and Anaesthsia Surgical Instrument; Special ed.; pp 2001-2384; **NLM** (W26 K74c).

1915   Illustrations of Surgical Instruments of Superior Quality, Carried by C. W. Alban Co.; 20th ed.; 5216 pp, index; **BLEL; UBML** (W26 K74l); **SLSC; NWUCML** (617.91 K782); **TMHM.**

1921   Surgical Instruments; 22nd ed.; pp 1001-5216; **MAH; UREGML; LON** (W26 K74i); **CS; HDM.**

1924   Supplement to the 22nd ed., Surgical Instrument Catalog; **CS.**

1926   Modern Aseptic Furniture and Sterilizers; 18th ed.; 240 pp; **HDM.**

1928   Instrument Catalog, Carried by C. W. Alban Co.; 23rd ed.; 5218 pp, index; **SLSC.**

1929   General Catalog, Hospital & Surgical Supplies, Scientific Apparatus, Sections A, B, C; **HDM.**

21-09 Bordon Lane, Long Island City, New York.

1935   Catalog of Surgical Instruments of Superior Quality; 24th ed.; **MCFM.**

n.d.   Sanitorium Supplies Including a Complete Line of Articles for Preventing the Spread of Tuberculosis, Treatment of TB, Sickroom Invalid Supplies,

Sect. P, Part 6a; 32 pp; **CPP.**

n.d. Galvano-Cautery, Endoscopy, and Diaphanoscopy Catalog, Section G, Part IV; 48 pp; **CPP.**

n.d. Electric Hot Air Douche; 4 pp; **CPP.**

n.d. New and Modern Appliances for Surgical Men, issued by *Annals of Surgery*; 7 pp; **CPP.**

n.d. A New Alternating Current Low Tension Transformer; 2 pp; **CPP.**

n.d. Dr. Killian's Instruments for Tracheoscopy, Bronchoscopy and Oesophagoscopy; 4 pp; **CPP.**

n.d. The Albee Electro-Operative Bone Set with Hearley-Kenyon Sterilizable Shells; 7 pp; **CPP.**

n.d. Bone Surgery with the Improved Albee Electro-Operative Instruments; 20 pp; **CPP.**

n.d. The Manning System for the Collection, Disinfection, and Disposal of Human Expectorations and Sputum; 4 pp; **CPP.**

n.d. Electro-Therapeutic Appliances; 7 pp; **CPP.**

n.d. Bier's Hyperemic Treatment, by Will Meyer and Victor Schmieden, 4 specimen pp from book; **CPP.**

n.d. The Iodine Vapor Spray; 4 pp; **CPP.**

n.d. Special Sheet, Dept. E, Referring to the Kny-Sprague Tubular Disinfecting Chambers; 4 pp; **CPP.**

n.d. Catalog no. 60, Chemical Apparatus, Department of Laboratory Supplies; 612 pp; **CTY-B** (Uai K788).

KOCH, F. A., & CO.
New York.
Est: 1874

n.d. Illustrated Catalogue, Surgical Dept.; 200 pp, illus.; **MAH.**

1932 Catalogue of Surgical Instruments; 12th ed.; **CS.**

KOCH & STERZEL
Zwickauer Strasse 42, Dresden, Germany.

n.d. Spezialfabrik wissenschaftlicher Apparate und Instrumente der Oscillodor; **NYAM; MF/MAH.**

KODAK
See: EASTMAN KODAK CO.

KOENIG, RUDOLPH
5 Place du Lycée Louis-Le-Grand, Paris, France.

1859 Catalogue des principaux appareils d'acoustique; 31 pp; **CTY/B** (Uai K 8185).

30 rue Hautefeuille, Paris, France.

1865 Catalogue des appareils d'acoustique; 52 pp; **CTY/B** (Uai K 8185).

1875 Catalogue des appareils d'acoustique; 51 pp; **CTY/B** (Uai K 8185).

1882 Catalogue des appareils d'acoustique; 54 pp; **CTY/B** (Uai K 8185).

27 Quai d'Anjou, Paris, France.

1889 Catalogue des appareils d'acoustique; 100 pp; **NYAM; CTY/B** (Uai K 8185).

KOENIGLICHE PORZELLAN-MANUFACTUR
Leipziger Strasse 2, Berlin, Germany.

Apr. 1, 1906 Catalog and Price List for Porcelain Supplies, no. V; 160 pp; **CTY/B** (Uai P 839).

KOEPPEN, WILLY
Rathenow, Germany.
Optische Industrie
　　　1927　Katalog; 46 pp; Price List; 47 pp; **URRR** (K-11).

KOHL, MAX
17 Becherstrasse, Chemnitz, Germany.
　　1897–99　The Instruments for Producing Roentgens X-Rays and Manner of Their
　　　　　　　Application; 30 pp; **CTY/B** (Uai K 822).
　　1897–99　Neueste Apparate fuer Roentgen-Photographie und Durchleuchtung und
　　　　　　　ihr Gebrauch; 31 pp; **CTY/B** (Uai K 822).
　　　1898　Novelties 1898 upon the Subject of Roentgen's X-Rays, Communication
　　　　　　　no. 5; 14 pp; **CTY/B** (Uai K 822).
　　ca 1907　Price List of X-Ray and High Frequency Apparatus; 149 pp; **BLEL.**
　　　1923　Catalog Acoustics; 464 pp; **NYAM; MF/MAH.**
　　　n.d.　Apparate fuer Roentgen-Photographie und Durchleuchtung zum Gebrauch
　　　　　　　fuer Aertze, Krankhaeuser, Kliniken, Universitäten; 14 pp; **CTY/B**
　　　　　　　(Uai K 822).
　　　n.d.　Physikalisch Apparate Preisliste Nr. 21; 882 pp; **URRR** (K-184).
Adorfer Strasse 20, Chemnitz, Germany.
　　　1928　Price List no. 100, Vol. I & II, Educational and Laboratory Furniture for
　　　　　　　Physics, Chemistry and Biology Class Rooms and Laboratories; 472 pp,
　　　　　　　Price List May 1928 and Oct 1928, 3 pp; **MAH.**
　　　n.d.　Price List Physical Apparatus, Catalogue 50; 70 pp; **NYAM; MF/MAH.**

KOHLBAUM, C. A. F.
Chemische Fabrik, 35 Schlesische Strasse, Berlin C 25, Germany.
　Oct. 1896　Preis-Liste wissenschaftlicher Praeparate von C.A.F. Kohlbaum; 38 pp;
　　　　　　　CPP.
　Oct. 1912　Preisliste wissenschaftlicher Praeparate; 171 pp; **CPP.**

KOHLBUSCH, HERMAN
59 Nassau Street, New York, New York.
Est: 1859
　　　1898　Catalogue Balances & Weights; 38 pp; **NYAM; MF/MAH.**

KOEHLER, FRITZ
Leipzig, Germany.
　　　1905　Katalog E, Apparate fuer physiologische Chemie und die medizinischen
　　　　　　　Wissenschaften nach Hamburger, Hofmann, Henry, Asher, und
　　　　　　　Balneologie nach Zoerkendoerfer; **CTY/B** (Uai K 816).
　　　1905　Katalog F, Apparate fuer Elektrochemie, insbesondere nach Luepke; cited
　　　　　　　by **CTY/B** (Uai K816).
　　　1905　Hauptkatalog D, Physico-Chemische Apparate besonders nach Ostwald;
　　　　　　　216 pp; **CTY/B** (Uai K816).
　Feb. 1906　Katalog E, Physiko-Chemische Apparate fuer Physiologie und die
　　　　　　　medizinischen Wissenschaften; 32 pp; **NYAM; MF/MAH.**
　　　1909　Katalog Apparate; 141 pp; **NYAM; MF/MAH.**

KOKEN COMPANIES
3400 Morganford Road, St. Louis, Missouri.
　　　1930　Catalog Physician's and Surgeon's Equipment; 15 pp; **NYAM;**
　　　　　　　MF/MAH.

KOLBÉ, D. W., & SON
15 South Ninth Street, 1207 Arch Street, Philadelphia, Pennsylvania.
Est: 1849

1868 Orthopaedic Apparatus and Description of the Mechanical Appliances Employed in the Treatment of Deformities and Deficiencies of the Body, with Directions for Taking Measurements for their Application; 37 pp; **BLEL.**

1869 Orthopaedic Apparatus and Description of the Mechanical Appliances Employed in the Treatment of Deformities and Deficiencies of the Body . . .; 37 pp; **NLM** (W26 K81).

1870 Description of the Orthopaedic Apparatus Employed in the Treatment of Deformities and Deficiencies of the Human Body, with Directions for Taking Measurements for Their Application; 2nd ed.; 57 pp; **CPP; NLM** (W26 K81).

1871 Description of the Orthopaedic Apparatus Employed in the Treatment of Deformities and Deficiencies of the Human Body; 60 pp; **MAH** (C617.3078K 3d).

1874 Description of the Orthopaedic Apparatus Employed in the Treatment of Deformities and Deficiencies of the Human Body, with Directions for Taking Measurements for Their Application; 3rd ed.; **MAH** (C 617.3078 K 3d).

1876 Description of the Orthopaedic Apparatus . . .; 4th ed.; 60 pp; **CPP.**

1877 Description of the Orthopaedic Apparatus . . .; 5th ed.; 62 pp; **CPP.**

1879 Description of the Orthopaedic Apparatus Employed in the Treatment of Deformities and Deficiencies of the Human Body; 6th ed.; 62 pp; **NLM** (W26 K81).

1879 Illustrated Catalog of Surgical Instruments; 202 pp; **CPP** (Ed/24); pp 25-202; **AFMM.**

1879 Illustrated Catalog of Surgical Instruments; 216 pp; **AFMM; MUM** (Ed24 1879).

ca 1880 Catalog of Surgical Instruments; 213 pp; **NLM** (W26 K81).

1880 Description of the Orthopaedic Apparatus . . .; 7th ed.; 62 pp; **CPP; AFMM.**

1881 Illustrated Catalog of Surgical Instruments; 202 pp; **CPP** (Bolenius Coll); **MUM** (Ed 119 v.2).

1881 Description of the Orthopaedic Apparatus Employed in the Treatment of Deformities and Deficiencies of the Human Body; 8th ed.; 62 pp; **CPP** (Bolenius Coll); **MUM** (Ed 119 200ff).

1882 Suggestions on the Treatment of Club-Foot; 23 pp; **CPP.**

1886 Description of the Orthopaedic Apparatus Employed in the Treatment of Deformities and Deficiencies of the Human Body . . .; 9th ed.; 62 pp; **AFMM.**

1887 Description of the Orthopaedic Apparatus Employed in the Treatment of Deformities and Deficiencies of the Human Body . . .; 10th ed.; 62 pp; **AFMM.**

n.d. Catalogue of Surgical and Dental Instruments, Elastic Trusses; **CPP** (Bolenius Coll).

Berlin, Germany

n.d. Preis-Verzeichniss Electro-Therapeutischer Apparate; 8 pp; **NYAM; MF/MAH.**

n.d. Brochure, Transportabler Apparat fuer constante Stroeme; 5 pp; **NYAM; MF/MAH.**

KONRAD, JARNUSZKIEWICZ i Ska
Spotka Akeyjna, Warsaw, Poland.
    1932   Szpitali, lecznic, Klinik, sal operacyjnych, Gabinetow Lekarskich oraz Sanatorjon; 120 pp; **MAH.**

KORISTKA, F.
Via S Vittore 47, Milano, Italy.
    1892   Catalogo Illustrato Descrittivo N. 6; 80 pp; **URRR** (K-193).

KRAUSS, E., & CO.
Luetzowstrasse no. 68, Berlin, Germany.
Est: 1882
    post 1890   Catalogue and Price List of the Optical Instrument Works of E. Krauss & Co.; 48 pp; **CTY/B** (Uai K 869); **CPP.**
    Dec. 1898   Microscopes and Accessories, Bausch and Lomb, no. 1; 48 pp; **URRR** (K-17E).
    1905   Krauss Microscopes and Accessories Microphotographie; 2nd ed.; 64 pp; **URRR** (K-22E).

KREMENTZ, FRANK
164 Emmet St., Newark, N.J.
Branch Offices: 13 Maiden Lane, New York City.
                  49 Geary Street, San Francisco.
                  31 N. State Street, Chicago.
Krementz & Co.
49 Chestnut Street, Newark, New Jersey.
Est: 1866
"We Dress the Eyes of the World"
    1923   The Optical Catalog, with 1923 Price List; 16 pp; **AO.**
    1924   The Optical Catalog, with 1924 Price List; 16 pp; **AO.**
    1925   Optical Catalog, Lorgnons, The Oxford Eyeglass, Shopping Oxford, Oxford Guards, One Piece Mountings; 16 pp unmarked; **AO**; photographs on folio size pages; **URRR** (K-247).
    1925   The Optical Catalog; **URRR** (K-243).
    1927–8   A Showing of Our New Optical Specialties for 1927–8 Quality Oxfords and Lornons; 4 pp, inserts; **AO.**
    1929   Frank Krementz Oxfords, Oxfords, Lornons, Chains; 9 pp, price List; **AO, URRR** (K-266).
    1930   Frank Krementz Oxfords, Oxfords, Lornons, Chains; 16 pp; **AO.**
    1932   Oxfords, Lorgnettes, and Chains, Temporary Price List; 15 pp; **AO.**
    1936   Lorgnons, Oxfords, Chains; 20 pp; **URRR** (K-268).

KROHNE & SESEMANN
8 Duke Street, Manchester Square W., 241 Whitechapel Road, London E, England.
Est: 1860
    1878   Catalog of Surgical and Orthopaedic Instruments; 312 pp; **NYAM; MF/MAH; WMScM; MUM; CPP** (Ed/26a); **ZUR.**
    14 Barrett Street, 152 Whitechapel Road E., London, England
    1901   Illustrated Catalog of Surgical Instruments and Appliances manufactured and sold by; 425 pp; **NYAM** (S 125); **WMScM.**
    1905   Illustrated Catalogue of Surgical Instruments and Appliances; 544 pp; **BLEL.**
    1908   Illustrated Catalog of Surgical Instruments and Appliances; **CPP** (Ed/26a).
    ca 1909   Catalog of Surgical Instruments and Appliances; **SBMC.**

KROMEL LABORATORIES
New York, New York.
    n.d.   Cast Lingual Bar and Clasps; Cast Partials and Partial Bar; **MAH.**

KROWER, LEONARD
536 and 538 Canal Street, New Orleans.
    1909,10   Optical Catalogue; 211 pp, index; **AO.**

KRUEGER, RUDOLPH
S. W. Simeon-Strasse no. 20, Berlin, Germany.
    n.d.   Preis-Verzeichniss electro-therapeutischer Apparate; 8 pp; **NYAM; MF/MAH.**
    n.d.   Brochure, transportabler Apparat fuer constante Stroeme; 5 pp; **NYAM; MF/MAH.**

KRUPP, FRIEDRICH
Essen, Germany.
    n.d.   Dental Instruments; 64 pp; **UPSDM** (617.604.K945).
    1939   Zahnärztliche Instrumente aus nichtrostendem D2 Stahl; 106 pp; **AFMM.**

KRUESS, A.
Adolphsbruecke 7, Hamburg, Germany.
Est: 1796; Inc: 1844
    Feb. 1890   Catalog Preis-Liste ueber Spectral Apparate angefertigt in den Werkstaetten des Optischen Instituts; **CTY/B** (Uai K 936).
    Mar. 1890   Catalog Verzeichniss von Glasphotogrammen fuer das Scioptikon; **CTY/B** (Uai K 936).
    Feb. 1893   Catalog Nachtrag no. 1 zum Verzeichniss von Glasphotogrammen fuer das Scioptikon; **CTY/B** (Uai K 936).
    1895   Catalog Preis-Liste ueber Spectral Apparate angefertigt in den Werkstaetten des Optischen Instituts; **CTY/B** (Uai K 936).
    1916   Kolorimeter; 9 pp; **URRR** (K-20).

KRYPTOK LTD.
31-33 High Holborn, London, W.C., England.
    1909   Profits in Kryptoks fused bifocal lenses; 12 pp; **URRR** (K-250).

KRYPTOK SALES COMPANY
KRYPTOK COMPANY
401-403-405 East 31st Street, New York (1908)
    (Executive Offices and Factory), 104 East 23rd Street, New York (1911), 50 East 42nd Street, New York (1917).
    Sales Offices: Heyworth Bldg., Chicago (1909). 150 Post Street, Jeweler's Bldg., San Francisco (1910). 140 Geary Street, Chicago (1915).
    1904   *Kryptok Bulletin*, published monthly, selected months through 1920; **AO.**

KUECHMANN, C.
Dorotheen Strasse 69, Berlin, N W 7, Germany.
    n.d.   Bandagist Spezial-Liste ueber Bruchbandagen und Leibbinden; 7 pp; **NYAM; MF/MAH.**

KUERMERLE, JOHN F., & KOLBE
45 S. 8th Street, below Chestnut Street, Philadelphia, Pennsylvania.
    1855   Illustrated Catalogue of Surgical and Dental Instruments and Syringes; 30 pp; **CPP; MUM** (2r-56 pam 27).

1858   Catalogue of Surgical and Dental Instruments and Syringes; 30 pp; **NLM** (W26 qK85).

KULLMEYER, RICHARD, & CO.
Berlin, Germany.

1880   Illustrirter Katalog ueber Apparate und Geraethschaften im Gesamtgebiete der Medizin, Chirurgie und Bacteriologie Disinfection Sterilisation, Nr. 12; 207 pp; **RCSL**.

KUNSTEHEN, A.
Berlin, Germany.

n.d.   Catalog; **RCSL**.

KUNZ, OTTO
Pittsburgh, Pennsylvania.

n.d.   A Guide for Dentists to Procure Teeth from Otto Kunz, Manufacturer of Mineral Teeth; 6 pp; **MF/MAH**.

KUTNOW, S., & CO., LTD.
41 Farington Road, London, E C.
66 Holborn Viaduct E C., London, England.
Kutnow Brothers Ltd.
853 Broadway at 14th St. and Union Sq., New York, New York.

ca 1893   Asthma, Bronchitis, Hay-Fever and Coughs; 12 pp; **CPP**.
1894   European Mineral Spring Treatment in America; 8 pp; **CPP**.
1898   Some Remarks on Errors of Metabolism in General; 14 pp; **CPP**.
ca 1907   An Essay on Faulty Metabolism; 18 pp; **CPP**.
n.d.   Kutnow's Anti-Asthmatic Powder; 1 pp; **CPP**.

LABORATOIRES LANCASME
71 Ac, Victor-Emmanuel III, Paris, France.

n.d.   Algocratine-1 cachet des les premières sensations de douleurs; 1 pp; **CPP**.

LABORATORY AND SCHOOL SUPPLY CO., LTD., THE
New York, New York.
See: KNY-SCHEERER CO.

ca 1904   Vereinigte Fabriken fuer Laboratoriumsbedarf . . . and for the Physical, Chemical Institute and Bureau of Standards of Dr. Heinrich Coeckel; **CTY/B** (Uai V 585).

LADD, WILLIAM
31 Chancery Lane, London, England.

1858   General Catalog of Optical, Philosophical & Mathematical Instruments; 10 pp, appendix; **CTY/B** (Uai L121).

11 & 12 Beak Street, Regent Street, London, England.

1860   Catalog of Optical Instruments; 5 pp; **CTY/B** (Uai L121).
1870   Catalog of Optical, Mathematical and Philosophical Instruments; 28 pp; **NLM** (W 26 L 154).
1872   Catalog of Optical, Mathematical and Philosophical Instruments; 23 pp; **CTY/B** (Uai L 121).

LAMBERT PHARMACAL CO.
2117 Franklin Ave., St Louis, Missouri.
Est: 1881

1897   Listerine in Dental Practice; 48 pp; **NYAM; MF/MAH**.

LAMBERT SNYDER CO.
10 & 12 West 22nd Street, New York, New York.
    n.d.   The Snyder Portable Exhilarator; 1 pp; **CPP.**

LA MOTTE CHEMICAL PRODUCTS
McCormick Building, Baltimore, Maryland.
Est: 1919
    1924   Standardized Chemicals and Special Apparatus; 24 pp; **NYAM; MF/MAH; CTY/B** (Uai L 19); **CPP.**
    1929   Lamotte Blood Chemistry Outfits for the General Practitioner's Routine Tests; **CTY/B** (Uai L 19).
    Jun. 1891   Instruments d'optique et de précision, Foro-uberrometre Laurent; Exposition universalle Paris 1889, Grand Prix; 23 pp; **RCSL.**
    n.d.   Colorimetre perfectionne; 4 pp; **CTY/B** (Uai L373).

LANDENBERGER, H.
25 & 27 North 13th Street, Philadelphia, Penn.
    1891   Illustrated and Priced catalog of Chemical Apparatus; 178 pp; **CPP.**

LANGLEY & MICHAELS CO.
34, 36, 38 and 40 First Street, San Francisco, California.
Est: 1850; Inc: 1888
    ca 1900   Prices, Current of Drugs, Chemicals, Proprietary Medicines, Pharmaceutical Preparations, Druggists' Sundries, etc., etc.; 560 pp; **UCSF.**

LAUNDY & SON
9 St. Thomas Street, London, England.
    1802   A Catalogue of Chirurigal Instruments; 19 pp, some prices inserted in ink; **NLM** (W 26 L 376).

LAURENT, LEON
21 rue de l'Odeon, Paris, France.
    1880   Saccarimètre et polarimètre Laurent, James W. Queen and Co. listed on cover; 24 pp; **CTY/B** (Uai L373).
    1881   Catalogue nouveaux miroirs magiques en cerre argent, Miroirs a creusures et comprimes, Miroirs chauffes de formes et d'épaisseurs quelconques, James W. Queen and Co., U. S. agents; 12 pp; **CTY/B** (Uai L 373).
    1882   Catalogue, saccramètre et polarimètre Laurent; 28 pp; **CTY/B** (Uai L373).
    1882?   Catalogue nouveaux miroirs magiques en cerre argent, Miroirs a creusures et comprimes, Miroirs chauffes de formes et d'épaisseurs quelconques; 12 pp; **CTY/B** (Uai L 373).
    Jun. 1891   Instruments d'optique et de précision, foro-uberromètre Laurent, Exposition universalle Paris 1889, Grand Prix; 23 pp; **RCSL.**
    n.d.   Colorimètre perfectionné; 4 pp; **CTY/B** (Uai L373).

LAURIE, THOMAS
28 Paternoster Row, London, England.
    L. 19 c   Catalog Laurie's Scientific and Technical Apparatus for Teaching Many Subjects, no. 14; 32 pp; **CTY/B** (Uai L375).

LAUNTENSCHLAEGER, F. & M.
24 Ziegel-Strasse, Berlin, N., Germany.
    n.d.   Catalogue Femel-Destillierapparate; 6 pp; **NYAM; MF/MAH.**

n.d.   Manometer-Regulator neuester Construction fuer Druck und Temperatur; **CPP.**

n.d.   Separat-Abdruck zur Darstellung leicht zersetzlicher chemischer Krankheitsstoffe; **CPP.**

n.d.   Preis-Verzeichniss ueber bacteriologische, microscopische und uroscopische Apparate und Instrumente; **CPP.**

n.d.   Sterilisations-Apparat fuer Metall-Instrumente nach Dr. Schimmelbusch; **CPP.**

n.d.   Neuster elektrischer Patent-Thermoregulator zum sofortigen Einstellen und beliebigen Veraendern der Temperaturen innerhalb 20-80 Grad C; **CPP.**

n.d.   Dr. H. Settegast's Steriliser for surgical purposes; **CPP.**

n.d.   Specialfabrik zur Herstellung wissenschaftlicher Apparate und Utensilien, speciell fuer Bakteriologie, Chemie, Mikroskopie, Physiologie und Technik; no. 60; **CPP** (ZEd/6).

n.d.   Sterilizing Oven for Dry Air, System of Dr. Koch; 4 pp; **CPP.**

LAWSON & JONES, LTD.
London, Ontario, Canada.

n.d.   Labels, Containers, Boxes, etc.; 152 pp, inserts; **UTP.**

LAWTON COMPANY, INC.
425 Fourth Avenue, New York 16, New York.

1927   Surgical Instrument Catalog; 577 pp; **MAH** (C 610.78085 L 187).

LEACH & GREENE
165 Tremont St., Boston, Massachusetts.

ca 1885   Illustrated Catalogue of Surgical Instruments, etc., etc., etc.; **CS.**

L. 19 c   Illustrated Catalog of Surgical Instruments, Orthopedic Apparatuses, Trusses, Microscopes (Bausch & Lomb), Batteries, etc.; 2nd ed.; 126 pp; **AFMM.**

Oct. 1888–
Nov. 1889   Two 4 page newspaper ads (flyers) for New Instruments; **AFMM.**

n.d.   Levis' Metallic Splints, designed by R. J. Levis, M.D.; 2 pp advertisement; **MAH** (16115).

LECLERC, T.
10 rue Vignon, Paris, France.
rue de Seze, 18, Paris, France.

1900   Catalogue produits aseptiques & antiseptiques; supplement de catalogue de pansements; 33 pp; **NYAM; MF/MAH.**

n.d.   Catalogue produits et éponges antiseptiques; 103 pp; **NYAM; MF/MAH.**

LEE, J. ELWOOD, CO.
Conshohocken, Pennsylvania.
Est: 1883; Inc: 1888

1893   Retail Catalogue of Surgical Instrument Specialties, Druggists' Sundries, Antiseptic Dressings, and Absorbant Cotton, for the Trade; **CS; CPP** (Ed/71).

1895   Surgical Instrument Specialties; **CPP** (Ed/71).

1897   Catalogue; **NYAM; MF/MAH.**

Sep. 1900   Catalogue Medicinal and Surgical Plasters; Absorbent Cotton, Antiseptic Dressings, Hospital and Physicians' Supplies, Druggists Sundries . . . Surgical Instrument Specialties, photographs in color of employees at work in various departments; 17th Annual ed.; 136 pp; **NYAM; MF/MAH.**

LEEDOM, CHARLES
1403 Filbert Street, Philadelphia, Pennsylvania.
1894   Nuclein Solution, formula of Dr. John Aulde, History and Scientific Position Source & Preparation, Physiological Properties; 19 pp; **CPP.**
1895   Nuclein Solution; 24 pp; **CPP.**

LEEDS & NORTHRUP CO., THE
259 North Broad Street, Philadelphia, Pennsylvania.
4970 Stanton Ave., Philadelphia 44, PA.
Est: 1899?
Successor to Morris E. Leeds & Co. in 1903
1899   Electro-Therapeutical Catalog Abridged; 19th ed.; 270 pp; **CPP.**
1903   Electrical Testing Instruments; 92 pp; **CPP.**
1914   Electro-Therapeutical Catalog; 192 pp; **CPP.**
n.d.   Electro-Therapeutical Catalog; 192 pp; 32nd ed.; **CPP.**

LEEMING, THOMAS, & CO.
73 Warren Street, New York, New York.
since 1891
1891   Baume Analgesique Bengue Made by Dr. B. Pharmacien de Première Classe, 47 rue Blanche, Paris, France; 4 pp; **CPP.**
1894   Summer Diarrhoea, A Suggestion for Its Prevention, Nestle's Foods; 4 pp; **CPP.**
1934   Calmitol, Dependable Antipruritic; 2 pp; **CPP.**
n.d.   A Cough Loosener Prunol Made by The Lotos Chemical Co., Danbury, Connecticut; 4 pp; **CPP.**
n.d.   Brief Notes on Diabetes and Its Treatment; 4 pp; **CPP.**
n.d.   Notes on the Preparation of Ethyl Chloride Bengue by Dr. Bengue; 6 pp; **CPP.**

LEHN & FINK
128 William Street, New York, New York.
192 Bloomfield Ave., Bloomfield, New Jersey.
Est: 1874
1887   Pamphlet, Neue Apparate und Instrumente zu Galvanokaustik; 5 pp, fragile; **CPP.**
Jan. 1889   Neue Beleuchtungs Apparate mit Zuhilfenahme des elektrischen Lichtes; 31 pp, fragile; **CPP.**
1895   Diphtheria Antitoxin and Other Biological Products; 34 pp; **CPP.**
1890   Chloralamid Schering Hypnotic; 2nd revised ed.; 32 pp; **CPP.**
1890   Chloralamid, by S. V. Clevenger; 11 pp, reprint; **CPP.**
1892   Iron: For Anaemia and Chlorosis; 14 pp; **CPP.**
1892   Chloralamid Schering, The New Hypnotic Discovered by Dr. J. von Mering of Strassburg; 64 pp; **CPP.**
1892   Thiol, An Antiseptic Reducing Agent for Dermatological Use; 23 pp; **CPP.**
1893   Phenocoll Hydrochloride Schering, Antipyretic, Analgesic, Antirheumatic, Nervine, Directions and Precautionary Measures for Gonorrhea Patients, Book of Tear Out Sheets; 2nd ed.; 40 pp; **CPP.**
1893   Chloralamid-Schering; 64 pp; **CPP.**

1893	Salipyrin, Its Use in Medicine, Antipyretic, Anti-neuraligic, Anti-rheumatic, Analgesin; 11 pp; **CPP.**
1895	Diphtheria Antitoxin and Other Biological Products; 34 pp; **CPP.**
ca 1895	Antitoxins, Vaccine Virus & Other Biological Products from the Biological and Vaccinal Department of the New York Pasteur Institute, 1, 3, 5 & 7 West 97th Street, New York; 28 pp; **CPP.**
1898	Papain; 24 pp; **CPP.**
1898	Chloralamid Schering, The New Hypnotic . . .; 52 pp; **CPP.**
1899	Vasogen, by Dr. M. Gallas, Hamburg; 68 pp; **CPP.**
ca 1899	Glandulen, A Specific Organic Remedy, by Dr. Hoffmann; 24 pp; **CPP.**
1900	Vasogen, Preparations and Indications for Their Use by Dr. M. Gallas, Hamburg, U.S. Agents: K-Lehn & Fink; 68 pp; **CPP.**
Jan. 1901	Brochure, Piperazine Water, A True Solvent for Uric Acid; 24 pp; **NYAM; MF/MAH.**
1901	Yohimbin, An Aphrodisiac of Particular Efficacy in Impotency; 19 pp; **CPP.**
1901	Impotentia Virilis, Its Significance and Its Treatment with Yohimbin-Spiegel, a New Aphrodisiac of Great Efficacy; 31 pp; **CPP.**
1902	Purgen; 5 pp; **CPP.**
1902	Purgen; A New Purgative; 16 pp; **CPP.**
ca 1902	Bromvicoll-Gelatine-Dibromo-Taunote; 6 pp foldout; **CPP.**
ca 1902	Bismatose-Bismuth Albuminate 21% Metallic Bismuth; Kalle & Co., Mfr. Biebrich; 14 pp; **CPP.**
1903	The Improvement of General Anaesthesia, the Basis of Schleich's Principle with Special Reference to Anaesthesiology, by Willey Meyer; 29 pp; **CPP.**
1904	The Medicinal Products Introduced by Lehn and Fink, New York, Abstracts from the Literature, Drugs: Lipol, Chloralamid-Schering, Phenocoll-Schering, Vasogin, Papain, Yohimbin, Salipyrin, Resorbin, Bromocoll, Tanocol, Periol, Chloroform as Anschiretz, Bishop's Granular Effervescent Salts and Varalettes, Beiersdorf's Gutte-perche Plastic Mulls, Mercolat Chest Pad, Beiersdorf's Aromatic Chloride-of-Potash Tooth-Paste, Anaesthol, Volesan, Piperozin-Schering, Lycetol; 87 pp; **CPP.**
ca 1904	Euguform-Condensation Product of Guaiacol & Formaldehyde, A New Dusting Powder for Women; 1 pp; **CPP.**
ca 1904	Yohimbin Spiegel, A New Alkaloid; 24 pp; **CPP.**
1906	Bornyval Antispasmodic & Sedative of Particular Efficacy in Functional and Psychic Neuroses; 16 pp; **CPP.**
1907	Taeschners Pertussin; 16 pp; **CPP.**
1907	Pertussin, An Excellent Remedy for Whooping Cough and Other Diseases of the Respiratory Tract; 14 pp; **CPP.**
ca 1907	Taeschners Pertussin; 16 pp; **CPP.**
1909	The Treatment of Ichthyosis, by P. G. Unna; 2 pp; **CPP.**
1911	Yohimbin Spiegel, Its Importance as a Nervorian and Tissue-Builder in Neurathenia, Functional Disturbances and Debility; 31 pp; **CPP.**
1911	Lysol, A Powerful and Reliable Antiseptic & Germicide; 16 pp; **CPP.**
1912	Yohimbin Spiegel; 31 pp; **CPP.**
1912	Ether-Basherville, A New Era in Anesthesia; 16 pp; **CPP.**
Jan. 1, 1926	in *Fortschritte der Medizin*; **CPP.**
n.d.	Eucerin, for Venereal Disease; 4 pp; **CPP.**

n.d. All the Good Points of Salipyrin, the Chemical Combination of Antipyrin & Salicylic Acid Briefly Told for Busy Doctors; 6 pp foldout; **CPP.**

n.d. The Kissinger and Vichy Treatment for Overfitness, by William T. Cathell; 24 pp; **CPP.**

n.d. Telephone Your Doctor, ad for Piperazine Water; 8 pp; **CPP.**

n.d. Schering's Piperazine Water; 4 pp; **CPP.**

n.d. Elixir Chloralamid-Schering, the Producer of Physiological Sleep; 15 pp; **CPP.**

LEIBE, H. L., CO.
276 New Jersey Railroad Ave., Newark, New Jersey.

1922 Oxfords and Onepiece Eyeglass Mountings in Gold, Silver and Allurium; 8 pp; **URRR** (L-249).

LEITER, JOSEF
Alserstrasse 16, frueher Hauptstrasse 150, Wien, Austria.

1862 Atlas und Preis-verzeichniss Chirurgie Intrumente und physikalische Apparate fuer Aerzte; 92 pp, 6 pp supplement describing Apparate zur Inhalation von Medicamenten in fluessiger und Dampfform von Jos. Leiter; **NLM** (W26 L 533).

1864 Ein nach dem Prinzipe von E. Siegle neukonstruierter Fluessigkeits-Zerstauber; **CPP.**

1867 Braum's Cephtrite, RCS Loan Coll no. 112; **RCSL.**

Mariannengasse 11, Wien IX, Austria.

1870 Catalog chirurgischer Instrumente, physikalischer Apparate, Bandagen, orthopaedischer Maschinen und kuenstlicher Extremitäten; 144 pp, 32 tafels; **NLM** (W26 L 533); **ZUR; BLEL; CS.**

1876 Catalog chirurgischer Instrumente, physikalischer Apparate, fuer Electrotherapie, Electrolyse und Galvanokaustic von Bandagen, orthopaedischen Maschinen und kuenstlichen Extremitaeten; 176 pp; **ZUR.**

1880 Elektro-endoskopische Instrumente, Beschreibung und Instruction zur Handhabung der von Dr. M. Nitze und J. Leiter Construirten Instrumente und Apparate zur direckten Beleuchtung menschlicher Koerperhöhlen durch electrisches Gluehlicht von Josef Leiter; 65 pp; **MAH** (RD 73. E 6L5).

Bezirk Alsergrund, Mariannengasse, Nr. 11, Wien, Austria.

1887 Catalog chirurgischer Instrumente, Bandagen, orthopaedischer Maschinen, kuenstlicher Extremitäten . . .; 138 pp; **NLM** (W26 1 533).

1887 Neue Apparate und Instrumente zu Galvanokaustik; 5 pp pamphlet; **CPP.**

Jan. 1889 Neue Beleuchtungs-Apparate mit Zuhilfenahme des electrischen Lichtes; 31 pp; **CPP.**

LEITZ, ERNST
Wetzlar, Germany.
Est: by Kellner in 1849

1877 Microscopes and Microscopical Accessories; 94 pp; **URRR.**

1891 Preisverzeichniss Mikroskope; 47 pp; **NYAM; MF/MAH.**

1894 Cataloge 35, Microscopes and Accessory Apparatus, 59 pp; **AFMM; CTY/B** (Uai L537); **URRR.**

Factory: Wetzlar, Germany.
Branch: 411 W. 59th Street, New York, New York.

1894   Microscopes and Accessory Apparatus; 59 pp; **NYAM; MF/MAH; MRLB.**

1896   Microscopes and Microscopical Apparatus, no. 36; 63 pp; **NYAM; MF/MAH; URRR.**

July 1899   Die mikrophotographischen Apparate der optischen Werkstätte; 2nd ed.; **MAH** (QH207 E71).

1899   Microscopes and Accessory Apparatus, no. 39; 99 pp; **NYAM; MF/MAH.**

659 W. Congress Street, Chicago, Illinois.

ca 1897   Catalog of Bacteriological Apparatus, Laboratory Supplies and Accessories; 98 pp; **CPP; MUM.**

1901   Microscopes and Accessory Apparatus, no. 39; 100 pp; **NYAM; MF/MAH; URRR; MRLB.**

1903   Microscopes and Accessory Apparatus, no. 40; 104 pp; **AFMM; HDM; URRR.**

1904   Hints on the Use of the Microscope; 16 pp; **URRR.**

1905   Hints on the Use of the Microscopes Made by Ernst Leitz; **AFMM.**

1906   Microscopes; 5 pp; **URRR.**

1906   Microscopes et appareils accessoires; no. 42; 118 pp, index; **MAH** (C 681.4085 L 25).

1907   Microscopes and Accessory Apparatus, no. 42; 116 pp; **NYAM; MF/MAH; URRR.**

May 1907   Catalog Microtomes; 38 pp; **NYAM; MF/MAH; URRR.**

ca 1908   Leaflet Reflecting Condenser for Observing Living Bacteria, etc., Under Dark Ground Illumination; 6 pp; **NYAM; MF/MAH.**

July 1908   Catalog Projection and Drawing Apparatus; 29 pp; **NYAM; MF/MAH.**

Oct. 1909   Catalog Microscopes; 2 pp; second copy 79 pp; **NYAM; MF/MAH; URRR.**

1909   Microscopes and Accessories; Cat 43 A; 77 pp; **MAH** (C 681.4085 L25 ma); **AFMM.**

Oct. 1909   Catalog Microscopes, no. 43 C; 16 pp; **NYAM; MF/MAH; URRR.**

1909?   Microscope Accessories, no. 43 D; 36 pp; **HDM.**

1909?   Stand II B Microscope; 7 pp; **URRR.**

1910   Price List of Microscopic Stains and Reagents; 20 pp; **URRR.**

post 1910   Catalog Reflecting Condensers for Dark Ground Illumination and Ultra-Microscopic Observations; 14 pp; **NYAM; MF/MAH; URRR.**

Jan. 1911   Catalog Photo-Micrographic Apparatus; no. 436; 28 pp, 12 plates; **NYAM; MF/MAH.**

30 East 18th Street, New York, New York.

324 Dearborn Street, Chicago, Illinois.

9 Oxford Street, London, England.

Luisenstrasse 45, Berlin N.W., Germany.

Neue Mainzerstrasse 24, Frankfurt am Main, Germany.

Woskressenskill, St. Petersburg, Russia.

May 1911   Catalog Microtomes, no. 44 F, 30 pp; **NYAM; MF/MAH; URRR; MRLB.**

1911   Photomicrographic Apparatus, no. 43 G; 28 pp; **MAH** (C 681.4085L); **AFMM.**

1911   Microscope Accessories; 34 pp; **URRR.**

1911   Leitz Pocket Price List; 31 pp; **URRR.**

30 East 18th Street, New York, New York.

360 Ogden Avenue, Chicago, Illinois.

1912   Microscopes; 78 pp; **URRR; MRLB.**

1913   Catalog, Microscope Accessories, no. 44 D; 46 pp; **MAH** (C 681.4085 L); **URRR.**

Jan. 1913   Projection and Projection Drawing Apparatus, no. 44 H; 38 pp; **NYAM; MF/MAH.**

1913   Catalog of Bacteriological Incubators, Sterilizers and Accessories; 58 pp; **URRR.**

1913   Hayen-Sahli Haemacytometer; 13 pp; **URRR.**

n.d.   Leaflet, Large Traveling Microscope; 1 pp; **NYAM; MF/MAH.**

Agents: Ogilon & Co., 18 Bloomsbury Square, London W.C. 1, England.

July 1923   Leitz Dissecting and Simple-lens Microscopes and Magnifiers; no. 47 C; 28 pp, inserts including 1924; **WMScM.**

1923   Pamphlet, Universal Photographic Apparatus for Micro and Macro Moving Pictures; 8 pp; **MAH** (C 681.4085 L); **AFMM.**

1924   Brochure, Photo-Micrographic Apparatus; no. 48 G; 27 pp; **AFMM.**

1924   Mon-Objective-Binocular Microscope LB; pp 1 and 2 from Pamphlet no. 1047; **AFMM.**

ca 1924   Catalogue III, A Microscopes, Objectives and Eyepieces, etc., with Leitz pamphlets inserted and bound within catalog; 64 pp; **MAH** (C 680.4085 L).

1925   Brochure, Small Epidiascopes, Vc and Vd; 7 pp; **AFMM.**

1925   Brochure, Micro-Projection Equipment with Special Collimator of Great Light Transmitting Power; 11 pp; **AFMM.**

1925   Brochure, Automatically Regulating Electrically Heated Stage as Devised by Walton; 4 pp; **AFMM.**

Aug. 1925   Catalog of Microtomes, no. 50 F; 39 pp; **MAH** (C 681.4085 M).

1925   Catalog IIB, Petrographical Microscopes of New Design With Wide Tube for Eyepieces with Enlarged Field, Petrographical Projection and Demonstration Apparatus; 36 pp; **MAH** (C 680.4085 L).

1924–25?   Brochure, Binocular Stereo Magnifiers; 12 pp; **AFMM.**

1925   Catalogue of Microscopes and Accessories Dissection Microscopes, no. IV-A; 161 pp; **MAH** (C681.4085 L247e); **AFMM.**

1925   Brochure, Micro Camera Attachment; 4 pp; **AFMM.**

60 East Tenth Street, New York, New York.

ca 1925   Brochure, Binocular Stereo Magnifiers; 15 pp; **AFMM.**

1926   Catalog of Microscopes, Microtomes and Accessories . . . for Educational Institutions; 59 pp; separate price list; **AFMM.**

1926   Catalog of Polarising Microscopes, IIIB; 66 pp, separate price list dated July 1929; **MAH** (C 681.4085 L 247).

1926   Catalog M of Microscopes, Microtomes and Accessories; Photo-Micrographic and Projection Apparatus, Colorimeters and Binocular Field Glasses for Educational Institutions; 60 pp; **MAH** (C 681.4085 L 247 mb).

Feb. 1927   Anleitung zum Gebrauch des Mikrotomes sowie zur Vorbehandlung der Objecte und zur Nachbehandlung der Schnitte, Liste 2221, 4th Auflage; 43 pp; **ZUR.**

1927   Pamphlet, List no. 2267, ORE Microscope MOP; 4 pp; **MAH.**

1927   Supplement Pamphlet no. 1099 to Catalog IIIB, Polarising Microscopes and Accessories; 8 pp; **MAH.**

1928   Pamphlet, Universal Chemical Microscope, Model CHEM, no. 1129; 16 pp; **MAH; AFMM.**

Aug. 1928   Catalog, Ore Microscope MOP; 4 pp; **CTY/B** (Uai L 537).
1928   Brochure, Wide Field Binocular Microscope, BSM; 8 pp; **AFMM**.
1928   Brochure, Binocular Microscope, Greenough Pattern; **AFMM**.
1929   Integrations-Tisch; 1 pp illustrated, Gebrauchsanweisung zum Integrations-Tisch; **MAH** (C 681.4085 L).
1929   Catalog of Biological, Polarising, Metallographic, Universal, Binocular, Special Models, etc.; 286 pp, price list dated 27 Dec. 1933; **MAH** (C 681.4085 L 247 mb).
1929   Brochure, Dissecting and Simple-Lens Microscopes and Magnifiers; 15 pp; **AFMM**.
1930   Brochure, Micrometer Eyepieces; 4 pp; **AFMM**.
July 1930   Catalog, Leitz Monochromator and Spectroscopes; 12 pp; **CTY/B** (Uai L 537).
1930   Brochure, Vertical Illuminators; 11 pp; **AFMM**.

304 Hudson Street, (New York).
1930   Brochure, Monochromator and Spectroscopes; 12 pp; **AFMM**.
ca 1930   Catalog, Metallographic Microscopes, Accessories and Grinding and Polishing Machines, 1B; 48 pp; **MAH**.
ca 1930   Pamphlet, Folder of Photomicrographs Showing Results Obtained With the Leitz Micro-Metallograph, no. 1042; 12 pp; **MAH**.
1931   Brochure Ultropaque Microscope Equipment; 12 pp; **AFMM; MAH** (C681.4085 L247).
1937   Brochure Simplified Metallographic Microscope MM, with Photomicrographic Camera; 15 pp; **AFMM**.
n.d.   Catalog Microscopes, Microtomes and Accessories, Photo-Micrographic and Projection Apparatus; Colorimeters and Binocular Field Glasses for Educational Institutions, no. M; 59 pp; **CTY/B** (Uai L 537).

730 Fifth Avenue, New York, New York.
Jan. 1938   Microscopes; 132 pp; **NYAM**.
1938   The Microscope and Its Application; **AFMM**.
1938   Catalog Mikroskopy Generalny reprezentant na Polske: C. Cegielske, Poznan-solacz ul Podolska 16/17; Warszawa; **AFMM**.
n.d.   Catalog 43 D, Microscope and Accessories; **HDM**.
n.d.   Appliances for Haematology, no. 43 E; 14 pp; **URRR**.
n.d.   Leaflet, Case of Microscope Accessories; 1 pp; **NYAM; MF/MAH**.
n.d.   Physicians Standard Instruments for Clinical Diagnosis; 8 pp; **URRR**.
n.d.   Price List of Microtome Knives; 8 pp; **URRR**.
n.d.   The Base Sledge Microtome; 4 pp; **URRR**.

LENNOX CHEMICAL CO.
1201-1215 East 55th Street, Cleveland, Ohio.
Est: 1881
See: DYNHAM-REIFEL CO., **MAH**.
ca 1915   Brochure, Compressed Gasss for Medicinal Use; 40 pp; **MAH** (C 617. 96085).

LENOIR, G. A.
Kaerntnerstrasse am Glacis 1019, Vienna, Austria.
post 1854   Katalog der Fabrik & Handlung chemischer, pharmaceutischer, physikalischer, meterologischer, etc.; 264 pp; **CTY/B** (Uai L 548).
Jan. 1, 1861   Katalog, Geraethscaften und Apparate; 32 pp; **NYAM; MF/MAH**.

LENTZ, CHARLES
27 S. 10th Street, Philadelphia, Pa.
Est: 1866

    1881   Illustrated Catalogue and Price List of Surgical Instruments and Appliances; 1st ed.; 73 pp; **CPP; MUM** (Ed 20 1881).

LENTZ, CHARLES, AND SONS
18 N. Eleventh Street, Philadelphia, Pennsylvania.
Est: 1866; Inc: 1906

    1881   Illustrated Catalog and Price List of Surgical Instruments, Hospital Supplies, Orthopedic Apparatuses, Trusses, etc.; **CPP** (Ed/20f).

1892, 1901, 1911   same as above.

    1885   Illustrated Catalogue and Price List of Surgical Instruments; 3rd ed.; 256 pp; **MAH** (C 610.78085 L); **AFMM; ZUR.**

    1890   New Instrument Catalogue; 48 pp; **WOC.**

    1890?   Illustrated Catalogue and Price List of Surgical Instruments; 490 pp; **AFMM.**

18 & 20 N. 11th Street, Philadelphia.

    1892   Illustrated Catalogue and Price List of Surgical Instruments, Orthopaedical Apparatus, Trusses, etc., Fine Microscopes, Medical Batteries, Physicians' and Hospital Supplies; 4th ed.; 500 pp; **MUM** (Ed 20c).

    1899   Special Agents for Bausch and Lomb Optical Co., Catalog of Microscopes and Accessories, Microtomes, Bacteriological Apparatus, Laboratory Supplies and Instruments for Clinical Diagnosis; 5th ed.; date on cover 1816; 133 pp; **AFMM.**

    1901   Illustrated Catalogue and Price list of Surgical Instruments, Orthopaedical Apparatus, Trusses, etc., Fine Microscopes, Medical Batteries, Physicians' and Hospital Supplies; 6th ed.; 598 pp; **MUM** (Ed 20e); **NLM** (W26 L574).

    1911   Illustrated Catalogue and Price List of Surgical Instruments, Orthopaedical Apparatus, Trusses, etc., Fine Microscopes, Medical Batteries, Physicians' and Hospital Supplies; 7th ed.; 610 pp; **MAH; CS; UVHSL** (RD 76. L4); **VM; MUM** (Ed 20f).

Lentz Bldg., 31, 33, 35 S. 17th Street, Philadelphia.

    1920   Lentz Noco Steel for the Medical Profession; 12 pp; **MAH.**

    1921   Abridged Illustrated Catalogue of Surgical & Scientific Instruments, Electro-Therapeutic & X-Ray Apparatus, Orthopedic Appliances; 9th ed.; 108 pp; **CPP; MUM** (Ed 114 1921 +).

    1922   Instrument Catalogue; 458 pp; **WOC.**

    1923   Illustrated Catalogue of Surgical & Scientific Instruments, Physicians' and Hospital Supplies, Electro-Therapeutic & X-Ray Apparatus, Orthopedic Appliances; 8th ed.; 416 pp; **CPP; HML.**

    1929–30   Illustrated Catalogue of Surgical & Scientific Instruments, Electro-Therapeutic, Orthopedic Appliances; 10th ed.; 458 pp; **MUM.**

    n.d.   The Arnold Steam Sterilzer; 17 pp; **CPP.**

    n.d.   Lentz's Improved Change-Gear Centrifuge; 15 pp; **CPP.**

LENZ & LOSSAU
623 Seventh Street, NW, Washington, D.C.

    n.d.   Wells' Trocar and Canula with Rasp, Surgical Instruments, Trusses, Orthopedic Apparatuses; 2 pp; **CPP.**

LÉPINE, PH.
14 Place de Terreaux, Lyon, France.
>1899 Catalogue, général, instruments pour toutes les opérations, chirurgicules; 144 pp; **UCSF.**

LEPLANQUAIS
76 rue du Temple, Paris, France.
>1869? Bandages, appareils, orthopédiques & autres instruments anatomiques; 69 pp, index pp 65-69, 22 plates; **RCSL.**
>
>n.d. Catalogue de bandages, appareils, orthopédiques, instruments de chirurgie, etc.; 44 pp, incomplete; **AFMM.**
>
>n.d. Instruments anatomiques, bound with 1865-66 Charriere and 1867 Mathieu; 63 pp, incomplete, fragile; **AFMM.**

LEPPIN & MASCHE
Alte Jacob-Strasse No. 83, Berlin, Germany.
>1885 Catalog Preis-Verzeichniss ueber physikalische Apparate, cover indicates they also make medical/surgical equipment; 96 pp; **CTY/B** (Uai L 558).

Brueder-Strasse 13, Berlin, Germany.
>n.d. Verzeichniss neu eingefuehrter Apparate und Utensilien fuer Chemie, Physik, etc.; 8 pp; **CTY/B** (Uai L 558).

LE PRINCE, M.
24 rue Singer, Paris, France.
>1896 Contribution to the Clinical Therapeutics of Cascarine by Doctor Tison; 2nd ed.; 16 pp; **CPP.**

LEREBOURS ET SECRETAN
Place de Pont-Neuf 13, Paris, France.
>1853 Catalogue et Prix des instruments d'optique, de physique, de chimie, de mathématiques, d'astronomie et de marine; 244 pp; **NYAM; MF/MAH.**
>
>n.d. Catalogue et Prix des instruments d'optique, de physique, de mathématiques, d'astronomie et de marine; **CTY/B** (Uai L 537).

LESLIE, A. M., & CO.
319 North Fifth Street, St. Louis, Missouri.
Est: 1856
>1870 Dr. E. A. Clark's Fracture Apparatuses, Manufactured and Sold by A. M. Leslie & Co.; 16 pp; **MAH** (22183).
>
>1874 Illustrated Catalogue of Surgical Instruments and Appliances, Orthopedic Apparatus, Trusses, Elastic Hose, Batteries, Saddle Bags and All Surgical Appliances; 104 pp; **AFMM.**
>
>1875 A Description of New Instruments for Making Examinations and Application to the Cavities of the Nose, Throat and Ear . . .; 3rd ed. revised by Thomas F. Rumbold; 24 pp; **CPP.**
>
>1875 Nose, Throat, and Ear Instruments, and Remarks by Thomas F. Rumbold; 24 pp; **CPP.**
>
>ca 1875 Illustrated Catalog of Dental Instruments, Furniture, Apparatus, Material and All Appliances for Dental Practice; 104 pp; **HML.**
>
>1879 Illustrated Catalog of Dental Instruments, Furniture, Apparatus, Materials and All Appliances for Dental Practice; 200 pp; **MAH** (C 617.6085 L); **ADA** (D 881 L 56).

1884   Illustrated Catalog of Surgical Instruments and Appliances . . .; 320 pp; **NYAM.**

1890   Illustrated Catalog of Surgical Instruments and Appliances . . .; viii, 374 pp; **NWUCML** (617.91 L56 in shelf list).

LEUNE ETABLISSEMENTS
28 rue du Cardinal Lemoine, Paris, France.
Est: 1785

1927   Catalogue des instruments de chirurgie, verrière pour dentiste, meubles et appareils pour hôpitaux, salles d'operations, pharmacies, laboratoires de cliniques, etc; 160 pp; **AFMM.**

LEVY, DAVID B., INC.
96 Warren Street, New York, New York.
Oct. 1916   Electro-Colloidal Iodine Therapy, vol 1, no. 4; House Organ, 100,000 copies with this issue; **CPP.**

LEVY, D. P.
New York, New York.
May 1926   Sterling Surgical Products; **CPP** (Ed/76).

LEWIS, BAILIE & CO.
Dec. 1892   *Southwestern Drug Current*, A Monthly Journal of Great Interest to Druggists and Physicians; 58 pp; **CPP.**

LEWIS, H. K., & CO.
136 Gower Street and 24 Gower Place, London W C 1.
n.d.   Anatomical Wall Charts, by G. H. Michel; 4 pp; **CPP.**

LEYDEN
See: DAVIS AND LEYDEN; **CPP.**

LICHTENBERGER
Strassburg, Germany.
n.d.   Farge's Mericourte in Nouvelle description de Strassburg of 1838 mentions Lichtenberger as outstanding instrument maker, WHM amputation set labelled Chirurgie militaire & D. no. 12 on front/lock plate, Lichtenberger was President of Corporation of Cutlers of St. M. 1789, Jean Daniel Lichtenberger was promoted to Master Cutler in 1784; **RCSL.**

LIEBEL-FLARSHEIM CO.
303 West Third Street, Cincinnati 2, Ohio.
See: GENERAL ELECTRIC X-RAY CORP. Publication 7B-460A, 1946; **ACR/MAH.**
410-416 Home Street, Cincinnati, Ohio.
ca 1930   Pamphlet, Dr. H. H. Young's Urological X-Ray Table; 3 pp; **ACR/MAH; MAH.**

ca 1931   Electro-Coagulation; 61 pp; **BLEL.**

1930s   Brochure, Kymograph and Kymoscope; 2 pp; **ACR/MAH.**

LIEBER, H., & CO.
1 Platt Street, New York, New York.
n.d.   Therapagen, the Antiseptic Without an Equal; 12 pp; **CPP.**

LIEBMANN'S, S., & SONS
36 Forest Street, Brooklyn, New York.
n.d.   Teutonic-Substitute for Solid Food; 16 pp; **CPP.**

LIFE SAVING DEVICES CO.
180 North Market Street, Chicago, Illinois.
    ca 1910   Directions for Using the Lungmotor, patented but no patent numbers provided; 6 pp foldout; **MAH** (C 617. 17085).
    1916   Mechanical Respiration; 36 pp; **CPP.**
565 Washington Boulevard, Chicago, Illinois.
1009 Times Building, New York, New York.
    n.d.   The Lungmotor Infant Model for Use of Obstetricians; 2 pp; **CPP.**
1008 Times Building, New York, New York.
53 Devonshire Street, Boston, Massachusetts.
    ca 1915   Booklet Mechanical Respiration, Historical, Physiological, Technical, Treating of Drowning, Electric Shock, Gas Poisoning, Hospital Cases, Asphyxia-Neonatorum, etc.; 36 pp; **MAH** (C 617.17085).
    n.d.   Catalogue, The Lungmotor; 6 pp, illustrations; **MAH** (C 617.17085).

LILLY, ELI, & CO.
740 S. Alabama St., Indianapolis, Indiana.
Est: 1876
    July 1923   Catalog, Pharmaceutical and Biological, no. 42; 228 pp, 3 pp insert; **NYAM; MF/MAH.**
    1938   Diabetes Mellitus; 80 pp; **CPP.**

LIMEBURNER, J. E., & CO.
1720 Chestnut Street, Philadelphia, Pennsylvania.
factory: 313-15 Vine Street.
    1910   Catalog of Ophthalmological Instruments; 42 pp; **URRR** L-150).
    n.d.   Catalog of Ophthalmological Instruments; 37 pp; **URRR** (L-151).
    n.d.   Catalog of Ophthalmological Instruments; 43 pp; **CPP.**
    n.d.   Catalog of Ophthalmological Instruments; 36 pp; **CPP.**
    n.d.   Catalog of Ophthalmological Instruments; 37 pp; **CPP.**
    n.d.   Catalog of Standard Optical Instruments, Oculists' Office Fittings and Accessories; 11 pp; **CPP.**
1407 Chestnut Street.
    n.d.   A Special at a Special Price; 4 pp; **CPP.**

LINCOLN, C. J., CO.
Little Rock, Arkansas.
    1892   General Price Current; 96 pp; **CPP.**

LINCOLN DENTAL MANUFACTURING CO.
1600 Chestnut Street, Philadelphia, Pennsylvania.
    n.d.   Catalog of Surgical, Orthopaedical Instruments and Apparatus, and Hospital Supplies; 115 pp; **BRML.**

LINCOLN & LUCHESI
143 & 145 E. 23rd Street, New York.
Formerly with J. Reynder and Co.
    L. 19 c   Fine Surgical and Orthopaedical Instruments, Trusses, Abdominal Supporters, Crutches, Suspensories, Elastic Stockings and Hospital Supplies; 115 pp; **MAH** (22534).
    L. 19 c   Catalogs of surgical and orthopedic instruments and apparautus; **NLM** (W26 L741c).

LINDEMANN, MAX
Rathenow, Prussia.
    n.d.   No cover, Eyeglasses; 24 pp; **URRR** (L-148).

LINDSAY LABORATORIES
344 Livingston Street, Brooklyn, New York.
    n.d.   Everything for the Sick; 16 pp; **CPP.**

LINDSTAEDT, FR.
Markstrasse 17 a, Bremen.
Dechenstrasse, Eckhausden.
    1882   Illustrirter Catalog chirurgischer Instrumente, Bandagen, orthopädischer
        Maschinen, kuenstlicher Glieder, galvanocaustischer und
        electrotherapeutischer Apparate, sowie saemmtlicher gebrauchlichen
        Artikel zur Krankenpflege; 189 pp, index viii pp; **NYAM** (S 125);
        fragile, in binder; **MF/MAH.**

LION OPTICAL CO., THE
Vine and Eighth Streets, Cincinnati, Ohio.
Wholesale Opticians
    Jan. 1923   *The Lion*, published monthly for the Optometrist, Optician, and Oculist,
        Vol. IV, no. 1; **AO.**

LIPOWSKY, EDUARD
Haupstrasse No. 16, Heidelberg, Germany.
Successor to von Friedrich Fischer & Cie
    1870-3   Des appareil de comfort et ustensiles (sic) sanitaires. Description of plates
        only, bound with Catalog saemmtlicher Apparate und Geraethschaften
        zu Heilzwecken; 32 pp, 39 tafel; **NLM** (W26 L 764).

LIT BROTHERS
Market & 8th Streets, Philadelphia, Pennsylvania.
Filbert and 7th Streets, Philadelphia, Pennsylvania.
Market & 9th Streets, Philadelphia 5, Penn.
Est: 1891; Inc: in New Jersey, dissolved Dec. 5, 1905
    n.d.   Physicians' and Hospital Supplies; 11 foldout; **CPP.**

LIVERNOIS, J. E., LIMITEE
Quebec, Canada.
    1922-23   Extrait du catalogue de J. E. Livernois; 18th ed.; 80 pp; **UTP.**

LLOYD BROTHERS
Cincinnati, Ohio.
    1909   Dose Book of Specific Medicines; **CPP.**
    May 1, 1914   A Condensed Pocket Booklet on Specific Medicine and Hypodermic
        Subculocyels; 64 pp; **CPP.**
    Mar. 1, 1914   Glyconda for Diarrhea and Bowel Troubles; 24 pp; introduced 1908; **CPP.**
    Mar. 1, 1914   Libradol, An External Remedy for Pain, introduced 1900; 32 pp; **CPP.**
    1921   Complete Dose Book of Fine Medicinal Specialties; 304 pp; **CPP.**
    Sep. 1921   Condensed Price List of Select Pharmaceutical Preparations; 72 pp; **CPP.**
    n.d.   Libradol, A Medicated Plasma for External Use, Relieves Pain and
        Congestion Without the Internal Administration of Opiates or Powerful
        Drugs; 16 pp; **CPP.**
    n.d.   Pamphlet, Genuine Specific Medicine; See Acc. no. 308730.05; **MAH.**

LLOYD, J. U.
    1892   Elixirs and Flavoring Extracts, their History, Formulae and Methods of
        Preparations; 191 pp, index pp 187-91; **MAH** (U 6152).

LOCHHEAD LABORATORY INC.
109 West 42nd St., New York, New York.
36 West Randolph Street, Chicago, Illinois.
120 Boylston Street, Boston, Massachusetts.
Est: 1907
n.d.   Brochure, Ceramic Dentistry; 9 pp; **NYAM; MF/MAH.**
n.d.   Catalog, Ceramic Dentistry; 39 pp; **NYAM; MF/MAH.**

LOCKWOOD, W. A.
618 Twelfth Street, N.W., Washington, D.C.
1901   Catalog, Dental Furniture, Instruments, and Material; 675 pp; **MAH.**

LOEWENSTEIN, LOUIS & H.
8 Sophia Strasse, (Berlin).
See: AMERICAN AGEMA CORP. 1927; **NYAM.**
L. 19 c   Illustrirer Preis-Courant der Fabrik chirurgischer Hartgummi und
Neusilber-instrumente, stamped E. Abramsky, 6 Warden's Place,
Clerkenwell Close, London, E. C.; 76 pp; **WMScM.**
Grosse Hamburgerstrasse 3, Berlin N., Germany.
n.d.   Katalog chirurgischer Instrumente; 51 pp; **NYAM; MF/MAH.**

LOEWY, HEINRICH
Dorotheen Strasse 92, Berlin N.W., Germany.
Est: 1859
1888   Special-Catalog fuer Bruchbaender ueber Bandagen, Verfertiger
chirurgisch-medicinischer Instrumente und Apparate; 43 pp; **NLM** (W
26 1 827s).

LOLLINI
Bologna, Italy.
n.d.   Exhibited Paris, 1867, RCS Loan Coll. no. 45-48, Razzoli's forceps, no.
103 stamped Fratelli Lollini; **RCSL.**

LONDON OPTICAL CO.
344-54 Gray's Inn Rd., King's Cross, London W. C.
n.d.   The Linfield Kerascope; 4 pp; **URRR** (L-70).

LONG, ADOLPH, CO.
1321 Arch Street, Philadelphia, Pennsylvania.
n.d.   The Philadelphia Fountain Cuspidor, Makers of High Grade Surgical
Instruments; 7 pp; **CPP.**

LONGDON, F., & CO., LTD.
Derby, England.
Est: 1823
Jan. 1927   Price List of Surgical Bandages; 20 pp; **WMScM.**
n.d.   Manufacturers of Elastic Hosiery, Abdominal Belts for Post Operations,
General Support, etc., Elastic Band Trusses, Suspensory Bandages,
Shoulder Straps; 62 pp, insert in May 1947 cover, 4 price lists;
WMScM.
n.d.   Illustrated Catalog; 40 pp; **WMScM.**

LOOMIS, L. J., & CO., INC.
17 West 60th Street, New York, New York.

ca 1926   Brochure describing The Janes Apparatus for Blood Transfusion Devised by Martin Lewis Janes, M.D.; **AFMM**.

LOOMIS-MANNING FILTER CO.
402 Chestnut Street, Philadelphia, Pennsylvania.
Loomis-Manning Filter Distribution Co.
Inc: in New Jersey, cancelled Jan. 26, 1915
    ca 1897   Loomis Filters; 40 pp; **CPP**.
    n.d.   Pamphlet, The Use of Filters; 21 pp; **NYAM; MF/MAH**.

LORD ELECTRIC CO.
81 Milk Street, Boston, Massachusetts.
    Sep. 1901   The Harvard Physiological Apparatus Made or Assembled by the Mechanics of the Harvard Laboratory of Physiology under the Direction of Prof. W. T. Porter, Catalog no. 7; 51 pp; **CPP**.

LORD, STOUTENBURGH & CO.
Nos. 72 & 74 Wabash Avenue, Chicago, Illinois.
    1881   Prices Current; Drugs & Druggists' Sundries, Chemicals, Proprietary Medicines, Paints, Oils, Glass, etc., etc.; 308 pp; **ABD**.

LORENZ, P. C.
354 Second Avenue, New York, New York.
    1923   Illustrated Catalog of Surgical Instruments, Hospital Furniture, Physicians' Equipment and Sickroom Supplies; 416 pp; **NYAM**.
    n.d.   Surgical Instruments and Hospital Supplies; 16 pp; **NYAM**.

LOUIS, O. T., CO.
59 Fifth Ave., New York, New York.
    n.d.   Catalog and Price List, Microscopical, Botanical and Entomological Supplies; 24 pp; **URRR** (L-149).

LOUIS, S.
See: WEST, WILLIAM; 1886; **MAH**.

LOWRES OPTICAL MFG. CO.
11-15 East Runyon St., Newark, N.J.
New Jersey Optical Co.
name changed Mar. 31, 1915
    n.d.   Eyeglasses; 32 pp; **URRR** (L-71).

LOWRY, H. S., D. D. S.
    Feb. 9, 1897   Lowry's System of Crown and Bridge Work; 16 pp; **NYAM; MF/MAH**.

LUCHESI
See: LINCOLN AND LUCHESI; **NLM**.

LÜER, MAISON
104 Boulevard St. Germain, Paris, France.
6 rue Antoine-Dubois, Paris, France.
Successor and Gendre H. Wulfing-Luer
Est: 1837
    1878   F. & Dr. W. Wulfing Lüer instruments de chirurgie et d'appareils de médicine, catalogue spécial illustré des instruments d'oto-rhin-laryngologie tracheo-broncho-oesphagosopie; 100 pp; **WMScM**.

1878   Chirurgie, médicine, hygiène et sciences, prix-courant de A. Lüer; 99 pp; **UCSF.**

1888   Catalogue, Général illustré des instruments de chirurgie, médicine; 188 pp, incomplete? fragile in 3-ring binder; **AFMM.**

1893   Catalogue, Appareils & instruments de chirurgie, partie ophtalmologique; 64 pp, index pp 63-64; **NYAM; MF/MAH.**

Aug. 1, 1894   Catalogue, Instruments pour les maladies des oreilles, du nez, de la bouche et de la gorge; 56 pp; **NYAM; MF/MAH.**

1896   Catalogue d'instruments de chirurgie; 167 pp; **UCSF.**

1901   Catalogue, Spécial illustré de 1489 figures ophtalmologie; **CPP** (Ed/11).

1904   Catalogue, Chirurgie, médecine, hygiène et sciences, Instruments de chirurgie; 328 pp; **NYAM; MF/MAH; BLEL.**

ca 1906   Fabrique d'instruments de chirurgie et d'appareils de médicine; 303 pp; **ZUR.**

1909   Catalogue, Special illustré des instruments d'ophtalmologie; 303 pp, inserts; **URRR** (L-36); **MUM.**

1922?   Catalogue, Special illustré des instruments d'oto-rhino-laryngologie, tracheo-broncho-oesophagoscopie; 507 pp; **TMHM.**

July 1922   Supplement A, Instruments d'oto-rhino-laryngologie, tracheo-broncho-oesophagoscopie; 96 pp, 8 pp price list; **NYAM; MF/MAH; TMHM.**

1926   Catalogue, Special illustré d'instruments pour sutures et pansements; **JHIHM** (RD 76.L 948).

1927   Catalogue, Special illustré d'instruments pour urologie; 181 pp; **JHIHM** (RD 76.L 94).

n.d.   Catalogue, Instruments de chirurgie; 3 pp; **NYAM; MF/MAH.**

n.d.   The Tachytoscope of Dr. Varela Santos of Santiago; 16 pp, in Spanish; **URRR** (L-359).

LUFKIN RULE CO.
1730 Hess St., Saginaw, Michigan.
Est: 1883

n.d.   RCS D. 40 palate measure; **RCSL.**

LUHME, J. F., & CO.
39 Landhausgasse, Vienna, Austria.
Kur-Strasse No. 51, Berlin, Germany.
Est: 1825

See: DR. HERMAN ROHRBECK; **AFMM; CTY/B** (Uai L 968).

1849   Catalog Preis-Verzeichniss chemischer, pharmaceutischer, physicalischer, meteorologischer, mineralogischer, geognostischer, etc, etc., Instrumente, Geraethschaften und Apparate; 108 pp; **CTY/B** (Uai L 968).

Pantheon Building, 343 Broadway, New York, New York.

1855   Catalogue of Scientific Apparatus and Instruments, claims to have best collection of chemical apparatus in the U.S. in variety, quality and cheapness, was in Berlin for past 31 years; 36 pp; **CTY/B** (Uai L968).

Neue Wieden Schmidt-Gasse, Wien.

1856   Preis-Verzeichniss chemischer, pharmaceutischer, physicalischer, meteorologischer, mineralogischer, medicinisch-chirurgischer Instrumente, Geraethschaften, und Apparate von W. J. Rohrbeck; 187 pp; **CTY/B** (Uai L 968).

556 Broadway, New York, New York.

1857 General Descriptive Catalog of Chemical and Philosophical Apparatus; 187 pp; **CTY/B** (Uai L 968).

1861 Nachtrag und Preis-veraenderungen zum Preis-Verzeichniss chemischer, pharmaceutischer und physikalischer Apparate, Instrumente, Geraethschaften, etc. von W. J. Rohrbeck; 56 pp; **CTY/B** (Uai R 6361).

n.d. Catalogue and Preis-Verzeichniss ueber Glasgefaesse fuer naturwissenschaftliche Museen Sammlungen Kliniken, etc.; **CTY/B** (Uai R636).

No. 9 Lafayette Place, near 8th St., New York, New York, crossed out, changed to 4 Murray St.

1868 List of Chemical Preparations, Pure Reagents, Minerals, etc.; 28 pp; **CTY/B** (Uai L 968).

1869 General Descriptive Catalog; 159 pp; **CTY/B** (Uai L 968)

1882 Illustrirter Catalog von Dr. Hermann Rohrbeck; **CTY/B** (Uai L 968).

1891 Catalog Dr. Hermann Rohrbeck Bauanstalt fuer Desinfectoren, bakteriologische und hygienische Apparate; **CTY/B** (Uai L 968).

Bureau 24 Karlstrasse, Fabrik Elsasserstrasse 52, Berlin, Germany.

1892 Glasutensilien fuer medicinisch-chirurgische Zwecke; 10 pp; **ZUR.**

n.d. Apparatus for sterilizing surgical instrument and sterilisable instrument cases; **CPP.**

4 Murray Street, New York, New York.

n.d. List of Chemical Preparations, Pure Reagents, Minerals, etc.; **CTY/B** (Uai L 968).

556 Broadway, (New York).

n.d. List of Chemical Preparations, Pure Reagents, Graduated Solutions, Minerals; 38 pp; **CTY/B** (Uai L 968).

n.d. General Descriptive Catalog of Chemical, Pharmaceutical and Physical Apparatus, Meteorogical & Mathematical Instruments, etc.; 160 pp; **CTY/B** (Uai L 968).

LUKENS, C. DE WITT CO.
4908 Laclede Avenue, St. Louis, Missouri.
13 Poland Street, London.
20 McGill College Avenue, Montreal, Canada.
Mexico City Avenue, San Francisco 12, California.

n.d. Lukens Sterile Catgut and Surgical Specialties Made Only for Those Who Appreciate and Demand the Best; 34 pp; **CPP.**

n.d. Catalog Lukens Sterile Specialties; 24 pp; **NYAM; MF/MAH.**

LUNEAU ET COFFIGNON
81 Blvd Malesherbes, Paris.

n.d. Javal-Schiotz ophtalmometre mires de couleurs complémentaires; 86 pp; **URRR** (L-73).

n.d. Opthalmoscope électrique summay; 6 pp; **URRR** (L-72).

LUNKEN WINDOW CO.
Cincinnati, Ohio.

n.d. Catalog Hospital Windows; 7 pp; **NYAM; MF/MAH.**

LUTTER, A.
Französische-Strasse Nr. 53, Berlin, Germany.

ca 1862 Preisverzeichniss und Atlas chirurgischer Instrumente, Apparate, etc.; 68 pp; **CPP; MUM** (Ed 51 pam 27a).

n.d. RCS A 32 Strabismus Book Loan Coll. no. 14, D. W. Busch's forceps, no. 42 Kristeller's dynamometrical forceps, no. 119 Cohen's cephalotrite; **RCSL.**

LUTZ, EDOUARD
49 Boulevard Saint-Germain, Paris, France.
49 rue des Noyers, Paris, France.
　　1872　Catalog des instruments d'optique; 39 pp; **CTY/B** (Uai L 979).

LUXTER PRISM CO.
24 Beekman Street, New York, New York.
　　1897　Catalog Luxter Prisms & Electric Glazing; 14 pp; **NYAM; MF/MAH.**

LYNCH & CO.
Aldersgate Street, London E.C., England.
　　n.d.　Catalogue, Illustrations of Druggists' Sundries and Surgical Instruments; 203 pp, index 23 pp; **NYAM; MF/MAH.**
　Jan. 1889　Catalog of Druggists' Sundries and Surgical Instruments; 14 pp; **NYAM** (S 125); **CPP** (Ed/28).
　July 1890　Catalog Surgical Instruments; 69 pp; **NYAM; MF/MAH.**

MACALASTER, WIGGIN CO.
210 Sudbury Building, Boston, Massachusetts.
Est: Jan. 1897
　See: VICTOR ELECTRIC CO.
　　1907　X-Ray Tubes and Electro-Therapeutic Goods, Glass Blowing, All Tubes Are Fitted With Automatic Regulating Devices, License under Queen patent no. 594036; 32 pp; **ACR/MAH.**
　　1908?　X-Ray Tubes and Accessories; 32 pp; **ACR/MAH.**
　　1909　X-Ray Tubes and Specialties; 32 pp; **ACR/MAH.**
　　1912　Catalog no. 15 X-Ray Tubes and Accessories; 32 pp; **ACR/MAH.**
　July 1913　Rules for X-Ray Protection Issued by the German Roentgen Society, Important, Hang in Operating Room; 1 pp; **ACR/MAH.**
　Aug. 1913　Tungsten Target Tubes, Penetration Type, Dr. Hampson's Roentgen Radiometer; 4 pp; **ACR/MAH.**
　May 1914　Tungsten Target Tubes, Penetration Type; 4 pp; Newton and Wright. Ltd., 72 Wigmore St., London, W. England are English representatives; **ACR/MAH.**
　605 Sudbury Building, Boston, Massachusetts.
　　n.d.　X-Ray Tubes and Accessories; 32 pp; **CPP.**
　79 Sudbury Street, Boston, Massachusetts.
　　1914　Catalog, X-Ray Tubes and Accessories; 35 pp; **ACR/MAH.**
　66 Broadway, Cambridge, Massachusetts.
　Nov. 1915　Brochure, Water-Cooled Tungsten Target Tubes; 4 pp; **ACR/MAH.**
　Jan. 1916　A Real X-Ray Tube, Newton and Wright British Representatives; 4 pp; **ACR/MAH.**
　Jun. 1916　Improved Hydrogen Tube, Tungsten Target; 4 pp; **ACR/MAH.**
　Mar. 1916　Water-Cooled Tungsten Tubes; 4 pp; **ACR/MAH.**
　May 1916　Improved Hydrogen Tube, Tungsten Target; 4 pp; **ACR/MAH.**

MACGREGOR INSTRUMENT CO.
Needham, Massachusetts.
　　n.d.　Catalog of the Thomas Intravenous Apparatus for Administering Anesthetic Agents and Other Solutions Intravenously, Designed by George J. Thomas, M.D. of Pittsburgh, patent applied for; 12 pp; **MAH** (C 617. 96085).

n.d. Manual for Use with the Vim-Sheftel Colorimeter; 55 pp; **MAH** (C 616.07561).

n.d. Thomas Intravenous Apparatus for Administering Anesthetic Agents and Other Solutions Intravenously; 11 pp; **MAH.**

MACHLETT, E., & SON
143-147 East 23rd Street, New York, New York.
220 East 23rd Street, New York 3, New York.
Est: 1897

1905 Catalog, X-Ray Tubes, Special Cancer Treatment Tubes, Violet Ray Tubes, Complete X-Ray Outfits, High Frequency Tubes; 3rd ed.; 24 pp; **ACR/MAH.**

153 East 84th Street, New York, New York.

Jan. 1914 Catalog X-Ray Tubes and Vacuum Electrodes; 19 pp; **ACR/MAH.**
Jun. 1914 Catalog X-Ray Tubes and Vacuum Electrodes; 19 pp; **ACR/MAH.**

MACLEAN, J. C.
1777 Broadway, New York, New York.
1893 The Quick Service Air Pump; 1 pp; **CPP.**

MADDOX, JAMES E.
19 University Street, London, England.
n.d. no title; **RCSL.**

MAGIC EARPHONE, THE
See: MEYROWITZ; **MF/MAH.**

MAHADY, E. F., CO.
671 Boylston Street, Boston, Mass.
ca 1915–20 Illustrated Catalogue of Surgical Instruments and Physicians Supplies, Distributor for Standard Surgical Instruments, section on Stille Hand-Forged Surgical Instruments follows index; 416 pp, index; **MAH** (8649).

851-857 Boylston St., Boston, Massachusetts.
1929 Illustrated Catalogue of Surgical Instruments and Physicians Supplies, Distributor for Standard Surgical Instruments; 458 pp, index, revised price list, 34 pp; **CS; MAH** (22728).

MAJOR, GENISSON & CO.
23 rue Racine, Paris, France.
1894 Fabrique d'instruments de chirurgie; 52 pp; **CPP.**
Apr. 1895 Catalog fabrique d'instruments de chirurgie; 187 pp; **NYAM; MF/MAH.**

MALES' METHOD COMPANY, THE
Aetna Building, Cincinnati, Ohio.
1892 The Family Ready Adviser, by Dr. Samuel Males; 64 pp; **CPP.**

MALLKINCKRODT CHEMICAL WORKS
St. Louis 7, Mo.
Est: 1867

1929 Oral Treatment of Genito-Urinary Disorders with Mallophene; 20 pp; **CPP.**

MALMSTEN, H. A.
Germantown, Pennsylvania.
Nov. 1871 Wilson Adjustable Chair; **CPP** (Bolenius Coll).

MANASSE, L., CO.
88 Madison St. Chicago, IL.
       1885   Optical and Electrical Instruments; 192 pp; **URRR** (M-2).
       1900   Illustrated Catalogue of Spectacles, Eyeglasses, Lenses and Material, etc.;
                3rd ed., Part 5; 174 pp; **AO; URRR** (M-287).
       1906   Illustrated Catalogue and Price List of Spectacles, Eyeglasses, Lenses and
                Material; 5th ed., Part 5; 170 pp; **URRR** (M-2).

MANDER AND WEAVER
Wolverhampton, England.
       1825   Instrument maker mentioned by John Read.

MANESTY MACHINES LTD.
Colege Lane, Liverpool 1, England.
"Proprietors—Thompson & Caper Wholesale Ltd."
       1920s?   Catalog Tablet Machines, Tablet Making Machinery, Chemical and
                Pharmaceutical Machinery, Automatic Water Stills; 40 pp; **MAH** (C
                615.43 M2).

MANHATTAN DENTAL CO.
New York, New York.
       ca 1900 Catalog of the Manhatten Dental Co., Specialties in Dental Goods of
                Platinoid; 8 pp; **HML**.

MANHATTAN ELECTRICAL SUPPLY CO.
New York, New York.
       n.d.   Catalog without title, no. 16; 78 pp, begins pp 3; **NYAM; MF/MAH**.
       n.d.   Catalogue 26, Something Electrical for Everybody; 212 pp; **BLEL**.

MANHATTAN SURGEONS' SUPPLY CO.
202 East 57th Street, New York, New York.
       ca 1895 Catalog of Medical and Surgical Instruments and Apparatus; 48 pp,
                tabloid newspaper size; **MAH** (C 610.78085); **NLM** (W26 M277c).
       ca 1916 Untitled, Assorted; 52 pp; **CPP**.
       ca 1920 Catalog; 416 pp; **WOC**.
       n.d.   Illustrated Catalog Medical and Surgical Instruments; 48 pp; **MAH** (C
                610.78085 M).

MANHATTAN SURGICAL INSTRUMENT CO.
New York City, New York.
       Feb. 1924 Illustrated Catalog of Surgical Instruments of Superior Quality, Distributor
                for Standard Surgical Instruments; 416 pp, index, revised price list 29
                pp; **MAH**.

MANLEY AND STONE, MESSRS.
Paternoster Row, London, England.
       1825   Instrument maker mentioned by John Read.

MANN ALFONS, SP. AKC.
Plac Malachowskiego Nr. 2, Warszawa, Poland.
       1930s   Przyrzadow i Narzedzi do Leczenia Alaman. Fabryka Narzedzi
                chirurgicznych, (orthopedic appliances and instruments), Catalog M; 23
                pp; **AFMM**.

MANNING SYSTEM, THE
   See: KYN-SCHEERER CO.; **MF/MAH**.

MAPPIN & CO.
121 New Street, Birmingham, England.
 1885 Catalog of Surgical Instruments and Appliances; 248 pp; **RCSL.**

MAREY, DR.
 n.d. Appareils et instruments de physiologie; **CPP.**

MARIAUD
(Maison Gueride et Mariaud Reunies), 41 Boulevard Saint-Michel, Paris, France.
 n.d. RCS Loan Coll no. 277; Vaginal Speculum Glass blades; **RCSL.**
 post 1873 Fabricant d'instruments de chirurgie orthopédie et membres artificiels, bandages, ceintures, instruments de vétérinaires, coutellerie, hygiène et sciences; 132 pp; **CTY/B** (Uai M 338).

MARIETTA APPARATUS CO.
Marietta, Ohio.
 Dec. 22, 1936 Psychological Equipment; stamp, unpaged; **MAH** (C 151.2 M2).

MARKS, A. A.
691 Broadway, New York, New York.
Est: 1853
 1884 Catalog of Patent Artificial Limbs with India Rubber Hands and Feet; 158 pp, fragile; **AFMM.**
701 Broadway, New York, New York.
 1894 A Treatise on Marks' Patent Artificial Limbs with Rubber Hands and Feet; 445 pp; **MAH** (C 617.57085 M164p).
 1898 A Treatise on Artificial Hands and Feet; 544 pp; **HDM.**
 1898–99 A Treatise on Artificial Limbs, Parts I & II; Special ed.; 530 pp; **AFMM; MF/MAH.**
 1904 Order Sheet for Artificial Legs and Arms; 1 pp; **NYAM; MF/MAH.**
 1907 Manual of Artificial Limbs; 430 pp; **MAH** (C 617.57085 M 164).
 1908 Manual of Artificial Limbs; 436 pp; **MAH** (C 617.57085 M 164).
 1913 Manual of Artificial Limbs; 415 pp; **MAH** owned by American Orthotics and Prosthetics Association, Washington, D.C.
 1917 Measuring Sheet for Artificial Legs and Arms; 1 pp; **NYAM; MF/MAH.**
 n.d. Catalog Artificial Limbs; 47 pp; **NYAM; MF/MAH.**

MARLOYE, CHEZ
161 rue Saint-Jacques et rue des Fosses-Saint-Jacques 1, Paris, France.
 1851 Catalogue des principaux appareils d'acoustique et autre objets; 3rd ed.; 56 pp; **CTY/B** (Uai M 3453).

MARSHALL, CARL
Solingen, Germany.
 n.d. Katalog, Chirurgie; 543 pp; **MF/MAH; ZUR.**

MARTIN, ALEXANDER, B. O. A.
128 South First Street, Philadelphia, Pennsylvania.
17 West 28th Street, New York, New York.
56 Flatbush Avenue Brooklyn, New York.
617 Main Street, Buffalo, New York.
 post 1902 Eyestrain, Cause and Correction; 23 pp; **CPP.**
 1906 Kon-tor-iks Give Clearer Vision, Wider Field, Greater Comfort, Improved Appearance; 4 pp; **CPP.**
 n.d. Eyestrain, Cause, Effect, Correction; 32 pp; **CPP.**

n.d.   Kromarck Lenses; foldout; **URRR** (M-239).

n.d.   Kontoriks, sold by A. Martin; 2 pp; **URRR** (M-238).

MARTIN-COPELAND CO.
101 Sabin, Providence, Rhode Island.

Est: 1880

Jun. 1, 1916   Price List for Solid Gold Frame Mountings and Material, assorted catalogs bound together; **URRR** (M-292).

Branches: Madison St. and Wabash Ave., Chicago, (IL). Post St. and Grant Ave., San Francisco, (CA). 37 Maiden Lane, New York City, (NY). 59 Hatton Garden, London, E. C. (not listed after this year). South American Offices: Galeria Guemes (or Casilla Correa 1312), Buenos Aires, Argentina (not listed after this year).

Nov. 11, 1918   Price List for Gold Filled, White Metal and Torshell Frames, Mountings and Materials; 8 pp; **AO.**

Nov. 11, 1918   Price List for Solid Gold Frames, Mountings and Material; 4 pp; **AO.**

1921   Optical Goods with 2 Price List inserted (21-22); 68 pp; **URRR** (M-341).

Mar. 7, 1927   Price List, Gold, Gold Filled and Zylonte Frames, Mountings, Oxfords and Materials; 29 pp; **AO.**

Branches: 29 E. Madison Street, Chicago, (IL).

210 Post St., San Francisco, (CA).

May 1, 1929   Price List, White Gold Filled Frames and Mountings; 26 pp; **AO; URRR** (M-371).

Branch: 529 Metropolitan Bldg., Los Angeles, (CA).

Nov. 1, 1930   Price List, Fawn-Tan Gold Filled Frames and Mountings; 13 pp; **AO.**

Sep. 1932   Duotone, The Two Tone Frame; 8 pp foldout; **URRR** (M-352).

Nov. 15, 1932   Price List, White and Fawn Tan Gold Filled Frames and Mountings; 19 pp; **URRR** (M-371).

Apr. 5, 1934   Price List, Rhodium Finished White Metal Frames; 6 pp; **URRR** (M-351).

Apr. 5, 1934   White and Fawn-Tan Gold Filled Frames and Mountings; 22 pp; **URRR** (M-349).

May 15, 1934   Price List, White and Fawn-Tan Gold Filled Solder Lock Mountings; 9 pp; **URRR** (M-350).

Branch: 126 Post St., San Francisco, (CA).

Oct. 1, 1935   Price List, Frames, Mountings, Material; 30 pp; **AO; URRR** (M-373).

MARTIN, JAMES
42 South Lansing, Albany, New York.

1843   Cutler listed in Albany City Directory.

MARTIN'S METHOD, INC.
105 East 30th Street, New York, New York.

n.d.   Colon Cleanliness, A Survey of the Newest Scientific Discoveries for Multiplying Physical Health and Mental Efficiency in the Human Organism; 59 pp; **CPP.**

MARVEL CO., THE
25 West 45th Street, New York, New York.

ca 1902   Vaginal Douche Therapy, The Advantages of and Indications for the Use of the Whirling Spray Syringe; 15 pp; **CPP.**

post 1904   Blood Circulation by Means of Vibration; 4 pp; **CPP.**

1922   A Brief Handbook of Gynecological Practice; 28 pp; **CPP.**

n.d.   Marvel Whirling Spray Syringe for Women; 11 pp; **CPP.**

n.d.   Marvel Whirling Spray for Women; 16 pp; **CPP.**

MARVEX X-RAY EQUIPMENT
See: MCFEDRIES X-RAY CO.; **ACR/MAH.**

MASON
See: SAVIGNY; 1810; **NLM.**

MASON, L. J., & CO., INC.
1323 South Michigan Avenue, Chicago, Illinois.
        n.d.   Catalog, Dental Operating Instruments; **UPL.**

MASON DETACHABLE TOOTH CO.
Redbank, New Jersey.
        n.d.   Catalog Detachable Porcelains for Crown and Bridge Work; 12 pp;
                NYAM; MF/MAH.

MASTER DENTAL CO., THE
Chicago, Illinois.
        1936   Cast Partials; **MAH.**

MATHESON, WILLIAM J., & CO., LTD.
New York, New York.
        n.d.   Amyloform Surgical Antiseptic; 32 pp; **CPP.**

MATHIEU FILS
16 Carrefour de l'Odeon, Paris, France.
        1878   Mathieu Fils, Fabricants d'instruments de chirurgie orthopédie, membres
                artificiels, bandages, ceintures, chirurgie vétérinaire et tout de qui a
                rapport à l'hygiène et aux sciences; 112 pp; **CTY/B** (Uai M 428).

MATHIEU, L.
28 rue de l'Ancienne Comédie, Paris, France.
Est: 1849
        1851   Atelier spécial pour les appareils orthopédiques et les membres artificiel,
                Fabricant des troussés et instruments de chirurgie générale; instruments
                pour dissection, autopsie, instruments de chirurgie vétérinaire, boîtes
                spéciales pour les maladies des yeux, des oreilles, lithotritie, taille,
                maladies des femmes, etc., membres artificiels, etc.; 62 pp; **AFMM.**
        1858   Catalogue des instruments de chirurgie; 64 pp, fragile; **AFMM.**
        1864   Catalogue des instruments de chirurgie; 96 pp; **CPP; MUM** (Ed 51 pam
                12).
        1867   Catalogue coutelleries fine, appareils de médecine et de chirurgie et tout ce
                qui a rapport à l'hygiène et aux sciences, bound with 1865–66 Charriere
                and undated Leplanquais; 192 pp, 8 pp supplement, fragile; **AFMM;**
                CTY/B (Uai M 427).
        1870   Coutellerie fine, appareils de médecine et de chirurgie et tout ce qui a
                rapport à l'hygiène et aux sciences, Appareils bonnet, de Lyon, pour
                immobiliser les hanches et le basin; 64 pp, supplement; **CPP; CTY/B**
                (Uai M 427).

MATHIEU, MAISON
Paris, France.
        ca 1907   Arsenal chirurgical; orthopédie, prothèse; 15th ed.; 484 pp; **BLEL.**

MATHIEU MAISON L.
113 Boulevard St.-Germaine, Paris, France.
Raoul Mathieu, fils and successor

1862 Catalogue d'instruments de chirurgie, orthopédie, membre
artificiels, bandages, ceintures, instruments de chirurgie
vétérinaire et tout ce qui se rapporte aux sciences et à l'hygiène;
138 pp; **AFMM.**
1883 Catalogue instruments de chirurgie; 143 pp; **NYAM; MF/MAH.**
1883 Catalogue d'instruments de chirurgie, orthopédie, membres
artificiels, bandages, ceintures, instruments de chirurgie
vétérinaire et tout ce qui rapporte aux sciences et à l'hygiène;
246 pp; **AFMM.**
1886 Catalogue instruments de chirurgie; 343 pp; **NYAM; MF/MAH.**
1887 Catalogue d'instruments de chirurgie, orthopédie, membres
artificiels, bandages, ceintures, instruments de chirurgie
vétérinaire et tout de qui se rapporte aux sciences et à l'hygiène;
246 pp, fragile; **AFMM.**
1895 Instruments de chirurgie, maladies de la bouche,
oesophage-larynx-nez-oreilles-dents-maladies des yeux; 432 pp;
ZUR.
1904? Arsenal chirurgical orthopédie, prothèse; 15th ed.; 484 pp; **NYAM;
MF/MAH; CTY/B; YML** (RD 76.906M).
Sep. 1909 Recueil des instruments de chirurgie, orthopédie et mobiliers; **ZUR.**

MATHIEU, RAOUL
Fils et Successeur, Paris.
1882 Fabricant d'instruments de chirurgie orthopédie; 143 pp; **AFMM.**
1883 Fabricant d'instruments de chirurgie orthopédie; 251 pp; **AFMM.**
1887 Fabricant d'instruments de chirurgie orthopédie; 172 pp; **AFMM.**
n.d. Fabricant d'instruments de chirurgie orthopédie; 206 pp; **CPP.**

MATSUMIOTO
Toyko, Japan.
n.d. RCS Catalogue 1901; **RCSL.**

MATTHEWS, W.
8 Portugal Street, London, England.
32 Carley Street, London, England.
1855 No title; **RCSL.**

MATTHEW BROTHERS
8 Portugal Street, London, England.
1851-2, Prize medal; moved to 27 Carey Street; **RCSL.**
27 Carey Street, Lincoln's Inn Fields, London, England.
1872 Illustrated Circular of Surgical Instruments; 19 pp; **YML** (RD 76 872M).
ca 1873 A Catalogue of Surgical Instruments; 136 pp; **NYAM; MF/MAH.**
1874? Catalogue of Surgical Instruments; 129 pp; **RCSL.**
1874? Catalogue of Surgical Instruments Manufactured and Supplied by
Matthews Bros; **ACS** (U 6a M 442c).
1875? Catalogue of Surgical Instruments; 136 pp, 10 pp Supplementary
Catalogue; **NYAM; MF/MAH.**
n.d. Catalogue of Surgical Instruments; 198 pp; **RCSL.**

MATTHEWS & WILSON, LTD.
No. 813 P. O. Croydon, 42a to 48a Portland Road, South Norwood, London, S.E., England.
n.d. Chemists' Counter Specialties, etc.; 56 pp; **CPP.**

MAUSSNER MANUFACTURING CO., INC.
312 North 3rd Street, Philadelphia, Pennsylvania.
    ca 1901   Sanitary Mattresses & Pillows Made of Interlaced Curled Hair; 6 pp; **CPP.**

MAW, GEORGE
Est: 1807
See: S. MAW, SON & THOMPSON; **NLM.**
    1822   A Catalogue of Surgical, Pharmaceutical and Veterinary Instruments . . .; **ABD.**
    1839   Catalog of Surgical Instruments; **BDA.**

MAW, S., AND SON
11 Aldersgate Street, London, England.
    1866   Catalog of Surgeons' Instruments, Air and Water Beds, Pillows, and Cushions, Bandages, Trusses, Elastic Stockings, Inhalers, Galvanic Apparatus and Other Appliances; 175 pp, fragile; **AFMM.**
    1869   Book of Illustrations to S. Maw and Son's Quarterly Price Current; 241 pp; **NYAM; UTP; TMHM.**
11 & 12 Aldersgate Street, (London).
Jan. 1, 1869   Book of Illustrations to Quarterly Price Current, Surgeon's Instruments and Appliances, Instruments for Veterinary Purposes, Pharmacy Apparatus and Shop Fittings; 232 pp, 9 pp of advertisements; **NLM** (W26 M462).
July 1, 1869   Quarterly Price Current; 100 pp; **NLM** (W26 M464).
    Oct. 1869   Quarterly Price Current of Surgeons' Instruments and Appliances; Pharmacy Apparatus and Shop Fittings; 90 pp, 10 pp advertisements; **NLM** (W26 M462).
Jan. 1, 1870   Book of Illustrations to Quarterly Price Current of Surgeons' Instruments and Appliances, Pharmacy Apparatus and Shop Fittings; 146 pp; **NLM** (W26 M462).

MAW, S., SON & THOMPSON
    1870   Book of Illustrations to S. Maw and Thompson's Quarterly Price Current; 154 pp; **YML** (RD 76 870M); **CTY/B** (Uai M 448); **HDM; UCSF.**
    Jan. 1872   Quarterly Price Current; 40 pp, 15 pp of advertisements; **NLM.**
    1882   Book of Illustrations, Surgeons' Instruments, etc., Quarterly Price Current; 448 pp; **NYAM; MF/MAH.**
    1891   Surgeons' Instruments, etc., Book of Illustrations to Quarterly Price Current; 217 pp; **NLM** (W26 M462); 235 pp; **FI** (617.91 gM 445); **ACS** (U 6a M462b).

MAW, S., SON AND SONS
7 to 12 Aldersgate Street, London, England.
    ca 1900   Separate brochure of Microscope, Bacteriological Apparatus, Dissecting Instruments, etc.; 22 pp; **AFMM** (filed with 1905 catalog).
    1903   Book of Illustrations to S. Maw & Sons Quarterly Price List; 292 pp; **UTP.**
    1905   Catalog of Surgical Instruments and Appliances, Aseptic Hospital

Furniture and Surgical Dressings, etc.; 508 pp; **BDA; NLM** (W26 M462); **AFMM.**

1909   Microscope, Bacteriological Apparatus, Dissecting Instruments, etc.; 19 pp; **AFMM; URRR** (M-293).

1913   A Catalogue of Surgical Instruments, Appliances, etc.; 657 pp; **AFMM; TMHM.**

1925   A Catalogue of Surgical Instruments, Appliances, Aseptic Hospital Furniture, Surgical Dressings, etc.; 606 pp; **BLEL.**

MAY MANUFACTURING CO.
146-152 West 29th Street, New York.
Est: 1919

pre–1934   Spectacles of Individuality; 23 pp; **AO.**

MAYER, ERNST W., & MELTZER, PERRY G.
71 Great Portland Street, London, England.
Est: 1863 by Joseph Mayer; Mayer and Meltzer, 1866; Mayer and Phelps, 1919.

1880   Catalog of Surgical Instruments & Appliances; 236 pp; **RCSL; TMHM.**

1885   An Illustrated Catalog of Surgical Instruments and Appliances; 425 pp; **RCSL.**

ca 1888   Catalog of Surgical Instruments and Appliances; 456 pp; **ZUR.**

ca 1895   Catalog of Instruments Used in the Practice of Laryngology, Rhinology and Otology; 120 pp; **NLM** (W26 M468c).

ca 1900   Catalog of Instruments Used in the Practice of Laryngology, Rhinology and Otology; 15 pp, bound with pp 139-282 of their general catalog; **NLM** (W26 M468c).

1911   An Illustrated Catalog of Instruments Used in the Practice of Laryngology, Rhinology and Otology; 272 pp; **MUM.**

ca 1917   Catalog of Surgical Instruments and Appliances, contains short account of the origin and history of the firm; 631 pp; **NLM** (W26 M468c).

233 & 235 Lansdale Street, Melbourne, Australia.
18 Plein Street, Capetown, Africa.

1913   Catalog of Surgical Instruments and Appliances, Aseptic Hospital Furniture and Surgical Dressings; 657 pp; **AFMM.**

n.d.   Supplementary Price List; 18 pp; **RCSL.**

n.d.   A Catalog of Instruments Used in the Practice of Laryngology, Rhinology & Otology; 282 pp; **NYAM; MF/MAH.**

n.d.   Catalog, Crouch's Microscopes & Accessories; **NYAM; MF/MAH.**

MAYER & PHELPS, LTD.
Chiron House, 59/61 New Cavendish Street, London W 1, England.
See: DOWN BROTHERS; **NLM.**

1925   A Catalog of Instruments Used in the Practice of Laryngology, Rhinology and Otology; 156 pp; **NYAM; MF/MAH; LACMA** (149 M45c); **HDM; WOC.**

1929   Addenda to Catalog of Instruments Used in the Practice of Laryngology, Rhinology and Otology; pp 157-192; **NYAM; MF/MAH.**

n.d.   Catalog Medical Instruments; 4 pp; **NYAM; MF/MAH.**

1931   An Illustrated Catalogue of Surgical Instruments and Appliances; 568 pp; **BLEL; ABD.**

MAYNARD, J. G., & CO.
Chicago, IL.
> ca 1910 Price List of J.G. M. Co., Mfrn. of Dental Supplies; folder, **HML.**

McALLISTER, T. H.
49 Nassau Street, New York, New York.
> 1870 Condensed List of Optical Goods; 32 pp; **CTY/B** (Uai M 117).
> post 1870 Illustrated Price List of Microscopes and Microscopic Apparatus; 2nd ed.; 28 pp; **CTY/B** (Uai M 117).
> post 1870 Illustrated Price List of Microscopes and Microscopic Apparatus, Lenses; 3rd ed.; 28 pp; **CTY/B** (Uai M 117).
> Jun. 1878 Illustrated Price List of Microscopes; 33rd ed.; 62 pp; **CTY/B** (Uai M 117).
> Aug. 1881 Illustrated Price List of Microscopes; 39th ed.; 88 pp; **CTY/B** (Uai M 117).
> Sep. 1881 Illustrated Price List of Microscopes; 40th ed.; 88 pp; **CTY/B** (Uai M 117).
> Apr. 1882 Illustrated Price List of Microscopes; 43rd ed.; 92 pp; **CTY/B** (Uai M 117).
> Jun. 1884 Illustrated Price List of Microscopes; 46th ed.; 92 p; **CTY/B** (Uai M 117).
> 1880's Reprint 1971 Condensed List of Optical Goods, reprinted by N.M. and M. A. Graver, Rochester, N.Y., includes family history; 31 pp; **ABD.**

McALLISTER, WILLIAM Y.
728 Chestnut Street, Philadelphia, Pennsylvania.
Est: 1783
Successor to John McAllister Sr. at Market St. (1783), Chestnut St. (1796), Chestnut St. (1854). John M., Sr. (1783-1811); John M., Sr. and Son (1811-1830); John M., Jr. and Co. (1830-1836); W.Y.? & Co. (1836-1853); McA. & Bros. (1853-1865); W. M. (1865-72?).
> July 1872 A Priced and Illustrated Catalog of Optical and Mathematical Instruments; 32nd ed.; 45 pp; **CPP.**
> 1873 A Priced and Illustrated Catalog of Meteorological and Philosophical Instruments and Chemicals, School Apparatus; 80 pp; **CTY/B** (Uai M 1173).
> 1881 Catalog of Spectacles, Microscopes, Thermometers and Other Scientific Instruments, Part First; 132 pp, fragile; **AFMM.**
> July 1881 A Priced and Illustrated Catalog of Optical Instruments, Spectacles, and Eyeglasses, Microscopes, and Microscopic Accessories, All Kinds of Thermometers, Aneroid & Mercurial Barometers . . .; 132 pp; **CTY/B** (Uai M 1173).
> 1919 Illustrated Catalogue of Optical, Mathematical and Philosophical Instruments; **MUM** (Ed119 v.2 p.1919ff).
> n.d. Our Eyesight; 24 pp; **CPP.**

McALLISTER & BROTHER'S
194 Chestnut Street, Philadelphia, Pennsylvania.
Est: 1796
> 1855 Illustrated Catalog of Optical, Mathematical, and Philosophical Instruments; 2nd ed.; 84 pp; **CTY/B** (Uai M 1174).

728 Chestnut Street, Philadelphia, Pennsylvania.
    1856-7   Illustrated Catalog of Optical, Mathematical, and Philosophical
                  Instruments; **CTY/B** (Uai M 1174).
    1858   Illustrated Catalog of Optical, Mathematical, and Philosophical
                  Instruments; 8th ed.; 108 pp; **CTY/B** (Uai M 1174).
    1859   Illustrated Catalog of Optical, Mathematical, and Philosophical
                  Instruments; 116 pp; **CTY/B** (Uai M 1174).
    1865   Illustrated Catalog of Optical, Mathematical, and Philosophical
                  Instruments; 116 pp; **CTY/B** (Uai M 1174).

McALLISTER, W. MITCHELL
728 Chestnut Street, Philadelphia, Pennsyvlania.
    n.d.   Catalog of Magnesium Stereopticans, Magnesium Lamps,
                  Oxy-Hydrogen Microscopes, Oxy-Hydrogen Polariscopes,
                  Oxy-Hydrogen Kaleidoscopes, Oxy-Hydrogen Stereopticans; 122
                  pp; **CTY/B** (Uai M 1172).
    n.d.   Illustrated Catalog of Optical, Mathematical, and Philosophical
                  Instruments; **CPP** (Bolenius Coll).

McILLROY, PROF. T.
New York.
    n.d.   Invalid and Fracture Bedsteads, Surgical Operating Tables and
                  Chairs, All Requirements for the Comfort of Invalids; **CPP**
                  (Bolenius Coll).
    n.d.   Speculum and Oculist Operating Chairs; **CPP** (Bolenius Coll).

McINTIRE, MAGEE AND BROWN
723 Sansom St., Philadelphia, PA.
Est: 1894
Wholesale Mfr. and Jobbing Opticians, Maker of Kachoo Eyeglasses
    1905   Illustrated Catalogue and Price List of Optical Goods, Prescription
                  Work; 235 pp; **AO.**
    1906   Illustrated Catalogue of Optical Goods; 254 pp; **URRR** (M-6).
    1908   Illustrated Catalogue of Optical Goods; 26 pp; **URRR** (M-?)
    1908   Illustrated Catalogue, Optical Goods, Opera and Field Glasses,
                  Ophthalmological Apparatus and Supplies, Artificial Eyes, Trial
                  Sets, Trial Frames, Machinery and Tools, Catalogue B; 254 pp;
                  AO; MUM.
    1910   Supplement to Our Regular Catalogue; 32 pp; **AO.**
Jul.-Aug. 1917   *Kachoo News*, Vol. IX, no. 2; 16 pp; **AO.**
Apr.-May 1918   *Kachoo News*, Vol. IX, no. 4; 16 pp; **AO.**
    1920   Prescription Catalog Presenting the Refractochart with Controlled
                  Illumination; 6 pp foldout, chart for testing eye; **URRR** (M-340).
    9-11 Nesbitt Court, Wilkes-Barre, PA.
    Aug. 1928   Lens Price List, Premier Brand Prescription Work, A Precision
                  Product; 12 pp; **AO.**
    n.d.   Prescription Price List; 39 pp; **URRR** (M-274).
    n.d.   Illustrated Catalogue and Price List of Optical Goods; 235 pp;
                  URRR (M-4).

McINTOSH BATTERY & OPTICAL CO.
521-531 Wabash Avenue, Chicago, Illinois.
Successor to McIntosh Electrical Corporation
Est: 1879

See: MCINTOSH GALVANIC AND FARADIC BATTERY
- 1893 Illustrated Catalog Batteries and Electro-Therapeutical Appliances; no. 16 revised; 200 pp; **MAH** (C 615.84085).
- 1897 Catalog of Batteries and Electro-Therapeutical Appliances; 18th ed.; 288 pp; **AFMM; ACR/MAH.**
- 1899 Electro-Therapeutical Catalogue; 19th ed.; 272 pp; **ACR/MAH.**

92-98 State Street, Chicago, Illinois.
- 1900 Illustrated Catalog of Batteries and Electro-Therapeutical Appliances; 21st ed.; 96 pp; **HDM; CPP.**

322 West Washington Street, Chicago, Illinois.
- ca 1905 Brochure, The Hogan Silent X-Ray Transformer; 10 pp (missing?); **ACR/MAH.**
- 1907 Catalog Electro-Therapeutical Apparatus; 29th ed.; 158 pp; **NYAM; MF/MAH.**
- 1909 Illustrated Catalog of Electro-Therapeutical Apparatus, no. 30; 158 pp; **MAH** (C 615.84085); **CPP** (Ed/94).
- 1911 Catalog Electro-Therapeutical Apparatus; 32nd ed.; 192 pp; **MAH** (C 615.84085); **NYAM; MF/MAH; URRR** (M-251); **TMHM.**
- n.d. Sinusoidal Technique, A Working Manual of the Sinusoidal Current; 20 pp; **CPP.**

217-223 North Desplaines Street, Chicago, Illinois.
- ca 1910 McIntosh Improved Alternating Current Rectifier with Potential Equalizer; 12 pp; **CPP.**
- ca 1912 Suggestions for Spondylotherapists; 24 pp; **CPP.**
- 1917 Simtech, A Simple Roentgen Testa-d'Arsonval Technique; 48 pp; **CPP.**
- n.d. Sinusoidal Therapy; 28 pp; **CPP.**

223-233 North California Avenue, Chicago, Illinois.
- 1922 The Therapeutics of High Frequency; 16 pp; **CPP.**
- Dec. 1923 The *Electron*, Monthly Bulletin of Electro-Medical and Physical Therapeutic Progress, The Industrial Hospital Number; 4 pp; **CPP.**
- ca 1926 A Compend of High Frequency Currents and Their Therapeutic Uses; 70 pp; **BLEL.**
- 1929 Catalog Physical Therapy Equipment; 48 pp; **NYAM; MF/MAH.**
- n.d. Alternating Current Therapeutics; 12 pp; **CPP.**

McINTOSH ELECTRICAL CORPORATION
Chicago, (IL).
- ca 1881 Illustrated Catalogue of McIntosh Combined Galvanic and Faradic Battery; 63 pp; **BLEL.**

McINTOSH GALVANIC & FARADIC BATTERY CO.
300 & 302 Dearborn Street, Chicago, Illinois.
See: MCINTOSH BATTERY AND OPTICAL CO.
- 1881 Illustrated Catalog of McIntosh Combined Galvanic and Faradic Battery; Office Battery, Electric Bath Apparatus, Electrodes, Solar Microscope, Stereoptican, etc.; 64 pp; **AFMM; MAH** (16117).

192 Jackson Street, Chicago, Illinois.
- ca 1885 Catalog, Dr. McIntosh's Solar Microscope and Stereopticon Combination, Microscopes, Achromatic Objectives, Optical

Lanterns, Stereopticons and New Ether Oxygen Lime Light; 13 pp, **MAH.**

McINTOSH'S NATURAL UTERINE SUPPORTER CO.
296 West Lake Street, Chicago, Illinois.
Est: 1871
      1875   Advertisement Pamphlet for Uterine Supporter; **MUM** (Ed199 v.2 p.410).

McKEE SURGICAL INSTRUMENT CO.
New York, New York.
      n.d.   Surgical Instruments . . . ; 18th ed.; **JHIHM** (RD 76.M15).

McKESSON
51 Wollwanhill, Aberdeen, Scotland.
11 Saville Row Newcastle-on-Tyne, England.
      n.d.   McKesson Nargraf, Surgical instrument maker to Army and Navy and most of the leading infirmaries throughout Scotland and North of England; 2 pp; **WMScM.**

McKESSON APPLIANCE CO.
2226-36 Ashland Avenue, Toledo, Ohio.
  Sep. 1, 1929   McKesson Appliances, Catalog no. 16; 80 pp; **MAH.**
  Dec. 1930   Description of and Photos of the Recording and Indicating Types; 24 pp; **MAH** (C 617.96085 M).
      n.d.   Vacuum and Pressure Pumps, Hamilton Dental Supply; **MAH.**

McKESSON & ROBBINS
91 & 93 Fulton Street, New York, New York.
80, 82 & 84 Ann Street, New York, New York.
McKesson & Robbins, Inc.
155 East 44th Street, New York 17, New York.
Est: 1833
      1873   Prices Current of Drugs and Druggists' Articles, Chemical and Pharmaceutical Preparations, Proprietary Medicines and Perfumery Sponges, Corks, Dyes, Paints, etc.; 160 pp; **MAH** (C 615.1373 M 124).
      1879   Prices Current Illustrated; 224 pp; **MAH** (C 615.1373 M 124).
  ca 1880   Price List Formula Card of Gelatin-Coated Pills; For Vest Pocket Containing . . . List Prices of Pills; 7 pp; **MAH** (C 615.1373 M).
      1883   Prices Current of Drugs, Chemical and Pharmaceutical Preparations, Proprietary Medicines, Corks, Dyes, Paints, etc., etc., etc.; 480 pp, pp 381 begins Surgical Instruments and Appliances; **MAH.**
      1883   Illustrated Catalogue of Druggist Sundries, Fancy Goods, Surgical Instruments, Syringes, Chamois; 244 pp; **HML.**
      n.d.   Compound Stearate of Zinc with Combinations as Insufflation and Dusting Powders or, Dry Ointments; 39 pp; **NYAM; MF/MAH.**

McNEIL LABORATORIES
2900 North 17th Street, Philadelphia, Pennsylvania.
      1931   Revised Notes on Sulphydryl Technique for Cell Growth & Wound Healing; 18 pp; **CPP.**
      n.d.   Dental Hemarestors, McNeil; **MAH.**

McNEIL, ROBERT
Front & York Streets, Laboratory and Warehouse: 2351-53-55 North Reese Street, Philadelphia, Pennsylvania.
1917–18   A Catalog of Surgical Dressings and Pharmaceuticals; 174 pp; **CPP.**

McNEIL & WASHBURN
New Haven, Connecticut.
1871   Commercial Catalog of Surgical Instruments, Trusses, Abdominal Supporters, Shoulder Braces, Elastic Hose, Crutches & Apparatus for the Treatment of Deformities of All Kinds, Physician's Supplies and Rubber Goods; 18 pp; **CHS** (74.62N 536 mw).

MEAD, JOHNSON & CO.
Evansville, Indiana.
Est: 1900
1929   Acterol Activated Ergosterol for the Prevention of Rickets; 31 pp; **CPP.**
1929   Rickets Dentition and Vitamin D; 24 pp; **CPP.**
n.d.   The Dental Value of Vitamin D in Pregnancy and Lactation with Special reference to Calcium and Phosphorus; 34 pp; **CPP.**

MEARS EAR PHONE CO., INC., THE
One West 34th Street, New York, New York.
ca 1908   Devices for the Deaf, Aurophones and Aurasage; 16 pp; **CPP.**

MEDICAL ARTS SUPPLY CO.
Huntington, West Virginia.
E. 20 c   Catalog of medical supplies and equipment; **NLM** (W26 M489c).

MEDICAL NOVELTY CO.
21 West 23 Street, New York, New York.
1895   External and Internal Antisepsis; 16 pp; **CPP.**

MEDICAL SUPPLY ASSOCIATION
12 Teriot Place, Edinburgh, Scotland.
Est: 1887
1887   Stamped on aneurism needle with cutting point; **RCSL.**
n.d.   Manufacturers of Surgical Instruments; 4 pp; **CPP.**

MEDICINISCHES WAARENHAUS AKTIEN-GESELLSCHAFT
Karlstrasse 31, Berlin N W 6, Germany.
Est: 1894
1929   Catalog Spezial-Unternehmen fuer Aerzte-und Krankenhaus-Einrichtungen; Nr. 213; Trilingual ed., Eng., Fr., Span.; 30 pp; **MAH.**
Friedrich Strasse 108, Berlin, Germany.
Postrasse 13, Odessa, Russia.
ca 1900   Catalog; 254 pp; **NYAM; MF/MAH.**
Mar. 1901   Katalog Apparate fuer physikalisch-Diätetische Therapie, Hydrotherapie; 28 pp; no. 6; **NYAM; MF/MAH.**
1930s?   Katalog A, Instrumentarium fuer die ärztliche Praxis und den gesamten Krankenhausbedarf; 12 sections each of 10-50 pp; **NLM** (W26 M 491k).

MEIER DENTAL & SURGICAL MANUFACTURING CO.
St Louis, Missouri.
Est: 1902
    1919   Catalog Orthodontic Appliances; 15 pp; **NYAM; MF/MAH.**
    1921   Catalog Orthodontic Appliances; 15 pp; **NYAM; MF/MAH.**
    1932   Usona Brand Bonds and Arches; **MAH.**

MEINECKE & CO.
48-50 Park Place, New York, New York.
    1902   Advanced Specialties for the Hospital and Sick Room; 16 pp; **CPP;**
          MAH (C 610.78085m).
 1904-05   High Grade Atomizers and Hot Water Bags and a Few Specialties
          for the Baby; 36 pp; **CPP.**
    1912   Suture Stitches; 24 pp; **CPP.**
    1924   Makers and Importers of Dependable Hospital Supplies; 224 pp;
          MAH (C 610.78085 M 514).
 1939-40   Dependable Hospital Supplies; 334 pp; **WOC.**
    n.d.   Sterile Sutures and Ligatures or Suture Stitches; 24 pp; **CPP.**
    n.d.   Simpler Sanitary Paper Sputum Cup; 1 pp; **CPP.**

MEISINGER, A.
Bohrer und Steine, Duesseldorf, Germany.
See: HAGER & MEISINGER; **AFMM.**
    n.d.   Catalog, Dental Instruments and Other Specialties manufacturered
          by the Deutsch-Amerikanische Zahntechnische Fabrik; 66 pp;
          UPSDM (D 617.604 M 479).
    n.d.   Wholesale Price List of Dental Engine Instruments Manufactured
          by the Deutsch-Amerikanische Zahntechische Fabrik, no. 3; 29
          pp; **UPSDM.**
    n.d.   Illustrirtes Preis-Verzeichniss von Instrumenten fuer die
          Bohrmaschine. Deutsch-Amerikanische Zahntechnische Fabrik,
          no. 4; 34 pp; **UPSDM** (D 617.604 M 479).

MELLIN'S FOOD CO.
177 State Street, Boston 9, Massachusetts.
See: DOLIBER-GOODALE CO.
    1892   Dietary for the Dyspeptic, by J. Milner Fothergill; 15 pp; **CPP.**
    1905   Diet after Weaning; 40 pp; **CPP.**
    1910   Formulas for Infant Feeding Based upon the Mellin's Food Method
          of Milk Modification; 80 pp; **CPP.**
 ca 1916   Mellin's Food for the Adult; 27 pp; **CPP.**
 ca 1916   Maltose and Dextrins in Infant Feeding; 21 pp; **CPP.**
 ca 1923   Formulas for Infant Feeding Based upon the Mellin's Food Method
          of Milk Modification; 80 pp; **CPP.**
    n.d.   The Feeding of Infants in Diarrhea; 6 pp; **CPP.**
    n.d.   Malnutrition Marasmus Atrophy; 4 pp; **CPP.**
    n.d.   Constipation in Infants; 5 pp; **CPP.**
    n.d.   A Manual for the Care of Feeding of Children Between One and
          Two Years of Age; **CPP.**
    n.d.   Diet for the Sick; 5 pp; **CPP.**
    n.d.   The Source, Nature and Amount of the Nutritive Elements in
          Mellin's Food; 14 pp; **CPP.**
    n.d.   The Artificial Feeding of the Well Infant; 7 pp; **CPP.**

n.d.   The Foundation of the Mellin's Food Method of Milk Modification; 12 pp; **CPP.**

MELER
France.
1806–70?   Signature appears on a microscope held by Ralph W. Bartlett, Medomak, Maine, which he dates from 1860–1870; correspondence in 1975 file; **MAH.**

MENNEN, G.
Newark, New Jersey.
n.d.   Treatise on Hygienic Infant Powder; 3 pp; **CPP.**

MERCK & CO.
New York, New York.
Rahway, New Jersey.
Est: 1818
1907   Merck Index; 3rd ed.; 472 pp, **MAH.**

MERKEL, EDWARD A.
22 South 17th Street, Philadelphia, Pennsylvania.
Merkel Building, 2013 Chestnut Street, Philadelphia, Pennsylvania.
Est: 1904
n.d.   Assorted Items; 3 pp; **CPP.**
n.d.   Maker Surgical Furniture, Instruments, & Supplies; 31 pp; **CPP.**
1922   Illustrated Catalog of Surgical Instruments, Furniture and of Allied Lines; 416 pp; **CPP** (Ed/100).

MERRELL, WILLIAM S., & CO.
Cincinnati, Ohio.
Amity Road, Reading, Ohio.
Est: 1828
Division of **Vick Chemical Co.**
1880   Revised Current Price List; 48 pp; **MF/MAH.**

MERRY OPTICAL CO.
Kansas City, Missouri.
ca 1910   Catalog of Refractive Instruments; 23 pp; **MAH** (C 617.75085).
n.d.   General Catalog Series 25; Eyeglasses, Spectacles, Cases; 288 pp; **URRR** (M-308).

MERWIN, HULBERT & CO.
26 West 23rd Street, New York, New York.
1891   Catalog, Gymnasium Apparatus and Fixtures; 40 pp; **CTY/B** (Uai M 559).

MERZ CAPSULE CO., THE
Detroit, Michigan.
1891   Revised Net Price List of The Merz Capsule Co., Gelatine Capsule Mfrs.; 23 pp; **CPP.**

MESSTER, ED.
Friedrichs-Strasse 99, Berlin, Germany.
1873   Preisverzeichniss . . . Optischen und Mechanischen Werkstatt; 18 pp; **NYAM; MF/MAH.**
1909   Preisliste ueber Mikroskope fuer Wissenschaftliche Zwecke; 88 pp; **URRR** (M-Box 31).

METALIX
See: C. H. F. MULLER, A. B., Hamburg; 1931; **ACR/MAH.**
PHILIPS METALIX CORP.; NORTH AMERICAN PHILIPS CO., INC.

METZ, H. A., LABORATORIES
122 Hudson Street, New York, New York.
See: WINTHROP-METZ; **NYAM.**
    1921   The Sal Varsans; 24 pp; **CPP.**
  Oct. 1931   Novocain, The Supraperiostal Injection; **MAH.**

METZGER, FERDINAND F.
145 North 7th Street, Philadelphia, Pennsylvania.
    189?   Manufacturer of Optical, Physical and Electrical Instruments; 1 pp; **CPP.**

MUENCKE, DR. ROBERT
Luisen Strasse, 58, Berlin N W.
Est: 1878
    1900   Katalog, Ueber bacteriologische, mikroskopische und hygienische Apparate; 360 pp; **URRR** (M-309).

MEYER, A., & CO.
1 Utostrasse Enge, Zurich.
    1891   Preis Verzeichniss ueber Mikroskope und Hilfs-Apparate aus der Optischen Werkstaette; 42 pp; **URRR** (M-297).

MEYER, BERNARD
151 Chambers Street, New York, New York.
Est. 1853
    1894   Catalog Drug, Pill & Powder Boxes; 32 pp; **NYAM; MF/MAH.**

MEYER BROTHERS & CO.
MEYER BROS. DRUG CO.
217 S. 4th Street, St. Louis, Mo.
Est: 1852
    1887   Annual Price Current of Meyer Bros. & Co., Importers and Wholesale Druggists; Reprint; **UTP.**

MEYER, CURT W.
New York.
    1886?   Illustrated Catalogue and Price-List of Physical and Chemical, Electro-Medical, Optical and Scientific Instruments, etc.; 64 pp; **BLEL.**

MEYER & KETSTING
Kaiserstrasse 106/8, Karlsruhe (Baden), Germany.
    n.d.   Wholesale and Export Catalog of Vulcanite & Metal Surgical Instruments, Paquelin's Thermo-Cauteries and Accessories of Platina and Platini-Iridium; 12 pp; loose cover; **RCSL.**

MEYER, MAX
18 West 27th Street, New York, New York.
    ca 1910   Dealer; Three Brochures advertising Spencer Microscopes: no. 20, 36, 40, 46, 66, 70, filed with Spencer Catalogs; **AFMM.**

MEYER, WILLIAM, CO.
825 West Washington Boulevard, Chicago, Illinois.
Est: 1904
ca 1910	X-Ray and Electro-Medical Apparatus; 10 brochures bound in Meyer binder; **ACR/MAH**.
ca 1910	X-Ray and Electro-Medical Apparatus; 15 brochures; **ACR/MAH**.
ca 1915	Brochure, X-Ray Tubes and High Frequency Electrodes; 12 pp; **ACR/MAH**.
1915?	Brochure, X-Ray Accessories; 36 pp; **ACR/MAH**.
ca 1916	Catalog, X-Ray & Electro-Medical Apparatus; 44 pp; **NYAM; MF/MAH**.

1644 North Girard Street, Chicago, Illinois.
ca 1920	Brochures, 5 clipped together, Transformers, Klinoscope, Vertical Radioscope, Wheatstone Stereoscope, Tubes and High Frequency Electrodes; 25 pp; **ACR/MAH**.
July 1920	Price List of Accessories Bulletin; single sheet; **ACR/MAH; MAH**.
ca 1920	Pamphlet, Meyer Multoscope, a Combination Stereo-Radiographic Table and Klinoscope; 11 pp; **ACR/MAH; MAH**.
ca 1920	Catalog, X-Ray Accessories; 32 pp; **ACR/MAH; MAH**.
ca 1930	Pamphlet, Meyer Improved Universal Klinoscope; 3 pp; **ACR/MAH; MAH**.
n.d.	X-Ray Tubes High Frequency Electrodes; 12 pp; **NYAM; MF/MAH**.
n.d.	Meyer Type E Apparatus; 2 pp; **NYAM; MF/MAH**.
n.d.	Meyer Type F Apparatus; 2 pp; **NYAM; MF/MAH**.
n.d.	Meyer Portable High Frequency Apparatus; 8 pp; **NYAM; MF/MAH**.
n.d.	Meyer no. 2 Interruptless X-Ray Apparatus; 5 pp, pp 3 & 4 missing; **NYAM; MF/MAH**.

56 Fifth Avenue, Chicago, Illinois.
n.d.	X-Ray and Electro-Therapeutic Apparatus; 32 pp; **CPP**.

MEYER-STEINEG, DR. THEODORE
Jena, Germany.
1912	Chirurgische Instrumente des Altertums von Dr. Theod. Meyer-Steineg; 49 pp; **MAH**.

MEYERSTEIN, ARTHUR
51 Maiden Lane, New York, New York.
1904?	Brochure, Bougies, Porgies, Catheters; 8 pp, covers missing; **NYAM**.

MEYROWITZ, E. B.
104 East 23rd Street, New York, New York.
no. 297 Fourth Avenue, New York, New York.
Est: 1875
See: AKOUPHONE MANUFACTURING CO.
1880	Illustrated Catalogue of Optical Goods, Manufactured and Imported by Meyrowitz Bros.; 134 pp; **CPP, CTY/B** (Uai M5781).
n.d.	Illustrated Catalog of Surgical Instruments; 26 pp; **CPP** (42/Ed).
ca 1887	Brochure, The Otophone, Patented 1887; 5 pp; **NYAM; MF/MAH; CPP**.
Jun.1892	Catalog, Instruments for Eye, Ear, Nose & Throat; 36 pp; **NYAM; MF/MAH**.
Mar. 1893	Bulletin, Instruments Used in Ophthalmology, Otology, Rhinology, Laryngology, and Microscopy, no. 13; 11 pp; **NYAM; MF/MAH**.

Nov. 1893	Bulletin, Instruments Used in Ophthalmology, Otology, Rhinology, Laryngology, & Microscopy, no. 14; 12 pp; **NYAM; MF/MAH**.
1893	The M.B. Storage Battery, Electrodes, Illuminators, Snares and Handles; 48 pp; **BLEL**.
1894	Illustrated Catalog of Ophthalmological Apparatus and Eye, Ear, Nose, and Throat Instruments; 3rd ed., Parts II & III; 154 pp; **CPP; MCFM**.
Jan. 1895	Catalog Eyeglasses; 4 pp; **NYAM; MF/MAH**.
Feb. 1895	Bulletin, Instrument Used in Ophthalmology, Otology, Rhinology, Laryngology and Microscopy; no. 17; 16 pp; **NYAM; MF/MAH**.
1898	Catalog of Dry Cell Batteries, Current Controllers, Part IV; 73 pp; **AFMM**.

125 West 42nd Street, New York.

1898	Optical and Meteorological Instruments and Projection Apparatus, Parts VI, VII, VIII & IX; 168 pp; **AFMM**.
ca 1898	Illustrated Catalogue of Ophthalmological Apparatus and Eye, Ear, Nose and Throat Instruments; 71-218 pp; **BLEL**.
Feb. 1900	Meyrowitz Bulletin, Ophthalmological Instruments and Appaatus, no. 22; 16 pp; **MAH** (C 617.75085).
Oct. 1900	Bulletin, Instruments Used in Ophthalmology, Otology, Laryngology, Rhinology and Microscopy, no. 23; 12 pp; **NYAM; MF/MAH**.
ca 1900	Illustrated Catalog of X-Ray Apparatus Used in Radiography and Fluoroscopic Demonstrations, Cardiographs, Lantern Slides, X-Ray Dry Plates, etc. Part X, 2nd ed.; 15 pp; **MAH** (C 616.0757M).
Jun. 1901	Bulletin of Instruments Shown at the Pan-American Exposition, no. 24; 12 pp; **NYAM; MF/MAH**.
1901	Meyrowitz Bulletin, Ophthalmological Instruments and Apparatus, Pan-American ed., no. 24; 11 pp; **MAH** (C 617.75085M).
1901	Illustrated Catalog of Ophthalmological Apparatus & Eye, Ear, Nose and Throat Instruments; 4th ed., Parts II & III with separate titles; 218 pp; **MAH** (C617.7085M); **AFMM**.
1902	Catarrhal Deafness, Being A Study of Its Treatment; 32 pp; **CPP**.
Jun. 1902	Bulletin, Instruments Used in the Practice of Ophthalmology, Otology, Rhinology, Laryngology & Microscopy, no. 25; 15 pp; **NYAM; MF/MAH**.
1903	Dry Cell Galvanic and Faradic Batteries, Mil = am = meters and Volt Limit Selectors, Current Controllers for the Constant and Alternating Electric Currents; 73 pp; **AFMM**.
May 1906	Bulletin, Instruments Used in the Practice of Ophthalmology, Otology, Rhinology, Laryngology, Electro-Therapy & X-Ray Sciences, no. 31; 15 pp; **NYAM; MF/MAH**.
Aug. 1906	Bulletin, Instruments Used in the Practice of Ophthalmology, Otology, Rhinology, Laryngology, no. 32; 28 pp; **NYAM; MF/MAH**.
Sep. 1906	Bulletin, Electro-Therapeutic Instruments; no. 1; 16 pp; **NYAM; MF/MAH**.
1906	Ophthalmological Apparatus, Eye, Ear, Nose and Throat Instruments; 5th ed., Parts II and III; 241 pp, index; **NYAM; MF/MAH; AFMM; MAH** (C 617.75085); **CPP**.
ca 1906	Brochure of High Frequency X-Ray Apparatus and Accessories; 8 pp; **AFMM**.
1906?	Brochure, X-Ray High Frequency Apparatus and Accessories; 6 pp; **ACR/MAH**.

1907   Catalog, The Sutcliffe Keratometer, A New Ophthalmometer containing description, direction, photos, illustrations of the use, ordering procedure and other items such as tables, chairs to be used with this object; 24 pp; **MAH** (C 617.75085 M).

Main Factory: 404, 406, 408, 410 E. 37th Street, New York, New York.

125 W. 42nd Street, New York, New York.

Mar. 1908   Meyrowitz Bulletin; 16 pp; **CTY/B** (Uai M 578).

Branches: 45 6th Street South, Minneapolis, Minnesota. 360 Saint Peter Street, St. Paul, Minnesota.

Mar. 1908   Price List; 7 pp; **URRR** (M-255).

Mar. 1908   *Meyrowitz Bulletin*, Published in the Interest of Ophthalmology, Otology, Rhinology, Laryngology and Microscopy, no. 34; **CTY/B** (Uai M 578).

Dec. 1908   Bulletin, Instruments Used in Ophthalmology, Otology, Rhinology, Laryngology & Microscopy, no. 35; 16 pp; **NYAM; MF/MAH**.

May 1909   Catalog, Instruments & Apparatus for Use in Ophthalmology, Otology, Rhinology, Laryngology & Microscopy, no. 36; 13 pp; **NYAM; MF/MAH**.

ca 1910   Catalog E, X-Ray Radiographic Plates, The Ilford Plate, Sec. 5; 2 pp; **ACR/MAH**.

520 Fifth Avenue, New York, New York.

ca 1910   Tendon Shortening Instruments; 1 pp; **MAH**.

ca 1910   The Klaar Headlight; 1 pp; **MAH**.

ca 1910   The Braun Adenotome and Curette and the New Meyrowitz Rheostat; 1 pp; **MAH**.

n.d.   Catalog, Optical, Meteorological Instruments and Projection Apparatus; 4th ed., Parts VI, IX; 168 pp; **NYAM; MF/MAH**.

n.d.   Catalog, Ophthalmological Apparatus, Eye, Ear, Nose & Throat Instruments; 6th ed.; 120 pp; **NYAM; MF/MAH**.

1911   Catalog, Ophthalmological Apparatus & Electro-Medical Equipment; 6th ed., Parts II, II, IV; 232 pp; **NYAM; MF/MAH; SLSC**.

post 1911   Ophthalmic Apparatus, Eye, Ear, Nose and Throat Instruments and Electro-Medical Equipment; 6th ed.; 232 pp; **MUM**.

Aug. 1913   Catalog Instruments Used in Ophthalmology, Otology, Rhinology, Laryngology and Microscopy; no. 39; 16 pp; **NYAM; MF/MAH**.

1914   Sterilizers Supplement to Catalog E; 3rd ed.; 11 pp; **CPP**.

Jun. 1915   Meyrowitz Brothers, no. 43; 16 pp; **CPP**.

May 1916   Meyrowitz Brothers, no. 44; 16 pp; **CPP**.

May 1, 1916   Ophthalmological Apparatus Price Change Note; 232 pp; **CPP**.

520 Fifth Ave., (NY).

Jun. 1917   Bulletin, Instruments Used in Ophthalmology, Otology, Rhinology & Laryngology, no. 45; 16 pp; **NYAM; MF/MAH; CPP; CTY/B** (Uai M 578).

Jun. 1919   Bulletin, Eye, Ear, Nose & Throat Instruments, no. 47; 16 pp; **NYAM; MF/MAH; MAH**.

Jun. 1921   Bulletin, Ear, Eye, Nose and Throat Instruments, no. 48; 15 pp, pp 2 & 3 are missing; **NYAM; MF/MAH**.

1921   Catalog, Ophthalmological Apparatus, Eye, Ear, Nose & Throat Surgical Instruments, Specialists' Equipment; Supplementary 6th ed.; 121 pp; **CUHSL** (RD 76 M 57), **URRR** (M-345).

1925   Bulletin, Instrument Used in Ophthalmology, Rhinology & Laryngology; no. 51; **MUM**.

Dec. 1927   Bulletin, Instrument Used in Ophthalmology, Rhinology & Laryngology, no. 52; 32 pp; **NYAM; MF/MAH**.

May 15, 1929	Bulletin Instruments Used in Ophthalmology, Otology, Rhinology & Laryngology; no. 53; 8 pp; **NYAM; MF/MAH**.
n.d.	Catalog, X-Ray, High Frequency Apparatus & Accessories; no. 6, Part V; 39 pp; **NYAM; MF/MAH**.
n.d.	Catalog, Hearing Aids; 20 pp; **NYAM; MF/MAH**.
n.d.	Brochure, The Sutcliffe Keratometer; 24 pp; **NYAM; MF/MAH**.
n.d.	Catalog, Instruments for the Eye, Ear, Nose & Throat; 55 pp; **NYAM; MF/MAH**.
n.d.	Brochure, The Magic Earphone; 9 pp; **NYAM; MF/MAH**.
n.d.	Physicians' Cabinet no. 101, Especially Adapted for Ear, Nose, Throat Practice; 4 pp; **CPP**.
n.d.	The First Rigid Spring Eyeglasses; 1 pp; **CPP**.
n.d.	Price List, Staining Fluids and Chemical Preparations for Microscopic Anantomy and Dr. Gruber's Aniline Dyes; 12 pp; **CPP**.
n.d.	New Model Masseur; 4 pp; **CPP**.
n.d.	Aids to Hearing; 16 pp; **CPP**.
n.d.	Portable X-Ray and High-Frequency Apparatus, Catalogue E, Sec. 3; 8 pp; **CTY/B** (Uai M 578).
n.d.	X-Ray High Frequency Apparatus and Accessories; 17 pp; **CTY/B** (Uai M 578).
n.d.	Unimount, A New Eyeglass; 1 pp, folded; **URRR** (M-314).
n.d.	Ophthalmological Apparatus, Eye, Ear, Nose and Throat Instruments; 232 pp; **URRR** (M-313); **MRLB**.

MEYROWITZ BROTHERS

303 Fourth Avenue, New York, New York.
78 N. Pearl St., Albany, New York.

| Dec. 6, 1879 | Advertisement in *Medical Records*; 1 pp; **MUM** (Ed 119 r2 p. 747). |

297 Fourth Avenue, New York.

| 1880 | Illustrated Catalog of Optical Goods; **CTY/B** (Uai M5781). |
| 1893 | The M.B. Storage Battery, Electrodes, Illuminators, Snares and Handles, M.B. Motors, Drills, and Trephines; 48 pp; **BLEL**. |

MICHAULT

Paris, France.

| ca 1775 | Instrument maker mentioned by the veterinary instrument maker Page, Vol. IV, in catalog at **RCSL**. |

MICHIGAN BIOLOGICAL SUPPLY CO.

324 South State Street, Ann Arbor, Michigan.

| 1923 | Jewell Models for Biology; 12 pp; **CPP**. |
| n.d. | Biological Supplies, Catalog no. 6; 32 pp; **CPP**. |

MICHIGAN OPTICAL COMPANY

83 to 93 Beacon Street, Detroit, Michigan.
Toronto, Canada.
Est: 1895
From 1895 to 1914, company distributed through jobbers. In 1915, they went to direct sales.

1912	Price List for Frames, Mountings, and Materials; 23 pp; **AO**.
1914	Quality; 56 pp; **AO**.
Mar. 1, 1915	Price List of Lenses; 24 pp; **AO**.
1915	Quality; 56 pp; **AO**.
Oct. 10, 1918	Catalogue, revised Prices, Styles and Qualities, Supplement C; 4 pp; **AO**.

MIDLAND DENTAL MANUFACTURING CO., LTD.
Birmingham, England.
      n.d.   Catalog; **BDA**.

MIDWEST OPTICAL SUPPLY
16 East Fourth St., Dayton, OH.
      1930   Prescription and Stock Price List; 35 pp; **URRR** (M-366A).
      1933   6 pp; **URRR** (M-336).
      1933?   Prescription and Stock Catalog, Lenses, Cases, Frames, Mountings, Goggles, Oxfords, Supplies; 86 pp; **AO**.
Prospect-Fourth Bldg., Cleveland, Ohio.
      1934?   Prescription and Stock Catalog, no. 21; 100 pp; **AO**.
      1936   Optical Supply Catalog no. 30; **URRR** (M-366B).
  May 3, 1937   56 pp; **URRR** (M-366).
  Nov. 30, 1938   Prescription Service and Stock Lenses, Mountings, Frames, Oxfords, Cases, Goggles; 67 pp; **URRR** (M-364).
      n.d.   Catalogue no. 45; 16 pp; **URRR** (M-365).

MIEHE, GUSTAV
Hildesheim.
      1895   Mikrotome und Nebenapparate, Preis-Verzeichniss ueber Instrumente und Apparate; 23 pp; **URRR** (M-12).

MILBURN, H. J., & CO.
Detroit, Michigan.
      n.d.   General Prices Current of Surgical Instruments and Appliances; 381 pp, illustrated; **TMHM**.

MILLER & BROTHERS
69 Nassau Street, New York, New York.
      1868?   Catalog Achromatic Microscopes, Telescopes, Opera and Field Glasses; **CTY/B** (Uai M6142).
1213 Broadway, New York, New York.
      1879   An Illustrated Description of First-Class Achromatic Microscopes, Apparatus, Specimens, etc.; 44 pp; **AFMM**.

MILLER, HORACE M.
Owsego, Oregon.
      1934   The Dental Office Guide; **LLU** (WU 26 M648d).

MILLER, O. E., HERNIA TREATMENT CO.
Tabor Opera Block, Denver, Colorado.
Est: ca 1885
      ca 1890   Rupture Cured Permanently or No Pay; 16 pp; **CPP**.

MILLER, J(ACOB) & D(AVID)
25 Canal Street, New York, New York.
36 Canal St. (1915), New York, New York.
1805-7 Bronxdale Ave., Cor: Morris Park Ave., Bronx, New York.
Est: 1909
      1923   Catalog of Current Prices, Circumcision Knives and Paraphernalia (English in transliterated Hebrew); **MAH** (divison of Community Life).

MILLER RUBBER MANUFACTURING CO.
Akron, Ohio.
      ca 1899   The Aseptic Hand; 4 pp; **CPP**.

Nov. 15, 1912   Scientific Spraying Devices; 23 pp; **CPP**.
1918   Catalog of Surgeon's Grade Rubber Goods; 49 pp; **NLM** (W26 qM652).

MILLIKEN, JOHN T., & CO.
St Louis, Missouri.
See: ABBOTT LABORATORIES, foreward, 1928; **NYAM**.
n.d.   Price List Products of the Bacteriologic Laboratory of John T. Millikin & Co.; 3 pp; **CPP**.

MILLIKIN, STRAND
1825   Instrument maker mentioned by John Read.

MILNE, JOHN
Ladywell, London.
Nov. 1, 1890   John Milne's Price List of Surgical Dressings; 22 pp; **CPP**.

MILVAY
n.d.   Trademark for Chicago Apparatus Company; **NLM**.

MILWAUKEE OPTICAL MFG. CO.
Milwaukee, Wisconsin.
Inc: 1920s
Oct. 1, 1912   Price List and Catalog;   pp; **AO; URRR** (M-13).
Oct. 1915   Price List and Catalog; 236 pp; **AO**.
1930   Instruments, Equipment, & Accessories for the Refractionist and Specialist; 64 pp; **AO**.

MINE SAFETY APPLIANCE CO.
Pittsburgh, Pa.
Aug. 15, 1933   MSA Goggle Price List; **AO**.

MION, JOSEF
Sagrado bei Goerz.
n.d.   Einzige Fabrik elektrischer Apparate System Alimonda, Appendix to the Prospectus of the Nature Cure of Drs. Alimonda Brothers; 15 pp; **CPP**.

MITCHELL, CHARLES L.
1016-18 Cherry St., Philadelphia, Pennsylvania.
1930's   Catalog, Mitchell's Gonocide Bougies for Gonorrhea, Gleet, etc.; 8 pp; **CTY/B** (Uai M 692).

MITCHELL, WILLIAM
10 Broad Street, Albany, New York.
1847   Surgical Instrument Maker listed in Albany City Directory.

MIX, JAMES
28 Beaver Street, Albany, New York.
18 Green, Albany, New York (1837).
1833–41   Jeweler and Spectacle Maker listed in Albany City Directory.

MOECKE, OTTO
Universitaetsstrasse 13, Leipzig, Vienna.
n.d.   Catalog, Chirurgischer Instrumente; 143 pp; **NYAM; MF/MAH**.

MOELLER, J. D.
Wedel in Holstein, Berlin, Germany.
Est: 1875

1883 Preisverzeichniss mikroskopischer Praeparaten, Utensilien und Materialien zur Anfertigung derselben; 40 pp; **CTY/B** (Uai M722).

MOHR, R., AND SONS
Mohr Bldg., 883 Mission St., San Francisco, CA.
    1924   Catalog of Optical Merchandise and Sundries; 47 pp; **URRR** (M-346).
150 Post Rd., San Francisco, CA.
    pre-1937   Spectacles, Eye Glasses, Colored Glasses, Goggles, Compasses, Magnifiers, Field Glasses, Spectacle Cases, etc., Optical Catalogue no. 2; 84 pp; **AO**.
    pre-1937   Spectacles, Eye Glasses, Colored Glasses, Goggles, Compasses, Magnifiers, Field Glasses, Spectacle Cases, etc., Optical Catalogue no. 3; 56 pp; **AO**.
    pre-1937   Motor and Sportsman's Glasses, Automobile Goggles and Eye Protectors Goggle Catalogue, no. 5; 24 pp; **AO**.
    1937   Optical Specialties, Catalog no. 9; 72 pp, index; **AO**.
    n.d.   A Catalog of Spectacles, Eye Glasses, Smoke Glasses, Eye Protectors, Automobile Goggles, Field and Opera Glasses, Magnifying Glasses, Eye Shades and Optical Material; **URRR** (M-236).

MOLINARI
Barcelona, Spain.
    n.d.   Fadesteran Molinari, 18th c. pocket set in WHM (R .3681/1936); **RCSL**.

MOLTENI, A.
44 rue de Chateau d'eau, Paris, France.
    n.d.   Brochure, Lumière oxy-étherique, no. 62; 3 pp; **NYAM; MF/MAH**.

MONEL METAL
See: INTERNATIONAL NICKEL CO., INC.

MONTAGUE, J. H.
London, England.
    1897   Illustrated Catalogue of Surgical Instruments, Appliances and Cutlery; 464 pp; **BLEL; TMHM**.

MONTGOMERY WARD & CO.
    1891-2   Catalog no. 50, photocopies from pertinent pages of catalog; **MAH**.

MOOCK-GUILLOT
See: GUILLOT, FERNAND; **AFMM**.

MOORE, JNO L., & SONS
Murphy Bldg., Auburn Ave. and Pryor Street, Atlanta, GA.
Originally located in the Prudential Bldg., company moved to above address in March 1908.
    1909   Price Prescription List; 40 pp; **URRR** (M-312).
    1912   Illustrated Catalog and Price List; 136 pp; **URRR** (M-311); **AO**.

MOORE, MAIDSTONE
    1825   Instrument maker mentioned by John Read.

MORETTE
Paris, France.
    ca 1835   Instrument maker mentioned by the Veterinary Instrument maker Pagé, Vol. IV, as the successor to M. Leruerer, in the catalog at **RCSL**.

MORIA, P.
Paris, France.
    1910   Catalog d'instruments et appareils ophtalmologiques; **CPP**.

MORITZ BOEHME
75 Oranienburger Strasse, Hof Part, Berlin North, Germany.
        n.d.   Verbandstoff-Fabrik und chirurgische Artikel zur Krankenpflege; 76 pp;
            CPP.

MORRIS & SCHRADER
8 Barclay Street, New York, New York.
        n.d.   Kissingen Rakoczy, the Genuine Kissingen Water; 4 pp; **CPP**.

MORRISON & PLUMBER
Chicago, Illinois.
        1887   Morrison & Plummer Prices Current; **UTP**.

MORSE & BURT CO.
1 Carlton Avenue, Brooklyn, New York.
        n.d.   Two Feet of Happiness; 8 pp; **CPP**.

MORTON, GEORGE, & CO.
19-21 Wilson Street, Finsbury, London, England.
        Jan. 1899   Catalog Anatomical, Pathological and Museum Jars Manufactured from
                  the finest White Soda Glass; 25th Ed; 4 pp; **CTY/B** (Uai M 842).
        Jan. 1900   Price List of Anatomical, Pathological amd Museum Jars, Lists all
                  customer supplied institutions; 27th ed.; 8 pp; **CTY/B** (Uai M 842).

MOTT, J. L., IRONWORKS
Fifth Avenue & 17th Street, New York, New York.
  Trenton, New Jersey.
Est: before 1901
        1921   Catalog, Hospital Plumbing & Hydrotherapeutic Equipment with Photos
             of Companies & Hospitals Which Use Mott Products; 33 pp; **NYAM;**
             MF/MAH.

MOYER, THE J. BIRD CO., INC.
1210-1214 Vine Street, Philadelphia, Pennsylvania.
Est: 1894
        ca 1905   The J. Bird Mfg. Co., Dental Chemists and Metallurgists, Mfrs. of Strictly
             High Grade Dental Products; 32 pp; **HML**.
        ca 1935   Catalog of Dental Products and Specialties, one log of development of
             company from 1894 when Desanno & Hussey formed a partnership;
             164 pp; **NLM** (W26 M 938).
  1211 Vine Street, Philadelphia, Pennsylvania.
        n.d.   Catalog Dental Products; no. 12; 200 pp; **NYAM; MF/MAH**.
        n.d.   Catalog no. 13; 168 pp; **UPSDM** (D 617.604 M 874).
        n.d.   Fliers (13) Mortar & Pestle, Scientific Proportioner for Mercury & Alloy,
             Heavy Service Mandrel, New Prices on Alloy, Amalgam Spoon, Electric
             Modeling Compound Heater, Nonabrasive Arbor Bands, the Holland
             Dental Chip Blower, Stainless Steel Mandrels, A Real Reversible
             Mandrel, Diamond Ruby Grooved Instrument Sharpener, Diamond
             Ruby Instrument Sharpeners, Wayne Wax Burs; 4 pp; **NYAM;**
             MF/MAH.

MU-COL CO., THE
Buffalo, New York.
Est: 1900
        n.d.   Mu-Col for Cleansing Mucous Membrances; 2 pp; **CPP**.

MUELHENS & KROPFF
113 West Broadway, New York, New York.
      n.d.   The New Superfatted Medicinal Soaps; 3 pp; **CPP**.

MUELLER, C. H. F.
Hammerbrookstrasse 93, Hamburg, Germany.
Est: 1865
    See: QUEEN & CO., INC., 1906 Catalog; **ACR/MAH**.
    July 1928   Catalog Mueller Helium X-Ray Tubes; 18 pp; **ACR/MAH**.
        1930   Von Werden Der Roentgen-Rohren Sonderheft Der Technischen
              Mitteilunger fuer Roentgenbetriebe, includes history of factory; 95 pp;
              ACR/MAH.
      1930s   Muller Media Line Focus X-Ray Tubes; 10 pp foldout; **ACR/MAH**.
    ca 1930   Catalog Original Muller X-Ray Tubes; 52 pp; **ACR/MAH**.

MUELLER, F. A. D., SOHNE
Taunustrasse 14, Wiesbaden, Germany.
        1906   Instruction for Ordering Artificial Eyes; 20 pp, tear out sheets to give
              patients; **NYAM; MF/MAH; CPP**.

MUELLER & CO.
405 W. 59th Street, New York, New York.
Fehrenback, Germany.
      n.d.   Catalog, Vaginal or Wound Washing Tube; **CTY/B** (Uai M 8875).
      n.d.   Catalog, Mueller and Company's Specialties: Mueller's Eye Washer &
              Spray, Mueller's Nose Douche or Tube, Mueller's Ear Tube; **CTY/B**
              (Uai M 8875).
      n.d.   Catalog of Mueller and Company's Scientific and Chemical Glass
              Manufacturers; 56 pp; **CPP**.

MUELLER-UNKEL, LOUIS
13 Rebenstrasse, Braunschweig, Germany.
    Apr. 1896   Catalogue, Nachtrag zum Hauptkatalog; **CTY/B** (Uai M 888).
    May 1896   Catalogue, absorptiometer nach Passow zum Studium der einwirkung von
              Gasen auf feste Koerper und Flussiguekeitten; **CTY/B** (Uai M 888).
    Dec. 1896   Catalogue, Neuste Constructionem aus dem Glastechnischen Institute,
              includes x-ray equipment; **CTY/B** (Uai M 888).

MUELLER, VINCENZ, & CO.
1775 to 1781 Ogden Avenue, Chicago, Illinois.
Est: 1895
    ca 1906   Makers of Surgical Instruments, Hospital and Office Furniture, Deformity
              Apparatus and Physicians' Supplies; 738 pp, index; **JHIHM** (RC
              76.M94); **SLSC**.
        1910   Makers of Surgical Instruments, Hospital and Office Furniture, Deformity
              Apparatus and Physicians' Supplies; **CPP** (Ed/67).
        1911   Catalog S, Electro Therapeutic X Ray and Other Physical Apparatus; 62
              pp; **ACR/MAH**.
    May 1913   Catalog M, Direct Laryngeal, Bronchial, Oesophageal and Stomach
              Instruments; 28 pp; **CPP**.
        1916   Surgeons' Instruments, Office and Hospital Equipment; 4th ed., no. 7;
              320 pp; **UCLABM** (W 26 M 887s); **NYAM; MF/MAH**.
    ca 1919   Surgical Instruments, Hospital and Office Furniture, Deformity Apparatus

and Physicians' Supplies; 730 pp; **VM**.

1924   Condensed General Catalog, Surgical Instruments and Equipment; 6th ed.; 612 pp; **NLM** (W26 M947); **VM; MAH**.

ca 1925   Compressed Air and Negative Pressure for Operating and Treatment Rooms; 24 pp; **VM**.

1928   Instruments for Oral and Plastic Surgery; 54 pp; **VM**.

1929   Surgeon's Instruments and Equipment for the Eye, Ear, Nose and Throat; 7th ed.; 328 pp; **CPP** (Ed/77); **VM**.

n.d.   Bulletin no. 3, New Instruments, Apparatus and Office Equipment; 35 pp; **CPP**.

n.d.   Bulletin no. 4; 51 pp; **CPP**.

n.d.   Supplement no. 2; 20 pp; **CPP**.

n.d.   Post Operative Hemorrhages; 1 pp; **CPP**.

264-266 Ogden Avenue, Van Buren and Honore Streets, Chicago, Illinois.

ea 20 c   Catalog of Medical and Surgical Instruments, Orthopedic Apparatus, Hospital and Sick Room Supplies; pp 3-591; **AFMM**.

ca 1915   Dr. J. F. Percy's Instruments for the Application of Heat, to Inhibit and Destroy Inoperable Carcinoma of the Uterus and Vagina; 4 pp; **MAH** (12692).

ca 1915   The Latest New Instruments for Eye, Ear, Nose and Throat Work; 20 pp; **MAH** (12693).

ca 1915   New Instruments and Office Equipment, Bulletin no. 3; 35 pp; **MAH** (12694).

ca 1915   New Instruments and Office Equipment, Bulletin no. 4; 51 pp; **MAH** (12695).

1930   Catalog no. 8, Hospital Supplies and Equipment, Surgeons' Instruments; 249 pp; **NLM** (W26 M 947).

1938   General Catalog of Surgical Instruments, Equipment, Furniture and Supplies; 600 pp; **NLM** (W26 M947).

1938   Hospital, Instruments, Equipment, Supplies; 680 pp; **AFMM**.

ca 1938   Complete General Catalog: Surgical Instruments, Equipment, Furniture and Supplies; 680 pp; **BLEL; MCFM**.

n.d.   The Latest New Instruments Invented and Found to be of Value to the Eye, Ear, Nose and Throat Specialist Since the Compilation of our Catalogue; 6 pp; **CPP**.

n.d.   Surgical Instruments, An Historical Sketch of the Development of the Surgeon's Instrumentarium; 48 pp; **YML** (RD 71 900m).

ca 1920   Condensed General Catalog Surgeons' Instruments, Office and Hospital Equipment; 5th ed.; 414 pp; **MAH**.

MUELLER X-RAY TUBES
See: AMERICAN VACUUM COMPANY; **ACR/MAH**.

MUENCKE, GEBRUEDER
Karlstrasse 18a, Berlin N W, Germany.

ca 1890   Abtheilung I, Chemische Apparate und Geräthschaften, Abtheilung II, Bacteriologische Apparate, Mikroskopische Utensilien, Sterilisir. Apparate, Abtheilung III, Electrische Apparate; 214 pp, **AFMM**.

1910   Catalogue Haupt-Preisliste no. 63 ueber allgemeine chemische Laboratoriums-Apparate und Geraetschaften. Fabrik und Lager von Apparaten und Geraetschaften fuer chemischen, bakteriologischen, physikalischen . . . .; **CTY/B** (Uai M 889).

MUENCKE, DR. ROBERT
58 Luisenstrasse, Berlin NW 6, Germany.
Est: 1878

    1910   Haupt-Preisliste no. 63 ueber Allgemeine chemische Laboratoriums-Apparate und Geraetschaften. Fabrik und Lager von Apparaten und Geraetschaften fuer chemischen bakteriologischen, physikalischen . . . .; 1224 pp; **CTY/B** (Uai M 889).

MUKERJI H. & CO.
39/1 College Street, Calcutta, India.
Est: 1905

    n.d.   Catalog of Hospital Furniture and Sterilizer; 16 pp; **AFMM; MAH**.

MULLER, C.
64 & 65 Holborn Viaduct, London E. C., England.
Berlin, N. O., Germany.
Est: 1875

    n.d.   Wholesale and for Export Only Illustrated Catalogue of Surgical Instruments; 2nd ed.; 186 pp; **RCSL**.

MUNRO, R. W., LTD.
103-149 Cornwall Rd, South Tottenham, London, N 15, England.

    n.d.   Improved Photomicrographic Camera and Microscope (Patented); 11 pp; **URRR** (M-375).

MURLEY-ROLLESTON CORPORATION
  See: MCFEDRIES X-RAY CO., Chicago; **ACR/MAH**.

MURRAY-BAUMGARTNER SURGICAL INSTRUMENT COMPANY, INC.
1421 Maryland Avenue, Baltimore, Maryland.

    1960   Jobbers Illustrated Catalogue, Surgical Instruments, Equipment & Supplies for Hospitals and Physicians; 28 pp, index; **MAH**.

MYERSON TOOTH CORPORATION
Cambridge, Massachusetts.

    n.d.   Porcelain Anteriors; **MAH**.

MYNOL CHEMICAL CO.

    1931   Dental Specialties; **UPSDM** (D 617.604. M 989).

NACHET ET FILS
16 rue Serpente, Paris, France.

    1856   Catalogue, descriptif des instruments de micrographie; 16 pp; **CTY/B** (Uai N 114).

    1863   Catalogue, descriptif des instruments de micrographie; **CPP**.

17 rue Saint-Severin, Paris, France.

    1863   Catalogue, descriptif des instruments de micrographie; **MUM** (Ed 51 pam 19).

  May 1872   Catalogue, instruments de micrographie; 29 pp; **NYAM; MF/MAH**.

    1892   Microscopes, objectifs & accessoires appareils de microphotographie construits par; 77 pp; **RCSL**.

    1898   Microscopes et accessoires; 82 pp; **URRR** (N-13).

    1904   Instruments d'optique et de précision construits par Nachet et fils; 93 pp; **URRR** (N-12).

    1913   Instruments d'optique et de précision; 93 pp; **URRR** (N-69).

    1924   Microscopes; 28 pp; **URRR** (N-14).

1979 Maison Nachet: Catalogues de Fonds de 1854 à 1910. Introd. par G. L'E. Turner; various pages; **MAH, BLEL**.

NAGASHIMA, R., CO.
No. 12 4-chome, Hongo, Hong-ku, Tokyo, Japan.
1920s Catalogue of Medical and Surgical Instruments and Laboratory Equipment; 81 pp, Japanese; **AFMM**.
n.d. Pamphlet, Gracious Illuminating Apparatus for Eye, Ear, Nose and Throat; 16 pp; **AFMM**.
n.d. Gracious; 4 pp, foldout; **AFMM**.
n.d. Brochure of Ear Trumpets and Hearing Aids; 8 pp; **AFMM**.

NAKAI DENTAL SUPPLY CO.
38 Awajimachi 4-chome, Osaka, Japan.
1927 Catalog Dental Furniture, Appliances, Instruments & Materials; 135 pp; 11th ed.; **NYAM; MF/MAH**.

NALDER BROTHERS & CO.
132 Horseferry Road, Westminster, London SW, England.
Apr. 20, 1888 Price List of Apparatus and Instruments Illustrated and Described in Professor W. E. Ayrton's Practical Electricity; 13 pp; **CTY/B** (Uai N 146).

NARRANGANSETT MACHINE CO.
Providence, Rhode Island.
1887 Pocket Manual on Home Exercise, Fine Gymnasium Goods for the Home, School, College, Association or Club; Holiday ed.; 48 pp; **CPP**.
1904 Catalog One, Medical and Anthropometric Apparatus; 47 pp; **NLM** (W26 N234).

NASHVILLE SURGICAL SUPPLY
1927 Catalog; 423 pp; **WOC**.

NATHAN ANKLET SUPPORT CO.
55 Fifth Avenue, New York, New York.
1919 Feet, Their Construction Ailments Correction; 1st ed.; 33 pp; **CPP**.

NATIONAL COLLEGE OF ELECTRO-THERAPEUTICS, THE
Chicago, Illinois.
n.d. Catalog, New Paris Model Microscope; **CTY/B** (Uai N 2187).
1930 Clinical and Chemical Laboratory Requirements: For Schools, Hospitals, Colleges, Physicians, Boards of Health; **CTY/B** (Uai N 219).

NATIONAL DRUG CO., THE
4679–4685 Stenton Avenue, Philadelphia, Pennsylvania.
Est: 1900
n.d. Diphtheria Toxin-Antitoxin; 7 pp; **CPP**.
n.d. The Injection Treatment of Varicose Veins and Varicose Ulcers; 35 pp; **CPP**.
n.d. Lukosine, National Vaginal Douche Powder; 4 pp; **CPP**.

NATIONAL OPTICAL CO.
7 Bleury St., Montreal, Quebec, Canada.
ca 1915 Catalog and Price List of Spectacles, Eye Glasses, Lenses, Oculists' and Opticians Supplies, Optical Instruments, Optical Machinery, Opera and Field Glasses, Readers, Magnifiers, Compasses, Barometers, etc.; 80 pp; **URRR** (N-1).

Holland Bldg., St. Louis, MO.
    ca 1916   Catalog no. 50; **URRR** (N-2).
    n.d.   Ophthalmic Equipment; 4 pp foldout; **URRR** (N-149).

NATIONAL OPTICAL COMPANY, THE
Denver, Colorado.
Salt Lake City, Utah.
Pocatello, Idaho.
    1920s   Catalog no. 33; 192 pp; **AO**.

NATIONAL PATHOLOGICAL LABORATORIES, THE
5 South Wabash Avenue, Chicago, Illinois.
18 East 41st Street, New York, New York.
The University Club Building, St. Louis, Missouri.
312 David Whitney Building, Detroit, Michigan.
302 South Jefferson Avenue, Saginaw, Michigan.
517 Industrial Savings Bank Building, Flint, Michigan.
    ca 1921   Diagnostic Aids; 60 pp; **CPP**.

NATIONAL SCHOOL FURNISHING CO.
Chicago, Illinois.
    n.d.   New Paris Model Microscope; 1 pp; **CTY/B** (Uai N 2187).

NATIONAL SCIENTIFIC CORP.
814 North Franklin Street, Chicago, Illinois.
    1930   Catalogue, Clinical & Chemical Laboratory Requirements, no. C-6; 54
          pp; **NYAM; MF/MAH; UCSF**.

NATIONAL STAIN AND REAGENT CO.
Norwood, Ohio.
    Apr. 1921   Biological Stains, Chemical Indicators and Organic Chemicals; Revised
           Price List; 23 pp; **CPP**.

NATURAL FOOD CO., THE
Niagara Falls, New York.
    1901   The Vital Question Devoted to Natural Food; 39 pp; **CPP**.

NEGRETTI & ZAMBRA
Holborn Viaduct, E. C., London, England.
    ca 1878   Encyclopedic, Illustrated, and Descriptive Catalogue of Optical,
           Mathematical, Philosophical, Photographic, and Standard Meteorological
           Instruments; 526 pp; **NYAM; MF/MAH**.
    1900?   Microscopes, Microscopical Apparatus and Stereoscopes; 24 pp; **URRR**
           (N-84).

NESTOR
    n.d.   Nestor Limerick stamped on pointed amputation knife 7 1/4 inches;
          RCSL.

NEW ENGLAND VACCINE CO., THE
294 Broadway, Chelsea Station, Boston, Massachusetts.
    n.d.   Variola and Vaccinia, History and Description; 59 pp; **CPP**.

NEW ERA OPTICAL CO.
17 Wabash Avenue, Chicago, Illinois.
123 W. Madison Street, Chicago, Illinois.
Est: 1912

1915	76 pp; **URRR** (N-87).
1927	Catalog no. 15; 159 pp; **URRR** (N-108).
Jan. 15, 1929	Bulletin no. 18, New Era Money-Savers; 12 pp; **URRR** (N-11).
n.d.	Catalog, Optical Supplies, no. 20; 28 pp; **NYAM; MF/MAH**.
n.d.	Catalog no. 25; 192 pp; **URRR** (N-112).
1930	Bargain Bulletin no. 26; 36 pp; **URRR** (N-109).
1931	Bulletin no. 31; 64 pp; **URRR** (N-111).
1931	Ophthalmic Instrument and Equipment Catalog; 39 pp; **URRR** (N- 114).
n.d.	Catalog no. 32; 68 pp; **URRR** (N-110).
1931	Catalog no. 36; 68 pp; **URRR** (N-113).
1931	New Era Real Buys Catalog no. 38; 68 pp; **URRR** (N-115).
1932	4 folio pages; **URRR** (N-116).
May 1932	4 folio size pages; **URRR** (N-117).
1932	New Era Overstock Cleanup Sale; 4 folio pages; **URRR** (N-118).
1932	Mid-Year Economy Bulletin no. 46; 84 pp; **URRR** (N-119).
1932	Money Saving Catalog, no. 51; 84 pp; **URRR** (N-120).
n.d.	Money Saving Catalog, no. 55; 84 pp; **URRR** (N-125).
1934	Solder Lock Frame and Mounting, Catalog no. 63; 32 pp; **URRR** (N-126).
1934	Catalog no. 65; 88 pp; **URRR** (N-134).
Nov. 1938	Catalog no. 70 C; 36 pp; **URRR** (N-150).
1938	8 pp; **URRR** (N-146).
1938	12 pp; **URRR** (N-147).
n.d.	12 pp; **URRR** (N-148).
n.d.	Real Buys Special Catalog no. 113; 20 pp; **URRR** (N-151).
1938	Catalog no. 101; 84 pp; **URRR** (N-152).

NEW JERSEY OPTICAL CO.
280 Badger Ave., Newark, New Jersey.

May 1, 1922	Realfit Optical Products; unpaginated; **URRR** (N-127).
Jun. 1, 1932	Gold Filled and Gold Spectacle Frames and Mountings; 16 pp; **URRR** (N-161).
1935	Book of single sheets; **URRR** (N-131).
n.d.	Style and Smartness Demand a Frame Which Is Adaptable; 5 pp; **URRR** (N-160).

NEW ORLEANS OPTICAL COMPANY
Canal and Exchange Place, New Orleans, LA (Home Office).
Branch Houses: City Bank Bldg, Mobile, Alabama. 206 Montgomery Street, Montgomery, Alabama. Dambly Bldg., Shreveport, LA. Renfroe Bldg., Meridan, Mississippi.

| 1920s | Stock Catalogue, Wholesale and Manufacturing Opticians; 103 pp; **AO**. |

NEWPORT NOVELTY MFG. CO., THE
89-91 Wallabout St., Brooklyn, New York.

| 1916 | Catalogue of Genuine Tortoise Shell and Zylonite Spectacles, Goggles, Eye Glasses, Materials and Zylo Cases; 20 unnumbered pages; **URRR** (N-158). |

NEWPORT OPTICAL MFG. CO.
22-24-26 Boerum St., Brooklyn, New York.
1762-1782 53rd Street, Brooklyn, New York (Factory no. 2).

| 1918–19 | Catalogue of Genuine Tortoise Shell and Zylonite Optical Goods; 16 pp; **URRR** (N-128). |
| 1923 | The Newport Price List, Frames, Oxfords, and Other Products; **AO**. |

1924	The Newport Price List, Frames, Oxfords, and Other Products; **AO**.
1925	The Newport Price List, Frames, Oxfords, and Other Products; **AO**.
1927	The Newport Price List, Frames, Oxfords, and Other Products; **AO**.
Mar. 10, 1927	Frames, Oxfords Cases, Rims Fronts, Eye Glasses, Lorgnettes; 15 pp; **URRR** (N-128A).

NEWTON AND CO.
72 Wigmore St., London W, England.
Est: over 200 years
"Scientific Instrument Makers to H. M. King George V."
1899	A Catalog of Microscopes, Telescopes, and Binoculars; 91 pp; **URRR** (N-94).
1908	Supplementary List of New X-Ray, High Frequency, and Electro-Medical Apparatus; 19 pp; **URRR** (N-90).
1915	Projection Microscopes, Catalog no. 4, Section G; 4 pp; **URRR** (N- 59).

3 Fleet Street, London E. C., England.
| 1920s | Leaflet, Dr. Hampsons' Roentgen Radiometer, Made Only by Newton & Co.; **ACR/MAH**. |

NEWTON & WRIGHT, LTD.
72 Wigmore Street, London W, England.
See: MACALASTER, WIGGIN CO., May 1914; **ACR/MAH**.

NEW YORK EDISON CO.
124 West 42nd Street, New York, New York.
| n.d. | Catalog Biological Supplies; pp 119-148; **NYAM; MF/MAH**. |

NEW YORK INTRAVENOUS LABORATORY
100 W. 21st Street, New York, New York.
Apr. 1920	Price List, Practical and Safe Intravenous Medication; 4 pp; **CPP**.
1924	Clinical Data and Case Reports on the Intravenous Injection of Calcium in the Treatment of Tuberculosis; 16 pp; **CPP**.
n.d.	Evolution in Drug Administration; 7 pp foldout; **CPP**.

22 West 26th Street, New York, New York.
| n.d. | Knights of the Crimson Stream, Loeser Laboratory; 15 pp; **CPP**. |

NEW YORK THERMOMETER CO.
36 East 23rd Street, New York, New York.
| ca 1918 | Catalog and Price List Containing Illustrations and Descriptions of Thermometers and Hydrometers; 23 pp; **CTY/B** (Uai N 4366). |

NEWINGTON AND TOMPSETT
24 Whitechapel, London, England.
| 1825 | Instrument maker mentioned bv John Read. |

NEY, J. M., CO.
Elm & West Sts., Hartford, Connecticut.
Est: 1812
1914	Ney Oro Casting Golds; 4 pp; **NYAM; MF/MAH**.
1913	Price list Ney's Dental Golds; 5 pp; **NYAM; MF/MAH**.
Oct. 1919	Brochure, Ney Oro Gold Alloys, Weinstein Formulae; 12 pp; **NYAM; MF/MAH**.
1920	Brochure, Ney Oro Gold Alloys; 63 pp; 2 cc; **NYAM; MF/MAH**.
1920	Leaflets, Clean Mercury; Ney's C. P. Mercury; **NYAM; MF/MAH**.
Jan. 1, 1921	Price List, Precious Metal Products; 11 pp; **NYAM; MF/MAH**.

n.d. Leaflet, How to Use Ney's Velvel Fold Cylinders; 1 pp; **NYAM; MF/MAH**.

n.d. Ney's High Fusing Clasp; **NYAM; MF/MAH**.

n.d. Brochure, Dialoy (trademark); 3 pp; **NYAM; MF/MAH**.

NICOLAY & CO.
Manufacturing Chemists, London and Zurich.
See: LEHN & FINK.

n.d. Dr. Hommel's Haematogen Natural . . . Organic Iron Evidence as to Its Therapeutic Value; 24 pp; **CPP**.

NITSCHE & GUENTHER
Rathenow.
66 Hatton Garden, London, England.

Sep. 1909 Katalog, Die letzten Erfolge bei der Verarbeitung von gold double, die altstaedtische optische Industrie-Anstalt; 56 pp; **URRR** (N-6).

1909 Menischen; 20 pp; **URRR** (N-140).

1913 Wholesale Catalog; 303 pp; **URRR** (N-99).

Diamond House, 37-38 Hatton Garden, London, EC 1.

n.d. Spectacle and Eyeglass Frames, List no. 160E; 40 pp; **URRR** (N- 137).

1924 Nachtrag zum Katalog; 31 pp; with Brillen und Klemmer- Preisliste zum NG Kat; 12 pp; **URRR** (N-136).

1924 Katalog Brillen, Klemmer, Zubehoerteile, Schutz und Automobilbrillen, Behaelter Kettchen und Schnuere Stielbrillen; 165 pp; **URRR** (N-139).

1926? Katalog; 35 pp; **URRR** (N-143).

NOE, CHARLES
8 rue Berthollet, Paris, France.

1893 Catalogue du matériel scientifique, physique, électricité-physiologie, chimie; 168 pp; **CTY/B** (Uai N 68).

NOELLNER, W. F.
Darmstadt, Germany.

1852 Preis-verzeichniss chemischer, pharmaceutischer, physikalischer, mineralogischer Apparate, Instrumente, und Geraethschaften, chemischer Praeparate, Reagentien, etc.; 38 pp; **CTY/B** (Uai N 682).

NOLDE, JOHN T., DENTAL MANUFACTURING CO.
St. Louis, Missouri.

1905 Illustrated Catalog and Price List of Dental Supplies; 808 pp; **ADA** (D 881 N 71).

NONPAREIL
See: FISCHER & CO., trademark.

NORIE, W. A.
77 Hutcheson Street, Glasgow, Scotland.

n.d. Stamped on bleeding lancets, WHM 125800; William Augustin Norie, cutler and surgeon's instrument maker; RCS Lister Collection, gum lancets, Holden 1805-F; **RCSL**.

NORRIS, ALISTER-BALL CO.
58 East Washington St., Garland Bldg., Chicago, Illinois.

1918 Catalog of Optical Goods; 940-973 pp; **URRR** (N-8).

NORTH AMERICAN PHILIPS CO.
See: PHILIPS METALIX CORP.

NORTH SPANISH LABORATORIES
Figueras, Spain.
n.d. Barraquer Erysiphac for the Complete Extraction of Cataract; 6 pp foldout; **MAH; CPP**.

NORTHERN X-RAY CO.
Minneapolis, Minnesota.
1930s Brochure Model X, Portable-Mobile Unit; 2 pp; **ACR/MAH**.

NORWICH PHARMACAL CO.
Norwich, New York.
Est: 1885
n.d. Norwich Vaginal Pessaries; 1 card; **CPP**.

NOVOCAL CHEMICAL MANUFACTURING CO.
Brooklyn, New York.
Oct. 1919 Conduction and Infiltration Anesthesia with Procaine Tablets; 2nd ed.; 48 pp; **CPP**.
n.d. Procaine Tablets; 4 pp; **CPP**.

NOWAKOWSKY, EDUARD
IX/2 Spitalgasse Nr. 25, Wien, Austria.
n.d. Catalog medicinischer und chirurgischer Instrumente und Apparate; 8 pp; **NYAM; MF/MAH**.

NOWELL, J., & SONS
Sheffield, England.
n.d. RCS Collection, Orthopaedic Appliances; **RCSL**.

NOYES BROTHERS & CUTLER
6th St. and Marquette Ave., St. Paul, Minnesota.
1892 Surgical, Dental and Veterinary Instruments, Galvanic Batteries, Artificial Limbs, Artificial Eyes, Deformity Apparatus, Elastic Stockings, Trusses, etc., etc., Part IV; 603 pp; **LACMA** (149 N 87C).
1891 Catalogue, Importers and Wholesale Dealers in Drugs, Chemicals, Patent Medicines, Paints and Oils, Varnishes, Window Glass, Druggists' Sundries, etc.; various pp; **BLEL**.
1895–96 Catalog of Surgical and Dental Instruments, Galvanic Batteries, Artificial Limbs, Artificial Eyes, Deformity Apparatus, Elastic Stockings, Trusses, etc, etc.; 772 pp; **NLM** (W 26 N 959); **LLU**.
1895–96 Catalogue Surgical and Dental Instruments, Microscopes, Physical and Histological Apparatus; **LACMA** (149 N 87 s).
1895–96 Surgical and Dental Instruments; 784 pp; **UPSDM** (D 617.604 N 874).
1900 Surgical and Dental Instruments, Electrical Apparatus, Artificial Limbs, Artificial Eyes, Deformity, Elastic Stockings, Trusses, etc., etc.; 4th ed.; 1200 pp; **NYAM; HDM**.
1913–14 General Catalog and Prices Current Patent Medicines, Pharmaceutical Preparations, Druggists' Sundries; 852 pp; **URRR** (N-101).
1916 Catalog, Optical Goods, Equipment and Instruments for Opticians and Specialists; 226 pp; **URRR** (N-10).
n.d. Catalog Surgeons' Instruments and Allied Lines; **LON** (W959c).
n.d. Druggists' Supplies, Section K; pp 703-922; **URRR** (N-103).

NUMOTIZINE INC.
220 West Ontario Street, Chicago, Illinois.

---

n.d.   Fever, A Simple and Scientific Method of Introducing The Control Factor in the Reduction of Excessive Fever Temperature; 22 pp; **CPP**.

post 1930   Diadermic Therapy; 22 pp; **CPP**.

NURNBERG THERMOMETER CO.
138 Street & Third Avenue, New York, New York.

1919   Report of Thermometer Rating; in Acc. no. 66863; **MAH**.

NYE, TUNBRIDGE

1825   Instrument maker mentioned by John Read.

NYROP, C.
Copenhagen, Denmark.

1862   Exhibit Paris 1867 RCS Loan Collection no. 51 Leny's forceps stamped Nyrop Kjobenham 1862; **RCSL**.

n.d.   Illustreret Katalog over Kirurgiske Instrumenter, Bandager, kinstige lemmer, operations-materiel, elektriske apparater og sygepleje-rekvisitter; **CPP** (ZEd/11).

NYSTROM, A. J., & CO.
2249-53 Calumet Avenue, Chicago, Illinois.

1922   Anatomical Charts for the Nurse Training Dept.; Booklet no. B 210, revised and augmented by Max Brodel; **CPP**.

OBERHAUSER, G., & HARTNACH, E.
Place Dauphine 21, Paris, France.

n.d.   Prix-Courant des Microscopes Achromatiques; 2 pp; **NYAM; MF/MAH**.

O'BRIEN WORTHEN CO.
St. Louis, Missouri; Des Moines, Iowa; Keokuk, Iowa; Sioux City, Dakota; Davenport, Iowa; Dubuque, Iowa; Joplin, Missouri; Iowa City, Iowa.

1912   Surgical Catalog; 2nd ed.; xvi, 576 pp, index; **SLSC**.

OCULUS UNIVERSAL-OPHTHALMOSKOP

n.d.   Das Ueberlegene; 8 pp; **URRR** (O-38).

ODELGA, J.
Schmalzhofgasse 18, Wien 15, Austria.

Feb. 1887   Fabrikant von Bandagen, Instrumenten, Apparaten und Utensilien fuer Chirurgie und Krankenpflege; 146 pp; **NLM** (W26 O23).

1906   Katalog ueber technische Hilfsmittel fuer Chirurgie Medizin u. Krankenpflege; 335 pp; **BLEL**.

IX Spitalgasse 1, Wien, Austria.

1930   Instrumente zur allgemeinen oder speziellen Chirurgie, Urologie, Gynäkologie und Geburtshilfe; 215 pp; **AFMM**.

ca 1935   Einrichtungsgegenstaende fuer Operations-Behandlungs-und Untersuchungsraeume; 50 pp; **MAH**.

Oct. 1937   Einrichtungsgegenstande fuer Laboratorien und Prosekturen; 35 pp; **MAH**.

Nov. 1937   Einrichtungsgegenstaende fuer Krankenzimmer und deren Nebenraeume; 40 pp; **MAH**.

ODOUX
France.

n.d.   Instrument maker mentioned by Page, veterinary instrument maker, Portiers 18c, Page IV, notes VII in catalog at **RCSL**.

OECHSLE, CHRISTIAN LUDWIG
Pforzheim, Germany.
Est: as early as 1825
        1855   Verzeichniss physikalischer und chemischer Instrumente, Apparate und
               Maschinen; 23 pp, photos; **CTY/B** (Uai Oe2).

OERTLING, AUGUST
Jerusalemer Strasse No. 1, Berlin, Germany.
   Mar. 1836   Preis-Courant ueber mathematische, physikalische, und optische
               Instrumente; 4 pp, 2 inserts; **CTY/B** (Uai Oe7).

OFFICINA COSTRUZIONI
Via Faentina 54, Firenza, Italy.
        1933   Catalogo N. 13; Istrumenti Precisione Societa Anonima; 60 pp; **URRR**
               (O-39).

OFFICINE GALILEO
Direction commerciale, via c. correnti 6, Milan, Italy.
Est: 1871
        1932   Microscopes and Accessories; in Russian; 127 pp; **URRR** (O-50).
        1945   Polarimetri e saccarimetri; 6 pp; **URRR** (O-56).
        n.d.   Ottica e meccanica de precisione; 51 pp; **URRR** (O-59a).

OGILVY & CO.
20 Mortimer Street, London, England.
        1928   Catalogue of Shop-Soiled and Second Hand Instruments & Apparatus at
               Reduced Prices (includes Microscopes, Haematological Apparatus, etc);
               35 pp; **URRR** (O-45).
   Jan. 1928   Pamphlet; 6 pp; **URRR** (O-2).
        n.d.   Students' Microscope Model L. O.; 1 pp; **URRR** (O-44).
        n.d.   Electric Microscope Lamps; 3 pp; **URRR** (O-43).

OHIO CHEMICAL & MANUFACTURING CO.
1177 Marquette Street, Cleveland, Ohio.
Est: 1910
   Oct. 1913   Catalog Compressed Gases & Equipment for Their Use; 20 pp; **NYAM;**
               MF/MAH.
        n.d.   The Ohio Monovalve no. 6 Model; flyer; 7 pp; **ABD.**

OHIO ELECTRIC WORKS
Cleveland, Ohio.
        189?   Illustrated Catalogue of the Leading Electric Novelties and Appliances; 32
               pp; **BLEL.**

OISO, J., & CO.
Nichome, Hongo, Tokyo.
  See: **AFMM.**

OLIVER & OGLE
Sycamore Street, Sheffield, England.
        n.d.   Lancet and phleme makers; **RCSL.**

OLIVER ELECTRIC & MANUFACTURING CO.
1020 Walnut Street, Philadelphia, Pennsylvania.
  See: BAKER ELECTRIC CO., Distributor, 1905 Catalog; **ACR/MAH.**

OMAHA OPTICAL CO.
Omaha, NE.
Manufacturers, Jobbers, Importers, no retail goods; picture of American Optical Factory on 2nd page of 1912 catalog.

        1909   Illustrated Price List of Optical Goods; 200 pp; **URRR** (O-24).

        1912   Illustrated Catalogue of Optical Goods, Instruments, Machinery and Accessories; **AO**.

ONEPIECE BIFOCAL LENS CO.
Onepiece Publishing Company
Indianapolis; IN.

    Nov. 1914   The *Ultex Hatchet*, Vol. 1, no. 2; **AO**.

        1917   Ultex Hand Book; 16 pp; **URRR** (O-49).

       1920s   How to Sell Ultex Onepiece Bifocals; **AO**.

O'NEILL & THOMPSON
See: NESTOR; **RCSL**.

OPERAY MULTIBEAM

        1928   Modern Surgical Illumination, stamped: Physicians and Hospitals Supply Co., 414 South Sixth St., Minneapolis, MN; 6 pp, foldout; **URRR** (O-3).

OPPLEM CO.
352 Fourth Avenue, New York 10, New York.
See: GALILEO, OFFICINE DE MILANO; Opplem is U. S. Distributor; **AFMM**.

OPTICAL CONVENTION

        1905   Catalog of Optical and General Scientific Instruments, Frank and Edward Murray, Edinburgh; 276 pp; **NYAM; MF/MAH**.

OPTICAL IMPORT CO.
Bellingham, Washington.

        1957   Summer Flyer and Sale Featuring the Newest Imported Ophthalmic Instruments; 24 pp; **URRR** (O-61).

OPTICAL PRODUCTS CO.
43-45-47 West 16th St., New York, New York.

        1921   Eye Glasses and Spectacle Frames; 20 pp, price list; **AO**.

        1922   Eye Glass and Spectacle Frames; 16 pp, 8 pp price list; **URRR** (O-38).

  Feb. 1, 1926   Tortex Shell Frames Oxfords and Rims; 37 pp, 4 pp price list; **URRR** (O-41); **AO**.

  Feb. 26, 1927   Tortex Shell Frames, Oxfords and Rims; 20 pp, 10 pp price list; **URRR** (O-42).

        1935   Supplemental Merchandiser; 12 pp; **URRR** (O-40).

        n.d.   Catalog, Price List no. 10; 32 pp; **URRR** (O-48).

   July 1937   Catalog and Price List no. 12, Spectacle Frames of Distinction; 46 pp; **URRR** (O-46).

        n.d.   The Viking, A Sturdy Frame of Exceptional Beauty; 12 pp foldout; **URRR** (O-47).

OPTICAL SPECIALTY MANUFACTURING CO.
Southbridge, MA.
Est: 1910

        1914   Catalog of Aristocrat Optical Specialties, Gold Filled Frames and Frame Attachments, etc.; 12 pp; **URRR** (O-1).

L'OPTIQUE COMMERCIALE
7 rue de Malte, Paris, France.

    1900   Paris Universal Exhibition; 44 pp; **URRR** (O-22).
    1900   Paris Universal Exhibition; 162 pp; **URRR** (O-23).
    1909   48 pp; **URRR** (O-21).

ORME, J., & CO.
65 Barbican, London E C, England.
Mfr. of Every Description of Apparatus for Use in Teaching or Experimenting in the Sciences of Chemistry, Electricity, Magnetism, Acoustics, Light, Heat, Hydrostatics, Mechanics, etc. M. JACKSON & CO., whom Orme succeeded.

    1886?   Baker's Patent Calorimeter; 7 pp; **CTY/B** (Uai Or 5).
    n.d.   Illustrated Price List of Chemical Apparatus; 476 pp; **RCSL**.

OSKAMP NOLTING & CO.
411-417 Elm Street, Cincinnati, OH.
26-28-30 West 7th Street, Cincinnati, Ohio.

    1909   Optical Goods, Catalog no. 25, Opera and Field Glasses, Barometers, Thermometers, Telescopes, Magnifiers, etc.; pp 626-721; **AO**.
    1910   Optical Goods; 95 pp; **URRR** (O-29).
    1911?   Optical Goods, Catalog no. 26, Opera and Field Glasses, Barometers, Thermometers, Telescopes, Magnifiers, etc.; pp 642-739; **AO**.
    1912   Optical Goods, Catalog no. 27, Opera and Field Glasses, Barometers, Thermometers, Telescopes, Magnifiers, etc.; pp 623-732; **AO**.
    1915   Optical Catalogue no. 31; 131 pp; **URRR** (O-25).
    1920   Optical Goods, Catalog no. 33, Opera and Field Glasses, Barometers, Thermometers, Telescopes, Magnifiers, etc.; 124 pp; **AO**.
    n.d.   64 pp; **URRR** (O-26).

OSTERMOOR & CO.
116 Elizabeth Street, New York, New York.
Ostermoor & Co., Inc.
2329 S. Columet, Chicago 17, Illinois.
Est: 1853

    1900   Bedsteads and Mattresses; 36 pp; **CPP**.

OSTEOPATHIC PUBLISHING SUPPLY CO.
Cincinnati, Ohio.

    n.d.   Catalog Hospital Supplies, no. 1; 16 pp; **NYAM; MF/MAH**.

OSTERTAG & WALTON
Late with Lentz and Sons.
135 South 10th Street, Philadelphia, Pennsylvania.

    L. 19 c   Surgical Instruments and Physicians' Supplies, abridged catalog; 32 pp; **CPP**.
    ca 1900   Sixty Years, Tycos Fever Thermometers; 8 pp; **CPP**.
    n.d.   Purchased Stock of Late E. Spellarge, 135 South 10th Street; Will Sell Surgical Instruments and Physicians Supplies, Trusses, Elastic Hosiery, Invalid's Requisites, Microscopes; 1 pp; **CPP**.
    n.d.   Catalogue of Surgical Instruments and Physicians' Supplies; 32 pp; **CPP**.

OSTRANDER-SEYMOUR CO.
Chicago, Illinois.
Eastern Office: 38 Park Row, New York City.

    1914   A Complete Catalogue of Every Requisite for Photo-Engraving and Allied Processes, no. 19; 331 pp; **URRR** (O-14).

O'SULLIVAN RUBBER CO.
131 Hudson Street, New York, New York.
    1913   Rubber Heels from the Medical Viewpoint; 8 pp; **CPP**.

OTTO, F. G., & SONS
64 Chatham Street, New York, New York.
    1884   Illustrated Catalog & Price List of Surgical Instruments, Electric Batteries, Orthopedic Appliances, etc., etc.; **NYAM**.
    n.d.   Catalog & Price List of Surgical, Orthopedical Instruments, Trusses, Bandages, etc.; 64 pp; **CPP** (Bolenius Coll); **MUM** (Ed 119 r.2 p.670).
    n.d.   Catalog Orthopedic Appliances, Surgical Instruments, Druggists' Sundries, Electro-Medical Apparatus, etc.; 47 pp; **NYAM; MF/MAH**.
    n.d.   Price List Orthopedic Appliances, Mfg. by F. G. Otto & Sons, 48 pp; **CPP**.
    n.d.   Portable Lung Forceps of Alexander S. Hunter, M.D., sold by F. G. Otto; **CPP**.

OTTO & REYNDERS
See: JOHN REYNDERS & CO.; **AFMM**.

OUIMETTER, J., JR., CO.
Hamilton Street, Southbridge, Massachusetts.
Est: 1895
    1901   Prescription Price List, J. Ouimetter, Jr., Manfacturing and Jobbing Optician; 16 pp; **AO**.
    1906   Presciption Price List, J. Ouimetter, Jr., Wholesale Opticians, 16 pp; **AO**.

OVINGTON MANUFACTURING CO.
Sudbury Building, 79 Sudbury Street, Boston, Massachusetts.
    1905   Catalog Standard & Special Apparatus; 55 pp; **NYAM; MF/MAH**.

OWENS, EDWARD
26 Beaver Street, Albany, New York.
    1833–41   Surgical and Dental Instrument Maker in Albany City Directory.

PADILLA, MARIO
16 Motolinia, Mexico.
    ca 1933   Instrumentos de cirugia; Aparatos para Laboratorio; Equipos para Hospitales; 190 pp; **ABD**.

PAGET, RICHARD
184 Picadilly, London, England.
Est: 1822
    n.d.   Dressing and General Series no. 12 A, 4 lancets with tortoise shell scales which belonged to Dr. W. Lewis who completed his apprenticeship in 1822; **RCSL**.

PAINE DRUG COMPANY, THE
24 E. Main St., Rochester, New York.
Est: 1820
    1922   Standard Surgical Instruments; **UREGML**.
    1928   Standard Surgical Instruments; **UREGML**.
    n.d.   Illustrations of Surgical Instruments; 15th ed.; **UREGML**.
    1935   Catalogue of Surgical Instruments of Superior Quality; 24th ed.; **UREGML**.

PALASCIANE, PROFESSEUR
Paris, France.

    1865   Notice sur l'appareil-Brancard pour le traitement des fractures compliqués de tronc et des membres ingénieurs et pour le transport des blessés de ce genre; **CPP**.

PALISADES MANUFACTURING CO.
Yonkers, New York.
245 Clinton Ave., West Hoboken, New Jersey.
Inc: in New Jersey, but dissolved Dec. 31, 1918.

    1895   Successful Essays in Borolyptol Prize Contest Germicides & Antiseptics in Dentistry; 230 pp; **NYAM; MF/MAH**.

    1900   The Essentials of Hematology, Makers of Hemaboloids; 48 pp; **CPP**.

    n.d.   Iron, Arsenic, and Strychnia: A Natural, Organic Embodiment of This Therapeutic Trinity; 7 pp; **CPP**.

    n.d.   Manual of Urinalysis, A Condensed Guide to the Clinical Examination of the Urine; 23 pp; **CPP**.

    1918   Blood Pressure as an Aid to Diagnosis, Prognosis and Treatment; 16 pp; **CPP**.

    1922   The *Bacillus acidophilus*; 16 pp; **CPP**.

    n.d.   Allergy and Food Idiosyncrasy; 4 pp; **CPP**.

PALMER
England.

    n.d.   Two fleams in long steel arms which close with a bone handle, stamped Palmer; veterinary?; **RCSL**.

PALMER, B. FRANK
376 Chestnut Street, Philadelphia, Pennsylvania.

    1855   The Bone and Antidote, A Surgical Adjuvant & Reporter of Artificial Limbs; 32 pp; **CPP** (Bolenius Coll).

PALMER, C. F., LTD.
London, England.

    1830   Catalogue Research and Students' Apparatus; **JHIHM** (RD 76. p17).

    1934   Research and Students' Apparatus for Physiology, Pharmacology, Psychology, Bacteriology, Phonetics, Botany, etc.; **UREGML**.

PALMER, EDWARD
London.

    1840   Palmer's New Catalogue, with Three Hundred Engravings of Apparatus, Illustrative of Chemistry, Pneumatics, Frictional and Voltaic Electricity, Electro Magnetism, Optics, etc.; 64 pp; **BLEL**.

PALMER SLIDE CO.
Cleveland, Ohio.

    n.d.   Price List of Slides and Covers of Microscope Objects; 8 pp; **URRR** (P-1).

PALO CO.
90-94 Maiden Lane, New York, New York.

    1916   Catalog A, Biological, Bacteriological, Chemical, Physical, Metallurgical and Astronomical Apparatus Instruments and Assayers' Materials; 319 pp; **CTY/B** (Uai P 186).

    1916   Catalog G, Gas Testing Apparatus . . . Calorimeter; 24 pp; **CTY/B** (Uai P 186).

ca 1916   Catalogue Spencer Microscopes Selected Models for Medical and Laboratory Use; **CTY/B** (Uai Sp 366).

PALO-MYERS, INC.
81 Reade Street, New York, New York.
See: TESCHNER-MYERS CO., INC.
ca 1916   Laboratory Supply Co.; **CTY/B** (Uai P 186).
1931?   Catalogue 40, Laboratory Supplies; **CUHSL** (Q 185 P 18).

PAN-PEPTOGEN CO., LTD.
Battle Creek, Michigan.
n.d.   Pan-Peptogen; 16 pp; **CPP**.

PAQUELIN-CAUTERY
See: BENAS' SON; **MF/MAH**.

PAPP & BECKER, DRS.
153 Fenchurch Street, London E C, England.
1893   The Sterilization of Milk, Soups, Fruit, and Other Substances and Apparatus Especially Constructed for This Purpose; 21 pp; **CPP**.

PARAGON
See: GEORGE W. BRADY & CO.; 1931–32; **ACR/MAH**.

PARDEE, L.
Cuyahoga Falls, Ohio.
n.d.   Chemical Laws of Life-Synopsis of the Uses and Effects of L. Pardee's Herbal Remedies; 16 pp; **CPP**.

PARKE, DAVIS & CO.
Joseph Campan Ave. and River, Detroit, Michigan.
Est: 1866
1916   Catalog of the Products of the Laboratories of Parke, Davis & Co.; 305 pp; **MAH** (C 615. 1373 P).
Mar. 15, 1917   Price Change A to Supplement no. 2; 16 pp; **MAH** (C 615. 1373).
1922   Price List Pharmaceutical Supplies; 224 pp; **NYAM; MF/MAH**.
1922   Price List Pharmaceutical Supplies; 8 pp; **NYAM; MF/MAH**.
1922   Price List Pharmaceutical Supplies; 16 pp; **NYAM; MF/MAH**.
1929–30   Physician's Catalog of the Pharmaceutical and Biological Products; xxxvi, 221 pp; **UCSF**.

PARKER, STEARNS & SUTTON
227, 228 and 229 South Street, New York, New York.
449, 451, 453 and 455 Water Street, New York, New York.
Parker, Stearns & Co., Inc.
288 Sheffield Ave., Brooklyn 7, New York.
Est: 1879
1895   Catalog Alpha & Omega Continuous Flow Syringes, Fountain Syringes with Self-Closing Neck, Hot Water Bottles, Depressed Eye Catheters, Elastic Bands, Erasive Rubber; **MAH**.

PARMELEE, SAMUEL B.
n.d.   The Parmelee Automatic Aerating Water Still and Sterilizer; 4 pp; **CPP**.

PARR, THOMAS
at the Golden Shears, Lombard Street, London, England.
n.d.   Surgical Instrument Maker, property of St. Mary Woolchurch, signs of Old Lombard Street; **RCSL**.

PARTRICK & CARTER
Philadelphia, Pennsylvania.
1880? Dr. Bonwill's Dental and Surgical Engines, Hand-pieces, Mallets & Directions for Operating . . . Dr. Bonwill's Dental and Surgical Engines . . .; 28 pp; **UPSDM** (D 617. 604 p 258).

PARTZ ELECTRIC BATTERY CO.
1723 Chestnut Street, Philadelphia, Pennsylvania.
1888 Catalog of Electric Batteries and Other Electrical Supplies; 32 pp; **CPP**.
n.d. Acid Gravity Battery, Circular no. 2; 4 pp; **CPP**.
n.d. Electric Light Bath Cabinets; 1 pp; **CPP**.

PASTORELLI & RAPKINS
London, England.
1895 Instrument makers listed in the catalog at **RCSL**.

PATCH, E. L., CO.
Stoneham 80, Dept. H-2, Boston, Massachusetts.
n.d. Acc. no. 109,835, date recieved 5/6/30; **MAH**.

PATHE-CINÉMA
Bureaux et Magasins de Vente, 20 bis rue Lafayette, Paris, France.
1924 Films radiographiques pathe rapides de sécurité emulsionnes sur les deux faces fabrication Française; 8 pp; **CPP**.

PATHO-CHEMICAL CO.
New York, New York.
n.d. Mukosan Modern Scientific Internal Prophylaxis; 3 pp; **CPP**.

PATTERSON, M. F., DENTAL SUPPLY CO.
Ryan Building, Seventh and Robert Streets, St. Paul, Minnesota.
See: STANDARD X-RAY CO., 1935. PATTERSON SCREEN CO.
1901 Catalogue, Dental Furniture, Instruments and Materials; 3rd ed.; 675 pp; **UPSDM** (D 616.604 P 277).
1911 Dental Catalog; 4th ed.; 775 pp; **ADA** (D 881 P 277).

PATTERSON SCREEN CO.
Towanda, Pennsylvania.
1919 Brochure, Fluoroscopic and Intensifying Screens for X-Ray Work; 16 pp; **ACR/MAH**.
1921 Leaflet Operating Fluoroscope; 1 pp; **ACR/MAH**.
1935? Brochure Detail Intensifying Screens; **ACR/MAH**.
1936? Hi-Speed and Par-Speed Combination Intensifying Screens; 2 pp; **ACR/MAH**.

PATTON, HENRY
n.d. Razor Maker at the Saw and Crown in Middle Row, Holborn, London, A Head in British Museum; **RCSL**.

PAUL, A.
n.d. RCS A 31; Case of C. B. Guthrie's Strabismus Instruments; **RCSL**.

PAUL-BRAGG PULSATOR MODEL II, THE
London, England.
1938 For Prolonged Artificial Respiration; 8 pp; **MAH**.

PAUL, BURY
1825 Instrument Maker mentioned by John Read.

PAUTAUBERGE, L.
9 bis rue Lacuee, Paris, France.
n.d.   The Rational Employment of Beech Wood Creosote by the Pautauberge Solution Prophylaxis and Curability of Pulmonary Tuberculosis; 20 pp; **CPP.**

PEACOCK
Newcastle, England.
n.d.   Instrument maker listed in the catalog at **RCSL.**

PEAKE, ALLEN & CO.
n.d.   Lithotomy Forceps in WHM; **RCSL.**

PEARCE & CO.
n.d.   WHM 215/1956 Twelve Blade Scarificator stamped Pearce; RCS Catalogue of Dressing and General Series, no. 13 M, a lancet; **RCSL.**

PEARSON, R. I., & CO.
Rialto Building, Kansas City, Missouri.
405 Main Street, Memphis, TN.
See: SHEPARD & DUDLEY; **AFMM.**
1891   Catalogue of Dental Instruments and Materials; 440 pp; **MAH** (C 617.6085P).

PEDERSON LUBRICATOR CO.
New York, New York.
ca 1907   Catalogue Electric Motor Instruments & Attachments; 14 pp; **NYAM; MF/MAH.**

PELLIN, PH. & F.
5 Avenue d'Orleans, Paris, France.
1913   Instruments d'optique et de précision; VIII fascicule polarimetrie; saccharimetrie, colorimetrie; 32 pp; **URRR** (p-9).

PELTON & CRANE
11-13 Raynor Street, Detroit, Michigan.
Est: 1899
1908   Catalog, Electrical Equipment; 36 pp; **NYAM; MF/MAH.**
Macomb & Beaubien Street, Detroit, Michigan.
Pelton & Crane Co.
632 Harper Ave., Detroit, 2 Michigan.
1912   Catalog, Electrical Equipment; 48 pp; **NYAM; MF/MAH.**
1913   Catalog, Electrical Dental Equipment for the Office; 52 pp; **MAH** (C 617. 6085 P).

PENN SURGICAL MANUFACTURING CO., INC.
909-915 Montgomery Avenue, Philadelphia, Pennsylvania.
Est: 1899
1911-12   Illustrated Catalogue of PSMCO, Dental Instruments, For the Trade Only; **CDMC.**
1407-09 North Eighth Street, Philadelphia, Pennsylvania.
1920   Illustrated Catalogue of Penn Surgical Manufacturing Co.; 261 pp; **WOC.**
1926   Illustrated Catalog of PSMCO Surgical Instruments For the Trade Exclusively, Price List no. 21; 6th ed.; 360 pp; **MAH.**
1930   Illustrated Catatalogue of a Complete Line of Surgical Instruments for the Retail Trade Exclusively; 367 pp; **HML.**

PENNOCK, EDWARD, IMPORTER
3609 Woodland Avenue, Philadelphia, PA.
See: RICHARD PIETZSCH.

PENNSYLVANIA OPTICAL CO.
234 South 8th Street, Reading, PA.
Est: 1886
    1909   Spectacles Eye Glasses, Goggles; 48 pp; **URRR** (P-3).
    1913   Spectacles Eye Glasses, Goggles; 52 pp; **URRR** (P-196).
    1916   Wholesale Price List Spectacles, Eye Glasses, Goggles; 16 pp;
         URRR (P-195).
    1922   Revised Net Wholesale Price List Spectacles, Eye Glasses, Goggles;
         20 pp; **URRR** (P-232).
    1927   Revised Net Wholesale Price List; 32 pp; **URRR** (P-237).

PEPYS, POULTRY
    1825   Instrument Maker mentioned by John Read.

PERFECTION INHALER CO., THE
South Bend, Indiana.
    n.d.   no title; 6 pp; **CPP**.

PERKINS BACON & CO., LTD.
69 Fleet Street, London, England.
    n.d.   Boron, Food Preservatives, and Their Influence on the Human
         Organism; 59 pp; **CPP**.

PERKINS, JONATHAN
15 Portland Street, Oxford Street, London, England.
    1826   Instrument maker listed by Pagé, veterinary instrument maker, in
         the catalog at **RCSL**.

PEROT, T. MORRIS, & CO.
19 N. Market Street, 612 St. James Street, Philadelphia, Pennsylvania.
    1857?   Wholesale Druggists, Prices Current for Druggists Only; **MUM**
         (2r.56 pam 40).
  621 Market Street & 612 Commerce Street.
    1857?   Importers & Wholesale Dealers in Drugs, Medicines, Chemicals,
         etc.; 52 pp; **MUM**.

PERRET, JEAN JACQUES
France.
    n.d.   Instrument maker mentioned by Pagé, Vol. I, RCS G 195 Le Cat,
         Stamped Perret à Paris surrounded by trade mark; modified Le
         Cat's urethrotome for lithotomy; **RCSL**.
  1771-72   L'Art du coutelier . . .; 2 Vol.; **UREGML**.

PERSONNE
France.
    1856   Instrument maker listed by Page, veterinary instrument maker, Vol.
         VI, at **RCSL**.

PETERS & ROST, DRS.
  See: The KNY-SCHEERER CO.
Chausse-Strasse 3, Berlin N, Germany.
    1900   Liste no. 29, Apparate und Utensilien fuer elektrochemische und
         elektrolytische Arbeiten; 48 pp; **NLM** (W26 P483).

1900   Liste no. 30, Apparate und Utensilien fuer Bakteriologie, Hygiene, Mikroskopie; 120 pp; **NLM** (W26 P483).

PETERSON, W. L.
2869-75 West 22nd Street, Chicago, Illinois.
1926   Price List Dental Supplies; 23 pp; **NYAM; MF/MAH**.

PETITDIDIER OPTICAL AND ASTRONOMICAL INSTRUMENTS
5423 Lake Ave., Chicago, Illinois.
Est: 1894
1909   Price List of Optical Parts; 12 pp; **URRR** (P-177).

PETROLAGAR LABORATORIES, INC.
8134 McCormick Boulevard, Chicago, Illinois.
1931   Illustrations of the Digestive Tract; **CPP**.

PETZOLD, WILHELM
1902   Illustrirtes Preis-Verzeichniss; 132 pp; **URRR** (P-167).

PEYER, FAVARGER & CO.
Neuchatel, Switzerland.
Est: 1860
1895   Price List, Appareils Scientifiques, IX parts, B; 16 pp; **NYAM; MF/MAH**.

PFALTZ & BAUER, INC.
300 Pearl Street, New York, New York.
n.d.   Sole Distributor of Reichert Microscopes through 1930s; **AFMM**.

PFAU, H., INH.
Proprietor L. Lieberknecht, Dorotheen-Strasse 67, Berlin N W 7, Germany.
Est: 1837
ca 1896   Spezial-Preis-Liste ueber Instrumente fuer Ohr, Nase, Hals; 339 pp; **NYAM; MF/MAH**.
1899   Spezial-Preis-Liste ueber Instrumente fuer Ohr, Nase, Hals; **CPP** (Ed/47).
ca 1904   Catalogue, Instrumente fuer Ohr, Nase, Hals; 339 pp, index, **MAH; NYAM; MF/MAH; SLSC**.
48 Luisenstrasse, Berlin N W 6, Germany.
May 1913   Catalogue, Surgical Instruments for Ear, Nose & Throat Diseases and Novelties; 64 pp; **NYAM; MF/MAH**.
n.d.   Spezial Preis-Liste ueber Instrumente fuer Ohr, Nase, Hals; 356 pp; **ZUR**.
n.d.   Katalog, Instrumente fuer Ohr, Nase, Hals; 306 pp; **NYAM; MF/MAH**.
n.d.   Spezial-Preis-Liste ueber Instrumente fuer Ohr, Nase, Hals; 356 pp; **JHIHM** (RF 87 P 523).

PFAU'S AMERICAN INSTRUMENT CO.
New York.
n.d.   Illustrated Catalog, Eye, Ear, Nose and Throat Instruments; 106 pp, Section C pp 169-272; **TMHM**.

PHILADELPHIA AUDIO LABORATORY, INC.
Suite 404, Weightman Building, 1524 Chestnut Street, Philadelphia, Pennsylvania.
1925   The Electrophone; 6 pp; **CPP**.
n.d.   Bulletin of Philadelphia Electric Co., Vol. 1, no. 3; 20 pp; **CPP**.

PHILADELPHIA ELECTRIC STORAGE BATTERY RENTING CO., THE
Agents: 1004 Walnut Street, Philadelphia, Pennsylvania.
1895   Stock Offerings Booklet; 43 pp; **CPP**.

PHILADELPHIA OPTICAL & WATCH CO., LTD., THE
916 Chestnut Street, Philadelphia, Pennsylvania.
n.d.   Catalogue and Price List of Optical Instruments Movements, Watch Case and Optical Repair Price List; 44 pp; **MAH** (C 617.75085 P).

PHILADELPHIA PURE OXYGEN CO.
625 Commerce Street, Philadelphia, Pennsylvania.
n.d.   Oxygen Therapy Emergency Service; 4 pp; **CPP**.

PHILADELPHIA SURGEON'S BANDAGE INSTITUTE
1842   Catalogue; 12 pp; **CPP** (Cage Pam A 130).
1854?   Catalogue; 12 pp; **CPP** (R 56 Pa, 35).

PHILADELPHIA TRUSS CO., THE
610 Locust Street, South Washington Square, Philadelphia, Pennsylvania.
Est: 1850
1875   Patent Combination Truss and Abdominal Supporter; 10 pp; **CPP** (Bolenius Coll).

PHILIPS
See: PHILIPS METALIX CORP.; NORTH AMERICAN PHILIPS.

PHILIPS METALIX CORPORATION
300 Fourth Avenue, New York, New York.
See: NORTH AMERICAN PHILIPS COMPANY, INC.; Philips, Holland.
1930s   Brochure, Radiographic Tubes, Catalog Section 3; Series H. A.; 6 pp foldout; **ACR/MAH**.
1930s   Brochure, the Rotalix Tube, Catalog Section 5; 6 pp; **ACR/MAH**.
1930s   Brochure, Therapy Tubes Series, Catalog Section 6; 6 pp; **ACR/MAH**.
1930s   Brochure, Deep Therapy Apparatus, Catalog Section 11; 11 pp; **ACR/MAH**.
1930s   Brochure, The Super Volt Generator, Catalog Section 14; 6 pp; **ACR/MAH**.

PHILLIPS, GEORGE P.
Boston, Massachusetts.
1927–30   Occulusoscope and Graphic Recorder; 15 pp; **UPSDM** (D 617. 604 P 543).

PHILLIPS, W. E., CO., LTD.
Oshawa, Ontario, Canada.
1927   Vioray, the Health Giving Glass for Hospitals, Sanitariums, Sick-Rooms for Greenhouses and Poultry Houses, for Schools, Office Buildings, Factories and Homes; 4 pp; **URRR** (P-224).
1931   Vioray Health Giving Glass; 6 pp foldout; **URRR** (P-220).
1931   Vioray Window Glass; 1 pp; **URRR** (P-227).
1931   Health by Way of Your Window; 4 pp; **URRR** (P-226).
44 rue de la Jonquière, Paris.
1931   Uses of the Panscope, la technique de l'ultra-violet scientifique et industrielle; 2 cards; **URRR** (P-229).

PHYSICIANS SPECIALTY CO., INC.
Leesburg, Virginia.
Est: Apr. 8, 1913, charter revoked 1920
        n.d.   When Your Sphygmomanometer Shows Your Patient Has High Arterial Pressure, What Are You Going To Do?; 4 pp; **CPP**.

PHYSICIANS' SUPPLY CO. OF PHILADELPHIA
116 South Sixteenth Street, Philadelphia, Pennsylvania.
1118-1120 Chestnut Street, Philadelphia, Pennsylvania.
        1908   Illustrated Catalog and Price List of Surgical Instruments; **CPP** (Ed/43).
        1911   Illustrated Catalog and Price List of Surgical Instruments, Physician's Hospital and Invalid Supplies; 2nd ed.; 337 pp; **CPP** (Ed/43); **JWL** (W26 P578i); **ISUM** (W 26 P578i).
  Apr. 1921   Special Catalog of Eye, Ear, Nose and Throat Instruments and Apparatus; 125 pp, price list; **MAH** (C 610. 78085).
        1928   Illustrated Catalog and Price List of Surgical Instruments; **CPP** (Ed/43).

PICKER, JAMES, INC.
See: PICKER X-RAY CORP.
See: ACME-INTERNATIONAL X-RAY CO., 1923 210 K.V. Leaflet; **ACR/MAH**.
686 Lexington Avenue, New York, New York.
     ca 1922   Catalogue Dental X-Ray Film Mounts; 16 pp; **NYAM; MF/MAH**.

PICKER INTERNATIONAL CORPORATION
See: PICKER X-RAY CORP.; **ACR/MAH**.

PICKER X-RAY CORPORATION
Est: 1879
See: ALLIS-CHALMERS BETATRON; **ACR/MAH**; PICKER X-RAY CORP., WAITE MFG. DIV. and WAITE and BARTLETT X-RAY MFG. CO.; CORP. PICKER INTER-AMERICANA; PICKER INTERNATIONAL CORP.; JAMES PICKER, INC.
Jun. 1, 1927   Catalog Price List, Accessories, corrected; 15 pp; **ACR/MAH**.
300 Fourth Avenue, New York 10, New York.
      1930s   Bulletin 3250, The Constellation X-Ray Table; the Serial Filmer Motor-Driven Serialgraph; 7 pp; **ACR/MAH**.
      1930s   Bulletin A-150, Waite Mobile Counter Balanced Bucky Unit; **ACR/MAH**.
373 Washington St., New York.
      1930s   Bulletin A-160, The New Picker Stainless Steel Cassette; 4 pp; **ACR/MAH**.
      1930s   Bulletin M-205, X-Ray Tube Unit, Shockproof, Oil Immersed; 7 pp; **ACR/MAH**.
      1930s   Bulletin Z-124, Picker-Waite Zephyr Shockproof X-Ray Apparatus Designed for Dermatology; 34 pp; **ACR/MAH**.
      1930s   Waite Flexible Shockproof Therapy Systems; 32 pp; **ACR/MAH**.
      1930s   Bulletin A-165, Picker Cassette Changer; 2 pp; **ACR/MAH**.
      1930   Catalog, X-Ray Accessories; 154 pp; **ACR/MAH**.
      1933   Brochure, X-Ray Equipment and Accessories; 32 pp; **ACR/MAH**.
      n.d.   Catalog, X-Ray Supplies & Accessories; 23 pp; **NYAM; MF/MAH**.

PIETZSCH, RICHARD
        n.d.   Slege Microtomes; 4 pp; imported by Edward Pennock, Philadelphia, PA; **URRR** (P-11).

PIERCE, HARVEY, AND CO.
1 South Pearl Street, Albany, New York.
1837   Instrument Maker listed in Albany City Directory.

PIERCE, RODNEY, OPTICAL COMPANY, INC.
Bessemer Bldg., Pittsburgh, PA.
Jan. 1923   The *Pierce OUTLOOK*, Vol. 1, no. 9; **AO**.

PIKE, BENJAMIN, JR.
294 Broadway, New York, New York.
1848   A Catalog of Mathematical, Optical, Chemical, and Philosophical Apparatus for 1848; **CTY/B** (Uai P 635).

PIKE MANUFACTURING CO., THE
Pike Station, New Hampshire.
Est: 1823; Inc: 1883 or 1889, charter repealed 1925
     1901   Catalog and Price List of Dental Wheels, Knife Sharpeners, Stones for Polishing, etc.; 7th ed.; 66 pp; **NYAM**.
131 Chambers Street, New York, New York.
     Feb. 1901   Catalog, Stones-Scythe, Oil, Razor, etc.; 66 pp; **NYAM; MF/MAH**.

PILLING, GEORGE P., & SON COMPANY
N. E. Corner 23rd and Arch Streets, Philadelphia, Pennsylvania.
Est: 1814
     ca 1901   Catalog, Faught Blood Pressure Apparatus; 24 pp; **MAH** (C 610.78085 P).
     1904   Illustrated Catalog to Jobbers and Exporters of Patented Wrought Metal Specula; 72 pp; **MAH** (C 610.78085 P 44i).
     ca 1905   Complete Guide for Domestic Treatment by Electricity; 32 pp; **BLEL**.
     1914   Surgical Instruments; 298 pp; **VM**.
     1920   Instruments for Exodentia Maxillo-Facial and Oral Surgery; **CDMC**.
     1920   Brochure Describing the Tait McKenzie Muscular Re-Educational Apparatus for Reclaiming the Maimed; 40 pp; **AFMM**.
     1921–22   Illustrated Catalog of G. P. Pilling, Manufacturers of American Made Surgical Instruments; 416 pp; **MAH** (RD 76 P64); **CPP; WOC**.
     1925   Catalog, Chevalier Jackson Endoscopic Instruments; 72 pp; **NYAM; MF/MAH; WOC**.
     1925   Pilling Made Chevalier Jackson Endoscopic Instruments and Supplement of New Instruments; 87 pp; **MAH**.
     1925   Pilling Made Chevalier Jackson Endoscopic Instruments, Broncho-Esophagology; 127 pp; **MAH**.
     1926   Pilling Made Favorite Brain Surgery Instruments of Charles H. Frazier, M. D.; 8 pp; **NYAM; MF/MAH**.
     Mar. 1927   Pilling Bulletin, Eye, Ear, Nose, Throat, no. 3, attached to Bulletin no. 2, Nov. 1926; 8 pp; **NYAM**.
     Mar. 1928   Pilling Bulletin, Eye, Ear, Nose, Throat, no. 4; 16 pp; **NYAM**.
     1928   Catalog, Pilling Made Chevalier Jackson Endoscopic Instruments; 88 pp, letter from Jackson 1925, Jan. 5; **NYAM; NLM** (W26 P641c); **MAH**.

1928   Cuspidors and Suction Pumps; 30 pp; **WOC**.
1928-29 Catalog and Price List Surgical Instruments; 32 pp; **MAH**.
1929   Pilling Made Pressure and Suction Pumps, Fountain Cuspidors; 47 pp; **NYAM**.
1932   Catalog of Eye, Ear, Nose, Throat and Bronchoscopic Instruments and Equipment, Catalog 37-E; 160 pp; **AFMM**.
1932   Catalog of Instruments and Equipment for Surgeons and Hospitals; 337 pp; **CS; NLM** (W26 P641c).
1937   Catalog of Instruments and Equipment for Surgeons and Hospitals; 352 pp; **AFMM**.
1930-37 Pages from catalogs, price lists all mostly undated, advertising instruments made by Pilling, particularly promoting Chevalier Jackson's instruments and publications; 30 pieces; **AFMM**.
1939   Catalog of Pilling Made Chevalier Jackson Endoscopic Instruments, Broncho-Esophagology; 124 pp; **NLM** (W26 P641c); **CS**.

Leesburg, Virginia.
n.d.   When Your Sphygmomanometer Shows Your Patient Has High Arterial Pressure, What Are You Going To Do?; 4 pp; **CPP**.

PILLISCHER, MORITZ
88 New Bond Street, London W, England.
1873   Catalog of Achromatic Microscopes, Telescopes, Opera, Race and Field Glasses and Other Optical, Philosophical, Mathematical, Surveying and Standard Meteorological Instruments; 124 pp, **MAH** (c 681.2085).

PILLOW INHALER CO., THE
1520 Chestnut Street, Philadelphia, Pennsylvania.
Patented 1880
n.d.   The Pillow-Inhaler; 40 pp; **CPP**.

PINCHES DENTAL MANUFACTURING CO.
1181 Broadway, New York, New York.
1908   Aschers Artificial Enamel; 78 pp; **MAH** (C 617.6085).

PINKHAM & SMITH CO.
292-294 Boylston Street, Boston, MA.
15 Bromfield Street, Boston, MA.
1931   Wolfe Artistic Lens; 4 pp; **URRR** (P-230).

PIPERAZINE WATER
See: LEHN and FINK.

PITTSBURGH ELECTRIC SPECIALTIES CO.
927 French Street, Pittsburgh, Pennsylvania.
post 1913 Flyer advertising the Dentoscope included in Columbia 1913 Catalog; **AFMM**.
n.d.   Dr. Ziegler's Surgical Photophore; 6 pp; **CPP**.
817 Penn Avenue, Pittsburg (sic), Pennsylvania.
1908   Illustrated Catalog, Surgeon's (sic) Instruments, Microscopes and Accessories, Laboratory Apparatus, Hospital and Office Furniture, Sterilizing Apparatus, Invalid's Furniture, Sick Room Utensils, Apparatus, Elastic Hosiery and Supporters, Trusses, Crutches, etc., etc.; 515 pp; **MAH** (C 610. 78085 P 477).

PIXII, PERE ET FILS
18 rue de Grenille St. Germain, Paris, France.
Est: 1780
Successors de Dumotiez
- 1835 Catalogue des principaux instruments de physique, chimie, optique, mathématiques et autres, à l'usage des sciences; 79 pp; **CTY/B** (Uai P 688).
- 1852 Catalogue des principaux instruments de physique, chimie, optique, mathématiques et autres, à l'usage des sciences; 48 pp; **CTY/B** (Uai P 688).

PLACE & THISTLEWAITE
31 Market, Manchester, England.
- n.d. An Ophthalmic set of Mr. Knaggs; **RCSL**.

PLATSCHICK, B.
51 bis, rue Sainte-Anne, Paris, France.
- 1907 Catalogue le four électrique pour blocs en coule, construit au laboratoire spécial de prothèse dentaire; 20 pp; **NYAM**.

PLOESSEL, SIMON
215 Schmoellerlgasse, Wein, Austria.
- July 1856 Verzeichniss der optischen Apparate; 14 pp; **NLM** (W 26 P765); **CTY/B** (Uai P 721).

PLUCKNETT, C. J., & CO.
London, England.
- 1899 Catalog Dental Requisites and Tools; **BDA**.

PLUM
- n.d. RCS Dressing and General Series no. 130 Lancet WHM Minor Operating Set no. 12345, Savigny on scalpel; **RCSL**.

PLUMBE PATENT
State and Market, Albany.
Offices in New York, Boston, Philadelphia.
- 1843 Surgical Instruments and Dental, Can Now Be Gilted or Silvered in the Most Durable Manner and to Any Thickness, Albany City Directory.

PNEUMACHEMIC CO., THE
120 Longworth Street, Cincinnati, Ohio.
- n.d. Robertson's Multiple Comminuter; 8 pp; **CPP**.

PNEUMO-CHEMIC VAPORIZER CO., THE
Columbus, Ohio.
- n.d. The Pneumo-Chemic Vaporizer; 5 pp; **CPP**.

POMEROY CO.
34 East 23rd St., New York, New York.
Est: 1867
- n.d. The Walkeasy Artificial Limbs; 18 pp; **NYAM; MF/MAH**.

PONDS EXTRACT CO.
60 Hudson St., New York 13, New York.
Est: 1878
- 1896 What Shall I have for Breakfast? Dinner? Supper?; **CPP**.

PONDS SPHYGMOGRAPH CO.
Rutland, Vermont.
    n.d.   Pond's New Phonographic Sphygmograph; **CPP** (Bolenius Coll).

PORGES, FERNAND AND JULES
12 Boulevard de Magenta, Paris, France.
    1906   Album illustre d'instruments de chirurgie en gomme et caoutchouc
        souple; 3rd ed.; **NYAM; MF/MAH; JHIHM** (RD 76 P 835).
    n.d.   Catalogue, catheters; 8 pp; **NYAM; MF/MAH.**

PORTABLE HYGIENIC VAPOR & DISINFECTOR CO.
40 Spruce Street, New York, New York.
    n.d.   New & Valuable Apparatus for Vapor Baths; 16 pp; **CPP.**

PORTER, GEORGE
Patroon Continued, Albany, New York.
    1841   Instrument Maker listed in Albany City Directory.

POULSON, GEORGE
Hamburg, Germany.
    1881   Catalog, Zahnaerztlicher Utensilien von George Poulson; 243 pp;
        UPSDM (D 617.604 P864).
Moenkendamm Nr. 14, Hamburg, Germany.
  Apr. 1889   Catalogue, Dental Instruments, no. 13; pp 562-600; **NYAM;**
        MF/MAH.
  Oct. 1889   Gebiete der Zahnheilkunde und Zahntechnik, Nr. 15; pp 682-800;
        NYAM; MF/MAH.
  Apr. 1890   Gebiete der Zahnheilkunde und Zahntechnik, Nr. 17; pp 722-760;
        NYAM; MF/MAH.
  Oct. 1890   Catalogue, Dental Supplies and Instruments, no. 19; pp 696-760;
        NYAM; MF/MAH.
  Jan. 1891   Medical Instruments, Dental Supplies, no. 20; pp 842-882; **NYAM;**
        MF/MAH.
    1891   Catalogue, Medical Instruments; 56 pp; **NYAM; MF/MAH.**
  Oct. 1891   Gebiete der Zahnheilkunde and Zahntechnik, Nr. 13; pp 641-680;
        NYAM; MF/MAH.
  Apr. 1896   Gebiete der Zahnheilkunde und Zahntechnik; Nr. 12; pp 762-824;
        NYAM; MF/MAH.
    1898   Preislisten; various pages; **UPSDM** (D 617.604. P 864.2).
Home Bleichen 20, Hamburg, Germany.
  Oct. 1901   Gebiete der Zahnheilkunde und Zahntechnik; pp 1082-1143;
        NYAM; MF/MAH.
    n.d.   Gebiete der Zahnheilkunde und Zahntechnik; pp 801-840; **NYAM;**
        MF/MAH.

POWELL, HUGH
    n.d.   RCS no. 12 F, Sir William Bowman's Microscope; **RCSL.**

POWELL & LEALAND
170 Euston Road, London, England.
    1871   Catalogue of Optical Instruments; 10 pp; fragile; **AFMM.**
    1875   Catalogue of Optical Instruments; 10 pp; fragile; **AFMM.**
    1899   Catalogue of Microscopes, Object Glasses and Apparatus; 9 pp;
        AFMM.
    1902   Price List of Apochromatic Object Glasses; 1 pp foldout; **AFMM.**

Emsdale Greenham Rd., Muswell Hill N., London, England.
     1909   Catalog of Microscopes, Object Glasses, and Apparatus; 8 pp, 2 pp price
             list; **URRR** (P-181).

POWERS & ANDERSON DENTAL CO., INC.
603 East Main Street, Richmond, Virginia.
Est: 1910
     n.d.   Illustrated Catalogue, Surgeon's Instruments, Physicians Supplies,
             Microscopes and Accessories, Laboratory Apparatus, etc.; 2nd
             ed.; 576 pp; **BLEL**.
     1920   Standard Surgical Instrument Catalogue; 4th ed.; 416 pp; **UVHSL**
             (RD76. P68); **MAH** (photocopy).

POWERS & ANDERSON SURGICAL INSTRUMENT CO., INC.
Norfolk, Virginia.
     ca 1930   Illustrated Catalogue of Standard Surgical Instruments and Allied
             Lines; 4th ed.; **CS**.

POWERS-WIGHTMAN-ROSENGARTEN CO.
Philadelphia, Pennsylvania.
Est: 1818
     1920   P-W-R Manual; 471 pp; **UTP**.

PRANG EDUCATIONAL CO.
7 Park Street, Boston, Massachusetts.
     Mar. 1884   Catalogue mentioned in letter of March 1884, Company has a
             catalogue of chemical and physical apparatus about to be
             published; 4 pp; **CTY/B** (Uai P 885).

PRATT, JOSEPH F.
420 Oxford Street, formerly at 10 Chestnut Street, London, England.
     1855-1861   Middlesex Hospital in 1852; RCS Loan Coll. no. 221 E Martin's
             Metrotome no. 224 Greenhalgh's metrotome; K 57B bone cutting
             scissors; London Directory; **RCSL**.

PRATT, T.
Boston, Massachusetts.
     ea 19 c   Made petit-style tourniquet; RCS I 76; **RCSL**.

PRAZMOWSKI, A.
1 rue Bonaparte, Paris, France.
     n.d.   Prix-Courant des microscopes objectifs photographiques
             longues-vues & telescopes; 12 pp; **CPP**.

PRECISION
     ca 1926   Pamphlet; Precision Bedside Unit Circular no. 9-A; 2 pp;
             ACR/MAH; MAH.

PRECISION CORONALESS
     See: ACME-INTERNATIONAL SALES CO.; **ACR/MAH**.

PRECISION THERMOMETER & INSTRUMENT CO.
1434-1436 Brandywine Street, Philadelphia, Pennsylvania.
     n.d.   Blood Pressure, the New Nicholson Pocket Sphygmomanometer; 16
             pp; **CPP**.

PRENTICE, JAMES, AND SON
New York, New York.
Est: 1842
    1884–85   Illustrated and Descriptive Catalog and Price List; 192 pp; **URRR**
                (P-257).

PRESTON
    n.d.   RCS Dressing and General Series no. 8 c; curved bistoury; **RCSL**.

PRICE
    n.d.   Lancet stamped; RCS A. 48 eye speculum handle stamped W.
            Pepy's and Price; **RCSL**.

PRINCE, L. M.
Opticians
Cincinnati, Ohio.
    ca 1876   Perfect Sight, How to Retain, Imperfect Sight, How to Restore; 12
            pp; **MF/MAH**.
    n.d.   Illustrated Price List of Microscopes, Microscopic Apparatus; 60
            pp; **MF/MAH**.
    n.d.   Priced and Illustrated Catalog of Spectacles and Eyeglasses, Lenses,
            Spectacles and Eye Glass Cases, etc.; 40 pp; **MF/MAH**.

PROCKTER, HENRY JAMES
12 Barton Street, Westminster, England.
    1826   Instrument maker mentioned by Pagé, veterinary instrument maker,
            in the catalog at **RCSL**.

PRYOR, THOMAS
67 Minories.
    1826   David Pryor (Johnstone 1817) is the new Pryor and Howard Ltd.,
            Willow Lane, Mitcham 1177–8, instrument maker mentioned by
            Pagé, veterinary instrument maker, in the catalog at **RCSL**.

PULVERMACHER, GALVANIC CO.
Cincinnati, Ohio.
    ca 1876   Pulvermacher's Electro-Galvanic Chain-Belts, etc., Self-Applicable,
            for the Cure of Nervous and Chronic Diseases without Medicine;
            32 pp; **BLEL**.
    1878   Electricity, Nature's Chief Restorer, Self-Applicable for the Cure of
            Nervous and Chronic Diseases; 32 pp; **MF/MAH**.
    ca 1882   Pulvermacher's Electric Belts, etc., Self-Applicable, for the Cure of
            Nervous and Chronic Diseases without Medicine; 30 pp; **BLEL**.
    ca 1887   Pulvermacher's Electric Belts, etc., Self-Applicable, for the Cure of
            Nervous and Chronic Diseases without Medicine; 30 pp; **BLEL**.
    ca 1889   Pulvermacher's Electric Belts, etc., Self-Applicable, for the Cure of
            Nervous and Chronic Diseases without Medicine; 30 pp; **BLEL**.
    n.d.   Pulvermacher's Self Restorable Electric Belts, Bands, etc.; **CPP**
            (Bolenius Coll).

PYE, W. G., & CO.
Montague Road, Cambridge, England.
    Jan. 1926   Catalogue of Scientific Apparatus, List no. 200; 157 pp; **CTY/B**
            (Uai P 992).

QUALITAS ELECTRIC CO.
Mulheim/Baden, Germany.
    d. Sole Manufacturers Provita Messeur Electric, Electrical Specialties; 1 pp foldout; **WMScM**.

QUECKSILBER LUFTPUMPE
See: GREINER and FRIEDRICHS.

QUEEN, JAMES W.
264 Chesnut (sic) Street, East of Tenth Street, Philadelphia, Pennsylvania.
924 Chestnut St., Philadelphia, Pennsylvania.
Est: 1853

    1854 Supplies Catalogue of Optical, Mathematical, and Philosophical Instruments; no. 264 (?); 18 pp; **MUM** (2r.56 pam26).

Jan. 1859 Illustrated Catalogue of Mathematical, Optical and Philosophical Instruments and School Apparatus; 7th ed.; 88 pp; **MUM** (2r.56 pam41).

    1862 Priced and Illustrated Catalogue of Optical Instruments; 13th ed., Part 2; 16 pp; **CTY/B** (Uai Q 31).

    1867 Priced and Illustrated Catalogue of Optical Instruments; 18th ed., Part 2; 54 pp; **MUM**.

    1870 Priced and Illustrated Catalogue of Optical Instruments; 20th ed., Part 2; 54 pp; **CTY/B** (Uai Q 31).

    1870 Priced and Illustrated Catalogue of Optical Instruments; 21st ed., Part 2; 68 pp; **CTY/B** (Uai Q 31).

    1871 Priced and Illustrated Catalogue of Optical Instruments; 23rd ed., Part 2; 103 pp; **CTY/B** (Uai Q 31).

    1876 A Condensed List Clinical Thermometers, Hygrometers, Urinometers, Trial Sights, Ophthalmascopes and Microscopes; 8 pp; **MUM** (Ed119 v.2 p.748).

    1878 Priced and Illustrated Catalogue of Optical Instruments; 40th ed., Part 2; 144 pp; **CTY/B** (Uai Q 31); **MUM** (p.792).

    1878 Philosophy of the Eye and Vision; 47 pp; **CTY/B** (Uai Q 31).

    1879 Priced and Illustrated Catalogue of Optical Instruments; 43rd ed., Part 2; 185 pp; **CTY/B** (Uai Q 31).

    1880 Catalogue of Chemicals Imported and For Sale by J. W. Queen & Co., no. 203; 48 pp; **MUM**.

    1880 Priced and Illustrated Catalogue of Optical Instruments; 44th ed., Part 2; 186 pp; **CTY/B** (Uai Q 31).

    1880 Priced and Illustrated Catalogue of Physical Instruments; 27th ed.; 188 pp; **CTY/B** (Uai Q 31).

    1881 Queen's Toepler-Holtz Electrical Machine for Medical Use; 29 pp, 3 pp advertisements; **MUM**.

Aug. 22, 1881 Supplementary Catalogue of Microscopes; 16 pp; **CTY/B** (Uai Q 31); **MUM** (Ed119 v.2 p.776).

    1882 Abridged Catalogue, Medical Batteries, Microscopes, Clinical Thermometers, Auzoux's Models, Spectacles and Eye Glasses, etc.; 952 pp; **MUM** (8d 5).

    1882 Priced and Illustrated Catalogue of Meterological Instruments; 2nd ed., Part 5; 129 pp; **MUM**.

    1882 Priced and Illustrated Catalogue of Optical Instruments; 55th ed., Part 2; 187 pp; **CTY/B** (Uai Q 31).

1883   Catalogue of Instruments of Precision for Use in Physiology and Medicine; 54 pp; **MUM**.

1883   Priced and Illustrated Catalogue of Optical Instruments; 56th ed., Part 2; 191 pp; **CTY/B** (Uai Q 31); **MUM** (AA60 pam10).

1883   Abridged Catalogue Optical Instruments; 32 pp; **CTY/B** (Uai Q 31).

1883   Supplementary Catalogue of Microscopes (New and second hand), Microscopic Object-Glasses, Microscopic Accessories and Sundries; 12th ed.; 16 pp; **CTY/B** (Uai Q 31); 8 pp; **MUM** (AA9e 60).

Feb. 25, 1885   Supplementary Catalogue of Microscopes, Objects, Accessories, Sundries; 15th ed.; 16 pp; **CTY/B** (Uai Q 31).

Apr. 1886   Reduced Price List of Microscopes, Objectives, Accessories and Sundries; 16th ed.; 14 pp; **CTY/B** (Uai Q 31).

1886   Catalogue of Anatomical Models, Charts and Osteopathy Preparations, Auzoux's Papier Mache Models, Bock-Steger models, . . ., no. 221; 24 pp; **MUM**.

1886   Priced and Illustrated Catalogue of Ophthalmic Instruments, Spectacles and Eyeglasses; 65th ed., Part D & E; 149 pp; **MUM**.

1886   Catalogue P, Photographic Guide, Classified and Illustrated Price List, and Catalogue of Photographic Lenses, Cameras, Apparatus and Materials; 135 pp; **MUM**.

1886?   Priced and Illustrated Catalogue of Ophthalmic Instruments, Spectacles and Eyeglasses; 68th ed., Part D & E; 164 pp; **MUM**.

1887   Catalogue 1-66, Catalogue and Price List of Electrical Testing Apparatus; **MUM**.

1887   Priced and Illustrated Catalogue of Physical Instruments, Chemical Apparatus and Chemicals; 37th ed.; 254 pp; **MUM**.

Apr. 1887   Clearance Sale of Microscopes, Objectives, Accessories and Sundries; 16 pp; **CTY/B** (Uai Q 31).

1888   Priced and Illustrated Catalogue of Meterological Instruments; 129 pp; **MUM**.

1888   Priced and Illustrated Catalogue of Chemical Apparatus, 1st ed.; 364 pp; **MUM**.

Feb. 1888   Clearance Sale of Microscopes, Objectives, Accessories and Sundries to Make Way for Our Acme Microscopes; 8 pp; **CTY/B** (Uai Q 31).

July 1889   Clearance Sale of Microscopes, Objectives, Accessories and Sundries; 12 pp; **CTY/B** (Uai Q 31).

1889   Catalogue of Electrical Testing Apparatus, Dept. 4, Catalogue 1-66; 208 pp; **MUM** (8d 5).

1889?   Priced and Illustrated Catalogue of Ophthalmic Instruments, Spectacles and Eyeglasses; 69th ed., Part D & F; 164 pp; **MUM**.

1890   Priced and Illustrated Catalogue of Ophthalmological Instruments, Spectacles, and Eye Glasses, from J. E. Reid Instrument Co., Inc., 255 N. 4th Street, Philadelphia; vi, 175 pp, index; **AO**.

1891   Catalogue and Price List of Electrical Measuring Instruments for Student's Use, Catalogue 1-70; 1st ed.; 16 pp; **MUM**.

May 1892   Circular 320, Reduced Price List of High Grade Scientific Apparatus; 15 pp; **CTY/B** (Uai Q 31).

1892   Circular 280, Queen's Patent Triple-Plate Toepler-Holtz Electric

Machine; 4 pp; **CTY/B** (Uai Q 31).

> 1892 New Toepler-Holtz Electric Machines, this machine first introduced into U.S. by Queen; 7 pp; **CTY/B** (Uai Q 31).
>
> 1892 Special Net Price List for Schools and Colleges of Microscopes, Magnifiers; 32 pp; **CTY/B** (Uai Q 31).
>
> 1892 Priced and Illustrated Catalogue of Microscopes and Accessories, Catalogue B; 76th ed.; 112 pp; **CTY/B** (Uai Q 31).
>
> Jun. 1896 Bargain List of Scientific Apparatus, Models, Charts, Books, etc., Circular 94; 16 pp; **CTY/B** (Uai Q 31).
>
> n.d. Supplementary Catalogue of New and Second Hand Microscopes, Microscopic Object Glasses, Microscopic Accessories and Telescopes; 31 pp; **CTY/B** (Uai Q 31).
>
> n.d. Circular 84, X-Ray Apparatus; 6 pp; **CTY/B** (Uai Q 33).
>
> n.d. Crooke's Radiant Matter Tubes; 4 pp; **CTY/B** (Uai Q 31).

QUEEN & COMPANY
Philadelphia.

> 1883 The Practical Examination of Railway Employees as to Color Blindness, Acuteness of Vision, and Hearing by William Thomson; 15 pp; **URRR** (Q-26).
>
> 1885 Priced and Illustrated Catalogue of Optical Instruments; 191 pp; **URRR** (Q-28).
>
> 1886 Priced and Illustrated Catalogue of Microscopes and Accessories, Magnifying Glasses, Stereoscopes, Graphoscopes, etc., Catalogue B; 104 pp; **URRR** (Q-29).
>
> 1886 Priced and Illustrated Catalogue of Ophthalmological Instruments Spectacles and Eye-Glasses, Parts D & E; 140 pp; **URRR** (Q-27).
>
> 1888 Microscopes and Accessories Prices and Illustrated Catalogue; 105 pp; **URRR** (Q-20).
>
> 1889 Complete Illustrated Wholesale Price List of Ophthalmological Instruments, Charts, Spectacles, Eye Glasses, Materials, etc.; 64 pp; **URRR** (Q-25).
>
> 1897 Priced and Illustrated Catalogue of Spectacles, Eye Glasses and Oculists' Prescription Lenses; 77th ed., Part E; 52 pp; **URRR** (Q-19); **MUM**.
>
> 1898 Illustrated Catalogue of Optical Lanterns & Accessories, Appartus for Projection; 63rd ed.; 16 pp; **MUM**.
>
> 1900 Catalogue of Microscopes and Accessories; 166 pp; **URRR** (Q-3).
>
> 1900 Electrical Testing Instruments; 117 pp; **BLEL**.
>
> 1903 Catalogue of Microscopes and Accessories; 161 pp; **URRR** (Q-21).
>
> 1904 Catalogue BM, Catalogue of Microscopes and Accessories; 161 pp, index 5 pp; **MUM**.
>
> 1906 High Grade Optical Instruments; 93 pp; **URRR** (Q-2).
>
> n.d. Priced and Illustrated Catalogue of Microscopes, Catalogue B; 79th ed.; 112 pp; **URRR** (Q-22).
>
> n.d. B & L listing of catalogs available; 4 pp; **URRR**.

QUIMBY, C. N.
373 Washington St., Boston, MA.

> 1907 The Handy Prescription Price List and Catalog of Optical Goods Wholesale; 80 pp; **URRR** (Q-9).

QUINEY

> n.d. Stamped on bleeding lancet in WHM 50303/7; **RCSL**.

QUINLAN, JEREMIAH CO.
136 & 138 William Street, New York, New York.
    ca 1878   Importers and Manufacturers of Druggists' Glassware, Sundries and Fancy Goods; **AFMM**.

RADELIN
See: UNITED STATES RADIUM CORP., Radelin is Trademark.

RADIGUET & MASSIOT
44 rue de Chateau-D'Eau (10e Arrt), Paris, France.
13 & 15 Boul des Filles-du-Calvaiere (3e Arrt), Paris, France.
    ca 1900   Lumière oxy-étherique, no. 62; 4 pp, insert in Catalog no. 117; **NYAM**.
    ca 1900   Étrennes scientifiques; 16 pp; **BLEL**.
    1903   Notice sur les applications médicales des machines électrostatiques, genre Wimshurst (modèle depose), contenant les instructions complètes et prix courant des machines; 64 pp; **BLEL**.
    ca 1910   Catalogue 117, les appareils de haute fréquence appliqués à la médecine; 1st ed.; 97 pp; **NYAM; MF/MAH**.
    ca 1910   Installations électriques privées pour L'Arc, Groupe électrogene de petite dimensions; 2nd ed.; 6 pp; **NYAM; MF/MAH**.
    ca 1910   Catalogue no. 106, appareil universel de projections, nouveau modèle R. & M.; 45 pp; **NYAM; MF/MAH**.

RADIUM COMPANY OF COLORADO, INC.
Denver, Colorado.
    1920   Catalog of Radium Applicators, Screens and Accessories; 53 pp; **NLM** (W26 R129).

RADIUM EMANATION CORPORATION, THE
250 West 57th Street, New York, New York.
    1924   Pamphlet, 8 pp; **CPP**.

RADU SURGICAL INSTRUMENT CO.
North Tonawanda, New York.
    n.d.   General Practitioners' Electrically Lighted Diagnostic Instruments; 11 pp; **URRR** (R-116).

RAEBURN, GEORGE
22 Little Queen Street, London, England.
    n.d.   Lincoln's Inn Fields (Holden 1805–7); **RCSL**.

RAINAL, LEON & JULES, FRERES
23 rue Blondel, Paris, France.
236-238 rue St.-Denis, Paris, France.
    1905   Catalogue générale; 426 pp, index; **MAH** (26818).

RANDALL-FAICHNEY CORP.
123 Heath Street, Boston, Mass.
Est: 1888
    n.d.   Ranfac, Dental Catalog, Quality Supreme; **CDMC**.

RANSOM & RANDOLPH CO.
Toledo, Ohio.
Est: 1872
    1897   Catalog, Modern Office Furnishings; 71 pp; **MAH** (C 617.6085 R).
    ca 1899   Catalog, Modern Office Furnishings; 72 pp; **MAH**.
    1899   Catalog, Dental Cabinets and Benches; 56 pp; **MAH**.

ca 1900 Modern Office Furnishings; 80 pp; **MAH**.

ca 1901 Practical Hints Pamphlet; 24 pp; **NYAM; MF/MAH**.

ca 1904 The Catalog, Dental Cabinets and Workbenches; 63 pp; **MAH**.

1907 Catalog of Dr. R. C. Brophy's Improved Gasoline Laboratory Appliances; 18 pp; **MAH**.

1907 Modern Office Furnishings; 79 pp; **MAH**.

1908 Modern Office Furnishing; 73 pp; **MAH**.

1908 Catalog, Dental Specialties; 56 pp; **MAH**.

1909 Catalog, Dental Specialties; 64 pp; **MAH**.

Branches: Cleveland, Ohio.

Grand Rapids, Michigan.

1909 Progessive Dentistry; 32 pp; **NYAM; MF/MAH**.

1911 Dental Catalog; 775 pp; **ADA** (D 881R 17, Case).

1911 Dental Specialties; 64 pp; **NYAM; MF/MAH**.

1916 Dental Specialties; 79 pp; **NYAM; MF/MAH; MAH**.

1916 Manufacturing and Wholesale Dental Products; **UPAL**.

1917 Catalog, Dental Specialties; 81 pp; **MAH**.

1920 Dental Specialties; 82 pp; **NYAM; MF/MAH**.

ca 1920 Brochure, The Elgin Vacuum Casting Appliance; 6 pp foldout; **MAH**.

1923 Dental Specialties; **UPSDM** (D 617.604 R 174).

1924 Dental Specialties; 56 pp; **NYAM; MF/MAH**.

1926–27 Dental Specialties; 40 pp; **NYAM; MF/MAH**.

n.d. Brochure, The Practical Crown Outfit and Swaging Device; 16 pp; **MAH**.

n.d. Illustrated Catalog Dental Casting; 6 pp; **MAH**.

n.d. Catalog, Dental Specialties; 32 pp; **MAH**.

n.d. Brochure, Seamless Crowns and Their Making; 20 pp; **MAH**.

RAPHAEL'S, LTD.

Hatton Garden, London E C 1, England.

n.d. Subjective Test Types (Mechanically Opened); **WMScM**.

ca 1925 Instruments for Objective Examination with Brief Notes on Some Technical Considerations; 7 pp; **WMScM** (P. M. 233/8/92k).

ca 1930s Pulzone Pocket Ophthalmoscope; 1 pp; **WMScM**.

RAPHAEL'S OPTICAL

Clerkenwell, London E.C., England.

1907 Optical Catalog; 112 pp; **URRR** (R-1a).

1907 Optical Catalog; pp 114-208; **URRR** (R-1).

RAPSCH OPTICAL CO., LTD.

1886–1926 58 pp; **URRR** (R-221).

RATERY

France.

n.d. Instrument maker mentioned by Pagé, Vol. IV, veterinary instrument maker, in the catalog at **RCSL**.

RATTI, GIUSEPPE, S.A.

n.d. Catalogo Perzol 29; 16 pp; **URRR** (R-127); Manifattura Italiana Occhiali di protezione.

1926 Occhiali Protettori Cicogna; 23 pp; **URRR** (R-210).

1935 Protector; 32 pp; Occiali per lo sport; **URRR** (R 126).

RAUSCHKE

n.d. RCS Spring Forceps stamped Rauschke Leeds; Late Mayer, Meltzer; **RCSL**.

RAYNOR, H. M.
25 Bond Street, New York, New York.
> n.d.   Platinum Sheet and Wire . . . Triangles, Spatulas, Tweezers, Crucibles; 1 pp; **CTY/B** (Uai R 218).

R-B COMPANY, THE
Minneapolis, Minnesota.
> ca 1922   Pamphlet, The Serialograph, An Apparatus for Serial Roentgenography of the Stomach and Duodenum; 5 pp; **ACR/MAH; MAH.**

READ, F. W., & SONS, LTD.
175-181 Gray's Inn Road, London W C 1, England.
> n.d.   Readson's Safety Universal Radiant Heat Bath, x/o 649, Catalog no. 114; 4 pp; **WMScM.**
> n.d.   Electro-Medical Apparatus and Accessories, Catalog no. 115; 51 pp; **WMScM.**

READ, JOHN
Bridge House Place, Newington Causeway, London.
> 1825   Patentee and Maker of the Stomach Pump and Horticultural Syringes and Veterinary Instruments; **RCSL.**

READ, THOMAS, & CO.
4 Parliament Street, Dublin, Ireland.
> n.d.   Aneurysm Needle, Bullet Extractor; Thomas Read in 1670 as Sword Cutlers in Blind Quay, nephew John Read (1717–76); **RCSL.**

REAY & ROBINSON
47 Church Street, Liverpool, England.
> n.d.   Amputation Set; WHM; **RCSL.**

REGNARD, CAMILLE
4 rue Antoine-Dubois, Paris, France.
Place de l'École-de-Médecine, Paris, France.
Est: 1864
> 1889   Catalogue illustre de appareil orthopédiques et bandages; 64 pp; **NYAM; MF/MAH.**

REICHARDT, F. ALFRED, & CO.
96 Liberty Street, New York, New York.
41 New Church, New York, New York.
> May 1885   Surgical Instruments and Physicians' Supplies, Price List no. 36; 37 pp; **MAH.**

REICHERT, CARL
Bennogasse 26, Vienna VIII, Austria.
Est: 1876
See: Reichert's American Agent James W. Queen, and Co.; James T. Doughtery, sole agent, lt 19 c; **NYAM; AFMM.** Pfaltz & Bauer, Inc. sole agent through 1930s, American Optical Corp., sole agent in the 1970s; **AFMM.**
> 1887   Manufacturers, Dealers and Importers Surgical Instruments and Physicians' Supplies; **CPP** (Ed/80).
> 1888   Catalog of Microscope Stands, Microtomes, etc.; iv, 55 pp; **AFMM; CTY/B** (Uai R 271).
> 1891   Extract from the Catalog no. XVII; Catalog of Microscopes, Microtomes, etc.; 67 pp; **MAH** (C 681.4085 M); **MUM** (8 d 5 1891).

1926   Catalog of Microscopes and Accessories, List E 7; 135 pp; **AFMM; HDM; NYAM; MF/MAH.**
ca 1928   Brochure, Presenting the Heimdal after Reinsch; 4 pp; **AFMM.**
1931   Brochure, Presenting the Epidiascope Pro K; 13 pp; **AFMM.**
1931   Brochure, Presenting Mirror Condensers or Incident Light, List 315 E; 8 pp; **AFMM.**
n.d.   Price List for Catalog E 7; 11 pp; **NYAM; MF/MAH.**
n.d.   Brochure, Microscopes, Stand II/C, III/B; 8 pp; **NYAM; MF/MAH.**
n.d.   Brochure, New High Power Microscope, Make C; 10 pp; **NYAM; MF/MAH.**
n.d.   Brochure, Microscopes, Microtomes; 4 pp; **NYAM; MF/MAH.**
n.d.   Brochure, Mikrophotographische Camera Kams; 7 pp; **NYAM; MF/MAH.**

REID BROS.
Seattle, Washington.
n.d.   Catalogue of Surgical Instruments; 368 pp, 2 pp, price list; **LLU** (WO R353).

REID AND READ
Regent's Circus, London, England.
n.d.   Known for Read's Stomach Pump; **RCSL.**

REID INSTRUMENT CO.
255 North 4th St., Philadelphia, PA.
n.d.   The Reid Improved Streak Retinoscope; 4 pp; **URRR** (R-14).

REILLY & CO.
8 rue Niepce et 11 rue de Paris, Nice, France.
n.d.   Catalogue spécialités et produits pharmaceutics; 63 pp; **NYAM; MF/MAH.**

REINER, H.
Fabrik: IX, Van Swietengasse 10, Wien.
1885   Catalog medicin-chirurgischer Instrumente und Apparate, Bandagen, orthopaedischer Maschinen, kuenstlicher Extremitäten, galvano-kaustischer und elektrotherapeutischer Apparate; 200 pp; **NYAM; MF/MAH; HDM.**
1894   Catalog medicinisch-chirurgischer Instrumente und Apparate, Bandagen, orthopaedischer Maschinen, kuenstlicher Extremitaeten, galvanokaustischer und elektrotherapeutischer Apparate; 1800 original illustrations; 281 pp; **BLEL.**
(Niederlage) I, Franzenspring 22.
1908   Verzeichnis der Instrumente Ohr, Laryngoskopie, Rhinoskopie, Tonsillotomie und Tracheotomie, Bronkoskopie und Oesophagoskopie; 117 pp; **ZUR.**
n.d.   Brochure Laryngoskopie und Oesophagoskopie; 2 pp; **NYAM; MF/MAH.**

REINIGER, GEBBERT & SCHALL
Erlangen, Germany.
See: SCHEU, C.L. 1924.
1894   Elektro-Medizinische Apparate, ihre Handhabung und Preise; 113 pp; **BLEL.**
1897   Elektro-Medizinische Apparate; 6th ed.; 165 pp; **BLEL.**
1898   Elektro-Medizinische Apparate und ihre Handhabung; 7th ed.; 195 pp;

NYAM; MF/MAH; HDM.

1902   Elektro-Medicinische Apparate und ihre Handhabung; 8th ed.; 338 pp; NYAM; MF/MAH.

1906   Catalogue, des appareil électro-médicine; 418 pp; NYAM; MF/MAH.

Aug. 1909   Nachtrag zur Kat-Abteilung IV, A Ophthalmofundoskop nach Dr. Fritz, Rom; 4 pp; NYAM; MF/MAH.

ca 1909   Katalog Abteilung VI, Erdschlussfreie Anschlussapparate fuer Starkstrom; 42 pp; NYAM; MF/MAH.

1909?   Nachtrag zur Katalog-Abteilung IV A, Elektro-Endoskopie und Diaphanoskopie, Pantoskop nach Dr. Schmuckert; 1 pp; NYAM; MF/MAH.

1909?   Katalog; 16 pp; NYAM; MF/MAH.

Dec. 1, 1911   Pantostaten; 8 pp; NYAM; MF/MAH.

Berlin, Hamburg, Koln, Munchen, Leipzig, Strassburg, Germany; Rome, Italy; St. Petersburg, Moskow, Russia; New York, New York; Tokyo, Japan; Hornerstrasse 12, Zurich, Switzerland.
General Representative: A.-B. Elema, Goteborg, Stockholm, Sweden.

n.d.   Den Moderna Diatermiapparaten och dess användning inom medicinen; 11 pp, Swedish; NYAM; MF/MAH.

RELEVAINE SOLUBLE TABLET MANUFACTURING CO., THE
36 North Sixth Street, Philadelphia, Pennsylvania.

n.d.   The Relevaine Soluble Tablet Manufacturing Co.; 4 pp; CPP.

RELIABLE OPTICAL CO.
1445 West Jackson Blvd., Chicago, Illinois.

1930   Amazing Optical Bargains; 24 pp; URRR (R-175).

RESINOL CHEMICAL CO.
517 W. Lombard St., Baltimore, Maryland.
Est: 1895

n.d.   Resinol, A Specific in Diseases of the Skin and a Valuable Surgical Dressing; 24 pp; CPP.

REYNDERS, JOHN, & CO.
303 and 309 Fourth Avenue, New York, New York.
56 Randolph St., Chicago.
closed Chicago operation May 1, 1884

1875   Illustrated Catalog and Price-List of Surgical Instruments, Orthopaedical Apparatus, Trusses, etc.; 184 pp; NYAM; AFMM; NLM (W26 R459).

187?   Illustrated Catalog and Price List of Surgical Instruments, Orthopaedical Apparatus, Trusses, etc.; 2nd ed.; 194 pp; NYAM.

1880   Illustrated Catalog and Price List of Surgical Instruments, Orthopaedical Apparatus, Trusses, etc.; 3rd ed.; 262 pp; NYAM; AFMM; CPP (Ed/29e); BLEL.

1882   Catalog of Osteological Preparations, Anatomical Charts & Models; 32 pp; MAH (C 611.078 R3).

ca 1882   Illustrated Catalog and Price List . . .; 4th ed.; 286 pp; NYAM; MF/MAH.

1884   Catalog of Surgical and Orthopaedical Instruments, Trusses, Bandages, etc., etc., Spectacles and Eyeglasses; 5th ed.; 386 pp; MAH (C 610.78085 R); NYAM.

1889   Catalog of Surgical and Orthopaedical Instruments, Trusses, Bandages, etc., etc., Spectacles and Eyeglasses; 6th ed.; 398 pp; AFMM; NYAM; CPP.

ca 1889 Illustrated Catalog and Price List of Surgical Instruments, Spectacles, Eyeglasses, Optical Goods, Orthopaedical Apparatus, Trusses, Supporters, etc.; 6th ed.; 398 pp; **CUHSL** (RD 76 R 33); **YML** (RD 76 889R).

    1895 Illustrated Compendium and Price List of Instrumentalities for Surgery, Therapeutics and Biology . . .; 7th ed.; 617 pp; **CS; NYAM** (S 125).

    n.d. The Manhattan Surgical and Gynecological Table; **CPP**.

REYNOLDS & BRANSON, LTD.
19 Hendon Lane, Finchley W 3, London, England.
Head Office and Works: Leodis Works, North West Road, Leeds, England.
13 Briggate, Leeds, England.
Est: 1816

    ca 1900 Catalog of Surgical Instruments and Appliances; 107 pp; **NLM** (W26 R466c).

    1909? Catalogue of Microscopes, Microscopical Accessories, Dissecting Instruments; 26 pp; Abridged from General Scientific Apparatus List; 550 pp; **URRR** (R-100).

    1909? Catalogue of X-Ray and High Frequency Appliances; 12 pp; **URRR** (R-97).

    n.d. Clinical Thermometers, RCS .0A-3; **RCSL**.

REYNOLDS, E. W., CO.
340-42 So. Broadway, Los Angeles, California.

    n.d. Illustrated Catalog and Price List, Wholesale Opticians; 152 pp; **URRR** (R-137).

REYNOLDS, JOHN
9 Rodney Street, Liverpool, England.
Formerly: 61 Renshaw Street, Liverpool, England.

    n.d. Dressing and G 41 B Proble-pointed Dressing Scissors stamped Reynolds; WHM; **RCSL**

RHENISH GLASS WORKS
Cologne-Ehrenfeld, Germany.

    ca 1910 Catalogue Rhenish Apparatus Glass for Laboratory Purposes; **CTY/B** (Uai R 343).

RHODES, CHAMPION & SON
Wicker, Sheffield, England.

    1818 Lancet and phleme makers mentioned by Pagé, veterinary instrument maker, in catalog at **RCSL**.

RICHARD, JULES

    1919 Instruments de précision de mesure et de controle pour les sciences et l'industrie; various pp; **BLEL**.

RICHARDS, SON & ALLWIN, LTD.
England.

    1930 List lc/199 lA/M, Models of the Original Patented Folding Invalid Chairs and Self-Propelling Carriages, on cover: The Chair Which Makes the Healthy Man Envy the Invalid; 8 pp, material on both sides of cover, on title page: The First Steel Folding Invalid Chair Was an Allwin Manufactured at Sidway Works, Granville St., Birmingham; **WMScM**.

RICHARDSON, EDWIN
n.d.   Scalpel, RR4, WHM in mixed case of scalpels; **RCSL**.

RICHARDSON, JOHN
92 South Bridge, Edinburgh, Scotland.
1832–33   Surgical Instrument Maker and Cutler; **RCSL**.

RICHARDSON, JOHN
at the Golden Key, Present Street, London, England.
n.d.   Goodman's Fields, Steel Spring Trusses and Other Instruments to help the Weak and Lame, Heal A. Trade; **RCSL**.

RICHARDSON, THOMAS
P. O. Place, Liverpool, England.
1800   31 Maguire Street, Bevington Bush; **RCSL**.
1805   121 Dale Street; **RCSL**.
1807   P. O. Place; **RCSL**.
1810   Thomas R., Cutler and Surgeon's Instrument Maker, P. O. Place; **RCSL**.
1825   P. O. Place; **RCSL**.
1825–27   William Thomas, Cutler, 74 Church Street; **RCSL**.
1829   Thomas, R., Senior, P. O. Place; **RCSL**.
1829   Thomas R. Junior, 72 Church Street; **RCSL**.
1832   Richards Street, 72 Lord Street; **RCSL**.
1841   Thomas, Junior; **RCSL**.
1862   18 South Road, Waterboro; **RCSL**.

RIDGEWAY, SUNDERLAND
n.d.   RCS Dressing and G Series no. 10C; Lancet; **RCSL**.

RIEBER LABORATORIES
667 Howard Street, San Francisco, California.
Charter suspended in 1923
ca 1920   Bulletin no. 101; X-Ray Converter Units; 6 pp; **ACR/MAH**.

RIGGS OPTICAL CO.
Appleton, Wisconsin; Wichita, Kansas.
n.d.   Illustrated Catatalog and Price List of Optical Goods; 11th ed.; 274 pp; **URRR** (R-168).
1920   Catalog and Price List of Optical Goods; 12th ed.; 56 pp; **URRR** (R-201).
1923   Prescription Catalog; 13th ed.; 128 pp; **URRR** (R-200); **AO**.
1928   Prescription Price List; 71 pp; **URRR** (R-211).
n.d.   Prescription Price List, goods sold at retail in many cities of the U.S.; 16th ed.; 52 pp; **URRR** (R-16).
1935   Prescription Price List; 76 pp, 20 pp price list; **URRR** (R-212).
1935   Riggs large foldout; School Campaign for Glasses, in form of newspaper forecasting big business in fall; **URRR** (R-213).
n.d.   Greatly Reduced Prescription Price List; 15 pp; **URRR** (R-15).
n.d.   Spectacle Frames Mountings and Materials; 56 pp; **URRR** (R-169).
n.d.   The Peerless B Bifocal; 4 pp; **URRR** (R-1991).

RIKER & SON CO.
6th & 23rd Streets, New York, New York.
n.d.   Catalog; Rubber Goods; 144 pp; **NYAM**.

RILEYCO, LTD.
56 City Road, London E C, England.
>1920s   Catalog of Trusses, Surgical Appliance Manufacturers; 12 pp; **WMScM**.

RIMMER BROTHERS
78 Turnmill Street, Clerkenwell, London E C 1, England.
>n.d.   Manufacturers of Surgical, Electro-Medical and Scientific Instruments; foldout; **WMScM**.

RIO CHEMICAL CO.
St. Louis, Missouri.
>*79 Barrow Street, New York, New York.*
>>ca 1891   Urethral Diseases; 12 pp; **CPP**.
>>ca 1923   Stabilization of the Pelvic Circulation; 23 pp; **CPP**.
>>1926   The Clinicist Devoted to the Everyday Clinical Problems of the General Practitioner; 22 pp; **CPP**.
>>n.d.   Medical Men in Nearly All the States and Countries in the World Testify to the Value of S. H. Kennedy's Extract of Pinus Canadensis in All Diseases of the Mucous Surfaces; 48 pp; **CPP**.
>>n.d.   The Anemic Woman; 3 pp; **CPP**.
>>n.d.   Uterine Weakness, Aletris Cordial, Uterine Tonic and Restorative; 32 pp; **CPP**.
>>n.d.   Aletris Cordial Celerina; 96 pp; **CPP**.
>>n.d.   *Cholera infantum*, Diarrhea, etc., by James T. Edwards; 12 pp; **CPP**.
>>n.d.   Diarrhea and Dysentery; 12 pp; **CPP**.
>>n.d.   Uterine Ulceration; 16 pp; **CPP**.
>>n.d.   Valuable Testimony for the Medical Profession Only; 12 pp; **CPP**.
>>n.d.   Vaginitis; 17 pp; **CPP**.
>>n.d.   Some Notes on the New Gynecology with a chapter on Neurology, From Surgery to Therapeutics and Plastic Measures, Physiological Gynecology Coming Into Its Own; 23 pp; **CPP**.

RISLEY, WILLIAM
18 Ray Street, Clerkenwell, London, England.
>1826   Instrument maker mentioned by Pagé, veterinary instrument maker, in catalog at **RCSL**.

RITCHIE, EDWARD S.
313 Washington Street, Boston, Massachusetts.
>1857?   Ritchie's Illustrated Catalogue of Philosophical Instruments and School Apparatus; **CTY/B** (Uai R 511).
>1860   Ritchie's Illustrated Catalogue of Philosophical Instruments and School Apparatus; **CTY/B** (Uai R 511).

RITCHIE, E. S., & SONS
149 Tremont Street, Boston, Massachusetts.
>1868?   Ritchie's Illustrated Catalogue of Philosophical Instruments and School Apparatus; 59 pp; **CTY/B** (Uai R 5111).
>*150 Tremont Street, Boston, Massachusetts.*
>1871   Ritchie's Illustrated Catalogue of Philosophical Instruments and School Apparatus; 60 pp; **CTY/B** (Uai R 5111).
>1875   Ritchie's Illustrated Catalogue of Philosophical and School Apparatus; 57 pp; **CTY/B** (Uai R 5111).
>1877   Ritchie's Condensed Catalogue of Physical Instruments and School Apparatus; 43 pp; **CTY/B** (Uai R 511).

Brookline, Massachusetts.
- 1889   Ritchie's Catalogue of Electrical Test Instruments; 10 pp; **CTY/B** (Uai R 5111).
- 1890   Ritchie's Catalogue of Electrical Test Equipment; 20 pp; **AFMM**.
- 1894   Laboratory and Experimental Apparatus for High Schools and Colleges; 10 pp; **CTY/B** (Uai R 5111).
- 1895   Ritchie's Catalogue of Laboratory Supplies; 22 pp; **CTY/B** (Uai R 511).
- 1896   Ritchie's Catalogue of Electrical Test Instruments; 22 pp; **CTY/B** (Uai R 511).
- n.d.   Ritchie's Patent Holtz Machine; 8 pp; **CTY/B** (Uai R 5111).

RITTER, F. A., CO.
310 Woodward Avenue, Detroit, Michigan.
- n.d.   Ritter Orthopedic and Surgical Appliances; 8th ed.; 52 pp; **MAH; LACMA** (149 R 510).

RITTER DENTAL DEPOT
10 East 23rd Street, New York, New York.
- n.d.   The Griswold System of Attachments for Retaining Removable Bridges and Partial Plates; 8 pp; Letter from Griswold Co.; **NYAM; MF/MAH.**

RITTER DENTAL MANUFACTURING CO.
563-565 North St. Paul Street, Rochester, New York.
Est: 1888
- Mar. 1898   Catalogue, New Columbia Dental Chairs, Electric Engines & Appliances; 16 pp; **MAH; NYAM; MF/MAH.**
- Jan. 1, 1901   Catalogue of Dental Furniture, Instruments and Materials; 675 pp; **MAH** (C 617.6085 R).
- Apr. 1901   Catalogue, Dental Chairs, Columbia Electric Dental Engine, Electric Laboratory Lathes and Various Other Dental Appliances; 36 pp; **UPAL; CPP** (pamphlet); **MAH.**
- 1901   Catalogue, Dental Chairs and Engines; 36 pp; **MAH** (C 617.6085 R).
- Jan. 1913   Catalog of Columbia Dental Chairs, Electric Dental Engines and Dental Lathes; 102 pp; **AFMM**.
- 1919   Catalog of Ritter Dental Equipment; 110 pp; **CUHSL** (RH 686 ?81); **UPSDM** (D 617.604 R 514); **ADA** (D 881 R 51).
- pre–1922   Catalog, Ritter Electrically Baked Enamel and Ritter Pyalin Finishes; **CTY/B** (Uai R 514).
- 1924   Electrolytic Medication, Ionization or Ionic Medication; 34 pp; **FI**.
- 1925   Brochure, The Ritter Tri-Dent; 20 pp; **MAH**.
- 1927   Dental Radiography, The Modern Application of X-Ray in Dentistry; 31 pp; **FI** (302/13).
- 1930   Intra-Oral Stereoscope, The New Eyes of Dentistry; 11 pp; **URRR** (R-183).
- n.d.   Catalog, Equipment & Service for Dentists; 28 pp; **NYAM; MF/MAH.**
- n.d.   New Ritter Unit Model C; **FI** (302/14).
- n.d.   Improved Methods for Dental Stereoscopic Radiography as an Aid in Accurate Localization and Diagnosis, by Samuel Wald; 12 pp; **URRR** (R-184).

RIZZOLI INSTITUTO DE BOLOGNA
Bologna, Italy.
- 1900?   Catalogo dell'officina ortopedica del 'Instituto Rizzoli de Bologna; 117 pp;

date on pp 11 is 1921; **NLM** (W26 B693c).
1932   Catalogo dell' officina ortopedica del Instituto Rizzoli de Bologna; 143 pp; **RCSL**; 180 pp; **TMHM**.

ROBERT & COLLIN
Rue de l'École-de-Médecine 6, Paris, France.
Successors Maison Charriere
1867   Fabricants d'instruments et appareil de chirurgie de tous modèles appareil d'orthopédie et d'hygiène, bandages herniaires, pulverisation d'eau, chirurgie vétérinaire, histoire naturelle, coutelleries fine, etc.; 160 pp; **NYAM; MF/MAH; CPP.**
1867   Catalogue avec planches, présente au Jury de l'Exposition Universelle, Fabricants d'instruments et appareil de chirurgie de tous modèles appareil d'orthopédie et d'hygiène, bandages herniaires, pulverisation d'eau, chirurgie vétérinaire, histoire naturelle, coutelleries fine, etc.; 160 pp; **AFMM.**
1867?   Nomenclature indiquant sommairement les instruments crées ou perfectionnes depuis 1862 par la Maison Charriere; 32 pp; **NYAM** (S 125).

ROBERTS, MILTON JOSIAH
1883   The Electro-Osteotome, A New Instrument for the Performance of the Operation of Osteotomy; 18 pp; **CPP**.

ROBINSON, C. M.
2231 Broadway, New York, New York.
ca 1920   C. M. Robinson's Therapeutic Lamp and Stand; 2 pp; **NYAM**.

ROBINSON, JOHN
19 Kingsland Road, London, England.
n.d.   RCS G 119; Sir Thomas Blizard's lithotomy knife; **RCSL**.
35 Northumberland Street, 10 North Court Strand, London, England.
n.d.   Surgeons' Machines, Artificial Limbs, etc.; **RCSL**.

ROCHESTER DENTAL MANUFACTURING CO.
75, 77, 79 and 81 East Main Street, Rochester, New York.
Est: 1893
1897   Catalog Dental Furniture, Instruments and Materials; 594 pp; **UPSDM** (D 617.604 R 586).

ROCHESTER SURGICAL APPLIANCE CO.
1909   Electrically Illuminated Surgical Instruments, Surgical and Electrical Specialties; **CPP** (Ed/78).
n.d.   Catalogue A; 43 pp; **BLEL**.

RODENSTOCK, JOSEF
Berlin W 8, Leipziger Strasse 101/102.
L. 19 c   Diaphragma-Augenglaeser. Wissenschaftlich einzig richtige Ausfuehrung der Brillen, Pince-nez und Lorgnetten; Preisliste Nr. 37; 80 pp with inserts; **URRR** (R-139).
1900?   Frage und Bestellbogen zur exakten schriftlichen Verordnung passender Augenglaeser, Optische-oculistische Anstalt von Josef R.; 16 pp; **URRR** (R-141).
1900?   Preisliste Nr. 6; Optisch-Oculistische Anstalt; 158 pp; **URRR** (R-20).
1909   Preisliste Nr. 44; 32 pp; **URRR** (R-143).

RODGERS & SON

n.d. A single blade scarificator stamped Rodgers and Son in small box stamped F. R. Schubeler; 1823 WHM 13559, **RCSL**.

ROENTGEN APPLIANCE CORPORATION

209-211 Tehama Street, San Francisco, California.

ca 1925 Pamphlet, Rieber Stabilizer A Stationary Magnetic System Which Will Maintain a Constant Filament Temperature Over Any Voltage . . . Model K-3; **ACR/MAH; MAH**.

ca 1925 Pamphlet Rieber Stabilizer Improved Model K-4, The Modern Means for the Exact Control of Coolidge Tubes; 3 pp; **ACR/MAH; MAH**.

ca 1925 Pamphlet, Rieber Fluoroscopic Unit; 8 pp; **ACR/MAH; MAH**.

ROENTGEN MANUFACTURING CO.

417 Mariner and Merchant Building, Philadelphia, Pennsylvania.
Est: 1903

See: SNOOK-ROENTGEN MANUFACTURING CO., **ACR/MAH**.

ca 1905 Catalog X-Ray Supplies; 30 pp; **ACR/MAH**.

ca 1909 Catalog X-Ray Apparatus, Induction Coils and Special Electric Appliances; Group of Brochures bound together in Roentgen binder; approx. 60 pp; **ACR/MAH**.

ROENTGEN X-RAY APPARATUS

See: KNY-SCHEERER CO., 1904; **MF/MAH**.

ROESSLER & HASSLACHER CHEMICAL CO., THE

100 William Street, New York, New York.

n.d. Citrophen; 24 pp; **CPP**.

ROGERS ELECTRIC LABORATORIES CO.

2015 East 65th Street, Cleveland, Ohio.

ca 1921 Pamphlet, Rogers Bedside X-Ray Unit for Surgical and Dental Use; 3 pp; **ACR/MAH; MAH**.

ROHRBECK & GOEBELER

4 Murray St., New York, New York.

1871 Catalogue of Galvano-Electric Apparatus, Instruments, Batteries, etc.; 52 pp; **CTY/B** (Uai R 6362).

Sep. 1, 1871 Catalogue of Apparatus, Instruments, etc., for Chemical Analysis; 30 pp; **CTY/B** (Uai R 6362).

Dec. 1871 List of Chemical Preparations, Pure Reagents, Minerals, etc.; 31 pp; **CTY/B** (Uai R 6362).

1871? List of Chemical Preparations, Pure Reagents, Minerals; 52 pp; **BLEL**.

ROHRBECK, W. J. OR HERMANN

See: J. F. LUHME & CO.

ROHRBECK, HERMANN, DR.

Late J. F. Luhme & Co., 24 Karl Strasse, Berlin, N W, Germany.
Est: 1825

1891 Catalog of Bacteriological, Chemical, Physical and All Kinds of Technical and Scientific Apparatus, Disinfectors; pp 33-142 in English, pp 196-295 in German, fragile; **AFMM**.

1891 Catalog of Bacteriological, Chemical, Physical and All Kinds of Technical and Scientific Apparatus and Disinfectors; 32 pp; **AFMM**.

Karlstrasse 20 A, Office: N W Karlstrasse 201, Factory: N Pflugstrasse, Berlin, Germany.
    1901   Catalog no. 80, Disinfektion, Sterilisation, Asepsis Bakteriologie, Hygiene, Mikroskopie; 222 pp, then Section no. 1300-3575 approx. 222 pp; **AFMM; NYAM; MF/MAH.**
    1902   Catalogue of Bacteriological and Hygienic Apparatus; **CPP** (S3/1).
    1903   Catalogue, Utensilien und Instrumente fuer Thierversuche, Nr. 83; 47 pp; **NYAM; MF/MAH.**
    n.d.   Special Preis-Verzeichniss Laboratorium-Geraethe; 4 pp; **NYAM; MF/ MAH.**

ROMF LIN
France.
    n.d.   Showed dental instruments at Paris exhibit 1867; **RCSL.**

ROSEBERRY METAL WORKS
149/153 Roseberry Ave. E.C., London, England.
    n.d.   Catalogue name and number covered with label Robt. Whitelaw, Surgical Instrument Maker; 51 Woolmanhill, Aberdenn, 109 pp; **WMScM.**

ROSENBAUM, J.
Michaelkirchstrasse 17, Berlin S.O. 16, Germany.
    1928   Preisliste Nr. 23; 16 pp; **URRR** (R-21).
    n.d.   Preisliste Nr. 25; 16 pp; **URRR** (R-190).
    1930   Presiliste Nr. 27; 16 pp; **URRR** (R-178).
    1931   Preisliste Nr. 29; 16 pp; **URRR** (R-187).

ROSS, ANDREW
See: JAMES SWIFT & SON.

ROSS LTD., MFG. OPTICIANS
7 Wigmore Street, Cavendish Square W, London, England.
Est: 1830
    Jan. 1875   Catalogue of Microscopes, Object Glasses, Accessories, etc., Part I; 48 pp; **CTY/B** (Uai R 7331); **MUM** (AA60 pam96).
112 New Bond Street, London, England.
    post 1891   Provisional Reduced Price List, Microscopes, Object Glasses and Accessories; 16 pp; **CTY/B** (Uai R 7331).
111 New Bond Street, London, England.
    Jan. 1895   Catalogue Revised Price List of Ross' Lenses and Cameras, Ross-Zeiss Anastigmatic Lenses, Ross-Goertz Double Anastigmatic Lenses; Ross' Improved Microscopes . . .; 8 pp; **CTY/B** (Uai R 7331).
    1901   Photographic Catalogue; 120 pp; **CTY/B** (Uai R 733).
    1908   Abridged Catalogue Photographic Lenses . . . Cameras and Accessories; 64 pp; **CTY/B** (Uai R 733).
    1910   The Latest Improvements in Microscope Construction of Special Interest to the Bacteriologist, Practitioner and Medical Student; 32 pp; **URRR** (R-147).
    n.d.   Circular of two new catalogues and their contents, includes microscopes and thermometers; **CTY/B** (Uai R 733).
    n.d.   Ross New Series Eclipse Microscopes and Apparatus; pp 113-128; **CTY/B** (Uai R 733).
    n.d.   Microscopes and Microscope Accessories; 32 pp; **URRR** (R-32).

ROTEX
Division of W.B. Snook Mfg. Co. Inc.
    n.d.   Silver and Hypo Recovery Units; **ACR/MAH.**

ROTHE, RUDOLF
Prague, Czechoslovakia.
    n.d. Brochure, Apparate zur Diagnose der Farbenblindheit; 8 pp; **NYAM;**
      MF/MAH.

ROWAN, EDWARD
837 E. 163rd Street, New York, New York.
Est: 1878
    1902 Decimal Gold Foil; 23 pp; **UPSDM** (D 617.604 R 782).
  Jan. 1895 Catalogue of Specialties; 20 pp; **MAH**.
 625 E. 163rd Street, New York, New York.
    n.d. Treatment of the Abnormal Ear with the Meyer-Rowan Instrument; 14
      pp; **CPP**.

ROWE TRUSS COMPANY
922 Broadway, New York, New York.
    1874 Catalogue of Trusses, Supporters, Elastic Stockings and Deformity
      Instruments; 17 pp; **NLM** (W 26 R879).

RUBENCAME & BARKER
825 Arch Street, Philadelphia, Pennsylvania.
    1871 Catalogue, Dental Instruments and Materials Manufactured and For Sale
      by Rubencame and Barker; 184 pp; **MAH** (C 617.6085 R); **UPSDM**
      (D 617.604.R823).
    n.d. Catalogue, Dental Instruments and Materials; **UPSDM**.

RUBINSON, B.
619 Spring Garden Street, Philadelphia, Pennsylvania.
    1914 B. Rubinson, Manufacturer, Jobber, and Importer, Wholesale Only,
      Premier Dental Specialties; **CDMC**.

RUDFORD
Manchester, England.
    n.d. Exhibited at RCP in 1866; **RCSL**.

RUEPRECHT, ALBERT
Favoritenstrasse 25, Vienna, IV Austria.
Est: 1858
    1903 Catalogue Precision Balances & Weights; 52 pp; **NYAM; MF/MAH**.

RU-KA (RATHEMAN)
GRAFTON OPTICAL CO., LTD.
40 Wilson Street, London E.C. 2, England.
    n.d. Frontoforimeter MA107 with Single New Eyepiece Reading; 4 pp;
      WMScM.

RUMBOLD, THOMAS F.
St. Louis, Missouri.
    1875 Description of New Instruments for Making Applications and
      Examinations to the Cavities of the Nose, Throat, Ear and Some
      Remarks about the Local and General Treatment of Affections in Which
      They are Applicable; 24 pp; **ZUR**.

RUPALLEY & CIE
Paris, France.
    1931? Le matériel medico-chirurgical moderne II, électricité médicale; 40 pp;
      BLEL.

RUSCH, A., & CIE
Rommelshausen, bei Stuttgart-Cannstatt.
　　　　1910　Fabrik Elastischer Chirurgie Instrumente und Weichgummiwaren, contains
　　　　　　　history of catheter industry; 94 pp; **ZUR**.

RUSSEL ELECTRIC CO.
　　　　n.d.　Brochure, Root Canal Drier; 2 pp; **NYAM; MF/MAH**.

RUSSENBERGER, THOMAS
35 Mittlere Bahnhofstrasse, Zurich.
Est: 1886
　　　　Mar. 1903　Preis-liste über chirurgische Verbandstoffe; 16 pp; **ZUR**.

RYLEY, JOHN WALKIN
4 Duke Street, West Smithfield.
　　　　n.d.　RCS D & G S. no. 83 Castration clamp, G 146 gorget; L 11 Neavus
　　　　　　　cautery; **RCSL**.

SABAJ, NECK
Austria.
　　　　n.d.　RCS Series A no. 7 Beer's cataract knife; **RCSL**.

SAGLER & HARTNESS
30 Beaver near Green, Albany, New York.
　　　　1830　Cutler and Surgical Instrument Maker listed in Albany City Directory.

ST. LOUIS DENTAL MFG. CO.
St. Louis, Missouri.
　See: HETTINGER BROTHERS, MFG.
　　　　1916　The White Line Office Equipment; 84 pp; **SLSC**.

SAINT PAUL OPTICAL CO.
　　　　1916　Catalog A, Price List of Lenses, Mountings, Frames, Oculist's and
　　　　　　　Optometrist's Supplies; 50 pp; **URRR** (S-452).

SALEM LEG CO.
Salem, Massachusetts.
　　　　1865　The Salem Leg under the Patronage of the U.S. Government, Patented
　　　　　　　Jun. 24, July 22, 1862 and Oct. 4, 1864; includes origin of invention;
　　　　　　　NLM (W26 S163).

SALMON, CHARLES, AND SON
London, Leigh-on-Sea, Norwich.
　　　　ca 1925　Manufacturers of Artificial Limbs, Specialists in Artificial Limbs,
　　　　　　　Orthopedic . . . and Surgical Appliances; 5th ed.; 40 pp, illustrated;
　　　　　　　WMScM.

SALT, RICHARD
4 Dale End, Birmingham, England.
21 Ball St., Birmingham.
5, 6, 7 Cherry St., Birmingham 2 (1856).
　　　　n.d.　Sword maker of Steelhouse Lane, exhibit at Brussels International
　　　　　　　Exhibition 1876; **RCSL**.

SALT, WILLIAM
　　　　Jun. 28, 1773　Advertised in *Birmingham Gazette*.

SALT & SON, LTD.
5, 6 & 7 Cherry Street, Birmingham, England.
Est: 1793
>1872 New Catalogue of Surgical Instruments, Artificial Limbs, Trusses, Abdominal and Umbilical Belts, Apparatus for All Kinds of Bodily Deformity, Improved Medical Syringes, Lint and Cutlery; 5th ed.; **MCFM.**

>ca 1920 Belts and Corsets, each page has tear-off order blank to order item advertised, Saltair Surgical Service, 9th List; 36 pp; **WMScM.**

SALT LAKE DENTAL DEPOT
Salt Lake City, Utah.
>1910 Illustrated Catalogue of Dental Furniture, Instruments and Materials; 675 pp; **UCSF.**

SAMSON
rue de l'École-de-Médecine, 50 Paris, France.
>n.d. Minor instrument set WHM R 6336; **RCSL.**

SAMPSON-SOCH CO.
731 Boylston Street, Boston, Massachusetts.
>1908 Catalogue Hospital Furniture and Surgical Supplies; 55 pp; **MAH.**

SANAX CO., INC., THE
125 East 23rd Street, New York, New York.
>n.d. Apparatus for Treating Obesity according to Nagelschmidt, M.D. and Bergonie, M.D.; 7 pp; **CPP.**

SANBORN CO.
79 Sudbury Street, Boston, Massachusetts.
>n.d. The Sanborn Blood Pressure Outfit Description and Directions; 19 pp; **CPP.**

>n.d. Instructions, Sanborn Electric-portocardiograph; 28 pp; **BLEL.**

SANDS, A. B., & CO.
139 & 141 William Street, New York, New York.
See: SHARP AND SMITH, 25th ed., 1930s; **NYAM.**
Importers and Jobbers of Drugs, Medicines, Chemicals, Proprietary Articles, Sponges, Perfumery, Druggists' Sundries, etc.; **NYAM.**

SANIRAS ELECTRICAL CO., LTD.
61 New Cavendish St., London, England.
>1909? Surgical Lamps; 40 pp; **URRR** (S-360).

SANITARIUM EQUIPMENT CO.
Battle Creek, Michigan.
>1927 Booklet, The Battle Creek Automatic Health Builder, Belt Exercise Machine, Electric; 23 pp; **NYAM; MF/MAH.**

SANITARIUM HEALTH FOOD COMPANY
Battle Creek, Michigan.
>n.d. Health Foods, 32 pp; **CPP.**

SANITAS
Friedrichstrasse 131d, Berlin N 24, Germany.
"Fabrik fuer elektromedizinische-u. Roentgenapparate"

1926–27   Price Lists and Brochures illustrating the
           Hochleistungs-Giathermie-Apparate/Penetrotherm,
           Pantotherm-Standard/Pantotherm, Novotherm/mit
           Metallodur-Dauer-Funkenstrecke; **AFMM; MAH**.

SANITUBE CO., THE
270 Thane Street, Newport, Rhode Island.
    1915   What Men Want to Know; 16 pp; **CPP**.

SAN-METHYL CAPSULE
    See: GRAPE CAPSULE CO.; **NYAM**.

SARGENT, E. H., & CO.
155-165 E. Superior Street, Chicago, Illinois.
    See: ZEISS, CARL, 1935; **AFMM**.
    1880   Illustrated Catalogue of Surgical Instruments; **CPP** (Ed/120).
    1922   Price list no. 25, Scientific Laboratory Apparatus and Bacteriological
            Supplies; 554 pp; **HDM**.

SARGENT'S, GEORGE F.
814 & 816 Broadway, New York, New York.
    pre–1888   Catalogue, George F. Sargent's Specialties; 32 pp; **CTY/B** (Uai Sa 735).
    289 Fourth Ave., New York, New York.
    spg 1888   Illustrated Catalogue of the Sargent Mfg. Co. Successors to George F.
                Sargent, Proprietors & Mfrs. of . . ., list of invalid's furniture; 96 pp;
                CTY/B (Uai Sa75).
    1899   The George F. Sargent Company's Rolling Chairs, Carrying Chairs, etc.,
            Catalogue B; 64 pp; **CTY/B** (Uai Sa 735).

SARTORIUS, F.
Goettingen, Germany.
    1906   Auszugs-Preisliste III ueber Aug. Becker's Mikrotome und Nebenapparate;
            24 pp; **URRR** (S-47).
    1904   Auszugs-Preisliste III Aug; Becker's Mikrotome und Nebenapparate; 24
            pp; **URRR** (S-566A).
    1909   Preisliste III ueber Mikrotome und Nebenapparate; 26 pp; **URRR** (S-566).
    ca 1920   Catalog of Microtomes, Mikro 3; 47 pp; **MAH** (C 681.4085M62).
    1925   Catalog of Microtomes and Accessories, Ref. no. Mikro 4; 32 pp; **CPP**.
    n.d.   Mikrotome und Nebenapparate; 46 pp; **URRR** (S-46).

SARTORIUS-WERKE, A. -G.
Goettingen, Germany.
    ca 1925   Catalog of Microtomes and Accessories, Mikro 4; 32 pp; **MAH** (C
               681.4085 M).

SASS, WOLF & CO.
Oranienburger Strasse 65, Berlin N 24.
    Buelowstrasse 56, Berlin W 57.
    ca 1925   Price of Lamps for Medical Instruments, Special Catalogue of the
               Sass-Wolf Instruments; 65 pp; **WMScM**.

SAVALLE, D., FILS & CIE
64 Avenue de l'Imperatrice, Paris, France.
    ca 1867   Savalle's Patent Distilling and Rectifying System; **CTY/B** (Uai Sa91).

SAVIGNY, JOHN H.
London, England.

1798   A Collection of Engravings Representing the Most Modern and Approved
        Instruments Used in the Practice of Surgery; 38 plates; **MAH**
        (photocopy); **UREGML**.

SAVIGNY, EVERILL, AND MASON
67 St. James Street, London, England.
1810   Catalogue of Chirurgical Instruments; 40 pp; **NLM** (W26 S267; reel
        72-38 no. 8).

SAVORY & MOORE, LTD.
143 New Bond Street, London, England.
See: ARNOLD AND SONS; **NLM**;
See: BELL & CROYDEN.
ca 1870 On the Remedial Agents for Consumption, Dyspepsia and the Wasting
         Diseases Prepared and Guaranteed by Savory and Moore; 30 pp; **CPP**.

SAWYER
n.d.   Stamped on a bleeding lancet, WHM 8849; **RCSL**.

SCANLAN-MORRIS CO.
Madison, Wisconsin.
Est: 1904?
"Manufacturers of the White Line"
1915   Hospital Furniture, Sterilizing Apparatus and Physicians' Office Furniture;
        304 pp; **UWL** (QW.ScA 6); **HDM; CS**.
1925   The White Line, Section A, Hospital Furniture, Section B, Sterilizing
        Apparatus; **LACMA** (149 Sca 6w).
July 1, 1929 Scanlon-Balfour Operating Table; 15 pp, 4 pp list of hospitals using the
        table; **CPP**.
n.d.   Catalogue Hospital Furniture, Sterilizing Apparatus, White Line Operating
        Tables, Monograph B; 16 pp; **CPP** (Pamphlet).
n.d.   Collection of publications; **NLM** (W26 S283).

SCHAEDEL, A.
Leipzig, Germany.
n.d.   Made Prof. Trendelenburg's instrument for pulmonary emboli; **RCSL**.

SCHAERER, M., A. -G.
Bern, Lausanne, Paris, Brussels.
Est: 1892
n.d.   Illustrierter Katalog ueber technische Hilfsmittel und Einrichtungen fuer
        die gesamte Medizin und Chirurgie; 866 pp; **ZUR**.
1905   Illustrierter Katalog ueber technische Hilfsmittel und Einrichtungen fuer
        die gesamte Medizin und Chirurgie; **HDM**.
ca 1906 Illustrierter Katalog ueber Artikel zur Krankenpflege; 136 pp; **ZUR**.
Place Bubenberg 13, Berne, Switzerland.
ca 1910 Fabrique d'instruments de chirurgie, mobilier, pour salles d'opérations et
        de tous les articles pour cliniques, hôpitaux, et sanatoriums ateliers
        spéciaux pour la fabrication des appareils orthopédiques, prothèses
        bandages, ceintures, ventrières, etc., no. 211; 100 pp; **ZUR**.
Jan. 1918 Fabrik fuer Chirurgie-instrumente Operations und Krankenhaus-mobiliar,
        Sterilisations und Desinfektions-anlagen, vollstaendige Einrichtungen
        fuer Laboratorien, no. 968; 36 pp; **ZUR**.
rue due Marche 12, 12 Marktgasse, Berne, Switzerland.
n.d.   Illustrierter Preis-Courant Catalogue Illustre; 128 pp; **ZUR**.
n.d.   Catalogue Illustre des Instruments Première Partie; 51 pp; **ZUR**.

SCHALL, K.
75 New Cavendish Street, London W, England.
Est: 1892?
>1902   Electro-Medical Instruments and Their Management and Illustrated Price List of Electro-Medical Apparatus; 8th ed.; 201 pp; **UWL** (W26 S298e).
>
>May 1905   Electro-Medical Instruments and Their Management & Illustrated Price List of Electro-Medical Apparatus; 9th ed.; 312 pp; **WMScM.**

SCHALL & SON
75 New Cavendish Street, London W, England.
>Dec. 1907   Brochure, Ultra Violet Therapy, no. 1008; 48 pp; **NYAM; MF/MAH.**
>
>Oct. 1908   Catalogue, Electro-Medical Apparatus; 10th ed.; 220 pp; **MAH.**

71 and 75 New Cavendish Street, London W, England.
>1913   Electro-Medical Instruments and Their Management and Illustrated Price List of Electro-Medical Apparatus; 15th ed.; 328 pp; **TMHM.**
>
>1914   Electro-Medical Instruments and Their Management; 51 pp; **ACR/MAH.**
>
>1914   Catalog, Electro-Medical Instruments and Their Management and Illustrated Price List of Electro-Medical Apparatus; 16th ed.; 356 pp; **ACR/MAH.**

74 Bath Street, Glasgow, Scotland.
>Oct. 1924   Electro-Medical Instruments and Their Management & Illustrated Price List of Electro-Medical Apparatus; 17th ed.; 143 pp; **WMScM.**
>
>Feb. 1928   Brochure, The Pantostat, no. 1009; 23 pp; **NYAM; MF/MAH.**
>
>1930   Catalogue of Electro-Medical Apparatus; 100 pp; **NLM.**

18 New Cavendish Street, London, England.
>ca 1930   Electro-Medical Apparatus; 84 pp; **WMScM.**

SCHALL, WILLIAM EDWARD
Bristol, England.
>1925   Electro-Medical Instruments and Their Management; 148 pp; **BLEL.**
>
>1925   X-Rays: Their Origin, Dosage and Practical Application; 2nd ed.; 260 pp; **BLEL.**
>
>1928   X-Rays, Their Origin, Dosage and Practical Application; 3rd ed.; 306 pp; **BLEL.**

SCHANZE, M.
>1893   Preis-Verzeichnis Mikrotome; 17 pp; **URRR** (S-55).

SCHAPER, WILHELM
Ferdinandstrasse No. 18, Dresden, Germany.
>1897   Catalog, zahnaerztliche und zahntechnische Bedarfsgegenstaende; **UPSDM** (D 617.604.Sch 16).

SCHARMANN, GUSTAV, DENTAL DEPOT
1181-1183 Broadway, New York, New York.
>n.d.   To the Dental Profession Relative to the Use of *Jodo-Formagen Cement*, and a Few Reprints from Items of Interest, patent 1898; 9 pp; **NYAM; MF/MAH.**
>
>n.d.   Catalogue, Imported Burs & Dental Specialties; 31 pp; **NYAM; MF/MAH; ADA** (D881 Sch l).

SCHEIDEL W., COIL CO.
171-173 W. Randolph Street, Chicago, Illinois.
Est: 1885 in Germany
Est: 1895 in America

See: SCHEIDEL-WESTERN X-RAY COIL CO.; **ACR/MAH**.
  ca 1905   Catalog of X-Ray Apparatus and Appliances; 32 pp; **ACR/MAH**.
  1906   Catalog X-Ray and Induction Coils, High Frequency and
      Electro-Therapeutic Instruments; 51 pp; **ACR/MAH**.

SCHEIDEL-WESTERN X-RAY COIL CO.
541-547 W. Jackson Blvd., Chicago, Illinois.
411 Jefferson St., stamped over above address on cover.
  See: SCHEIDEL W., COIL CO.
  ca 1908   Bulletin no. 8, Radiographic Coils, X-ray Equipment and Apparatus; 40
      pp; **ACR/MAH**.
  ca 1908–09   Catalogue, Radiographic Coils; 40 pp; **ACR/MAH**.
  ca 1910   Catalogue, Tables, Tube Stands and Trochoscopes; 32 pp; **ACR/MAH**.
  411-19 South Jefferson Street, Chicago, Illinois.
  Sep. 1913   Catalogue no. 400, Improved Interrupterless Transformer; 16 pp;
      ACR/MAH.
  ca 1913   Pamphlet, Pocket Perfection Radioscope; 3 pp; **ACR/MAH**.
  737-739 West Van Buren St., Chicago, Illinois.
  1914–15?   X-Ray Accessories and Tubes; 48 pp; **ACR/MAH**.

SCHEIDIG, JOHN, & CO.
43 Maiden Lane, New York, New York.
  n.d.   Condensed and Illustrated Net Trade Price List of Optical Specialties; 24
      pp; **URRR** (S-359).

SCHERER, R. L., CO.
Los Angleles, California.
  1925   Illustrated Catalog of Standard Surgical Instruments and Allied Lines; 416
      pp; **LACMA** (149 Sch Zs); **UCLABM** (W 26 S326i).

SCHERING E. GLATZ
55 Maiden Lane, New York, New York.
  1893   Brochure; 112 pp; **NYAM; MF/MAH**.

SCHERMERHORN, J. W., & CO.
New York, New York.
  n.d.   Dr. Johnson's Portable Parlor Health Lift and Lift Exercise; **CPP** (Bolenius
      Coll).

SCHEU, C. L.
217 E. 23rd Street, New York, New York.
  Jun. 1924   Catalogue, X-Ray Deep Therapy Outfits Latest Models 1924, Ninth
      Annual Meeting of the Radiological Society of North America and of
      the American Radium Society, 8 pamphlets of companies Scheu
      represented in the U.S., Companies were Reinger, Gebbert & Schall,
      A.-G., and Veifa-Werke, A. -G., Frankfort; **ACR/MAH; MAH**.

SCHMIDT, FRANZ, AND HAENSCH
Stallschreiber Strasse Nr. 4, Berlin.
  1893   Catalogue of Optical Instruments Exhibited at the World's Columbian
      Exposition, Chicago; 27 pp; **URRR** (S-396).

SCHOONMAKER, P., BRONCHOSCOPE, THE
  n.d.   Sold by Euclid Rubber Co., 2245 Broadway, New York; 2 pp; **CPP**.

SCHIEFFELIN, W. H., & CO.
170-172 William Street, New York, New York.
211 Cooper Square, New York 3, New York.
Est: 1794
   See: **MAH** bibliography *One Hundred Years of Business Life: 1794–1894*; New York, 1894. (C 615.1373 S).
   See: LEDERLE ANTITOXIN LABORATORIES; **MAH**.
      1887   General Prices Catalog, Drugs, Chemical and Pharmaceutical
              Preparations; 606 pp; **MAH** (C 615.1373s234).
      1891   General Prices Current of Drugs, Chemical and Pharmaceutical
              Preparations; 671 pp; **NYAM** (S 125).

SCHIEK, FRIEDRICH WILHELM
Marienstrasse 1, Berlin, Germany.
      19 c   Preis-Verzeichniss der Microscope; 3 pp; **CTY/B** (Uai Sch 325).

SCHILDKNECHT & CO.
16 Long Lane, London W.C., England.
      n.d.   Catalogue of Surgical Instruments; 58 pp; **RCSL**.

SCHIMMEL & CO.
(Fritzsche Brothers), Mililitz (near Leipzig).
London.
New York.
      1911   Semi-Annual Report of Schimmel and Co.; 192 pp; **CPP**.

SCHLAG & BEREND
Alexander-Strasse 70, Berlin, Germany.
      1870   Preis-Verzeichniss pharmaceutischer chemischer Utensilien und Apparate,
              etc. 74 pp; **CTY/B** (Uai Sch 36).

SCHLEICHER, CARL, & SCHUELL
   See: EIMER & AMEND, U.S. Agents.

SCHLOTTERBECK & FOSS CO.
Portland, Maine.
      n.d.   Schlotterbeck's Elegant Preparations; **CPP**.

SCHOTT & GENOSSEN
Jena.
      July 1886   Catalogue Glasschmelzerei fuer optische und andere wissenschaftliche
                  Zwecke. . . .; **CTY/B** (Uai Sch 67).

SCHMEINK, A. & B.
      1900–02   Geillustreerde prijscourant van A.B. Schmeink heelkundige
                  instrumentenmaakers; **CPP** (Ed/38).

SCHMIDT
Ziegel Strasse Nr. 3, Berlin N, Germany.
      n.d.   Preis Courant Fabrik chirurgischer, anatomischer, geburtshuelflicher
              Instrumente, no. 7; 127 pp; **NYAM; MF/MAH**.
      n.d.   Loan Collection no. 113; Martin's cephalotrite; **RCSL**.

SCHMIDT, CHARLES A.
St. Louis, Missouri.
- n.d.   Surgical Instruments and Apparatus; pp 521-522 missing; **NWUCML** (617.91 Sch 5).

SCHMIDT, CHR.
Friedrich-strasse Nr. 105c, Berlin N, Germany.
- 1880   Preis-Courant der Fabrik chirurgischer, anatomischer geburtshuelflicher Instrumente, orthopaedischer Maschinen und kuenstlicher Glieder; 112 pp; **ZUR**.
- n.d.   Preis-Courant Nr. 8, der Fabrik chirurgischer, anatomischer, geburtshulflicher Instrumente, orthopaedischer Maschinen und Glieder; **CPP**.

SCHMIDT & ROBINSON CO.
267 Strand, London, England.
- n.d.   Hooks in WHM case of scalpels no. 154132; **RCSL**.

SCHOEDINGER, F. O.
322-358 Mt. Vernon Avenue, Columbus, Ohio.
- 1922   Aseptical Hospital & Surgical Furniture; 40 pp; **NYAM; MF/MAH**.

SCHOLL MFG. CO.
182-204 St. John Street, London E.C. 1, England.
Scholl Mfg. Co., Inc.
213 W. Schiller St., Chicago 11, Ill.
Est: U.S., 1909
- n.d.   Catalog Orthopedic Appliances; **RCSL**.
- n.d.   Sections from catalog: Surgical Instruments, pp 5-62; Aseptic Furniture, pp 63-78; Physical Therapy Equip., pp 79-84; Chiropody Equip., pp 85-92; Consulting Room Furniture, pp 93-96; **RCSL**.

SCHOENFELDT, HERMANN
Luisenstrasse 18, Berlin N.W. 6, Germany.
- 1927   Catalogue, Mikroskope und Nebenapparate; 15 pp; **NYAM; MF/MAH**.

SCHOTT & GEN
Jena, Germany.
- July 1886   Glasschmelzerei fuer optische und andere wissenschaftliche Zwecke; 20 pp; **CTY/B** (Uai Sch 67).

SCHROEDER, J.
179 Sandstrasse, Darmstadt, Germany.
Est: 1837
- n.d.   Verzeichniss fuer Unterrichts-modelle, Apparate und Instrumente jeder Art; 32 pp; **CTY/B** (Uai Sch 76).

SCHROETER, THEODOR
Leipzig-Connewitz, Germany.
  See: RICHARD KNY and CO.
- 19 c   Price-List of Microscopical Object Slides, Cover Glasses and Microscopical Slide Cases and Cabinets; 7 pp foldout; **CTY/B** (Uai Sch 77).

SCHUEMANN-JONES CO.
Cleveland, Ohio.
    1929   Standard Surgical Instruments; 458 pp; **HDM**.

SCHWABE, F.
Moskva, Russia.
    1890   Illustrated Catalogue of Medical Surgical and Orthopedic Instruments and Apparatus; **CPP** (Zed/2).

SCHWARTZ, DR. M.
    Apr. 1884   Apparat zum Ersatz des Ausschüttelns mit Aether, Ligroin, etc.; 2 pp; **NYAM; MF/MAH**.

SCHWEICHARDT, ADOLF
Tuttlingen, Germany.
Est: 1896
    1928   Katalog Nr. 4, über zahnaerztliche Instrumente u. Gebrauchsgegenstände; 131 pp; Trademark: Schwert; **NLM** (W26 S413k); Extra price list 40 E/S; 8 pp; **WMScM**.
    n.d.   Catalogue, Dental Instruments and Utensils; 131 pp; **UPSDM** (D 617.604. Sch 97).

SCHWINDT, HENRY
610 Eighth Avenue, New York, New York.
    n.d.   Advertised by The R. Heyde Co., Corner 3rd and Prairie St., Milwaukee, Wisconsin; **NYAM**.

SCIENTIFIC MATERIALS CO.
717-719 Forbes Street, Pittsburgh, Pennsylvania.
Est: 1884; Inc: 1902
    1909   Apparatus Catalogue Illustrating and Describing Scientific Instruments, Assayers' Materials, and Laboratory Supplies; 534 pp; **CTY/B** (Uai Sci 28).
Factory: 714 Watson Street
    1912   Apparatus Catalogue Illustrating and Describing Scientific Instruments, Assayers' Materials and Laboratory Supplies; 535 pp; **CPP** (Ed/66).
    1919   Scientific Materials Blue Book, Equipment and Supplies for Chemical, Metallurgical and Biological Laboratories; 663 pp; **AFMM; CTY/B** (Uai Sci 28); **CPP**.
    n.d.   Catalogue, Analytical Balance, American College Model; **CTY/B** (Uai Sci 28).
    n.d.   Catalogue, Pocket Test Cases and Tablet Stains; 4 pp; **CTY/B** (Uai Sci 28).
    n.d.   Manufacturers and Importers of Everything for the Laboratory, picture of building; **CTY/B** (Uai Sci 28).
    n.d.   Catalogue of Spencer Microscopes; 11 pp; **CTY/B** (Uai Sci 28).

SCUDDER, DOCTOR
222 North Market, Albany, New York.
1839 Home Troy, Albany, New York.
    1839   Oculist, Aurist and Surgeon listed in Albany City Directory; in 1838 as Oculist.

SCULLY STEEL & IRON CO.
Chicago, Illinois.
    1909   Stock list; 95 pp; **MAH** (C 670.85 S).

SEABURY & JOHNSON
59 & 61 Maiden Lane, Seabury Bldg., New York.
32-33 Snow Hill, London, E.C.
Catherinenhof, Hamburg, Germany.
53 St. Sulpice St., Montreal.
Proprietors: **Seabury Pharmacal Laboratories.**
  East Orange, New Jersey.
    1897   Physicians' Catalogue; 36 pp; **MAH** (29503).
    n.d.   The New York Sanitary Supply Co.'s Spitting Cup; 8 pp; **CPP**.

SEARLE
Leeds, England.
    1825   Instrument Maker mentioned by John Read.

SEARLE & HERETH CO.
See: WM. R. WARNER AND CO., Price List 1910-1911; **MAH**.

SEARS, ROEBUCK AND CO.
New York, New York.
925 Homan Ave., Chicago 7, Ill.
Est: 1886
    1902   The 1902 Edition of the Sears Roebuck Catalogue; medical pp 127, 128, 227, 245, 440-476; facsimile ed., 1969; **LACMA** (149 Se1n).
    1902?   Electrical Goods and Supplies; 5th ed.; 44 pp; **BLEL**.
    1903   Catalog of Surgical Instruments and Physician's Supplies; 144 pp; **CS; NLM** (W26 S439c); **CPP** (Ed/73); **UCSF**.
  1904-05 Surgical Instruments and Physicians' Supplies, Hospital Furniture, Enamel Ware, Orthopedic Apparatus, Artificial Limbs, Invalid Chairs; 232 pp; **YML** (R 717 S 42); **NYAM; MF/MAH; ACS** (U-6-a S-439-s).
    1906   Surgical Supply; 232 pp; **WOC**.
    1907   Surgical Instruments, Deformity Apparatus, Physicians' Hospital and Invalid Supplies, Drugs, Medicines, Chemicals; **CS**.
  ca 1918 Electrical Goods; 37 pp; **BLEL**.

SEELEY'S, I. B.
1347 Chestnut Street, Philadelphia, Pennsylvania.
737 Broadway, New York, New York.
    1873   Illustrated Catalogue of Hard Rubber Trusses, Abdominal Supporters, Pile Instruments, Elastic Stockings, Bandages; 48 pp; **MAH** (C 610.78085 S).

SEIBERT, E. J.
New York, New York.
    1875?   The Voltaic Armadillo, Electric Bands and Soles, A Reliable and Safe Remedy for Nervous Diseases, For Sale by Max Wocher & Son, 105 W. Sixth St., Cincinnati, Ohio; 15 pp; **MF/MAH**.

SEIBERT, W. & H.
Luisenstrasse 52, Berlin N W.

n.d.   Preisverzeichnis der Apparate fuer Projection und Mikrophotographie; 30 pp; **URRR** (S-571).

1900   No. 28 Mikroskope und mikroskopische Hilfsapparate; 71 pp; **URRR** (S-437).

1905   Mikroskope, no. 32; 91 pp; **URRR** (S-438A).

1909   Preis-verzeichnis der Mikroskope und mikroskopischen Hilftsapparate, no. 34; 88 pp; **URRR** (S-49).

1910   No. 35 Preis Verzeichnis; 83 pp; **URRR** (S-438).

1915   Mikroskope Nr. 39; Preis-Verzeichnis; 91 pp; **URRR** (S-389).

n.d.   Preisverzeichnis der Mikroskope und mikroskopischen Hilfsapparate no. 26; 57 pp; **URRR** (S-438A).

SELPHO, WILLIAM
516 Broadway, New York.

n.d.   Patent Anglesey Leg and Artificial Hand (charged $100-150, gave reduction to the poor); 16 pp; **CPP** (Bolenius Coll).

SEXTON, L. R.
Rochester, New York.

1879?   Catalogue Gundlach's Microscopes and Objectives and Other Optical Instruments; **CTY/B** (Uai G 956).

SHAFER-PIERCE CO.
608 Nicollet Avenue, Minneapolis, Minnesota.

Jan. 1, 1905   Catalogue of Dental Furniture Instruments and Materials; 808 pp; **MAH**.

SHAFFNER, PHILIP FRANK
30 North Michigan Avenue, Chicago, Illinois.

n.d.   The Vaccine Treatment of Acne Vulgaris; 7 pp; **CPP**.

SHARLAND AND CO., LTD.

1903   Catalogue of Microscopes and Accessories; 23 pp; **URRR** (S-452).

SHARP, W. M., MFG. CO., INC.
Philadelphia, Pennsylvania.
factory: 243 Water St., Binghamton, New York.
Est: 1908

1912   Instructions for Using the Sharp Seamless Crown Outfit; **BDA**.

n.d.   Dr. W. M. Sharp's Crown and Bridge System and Other Dental Specialties; 32 pp; **NYAM; MF/MAH**.

n.d.   Catalogue, Dr. W. M. Sharp's Crown and Bridge System; 28 pp; **MAH**.

SHARP & DOHME
422 Gravier Street, New Orleans, Louisiana.
221 Randolph Street, Chicago, Illinois.
New York, New York.
Est: 1860

Jan. 1, 1901   Price List, Chemical and Pharmaceutical Preparations; 185 pp; **NYAM; MF/MAH**.

Jan. 1927   Price List, Chemical and Pharamceutical Preparations; 224 pp; **NYAM; MF/MAH**.

SHARP & SMITH
73 Randolph Street, Chicago, Illinois.

Est: 1844; Inc: 1904

      1889   Catalogue Surgical Instruments, Deformity Apparatus, Artificial Limbs, Artificial Eyes, Elastic Stockings, Trusses, Crutches, Supporters, Galvanic and Faradic Batteries, Surgeons' Appliances of Every Description; 924 pp; **MAH; NLM** (W 26 S531); **NWUCML** (617.91 Sh2); **CPP** (Ed/30); **LLU** (W S532c).

      1889   Catalogue Surgical Instruments and Apparatus . .; 12th ed.; 963 pp; **NWUCML**.

   ca 1890   Surgical Instruments, Deformity Apparatus, Artificial Limbs, Artificial Eyes, . . .; 987 pp; **MAH** (RD 76S 531).

   ca 1895   Catalogue of Surgical Instruments, Deformity Apparatus, Galvanic and Faradic Batteries, Surgeons' Appliances of Every Description; 14th ed.; 915 pp; **NLM** (W26 S531c, has catalogued as 1889).

   ca 1895   Catalogue of Surgical Instruments, Deformity Apparatus, Artificial Limbs, Artificial Eyes, Elastic Stockings, Trusses, Crutches, Supporters, Galvanic and Faradic Batteries; 1014 pp; **MAH** (Rd 76 S 53); **VM**.

      1903   Catalogue G, Veterinary Instruments, Cattle and Poultry Specialties; 8th ed., revised and enlarged, 262 pp, illustrated; **HDM**.

      1905   Catalogue of Surgical and Veterinary Instruments & Hospital Supplies; 20th ed.; **HDM**.

     n.d.   Illustrated Catalogue of High Grade Surgical Instruments and Physicians' Supplies; 20th ed.; pp 1-6, 200-769; **TMHM**.

   ca 1908   Surgical Instruments and Physician's Supplies; 590 pp; **WOC**.

   ca 1912   Manufacturers of Surgical Instruments; 48 pp; **MAH**.

      1916   Illustrated Catalog of Eye, Ear, Nose and Throat Instruments, Electrical Apparatus and Office Furniture; 2nd ed.; 306 pp; **UCLABM** (W 26 S 531i).

      1925   Catalogue of General Surgical Supplies, Instruments and Apparatus . . .; 22nd ed.; **NWUCML; ACS** (U 6a S531c); **JHIHM** (Rd 76. S 53).

      1926   Catalog of General Surgical Supplies; 23rd ed.; 865 pp; **ACS** (U 6a S 531c); **VM; LACMA** (149 Sh2c).

      1927   Modern Instruments for Bone and Joint Surgery; 24 pp; **LACMA** (149 Sh2m).

65 E. Lake Street, Chicago, Illinois.

      1929   Catalog, Surgical Instruments; 48 pp; **CS; NYAM; MF/MAH**.

      1929   Catalog of General Surgical Supplies; 24th ed.; 865 pp; **MAH** (C610.78085); **SLSC; VM**.

      1929   Supplement to the 24th ed.; General Surgical Instrument Catalog; 48 pp; **MAH**.

      1930   Catalog Surgical Instruments, Equipment, Supplies; 25th ed.; 404 pp; **NYAM; CS; SLMS; MUM; UCSF**.

103 North Wabash Avenue, (Chicago, IL).

     n.d.   Chiropody Instruments; 3rd ed.; 60 pp; **MAH**.

SHARPLESS & WATTS
Philadelphia, Pennsylvania.

     n.d.   Sanitary Medicine Closet; 5 pp; **CPP**.

SHAW SUPPLY CO., INC.
Tacoma, Washington.

     n.d.   Catalog of Medical Supplies, Surgical Instruments and Equipment, etc.; **NLM** (W26 S961c).

SHAWSPLY
See: SHAW SUPPLY CO., Trademark; **NLM**.

SHELTON ELECTRIC CO.
16 E. 42nd Street, New York.
30 E. Randolph Street, Chicago.
Factory: Fort Wayne, Indiana.
      1917   Catalogue Electric Vibrator; 30 pp; **NYAM; MF/MAH**.
  ca 1905   Catalogue Shelton Electric Vibrator, The Relief of Pain and the Treatment
             of Disease by Vibration; 24 pp; **MAH** (C 615.84085).

SHEPARD & DUDLEY
150 William Street, New York, New York.
  Jan. 1873   Catalog of Apparatus for the Mechanical Treatment of Deformities,
             Deficiencies, etc. of the Human Body, Inhalers, Atomizers,
             Electromagnetic Devices; 128 pp; **NYAM; MF/MAH; AFMM**.
      1876   Illustrated Catalogue of Surgical Instruments; pp 501-926; **NYAM** (S 125).
      1878   Catalogue of Surgical Instruments; pp 501-926; bound with:
  Jan. 1879   Catalogue of Apparatus for Deformities and Deficiencies, Elastic Stockings,
             Galvanic Batteries, Inhalation Apparatus, etc.; 133 pp; **AFMM**.
      1886   Illustrated Catalogue of Surgical Instruments, Part II; pp 501-977; **NYAM;**
             MF/MAH.
      1886   Catalogue of Surgical Instruments mfg. by R. I. Pearson & Co., Part II;
             pp 501-986; **AFMM**.
      1889   Title page: January 1889 Illustrated Catalogue of Surgical Instruments
             Manufactured by R.I. Pearson & Co., Kansas City, Missouri, Part II;
             reverse side: Preface signed by Shepard and Dudley; 501-986 pp, fragile;
             AFMM.
      n.d.   Catalog of Surgical Instruments; 40 pp; **NLM** (W26 H136).

SHERMAN, G. H., M.D.
Detroit, Michigan.
      n.d.   Vaccine Therapeutics; 12 pp; **CPP**.

SHOTEN, K. YAWATA, INC.
No. 5, 7-Chome, Ginza, Kyobashi, Tokyo, Japan.
  ca 1936   Catalogue no. 1, Surgical Instruments, Gynecological and Obstetrical
             Instruments; 18 pp; **AFMM**.
    1930s   Catalog of X-Ray Apparatus, Giba; 22 pp; **AFMM**.
      1936   Brochure Hypodermic and Serum Syringes; 6 pp; **AFMM**.
    1930s   Catalog Laboratory Apparatus; 29 pp; **AFMM**.

SHRIMPTON, ALFRED, & SONS, LTD.
Britannia Works, Redditch, England.
  ca 1915   Surgical Needles of Every Description, Surgical Safety Pins, etc.;
             WMScM.

SHUR-ON STANDARD OPTICAL COMPANY, INC.
  Shuron Optical Company, Inc. (1931)
Geneva, New York.
  Rochester, New York (listed in one 1929 catalog).
  Branches: 1112 Pershing Square Bldg., New York; 1211 Chestnut St., Philadelphia; 128 E. Sixth St.,
  Cincinnati (1925, removed from 1926 list); 5 South Wabash Ave., Chicago; 278 Post St., Chicago; 333
  Washington St., Boston.
  Factories at Geneva, N.Y.; Mt. Vernon, N.Y.; Rochester, N.Y.; Southbridge, Mass.

Est: 1864 as Standard Optical Co.

    1915–   *Shur-On Chronicle*, Vol X, various Issues through 1920; **AO**.

Sep. 1, 1925   Shur-On Cases, America's Dominant Line of Spectacle and Eyeglass Cases, Price List; 28 pp; **AO**.

Sep. 1, 1925   Shur-On Ophthalmic Lenses, Price List; 33 pp; **AO**.

Sep. 1, 1925   Genothalmic Equipment, Complete Refracting Room Equipment, Price List; 24 pp; **AO**.

Sep. 1, 1925   Shur-On Frames and Mountings, Price List; 100 pp, index; **AO**.

Mar. 1, 1926   Shur-On Frames, Mountings, and Lenses, Price List; 104 pp; **AO**.

Mar. 1, 1926   Stoco Optical Machinery, Built by the Largest Manufacturers of Optical Machinery in the World, Price List; 104 pp; **AO**.

    1926   The Genothalmic Visual Test Apparatus, A Simple, Practical, Mathematically Precise Test Chart; 53 pp; **AO**.

Feb. 26, 1927   Shur-On Ophthalmic Lenses, Stock Price List; 26 pp; **AO**.

Feb. 26, 1927   Shur-On Cases, America's Dominant Line of Spectacle and Eyeglass Cases, Price List; 38 pp; **AO**.

Feb. 26, 1927   Shur-On Frames and Mountings, Price List; 78 pp; **AO**.

Branches: 122 E. 42nd St., New York; Main and E. 5th St., Cincinnati; 110 Tremont St., Boston.

Sep. 1929   Shur-On Imperial Frames and Mountings, Price List; 36 pp; **AO**.

pre–1930   Spectacle and Eyeglass Frames, Mountings and Cases; 42 pp; **AO**.

    1930   Introducing the New Shur-On Ronlite Cases, Featherweight, Genuine Leather, Featuring the Ronlite Mograin, Snakegrain, Lizardgrain; 4 pp; **AO**.

    1930   Shur-On Standard Chronicle for March, Spring and Summer Styles ed.; 32 pp; **AO**.

May 15, 1931   Stoco Optical Machinery, Price List; 30 pp; **AO**.

    1933   The Shuron Lens Book; 32 pp; **AO**.

SIBER HEGNER & CO., LTD.
Talstrasse 14, Zurich 8022, Switzerland.
8 West 30th Street, New York, New York.

    n.d.   Anthropological Instruments for Somatology and Osteology; **RCSL**.

SIBLEY, GIDEON
Thirteenth and Filbert Streets, Philadelphia, Pennsylvania.
Est: 1869

    1887   Catalogue Artificial Teeth; 32 pp; **MAH** (C 617.6085 S).

    1900?   Catalogue the Sibley Dental Chair, Fountain Cuspidor, Dental Engine and Specialties; 32 pp; **MAH** (C617.6085 S).

N. W. Corner State and Quincy Streets, Chicago.

    1903–04   School of Dentistry, University of Illinois, Equipment List for Freshman Students in Operative Technics; **CDMC**.

SIDLE, JOHN W., & CO.
Lancaster, Pennsylvania.

    1880   Catalogue of the Acme Optical Goods; 1st ed.; 36 pp; **CTY/B** (Uai Si 13).

    1881   Condensed Price List of the Acme Optical Goods; 2nd ed.; 16 pp; **CTY/B** (Uai Si 13).

Sep. 1881   Condensed Price List of the Acme Optical Goods; 3rd ed.; 16 pp; **CTY/B** (Uai Si 13).

SIEMENS, FRIEDRICH
Alserstrasse 20, Wien, Austria.
    n.d.   Catalogue Heisswasserapparate; 8 pp; **NYAM; MF/MAH**.

SIEMENS & HALSKE, A. -G.
Wernerwerk Nonnendamm, Berlin, Germany.
See: SIEMENS-REINIGER-WERKE, SIEMENS-REINIGER-VEIFA CO.; **ACR/MAH**.
    1911–12   Preisliste 52, Elektromedizinische Apparate; 7 plates; **BLEL**.
    1911   Preisliste Nr. 53, Apparate und Einrichtungen fuer Untersuchungen mit Röntgenstrahlen; 166 pp; **ACR/MAH**.
    1912   Presliste Nr. 53, 15 Teil Gynäkologisches Universalinstrumentarium nach Dr. Albers-Schonberg; 7 pp; **ACR/MAH**.
    1913   Preisliste Nr. 53, 16 Teil; Apparate und Einrichtungen fuer Untersuchungen mit Röntgenstrahlen; 9 pp; **ACR/MAH**.
    1920–20s   Brochure, Tiefentherapie-Bestrahlungsgeräte nach dem Siemens-Tuto-System; 6 pp foldout; **ACR/MAH**.

SIEMENS-REINIGE
Berlin W 8, Germany.
    n.d.   Brochure Dosis und Spektramessgeraete fuer Roentgenstrahle; 10 pp; **NYAM; MF/MAH**.

SIEMENS-REINIGER-VEIFA CO.
54 Lafayette Street, New York, New York.
Manufacturers of Electro-Medical Apparatus
    See: SIEMENS & HALSKE, A.B., SIEMENS-REINIGER-WERKE; **ACR/MAH**; ADLANCO INDUSTRIAL PRODUCTS CORP.; **NYAM**.
    ca 1910   Helidore Roentgenapparate fuer Diagnostik, Oberflaechen und Tiefentherapie; 22 pp; **NYAM; MF/MAH**.
    ca 1910   Catalog, Deep Therapy Apparatus, The Stabilivolt, no. 455; 15 pp; **ACR/MAH**.

SILVERDALE MFG. CO.
110 Cheapside, London E C 2, England.
    E. 20 c   Hospital and Invalid Furniture, Self-Propelled and Auto Propelled Invalid Tricycles; 3 pp; **WMScM**.

SILVERMAN, L.
1033 Chestnut Street, Philadelphia, Pennsylvania.
Est: 1896
    ca 1914   Illustrated Catalog of Dental Supplies of Every Description; 111 pp; **HML**.
    n.d.   Catalogue Dental Supplies, no. 15; 49 pp; **NYAM; MF/MAH**.

SIMAL, D.
5 rue Monge, Paris, France.
    n.d.   Fabricant d'instruments de chirurgie; Supplément au catalogue illustré; 32 pp; **NYAM**.

SIMMONS CO.
Kenosha, Wisconsin.
Newark, New Jersey.
San Francisco, California.
    n.d.   Catalogue Institution Beds, no. 11; 55 pp; **NYAM; MF/MAH**.
    110 East 42nd Street, New York, New York.
    n.d.   Catalogue Beds, Mattresses, Springs, no. 12; 40 pp; **NYAM; MF/MAH**.

SIMMONS, JOHN
106, 108, 110 Centre Street, New York, New York.
    Jan. 1885   Catalogue no. 3; Malleable and Cast Iron Gas, Steam and Water
              Fittings . . .; 243 pp; **NYAM; MF/MAH.**

SIMON, CHARLES E., M.D.
    1906   A New Counting Chamber for the Enumeration of Blood Corpuscles, 3
              pp; AMA reprint; **NYAM; MF/MAH.**

SIMONDS MACHINE CO., INC.
Southbridge, MA.
    n.d.   Prescription for Precision Economy Speed; Lensmaster Optical Accessories
              Equipment; 4 pp; **URRR** (S-676).
    n.d.   Prescription for Precision Economy Speed; 4 pp; **URRR** (S-675).
    n.d.   Advertisement for lens block; 1 pp; **URRR** (S-674).

SIMONIS
Jodo-Formagen-Cement
    See: SCHARMANN, GUSTAV; **MF/MAH.**

SIMPLEX LAMP MFG. CO.
366 Ninth Street, Brooklyn, New York.
    n.d.   Steam Vaporizer, Formaldehyde Sterilizer, Complexion Steamer; 1 pp;
              CPP.

SIMPSON AND SMITH
Strand, London.
    1825   Instrument maker mentioned by John Read.

SINDERIE OF LANGRES
    18 c   Instrument maker mentioned by Pagé, veterinary instrument maker, Vol.
              I, Pl xxxvi, in catalog at **RCSL.**

SINGER SEWING MACHINE COMPANY
149 Broadway, New York 7, New York.
Est: 1851
    ca 1942–43   The Singer Surgical Stitching Instrument for Better Surgical Technique; 32
              pp; **BLEL.**

SIOUX CITY OPTICAL CO.
Corner 5th and Nebraska Streets, Sioux City, Iowa.
    1916   Catalogue of Optical Goods; 77 pp; **URRR** (S-15).

SISCHO & BEARD
512-529 Ryan Bldg., St. Paul, MN.
    ca 1910   Illustrated Catalog and Price List of Optical Goods; 176 pp; **URRR** (S-16).
    1913   20th Anniversary Catalog, Lenses, Frames and General Optical
              Merchandise; **URRR** (S-17).
    1916   Goggles; 27 pp; **URRR** (S-18).
    1915   Goggles, 24 pp; **URRR** (S-19).

SITTEL, HEINRICH
Heidelberg, Germany.
    1876   Preis-verzeichniss physiologisch-chemischer Präparate; 11 pp; **NYAM;**
              MF/MAH.

SKLAR, J., MFG. CO., INC.
38-04 Woodside Ave., Long Island City, New York.
133-143 Floyd St., Brooklyn, N.Y.
Est: 1892
   1917 Catalogue, Surgical, Dental, and Veterinary Instruments; **CDMC**.
   1938 Catalog Surgical Instruments; 12th ed.; 463 pp; **AFMM**.
   n.d. Catalogs of surgical instruments, physicians' supplies, apparatus, etc.;
      NLM (W26 S628c).

SLACK, ALFRED M.
Central P.O. Box 160, Osaka, Japan.
   n.d. Price List; 10 pp; **NYAM; MF/MAH**.

SMALE BROTHERS
London, England.
   1862 Catalog and Price List of Teeth and Dental Materials; **BDA**.

SMIT ROENTGEN N.V.
Leiden, Holland.
   See: PHYSICIANS' TECHNICAL EQUIPMENT CO.; **ACR/MAH**.

SMITH, A. & J.
Maxwell House, Aberdeen, Scotland.
   1930s Apparatus for Physical Measurements; 14 pp; **WMScM**.

SMITH & BECK
6 Coleman St., London, England.
   1851 Catalogue of Achromatic Microscopes; 8 pp; **CTY/B** (Uai Sm 675).

SMITH, BECK & BECK
6 Coleman Street, London, England.
   See: R. & J. BECK LTD.; **AFMM**.
   1851 Catalogue of Achromatic Microscopes, etc.; **CTY/B** (Uai Sm653).
  Jan. 1859 A Catalogue of Acromatic Microscopes, etc.; 20 pp; **CTY/B**
      (Uai Sm 675).
   1859 Description, Price etc. of the Educational Microscope; 5th ed.; 14 pp;
      CTY/B (Uai Sm 675).
  31 Cornhill, London, England.
   1864 Description, Price, etc. of the Educational Microscope; 13 pp; **NLM**
      (W26 S643).
  Mar. 1866 Catalogue of Achromatic Microscopes, dissecting instruments, etc.; 23 pp;
      NLM (W26 S643).
   1865 A Treatise on the Construction, Proper Use, and Capabilities of Smith,
      Beck, and Beck's Achromatic Microscopes; 144 pp; **AFMM**.
  Apr. 1865 Catalogue of Scientific Instruments; 39 pp; **AFMM**.
   1866 An Illustrated Description of the Popular Microscope; 16 pp; **NLM** (W26
      S643).
  Jun. 1866 Catalogue of Scientific Instruments, Stereoscopes . . . Hand Magnifiers,
      Reading Glasses, Part VI; **NLM** (W26 S643).

SMITH, BENJAMIN
68 Cromer Street, Brunswick Street, London.
   1826 Instrument maker mentioned by Pagé, listed in catalog at **RCSL**.

SMITH & DAMPER
   1904 From 1904 catalogue of Peter Van Schaak & Sons, Successors to the

following series of companies: Peter Van Schaack & Sons, 1885; Van Schaack & Stevenson & Co., 1877; Van Schaack, Stevenson & Reid, 1870; E.P. Dwyer, 1860; Penton, Robinson & Smith, 1859; Penton & Robinson, 1857; Brickerhoff & Penton, 1844; **NYAM**.

SMITH, GEORGE A., & CO.
7 Park Street, Boston, Massachusetts.
        n.d.   Educational Supplies Chemical, Microscopical and Philosophical Apparatus, Laboratory Department; 10 pp; **CTY/B** (Uai Sm57).
        n.d.   Catalogue, Hartnack Microscopes and Objectives, Selling Agents for Chance's Slides and Cover Glasses; **CTY/B** (Uai Sm 6775).

SMITH, HERBERT S.
162 William Street, New York, New York.
    1867-78   Descriptive Price List of Wheel Chairs; **CPP** (Bolenius Coll).
    1878   Catalogue of Wheel Chairs; **CTY/B** (Uai Sm 69).

SMITH & HODSON
See: BULLOCK & CRENSHAW; **NLM**.

SMITH, JOHN, & SON
26/30 Gibson Street, Hillhead, Glasgow, Scotland.
Est: 1751
        n.d.   Makers of Electric Diagnostic Instruments; set of 13 single sheets; **WMScM**.
        n.d.   Improved May Electric Ophthalmoscope; **WMScM**.
        n.d.   Klinostik diagnostic set; 4 pp; **WMScM**.

SMITH, LEE S., & SON
Keenan Building, Pittsburgh, Pennsylvania.
    1905   Illustrated Dental Catalogue no. 2106; 5th ed.; 780 pp; **MAH**.
  Apr. 1, 1914   Catalogue Dental Products; 132 pp; **NYAM; MF/MAH**.
    1915   Catalog of Dental Furniture, Instruments and Materials; 6th ed.; 982 pp; **MAH** (C 617.6085 S); **UPSDM** (D 617. 604. Sm61).
  Aug. 1917   Brochure, Dental Supplies for Students; 20 pp; **NYAM; MF/MAH**.
  Aug. 1, 1925   Catalogue, Dental Products; 24 pp; **NYAM; MF/MAH**.
        n.d.   Science Progresses; 8 pp; **NYAM; MF/MAH**.
Sharpsburg Station, Pittsburgh, Pennsylvania.
        n.d.   Brochure, The Effect of Thoro Mixing on Silicate Cements; 8 pp; **NYAM; MF/MAH**.
        n.d.   The Weber Fountain Spittoon; 4 pp; **MAH** (C 617.6085 S).
        n.d.   Catalogue Weber Spittoons; 24 pp; **MAH** (C 617.6085S).

SMITH, LEE S., & SONS DENTAL DEPOT
524 Penn Avenue, Pittsburgh, Pennsylvania.
Est: 1866
    1894   Catalogue of Dental Instruments and Materials; 558 pp; **MAH** (C 617.6085).
    1897   Illustrated Catalogue of Dental Furniture, Instruments and Materials; 2nd ed.; 594 pp; **UBML** (WU 26 S654i); **HML**.
        n.d.   The Weber Fountain Spittoon; 4 pp; **CPP**.
    1901   Catalogue, Dental Furniture, Instruments and Materials; 3rd ed.; 675 pp; **UPSDM** (D 617.604 Sm61).
    1902   Catalogue, Dental Furniture, Instruments; 4th ed.; 808 pp; **UBML**.

SMITH, MARTIN H., CO.
New York, New York.
>n.d.   Ergoapiol, In the Successful Treatment of Menstrual Disorders; 16 pp; **CPP**.

SMITH OPTICAL CO.
8 Winter Street, Boston, MA.
>Mar. 1, 1921   Prescription Catalog, Prices Revised; 16 pp; **URRR** (S-555).

SNOOK, W. B., MFG. CO., INC.
See: SNOOK-ROENTGEN MFG. CO.; **ACR/MAH**.

SNOOK-ROENTGEN MANUFACTURING CO.
1210 Race Street, Philadelphia, Pennsylvania.
See: GENERAL ELECTRIC CORP., ca 1927; **ACR/MAH**.
>ca 1915   Sweet's Eye Localizer, Bulletin 103; 15 pp; **ACR/MAH**.
>ca 1915   The Hydrogen Tube, Bulletin 105; photocopy; 11 pp; **ACR/MAH**.
>1916   X-Rays and Snook, A Brief History of Roentgenology and the Part Played by the Snook-Roentgen Manufacturing Co., in its Development and Perfection; 23 pp; **ACR/MAH**.

SNOW DENTAL CO.
Buffalo, New York.
>1925   Catalogue; **CDMC**.

SNOWDEN & BROTHER
(Late Wiegan & Snowden)
15 North Fifth Street, Philadelphia, Pennsylvania.
Est: 1821
>1860   Catalogue of Surgical and Dental Instruments, Elastic Trusses, Medical Saddle Bags, Abdominal Supporters, Shoulder Braces and Druggists Sundries; 89 pp; **AFMM**.
23 South Eighth Street, Philadelphia, Pennsylvania.
>1866   Copy with handwritten corrections made throughout catalogue; 87 pp, covers missing; **AFMM**.

SNOWDEN, (WILLIAM), COMPANY
7 South 11th Street, Philadelphia, Pennsylvania.
>n.d.   The New Medical Centrifuge and the Purdy Electric Centrifuge; 8 pp; **CPP** (Cage Pam A 107).
>n.d.   John A. Barrett's New Chloride of Silver Galvanic Battery and Absolute Galvanometer; 12 pp; **CPP**.
>n.d.   Pamphlet on new centrifuge; **MUM** (Page Pam A 107).

SOCIÉTÉ BELGE D'OPTIQUE & D'INSTRUMENTS DE PRÉCISION BRUXELLES
35 rue de l'Hôpital Bruxelles, Bruxelles, Belge.
>n.d.   Catalog, Optical Instruments; 51 pp; **URRR** (S-11).

SOCIÉTÉ D'ÉTUDES SCIENTIFIQUES
8 rue du Centre, Neuilly-Sur-Seine.
>n.d.   Médication Anesthesique le Coryl et le Coryleur; 4 pp; **CPP**.

SOCIÉTÉ FRANÇAISE DES INSTRUMENTS D'OPTIQUE
>1925   Microscope Type no. 1; 11 pp; **URRR** (S-626).
>1926   Microscope Type 3, 2 pp bound with Microscope no. 5, bound with

Microscope Binocular Type 1925, 7 pp bound with Instruments optiques d'examen de mesure & de controle appliqués à l'industrie; 12 pp; **URRR** (S-624).

1929   Microscope Standard no. 2; 4 pp; **URRR** (S-625)

SOCIÉTÉ GENEVOISE
5 Chemin Gourgas, Genève, Switzerland.
Est: 1861
See: QUEEN & CO., INC.; Agents in U.S.

1886   Catalogue Société Genevoise pour la construction d'instruments de physique, supplement au catalogue de 1883; **CTY/B** (Uai So 126).

1909   Catalogue Prix-courant illustré de la Société Genevoise pour la construction des instruments de physique et de mécanique; 158 pp; **CTY/B** (Uai So 126).

n.d.   Queen and Co. Instruments of Precision, Circular 104; 14 pp; **CTY/B** (Uai So 126).

n.d.   Nouveau microscope universel; 6 pp; **URRR** (S-477).

1928   Elsi Pedometers; 4 pp, 1 pp price list; **URRR** (S-495).

SOCIÉTÉ DES LUNETIERS
56 Hatton Garden, London E.C. 1, England.
Est: 1849
Head Office: 6 rue Pastorelle, Paris, France.

1929?   No title; 366 pp, separate price list of Sets of Drawing Instruments, Loose Compasses and Protractors, Mar. 1929; **WMScM**.

1936?   Fronco-Focometer no. 2 Model for Opticians and Prescription Houses; 4 pp; **URRR** (S-363).

SOFT-LITE LENS CO.
New York, New York.

Aug. 1934   The Dualens; 4 pp; **URRR** (S-551).

1934   14 pp; **URRR** (S-551-a).

1935   Glare Filtering Lenses Optical Service Corp., 119 W. 57th St., New York, New York, advertisements for Soft Lite Lenses; 12 pp; **URRR** (S-567).

Apr? 1936   Series of advertisements for lenses in large hard cover binder, one dated Apr. 1936; **URRR** (S-604).

1936-37   Soft-Lite presents; 1 pp; **URRR** (S-684).

n.d.   New Soft-Lite HT 51, Product of a Decade of Research; 4 pp; **URRR** (S-683).

SOHNGEN, W., & CO.
Waldstrasse 25, Wiesbaden, Germany.

1930s   Katalog, Fabrik fuer Sanitätsausruestungen und Verbandstoffe; 320 pp; **NLM** (W26 S681k).

SOLEIL, H.
Rue de l'Odeon, 21, Paris, France.
Est: 1825
Son of Founder

1867   Catalogue des appareils d'optique; 13 pp; **CTY/B** (Uai So 43).

SOLILA TEETH
See: DENTIST'S SUPPLY CO.

SORENSEN, C. M., CO., INC.
444 Jackson Avenue, Long Island City, New York.
    1928   Catalogue Tankless Apparatus for the Nose & Throat Specialists and Hospital; 55 pp; **NYAM; MF/MAH.**
117 East 87th Street, New York, New York.
    n.d.   Sorensen's Standard Small Floor-Type Tankless Air Compressor Combinations; 7 pp; **CPP.**
    n.d.   Sorensen's Universal Specialist's Chairs; 10 pp; **CPP.**

SORENSEN SCIENTIFIC CORPORATION
    ca 1923   Apparatus for Determination of Patency of Fallopian Tubes in Sterility as Devised by Dr. Gilman S. Currier; 6 pp; **CPP.**
    n.d.   Sorensen's Universal Specialist's Chairs; 10 pp; **CPP.**

SOUTHEASTERN OPTICAL CO., THE
737 E. Main St., Richmond, VA.
    1933   Catalog of Prescription Work; 47 pp; **URRR** (S-603).

SOUTHERN OPTICAL CO.
Louisville, KY.
    n.d.   Price List; 60 pp; **URRR** (S-20).

SPALTEHOLZ, PROF. DR.
    May 1929   Catalogue, Human & Zoological Specimens; 4 pp; **NYAM; MF/MAH.**
    n.d.   Transparent Anatomical Preparations in Museum Glass Jars; 2 pp, 30 price lists; **MAH.**

SPARKLETS, LTD.
London, England.
    1934?   Handbook on the Use of the Sparklet Pocket Resuscitator; 10 pp; **WMScM.**
    n.d.   The Use of Carbon Dioxide in General Practice; 12 pp; **WMScM.**

SPEAKMAN, WILLIAM M.
6 South 10th Street, Philadelphia, Pennsylvania.
    n.d.   Assorted Ads; 4 pp; **CPP.**

SPECIALTY OPTICAL CO.
1009-1017 McGee, Kansas City, MO.
    Aug. 1929   Price List; 24 pp; **URRR** (S-546a).
    1932   Price List; 32 pp; **URRR** (S-513).
    1932   Price List; 6 pp foldout; **URRR** (S-510).
    1932   Price List; 32 pp; **URRR** (S-511).
    1932   Price List; 13 pp; **URRR** (S-519).
    1933   Catalog; 10 pp; **URRR** (S-525).
    1933   Price List; 14 pp; **URRR** (S-527).
    1933   Price List; 32 pp; **URRR** (S-523).
    1934   Price List; 22 pp; **URRR** (S-545).
    Feb. 1934   Price List; 24 pp; **URRR** (S-543).
    1934   A Trip Through the Factory of Specialty Optical Company; 16 pp; **URRR** (S-546).
    1935   Logic System; 24 pp; **URRR** (S-686).
    1936   8 pp foldout; **URRR** (S-685).
    Apr. 1937   Optical Goods; 8 pp foldout; **URRR** (S-546b).
    n.d.   Price List; 15 pp; **URRR** (S-529).

n.d.   Price List; 18 pp; **URRR** (S-532).
n.d.   Price List; 31 pp; **URRR** (S-506).

SPECIALTY MANUFACTURING COMPANY
Brooklyn, New York.
    n.d.   DeLuxe Products, dental; **CDMC**.

SPENCER & CROCKER
117, 119, 121 West Fifth Street, Cincinnati, Ohio.
See: SAMUEL A. CROCKER & CO.; **AFMM**.
    1884   Catalogue, Dental Materials, Furniture, Instruments, etc.; 260 pp; **MAH**
            (C 617.6085).

SPENCER LENS CO.
Buffalo, New York.
See: AMERICAN OPTICAL COMPANY, MAX MEYER, J. F. HARTZ; **AFMM**.
    1896   Catalog of Optical Instruments; 29 pp; **AFMM**.
 ca 1898   Brochure advertising Spencer's New Microscope Stand, Continental Form
            no. 1; 4 pp; **AFMM**.
 ca 1898   Brochure advertising Spencer's New Microscope Stand, Continental Form
            no. 3; 4 pp; **AFMM**.
    1900   Catalog of Microscopes for School, Laboratory and Medical Work with
            Microscopic Accessories, Laboratory Supplies and Scientific Apparatus;
            32 pp; **AFMM**.
 ca 1900   Spencer Microscopes, Selected Models for Medical and Laboratory Use; 7
            pp; **CTY/B** (Uai Sp 366).
 ca 1900   Brochure, Bloodtesting Apparatus Supplied by Spencer, includes
            Thoma-Zeiss Haemacytometer; 4 pp; **AFMM**.
 ca 1900   Brochure advertising Spencer's New Laboratory Microtome and
            Microtome Accessories; 9 pp; **AFMM**.
    1902   Some Facts about Spencer Microscopes in Their Relation to Medical
            Work; 2nd ed., 9 pp; 3rd ed., 11 pp; **AFMM**.
 ca 1902   Pamphlet, How to Use and Care for the Microscope; 27 pp; **MAH**.
Jan. 1, 1904   Catalogue of Microscopes and Accessories, Microtomes, Bacteriological
            Apparatus and Laboratory Supplies; 157 pp; **MAH** (578.08 S 745).
Jan. 1, 1905   Catalogue Microscopes, Microtomes, Bacteriological Apparatus & Labora-
            tory Supplies; 72 pp; **NYAM; MF/MAH**.
    1905   Spencer Microscopes and Accessories; 72 pp; **CPP** (Pam 7540).
    1906   Catalog of Microscopes and Accessories, Microtomes, Bacteriological Appa-
            ratus and Laboratory Supplies; 200 pp; **AFMM**.
    1908   Brochure advertising Spencer Lens Company's New No. 10 Microscope; 4
            pp; **AFMM**.
 ca 1908   Brochure advertising Spencer's New no. 16 Microscope; 4 pp; **AFMM**.
    1910   Catalog of Microscope and Accessories, Microtomes and Bacteriological
            Apparatus and Laboratory Supplies; 190 pp; **AFMM; HDM**.
 ca 1910   Brochure Spencer's Capillary Rotator; 4 pp; **AFMM**.
 ca 1910   Brochure Spencer's New Microscope no. 36; 4 pp; **AFMM**.
    1911   Brochure advertising New Spencer Microscopes, nos. 45, 65, 66; 6 pp;
            AFMM; MAH (C 681.4085 S 625mm).
    1914   Catalog of Microscopes and Accessories, Microtomes, Bacteriological Appa-
            ratus and Laboratory Supplies; 226 pp; **MAH** (C681.4085 S625).
 ca 1914   How to Use and Care for the Microscope; 27 pp; **MAH**.

1914   Catalog of Spencer Microscopes and Accessories, Microtomes, Bacteriological Apparatus and Laboratory Supplies; 226 pp; **AFMM**.

ca 1915   Brochure advertising Spencer's New Binocular Types, Covertible; 12 pp; **AFMM**.

1915   Catalog of Spencer Delineascopes for Transparent, Opaque, Vertical, Microscopic Projection; 32 pp; **AFMM**.

1919–20   Catalog of Spencer Microscopes, Microtomes and Accessories; 114 pp; **AFMM**.

ca 1922   Catalogue, A Selection of Spencer Products for Commercial and Industrial Laboratories; 24 pp; **MAH** (C 681.4085 S625).

Aug. 1923   Catalogue, the Delineascope; 28 pp; **NYAM; MF/MAH**.

1924   Catalog of Microscopes, Microtomes, Delineascopes and Their Accessories, and Other Scientific Optical Instruments; 117 pp; **AFMM**.

1926   The Microscope, Construction, Use and Care; 59 pp; **AFMM**.

1928   Corrected Price List to 1924 Catalog; **AFMM**.

1929   Catalog, Of The More Popular . . . Spencer Microscopes, Microtomes and Accessories; 79 pp; **MAH** (C 681.4085 S 625mm).

1930   Catalog, . . . Of The More Popular Microscopes, Microtomes, Delineascopes, Optical Measuring Instruments and Accessories; 102 pp; **MAH** (C 681.4085 S 625mm).

1930s   Brochure, Spencer New Binocular Types, Convertible; 11 pp; **AFMM**.

1935   Brochure, A Selection of Spencer Instruments; 15 pp; **MAH**.

May 1935   Spencer Research Microscopes; 26 pp; **AFMM; MAH**.

Dec. 1935   A Selection of Spencer Instruments; 15 pp; **CTY/B** (Uai Sp 366); **MAH** (C681.4085 S625).

n.d.   Catalogue, Microtomes and Microscopes; 79 pp; **NYAM; MF/MAH**.

546 Main St., Buffalo, New York.

367-373 Seventh St., Buffalo, New York.

Aug. 15, 1896   Catalogue & Price List of Microscopes, Telescopes and Accessories; 29 pp; **CTY/B** (Uai Sp 366).

n.d.   Catalogue Spencer Microscopes for School, Laboratory and Medical Work with Microscopic Accessories, Laboratory Supplies, and Scientific Apparatus; 32 pp; **CTY/B** (Uai Sp 366).

70 Fifth Ave., New York, New York.

pre–1930   Illustrated Catalogue of Spencer Products for Commercial & Industrial Laboratories; 24 pp; **MAH** (C 681.4085 S 625).

1931   Brochure featuring the New Spencer Combination Binocular and Monocular Body, Patented; 8 pp; **AFMM**.

1935   Brochure, Spencer Medical Microscopes; 11 pp; **AFMM**.

1935   Brochure, Spencer Research Microscopes; 26 pp; **AFMM**.

SPENCER, M. A., CO.
134 West Seventh Street, Cincinnati, Ohio.
16 E. Fourth St., Cincinnati, OH.
Est: 1871; Inc: in Tennessee, charter cancelled Nov 13 1920

post 1893   Condensed Price List, Optical Goods; 108 pp; **URRR** (S-30).

SPENCER MICROTOMES
See: CENTRAL SCIENTIFIC CO., ca 1922; **NYAM**.

SPENCER OPTICAL CO.
21 Seneca Street, Cleveland, Ohio.

1889? Catalogue Price List of Microscope Objectives, Telescopes and Accessories; **CTY/B** (Uai Sp 34).

1898 Manufacturing and Importing Opticians, Catalogue 15; 160 pp; **URRR** (S-27).

1906 Catalog 17; 192 pp; **URRR** (S-29).

5 & 7 Maiden Lane, New York, New York.

1921 Optical Goods; 25th ed.; 96 pp; **URRR** (S-553).

SPENCER SCIENTIFIC INSTRUMENTS
See: AMERICAN OPTICAL CO.

SPENCER, THOMAS D.
Rochester, New York.

Oct. 1892 Spencer's Fumigating Diphtheritic Pastilles; 7th ed.; 16 pp; **CPP**.

SPILLER, GEORGE, LTD.
32 Wigmore St., London W.
Est: 1874

n.d. Ophthalmoscopes, Supplementary List; 5 pp; **URRR** (S-31).

SPINDLER & HOYER
Goettingen, Germany.

1900 Preisliste XX Apparate fuer psychologische Untersuchungen; 48 pp; **CTY/B** (Uai Sp 46).

1904 Price List Nr. XXII for Miscroscopes for the Use in the Laboratories of Universities, Colleges, Other Educational Institutions, for Pharmaceutical Chemists, etc.; 17 pp; **URRR** (S-370A).

1904 Katalog, ueber Physikalische, psychologische und physiologische Instrumente; 41 pp; **URRR** (S-365).

post 1904 Price List Nr. XIII, Microscopes; 12 pp; **CTY/B** (Uai Sp 46).

Arthur Thomas Importers
1200 Walnut St., Philadelphia, PA.

1909? Apparate fuer psychologische Untersuchungen; 48 pp; **URRR** (S-369).

SPIRELLA CO., THE
Meadville, Pennsylvania.

ca 1915 The Spirella Surgical Belt; 4 pp; **CPP**.

n.d. Spirella Service for Physicians and Surgeons; 24 pp; **CPP**.

SPLIT BAR CO.
17 West 42nd Street, New York, New York.
Inc: in New Jersey, charter void in 1922

n.d. Brochure, The Split Bar Attachment for Removable Bridge Work; 10 pp; **NYAM; MF/MAH**.

SPRAGUE APPARATUS CO.
33 West 42nd Street, New York, New York.

post 1898 For the Medical Profession; 11 pp; **CPP**.

SPRAGUE INSTITUTE, THE
141-3-5 West 36th Street, New York, New York.

n.d. Sprague Methods of Applying Superheated Dry Air in the Treatment of Rheumatism, Gout, Sciatica, Lumbago, Neuritis, The Arthrometer, the Most Ingenious Swiss Instruments; 48 pp; **CPP**.

SPURLOCK NEAL CO.
Nashville, Tennessee.
    1897   Wholesale Druggists; 128 pp; **CPP**.

SQUIBB, E. R.
36 Doughty Street, Brooklyn, New York.
Est: 1858
E. R. Squibb and Sons
745 5th Ave., New York 22, New York.
Div. **Mathieson Chemical Corp.**

Jan. 1, 1884	Price List Pharmaceutical Preparations & Pharmacopoeial Reagents, no. 51; 26 pp; **NYAM; MF/MAH**.
July 1, 1884	Price List Pharmaceutical Preparations & Pharmacopoeial Reagents, no. 52; 26 pp; **NYAM; MF/MAH**.
Jan. 1, 1885	Price List Pharmaceutical Preparations & Pharmacopoeial Reagents, no. 53; 25 pp; **NYAM; MF/MAH**.
July 1, 1885	Price List Pharmaceutical Preparations & Pharmacopoeial Reagents, no. 54; 25 pp; **NYAM; MF/MAH**.
July 1, 1886	Price List Pharmaceutical Preparations & Pharmacopoeial Reagents, no. 56; 25 pp; **NYAM; MF/MAH**.
Jan. 1, 1887	Price List Pharmaceutical Preparations & Pharmacopoeial Reagents, no. 57; 25 pp; **NYAM; MF/MAH**.
July 1, 1887	Price List Pharmaceutical Preparations & Pharmacopoeial Reagents, no. 58; 27 pp; **NYAM; MF/MAH**.
Jan. 1, 1889	Price List Pharmaceutical Preparations & Pharmacopoeial Reagents, no. 61; 32 pp; **NYAM; MF/MAH**.
July 1, 1890	Price List Pharmaceutical Preparations & Pharmacopoeial Reagents, no. 64; 32 pp; **NYAM; MF/MAH**.
Jan. 1, 1892	Price List Pharmaceutical Preparations & Pharmacopoeial Reagents, no. 67; 28 pp; **NYAM; MF/MAH**.
July 1, 1892	Price List Pharmaceutical Preparations & Pharmacopoeial Reagents, no. 68; 28 pp; **NYAM; MF/MAH**.
Jan. 1, 1893	Price List Pharmaceutical Preparations & Pharmacopoeial Reagents, no. 69; 41 pp; **NYAM; MF/MAH**.
July 1, 1893	Price List Pharamceutical Preparations & Pharmacopoeial Reagents, no. 70; 41 pp; **NYAM; MF/MAH**.
Jan. 1, 1894	Price List Pharmaceutical Preparations & Pharmacopoeial Reagents, no. 71; 40 pp; **NYAM; MF/MAH**.
July 1, 1894	Price List Pharamceutical Preparations & Pharmacopoeial Reagents, no. 72; 54 pp; **NYAM; MF/MAH**.
Jan. 1, 1895	Price List Pharmaceutical Preparations & Pharmacopoeial Reagents, no. 73; 54 pp; **NYAM; MF/MAH**.
July 1, 1895	Price List Pharmaceutical Preparations & Pharmacopoeial Reagents, no. 74; 60 pp; **NYAM; MF/MAH**.
Jan. 1, 1896	Price List Pharmaceutical Preparations & Pharmacopoeial Reagents, no. 75; 60 pp; **NYAM; MF/MAH**.
July 1, 1896	Price List Pharmaceutical Preparations & Pharmacopoeial Reagents, no. 76; 58 pp; **NYAM; MF/MAH**.
Jan. 1, 1897	Price List Pharmaceutical Preparations & Pharmacopoeial Reagents, no. 77; 60 pp; **NYAM; MF/MAH**.
July 1, 1897	Price List Pharmaceutical Preparations & Pharmacopoeial Reagents, no. 78; 60 pp; **NYAM; MF/MAH**.

Jan. 1, 1898	Price List Pharmaceutical Preparations & Pharmacopoeial Reagents, no. 79; 60 pp; **NYAM; MF/MAH**.

Jan. 1, 1898   Price List Pharmaceutical Preparations & Pharmacopoeial Reagents, no. 79; 60 pp; **NYAM; MF/MAH**.

July 1, 1900   Price List Pharmaceutical Preparations & Pharmacopoeial Reagents, no. 84; 63 pp; **NYAM; MF/MAH**.

Jan. 1, 1901   Price List Pharmaceutical Preparations & Pharmacopoeial Reagents, no. 85; 64 pp; **NYAM; MF/MAH**.

July 1, 1901   Price List Standard Pharmaceutical Preparations & Pharmacopoeial Reagents, no. 86; 64 pp; **NYAM; MF/MAH**.

Jan. 1, 1902   Price List Pharmaceutical Preparations & Pharmacopoeial Reagents, no. 87; 62 pp; **NYAM; MF/MAH**.

Jan. 1, 1903   Price List Pharmaceutical Preparations & Pharmacopoeial Reagents, no. 89; 63 pp; **NYAM; MF/MAH**.

Jan. 1, 1904   Price List Pharmaceutical Preparations & Pharmacopoeial Reagents, no. 91; 69 pp; **NYAM; MF/MAH**.

Jun. 1922   Price List Pharmaceutical Preparations; 157 pp; **NYAM; MF/MAH**.

80 Beckman Street, New York, New York.

n.d.   Ethyl Chloride and Ethyl Bromide, by Robert H. Thompson; 16 pp; **CPP**.

STAIMAN, J.

n.d.   The Universal Ophthalmometer; 13 pp; **MAH**.

STAINLESSFRANCE

38 Boulevard Saint-Michel, Paris, France.

Jan. 1930   Catalog no. 1, Instruments de chirurgie inoxydables; 82 pp; **AFMM**.

STALEY, CHARLES

45 Gayette, Albany, New York.

1841   Instrument maker listed in Albany City Directory.

STANDARD CHEMICAL CO., INC., THE

1016 Cherry Street, Philadelphia.
Pittsburgh, Pennsylvania.

n.d.   Soluble Medicated Intra-Uterine Crayons; 1 pp; **CPP**.

STANDARD COMFORT WINDOW CORP.

426 Broome Street, New York, New York.

n.d.   Brochure, Physicians Were the First to Adopt Comfort Windows, no. 2; 12 pp; **NYAM; MF/MAH**.

STANDARD ENGELN CORPORATION
THE ENGELN ELECTRIC CO.

Cleveland, Ohio.
Chicago, Illinois.

See: STANDARD X-RAY CO.

ca 1931   Deep Therapy Tilting Tube Container, unsigned, reads: from the desk of Byron Hess, Cenco Medical/Health Co., this company never produced anything, literature published, stock issued, etc.; 2 pp; **ACR/MAH**.

STANDARD FOUNTAIN CUSPIDOR, THE

P.O. Box 177, Canton, Ohio.

pre–1898   Pamphlet, The Standard Fountain Cuspidor; 6 pp; **MAH** (C 617.6085 S).

STANDARD OPTICAL CO.
Geneva, New York.
Est: 1864
        1903   Ophthalmoscopes, Retinoscopes, Ophthalmologic Apparatus; 28 pp; **CPP** (Pam A 99).
Jan. 1, 1910   Machinery and Instruments for Optical Rx Work, Catalog E, issued 24 Nov 1909; 52 pp; **AO**.
London Office: 62 Hatton Garden, London, E.C., England.
        1914   Stoco, Optical Machinery for Optical Rx Work, Catalog F; 127 pp; **AO**.
Chicago Office: 37 South Wabash Ave.
        1917   Stoco, Optical Machinery for Optical Rx Work, Catalog G; 123 pp; **AO**.
May 1, 1923   Catalog H, Stoco Optical Machinery for Optical Rx Work; 147 pp; **AO**; inserted in catalog: Barney Oldfield brings a great machine to Stoco advertising the Stoco-Oldfield die cutting machine, and The Stoco Invincible Lens Cutter; price list; **MAH** (C 617.75085 S 715).

STANDARD SCIENTIFIC COMPANY
147-153 Waverly Place, New York, New York.
        1920   Catalogue Scientific Instruments and Laboratory Supplies, no. 3; 240 pp; **CTY/B** (Uai St 247).
186-192 West Fourth Street, New York, New York.
        1921   Catalogue Laboratory Apparatus Chemistry, Biology, Photography, Microscopes, Projection Lanterns, Chemicals, Minerals, etc., no. 4; 192 pp; **CTY/B** (Uai St 247).

STANDARD SURGICAL MANUFACTURING CO., LTD.
London W 3, England.
        1933   Electric Automatic Sterilizer & Equipment, Stainless Steel Instruments; 57 pp, first 6 pp missing; **WMScM**.

STANDARD X-RAY COMPANY
1932 North Burling Street, Chicago, Illinois.
Est: 1911
    See: STANDARD ENGELN CORP.; **ACR/MAH**.
    ca 1920   Iontoquantimeter for Measuring Relative Intensities of X-rays; 2 pp; **ACR/MAH**.
    ca 1920   Type D X-Ray Transformer, Type A X-Ray Transformer; 7 pp; **ACR/MAH**.
    ca 1920   Some Data on Wave Lengths; 3 pp; **ACR/MAH**.
    ca 1920   The Story of Standard; 15 pp; **ACR/MAH**.
    ca 1920   De Luxe Model H X-Ray Machine; 2 pp; **ACR/MAH**.
    ca 1920   Type KSV 100 PKV Machine; 5 pp foldout; **ACR/MAH**.
    ca 1920   De Luxe 100 Peak Kilovolt X-Ray Machine; 5 pp foldout; **ACR/MAH**.
    ca 1920   220 Peak Kilovolt Valve Rectified X-Ray Machine; 2 pp; **ACR/MAH**.
    ca 1924   De Luxe Type X-Ray Transformers, Models F, J, E, and I; 6 pp; **ACR/MAH**.
    ca 1925   Pamphlet, 11 photos of X-Ray equipment; 11 pp; **ACR/MAH; MAH**.
    Feb. 1927   The Standard Stereoscope; 2 pp; **ACR/MAH**.
    Mar. 1927   Vertical Fluoroscope; 6 pp; **ACR/MAH**.
    Apr. 1927   Radiographic and Fluoroscopic Bucky Table; 2 pp; **ACR/MAH**.
    May 1927   Pamphlet, The Standard Cassette Changer; 6 pp; **ACR/MAH; MAH**.
    Jan. 1928   Radiographic and Fluoroscopic Bucky Table; 2 pp; **ACR/MAH**.
    ca 1928   Roentgenometer; 5 pp; **ACR/MAH**.

Jan. 1928	De Luxe Type K Special X-Ray Machine; 6 pp; **ACR/MAH**.
Jan. 1928	DeLuxe 95 Peak Kilovolt X-Ray Machine; 6 pp; **ACR/MAH**.
Feb. 1928	Unrectified Units; 10 pp; **ACR/MAH**.
July 1928	De Luxe 155 Peak Kilovolt X-Ray Machine; 6 pp; **ACR/MAH**.
May 1929	Type H 125 P.K.V. Machine; 5 pp; **ACR/MAH**.
Mar. 1929	Motor Driven Radiographic and Fluoroscopic Bucky Table; 10 pp; **ACR/MAH**.
1929?	Combination Two-Way Tilt Table; 2 pp; **ACR/MAH**.
ca 1930	Pamphlet, Tables, Vertical Fluoroscope Tube Stand; 13 pp; **ACR/MAH; MAH**.
Oct. 1931	Bulletin no. 32, Deep Therapy Tilting Tube Container; 6 pp; **ACR/MAH**.
1932	Fluoroscopic and Radiographic Bucky Table; 2 pp; **ACR/MAH**.
1932?	Tilting Radiographic and Fluoroscopic Bucky Table; 5 pp foldout; **ACR/MAH**.
1930s	Double Diaphragm Radiographic X-Ray Cones; pp 48 from brochure; **ACR/MAH**.
1930s	Shockproof Model EBRF, Diagnostic X-Ray Units, Series 60MA, 100MA, 200MA; 11 pp; **ACR/MAH**.
1930s	Standex Radiographic and Fluoroscopic Unit; 4 pp; **ACR/MAH**.
1930s	Shockproof Portagraph, B&W 8 x 10 inch glossy photo; **ACR/MAH**.
1930's	Model HCC Cassette Changer with Bucky; 8 x 10 inch glossy photo; **ACR/MAH**.

STEARNS, FREDERICK, & CO.
Detroit, Michigan.

| n.d. | Catalogue no. 89, Popular Non-Secret Medicines, American ed.; 78 pp; **UCSF**. |

STEEG, DR., AND REUTER
Homburg vor der Höhe, (Bad Homburg), Germany.

| 1884 | Preis-Verzeichniss optischer Instrumente, Apparate und Praeparate besonders zur Polarisation des Lichtes; 56 pp; **NYAM; MF/MAH**. |

STEELE, A. J.

| 1899 | Pointers on the Leather Splint read before the American Orthopedic Association at New York Meeting; 24 pp; **CPP**. |

STEELE'S
See: COLUMBUS DENTAL MFG. CO., 1916; **NYAM**.

STEINMANN, FRED C., & CO.
102-104 Fulton Street, New York, New York.

| 1900 | Catalogue Dental Specialties; 94 pp; **MAH** (C 617.6085S). |

STEINHEIL, C. A.
7 Theresienhoehe, Munich, Germany.
Est: 1855

1857	Preis Courant der Optischen und Astronomischen Werkstatter; 1 pp; **CTY/B** (Uai St 36).
1860	Preis Courant der Optischen und Astronomischen Werkstatte; 1 folded pp; **CTY/B** (Uai St 36).
1866	Preis Courant der Optischen und Astronomischen Werkstatte; **CTY/B** (Uai St 36).

1867   Preis Courant der Optischen und Astronomischen Werkstatte; 10 pp;
CTY/B (Uai St 36).

1907?   Price List of Astronomical and Physical Instruments; 84 pp; **CTY/B** (Uai
St 361).

STEINMETZ & KNETSCH
Kassel, Germany.
Stonecutter 4 & 5, London E.C., England.
Sodergatan 32, Malmo.

1903   Preis-Verzeichniss über chirurgische Instrumente; 13 ed.; 193 pp;
WMScM.

STELZIG, JONAS
Prague, Czechoslovakia.

ca 1850   Name appears on Ritgen type of forceps; Acc. no. 316358; **MAH**.

STEMMLE, THEO. E.
95 Lakeside Avenue, Orange, New Jersey.

ca 1900   Illustrated Catalogue and Price List of Surgeons' Instruments and
Physicians' Supplies, Electric Batteries, Orthopedic Appliances, etc.,
etc.; 328 pp, index, appendix; **MAH** (22487).

STENDICKE, AUGUST
240 Pearl Street, formerly 96 & 98 Fulton St., New York, New York.

19 c   Illustrated and Descriptive Catalogue of Optical Instruments; **CTY/B** (Uai
St 425).

STERLING SURGICAL PRODUCTS
34 Warren Street, New York, New York.

Feb. 1927   Wholesale Catalog; 32 pp; **NYAM; MF/MAH**.

STEVENS & CO., INC.
Providence, Rhode Island.

n.d.   Complete List Showing Correct and Satisfactory Combinations of S-Q
Finger Piece Guards and Mountings; 6 pp foldout; **MAH**.

STEVENS PHYSICIANS SUPPLY CO.
301-02-03-17 Odd Fellows Temple, Philadelphia, Pennsylvania.

n.d.   The Simplex Spirometer; 4 pp; **CPP**.

STEWARD, J. H.
406 Strand W.C., London, England.

1862   Catalogue of Opera and Field Glasses, Telescopes, Microscopes and other
Optical Instruments; 3rd revised ed.; 48 pp; **CTY/B** (Uai St 49).

1871   Catalogue of Optical, Philosophical, Mathematical, Surveying,
Meteorological Instruments, etc.; 81 pp; **NLM** (W26 S849).

1899   Catalog of Microscopes and Apparatus, Dissecting Instruments, Objects,
etc.; 36 pp; **URRR** (S-36).

STIASSNIE, MAURICE
Maison Verick is successor
204 Blvd. Raspail, Paris, France.

1907   Microscopes appareil accessories; 108 pp; **URRR** (S-53).

n.d.   Microtome du Prof Radais, stamped on cover Uhler Optical Instrument

Co., Allan H. Uhler, M.D., Microscope and Optical Apparatus, 1581 McCulloh St., Baltimore, MD; 4 pp; **URRR** (S-382).
1938 Microscopes de recherches etc; several pamphlets 16 pp each; **URRR** (S-634).

STILLE, ALB.
Kaplansbacken no. 3, Central-Tryckeriet, Stockholm, Sweden.
Est: 1841
1901 Preisliste ueber chirurgische Instrumente, Bandagen, Prosthesen Geraethe fuer Operationssaele und fuer Krankenpflege von Alb. Stille; 55 pp; **MAH; ACS** (U 6 A/ 5857i); **CPP** (ZEd/7); **ZUR** (Regeringsgatan 19).
1926 Catalog of Surgical Instruments; 178 pp; **AFMM; ZUR.**
ca 1937 Mobler for operationssalar och undersokningsrum, Transport vagnar for patienter Sangar, Matlador M.M.; 61 pp; **AFMM.**

STILLE-SCANLAN COMPANY
8 West 40th Street, New York, New York.
1920s International Hospital Equipment Corp. of New York, Stille-Scanlan Non-Rustable Steel Surgical Instruments; 26 pp; **NYAM; MF/MAH.**

STOCO
See: STANDARD OPTICAL CO.

STODART, STRAND
1825 Instrument maker mentioned by John Read.

STODDARD, G. S., AND CO., INC.
121-123 East 24th Street, New York, New York.
1928 Catalogue of Pharmaceutical Specialties; 39 pp; Price list Apr 1 1929; 4 pp; **NYAM; MF/MAH.**

STODDER, CHARLES
Rialto, Roo, 36, 131 Devonshire, Boston Massachusetts.
See: BOSTON OPTICAL WORKS; **NLM.**
1879 Catalogue Microscopes, Sole Agent for the Sale of Microscopes and Telescopes, Made by R. B. Tolles; 15th ed.; **CTY/B** (Uai T 578).

STOELTING, C. H., CO.
121 N. Green Street, Chicago, Illinois.
Est: 1886
Dec. 1909 Price List of Psychological Apparatus Manufactured by C.H. Stoelting Co.; 22 pp; **CTY/B** (Uai St 67).
424 North Homan Avenue, Chicago, Illinois.
1930 Apparatus, Tests and Supplies for Psychology, Psychometry, Psychotechnology, Psychiatry, Neurology, Anthropology, Phonetics, Physiology and Pharmacology; 227 pp; **MAH; LACMA** (149 St6a).
31-45 West Randolph St., Chicago, IL.
n.d. Optical Disk; 15 pp; **URRR** (S-339).

STOEHRER, EMIL JUN.
Grimmaische Strasse 26, Leipzig, Germany.
L. 19 c Preisverzeichniss von Instrumenten, Apparaten u. Geraethschaften der Physik und Chemie; 80 pp; **CTY/B** (Uai St 66).

STOHRER, DR., & SOHN
West-Strasse 10, Leipzig, Germany.

1892   Preis-Verzeichniss von Apparaten und Instrumenten fuer den
        physikalischen Unterricht; 148 pp; **NYAM; MF/MAH**.
1897   Nachtrag zur Preisliste physikalischer Apparate; 48 pp; **NYAM;
        MF/MAH**.

STOKES, F. J., MACHINE CO.
Tabor Road at Cedar Grove Station, Philadelphia, Pennsylvania.
5900 Tabor Rd., Philadelphia 20, Pa.
Est: 1900
        n.d.   Pharmaceutical & Chemical Machinery & Apparatus, no. 27; 112 pp;
                NYAM; MF/MAH.
        1928   Catalog no. 28T, Tablet Making Machinery; 48 pp; **MAH**; (C 615.43
                S7).

STORZ, ADAM
Tuttlingen, Germany.
Philadelphia office: 927 Chestnut Street.
        Sep. 1895   List of Surgical Instruments; 3 pp; **CPP**.

STORZ, G. ALBERT
Bahnhofstrasse 81-81a, Tuttlingen-Wuertt, Germany.
Est: 1889
        1920s   Fabrik fuer Chirurgie und zahnaerztliche Instrumente, Katalog C; 15 pp,
                 2 pp preisliste; **WMScM**.

STORZ INSTRUMENT CO.
St. Louis, Missouri.
        n.d.   Surgical Instrument Catalog; **LLU** (W 26 S888).

STRASENBURGH, R. J., CO.
195 Exchange St., Rochester, New York.
Est: 1886
        192?   Catalogue of Surgical Instruments, Physicians' and Hospital Supplies; 416
                pp; **NYAM** (S.125).
        1925   Catalogue of Surgical Instruments, Physicians' and Hospital Supplies; 35
                pp; **NYAM**.

STRATFORD-COOKSON CO.
42nd and Ludlow Streets, Philadelphia, Pennsylvania.
4058 Haverford Ave., Philadelphia, Pennsylvania.
Successor to E. deTrey & Sons
Est: 1913
        1919   Pamphlet, Somnoform or Analgesia and Surgical Anesthesia, Compiled
                with the Aid of Expert Anesthetists and from the Most Authoritative
                Writings on Anesthesia and Anesthetics; 23 pp; **MAH** (C 617.96085 S).

STRAUSS, LEO
317 East 34th Street, New York.
        1928   Wholesale Price List of Optical Goods, Goggles, Spectacles, Magnifying
                Glasses; 18 pp; **AO**.

STRAUSS OPTICAL CO.
44 West 18th St., New York, N.Y.
        1931   Protex Goggles, Sun Glasses and Magnifiers; 42 pp; **URRR** (S-12).
        1932   Catalogue, Protex, Everready, Readers, and Magnifiers; 16 pp; **AO**.

STREET, LINDER, AND PROPERT
20th and Chestnut St., Philadelphia.
    1930s   Ophthalmic Instruments; 22 pp; **AO.**

STREISGUTH, C. & E.
Gutenbergplatz Nr. 12, Strassburg I E.
    1920s   Illustrated Catalogue of Urethral Instruments, Spezial-Preisliste; **NYAM;**
        MF/MAH.

STURDY'S, J. F., SONS CO.
Attleboro Falls, Massachusetts.
Est: 1860s
    1919   Eye Glass Chains, Hairpins, Hooks, Earloops, Automatic Eye Glass
        Holders; 30 pp; **AO.**

SUNBEAM ULTRA-VIOLITE
   See: CHICAGO FLEXIBLE SHAFT CO; **NYAM.**

SUNIC RECORD
   See: WATSON & SONS; **MAH.**

SUPERIOR OPTICAL CO.
   Oct.–Nov. 1935   24 pp; **URRR** (S-687).
   Feb.–Mar. 1936   Glasses; 24 pp; **URRR** (S-688).
   Apr.–May 1937   8 pp foldout; **URRR** (S-689).

SUPPLEE & CO.
17-19 Union Square, New York, New York.
    1926   Brochure, Akers Technique of Partial Denture Restorations, Specimens of
        Cast Partial Dentures, together with the Preparatory, Fitting and
        Cleansing Techniques; 8 pp; **NYAM.**

SUPPLEE, SAMUEL G., & CO.
17-19 Union Square, New York, New York.
   See: AKER'S.
    1926   Aker's Technique, Partial Denture Restorations; **NYAM; MF/MAH.**

SUREX
    ca 1920   Trademark of Campbell Electric Co., Lynn, Mass, for Transformers.

SURGICAL MANUFACTURING CO., LTD.
83-85 Mortimer Street, London W 1, England.
"Surgical Instrument Makers to the War Office"
    E. 20 c   Supplementary List of Orthopedic and Fracture Apparatus, Artificial
        Limbs, Colotomy Appliances, Abdominal Belts, etc.; 51 pp; **NLM**
        (W26 S961c).
    1925   Catalogue of Surgical Instruments; 6th ed.; 1072 pp; **WOC.**
    1928   Catalogue of Surgical Instruments; 7th ed.; 1312 pp; **WOC.**

4 Park Terrace, Glasgow, Scotland.
Works: Cricklewood, London N W 2.
    1930s   Diagnostic Instruments etc.; 16 pp; **NYAM; MF/MAH.**

SURGICAL PRODUCTS
118-120 East 25th Street, New York, New York.
   Sep. 1927   Catalogue Surgical Products; 33 pp; **NYAM; MF/MAH.**

SURGICO
11 Red Lion Square, London W C 1, England.
        n.d.   Surgical and Medicinal Sundries, Section V; 44 pp; **WMScM**.

SUSSFELD, LORSCH & CO.
Sussfeld, Lorsch & Schimmel (1923)
90-94 Maiden Lane, New York, New York.
Branches: Paris, Berlin.
        1915   Automobile Goggles, Sportsmen's Glasses Driving Spectacles and Cases;
                    28 pp; **URRR** (S-648).
        1915   Safety First Guardian Eye Protectors; 20 pp; **AO**.
        1916   Crown Lorgnettes with Pupillary Distance Adjustable Patented; 6 pp
                    foldout; **URRR** (S-647).
153 West 23rd St., New York.
        1923   Opera, Field and Prism Glasses of Lemaire, Paris, Sole Distributors for
                    the U.S. and Canada; **AO**.
        1927   Microscopes, Stamped Selsi Co., N.Y.; 15 pp; **URRR**.

SUTCLIFFE KERATOMETER
See: MEYROWITZ; **MF/MAH**.

SWAN-MYERS
See: ABBOTT LABORATORIES, 1931; **NYAM**.

SWETT AND LEWIS COMPANY
18 Boylston Street, Boston, Massachusetts.
        1902?   The Kinraide Coil, High Frequency Coil, Direct Current; 23 pp;
                    ACR/MAH.
        1903   Bulletin 33, Coils and Tubes; 32 pp; **ACR/MAH**.
        n.d.   The Kinraide Coil; 16 pp; **BLEL**.
        n.d.   Bulletin no. 28, The Kinraide Coil; 23 pp; **BLEL**.

SWIFT, JAMES
15 Kingsland Road, London N.E., England.
formerly with the Late Andrew Ross
Est: 1853
        1860–70   Catalogue of Microscopes and Other Optical Instruments; 10 pp; **NLM**
                    (W26 S977).
        1892   A Catalogue of Microscopes; 71 pp; **URRR** (S-37).
        1899   Catalogue of Microscopes, Object Glasses, Eye-Pieces and Microscopic
                    Apparatus; 19th ed.; 56 pp; **MAH** (C 681.4085 S 84).
        1901   A Catalogue of Microscopes; 55 pp; **URRR** (S-39).
        1904   A Catalogue of Microscopes; 21st ed.; 72 pp; **URRR** (S-392).
        1906   A Catalog of Microscopes; 22 ed.; 72 pp; **URRR** (S-42).
        1910   Catalogue of Microscopes, Objectives, Oculars and Microscope Apparatus;
                    23rd ed.; 92 pp; **MAH** (C 681.4085 S 84).
81 Tottenham Court Road, London W, England.
        1910   Catalogue of Microscopes, Objectives, Oculars and Microscopic Apparatus;
                    23rd ed.; 92 pp; **AFMM; URRR** (S-393).
        1913   Catalogue of Microscopes, Objectives, Oculars and Microscope Apparatus;
                    25th ed.; 70 pp; **MAH** (C 681.4085 S 84); **URRR** (S-39).

n.d.   Catalogue of Microscopes, Objectives, Oculars, Microscope Apparatus; 26th ed.; 44 pp; **URRR** (S-40).

n.d.   A Series of High Grade Microscopes for Advanced, Routine and Research Work, Research 28521; 16 pp, 1 pp price list; **URRR** (S-41).

1928   Microscopes and Other Optical and Scientific Instruments; assorted pamphlets; **URRR** (S-627).

1928   A Catalog of Microscopes, Objectives, Oculars and Accessory Apparatus for Biological and Medical Research, Students' Use and all General Purposes; 27th ed.; 40 pp; **URRR** (S-582).

SWIGART, E. & J., CO.
Nos. 15 and 17 West Fifth Street, Cincinnati, Ohio.

1904?   E. & J. Swigart, Importers and Wholesale Dealer's in Jewelers, Watchmakers, Engravers, Optician's Tools, Materials, Optical Goods; 66 pp, index; **AO**.

1906   E. & J. Swigart, Manufacturers and Importers of Optical Goods, pp 501-568; **AO**.

Merchant's Bldg., 28-34 Sixth St., Cincinnati.

1908?   Jewelers' Supplies and Optical Goods, Prescription Price List; **AO**.

Northwest Corner, Sixth and College St., Cincinnati (1911 only).

1911   Jewelers', Watchmakers', and Engravers' Supplies and Optical Goods; 803 pp; **AO**.

1924   Spectacles; 32 pp; **URRR** (S-476).

1931   Ophthalmic Prescription Price List; collection of Shur-On booklets; **AO**.

SWIGART WATCH AND OPTICAL CO.
328-32 Superior St., Toledo, OH.

1901   Illustrated Wholesale Catalog; 127 pp; **URRR** (S-474).

Apr. 1, 1910   Vest Pocket Prescription List; 38 pp; **URRR** (S-475a).

SYDOW, EMIL
No. 17 Albrecht-Strasse, Berlin NW 6.

1900   Specialitaet, Ophthalmologische Instrumente; 90 pp; **URRR** (S-372).

SYKES, WALTER F., & CO.
85 Water Street, New York, New York.

n.d.   Stovaine Chlorohydrate of Amylene; 12 pp; **CPP**.

1903   Oro-lecithin, A General Bibliographical Study, by F. Billon; **CPP**.

132 Chestnut Street, Philadelphia, Pennsylvania.
396 Atlantic Avenue, Boston, Massachusetts.

n.d.   R. B. Waite's Antiseptic, Local Anaesthetic; 6 pp; foldout; **CPP**.

SYMONS, BRYANT CO.
320 St. John St., London E.C.

1932   Lens Surfacing Machinery for Ophthalmic Work; 8 pp; **URRR** (S-657).

SYNCHRONOUS MANUFACTURING CO.
31-33 East Twenty-Seventh Street, New York, New York.

ca 1920   A Resume of the Uses of the Hyfrex Coils in High Frequency & X-Ray Therapy; 20 pp; **ACR/MAH**.

SYNDICAT DES CONSTRUCTEURS EN INSTRUMENTS D'OPTIQUE & DE PRÉCISIONS
28 rue Serpente, Paris, France.

1901–02   Catalogue, l'industrie Française des instruments de précision; 271 pp; **NYAM; MF/MAH**.

TABLE ROCK LABORATORIES, INC.
Greenville, South Carolina.
        n.d.   The Treatment of Hypertension with Citrin, Cucurbocitrin; 6 pp; **CPP**.
        n.d.   Bismuth-Violet, a Contribution to Chemotherapy; 6 pp; **CPP**.

TAEFEL, THEO, CO.
319 Third Street, Louisville, Kentucky.
        1922   Catalogue and Price List, distributor for Standard Surgical Instruments;
                416 pp, index; **CS; MAH** (21376).
        1941   Surgical Instruments; 619 pp; **WOC**.

TALBOTT, W. A., MICAJAD & CO.
Warren, Pennsylvania.
Est: June 1883
        1899   Non-Surgical Gynecology in a Nut Shell, A Useful Adjuvant to Local
                Gynecological Treatment; 6 pp foldout; **CPP**.

TALRICH
97 Boulevard St., Germaine, Paris, France.
        ca 1900   Catalogue, Modèles anatomiques; 44 pp; **NYAM; MF/MAH**.

TAUBER, M.
Leipzig, Dresden.
        1872   Preisverzeichniss ueber physikalische, optische, mathematische Instrumente
                und Apparate; 70 pp; **CTY/B** (Uai T191).

TAYLOR, F. H., & SONS, LTD.
131 Seven Sisters Road, London N 7, England.
        Nov. 1933   Graduated Glassware, Measures, Medicine Tumblers, etc., Medical Glass;
                13 pp; **WMScM**.

TAYLOR BROS. CO.
Rochester, New York.
        1896   Catalogue Thermometers; 7 pp; **NYAM; MF/MAH**.

TAYLOR INSTRUMENT COMPANIES
95 Ames St., Rochester, New York (Executive offices and Factory).
Est: 1849
        1911   The Sphygmomanometer, Dr. Rogers' Tycos; 16 pp; **CPP**.
        Jan. 1918   Catalogue; Tycos-Rochester; 28 pp; **CTY/B** (Uai T2184).
Other cities: New York, Chicago, Boston, Philadelphia, Washington, St. Louis, Toronto.
        1918   Tycos Meteorological and Other Scientific instruments, 37 pp; **AO**.
        1919   Short and Mason Meteorological and Other Scientific Instruments,
                Manufactured by Short and Mason, Ltd, London; 36 pp; **AO**.
Other cities: above and Baltimore, Pittsburgh, San Francisco.
        1920   Tycos Meteorological and Other Scientific Instruments, Barometers,
                Compasses, Rain Gauges, Stormographs, Thermometers,
                Anemometers, etc.; 39 pp; **AO**.
        1921   Prices and Code Words for Use with Catalog of Tycos Scientific
                Instruments of Domestic Manufacture; 4 pp; **AO**.
Other cities: above and Milwaukee, Seattle, Cleveland, Los Angeles, Indianopolis, Atlanta, Cincinnati, Tulsa, Detroit, Minneapolis.
        1923   Brochure, Urinalysis & Reagents, Hydrotherapy, etc.; 63 pp; **NYAM;
                MF/MAH**.
        1923   Thermometers, a Profitable Line; 24 pp, discount sheet included; **AO**.

1923   Tycos Thermometers, Hygrometers, Urinary-Analysis Instruments,
        Sphygmomonometers, Hydrometers, Lactometers, Chargometers,
        Barometers, Compasses, etc.; 101 pp; **AO**.

1923   Bulletin, Reprints of The Sphygmomanometer Question, Urinalysis with
        Reagents, Humidity and the Physician, Hydrotherapy; 63 pp; **CPP**.

1924   The Tycos Book, Its Just Everyday Things That Make Thermometers a
        Profitable Line; 24 pp; **AO**.

1925   The Tycos Book, Its Just Everyday Things That Make Thermometers a
        Profitable Line; 24 pp; **AO**.

Branch Offices: above except Milwaukee, Seattle.
Canadian Plant: Tycos Bldg., Toronto.

1926   The Tycos Book, Simple Everyday Things That Make Thermometers a
        Profitable Line; 24 pp, discount to the trade page included; **AO**.

pre–1926 Tycos Instruments for Educational Institutions, also tables and much other
        valuable data; 68 pp; **CTY/B** (Uai T2184).

1926   Tycos Meteorological and Other Scientific Instruments, Barometers,
        Compasses, Rain Gauges, Stormographs, Thermographs,
        Anemometers, etc.; 76 pp; **AO**.

1926   Tycos Thermometers, Hygrometers, Urinary Glassware, Hydrometers,
        Lactometers, Sphygmomonometers, Chargometers, Barometers, Pocket
        Compasses, etc.; 92 pp; **AO**.

1927?   Catalogue Six's Combination Maximum and Minimum Self-Registering
        Thermometers; **CTY/B** (Uai T2184).

1927   Tycos Meteorological and Other Scientific Instruments, Barometers,
        Compasses, Rain Gauges, Stormographs, Thermographs,
        Anemometers, etc.; 72 pp; **AO**.

1929   The Clinical Use of the Tycos Recording Sphygmomanometer by Daniel
        R. Barr, Medical Dept.; 44 pp; **CPP**.

1929   The Tycos Book; 31 pp; **AO**.

1931   Tycos Sphygmotonograph; 20 pp; **CPP**.

n.d.   Catalogue Recording & Index Thermometers; 29 pp; **NYAM; MF/MAH**.

n.d.   Daniel R. Barr patent 7 Apr 1925, no. 1,532,705, A Levin Method for
        Measuring Pulsating Pressures; **CPP**.

T-E X-RAY LABORATORY
Bethlehem, Pennsylvania.

1920–30s Pamphlet T-E Intensifying Screens, Dr. H. Threlkeld-Edwards, South
        Bethlehem, Pa; 6 pp foldout; **ACR/MAH**.

TELLER OPTICAL CO., THE
Providence, Rhode Island.

1927   Premier, All Zylo Frames, Guarenteed and Patented; 9 pp; **AO**.

TERMAX
Warsaw, Poland.

1938   Polskie aparaty do terapii falami ultrakrotkimi; 6 pp; **MAH**.

TERPITZ, ARTHUR VON, & CO.
Sprengelstrasse 15, Berlin N 65, Germany.

1920s   Makers of Electro-Medical Apparatus, Catalogue no. 30; 24 pp;
        WMScM.

TERRAPLASTICA MANUFACTURING CO.
Newark, New Jersey.

ca 1910 Dr. J. C. Graft's Dental Specialties; 16 pp; **HML**.

TERRY HEATER CO., THE
Cleveland, Ohio.
Inc: ca 1904
       n.d.   Super Heated Air in Medicine; 2nd ed.; 6 pp; **CPP**.

TESCHNER-MYERS CO., INC.
See: PALO-MYERS, INC.

TESTRITE INSTRUMENT CO.
40-44 West 20th Street, New York.
101 5th Ave., New York, New York.
       1920s   Testrite Intrument Co., Optical Specialties Co., Manufacturers and
                  Importers, Exclusive Manufacturers and Importers of Petite Display
                  Stands, Testcard Mirrors, Seerite Readers and Magnifiers, Snugfit
                  Goggles and Eye Protectors, Testrite Thermometers, Hydrometers &
                  Urinometers, Battery Syringes, Barometers and Hygrometers, Field
                  Glasses, Telescopes and Microscopes, Compasses, Stop Watches,
                  Pedometers, and Counters; 16 pp; **AO**.

TETER MFG. CO.
1108 Williamson Bldg., Cleveland, Ohio.
       1907   Catalog of the Teter Apparatus; 19 pp; **MAH** (C 617.96085 T).
       1912   Catalog of the Teter Gas-Oxygen Apparatus; 32 pp; **MAH**
                  (C 617.96085 T).
       1915   Catalog, The Teter Gas-Oxygen Apparatus; 15 pp; **MAH**
                  (C 617.96085 T).
       1915   The Teter Gas-Oxygen Obstetrical Apparatus, Sunrise Slumber; 8 pp;
                  MAH (C 617.96085 T).
       1915   Teter Gas-Oxygen Apparatus; 15 pp; **MAH**.
       1928   Teter Mercury Column Gas Oxygen Apparatus; 15 pp; **MAH** (C
                  617.96085 T).

TEUFEL, WILHELM JUL.
Stuttgart, Germany.
       ca 1910   Ophthalmic Electrodes, After the Method of Dr. Wirtz; 18 pp; **CPP**.

THAMM, J.
Berlin, Germany.
       1900   Illustriertes Preis-Verzeichniss chirurgischer Instrumente; **CPP** (Ed/41).

THATE, PAUL
Luisen-Strasse 58, Berlin NW, Germany.
       1890   Preis-Verzeichnis ueber Mikroskope und mikroskopische Neben Apparate
                  der Optischen und Mechanischen Werkstaette; 23 pp; **URRR** (T-84).

THAYER, HENRY, & CO.
Cambridgeport, Massachusetts.
Inc: in Maine, dissolved Mar 1916
       1866   Descriptive Catalogue of Fluid and Solid Extracts in Vacuo; **MAH** (C
                  615.1373 T319).
       1870   Catalogue, Fluid and Solid Extracts in Vacuo, also Concentrations and
                  Official Pills; 218 pp; **UTP**.
       1879   Descriptive Catalogue of Fluid and Solid Extracts, also Pills, Resinoids,
                  and Alkaloids; **MAH** (27423).

Boston, Mass.
> 1906   Thayer's Self Sellers and Druggists Proprietaries With Your Name on
>   Package; **MAH** (C 615.1373).

THERMALITE CO., THE
161-165 Elm Street, New York, New York.
> n.d.   The Thermalite Bag, Better Than a Hot Water Bag; 12 pp; **CPP**.

THERMO ELECTRIC INSTRUMENT CO. THE
10 Johnson Street, Newark, New Jersey.
> n.d.   Catalogue Freas, Electric Constant Temperature Drying Ovens, Vacuum
>   Drying Ovens, Conditioning Ovens, Incubators, Sterilizers, Water
>   Thermostats, Steam Water Mixers, Steam Hot Plates; **CTY/B** (Uai T
>   3431).

THOMAS, ARTHUR H., CO.
12th and Walnut Streets, Philadelphia, Pennsylvania.
Est: 1899; Inc: 1900
> 1904   Catalog F, of Laboratory Apparatus, Especially Selected for Laboratories
>   of Chemistry and Biological Sciences; 438 pp; **AFMM**.
> 1905   Das Pantomikrotom des Neurobiologischen Laboratoriums by Oskar Vogt,
>   reprint from *J. fuer Psychologie und Neurologies*.
> ca 1905   Brochure, Uskoff Sphygomotonograph; **AFMM**.
> ca 1910   Brochure, Instruments of Precision for the Study of Circulation after
>   Jaquet, Uskoff, Makenzie and Einthoven; 8 pp; **AFMM**.
> ca 1910   Brochure, Analytical Balances of German, Dutch and American
>   Manufacture; 8 pp; **AFMM**.
> ca 1910   Patent Cool Biological Incubator Model C for Gelatin Cultures; 1 pp;
>   **AFMM**.
> ca 1910   Brochure, Preparation Jars Especially Selected for Laboratories and
>   Museums of Anatomy, Pathology, Zoology, Botany, etc.; **AFMM**.
> ca 1910   Brochure, Hearson Bacteriological Incubators, etc. with Patent
>   Temperature Control; 12 pp; **AFMM**.
> ca 1911   Brochure, Zeiss Dissecting Microscope, after Prof Mayer and Binocular
>   Microscope XA; 4 pp; **AFMM**.
> 1912   Catalog F, of Laboratory Apparatus Especially Selected for the Laboratories
>   of Chemistry and the Biological Sciences; 4th ed.; 459 pp; **AFMM**.
> ca 1914–16 Laboratory Apparatus and Reagents . . .; 2 parts, iv, 76 pp; vi, 579 pp;
>   **UWL** (W26 T454L).
> 1914   Catalogue of Microscopes and Accessories; **MAH**.
> *West Washington Square, 230 South Seventh Street, Philadelphia, Pennsylvania.*
> 1914   Catalogue of Laboratory Apparatus and Reagents; 579 pp; **NLM** (W26
>   A788s); **MAH**.
> 1914   Catalogue Microscopes and Accessories of 1914 ed.; 32 pp, reprint; **MAH**
>   (C 681.4085 T).
> 1918   Price List Readjustment List no. 1 . . .; **AFMM**.
> ca 1918   Bockemann Thermometers, Either With or Without Bureau of Standards
>   Certificate; 1 pp; **AFMM**.
> ca 1918   Brochure, Apparatus for the Manufacture of Lipovaccines; 4 pp; **AFMM**.
> ca 1918   Bureau of Standards Volumetric Glassware; 1 pp; **AFMM**.
> 1919   Microscopes, Microtomes, Photo-Micrographic Apparatus and Accessories;
>   24 pp; **URRR** (T-97).

1921　Laboratory Apparatus and Reagents Selected for Laboratories of
Chemistry, Metallurgy, and Biology in Their Application to Education,
the Industries, Medicine, and the Public Services; 619 pp, code, reagent
index; **LACMA** (149 T 36L); **MAH**.

1921　Catalogue of Laboratory Apparatus and Reagents; 619 pp, 71 pp code
price index; **NLM** (W26 A788s); **MAH**.

1926　Catalog of Pyrex Laboratory Glassware; 26 pp; **AFMM**.

1928　Fanz Automatic Microtome Knife Sharpener; 4 pp; **URRR** (T-126).

1930　Haemacytometers with Levy and Levy-Hauser Counting Chambers and
Accessories; 16 pp; Stamped on cover: E. F. Mahady Co., Lab.
Apparatus and Supplies, 851-857 Boylston St., Boston, MA; **URRR**
(T-100).

1931　Catalogue of Laboratory Apparatus and Reagents; 824 pp; **NLM** (W 26
A 788s).

THOMAS, A. W.
n.d.　Nutritional Report on Dovitam; 14 pp; **CPP**.

THOMPSON
Great Windmill-Street.
1825　Instrument maker mentioned by John Read.

THOMPSON, A. T., & CO., MANUFACTURERS
25 Bromfield Street, Boston, Massachusetts.
15 Tremont Place, Boston (Salesroom) (1903).
No. 1 Madison Ave., Corner 23rd St., New York (Salesroom).
1903　Catalogue Optical Projection Apparatus; 72 pp; **AO**.
n.d.　Brochure, The Carman Projector; 4 pp; **NYAM; MF/MAH**.
n.d.　Catalogue, Optical Projection Apparatus; pp 11-52; **NYAM; MF/MAH**.
n.d.　Catalogue Electric Optical Apparatus; pp 20-; **NYAM; MF/MAH**.
n.d.　New Perfection Reflectoscope, model K, Equiped with 1000 Watt Gas
filled Mazda Lamp, Automatic, Noiseless, Efficient; 8 pp; **AO**.

THOMPSON AND PLASTER CO., INC., THE
Leesburg, Virginia.
ca 1921　Catalog of Accessories, X-Ray and Electrotherapeutic; 70 pp; **BLEL**.
n.d.　Electric Cabinet; 1 pp; **CPP**.
n.d.　Model HH; 1 pp; **CPP**.

THOMSON, SIR WILLIAM
Jan. 1892　Catalogue, Sir William Thomson's New Standard Electric Instruments;
8th ed.; **CTY/B** (Uai?).

THOMPSON & CAPPER WHOLESALE LTD.
See: MANESTY MACHINES LTD.; **MAH**.

THREE DIMENSION CO.
500 North Dearborn St., Chicago, IL.
n.d.　Three Dimension Tachistoscope; 4 pp foldout; **URRR** (T-141).

THUM, ED., INSTITUT FUER MIKROSKOPIE
Leipzig, Germany.
Mar. 1888　Spezial-Preis-Verzeichnis der Salonpraeparate Diatomen-Typenplatten,
Testpraeparate und Testplatten, Instrument Utensilien und Materialien
fuer mikroskopische Zwecke, Katalog V; 20 pp; **CTY/B** (Uai T423).

THURWACHTER, L. L., & SONS
215 West Fayette Street, Syracuse, New York.
114 Walton Street, Syracuse, New York.
    n.d.   Adirondack Adjustable Reclining Chair; 7 pp; **CPP**.

TIEMANN, GEORGE, & CO.
67 Chatham Street, New York, New York.
Est: 1826; Inc: 1902
    See: ALOE AND HERNSTEIN

    ca 1870   A group of 25 single page and pamphlet advertisements and descriptions of instruments made by Tiemann; **NLM** (W26 T562c).

    1872   The American Armamentarium Chirurgicum, A Representation of Modern, Chiefly American, Patterns of Surgical Instruments; 54 pp; **MAH** (C 610.78085 T).

    1872   Catalogue of Surgical Instruments, Illustrated Apparatus for Deformities and Fractures, Bandages, Trusses, Spine Braces, etc., Parts I-IV; **MAH** (C 610.78085 T).

    1872   Catalogue of Surgical Instruments; **UREGML; LLU** (W C357 1872); **TMHM**.

    ca 1872   Catalog of Surgical and Dental Instruments; 496 pp; **CUHSL** (RD 76 I 44); **WOC**.

    1872   General Operating, Amputating, Bone, Bullet, Artery and Minor Operating Instruments, Part I; 64 pp; **MAH** (C 610.78085); **NLM** (W26 T562c).

    1874   Catalogue of Surgical Instruments, Apparatus for Deformities and Fractures, Bandages, Trusses, Spine Braces, etc., part II; 144 pp, fragile; **AFMM; NLM** (W26 T562c).

    1872-74   Catalogue of Surgical Instruments, 5 sections bound together; Part I, 64 pp; Part II, 115 pp; Part II, 144 pp; Part IV, 88 pp; Dental sect., 16 pp; **UBML** (W 26T5625).

    1872-75   Catalogue of Surgical Instruments, Manufactured and Sold by Geo. Tiemann & Co. . ., 4 parts, 1872, 74, 75; **YML** (Rd 76.872T).

    1872-76   Catalogue of Surgical Instruments . . ., 4 parts; **NYAM** (S 125); **LACMA** (149 T 44c).

    1874   Otorhinolaryngological Instruments; 116 pp; **MAH** (C 610.78085).

    1875   Instruments used in Treatment of Diseases of Urinary Organs, Anus and Rectum and Ob-Gyn Instruments, Part III; 144 pp; **MAH** (C 610.78085).

    ca 1875   Catalogue of Dental Instruments; 16 pp; **MAH** (C 610.78085).

    1876   Apparatus for Deformities and Fractures; 124 pp; **MAH** (C 610.78085).

    1879   Catalogue Surgical Instruments, Part 1, 64 pp; Part 2, 116 pp; Part 3, 144 pp; Part 4, 124 pp; **NYAM; MF/MAH**.

    1879   The American Armamentarium; 530 pp, 36 pp price list; **WOC; MRLB; HDM; UREGML; MUM** (1879 Ed 17).

    1879   The American Armamentarium Chirurgicum; Part I, 134 pp; Part II, 102 pp; Part III, 126 pp; Part IV, 136 pp; Part V, 14 pp; Supplement 32 pp; Price List 36 pp; **JHIHM** (Rd 76.T56); **LACMA** (149 T.44); **MCFM; NLM** (W26 T562c); **NYAM** (S 125); **MAH** (C 610.78085); **CPP** (Ed/17a).

    1889   The American Armamentarium Chirurgicum; 846 pp, index; **MAH; MCFM; NLM** (W26 T562c); **CPP; UWL** (QGX.T44); **UPSDM** (D

617.604. T443); **RCSL; YML** (RD 76 T54); **LACMA** (149 T 44c); **VM; WOC; AFMM**, fragile; **HDM; UVHSL** (RD 76.T56); **MRLB; CUHSL** (RD 76 T 44); **HML; LLU** (WO T562a 1889); **MUM** (ZZEd 4 1889); **TMHM**.

ca 1889   The American Armamentarium Chirurgicum; 846 pp; **AFMM; BLEL**.

1894?   The American Armamentarium Chirurgicum; **JHIHM** (RD 76.T 56)

1894   Soft Rubber Goods with Patent Velvet Eyes; 8 pp; **MAH; CPP**.

1899   The American Armamentarium Chirurgicum; **ACS** (U 6a T562a).

n.d.   Formaldehyde Gas Generator; 4 pp; **CPP**.

n.d.   Pedersen's Ether & Chloroform Dropper; 1 pp; **CPP**.

n.d.   Prof. Currier's Conico-Cylindrical Tubes; 4 pp; **CPP**.

n.d.   A New Knot-Tier by Charles D. Scudder, New York; 1 pp; **CPP**.

n.d.   A New Instrument for Tracheotomy; 1 pp; **CPP**.

n.d.   Gas and Ether Inhaler by Thomas L. Bennett; 4 pp; **CPP**.

107 Park Row, New York, New York.

n.d.   Surgical Knives for General Operations; 9 pp; **MAH**.

Branch Store: Stohlmann, Pfarre and Co., 107 East 28th St., New York, New York.

1924   Catalogue of Special and General Surgical Instruments, Office Accessories, Laboratory and Hospital Equipment, Splints and Orthopedic Appliances; 176 pp; **AFMM; MUM** (1924 Ed17).

1926   Catalog of Surgical Instruments; 96 pp; **ACS** (U 6 A/T 562 c); **NYAM; MF/MAH; UCSF**.

1927   Price List; 9 pp; **AFMM**.

1928   American Armamentarium Chirurgicum; **CPP** (Ed/17a).

Jan. 1928   Centennial Catalogue; 96 pp; **WOC**.

1928   Catalogue, Surgical Instruments, no. 8; 32 pp; **NYAM; MF/MAH; MUM** (1928 ED17).

1929   Catalogue, Surgical Instruments; 24 pp; **NYAM; MF/MAH**.

1931   Supplement no. 10, Surgical Instruments; 16 pp; **AFMM**.

1931   Brochure, Chromium Plated Quality Instruments at Unusual Prices; 4 pp; **AFMM**.

n.d.   Illustrated Catalogue of Dental Instruments; 16 pp; **NYAM; MF/MAH**.

n.d.   Catalogue Medical Batteries; 4th ed.; 23 pp; **NYAM; MF/MAH**.

n.d.   Brochure Lockwood Colon Tube; 3 pp; **NYAM; MF/MAH**.

n.d.   Illustrated Catalogue of Surgical Instruments; Part I, 64 pp; Part II, 124 pp; **NYAM; MF/MAH**.

TILLYER

See: AMERICAN OPTICAL CO., Oct. 1928 price list; **NYAM**.

TIMKEN-DETROIT CO.
Detroit, Michigan.

1931   Timken Airlux Humidifier; 14 pp; **CPP**.

TOKYO IKA-KIKAI DOGYO-KUMIAI
Tokyo Medical Instrument Dealers' Association.

Mar. 1934   Index to the Standard Catalog of TI-K-D-K; 2nd ed.; 129 pp; **MAH**.

TOLAND, JOHN T.
38 West Fourth Street, Cincinnati, Ohio.
Dental Depot: 302 Main Street, Memphis, Tennessee.

ca 1860   Illustrated Price Catalogue of Dentists' Materials Consisting of Porcelain Teeth, Gold and Tin Foils, Gold, Silver and Platina Plate, Dental Instruments, Chairs, Cases, Lathes, Rolling Mills, and All Other

Articles Used by the Dental Profession; 72 pp; **MAH; MF/MAH; HML**.

TOLEDO TECHNICAL APPLIANCE CO.
2226-2236 Ashland Avenue, Toledo, Ohio.
>   1918   Catalogue of McKesson Anesthetic Appliances, The McKesson Model G
>   Apparatus; 32 pp; **MAH** (C 617.96085 T).
>   1923   McKesson Anesthetic Appliances Catalog no. 12, Illustrating and
>   Describing Three Standard Models; 58 pp; **MAH** (C 617.96085 T).
> Feb. 1926 McKesson Anesthetic Appliances; No 15; 79 pp; **MAH** (C 617.96085 T).
> Mar. 1928 McKesson Appliances no. 16; 80 pp; **MAH** (C 617.96085 T).
>   n.d.   McKesson Model D, Automatic Surgical, Automatic Dental &
>   Non-Automatic Appliances for Analgesia and Anesthesia giving
>   description, photos and uses; 16 pp; **MAH** (C 617.96085 T).

TOLLES, R. B.
See: BOSTON OPTICAL WORKS; **NLM**.
>   1879   Microscopes, Sole Importer of Microscopes and Telescopes by R. B. Tolles
>   15th ed.; 23 pp; **CTY/B** (Uai T 578).

TORBAY FRÈRES
Paris, France.
>   n.d.   Coqueluche (Jos. Fernia, Span.); 1 pp; **CPP**.

TORIC OPTICAL CO., INC.
110 East 23rd Street, New York City.
>   1923   *Toric Tips*, a Magazine of Ideas and Ideals; 8 pp; **AO**.

TORIL MFG. CO.
St. Paul, Minnesota.
>   n.d.   Catalogue Toril Products for the Dentist & Dental Laboratory, no. 8; 28
>   pp; **NYAM; MF/MAH**.

T & P OPTICAL MFRG. CO.
>   n.d.   Frames and Rimless Mountings; 8 pp foldout; **URRR** (T-144).
>   n.d.   T & P Illustrated Price List; 2 pp; **URRR** (T-145).
>   1928   Tried and Proved Oxfords that Grace the Face, Styles in Eyeglasses; 59
>   pp; **URRR** (T-145a).

TORTALINE MFG. CORPORATION
257 Ely Avenue, Long Island City, NY.
>   1930   Price List; 16 pp; **AO**.

TREFFURTH, A.
Ilmenau in Thueringen.
>   n.d.   Illustrierter Catalog ueber chemische Glas-und Porzellanwaaren Apparate,
>   Instrumente, etc, no. 2; 23 pp; **CTY/B** (Uai T 716).

TRENAMAN DENTAL CO.
New York, New York.
>   n.d.   Catalogue Electric Dental Appliances; 6 pp; **NYAM; MF/MAH**.

TRENKMANN BROS.
181 Lafayette Street, New York (Office and Salesroom).
409 Broome St., New York (Factory).
>   1917   Trenkmann Bros., Manufacturers, Real and Imitation Tortoise Shell
>   Optical Goods; 24 pp; **AO**.

TREY, E. de, & SONS
28 So. 40th St., Philadelphia, Pennsylvania.
        n.d.   Somnofore, The Ideal General Anesthetic for Minor Surgery and Dental Operations; 8 pp, prices given; **NYAM; MF/MAH**.

TRITON CO., THE
21 Cliff Street, New York, New York.
        n.d.   Manual of the Nanheim Treatment; 24 pp; **CPP**.

TROEMNER, HENRY
911 Arch Street, Philadelphia, Pennsylvania.
Est: 1840
    ca 1924   Catalogue Balances, Scales & Weights, no. 31; 63 pp; **NYAM; MF/MAH**.

TROUGHTON AND SIMMS
136 Fleet Street, London, England.
        n.d.   Catalogue of Instruments made by Troughton and Simms; 7 pp; **CTY/B** (Uai T 757).
        n.d.   Catalogue of Instruments made by Troughton and Simms, Opticians and Mathematical Instrument Makers to the Honourable Board of Ordnance; 15 pp; **CTY/B** (Uai T 757).

TROUVE, M. G.
rue Therese 6, Paris, France.
    ca 1873   Nouveaus appareil à l'usage des médecine et des chirurgiens, Estrait du Journal *les Mondes* 15 Juillet 1869, Describing his Electrode Laryngien; 8 pp; **AFMM**.
        n.d.   Extrait du Journal *les Mondes* des 9 et 16 Mai 1872, Describing his Pile Trouve; 8 pp; **AFMM**.

TRUAX, CHARLES, & CO.
75-77 Wabash Avenue, Chicago, Illinois.
Est: 1877
  See: TRUAX; **YML**; 1910, 12th ed., may be typo on their card.
    1885   Price List of Physicians' Supplies; 4th ed.; 700 pp; **UBML** (W 26 T8); **UCSF**.
    1889   Catalogue featuring the Allen Surgical Pump, patented Jun. 21, 1887; 32 pp; **NLM** (W26 T865); **MAH**.
    1890   Price List of Physicians's Supplies; 5th ed.; 1080 pp; **NWUCML** (617.91 T 76); **UBML** (W 26 T8); **UVHSL** (RD71 C53).
    1890   Physicians' Supplies, Surgical Instruments Description, Uses and Photos; 32 pp; **MAH**.
    1893   Price List of Physicians' Supplies, Surgical Instruments, Pharmaceutical Preparations and Strictly Pure Drugs; 6th ed.; 1568 pp; **MAH** (C 610.78085 T); **ACS** (U 6 A/T 865 P); **VM; CPP** (QC/4k); **NYAM** (S.125); **HDM; UBML** (W 26 T8); **UREGML**.
    1899   The Machanics of Surgery, Comprising Detailed Descriptions, Illustrations and Lists of the Instruments, Appliances and Furniture Necessary in Modern Surgical Art; 1024 pp; **MAH** (RD 71 T 77 c.2); **VM; LLU** (WO T865m 1899).
  Chas. Truax, Greene & Co.
    ca 1893   Price List of Physicians' Supplies; 6th ed.; various pp; **BLEL**.
    1900   Catalogue of Physicians' and Hospital Supplies . . .; 451 pp; 7th ed.; **CPP** (QC/4k); **AFMM; RCSL**.

1910 Catalogue of Physicians' and Hospital Supplies; 640 pp; 12th ed.; **CPP** (QC/4k); **SLSC; YML**.

1911 Physicians and Hospital Supplies, Wholesale Drugs, Surgical Instruments; 744 pp; 13th ed.; **AFMM; LACMA** (149 T 76c); **URRR** (T-144).

n.d. Special Sale of Buggy Cases; 7 pp; **LACMA** (149 T 76s).

n.d. The Truax Nebulizer; 4 pp; **CPP**.

42, 44, 46 Wabash Ave., Chicago, Illinois.

n.d. Price List of Physicians' and Hospital Supplies; 8 pp; **ZUR**.

n.d. Catalogue Medical Instruments; pp 3-30; **NYAM; MF/MAH**.

TRUBYTE
See: DENTIST'S SUPPLY CO.

TRUEBNER & CO.
60 Paternoster Row, London.

1873 The Warburg Tincture; 88 pp; **CPP**.

T. S. BROTHERS & CO.
Singapore.

1933 Catalogue of Dental Equipment, Appliances, Instruments and Materials; 130 pp; **BLEL**.

TUCK, BATH

1825 Instrument maker mentioned by John Read.

TUCKER, EDWARD
Fairfax, above Prince Street, Alexandria, Virginia.

1793 Photo, 8 X 10 inch B&W of ad in trade catalogue file, Cutler, Surgeons' Instrument Maker and Lock-Smith; **MAH**.

TURTON, GEORGE, AND SONS
Victoria St. & Portobello, Sheffield, England.
Est: 1875

1927 Catalogue of Surgical and Dental Instruments; 49 pp; **WMScM**.

TWIN CITY OPTICAL CO.
Minneapolis, MN.

1916 Price List Wholesale and Mfg. Opticians; 71 pp; **URRR** (T-11).

TYCOS
TYCOS-ROCHESTER
See: TAYLOR INSTRUMENT COMPANY.

UHLEMANN OPTICAL CO.
Pittsfield Bldg., 55 East Washington St., Chicago, Illinois.
Est: 1907

1927 An Old Friend in a New Form, Personalized Bifocals; 11 pp; **URRR** (U-79).

1929? The Dominant Factor in Human Vision; 16 pp; **URRR** (U-76).

1935 Prescription Catalog, Glasses by Universal; 72 pp; **URRR** (U-77).

ULTEK CORPORATION
See: PERKIN-ELMER; **MAH**.

UNDERWOOD, ARTHUR S.

1885 Notes on anaesthetics with an appendix containing illustrative cases and engravings of anaesthetic apparatus; Claudius Ash and Sons, London; pp 100-116; **MAH** (photocopy).

UNDERWOOD, O. B., & CO.
15 East 14th Street, New York, New York.
      1849   Catalogue Pulmonary Inspirator; 37 pp; **NYAM; MF/MAH.**

UNI-BIFOCAL CO., LTD.
188 Strand, London, England.
      1910   The Luxe Solid Invisible Bifocals; 28 pp; **URRR** (U-68).
      1914   Solid Onepiece Bi-Focals; 8 pp; **URRR** (U-69).

UNION ARTIFICIAL LIMB CO.
138 Westminster, Providence, Rhode Island.
    ca 1860s   Proprietors & Mfrs. of Gregory's Patent Artificial (paper) Limbs, the Lightest, Cheapest, Least Complicated and Most Durable Limbs in the World; 13 pp; **CPP.**

UNION DENTAL INSTRUMENT MANUFACTURING CO.
148 North Fourth Street, Philadelphia, Pa.
      1903   Catalogue of Instruments; **CDMC.**
530 Arch Street, (Phila., Pa.).
      1907   Catalogue of Instruments; **CDMC.**

UNITED FACTORIES FOR HOSPITAL SUPPLIES
    See: VEREINIGTE FABRIKE FUER LABORATORIUMSBEDARF; **MAH.**

UNITED FRUIT CO.
Home Economics Department, Pier 3 North River, New York, New York.
      1934   Banana and Skimmed Milk Reducing Diet; 2nd ed.; **CPP.**

U.S. ARMY MEDICAL DEPARTMENT
Washington, D.C.
      1920   Catalogue of Standard Surgical Instruments; 431 pp; **NLM** (W26 U567c).

UNITED STATES CATHETER & INSTRUMENT CO.
    See: C. R. BARD, INC.

U.S. COUNCIL OF NATIONAL DEFENSE
Washington, D.C.
    May 1917   List of Staple Medical and Surgical Supplies Selected to Meet War Conditions by the Committee on Standardization . . .; 71 pp; **NLM** (W26 U571L); **NWUCML** (613.67 Un31); **CUHSL.**

UNITED SURGICAL SUPPLIES CORP.
799 Eighth Avenue, New York, New York.
    Mar. 1928   Brochure, Colonization, A New Contribution to Materia Medica; 4 pp, inserted in Pilling Bulletin; **NYAM; MF/MAH.**

UNITRON INSTRUMENTS
Newton Highlands, Massachusetts.
      n.d.   Catalog Microscopes, A Complete Range of Models and Accessories for Education and Research Industries; **MAH.**

UNIVERSAL OPHTHALMOMETER
      n.d.   Booklet, How to Use the Universal Ophthalmometer, Will Increase Your Efficiency; 13 pp; **MAH** (C617.75085U).

UNIVERSAL PHYSIOTHERAPY EQUIPMENT
2824-30 S. Albert Street, Chicago, Illinois.
      n.d.   Brochure Universal Lamps and Their Therapeutic Use; 50 pp; **NYAM; MF/MAH.**

UNIVIS LENS CO.
Dayton, OH.

    1912   Universal Fingerpiece Mountings; 4 pp; **URRR** (U-3).

    1926   Twinsight Toric Onepiece Bifocals; 3 pp foldout, price list; 4 pp; **URRR** (U-80).

USONA BIOCHEMICAL CHEMICAL LABORATORIES, INC.
1930 Chestnut Street, Philadelphia, Pennsylvania.

    n.d.   The Place of Acidophilus in the Treatment of Toxic Conditions Due to Intestinal Absorption; 5 pp; **CPP.**

VALLEY CHEMICAL CO., THE
Danbury, Connecticut.

    ca 1902   Apetol; 4 pp; **CPP.**

    1903   It Will Make You Eat, An Old Time Combination Is a New Garb through Superior Pharmaceutical Manipulation, Apetol; 4 pp; **CPP.**

    ca 1914   Apetol Tonic Appetizer; 4 pp; **CPP.**

VALZAHN CO., THE
132 South 11th Street, Philadelphia, Pennsylvania.

    1902   Illustrations of Surgical Instruments; **CPP** (Ed/34).

    1904   Illustrations of Surgical Instruments; **CPP** (Ed/34).

    July 1907   New Instruments no. 4, Vol. 1, A Bulletin Published as a Current Appendix to Our Illustrated Catalogue; pp 86-115; **CPP.**

    Oct. 1910   The Bulletin of Medical and Surgical Technics Published by Kny-Scheerer Co., New York, Devoted to the Promulgation of Original and Improved Patterns of Surgical Instruments, Hospital Furnishings and Kindred Scientific Apparatus; 24 pp; **CPP.**

    n.d.   Asta Instrument Sterilizers, Seamless; 2 pp; **CPP.**

    n.d.   Modern Hospital Supplies, Catalog no. 7; 311 pp; **CPP.**

    n.d.   Vacuum Apparatus for the Induction of Artificial Hyperemia, Sect. A, Part 9; 32 pp; **CPP.**

1129 Chestnut Street, Philadelphia, Pennsylvania.

    n.d.   Sputum Flasks; 4 pp; **CPP.**

VAN ABBOTT, G., & SONS
6 Duke Street Mansions, Grosvenor Square, London W.

    1893   Dietary Tables, Menu Cookery Receipts for Diabetics and Price List of Diabetic Foods; 28th ed.; 24 pp; **CPP.**

VAN HORN & SAWTELL
15-17 East 40th Street, New York, New York.

    Feb. 1908   Catalogue Surgical Supplies; 52 pp; **NYAM; MF/MAH.**

    1910   Catalogue of Sterilized Sutures and Surgical Supplies; **CPP** (Ed/44).

    ca 1913   Catgut Dialogues, no. 1; 8 pp; **CPP.**

    ca 1914   Some Additional Uses of K-Y Lubricating Jelly; 4 pp; **CPP.**

    ca 1914   Interol, What It Is and What It Does; 24 pp; **CPP.**

    1914   Catalogue Sutures; 56 pp; **NYAM; MF/MAH.**

    ca 1915   *Pruritus Vulvae*; 4 pp; **CPP.**

    ca 1915   K-Y Additional Uses, Scarlet Fever, Measles and Chicken-Pox; 4 pp; **CPP.**

    n.d.   K-Y The Greaseless Anodyne (K-Y Analgesic is made of K-Y lubricating jelly as the base in combination with camphor menthol and methyl salicylate); 4 pp; **CPP.**

VAN HOUTEN & TEN BROECK
214-216 East 23rd Street, New York, New York.
Went into receivership in 1914, no value found for stock Mar. 28, 1916.
<blockquote>

189? The Morton-Wimshurst-Holt Influence Machine for X-Ray Purposes and Therapeutical Use; 15 pp; **NYAM** (135701).

1911 Catalogue, Therapeutic Apparatus; 45th ed.; 48 pp; **NYAM; MF/MAH.**
</blockquote>

300 4th Avenue, New York, New York.
<blockquote>

n.d. Catalogue, Batteries; 31 pp; **NYAM; MF/MAH.**
</blockquote>

VAN LAER, J.-B.-P.
43 rue de Flandre, Bruxelles.
<blockquote>

1896 Catalogue, Fabrique de balances de haute précision & de précision, poids, appareils, & ustensiles à l'usage des sciences, chimistes, pharmaciens, analystes, essayeurs, droguistes, bijoutiers . . .; 16 pp; **CTY/B** (Uai V 322).
</blockquote>

VAN ORDEN CORSET CO.
1204 Chestnut Street, Philadelphia, Pennsylvania.
New Jersey charter cancelled Jan. 18, 1916.
<blockquote>

1914 Radiographs Showing Effect of La Greque Surgical Corset; 10 pp; **CPP.**

1914 Surgical and Maternity Corseting, La Greque as an Aid to the Physician and Surgeon; 14 pp; **CPP.**
</blockquote>

45 West 34th Street, 101 Market Street, Newark, New Jersey.
<blockquote>

n.d. La Greque Corsets as an Aid to the Physician and Surgeon; 12 pp; **CPP.**
</blockquote>

VAN SCHAACK, PETER, & SONS
138 & 140 Lake Street, Chicago, Illinois.
Est: 1885, as above; originally in 1844.
Successors to: Van Schaack & Stevenson & Co., 1877. Van Schaack, Stevenson & Reid, 1870. E.P. Dwyer & Co., 1865. Smith & Dwyer, 1860. Penton, Robinson & Smith, 1859. Penton & Robinson, 1857. Brickerhoff & Penton, 1844.
<blockquote>

1874 Annual Price Current, Drugs, Chemicals, Medicines; 378 pp; **HDM.**

1888 Price Current & Illustrated Catalogue, Vol. xviii; 739 pp, index; **ISUM** (W 26 P478p).

1895 Price Current & Illustrated Catalogue, Vol. xxv; 1042 pp; **HDM.**

1904 Annual Price Current, Drugs, Chemicals, Medicines, Vol. xxxiv; 1353 pp; **NYAM** (125).
</blockquote>

VAN STEENBRUGGHE
See: DRAPIER et FILS; **NLM.**

VAROMA MEDICAL CO.
New York, New York.
<blockquote>

n.d. Varoma; 4 pp; **CPP.**
</blockquote>

VASS CHEMICAL CO., INC., THE
Danbury, Connecticut.
<blockquote>

1898 Thialion, A Laxative Salt of Lithia; 16 pp; **CPP.**

1898 Neurotic Lithemia, by Charles F. Craig; 3 pp; **CPP.**

1898 Treatment of the Uric Acid Daithese, by F. E. Hale; 7 pp; **CPP.**

1898 Uricadidemia, by L. H. Watson; 3 pp; **CPP.**

1900 Uric Acid, Its Literature and Therapeutics; 190 pp; 10th ed.; **CPP.**

1906 A Practical Treatise on Uric Acid Toxemia, In All Its Cases Including Its Treatment With Thialion, a Laxative Salt of Lithia; 15th ed.; 153 pp; **CPP.**
</blockquote>

n.d. The Kidneys Are Made Scapegoats for Gastro-Intestinal-Hepatic Insufficiency; 6 pp; **CPP.**

n.d. When the Body Gets Too Much Acid; 7 pp; **CPP.**

n.d. The Skin is a Page Upon Which are Written the Sum of the Digestive and Eliminative Systems; 6 pp; **CPP.**

n.d. Intestinal Autointoxication and its Sequelae, A Typical Case; 8 pp; **CPP.**

n.d. Acid Waste; 7 pp; **CPP.**

n.d. Diet in Hyperacidity; 7 pp; **CPP.**

n.d. The Vicious Circle and Its Efficient Treatment; 24 pp; **CPP.**

n.d. Rheumatism and Gout Treatment; 48 pp; **CPP.**

n.d. A Harbinger of Evil Import, High Blood Pressure; 7 pp; **CPP.**

n.d. The Price We Pay for Modern Civilization is Drawn Out of the Nervous System; 6 pp; **CPP.**

VEIFA-WERKE, A. -G.
Frankfort, Germany.
See: C. L. SCHEU, 1924.

VERBEEK, A., & PECKHOLDT
Gaertnergasse Nr. 4, Dresden.

1880 Catalogue Preis-Verzeichniss ueber Wagen mit constanter Empfindlichkeit fuer wissenschaftliche und technische Zwecke; **CTY/B** (Uai V 581).

1895 Price List of Balnaes of Constant Sensibility; 7 pp; **CTY/B** (Uai V 581).

VERDIN, CHARLES
11 rue Git-le-Coeur, Paris, France.
Est: 1875

1882 Catalogue des instruments de précision servant en physiologie et en médecine; 51 pp; **NLM** (W 26 V485).

Rue Linné 7, Paris, France.

Nov. 1890 Catalogue, Instruments de précision pour la physiologie et la médicine; 95 pp; **NYAM; MF/MAH; BLEL.**

G. Boulite successeur

1913 Catalogue microtomes, centrifugeuses; électrocardiographes, etc., no. D; pp 1-40, 101-188, 301-380, index; **NYAM; MF/MAH.**

New York Branch: 342 Madison Avenue.

1924 Scientific Instruments for Medicine and Physiology; **CPP.**

VEREINIGTE FABRIKEN FUER LABORATORIUMSBEDARF
3 Chaussenstrasse, Berlin, Germany.
See: MAX KAEHLER & MARTINI; Dr. Peters & Rost who incorporated to form VFL.
See: The KNY-SCHEERER CO.

1905 Preis-Verzeichniss ueber Apparate und Geraethschaften; **HDM.**

Scharnhorststr 22, Berlin N. 39, Germany.

1912 Catalogue, Apparate und Praeparate fuer medizinische Chemiie, klinische Diagnostic, etc.; 28 pp; **NYAM; MF/MAH.**

n.d. Hospital Furniture and Fittings, Part II, Hospital Laboratory Fittings; 156 pp; **MAH** (C 610.78085 V3, no. 94).

n.d. Catalogue, Hospital Furniture & Fittings, Hospital Laboratory Fittings, List 94; 167 pp; **MAH** (C 610.78085).

VERGNE, M.
116 rue de Rivoli, Paris, France.
Est: 1865

1888 Catalogue instruments de chirurgie; 56 pp; **NYAM; MF/MAH.**

VERICK, C.
2 rue de la Parcheminerie, Paris, France.

1885   Catalogue et Prix-Courant des microscopes et accessoires pour les études micrographiques; 51 pp; **URRR** (V-121).

VEROFORM HYGIENIC CO.

1906   How Best to Prevent Pathogenic Infection; 24 pp; **CPP.**

VETTER, J. C., & CO.
New York.

ca 1905   Illustrated Catalogue of Dry Leclanche Galvanic and Faradic Batteries and Standard Electro-Medical Apparatus; 52 pp; **BLEL.**

VIBRATOR INSTRUMENT CO.
Chattanooga, Tennessee.

ca 1904   The Chattanooga Vibrator; 30 pp; **BLEL.**

VIBROMETER CO., THE
210 North Holliday Street, Baltimore, Maryland.

n.d.   The Vibrometer; 15 pp; **CPP.**

VICTOR ELECTRIC CORPORATION
Jackson Blvd. and Robey Street, Chicago, Illinois.
55-59-61 Market Street, Chicago, Illinois.
110 East 23rd Street, New York, New York.
711 Boylston Street, Boston, Massachusetts.
California charter suspended Mar 5 1921, no further information.

See: VICTOR X-RAY CORP.; MACALASTER, WIGGIN CO., GENERAL ELECTRIC CO.

ca 1903   Electro-Surgical Apparatus Catalog no. 23; 64 pp; **CPP.**
Mar. 1914   High Frequency Apparatus no. 8, Bulletin no. 11-S; 8 pp; **CPP.**

66 Broadway, Cambridge, Massachusetts.

Oct. 1917   The Victor Calendar; 6 pp; **CPP.**

VICTOR ELECTRIC COMPANY
55-61 Market Street, Chicago, Illinois.
110 East 23rd Street, New York, New York.

1900   Victor Electro Surgical Specialties, no. 19; 32 pp; **BLEL.**
ca 1901   Catalogue no. 26 of Victor Electro-Surgical Apparatus; 92 pp; **BLEL.**
ca 1902   Catalogue no. 28 of Victor Electro-Surgical Apparatus; 114 pp; **BLEL.**
1904?   Catalogue no. 32, Victor Electro-Surgical Apparatus; 178 pp; **MAH** (C 615.85085 C); **MCFM** (De.V642v).

Jackson Blvd. & Robey Street, Chicago, Illinois.

ca 1910   Catalog, Roentgen Apparatus and High Frequency Outfits; 6th ed.; 51 pp; **ACR/MAH.**
May 1914   Bulletin no. 16-s, Teleflasher, The New Wantz Automatic X-Ray Timer; 7 pp; **ACR/MAH.**
Sep. 1914   Bulletin no. 24-s, Roentgen-Therapy Specialties; 7 pp; **ACR/MAH.**
Nov. 1914   Bulletin no. 31-s, X-Ray Sundries; 16 pp; **ACR/MAH.**
Dec. 1914   Bulletin no. 32-s, Electric Tray Rocker; 1 pp; **MAH** (C616.0757v).
1914   Illustrated Bulletin no. 32-s, Electric Tray Rocker; 2 pp; **MAH** (C 616 .0757 v).
Jan. 1915   Bulletin no. 18-s, Catalogue of Interrupterless X-Ray Transformers; 11 pp; **MAH** (C 616.0757v).
Mar. 1915   Bulletin no. 40-s, Roentgenoscopes Designed Exclusively for Fluoroscopy; 8 pp; **MAH** (C 616.0757v).

May 1915	Victor High Frequency Apparatus, Bulletin no. 15-s; 32 pp; **MAH** (C 616.0757).
Jun. 1915	Bulletin no. 41-s, Catalogue of Roentgen-Therapy Specialties; 8 pp; **MAH** (C 616.0757 v).
Jun. 1915	Bulletin no. 45-s, Roentgen Stands and Tables; 24 pp; **MAH** (C 616.0757v).
Oct. 1915	Illustrated Bulletin no. 39-s, Victor no. 9 High Frequency Apparatus; 2 pp; **MAH** (C616.0757 v).
Mar. 1915	Teleflasher, The New Wantz Automatic X-Ray Timer, Bulletin no. 16-s; 7 pp; **MAH** (C 616.0757 v).
1915	Interrupterless X-Ray Transformers; 11 pp; **MAH** (C 616.0757v).
1915	High Frequency Apparatus; 32 pp; **MAH** (C 616.0757 v).
Aug. 1916	Brochure Tungsten Target Tubes, Penetration Type for Transformers and Coils; 2 pp; **ACR/MAH.**
Sep. 1916	Tungsten Target Tubes, Penetration Type for Transformers and Coils; 2 pp; **ACR/MAH.**
Dec. 1916	Brochure, Improved Hydrogen Tube; 2 pp; **ACR/MAH.**
Feb. 1917	Brochure, Tungsten Target Tubes, Penetration Type for Transformers or Coils; 2 pp; **ACR/MAH.**
May 1917	Catalogue, Dental X-Ray Apparatus, no. 202; 24 pp; **NYAM; MF/MAH.**
May 1917	Leaflet, Model Snook, Roentgen Apparatus, no. 203; 4 pp; **NYAM; MF/MAH.**
Nov. 1917	Catalogue, Roentgen Stands, Tables & Fluoroscopic Apparatus, no. 206; 23 pp; **NYAM; MF/MAH.**

236 S. Robey Street, Chicago, Illinois.
66 Broadway, Cambridge, Massachusetts.
131 E. 23rd Street, New York, New York.

Oct. 1917	Brochure, Hydrogen Tubes, 6 pp foldout; **ACR/MAH.**
Nov. 1917	Brochure, Tungsten Target Tube, Penetration Type; 2 pp; **ACR/MAH.**
Dec. 1917	Leaflet, Roentgen Apparatus; Model New Universal, no. 207; 4 pp; **NYAM; MF/MAH; ACR/MAH.**
Aug. 1918	Brochure, Tungsten Target Tubes for Transformers or Coils; 6 pp foldout; **ACR/MAH.**
Nov. 1918	Brochure, Tungsten Target X-Ray Tubes, Penetration Type; 6 pp foldout; **ACR/MAH.**
Dec. 1918	Brochure, Tungsten Target X-Ray Tubes, Penetration Type; 6 pp foldout; **ACR/MAH.**
May 1919	Bulletin no. 232, Vertical Stereo-Plate Shifter; 2 pp; **ACR/MAH.**
July 1919	Brochure, A New Tube A Joyful Message to All Gas Tube Users; 6 pp foldout; **ACR/MAH.**
May 1920	Catalogue, Victor Roentgen Tables, Roentgenoscopes, and Tube Stands, Bulletin no. 206; 38 pp; **ACR/MAH; MAH.**
Dec. 1920	Pamphlet, Victor Combination Stereo Plate Shifter, Vertical-Horizontal, Bulletin no. 241; 3 pp; **ACR/MAH; MAH.**
Oct. 1921	Pamphlet, Victor Bucky Diaphragm Table, It Serves a Double Purpose; 3 pp; **ACR/MAH; MAH.**
Mar. 1923	Bulletin no. 257, Snook Special Combination Deep Therapy-Diagnostic Roentgen Apparatus; 11 pp; **ACR/MAH.**
Jan. 1925	Bulletin no. 264; 81 pp; **ACR/MAH.**
1925?	Bulletin no. 264; 95 pp; **ACR/MAH.**

2012 Jackson Blvd., Chicago, Illinois.
　　1928?　Bulletin no. 256, Victor Truvision Stereoscope; 7 pp; **ACR/MAH.**
　　1928?　Bulletin no. 214, Victor Model Dr. Sweet's Eye Localizer; 11 pp;
　　　　　　ACR/MAH.
　　1929?　Boletin no. 212-E, Aparatos Snook para rayos X 140 KV Cresta de Onda
　　　　　　para diagnostico y terapia superficial; 31 pp; **ACR/MAH.**
　　1920s?　Pamphlet, Roentgen Ray Measurement; 24 pp; **ACR/MAH.**
　　n.d.　　Catalogue, Roentgen Apparatus & High Frequency Outfits; 51 pp;
　　　　　　NYAM; MF/MAH.
　　M. 20 c　X-Ray and High Frequency Section; 4th ed.; 43 pp; **MAH** (C 615.0757).
　　n.d.　　Catalogue, Electrical Surgical Apparatus, no. 34; 186 pp; **NYAM;**
　　　　　　MF/MAH.
　　n.d.　　Instruction Manual CDX-LTMJ-Victor Dental X-Ray Unit; 23 pp;
　　　　　　NYAM; MF/MAH.
　　n.d.　　Catalogue, Roentgen Apparatus & High Frequency Outfits; 7th ed.; 56
　　　　　　pp; **NYAM; MF/MAH.**
　　n.d.　　Victor Electrical-Surgical Apparatus; 166 pp, no. 30; **CPP (Ed/121).**

VICTOR X-RAY CORPORATION
Est: 1895
　See: MACALASTER, WIGGIN CO., VICTOR ELECTRIC CO., GENERAL ELECTRIC CO.
　　1932　Formerly Victor X-Ray Corp. on General Electric Catalog; **ACR/MAH.**

VIDEX
　See: HOWDEN VIDEX PRODUCTS CORP., WRIGHT ENGINEERING CO.; **ACR/MAH.**
　　1907　Hauptkatalog ueber Krystallographisch-optische Instrumente; 59 pp;
　　　　　CTY/B (Uai V 871).

VOIGHT & HOCHGESANG
Untere Maschstrasse 26, Goettingen, Germany.
　　1896　Katalog ueber Krystallographische-optische Instrumente; 42 pp; **URRR**
　　　　　(V-120).
　　1903　Katalog ueber Krystallographische-optische Instrumente; **CTY/B** (Uai
　　　　　V871).

VOIGHTLANDER & SON, A. -G.
225 Fifth Avenue, New York, New York.
12 Charterhouse Street, London, E.C., England.
Est: 1756
　　ca 1908–09　Catalog of Microscopes and Microscopical Accessories, Temporary Catalog;
　　　　　　　56 pp; **AFMM.**

VOIGHTLANDER & SON OPTICAL CO.
New York, New York.
　467 East 14th Street, New York, New York.
Est: 1756
　　1896?　Catalogue of Collinear Doppel-Anastigmat and Telephoto Lenses; **CTY/B**
　　　　　(Uai V872).
　12 Charterhouse St., Holborn Circus, London.
　　1906　Mikroskope fuer Fleischbeschau; 4 pp; **URRR** (V-125).
　　1908　Microscopical Lenses and Apparatus; 56 pp; **URRR** (V-107).
　Brunswick Bldg., 225 Fifth Ave., New York, New York.
　　E. 20 c　Microscopical Lenses and Apparatus; 54 pp; **NYAM; MF/MAH.**

VOLTA BELT CO.
Cincinnati, Ohio.
    ca 1875   Medicine Rendered Useless, Electricity, Nature's Chief Restorer, Volta's
                Electro Magnetic Chain Belts and Bands; 40 pp; **MAH; MF/MAH.**

VOLTAIC BELT AND APPLIANCE CO.
Marshall, Michigan.
    189?   Beskrivelse af the Voltaic Belt and Appliance Co's elektriske baelter og
           apparater, bestaaende af baelter og baerebind, brystplader, indsaaler,
           hovebaand, ryg-, skulder-og laendebaand; 30 pp; **BLEL.**

WAARENHAUS, MEDICINISCHES
Friedrich-Strasse 108, Berlin North, Germany.
    Oct. 1894   No title; **ZUR.**

WAECHTER, PAUL
Friedenau bei Berlin. Berlin S.O., Koepenicker Strasse No. 112, Germany.
Est: 1872
    1889   Mikroskope und mikroskopische Hilfsapparate, Nr. 14; 48 pp; **URRR**
           (W-229).
    1904   Mikroskope und Nebenapparate; 64 pp; **URRR** (W-230).
    1909   Mikroskope und Nebenapparate; 64 pp; **URRR** (W-228).

WAGNER, R. V., & CO.
308 Dearborn Street, Chicago, Illinois.
    1899   Catalogue of Physicians and Surgeons Electrical Supplies; 5th ed.; 111 pp;
           ACR/MAH.
    ca 1900   Catalogue of Electrical Instruments for Physicians and Surgeons; 6th ed.;
           125 pp; **BLEL.**
   138-140 Wabash Ave., Chicago, Illinois.
    1905   Catalogue of Electrical Instruments for Physicians and Surgeons; 160 pp;
           MAH (C 615.84085w).

WAHMANN, GEORGE H., MFG. CO.
Baltimore, Maryland.
    1930?   Laboratory Apparatus Catalog; **CPP** (ZZooh/1).
    pre–1939   Circular no. 127, Animal Cages and Animal Room Equipment,
           Laboratory Apparatus; 12 pp; **NLM** (W26 W137).

WAITE & BARTLETT X-RAY MFG. CO.
143 East 23rd St., New York, New York.
Est: 1879 or 1881
   See: PICKER X-RAY CORP.; **ACR/MAH.**
    1885   Ranney, Ambrose L. M.D. *Practical Suggestions Respecting the Varieties of Electric*
           Currents and the Uses of Electricity in Medicine, New York; **MAH.**
    1890?   Illustrated Price List, Electro-Medical and Electro-Surgical Instruments; 48
           pp; **BLEL.**
    ca 1892   Catalogue of Electro-Medical and Electro-Surgical Instruments; 48 pp;
           NLM (W26 W145c).
    1893   Catalogue, Electro-Medical and Electro-Surgical Instruments; 47 pp;
           NYAM (135700); **MF/MAH.**
    1895–96   Catalog of Electro-Medical and Electro-Surgical Instruments for Physicians
           and Surgeons; 59 pp; **CS; NLM** (qW26 W145c).

108 E. 23rd Street, New York, New York.
    1901   Catalogue of Electro-Medical, Electro-Surgical, Static Machines, Galvanic Batteries for Physicians and Surgeons; 20th Annual ed.; 80 pp; **NLM** (W26 W145c); **NYAM; MF/MAH.**

Jan. 1905   Illustrated Catalogue & Price List, Mfrs. of Static Machines, X-Ray Coils and Tubes, Ultra Violet Ray Lamps, High Frequency Apparatus, Electric Light Heat Radiators, Galvanic, Faradic and Cautery Batteries, Cabinet Combinations for Office and Hospital Use; 21st ed.; 117 pp; **MAH** (C 615.84085 W); **ACR/MAH.**

113-115-117 W. 31st Street, New York, New York.
    1910   Illustrated Catalogue & Price List of Static Machines, X-Ray Coils and Tubes, High Frequency Apparatus, Therapeutic Lamps, Compression Diaphragms and X-Ray Tables and All Electro-Medical & Surgical Instruments for Physicians and Surgeons; 22nd ed.; 72 pp; **MAH** (C 615.84085).

    1910   Catalogue Electro-Medical and Surgical Instruments for Physicians and Surgeons; 23rd ed.; 48 pp; **MAH** (C 615.84085).

    1911   Brochure Silent Solace Interrupterless; 20 pp; **ACR/MAH.**

252-258 West 29th Street, New York, New York.
    1912   Brochure, Silent Solace Interrupterless; 16 pp; **ACR/MAH.**

    1913   Brochure, Solace Interrupterless; 2 pp; **ACR/MAH.**

    1913?   Brochure, Modified German Fluoroscopic Stand; 2 pp; **ACR/MAH.**

    1913?   Brochure, Solace Radiographic Tube Stand and Modified German Fluoroscopic Stand; 8 pp; **ACR/MAH.**

    1916   Catalogue, Electro Medical and Surgical Instruments for Physicians and Surgeons; 24th ed.; 36 pp; **ACR/MAH.**

ca 1917   Brochure, The U.S. Army Bedside Unit and New X-Ray Devices; 32 pp; **ACR/MAH.**

ca 1920   Brochure, The New Solate Portable X-Ray Outfit; 2 pp; **ACR/MAH.**

    1922   Bulletin no. 12, New Apparatus, X-Ray; 8 pp; **ACR/MAH.**

53 Jackson Avenue, Long Island City, New York.
Sep. 1923   Pamphlet, Oil Immersed Apparatus, Bulletin no. 14; 8 pp; **ACR/MAH; MAH.**

ca 1925   Leaflet, Solomon Iontoquantimeter; 1 pp; **ACR/MAH.**

ca 1925   Pamphlet, The New Solace Portable X-Ray Outfit; 4 pp; **ACR/MAH; MAH.**

ca 1925   Flyer, The Mackee Treatment Tube Stand; **ACR/MAH; MAH.**

ca 1925   Flyer, Solace Waugh Unit Type Oil Immersed Dental X-Ray Unit; **ACR/MAH; MAH.**

Mar. 1929   Pamphlet, Oil Immersed Hot Cathode Valve Tube, Kenotron; 5 pp; **ACR/MAH; MAH.**

    n.d.   Flyer, Solar Shock Proof Biplane Fluoroscopic and Radiographic Table; **ACR/MAH; MAH.**

E. 20 c   Pamphlet, Modified German Fluoroscopic Stand; 4 pp; **MAH** (C 616.0757w).

E. 20 c   Pamphlet, Solace Radiographic Tube Stand, Modified German Fluoroscopic Stand; 8 pp; **MAH** (C 616.0757).

WALB, WILHELM
5 Hauptstrasse, Heidelberg, Germany.
July 1888   Illustriertes Spezial-Preiscourant ueber Mikrotom-Messer und Mikroskopie-Instrumente; 15 pp; **CPP.**

1892   Illustriertes Special-Preisverzeichniss der Fabrik chirurgischer Instrumente von Wilhelm Walb in Heidelberg; 92 pp; **CPP** (Cage Pam A/129).

WALE, GEORGE, & CO.
Hoboken, New Jersey.
Formerly Hawkins & Wale.
  1877? Price List no. 1; 16 pp; **CTY/B** (Uai W 148).
 Jan. 1877? Price List no. 2, Philosophical Instrument Makers . . . Spectroscopes, Magic Lanterns and Attachments, and Blowpipe Apparatus; 4 pp; **CTY/B** (Uai W 148).
  n.d. Spectroscopes, Magic Lanterns and Attachments, and Blowpipe Apparatus; **CPP** (Bolenius Coll).
  1878 Price List no. 6, New Apparatus including Singing Telephone, Motophone, etc.; 12 pp; **CTY/B** (Uai W 148).

WALES, PHILIP SKINNER
Philadelphia.
  1867 A Practical Treatise on Surgical Apparatus, Appliances, and Elementary Operations, Embracing Bandaging, Minor Surgery, Orthopraxy and the Treatment of Fractures and Dislocations; xxiv, 685 pp; **LLU** (WO W173s 1867).

WALFORD, D. N.
477 Pennsylvania Avenue, N. W., Washington, D.C.
 May 1893 Descriptive Price List of Physicians' Pocket Medicine Cases, Buggy Cases, Satchels, etc.; 29 pp; **MAH** (C 610.78085 D).

WALL & OCHS
1716 Chestnut Street, Philadelphia, Pennsylvania.
  E. 20 c Physicians Net Price List of Ophthalmological and Laryngological Apparatus; 24 pp; **MAH** (C 617.7085).

WALLACH, MARTIN, NACHFOLGER
Kassel, Germany.
Successors to Martin Wallach
Est: 1848
  1888 Catalogue of Medical and Surgical Instruments and Apparatus; 92 pp; **NLM** (W 26 W 195c).

WALLAU, GEORGE J.
6 Cliff Street, New York, New York.
  1918 Mistletoe, Its Pharmacology and Therapeutic Use; **CPP.**
2- 4- 6 Cliff Street, New York.
  n.d. A Notice on the Medicinal and Curative Properties of Urodonal, Jubal, Globeal and Filudine, J. L. Chatelain, 207 Boulevard Pereire, Paris; 48 pp; **CPP.**

WALMSLEY, W. H., & CO.
1016 Chestnut Street, Philadelphia, Pennsylvania.
Successors to R. & J. Beck
Dealer for Zentmayer, Tolles and Wales
 ca 1900 Condensed List of a few of the Most Desirable Microscopes of Moderate Cost . . . Clinical Thermometers, Telescopes, Barometers, etc.; 32 pp, fragile; **MAH.**
  M. 19 c A Classified List of First Class Microscopic Objects . . .; 15 pp, fragile; **NLM** (W26 W216).

n.d.   Catalogue, A Classified List of First Class Microscopic Objects; 32 pp;
CTY/B (Uai W 162).

n.d.   A Classified List of First Class Microscopic Objectives with Many New,
Rare and Interesting Specimens in Anatomy, Physiology, Botany . . .;
CTY/B (Uai W 162).

1022 Walnut Street, Philadelphia, Pennsylvania.

n.d.   Catalogue Opticians and Photographic Stock Merchants; **CTY/B** (Uai W
162).

2225 Vine St., Philadelphia, PA.

n.d.   Educational Series of Microscopic Objects at Low Price; 14 pp; **CTY/B**
(Uai W 162).

WALTER, ANDRÉ, ÉTABLISSEMENTS
Paris, France.

1929   Haute fréquence, diathermie . . .; 25 pp; **BLEL.**

1929   Le Bistouri électrique et la diathermie; 7 pp; **BLEL.**

1936   La d'Arsonvalisation: Diathermie, ondes courtes, hautes fréquence, bistouri
diatherma; 12 pp; **BLEL.**

1936   La d'Arsonvalisation ondes courtes; 19 pp; **BLEL.**

WALTER-BIONDETTI, C.

1902   Ein Wink fuer bruchlediende und ein blick in das kurpfuschertum; 28 pp;
ZUR.

WALTON, ALFRED
280 Fourth Avenue between 21 and 22 Streets, New York, New York.

n.d.   Oxygen and Nitrogen Therapeutic Agents in the Treatment of Pulmonary
and Other Chronic Diseases; 17 pp; **CPP.**

WANAMAKER, JOHN
1300 Market St., Philadelphia, Pennsylvania.
Est: 1861
Department Store

n.d.   Illustrated Catalogue of Rolling, Reclining and Carrying Chairs; 96 pp;
CPP.

WANDER & SON X-RAY TUBE CO.
160 North Fifth Avenue, Chicago, Illinois.
See: HEINZE-WANDER X-RAY TUBE CO.

ca 1910   Midget High Frequency Apparatus; 8 pp; **ACR/MAH.**

WAPPLER ELECTRIC CO.
177 East 87th Street, New York, New York.
Est: 1898
See: AMERICAN CYSTOSCOPE MAKERS.

ca 1900   Catalogue of Galvanic, Faradic, Sinusoidal Cabinets, Switchboards and
Accessories; 27 pp; **MAH** (C 615.84085W).

1900?   Brochure no. 3, Cautery Generator for the 110 Volt Direct Current; 3 pp;
NYAM; MF/MAH.

ca 1900   Brochure, The Dental X-Ray and High Frequency Outfit; 3 pp; **NYAM;
MF/MAH.**

173 East 87th St., New York, New York.

ca 1905   Bulletin no. 76, Dental, X-Ray, High Frequency and Ionization
Apparatus; 16 pp; **NYAM; MF/MAH.**

173-175 East 87th St., (New York).

1911   Electro-Medical and Surgical Instruments, Catalog no. 1; 36 pp; **BLEL.**

1913   Catalogue of Electrically-Lighted Diagnostic Instruments and Accessories; 2nd ed.; 80 pp; **NYAM; MF/MAH.**

ca 1913   Catalogue of Cystoscopes, Endoscopes, Urethroscopes, Bronchoscopes, Pharyngoscopes, Laryngoscopes, Headlights, Controllers, Lamp Brackets, Light Batteries, High-Frequency Apparatus, etc.; 2nd ed.; 80 pp; **BLEL.**

1913?   Brochure, Excell High Frequency Apparatus; 2nd ed.; 16 pp; **ACR/MAH.**

ca 1914   Interrupterless Transformers and Upright Fluoroscopic Apparatus; 28 pp; **BLEL.**

ca 1914   Catalogue of Pneumo-Massage Apparatus, Multostats, Cautery Motors and Transformers, Surgical Drills, Headlights, etc.; 2nd ed.; 64 pp; **BLEL.**

ca 1915   Catalogue, Electro-Medical Apparatus; 16 pp; **NYAM; MF/MAH.**

ca 1915   Catalogue Electro-Medical and Surgical Apparatus, X-Ray and High-frequency Apparatus and Accessories; 125 pp; **NYAM; MF/MAH; FI** (636/4).

ca 1915   Bulletin no. 54, Water Circulating Pump and Water Cooled X-Ray Tubes; 2 pp; **ACR/MAH.**

ca 1915   Bulletin no. 55, Timers, Coolidge Transformer, Aerial Systems, Indicating Sparkgap; 7 pp; **ACR/MAH.**

1915   Catalogue no. 56, X-Ray and High Frequency Apparatus and Accessories; 2nd ed.; 160 pp; **NYAM; MF/MAH; MAH** (C 615.84085W); **ACR/MAH.**

ca 1915   Bulletin no. 57, Some Items of Interest to Dentists; 2 pp; **ACR/MAH.**

ca 1915   Bulletin no. 61, Dental X-Ray, High Frequency and Ionization Machines; 2 pp; **ACR/MAH.**

ca 1915   Catalogue no. 4, The Wappler Interrupterless X-Ray and Treatment Apparatus; 9 pp; **MAH** (C 617.7085 W).

1919   Wappler Electro-Medical Apparatus, Telatherm and Portable Telatherm, Bulletin no. 80; **FI** (1594/23).

ca 1920   Electro Medical Apparatus, Price list dated Apr 1 1920; **ISUM** (W 26 W252e).

1921   Wappler Galvanic, Faradic and Sinusoidal Apparatus, Bulletin no. 500; 11 pp; **FI** (1427/28).

Jun. 1921   Bulletin no. 89, Medical X-Ray Accessories; 2nd ed.; **ACR/MAH.**

Aug. 1 1922   Bulletin no. 87, Bellevue Model Roentgen Ray Machine; 2nd ed.; 4 pp; **ACR/MAH.**

1922   Bulletin no. 90, 3rd ed., Portable X-Ray Unit; 4 pp; **FI** (217/12).

Sep. 1922   Bulletin no. 98, Number Six Composite X-Ray Unit; 12 pp; **ACR/MAH.**

1923   Bulletin no. 95, Wappler Senior Dental X-Ray Unit; 4 pp; **FI** (314/7).

Apr. 1923   Bulletin no. 100, Duplex Model Roentgen Ray Machine; 6 pp foldout; **ACR/MAH; FI** (217/16).

1923   Bulletin no. 101, Senior Vertical Fluoroscope and Vertical Fluoroscope Unit; 4 pp; **FI** (217/17).

1923   Bulletin no. 102, X-Ray Aerial System; 12 pp; **FI** (217/18).

Nov. 1923   Bulletin no. 103, Number Xi Mobile X-Ray Unit Office and Hospital; 4 pp; **ACR/MAH; FI** (217/19).

n.d.   The Schoonmacher ACMI Headlight; 4 pp; **CPP.**

General Offices and Factory: Long Island City, NY.
    Mar. 1923   Wappler Cystoscopes and Cysto-Urethropscopes, Bulletin no. 200; 3rd ed.;
             20 pp; **AO; FI** (1418/35).
        1923   Bulletin no. 300, Cautery Appliances; 6 pp; **FI** (1524/40).
        1924   Infant Examining Cystoscope with Single Catheterizing Attachment,
             Supplement, no. 1 to Bulletin 200; 2 pp; **AO.**
        1924   Bulletin no. 104, Vertex Roentgen Ray Machine; 8 pp; **FI** (217/20).
        1925   Bulletin no. 82, King Model Roentgen Ray Machine; 8 pp; **FI** (217/9).
        1925   Bulletin no. 87, 3rd ed., Bellevue Model Roentgen Ray Machine; 8 pp;
             FI (217/10).
        1925   Bulletin no. 89, 3rd ed., Medical X-Ray Accessories; 20 pp; **FI** (217/11).
        1925   Bulletin no. 91, 3rd ed., Wappler Radiographic and Fluoroscopic
             Transformer and Control Unit; 4 pp; **FI.**
        1925   Bulletin no. 92, 6th ed., Junior Dental X-Ray Unit; 4 pp; **FI** (217/14).
        1925   Bulletin no. 99-A, Deep Therapy X-Ray Equipment; 4 pp; **FI** (217/15).
        1925   Bulletin no. 105, J. Bentley Squire, Cystoscopic X-Ray Table; 4 pp; **FI**
             (217/21).
    July 1926   Pamphlet, Wappler Monex Bulletin no. 107; 8 pp; **ACR/MAH; MAH.**
    ca 1930   Brochure, Britesun Carbon Arc Ultra Violet Lamps; 13 pp; **NYAM;**
             MF/MAH.
        n.d.   X-Ray and High Frequency Accessories; 52 pp; **BLEL.**
        n.d.   Eye, Ear, Nose and Throat Instruments; 16 pp; **URRR** (W-328).

WAPPLER ELECTRIC CONTROLLER CO.
173-75 East 85th Street, New York, New York.
   177 East 87th Street, New York, New York.
      E. 20 c   Brochure, Rotary Mechanical Interrupter for X-Ray and All High
             Frequency Apparatus; 4 pp; **NYAM; MF/MAH.**
      E. 20 c   Section 6, Galvanic, Faradic, Sinusoidal Cabinets, Switchboards and
             Accessories; 34 pp; **MAH** (C 615.84085).

WAPPLER ELECTRIC MANUFACTURING CO.
    ca 1910   Catalogue no. 2, Pneumo-Message Apparatus, Multostats, Cautery
             Motors and Transformers, Surgical Drills, Spray and Pressure Pumps,
             Cautery Knives, Otoscopes, Centrifuges, Vibrators; 26 pp; **MAH** (C
             615.85085W); **CPP.**
        n.d.   Brochure Electromedical Apparatus; 3 pp; **NYAM; MF/MAH.**
        n.d.   Brochure Apparatus & Devices for Surgeons; 7 pp; **NYAM; MF/MAH.**

WARD, CHARLES HOWELL
45-47 Mt. Hope Avenue, Rochester, New York.
Est: 1899; Inc: 1926
        1902   Price List of Fractures, Dislocations and Pathological Bones; 2nd revised
             ed.; 14 pp; **NYAM; MF/MAH.**
        1902   Catalogue of Human and Comparative Skeletons, Osteological Specialties
             and Anatomical Models Prepared and Imported by Charles H.
             Ward . . .; 136 pp; **LC.**
   17 East Main St., Rochester, New York.
        1913   Catalogue of Human Skeletons, Anatomical Models, Human Comparative
             Anthropology, Ethnology; 114 pp; **AFMM.**
        1937   Models Illustrating Human Anatomy & Zoological Models; 88 pp;
             AFMM.

WARD, HENRY A.
2 College Avenue, Rochester, New York.
Est: 1862; Inc: 1890

Sep. 1880   Catalogue of Specimens of Comparative Osteology; 54 pp; **NLM** (W26 W264).

ca 1883   Catalogue of Human Skeletons and Anatomical Preparations; 25 pp; **NLM** (W26 W264).

16-26 College Avenue, Rochester, New York.

1893   Catalogue of Human Skeletons, Human and Comparative Anatomical Models, Botanical Models, Busts and Masks; 6th ed.; 79 pp; **NLM** (W26 W264).

WARD, MONTGOMERY AND CO.
619 W. Chicago Ave., Chicago, Illinois.
Est: 1872

1895   Reprint by Dover Publications of Catalogue and Buyers' Guide no. 57; 624 pp; **BLEL.**

WARMBRUNN, QUILITZ & CO.
40 Rosenthaler Strasse, Berlin C, Germany.

1889   Artikel fuer Chirurgie, Krankenpflege, Nr. 63; **CPP** (lab/313).

Nov. 1893   Thermometer aus Jenaer Glas, Nr. 90; 13 pp; **CTY/B** (Uai W 237).

WARNER, W. R., & CO.
1228 Market Street, Philadelphia, Pennsylvania.

n.d.   Reliable Specialties; 24 pp; **CPP.**

WARNER-CHILCOTT LABORATORIES
Morris Plains, New Jersey.

n.d.   Catalog with insertible brochures and new brochures added as available, instruments division; **LACMA** (149 W 24C).

WARRING, C. B.
Poughkeepsie, New York.

1852   Catalogue of Chemical and Philosophical Apparatus; 16 pp; **CTY/B** (Uai W 258).

1856   Catalogue of Chemical and Philosophical Apparatus; 3rd ed.; 22 pp; **CTY/B** (Uai W 258).

WARRINGTON AND PENNYPACKER
NW Corner Fifth and Calowhill Streets, Philadelphia, Pennyslvania.

Jun. 1, 1892   Papillary Lotion of Nipple Wash; 8 pp; **CPP.**

n.d.   McClintock's Nipple Wash; 8 pp; **CPP.**

WATERBURY CHEMICAL CO.
Des Moines, Iowa.

n.d.   Pharmaceutical Chemists Price List; 24 pp; **CPP.**

WATKINS, G. A., & CO.
Springfield, Vermont.

1858   Circular Apparatus for Fractures, etc., List of Surgical Instruments made by Watkins; 8 pp; **NLM** (W 26 W335).

WATKINS AND HILL
London, England.

1838 A New and Enlarged Descriptive Catalogue of Optical, Mathematical, Philosophical, and Chemical Instruments and Apparatus; 112 pp; **BLEL.**

WATSON AND SONS
London.

1909 Catalogue of Microscope Objectives, Stage Condensors and Accessories; 162 pp; **HDM.**

1920 Catalogue of Microscopes and Accessories, Part 1, Student Instruments; 27th ed.; 40 pp; **HDM.**

1920 Catalog of Watson Microscopes, Part 2, Microscope Accessories for the Biological Sciences; 36th ed.; 258 pp. index; **HDM; MAH.**

n.d. A Modern X-Ray Department; 16 pp; **CPP.**

WATTERS LABORATORIES
35-37 East 20th Street, New York, New York.
See: HOSPITAL SUPPLY CO.; **NLM.**

1908? Illustrated Catalogue of Watters Hospital and Surgical Supplies; **CPP** (ZZSr/14).

n.d. Catalogue of Hospital Supplies; 93 pp; **NYAM; MF/MAH.**

WEBER DENTAL MANUFACTURING CO.
400 Cherry St., Canton, Ohio.
Est: 1897

1925 Catalog; 55 pp; **MAH** (C 617.6085).

n.d. Catalog Weber Fountain Cuspidors; 24 pp; **MAH** (C 617.6085 W).

n.d. Booklet Weber Fountain Cuspidors; 27 pp; **MAH** (C 617.6085).

WEED, W. A., & CO.
Chicago, Illinois.

1872 Illustrated Yearbook of Pharmacy and General Information; **HDM.**

WEICHERT, GEORGE A., & CO., INC.
247 West 42nd Street, New York, New York.

n.d. The Weichert-Glycene Denture; 1 pp; **NYAM; MF/MAH.**

WEINHAGEN, H.
152 Williams Street, New York, New York.
Est: 1855

1876 Illustrated Catalogue of Chemists' Physicians' Druggists' Brewers', Distillers' and Dairymens' Glassware, etc.; **CPP** (Bolenius Coll); **MUM.**

WEINSTEIN FORMULAE
See: J. M. NEY CO.; **MF/MAH.**

WEISS, JOHN M.
62 Strand, London, England.
Est: 1787

1823 Catalogue, Chirurgical Instruments Invented and Improved by Mr. Weiss to Which Are Added Various Accounts and Testimonials . . .; 80 pp; **YML; NWUCML** (617.91 W43s).

1825 Catalog of Chirurgical Instruments Invented and Improved by John Weiss; **SBMC; CPP** (Ed/13 G).

1831 An Account of Inventions and Improvements in Surgical Instruments made by John Weiss; 2nd ed.; 110 pp, appendix, plates; **NYAM** (s.125); **MF/MAH; AFMM; MAH** (RD 71 W 431); **LLU** (WO W531a 1831).

1836   Weiss and Son's Catalogue of Surgical Instruments for 1836; 8 pp; **NYAM; MF/MAH.**

1830s   Weiss's Screw Lithotrite; 23 pp; **NYAM; MF/MAH.**

John Weiss & Son

1863   Catalogue of Surgical Instruments, Apparatus, Appliances, etc.; 72 pp; **NYAM** (S. 125); **MF/MAH; CPP** (Ed/2); **MCFM; TMHM.**

1863   Catalogue of Surgical Instruments; 66 pp, appendix of Veterinary Instruments, **NLM** (W26 W431c, Reel 73-5-4).

1873   Description of Apparatus for Medical Electrisation, made and sold by John Weiss & Son; 17 pp; **CPP** (Cage Pam A/117).

1882   A Price List of Surgical Instruments, Apparatus, Appliances & Co.; 196 pp; **JHIHM** (RD 76.W 431).

WEISS, JOHN, & SONS, LTD.
287 Oxford Street, London W.
42 King Street, Manchester, England.

1898   A Catalogue of Ophthalmic Instruments and Appliances . . .; 103 pp; **NYAM; MF/MAH; NLM** (W26 W431c).

ca 1910   Catalogue Instruments for General Surgery, Section 2; 337 pp; **JHIHM** (RD 76.W 43); **NWUCML** (617.91 W 43).

1911   Catalogue of Ophthalmic Instruments and Appliances; 135 pp; **CPP** (Ed/72); **MAH** (photocopy).

1925   Catalogue of Instruments for General Surgery, Section 2; **CS.**

1927   Catalogue, Ophthalmic Instruments and Appliances; **LACMA** (149 W 43c).

1927–29   Catalogue of Ophthalmic Instruments and Appliances; 294 pp; **AFMM.**

1929   Supplement to the Catalogue of Ophthalmic Instruments and Appliances; 30 pp; **AFMM.**

WEISS, M., & CO.
1140-1154 Springfield Ave., Newark, New Jersey.
Charter revoked in 1925.

n.d.   Hospital and Physicians' Equipment, High Grade Aseptic Steel Furniture for Physicians, Surgeons and Hospitals, no. 6; 428 pp, index; **NYAM; MF/MAH.**

WEISS, PAUL
1620 Arapahoe Street, Denver, Colorado.

ca 1915   Catalogue Microscopes, Laboratory Requisites, Mounting Materials, Glassware, Capsule Stains, Dry Stains, Solutions and Reagents; 56 pp; **NYAM; MF/MAH; CPP.**

1922   Catalog of Microscopes, Laboratory Requisites, Mounting Materials, Glassware, Capsule Stains, Dry Stains, Solutions and Reagents; 56 pp; **NLM** (W26 W436m).

n.d.   The Wellsworth Lensmeter and Your Prestige; 5 pp; **CPP.**

n.d.   Microscopes, Laboratory Requisites, Mounting Material, Glassware, Capsule Stains, Dry Stains, Solutions and Reagents; 56 pp; **CPP.**

WELCH, BENJAMIN, M.D.
New York, New York.

1852   Surgeons' Splints and Improved Apparatus for Fractures; 23 pp; **YML.**

1858   Surgeons' Splints and Improved Apparatus for Fractures; 37 pp; **YML.**

WELCH, JAMES
21 Store Lane, Albany, New York.
      1833   Instrument Maker listed in Albany City Directory and listed as
              Mathematical Instrument Maker in 1835.

WELCH, W. M., MFG. CO.
100 Lake St., Chicago, Illinois.
1515 N. Sedgwick St. Chicago, 10, Ill.
Est: 1880
      n.d.   Biological Apparatus and Supplies, Catalog B; 48 pp; **URRR** (W-197).

WELLCOME CHEMICAL RESEARCH LABORATORIES, THE
      1914   Description of the Exhibits of the Laboratories at the Anglo-American
              Exposition; 80 pp; **CPP.**

WELLSWORTH
See: AMERICAN OPTICAL CO., Oct 1928 price list; **NYAM.**

WELLSWORTH PRODUCTS
      n.d.   Delightfully Restful for the Eyes; Wellsworth Cruxite Lenses; **YB.**

WEST DISINFECTING CO., INC.
9 East 59th Street, New York, New York.
42-16 West St., Long Island City 1, New York.
Est: 1882
      1905?   The Largest Manufacturers of Disinfectants, Disinfecting Appliances &
              Fumigating Apparatus in America; 16 pp; **CTY/B** (Uai W52).

WEST GRAVITISER CORP., THE
450-452 East 148 Street, New York, New York.
      1922   Directions for the Mechanical Operation of the West Gravitiser as used for
              Oscillatory-Gravity Treatment, in Acc. file no. 92249; 8 pp; **MAH.**

WEST, WILLIAM
15, Horton Lane, Bradford, England.
      1886   S. Louis' Catalogue of 43 Series of Mounted Slides and 57 Series of
              Unmounted Objects for the Microscope . . .; 36 pp; **MAH.**

WESTERN DENTAL MANUFACTURING CO.
London, England.
      ca 1924   Looseleaf, parts separately paginated; **BLEL.**

WESTERN ELECTRIC CO., LTD.
Bush House, Aldwych, London W.C. 2, England.
      1924   Information for the Cure and Operation of the 3-A Audiometer; 8 pp;
              CPP.
      n.d.   Bulletin no. 102; **CPP.**
      1920's   Bulletin no. 812, Instruction for Use of Audiphones nos. 36, 37 and 38;
              24 pp; **AFMM.**
      1936   Brochure describing Western Electric's 3A Electrical Stethoscope; 12 pp;
              AFMM.

WESTERN ELECTRICAL INSTRUMENT CO.
Newark, New Jersey.
      n.d.   Western Standard Direct Reading Voltimeters and Ammeters; 32 pp;
              CPP.

WESTERN ELECTRIC MANUFACTURING CO.
Chicago, Illinois.
        n.d.   Electro-Medical and Surgical Apparatus; 32 pp; **BLEL.**

WESTERN PASTEUR FILTER CO., THE
Springfield, Ohio.
        n.d.   The Pasteur Filter; 29 pp; **CPP.**

WESTERN SURGICAL INSTRUMENT HOUSE
West 59th Street, Chicago, Illinois.
      Aug. 1903   Bargain Bulletin, Illustrated Catalogue of Surgical Instruments; 4 pp; **MAH.**
        1904   Wholesale Price List of Surgical Instruments and Supplies; **MAH.**

WESTERN SURGICAL SUPPLY CO.
Los Angeles, California.
        1915   Surgical Instruments, Physicians' Equipment, Hospital and Invalid Supplies; **UCLABM** (W 26 W525s); **LLU** (W 26 W526).

WESTERN WHOLESALE DRUG CO.
Los Angeles, California.
        1911   Catalogue Drugs, Chemicals, Patent Medicines, Show Cases, Glassware; 1232 pp; **LACMA** (149 W 52g).

WESTERN X-RAY & COIL CO.
1007 Filmore Street, Chicago, Ill.
      post 1904   Surgical Instruments and Hospital Equipments, Ruf. M. Brady, M.E., The X-Ray Man; 61 pp; **UCSF.**

WESTINGHOUSE
Pittsburgh, PA.
      ca 1918   Catalogue Westinghouse Type U Graphic Meters; **CTY/B** (Uai W 5282).

WESTINGHOUSE ELECTRIC AND MANUFACTURING CO.
  See: WESTINGHOUSE X-RAY CO., INC.

WESTINGHOUSE X-RAY COMPANY, INC.
Long Island City, New York.
      post 1933   Dental X-Ray Unit, Model B; **MAH.**

WHEELER, EDMUND
48 Tollington Road, London, England.
        1876   A Classified List of First-Class Microscopic Objects with Many New, Rare, and Interesting Specimens Affording Instructive Illustration in Anatomy, Physiology, Botany.; 7th ed.; 27 pp; **CTY/B** (Uai W562).

WHITALL, TATUM & CO.
410 Race St., P.O. Box 1633, Philadelphia.
P.O. Box 1866, 46 & 48 Barclay St., New York.
41 & 43 Broad St., Philadelphia, Pennsylvania.
No. 79 South's Wharf, Baltimore.
91 Washington Street, North, Boston, Massachusetts.
45 Stevenson Street, San Francisco, California.
12 Barrack Street, Sydney, N.S.W., Australia.
Est: 1837
        1876   Chemical and Other Glassware; 10 pp; **CTY/B** (Uai W 58).

1878	Catalogue of Special Prices Chemical Glassware for Colleges, Institutes of Technology, Laboratories, Assaying Offices, etc.; **CTY/B** (Uai W 58).
1880	Catalogue of Druggists', Chemists, and Perfumers' Glassware, Reproduction of Catalog published by the Pyne Press, New Jersey as part of their American Historical Catalog Collection with a history of the company; 71 pp; **MAH** (TP 865 W578).
1882	Catalogue Glass Manufacturers, Druggists, Chemists, and Perfumers Glassware, Druggists' Sundries; **CTY/B** (Uai W58).
1885	Catalogue Manufacturers of Druggists', Chemists' and Perfumers' Glassware, Manufacturers and Jobbers of Druggists' Sundries; 106 pp; **CTY/B** (Uai W 58).
1889	Catalogue of Chemical and Philosophical Glassware; **CTY/B** (Uai W 58).
1892	Annual Price List; reprint 1969; **MSL** (HD 9999 G5.7W5).
1895	Supplemental Price List; 24 pp; **CPP.**
Apr. 27, 1896	Specialties for Physicians; 4 pp; **CPP.**
1898	Catalogue, Mfrs. of Druggists', Chemists' and Perfumers Glassware, Druggists' Sundries; 206 pp; **NYAM; MF/MAH.**
1898	Discounts from Price List of Laboratory Glassware and Sundries; 4 pp; **CTY/B** (Uai W 58).
1904	Annual Price List; 208 pp; **CPP.**
July 1905	Catalogue; 2 pp; **CTY/B** (Uai W 581).
n.d.	Catalogue of Special Prices Chemical Glassware; 16 A & B pp; **CTY/B** (Uai W 58).

964 Eddy Street, San Francisco, California.

| 1907 | Annual Price List; **MAH.** |
| 1908 | Catalogue Laboratory Glassware and Apparatus; 64 pp; **NYAM; MF/MAH.** |

10 Barrack Street, Sydney, New South Wales.

1908	Price List of Laboratory Glassware and Apparatus; 64 pp; **CTY/B** (Uai W 58).
Mar. 15, 1910	Price List Laboratory Glassware and Apparatus; 4 pp; **NYAM; MF/MAH.**
Mar. 15, 1911	Price List Laboratory Glassware and Sundries; 5 pp; **NYAM; MF/MAH.**
Sep. 1 1921	Catalog of Druggists', Chemists' and Perfumers' Glassware, Druggists' Sundries; 156 pp; **NLM.**

WHITCOMB METALLIC BEDSTEAD CO.
Shelton, Connecticut.
"Pioneer Works"

| Sep. 1909 | Brochure; 2 pp; **NYAM; MF/MAH.** |
| n.d. | Catalogue Iron Beds, List of hospitals using these beds, no. 8; 63 pp; **NYAM; MF/MAH.** |

WHITE, SAMUEL STOCKTON
See: MONOGRAPHS, DR. J. A. MALCOLM.

WHITE, SAMUEL S., DENTAL MFG. CO.
528 Arch Street, Philadelphia, Pennsylvania.
Est: 1844

1862	Catalogue Dental Materials; 98 pp; **MAH** (C 617.6085 W).
Jun. 1865	Condensed List of Retail Prices, 40 pp; **HML.**
Jan. 1, 1867	Catalogue of Dental Materials, Furniture, Instruments, etc.; 226 pp; **MAH** (C 617.6085 W); **HDM; LC** (RK 686.W58); **AFMM;**

UPSDM (D 617.604 W581); **FI** (617.6 W 583); **BDA; HML** (2nd copy with ms additions in rear).

1867　Dentist's Microscope for the Investigation of the Organic Structure of the Dental Tissues, etc.; 24 pp; **UPSDM** (D 617.604 W 586).

1867　Apparatus for Producing Local Anaesthesia, by Narcotic Spray, Applicable to General and Dental Surgery; 7 pp; **YML** (RK 686 867w).

Chestnut St., Corner of Twelfth, Philadelphia, Pennsylvania.

Jan. 1870　Price List of Instruments, etc., from the *Dental Cosmos*; 56 pp; **NLM** (W26 W588).

1873　List of Changes in Price; 80 pp; **MAH** (C 617.6085 W); **UPSDM** (D 617.604.W 5812).

1874　Catalogo de Materials Para Dentistas, Meubles, Instrumentos; **FI** (617.6 W 583).

1874　Fabricante de dientes de porcelana y materiales para dentistas; 255 pp; **UPSDM** (D 617.604 W579sp).

1874　Catalogo completo con ilustraciones, dientes, instrumentos, materiales, equipos-combinado; 255 pp; **UPSDM** (D 617.604.W581sp).

1875　Catalogue, Dental Engine; 24 pp; **MAH** (C 617.6985 W).

1876　Catalogue, S. S. White Dental Engine and Equipment; 40 pp; **MAH** (C 617.6085).

1876　Catalogue of Dental Materials; 408 pp; **MAH** (C 617.6085 W); **BLEL; HDM; BDA; UPSDM** (D 617.604 w581); **UCLABM** (W 26 W 585c); **BLEL; HML** (with ms additions).

1876?　Booklet, Testimonials to the S. S. White Dental Engine and the S. S. White Engine Plugger; 16 pp; **MAH** (C 617.6085 W).

1876?　Catalogue, Lathes and Equipment; 16 pp; **MAH** (C 617.6085 W).

1877　Catalog of Dental Materials, Furniture, Instruments, etc.; 408 pp; **HML; BDA; ADA; UPSDM** (D 617.604. W581).

1877?　Catalogue, The Improved Wilkerson Dental Chair; 8 pp; **MAH** (C 617.6085).

1878　Appendix to Catalogue of Dental Materials, Furniture, Instruments, etc.; 72 pp; **MAH** (C 617.6085 W); **UPSDM** (D 617.604.W 581).

Dec. 1879?　The S. S. White Improved Pedal-Lever Dental Chair; 14 pp; **MAH.**

1879　Coffer-Dam Rubber and Appliances; 16 pp; **HML.**

Mar. 1880　Catalogue, The S. S. White Improved Dental Engine and Equipment; 28 pp; **MAH** (C 617.6085 W).

1880?　Catalogue, Dental Equipment; 16 pp; **MAH** (C 617.6085 W).

1880?　Brochure, Improved Pedal Lever Dental Chair; 15 pp; **MAH** (C 617.6085 W).

1882　Price List, Dental Engines and Equipment; 40 pp; **MAH** (C617.6085 W).

1882　Price List Dental Engines and Equipment; 32 pp; **HML.**

Aug. 1, 1883　Revised List of Cone-Socket Instruments; 36 pp; **HML.**

Dec. 1883　Catalogue, Liquefied Nitrous Oxide and Gas Apparatus; 12 pp; **MAH** (C 617.6085 W).

Sep. 1884　Dental Furniture; 40 pp; **MAH** (C 617.6085W).

Sep. 1884　Catalogue, Coffer-Dam Rubber and Appliances; 18 pp; **MAH** (C617.6085 W).

Sep. 1884　Catalogue, Dental Furniture; 40 pp; **MAH** (617.6085 W).

Nov. 1885　Catalogue, Impression Trays; 24 pp; **MAH** (C 617.6085 W).

Dec. 1885　Catalogue, Dental Engines and Equipments; 47 pp; **MAH** (C617.6085 W).

1885	Catalogue, Specialties for the Mouth; 20 pp; **MAH** (C617.6085 W).
1885?	Dental and Surgical Electric Illuminating and Cauterizing Apparatus, Batteries, etc.; 15 pp; **HML**.
Apr. 1886	Brochure, Liquefied Nitrous Oxide and Gas Apparatus; 18 pp; **MAH** (C 617.6085 W).
Apr. 1886	Lathes and Equipment for Office and Laboratory; 26 pp; **HML**.

767 & 769 Broadway, New York, New York.
1260 Broadway, New York, New York.
14 & 16 E. Madison St., Chicago.
16 Tremont St., Boston.

July 1886	Condensed Price List of Dental Goods; 62 pp; **HML**.
Aug. 1886	Coffer-Dam Rubber and Appliances; 21 pp; **MAH** (C 617.6085 W).
Nov. 1886	Cone-Socket Instruments; 28 pp; **MAH** (C 617.6085 W); **HML**.
1886	Catalogue Specialties; 20 pp; **MAH** (C 617.6085 W).
Jan. 1887	Catalogue Impression Trays and Other Articles for Use in Taking Impressions; 40 pp; **MAH** (C 617.6085 W).
Jan. 1887	Dental Furniture and Cases; 44 pp; **MAH** (C 617.6085 W).
Jan. 1887	Price List of Long (fixed) Handle Instruments; 80 pp; **MAH** (C 617.6085 W).
Mar. 1887	Electrical Apparatus for Dentists and Physicians; 36 pp; **MAH** (C 617.6085 W).
May 1887	Catalogue Dental Engines and Equipments; 54 pp; **MAH** (C 617.6085 W).
Jun. 1887	Catalogue Filling Materials and Appliances Pertaining Thereto; 28 pp; **MAH** (C 617.6085 W).
July 1887	Catalogue Liquefied Nitrous Oxide and Gas Apparatus; 16 pp; **MAH** (C 617.6085 W).
Aug. 1887	Catalogue of Gum Sectional Teeth; 75 pp; **MAH** (C 617.6085 W).
Aug. 1887	Catalogue Forceps; 70 pp; **MAH** (C 617.6085 W).
Aug. 1887	Catalogue Gum Sectional Teeth; 72 pp; **MAH** (C 617.6085 W).
Nov. 1887	Catalogue Lathes and Equipments; 28 pp; **MAH** (C 617.6085 W).
1887	Impression Trays and Other Articles for Use in Taking Impressions; 40 pp; **MAH** (C 617.6085 W).
1887	Catalogue Porcelain Teeth; **UPSDM** (D 617.604.w579).
Feb. 1888	Catalogue Cone-Socket Instruments; 28 pp; **MAH** (C 617.6085 W).
Apr. 1888	Catalogue Dental Engines and Equipments; 65 pp; **MAH** (C 617.6085 W).
Apr. 1888	Catalogue Coffer-Dam Rubber and Appliances; 20 pp; **MAH** (C 617.6085 W).
Feb. 1889	Revised Catalog Long (fixed) Handle and Cone-Socket Instruments; 68 pp; **HML**.
Mar. 1889	Catalogue Liquefied Nitrous Oxide; 20 pp; **MAH** (C 617.6085 W).
Mar. 1889	Catalogue Impression Trays and Other Articles for Use in Taking Impressions; 40 pp; **MAH** (C 617.6085 W).
May 1889	Catalogue Dental Furniture and Cases; 42 pp; **MAH** (C 617.6085 W).
Sep. 1889	Catalogue Dental Engines and Equipment; 72 pp; **MAH** (C 617.6085 W).
Sep. 1889	Catalogue of Porcelain Teeth; 158 pp; **MAH** (C 617.6085 W); **HML**.
Sep. 1889	Catalogue of Compressed Oxygen and Liquefied Nitrogen Monoxide; 10 pp; **MAH** (C 617.6085 W).
1889	Porcelain Teeth Index; 194 pp; **MAH**.
1889	Catalogue Porcelain Teeth; **UPSDM** (D 617. 604.w579).

1889	Price List Liquified Nitrogen Monoxide and Compressed Oxygen and Apparatus for Their Therapeutic Administration; 10 pp; **CPP; FI** (405/8).
Apr. 1890	Lathes and Equipments; 28 pp; **HML.**
Apr. 1890	Revised Catalog Cone-Socket and Long (fixed) Handle Instruments, 2nd ed.; 72 pp; **HML.**
May 1890	Catalogue Dental Furniture and Cases; 48 pp; **MAH** (C 617.6085 W).
Aug. 1890	Price List Dental Engines and Equipments; 76 pp; **HML.**
Aug. 1890	Impression Trays and Other Articles for Use in Taking Impressions; 40 pp; **MAH** (C 617.6085W); **HML.**
1890	Illustrations of the Forms and Arrangement of the Natural Teeth, Their Relations and the Movement of the Jaw in Occlusion; 100 pp; **UPSDM** (D 617.604 W581.2); **HML.**
Jan. 1891	A Revelation in Burs; 12 pp; **HML.**
Apr. 1891	Catalogue Dental Furniture and Cases; 45 pp; **MAH** (C 617.6085 W).
July 1891	Catalogue Impression Trays and Other Articles for Use in Taking Impressions; 38 pp; **MAH** (C 617.6085 W).
Nov. 1891	Price List Dental Engines and Equipments; 80 pp; **HML.**
1891	An Eventful Year in Dentistry; 6 pp; **HML.**
Dec. 1892	Illustrated Catalogue of Dental Engines and Equipment; 84 pp; **MAH** (C 617.6085 W); **HML.**
Feb. 1893	Dental Forceps; 73 pp; **MAH** (C 617.6085 W).
Mar. 1893	Catalogue, Revised, Cone-socket and Long (fixed) Handle Instruments; 76 pp; **MAH** (C 617.6085 W).
May 1893	Catalogue Lathes and Equipments; 30 pp; **MAH** (C 617.6085 W).
Aug. 1893	Catalogue, Liquefied Nitrous Oxide; 16 pp; **MAH** (C 617.6085 W).
1893	Dentists' Supplies, Porcelain Teeth; notebook advertisement; **HML.**
Jan. 1894	Catalogue Dental Furniture and Cases; 44 pp; **MAH** (C 617.6085 W).
Apr. 1894	Revised Catalog Cone-Socket and Long Handle (fixed) Instruments; 76 pp; **HML.**
May 1894	Catalogue, Lathe and Equipments; 28 pp; **MAH** (C 617.6085 W); **HML.**
Oct. 1894	Brochure, Nitrous Oxide, liquefied; 16 pp; **MAH** (C 617.6085 W).
Oct. 1894	Catalogue of Porcelain Teeth; 204 pp; **MAH** (C 617.6085 W).
Oct. 1894	Catalogue Coffer-Dam Rubber and Appliances; 42 pp; **MAH** (C 617.6085 W).
Oct. 1894	Catalogue, The Hollingsworth System for Crown-and Bridge-Work, including the Method of Contouring Crowns; 17 pp; **MAH** (C 617.6085 W).
Nov. 1894	Catalogue, Dental Furniture and Cases; 48 pp; **MAH** (C 617.6085 W).
1894	Catalogues, Dental Materials, Furniture, Instruments, etc., 14 vols: 1862, 1917, 1921–25, 1935, 1937, 1939, 1943, unbound; **UPSDM** (D 617.604 W581).
1894	Instruments, Appliances, etc., for Crown-and Bridge-Work; 64 pp; **ADA** (D 881 W 58i).
1894	Catalogue, Porcelain Teeth; **UPSDM** (D 617.604.W579).
1894?	Catalogue, Porcelain Teeth; 204 pp; **UPSDM** (D 617.604. W 579).
May 1895	Catalogue, Lathes and Equipment; 24 pp; **MAH** (C 617.6085 W).
Jun. 1895	Illustrated Catalog, Dental Engines and Equipments; 104 pp; **HML.**
July 1895	Partz Batteries and Accessories; 20 pp; **HML.**
July 1895	Catalogue, Vulcanizers, Celluloid Presses, and Accessories; 42 pp; **MAH** (C 617.6085 W).
July 1895	Revised Catalog Cone-Socket and Long (fixed) Handle Instruments; 76 pp; **HML.**

1895	Coffer Dam Rubber (no cover); 44 pp; **HML**.
Jan. 1896	Dental Furniture and Cases; 58 pp; **HML**.
Mar. 1896	Illustrated Catalog Dental Engines and Equipments; 88 pp; **HML; FI** (317/1).
Apr. 1896	Catalogue, Lathe and Equipments; 32 pp; **MAH** (C 617.6085 W).
Sep. 1896	Liquefied Nitrous Oxide; 20 pp; **HML**.
Sep. 1896	Catalogue, Electrical Dental Outfits and Accessories; 24 pp; **MAH** (C 617.6085 W).
1896	Catalogue, Filling Materials; 37 pp; **MAH** (C 617.6085 W).
Jan. 1897	Coffer-Dam Rubber and Appliances-Separating & Wedging Devices Matrices-Regulating Apparatus; 44 pp; **HML**.
Feb. 1897	Files and Carriers, Saws and Saw Frames, Operative and Mechanical; 16 pp; **HML**.
Feb. 1897	Miscellaneous; 48 pp; **HML**.
Apr. 1897	Cone-Socket and Long (fixed) Handle Instruments; 84 pp; **HML**.
Jun. 1897	Dental Engines and Equipments; 92 pp; **UCSF**.
July 1897	Catalogue Vulcanizers, Celluloid Presses and Accessories; 47 pp; **MAH** (C 617.6085 W).
July 1897	Instruments, Appliances, etc., for Crown-and Bridge-Work; 112 pp; **HML**.
Aug. 1897	Catalogue Liquefied Nitrous Oxide; 20 pp; **MAH** (C 617.6085 W).
Nov. 1897	Catalogue Lathes and Equipment; pp 5-28; **MAH** (C 617.6085 W).
Apr. 1898	S. S. White's Die-Sinker's Engine; 12 pp; **HML**.
May 1898	Catalogue, Dental Furniture and Cases; 56 pp; **MAH** (C 617.6085 W).
Jun. 1898	Catalogue, Rubber Dam and Appliances, Separating and Wedging Devices, Regulating Apparatus; 40 pp; **MAH** (C 617.6085 W).
Aug. 1898	Dental Engines and Equipment; 100 pp; **UCSF**.
Aug. 1898	Files and Carriers, Saws and Saw Frames, Polishing Materials; 28 pp; **HML**.
Aug. 1898	Catalogue, Cone-Socket and Long (fixed) Handle Instruments; 95 pp; **MAH** (C 617.6085 W).
Nov. 1898	Catalogue, Lathes and Vulcanizers; 80 pp; **MAH** (C 617.6085 W).
1898	Confidential Trade Price List; **UPSDM** (D 617.604.W585).
Mar. 1899	Instruments, Appliances, etc., for Crown-and Bridge-Work; 144 pp; **HML**.
May 1899	Dental Engines and Equipments; 100 pp; **HML**.
Aug. 1899	Catalogue, Liquefied Nitrous Oxide and Compressed Oxygen; 18 pp; **MAH** (C 617.6085 W).
Sep. 1899	Catalogue, Porcelain Teeth; 156 pp; **MAH** (C 617.6085 W).
Oct. 1899	Catalogue, Cataphoresis and Cataphoric Appliances; 30 pp; **MAH** (C 617.6085 W).
1899	Some New Things of 1899; 64 pp; **ADA** (D 881 W58s).
1899	Partz Batteries and Accessories; 20 pp; **HML**.
1900	Advertising Circulars; 21 pp; **MAH** (C 617.6085 W).
Feb. 1900	Catalogue Dental Office Furniture; 64 pp; **MAH** (C 617.6085 W); **HML**.
Apr. 1900	Catalogue Nitrous Oxide, liquefied; 18 pp; **MAH** (C 617.6085 W); **HML**.
Apr. 1900	Catalogue, Miscellaneous; 52 pp; **MAH** (C 617.6085 W).
Apr. 1900	Rubber Dams & Appliances, Regulating Apparatus, Separating and Wedging Devices; 48 pp; **HML**.
Oct. 1900	Catalogue of Porcelain Teeth; 152 pp; **MAH** (C617.6085 W); **UPSDM**

(D 617.604. W579).

1900 Catalogue, Filling Materials; 52 pp; **MAH** (C 617.6085 W); **HML.**

ca 1900 S. S. W., Successor to Jones and White Dentists' Superior Gold, Tin Foil; 3 leaved books, no materials; **HML.**

Mar. 1901 Instruments, Appliances, etc., for Crown-and Bridge-Work; 148 pp; **HML.**

May 1901 Catalogue, Dental Office Furniture; 80 pp; **MAH** (C 617.6085 W); **HML.**

Jan. 1902 Catalog of Books Dental and Medical; 50 pp; **HML.**

Apr. 1902 Files and Carriers, Saws and Saw Frames, Polishing Materials; 24 pp; **HML.**

May 1902 Our Drug Store, Pharmaceutical and Laboratory Preparations for Dental Purposes; **CDMC.**

Jun. 1902 Operative Instruments Long-Handle and Cone-Socket Matrices, etc.; 96 pp; **HML; CDMC.**

July 1902 The S. S. W. no. 3 Engine Wall Bracket Outfit; 4 pp; **HML.**

Nov. 1902 Instruments, Appliances, etc., for Crown-and Bridge-Work; 156 pp; **HML.**

Nov. 1902 Catalogue, Dental Office Furniture; 80 pp; **MAH** (C 617.6085 W); **HML; CDMC.**

Dec. 1902 Lathes and Their Equipment for the Dental Laboratory; 24 pp; **HML.**

1902 Filling Materials; 44 pp; **HML; CDMC.**

1902 Catalogue Porcelain Teeth; 187 pp; **UPSDM** (D 617.604.W579); **HML.**

ca 1902 Directions for Using and Repairing Hammond Electric Furnaces nos. 3 & 4; 10 pp; **HML.**

Jun. 1903 Catalogue, Dental Engines and Equipments; 80 pp; **MAH** (C 617.6085 W); **HML.**

Sep. 1903 Condensed Price List; 106 pp; **HML.**

1903 Catalogue, Porcelain Teeth; 194 pp; **NYAM; MF/MAH.**

1903 The Selection and Adaptation of Porcelain Teeth with a Catalogue of Porcelain; 174 pp; **UPSDM** (D 617.604.W 579); **HML.**

ca 1903 Directions for Using and Repairing Hammond Electric Furnaces nos. 3 & 4; 10 pp; **HML.**

Feb. 1904 Files, Saws and Saw Frames, Polishing Materials; 12 pp; **HML.**

Mar. 1904 Rubber Dam and Appliances; 36 pp; **HML.**

Apr. 1904 The Hammond Electric Furnace nos. 1-4; 8 pp; **HML.**

Apr. 1904 Filling Materials, Gold, Alloys, Guta-Percha, Stoppings, Cements, Root Fillings, etc.; 28 pp; **HML.**

Apr. 1904 Confidential Trade Price List, revised; **UPSDM** (D 617.604.W 585).

1904 Catalogue, The Knapp Teeth Regulating Devices; 17 pp; **NYAM; MF/MAH.**

Jun. 1904 Illustrated Catalogue of Extracting, Operating and Mechanical Forceps; 100 pp; **HML.**

Jun. 1904 Miscellaneous, Lamps and Gas Burners, Mallets and Hammers, Mouth-Mirrors, Spatulas, Syringes, Mortars, Mixing Tablets, etc.; 36 pp; **HML.**

July 1904 Operative Instruments Long Handle and Cone-Socket Matrices, etc.; 72 pp; **HML.**

July 1904 Catalogue, Cone-Socket and Fixed (long-handle) Instruments; 72 pp; **MAH** (C 617.6085 W).

Aug. 1904 Foot-Controlled Electric Dental Engines; 16 pp; **HML.**

Sep. 1904 Catalogue of Individual Porcelain Work; 16 pp; **HML.**

Dec. 1904 Instruments, Appliances, etc. for Crown-Bridge & Palte-Work; 100 pp; **HML.**

Aug. 1904 Historical Exhibit of Dental Engines Hand-Pieces and Mallets; 10 pp; **HML.**

Mar. 1905 Die-Sinker's Engine and Machinist's Outfit for Countershaft and Electric Motor; 24 pp; **HML.**

Mar. 1905 Catalogue, Dental Office Furniture; 60 pp; **HML.**

May 1905 Catalogue, Dental Engines, Handpieces, Angle Appliances, Revelation Burs, Engine Mallets, etc.; 80 pp; **MAH** (C 617.6085 W); **NYAM; MF/MAH; HML.**

Jun. 1905 Vulcanizers and Lathes with Their Appurtenances; 40 pp; **HML; CDMC.**

1905 Catalogue of Porcelain Teeth; 157 pp; **MAH** (C 617.6085 W).

1905 Catalogue, Dental Engines, Handpieces, Angle Appliances, Revelation Burs, Engine Mallets, etc.; 78 pp; **ADA** (D 881 W 58d).

ca 1905 Directions for Cleaning, Oiling and Adjusting the S. S. White Automatic Mallet; 4 pp; **HML.**

Mar. 1906 Operative Instruments Long Handle and Cone-Socket and Automatic Matrices, etc.; 76 pp; **HML.**

Mar. 1906 Rubber Dams and Appliances; 36 pp.

Jun. 1906 Catalogue, The Precious Metals in Dentistry, no. 662; 24 pp; **MAH** (C 617.6085W); **NYAM; MF/MAH; HML.**

July 1906 Catalogue Extracting, Operating & Mechanical Forceps; 102 pp; **NYAM; MF/MAH.**

Dec. 1906 Dental Office Furniture; 44 pp, pages missing; **HML.**

Jun. 1907 Miscellaneous; 36 pp; **HML.**

July 1907 Filling Materials; 24 pp; **HML.**

Aug. 1907 Catalogue, Individual Porcelain Work, A Catalogue of Materials & Appliances for the Making of Porcelain Inlays, Crowns and Bridges; 28 pp; **MAH** (C 617.6085 W); **NYAM; MF/MAH; HML.**

Oct. 1907 Catalogue, Porcelain Teeth; 198 pp; **NYAM; MF/MAH.**

1907 Booklet E, Dental Rubbers; 19 pp; **MAH** (C 617.6085 W).

Feb. 1908 Catalogue, Dental Engines, Handpieces, Angle Appliances, Revelation Burs, Engine Mallets, etc.; 72 pp; **HML.**

Jun. 1908 Catalogue, Dental Operative Instruments; 68 pp; **NYAM; MF/MAH.**

Aug. 1908 Catalogue, Vulcanizers and Lathes with Their Appurtenances; 36 pp; **NYAM; MF/MAH.**

37 Lindenstrasse, Berlin S W, Germany.

Dec. 1908 Brochure, Electric Furnace A, no. 878; 12 pp; **NYAM; MF/MAH.**

Mar. 1909 Catalogue of Extracting, Operating, and Mechanical Forceps, Lancets, Root Extractors, Scissor, Shears, Pliers, etc.; 88 pp; **MAH** (C 617.6085 W).

Jun. 1909 Catalogue Liquefied Nitrous Oxide and Compressed Oxygen and Apparatus for Their Administration; 16 pp; **MAH** (C 617.96085 W); **HML.**

July 1909 Catalog of the World's Premium Porcelain Teeth; 199 pp; **MAH** (C 617.6085 W).

Aug. 1909 Instruments, Appliances, etc., for Crown-Bridge-and Metal-Work; 94 pp; **MAH** (C 617.6085 W); **HML.**

Sep. 1909 Dental Engines & Equipments; 68 pp, Spanish; **HML.**

1909 Catalogue, Porcelain Teeth; 199 pp; **NYAM; MF/MAH.**

Oct. 1909 Kat-Abteilung X Extraktions-Zangen; 94 pp; **HML.**

Feb. 1910	Pamphlet B, Dental Engines, Handpieces, Angle Appliances, Revelation Burs, Engine Mallet, etc.; 64 pp; **MAH** (C 617.6085 W); **HML**.
Mar. 1910	Catalogue, Filling Materials, Gold Alloys, Gutta-Percha Stoppings, Porcelains, Cements, Root Fillings, etc.; 24 pp; **MAH** (C 617.6085 W).
Mar. 1910	Catalogue, Miscellaneous; 63 pp; **MAH** (C 617.6085W).
Mar. 1910	Catalogue, Filling Materials; 24 pp; **NYAM; MF/MAH**.
Mar. 1910	Catalogue, Miscellaneous, no. 6; 63 pp; **NYAM; MF/MAH**.
Apr. 1910	El Horno Electrico A; 20 pp; **HML**.
Jun. 1910	Catalogue, Dental Operative Instruments, no. 1; 73 pp; **NYAM; MF/ MAH**.
Jun. 1910	Zahnaerztliche Instrumente fuer das Operationszimmer Kat-Abteil II; 3 Ausgabe; 68 pp; **HML**.
Jun. 1910	Vulkanisier-Apparate und Apparate und Materialien fuer die Zahntechnische Werkstett; 36 pp, 16 pp insert; **HML**.
July 1910	Fluessiges Stuckstoff oxydal komprimierter Sauerstoff Kat-Abt. XIII; 16 pp; **HML**.
Aug. 1910	Spezialitaten fuer den Mund: Zahnpulver, Zahnbuersten, Zahnseife, Zahnpaste, Zahnseide, Mundwasser; 16 pp; **HML**.
Aug. 1910	Pamphlet E, S. S. White Dental Office Furniture; 52 pp; **MAH** (C 617.6085 W); **HML**.
Sep. 1910	Instrumentos Dentales para Trabajos de Operatoria; 72 pp; **HML**.
Sep. 1910	Catalogue, Taking Impressions of the Mouth, no. L; 9th ed.; 76 pp; **NYAM; MF/MAH; MAH** (C 617.6085 W).
Dec. 1910	Catalogue S. S. White's elektrische Ofen; 48 pp; **MAH** (C 617.6085 W).
1910	Pamphlet F, Dental Operative Instruments; 73 pp; **MAH** (C 617.6085 W).
1910	Confidential Trade Price List; **UPSDM** (D 617.604.W585).
1910	Instruments, Accessories, etc. para Trabajos de Corona, Pirate y Metal; 95 pp; **HML**.
ca 1910	What to Look for in Equipment; 4 pp; **HML**.
Apr. 1911	Catalogue, Vulcanizers & Lathes with Their Appurtenances, no. N; 37 pp; **NYAM; MF/MAH**.
July 1911	Catalogue, Extracting Operating & Mechanical Forceps; 90 pp; **NYAM; MF/MAH**.
July 1911	Catalogue, Absorbents & Accessories Wedging & Separating Devices Orthopedic Appliances, no. K; 56 pp; **NYAM; MF/MAH**.
July 1911	Rubber Dam & Appliances, Absorbents and Accessories, Wedging and Separating Devices, Orthodontic Appliances, Pamphlet K; 56 pp; **HML; CDMC**.
July 1911	Zahnaerztliche Einrichtungs-Gegenstaende fuer das Operationszimmer, Liste B; 56 pp; **HML**.
Sep. 1911	Liquified Nitrous Oxide and Compressed Oxygen & Apparatus for Their Administration, Pamphlet H; 16 pp; **HML**.
Sep. 1911	Furniture for the Dental Office, Pamphlet E; 53 pp; **HML**.
Sep. 1911	Brochure, Liquefied Nitrous Oxide, no. H, 16 pp; **NYAM; MF/MAH**.
Oct. 1911	Catalogue, Instruments, Appliances, etc., Crown, Bridge & Metal Work, no. A; 98 pp; **NYAM; MF/MAH; HML**.
Oct. 1911	Zahnaerztliche Bohrmaschinen Handstuecke Winkelstuecke, Bohrmaschinen-Hammer, Revelation Bohrer, Liste C; 64 pp; **HML**.
1911	Catalogue, Porcelain Teeth; 215 pp; **NYAM; MF/MAH**.
1911–12	Collection of Illustrated Catalogues; **FI** (617.6 W 583).
1911?	Brochure, Electric Dental Apparatus; 16 pp; **MAH** (C 617.6085 W).

Jan. 1912	Catalogue, Practical Dental Helps of Genuine S. S. White Quality, no. 13; 24 pp; **NYAM; MF/MAH.**
Jan. 1912	Catalogue, Dental Engines, Pamphlet B; 65 pp; **NYAM; MF/MAH; HML.**
Feb. 1912	Dental Operative Instruments, Long Handle, Cone-Socket and Automatic, Pamphlet F; 75 pp; **HML.**
Aɼ '912	Filling Materials, Pamphlet C; 32 pp; **HML.**
Ju. '2	Impression Trays, Articulators and Accessories, Pamphlet L; 48 pp; **HML.**
Jun. 1912	Electric Furnaces for Porcelain Work, Pamphlet O; 32 pp; **HML.**
July 1912	Catalogue, Practical Dental Helps of Genuine Quality, no. 15; 24 pp; **NYAM; MF/MAH.**
Dec. 1912	Maquinas Dentales; 70 pp; **HML.**
Dec. 1912	Impression Trays, Pamphlet LN; 88 pp; **HML.**
1912	Electric Dental Apparatus; 16 pp; **HML.**
Feb. 1913	Impression Trays; 88 pp, Spanish, no cover; **HML.**
Apr. 1913	Catalogue, S. S. White Dental Office Furniture, no. E; 60 pp; **MAH** (C 617.6085 W).
Apr. 1913	Illustrated Catalogue Extracting, Operating and Mechanical Forceps, Lancets, Root Extractors, Scissors, Shears, Pliers, etc.; 94 pp; **MAH** (C 617.6085 W); **HML.**
Jun. 1913	Dental Operative Instruments, Long Handle, Cone-Socket and Automatic Matrices, etc., Pamphlet F; 80 pp; **HML.**
Jun. 1913	The S. S. White Dental Engines, Pamphlet; 53 pp; **HML.**
Jun. 1913	Filling Materials, Pamphlet C; 32 pp; **HML.**
July 1913	Instruments, Appliances, etc., for Crown-, Bridge-, and Metal-Work, Pamphlet A; 128 pp; **HML.**
July 1913	Catalogue Miscellaneous, no. G; 64 pp; **NYAM; MF/MAH.**
Oct. 1913	Mouth and Toilet Preparations; 14 pp; **HML.**
Dec. 1913	Miscellanea; 60 pp; **HML.**
1913	Electric Dental Apparatus; 16 pp; **HML.**
1913	Catalogo S-A Instumentos, Accessorios, etc., para Trabajos de Corona, Puente y Metal; 103 pp; **HML.**
Jan. 1914	Catalogue, Practical Dental Helps of Genuine Quality, no. 21; 24 pp; **NYAM; MF/MAH.**
Apr. 1914	Dental Operative Instruments, Long-Handle, Cone-Socket and Automatic Matrices, etc., Pamphlet F; 60 pp; **HML.**
Apr. 1914	Catalogue, Dental Operative Instruments, no. F; 59 pp; **MAH** (C 617.6085 W); **NYAM; MF/MAH; UBML** (WU 26W582).
May 1914	Pamphlet LN, Extracting, Operating, Mechanical Forceps, no. D; 44 pp; **NYAM; MF/MAH.**
May 1914	Catalogue, Impression Trays, Articulators, Spatulas, Pamphlet LN; 65 pp; **NYAM; MF/MAH; UBML** (WU 26 W 582); **HML.**
May 1914	Furniture for the Dental Office, Pamphlet E; 59 pp; **UBML** (WU 26W582); **HML.**
Aug. 1914	Catalogue Rubber Dam and Appliances, Absorbents and Accessories, Wedging and Separating Devices, Orthodontic Appliances; 48 pp; **MAH** (C 617.6085 W); **NYAM; MF/MAH.**
Aug. 1914	Rubber Dam and Appliances, Pamphlet K; 48 pp; **UBML** (WU 26 W582); **HML.**
Dec. 1914	Electric Dental Engines and Lathes, Catalog P; **UBML** (WU 26W582).
ca 1914	Catalog, Hand Book of First Aid, Suggestions for First Aid to the Injured in Accidents and Emergencies, How to Care for the Sick and Prevent

Spread of Disease, Household & Toilet Hints; 4th ed., revised; **CTY/B** (Uai J636).

1914? Confidential Price List Mouth and Toilet Preparations; 4 pp; **HML.**

1914 The S. S. W. Nitrous Oxide and Oxygen Apparatus no. 3, for the Induction and Control of Non-Asphysical Anesthesia in Dentistry and Surgery; 20 pp; **HML.**

Jan. 1915 Catalogue Miscellaneous Goods, no. G; 96 pp; **NYAM; MF/MAH; MAH** (C 617.6085 W); **UBML** (WU 26W582); **HML.**

Mar. 1915 Catalogue Dental Engines and Handpieces, Angle Appliances, Revelation Burs, Engine Mallets, etc., no. B; 56 pp; **MAH** (C 617.6085 W); **UBML** (WU 26W582).

Apr. 1915 Extracting and Operating Forceps, Lancets, Root Extractors, Scissors, Shears, Pliers, etc., Catalog D; 40 pp; **UBML** (WU 26W582); **HML.**

Sep. 1915 Catalog R, Nitrous Oxide & Oxygen Equipments; 38 pp; **MAH; HML.**

1915 Catalogue, World's Premium Porcelain Teeth; 100 pp; **MAH** (C 617.6085 W); **HML.**

1915 Catalog, Dental Materials, Furniture, Instruments, etc.; **UPSDM** (D 617.604.W 581).

1915 The Forsyth Limit; 1 pp; **HML.**

1915 Electrical and Compressed Air Instruments of the S. S. White Equipment Unit; 30 pp; **HML.**

1915 Physicians Descriptive Catalog, no. 21; 116 pp; **NLM** (W 26 J66d).

1915 The S. S. W. Equipment Combinations, The New Idea in Dental Equipment for Dental Offices, Colleges and Infirmaries; 51 pp; **HML.**

1915 Modern Dental Equipment; 16 pp; **HML.**

ca 1915 Dental Cements, The Chemistry and Physics of Oxyphosphates; 40 pp; **HML.**

Apr. 1916 Catalogue, Electric Engines and Lathes; 44 pp; **MAH** (C 617.6085 W); **HML.**

Oct. 1916 Catalogue D, Forceps, Root Elevators, Scissors, Shears, Pliers, etc.; 40 pp; **MAH** (C 617.6085 W); **HML.**

Oct. 1916 Catalogue E, Modern Equipment for the Dental Office, College and Infirmary; 71 pp; **MAH** (C 617.6085 W); **HML.**

Oct. 1916 Catalogue F, Dental Operative Instruments; 63 pp; **MAH** (C 617.6085 W); **HML.**

211-17 South 12th St., Philadelphia, Pennsylvania.

1916 Operative Instruments, Accessories, Appliances and Materials, Catalog F; 152 pp; **HML.**

Mar. 1917 Catalogue R, Dental and Surgical Nitrous-Oxide-and-Oxygen Apparatus nos. 3 & 4; 34 pp; **MAH** (C 617.96085 W); **HML.**

1917 The White Book Catalogue New Dental Products; 24 pp; **NYAM; MF/ MAH.**

1917 Catalog, Dental Materials, Furniture, Instruments, etc.; **UPSDM** (D 617.604.W 581).

1917 Brochure, Planning the Modern Dental Office; 20 pp; **MAH** (C 617.6085 W).

1917 Dental Engines and Appliances; 53 pp; **HML; LLU** (W 26 W588).

1917? Leaflet, S. S. White Pointed Pin Facings; 2 pp; **MAH** (C 617.6085 W).

ca 1917 S. S. W. Dental Rubbers; 19 pp; **HML.**

May 1918 Filling Materials Operating Accessories, Catalog G; 70 pp; **HML.**

Jun. 1918 Pamphlet, Lyon Adjustable Operating Stool; 6 pp foldout; **MAH** (C 617.6085 W).

July 1918	Prosthetic Appliances, Tools and Materials Catalog L; 103 pp; **HML.**
1918	Catalog, Filling Materials, Operating Accessories; 70 pp; **MAH** (C 617. 6085 W).
1918	Condensed Price List; 98 pp; **HML.**
1919	Catalogue E, Dental Chairs, Engines, Spittoons, Equipment Stands, Vulcanizers, Electric Furnaces, and Anesthesia Apparatus; 155 pp; **MAH.**
1919	S. S. White Equipment for the Dental and Oral Surgeon, Public or Private Infirmary, College, Clinic, Hospital and Specialist, Catalog G; **UPSDM** (D 617.604. W581).
Oct. 1920	Catalog, Aseptic Cotton Preparations and Appliances for Dentists; 9 pp, 4 pp price list; **NYAM; MF/MAH.**
Dec. 1920	Price List for Catalogue E; 12 pp; **NYAM; MF/MAH.**
1920	The Modern Way to Vulcanize; 6 pp; **HML.**
1920	S. S. W. Pointed-Pin Facings and Detached Post Crowns for Crown and Bridge Work; Catalog M, Section 2; 40 pp; **HML.**
1920	The S. S. W. Impression-Tray Compound after Method of Dr. Rupert S. Hall; 46 pp, Span., Fr.; **HML.**
ca 1920	S. S. W. Equipment Stand no. 3 with the Reid Distributing Unit; 12 pp, 4 pp price list; **HML.**
ca 1920	S. S. W. Revelation Handpieces; 1 pp; **HML.**
ca 1920	Samples of S. S. W. Paper Disks, Perfection Cloth Disks, Perfection Polishing Strips; 4 pp; **HML.**
ca 1920	Vulolax Locked in Vulcanite; 28 pp; **HML.**
ca 1920	Directions for the Care of Doist Handpiece no. 4; 4 pp, English, Spanish, and French; **HML.**
ca 1920	Kryptex; 36 pp; **HML.**
ca 1920	Higher Standards in Dental Rubbers; 16 pp; **HML.**
1921	Flexible Shaft Driven Tools, Catalog T; 30 pp; Price list dated Sep. 1 1920; 6 pp; **HML.**
1921	Catalogue F, Operative Instruments, Appliances, Materials & Accessories; 152 pp; **MAH** (C 617.6085 W); **NYAM; MF/MAH; HML.**
1921	Catalogo completo con illustraciones; 582 pp; **UPSDM** (D 617.604.W 581 sp).
1921	Catalogue R, Dental and Surgical Nitrous-Oxide-and Oxygen Equipment; 36 pp; **MAH** (C 617. 96085 W); **UBML** (WU 26W582); **HML.**
1921	Price List; 7 pp; **MAH** (C 617.96085W); **HML.**
ca 1921	The Precision Dental Shell Machine no. 2; 5 pp; **HML.**
1922	Catalogue, Operative Instruments, Appliances, Materials & Accessories, Catalog F; 176 pp; **NYAM; MF/MAH; MAH** (C 617.6085 W); **CTY/ B** (Uai W 5828); **HML.**
1922	S. S. W. Natural Porcelain Teeth; 38 pp; **HML.**
Jan. 1923	Catalog, Dental and Surgical Nitrous-Oxide-and Oxygen Equipment, Catalog R; 40 pp; **MAH** (C 617.96085 W), Price List, Aug 1924; **HML.**
Mar. 1923	S. S. W. Electric Pyrometer Furnace B; 10 pp; **HML.**
1923	Modern Dental Equipment; 37 pp; **HML.**
1923	The White Book, Catalogue New Dental Products; 38 pp; **NYAM; MF/MAH.**
1923	Catalogue M, Pointed-Pin Facings and Detached Post Crowns for Crown and Bridge Work; 42 pp; **MAH** (C 617.6085 W).
1923?	S. S. W. Corona Teeth for Vulcanite Work; 11 pp; **HML.**

1923?	Catalogue, Natural Porcelain Teeth; 41 pp; **MAH** (C 617.6085 W).
ca 1923	The Stone Age in Dentistry; 41 pp; **HML.**
May 1924	Prosthetic Appliances Tools and Materials, Catalog L; 100 pp; **MAH** (C 617.6085 W).
July 1924	Prosthetic Appliances, Tools and Materials; 18 pp; **MAH.**
Oct. 1924	Catalog G, Orthodontic Appliances and Accessories; 67 pp; **MAH** (C 617.6085 W).
1924	Condensed Catalog of Dental Supplies; 260 pp; **MAH** (C 617.6085 W).
1924	Catalog F, Operative Instruments, Appliances, Materials and Accessories; 167 pp; **MAH** (C 617.6085 W).
1924	Pamphlet, Wadsworth Universal Articulator; 58 pp; **MAH** (C 617.6085 W).
1924	Prosthetic Appliances, Tools and Materials, Catalog L; 100 pp; **HML.**
Oct. 1924	Orthodontic Appliances & Accessories, Catalog G; 67 pp; **HML.**
1924	Physicians Descriptive Catalog, no. 22; 128 pp; **NLM** (W26 J66d).
1924	S. S. W. Precious Metals for Dentistry; 4 pp; **HML.**
1924	S. S. W. Detached Post Crown Assortments; 3 pp; **HML.**
1924	Utility Combined with Economy Assortment A; 2 pp; **HML.**
1924	Two Essentials for Perfect Amalgam Fillings; 4 pp; **HML.**
1924?	S. S. W. Pointed Pin Facings and Detached-Post Crowns, Catalog M, Section 2; 42 pp; **HML.**
July 1925	Orthodontic Appliances and Accessories; 67 pp; **HML.**
1925	Catalogue F, Operative Instruments, Appliances, Materials and Accessories; 167 pp; **MAH** (C 617.6085 W); **HML.**
1925	Johnson's Standard First Aid Manual, Fred B. Kilmer, Ed., 9th rev. ed.; 144 pp, index; **UTP.**
Nov. 1926	S. S. W. Natural Porcelain Teeth; 41 pp; **HML.**
1926	S. S. W. Precious Metals for Dentistry Price List; 4 pp; **HML.**
ca 1926	Catalogue, The Stone Age in Dentistry; 41 pp; **MAH** (C 617.6085 W).
1926	S. S. White Filling Porcelain; 4th ed.; 79 pp; **MAH** (C 617.6085 W).
Jan. 1927	Operative Instruments, Appliances, Materials and Accessories; 26 pp; **MAH.**
1927	S. S. W. Flexible Shafts for Efficient Transmission of Power around Curves and Other Obstacles, Handbook for Engineers; 33 pp; **HML.**
1927	Catalogue, Wadsworth Universal Articulator, patented; 92 pp; **MAH** (C 617.6085 W).
1927	Catalog of Dental Supplies; 292 pp; **MAH** (C 617.6085 W); **NYAM; MF/MAH.**
1927?	Brochure, Appliances and Materials for the Wadsworth Technique; 28 pp; **MAH** (C 617.6085 W).
1927?	Brochure no. 2460B, Appliances and Materials for the Wadsworth Techniques; 28 pp; **MAH** (C 617.6085 W).
1927?	Brochure, Porcelain and Accessories for Dental Ceramics; 32 pp; **MAH** (C 617.6085 W).
1927	Catalogue G, Orthodontic Appliances and Accessories; 66 pp; **MAH.**
ca 1927	Directions for Using the S. S. White Nitrous Oxide and Oxygen Apparatus; 16 pp; **HML.**
1929	Catalog of Dental Supplies; 291 pp; **MAH** (C 617.6085 W); **UPSDM** (D 617.604.W 581).
1929	Flexible Shaft Handbook; 119 pp; **UPSDM** (D 617.604.W 588).
ca 1929	Directions for Setting Up and Operating the S. S. White Spiral Flush Spittoon, no. 7; 7 pp; **HML.**

ca 1930   S. S. W. Laboratory Lathes; 4 pp; **HML.**

ca 1930   Kryptex K, Germicidal K, Model K; 46 pp; **HML.**

ca 1930   S. S. W. Equipment Unit no. 6, How to Use It and Other Important Information, Combinations nos. 60 & 61; 14 pp; **HML.**

1931   S. S. W. Equipment for the Modern Dental Operating Room; 31 pp; **HML.**

1934   Dealer's Condensed Price List; 240 pp; **HML.**

1935   Nuggets, S. S. W. Gold Casting Alloys Systemized Simplified; 23 pp; **HML.**

ca 1935   Sorgfaeltige Auswahl, richtiger Gebrauch und Festhalten am Besten ist guter und nuetzlicher Rat; 16 pp foldout; **HML.**

ca 1935   S. S. W. Low Type Air Compressor; 4 pp; **HML.**

ca 1935   S. S. W. Fusing Porcelains, Stains, Accessories for Dental Ceramics; 40 pp; **HML.**

ca 1935   S. S. W. Carborundum Disk-Points Wheels; 16 pp foldout; **HML.**

ca 1935   S. S. W. Filling Porcelain Improved; folder with two inserts; **HML.**

1935?   S. S. W. Electric Pyrometer Furnace no. 3; 9 pp; **HML.**

1935?   Character in Porcelain Teeth; 37 pp; **HML.**

1938   S. S. W. Flexible Shafts for Remote Controls, English Bulletin no. 38; 27 pp; **HML.**

n.d.   S. S. White Filling Porcelain; 80 pp; **UPSDM** (D 617.604.W 581.3).

n.d.   Catalogue Lathes and Equipments; 17 pp; **MAH** (C 617.6085 W).

n.d.   Brochure Laboratory Lathe; 3 pp; **MAH** (C 617.6085 W).

n.d.   Spiral Flush Spittoon, no. 7; 3 pp; **MAH** (C 617.6085 W).

n.d.   Leaflet, S. S. White Electric Engine; 2 pp; **MAH** (C 617.6085 W).

n.d.   Leaflet, S. S. White Child's Chair; 3 pp; **MAH** (C 617.6085 W).

n.d.   Leaflet, S. S. White Spray Bottle Heater; 3 pp; **MAH** (C 617.6085 W).

n.d.   Booklet, Directions for the Care of Doriot Handpiece no. 3; 15 pp; **MAH** (C 617.6085 W).

n.d.   Brochure, Impression-Tray Compound; 23 pp; **MAH** (C 617.6085 W).

n.d.   Brochure, Dental Cements; 40 pp; **MAH** (C 617.6085 W).

n.d.   Brochure, Equipment Stand no. 3; 16 pp; **MAH** (C 617.6085 W).

n.d.   Brochure, Equipment a Matter of Essential Economy; 8 pp; **MAH** (C 617.6085 W).

ca 1896   Catalogue of Books published by S. S. White; 40 pp; **MAH** (C 617.6085 W).

n.d.   Brochure, Instructions for Using the S. S. White N2O and O Apparatus; 16 pp; **MAH** (C 617.96085 W).

n.d.   Catalog, Sterilized Absorbant Preparations for Dentists; 10 pp; **NYAM; MF/MAH.**

n.d.   Suggestions for the Use of Aseptic Dental Absorbents, Cotton, Rolls, Napkins . . .; 5th ed.; 19 pp; **NYAM; MF/MAH.**

n.d.   Revelation Burs; **MAH.**

n.d.   S. S. White Corborundum Wheels, Disks, Points; **MAH.**

n.d.   World's Premium Porcelain Teeth; **UBML** (WU 26W582).

WHITE, W. B., & SON
Quincy, Mass.

n.d.   Illustrated Catalogue of Optical Glass and Fancy Leather Cases; 24 pp; **URRR** (W-25).

WHITE-HAINES, O. C.
Many addresses including Columbus, OH, Tampa FL, Wheeling, W. VA.

1909	The Prescription House of Ohio; 7th ed.; 159 pp; **URRR** (W-268).
Aug. 1928	Price List, Prescription Blue Ribbon Rx Lenses, 28-B; 15 pp; **URRR** (W-41).
Apr. 1930	Frame and Mounting Supplement; 16 pp; **URRR** (W-305).
Apr. 1930	Blue Ribbon Prescription Lenses; 16 pp; **URRR** (W-306).
Aug. 1931	Blue Ribbon Bifocal Prescription Price List; 15 pp; **URRR** (W-307).
May 1932	Price List, Panoptik Bifocal Natural Vision; 4 pp; **URRR** (W-291).
n.d.	Modern Eyewear Featuring White Solid Gold, Gold Filled and Xylonite; 32 pp, Price List supplement to 29A; **URRR** (W-308).
n.d.	Blue Ribbon Prescription Book, A New Way To Buy; 47 pp; **URRR** (W-309).
n.d.	4 pp; **URRR** (W-331).
n.d.	Style Selections; 25 pp; **URRR** (W-311).

WHITESIDE, H. A.
New York.
| 1914 | The Miniature Electric Dental Engine; 17 pp; **BLEL.** |

WIGHTMAN, JOSEPH M.
Nos. 33 Cornhill & 34 Brattle St., Boston, Mass.
1853	Catalogue and Prices of Philosophical Apparatus; 44 pp; **CTY/B** (Uai W 639).
1855	A Catalogue of Philosophical, Astronomical, Chemical and Electrical Apparatus; 40 pp; **CTY/B** (Uai W 639).
1858	A Catalogue of Philosophical, Astronomical, Chemical and Electrical Apparatus; 40 pp; **CTY/B** (Uai W 639).

WILDER, CHARLES, COMPANY
Troy, New York.
Est: around 1860
Begun in Petersboro, NH. Purchased by W. & L. E. Gurley and removed to Troy, NY.
| 1911 | Wilder Accurate Thermometers, Catalogue and Price List; 32 pp; **AO.** |

WILFORD, LABORATORIES
Port Chester, New York.
| 1918 | Catalogue Revised List Prices Supplementing Price List no. 17, Mfrs. of Medicinal and Surgical Plasters, Surgical Dressings, Absorbent Cotton, Suspensory Bandages, Medicaid Soaps . . .; **CTY/B** (Uai H 147). |

WILKINSON, C. A., CO.
Providence, R. I.
616 W. 137th St., New York City.
Started as a Partnership by Charles A Wilkinson and Dutee Wilcox under the name of C. A. Wilkinson & Co., in 1896. Subsequently incorporated in 1921 under name of C. A. Wilkinson Co. Manufacturered solely Gold Filled Optical Goods.
1918	Price List, Frames, Mounting and Parts; 4 pp; **AO.**
1921	Society Optical Goods, Frames, Mountings, Optical Specialties, and Lorgnons; 36 pp, includes 1921, 22, and 23 price list; **AO.**
1922	Society Optical Goods, Frames, Mountings, Optical Specialties and Lorgnons; 36 pp; **URRR** (W-313).

WILL CORPORATION
Rochester, New York.
| 1920 | Catalog of Bacteriological Apparatus, Pathological, Biochemical; 569 pp; **MAH; NLM** (W26 W689). |
| 1928 | Catalog of Laboratory Apparatus and Chemicals, no. 4; 637 pp; **AFMM.** |

WILLIAMS, BROWN & EARLE
918 Chestnut Street, Philadelphia, Pennsylvania.
Est: 1885

ca 1897 Catalogue of Microscopes, Objectives, Centrifuges and Microscopical Supplies; 54 pp; **URRR** (W-30).

1898 The Purdy Electric Centrifuge; 16 pp; **CPP.**

ca 1900 Catalogue of Microscopical, Bacteriological, Optical, Electrical and Scientific Instruments and Supplies, sole agent for R. & J. Beck; 93 pp, fragile; **MAH.**

ca 1905 Catalogue and Price List of X-Ray Supplies; 32 pp; **ACR/MAH.**

ca 1905 Catalogue interleaved with ledger paper and bound in black binder with name: N. H. Brown, X-Ray; **ACR/MAH.**

n.d. Section D, Dissecting Instruments and Entomological Supplies; 11 pp; **CTY/B** (Uai W 6755).

1909 Catalog of Microscopes, Objectives, Centrifuges and Microscopical Supplies; 100 pp; **URRR** (W-218).

1910? Catalog of Microscopes, Chemical Apparatus, Laboratory Supplies; 120 pp; **URRR** (W-219).

33, 35 & 39 S. Tenth St., Philadelphia, PA.

n.d. List of Microtomes, Sterilizers, Incubators, etc., Circular no. 4; 8 pp; **CTY/B** (Uai W 6755).

WILLIAMS AND WILKINS CO., THE
Baltimore, Maryland.

n.d. The Young-Didusch Urological Outline-Charts; 8 pp; **MAH.**

WILLIS, W. V., & CO.
Philadelphia, Pennsylvania.

ca 1900 Illustrated Catalogue, Surgeon's Instruments, Physicians Supplies, Microscopes and Accessories, Laboratory Apparatus, Hospital and Office Furniture, Sterilizing Apparatus; 2nd ed.; 576 pp; **HML.**

1901 Illustrated Catalogue of Surgical Instruments; **CPP** (Ed/33).

1917 Illustrated Catalogue of Surgical Instruments; 672 pp, 19 pp index; **CPP** (Ed/33); **WOC.**

WILLMS, CHARLES, SURGICAL INSTRUMENT CO., THE
300 North Howard Street, Baltimore, Maryland.
Est: 1869

pre–1895 Catalog of Surgical Instruments, Orthopedic Apparatus, Laboratory Equipment, Office Furniture, etc.; 503 pp, fragile; **AFMM.**

1895 Catalogue and Price List; **CPP** (Ed/70).

1895 Catalogue and Price List of Surgical Instruments, Orthopedic Apparatus, Elastic Hosiery, Trusses, etc.; 503 pp; **MAH** (C 610.78085 W 444).

1905 Catalogue of Surgical Instruments, Orthopedic Appliances, Microscopes, Trusses, Abdominal Supporters, Elastic Hosiery, Suspensories, Supplies, Physicians', Hospital and Invalids' Supplies, Artificial Limbs, Crutches, Hospital Furniture; 365 pp; **JHIHM** (RD 76 C 47).

n.d. Illustrated and Descriptive Catalogue and Price List of Surgical Instruments, includes Price List dated Feb 1924; 4th ed.; **UREGML.**

190? Surgical instruments; **NYAM** (S 125).

n.d. Catalogue of Surgical Instruments; 3rd ed.; **JHIHM** (RD 76. C 47).

WILLSON, T. A., & CO.
WILLSON GOGGLES, INC. (1920)
2nd and Washington, Reading, PA (factory and Main Office).
Est: 1870
    See: JOHN REYNDERS & CO., 1875; **NLM.**
        ca 1877   Reasons Why the Arundell Tinted Spectacles Should Be Preferred; 13 pp;
                    MAH.
        1907   Descriptive Catalogue of Spectacles and Eye Glasses, Low Priced and
                    Medium Grades; 27 pp, price list; **AO.**
Branch offices: Chicago, Toronto, San Francisco, London, Bueno Aires.
        1918   Price List for . . ., Willson Goggles, Glasses and Safety Goggles; 33 pp;
                    AO.
        1920   Willson Goggles, Safety Flange Goggles and Other Protective Types for
                    Industrial Eye Safety; 16 pp; **URRR** (W-322); **AO.**
        1920   Goggles; 21 pp; **URRR** (W-321).
        n.d.   Goggles for Sun, Wind, Dust, Glare; 8 pp; **URRR** (W-320).
        1921   Style List of Willson Goggles; 22 pp, price list; **AO.**
        1921   Willson Goggles; Safety Flange Goggles and Other Protective Types for
                    Industrial Eye Safety; 16 pp; **AO.**
        1922   Style List of Willson Goggles; 22 pp, price list; **AO.**
        1923   Willson Safety Goggles, Dustrite Respirators, Welding Helmets and
                    Handshields; 20 pp; **AO.**
        1923   Style List of Willson Goggles; 22 pp, price list; **AO.**
Branch Offices above and New York, Pittsburgh, Kansas City, Dallas, New Orleans, Mexico City,
    Havana, Sydney.
British Office and warehouse: S. Pulzer, 45 Hatton Garden, London, ECI.
        1924   Style List of Willson Goggles; 22 pp; **AO.**
        1925   For Sun, Dust, Wind, Glare, The Standard of the World; 22 pp, price
                    list; **AO.**

WILLYOUNG & CO.
Philadelphia, Pennsylvania.
    See: ELMER G. WILLYOUNG, New York; **ACR/MAH;** WILLYOUNG & GIBSON CO.

WILLYOUNG, ELMER G.
New York, New York.
    See: WILLYOUNG & GIBSON CO; **ACR/MAH.**
        1902   Catalog, Induction Coils X-Ray Machines and Acessory Apparatus; 4th
                    ed.; 32 pp; **ACR/MAH.**
        n.d.   Catalogue, Electrical & Scientific Instruments; **CTY/B** (Uai W 6755).

WILLYOUNG & GIBSON CO., THE
40 West 13th Street, New York, New York.
    Apr. 15, 1904   Leaflet no. 522A, Improved 1904 type of Cunningham Mercury Jet
                    Interrupter; 1 pp; **ACR/MAH.**
    Apr. 15, 1904   Leaflet no. 529, Improved Wehnelt, Electrolytic, Interrupter; 1 pp;
                    ACR/MAH.
        1905   No. 534, Model Q, 1905 Style X-Ray Coil; 1 pp; **ACR/MAH.**
    Apr. 20, 1905   Brochure no. 535, Supplementary to 507AA of Nov 20 1903,
                    Inducto-Oscillo-Resonator and Other New High Frequency Apparatus
                    and Accessories; 16 pp; **ACR/MAH.**
    Aug. 1, 1905   No. 528 X-Ray Tubes, T.E. Focus Tubes; 2nd ed.; **ACR/MAH.**

ca 1910   Brochure, Continuous Current Voltmeters, Ammeters and Volt-Ammeters, Pignolet's; 2 pp; **ACR/MAH.**

WILMINGTON DENTAL MFG. CO., THE
1413 Filbert Street, Wilmington, Delaware.
Nov. 1890   Catalogue, Dental Instruments and Teeth; 376 pp; **MAH** (C 617.6085 W); **NYAM; MF/MAH; UPSDM** (D 617.604.W 688); **HML.**
1890   Illustrated Catalogue; 376 pp; **HDM.**
Jun. 1, 1894   Catalogue Impression Trays; 50 pp; **MAH** (C 617.6085 W).
Jun. 1894   Pamphlet no. 5, Steel Instruments; 78 pp; **MAH** (C 617.6085 W).

WILMOT CASTLE COMPANY
Rochester, New York.
19 c   The Arnold Steam Sterilizer; 1 pp; **CTY/B** (Uai W 689).
1925   Catalog of Sterilizer Equipment for Hospitals; 75 pp; **NLM** (W26 W744).

WILSON LABORATORIES, THE
4221-25 South Western Avenue, Chicago, Illinois.
Jan. 1923   Price List Gland Substances, Animal Derivatives, Digestive Ferments, Specialties; 24 pp; **CPP.**
ca 1923   Pluriglandular Therapy; 12 pp; **CPP.**
ca 1923   Orchic Therapy; 8 pp foldout; **CPP.**
ca 1923   Suprarenal Therapy; 12 pp; **CPP.**
ca 1923   Endocrine Therapy; 12 pp; **CPP.**
n.d.   On back page, Wilson's Endocrine Products Prepared from Selected Raw Glands, Pluriglandular Therapy with Suggested Formulas; 8 pp foldout; **CPP.**

WINCHESTER SURGICAL SUPPLY CO.
Winchester-Ritch Surgical Co.
Charlotte, North Carolina.
1924   Illustrated Catalogue of Domestic and Imported Surgical Instruments; 1st ed.; **CS.**

WINDLER, H.
Dorotheen-Strasse Nr. 3, Berlin, Germany.
Est: 1819
1866   Haupt-Preisliste: chirurgische Instrumente, Bandagen, orthopaedische Apparate; **CPP** (Ed/3).
1870   Fabrik chirurgischer Instrumente, Bandagen, Spritzen, Apparate zur Krankenpflege; 130 pp; **NLM** (W26 G6240).
1877   Preis Courant Chirurgischer Instrumente, Bandagen, Spritzen, Apparate zur Krankenpflege; 188 pp; **NYAM; MF/MAH.**
187?   Instrumenenmacher und Bandagist; **YML** (RD 76 870W).
1882   Preis-Verzeichniss der Fabrik chirurgischer Instrumente und Bandagen; 261 pp; **NYAM; MF/MAH; CPP** (Ed/3).
1888   Preis-Verzeichniss der Fabrik chirurgischer Instrumente und Bandagen; 247 pp; **MAH** (C 610.78085); **CPP** (Ed/5); **BLEL.**
1892   Preis-Verzeichniss der Fabrik chirurgischer Instrumente und Bandagen von H. Windler; 288 pp; **YML** (RD 76 888W); **JHIHM** (RD 76 W 765); **CPP** (Ed/5).
n.d.   Preis-Verzeichniss der Fabrik chirurgischer Instrumente und Bandagen von H. Windler; 252 pp; **UCSF.**

Nr. 24 Friedrichstrasse 133a, Berlin, Germany.
Colonaden 41, Hamburg, Germany.
Ulitzagogol 4, St. Petersburg, Russia.

1900	Haupt-Preisliste, chirurgische Instrumente, Bandagen, Apparate zur Orthopaedie, Sterilization und Krankenpflege, Nr. 41; 112 pp; **ZUR.**
1904	Haupt-Preisliste, chirurgische Instrumente, Bandagen, orthopaedische Apparate; **CPP** (Ed/5).
1909	Haupt-Preisliste: chirurgische Instrumente, Bandagen, orthopaedische Apparate; **CPP** (Ed/5).
ca 1910	Brochure Surgical Instruments and apparatus; 4 pp; **NYAM; MF/MAH.**
1912	Haupt-katalog 50; Chirurgie-Instrumente, Krankenhaus-Moebel, Bandagen, Apparate zur Orthopaedie, Sterilisation und Krankenpflege . . .; 1061 pp; **NYAM** (S 125).
1930	Chirurgie-Instrumente, Krankenpflege-Artikel, kuenstliche Glieder und Bandagen, Krankenhaus-Einrichtunger, Sterilisier-Anlagen, Operationssaal Vorbauten, Eigene Herstellung; 181 pp; **NLM** (W26 W765).

WINKEL

See: ZEISS-WINKEL; **AFMM.**

1908	Mikroskope und Hilfs-apparate; 42 pp; **URRR** (W-50).
1913	Mikrophotographische Apparate; 23 pp; **URRR** (W-177).
1937	6 pp foldout; **URRR** (W-371).

WINKEL, R.

Goettingen, Germany.
Est: 1857

1895	Microskope und zugehoerige Apparate aus der Optischen und Mechanischen Werkstaette; 47 pp; **URRR** (W-339).
1903	Mikroskope und zugehoerige Apparate aus der Optischen und Mechanischen Werkstaette; 63 pp; **URRR** (W-263).
1907	Mikroskope und Huelfsapparate; 63 pp; **URRR** (W-266).
1908	Microscopes and Optical Accessory Apparatus for Micro-Photography, Magic Lanterns, etc.; 19 pp; **URRR** (W-264).
1909	Mikrophotographische Apparate; 19 pp; **URRR** (W-265).
1909	Catalog of Microscopes and Microscopical Accessories, Represented by Dr. O. K. Zwingenberger, 106 Fulton St., New York City; 50 pp; **AFMM; NYAM; MF/MAH.**
1910	Microscopes and Accessory Apparatus, London agents: H. F. Angus Co., 83 Wigmore St.; 61 pp; **URRR** (W-372).
1912	Microscopes for Mineralogists, Microtomes and Grinding Apparatus Accessories; 23 pp; **URRR** (W-351).
1913	Mikroskope und Hilfsapparate; 72 pp; **URRR** (W-373).
1929	Microscopes et appareils auxiliaires pour examens à la lumière réfléchie; 56 pp; **URRR** (W-370).
n.d.	Stand LTB Microscopes; 8 pp; **URRR** (W-348).
n.d.	University Class and School Microscopes; 8 pp; **URRR** (W-347).
n.d.	Mikroskope und Huelfsapparate; Nr. 52; 95 pp; **URRR** (W-294).

WINKLEY ARTIFICIAL LIMB COMPANY

1326-1330 Washington Avenue, North, Minneapolis, Minnesota.

ca 1910	Catalog of Artificial Legs with the Patent Adjustable Double Slip Socket;

159 pp; **NLM** (W26 W775).

1927? Catalogue Miembros Artificiales Winkley con doble encaje ajustable de deslizamiento patentado; 96 pp; **MAH.**

WINTHROP CHEMICAL CO.
170 Varick Street, New York, New York.

n.d. Cardiac Distress Recent Therapeutic Advance; 4 pp; **CPP.**

n.d. Luminal; 6 pp foldout; **CPP.**

1923 Theocin, Soluble Powerful Diuretics; 12 pp; **CPP.**

ca 1927 Novocain, Luminal, Luminal-Sodium-Sedatives and Hypnotics; 48 pp; **CPP.**

ca 1929 Vigantol Irradiated Ergosterol; 16 pp; **CPP.**

ca 1932 Avertin; 5 pp; **CPP.**

ca 1933 A Dramatic Event in the History of a Distressful Disease; 4 pp foldout; **CPP.**

n.d. Increasing the Rate of Basal Metabolism, Thyractin; 3 pp; **CPP.**

n.d. Myorgal, Improved Cardiac Nutrition; 2 pp; **CPP.**

n.d. Theominal, When Storm Threatens; 2 pp; **CPP.**

n.d. Angina Pectoris, a New Idea in Treatment; 2 pp; **CPP.**

n.d. Thyroid Obesity; 2 pp; **CPP.**

n.d. Viosterol in Oil 250 D, Licensed by WARF; 3 pp; **CPP.**

n.d. A New Method of Treating Angina Pectoris; 2 pp; **CPP.**

n.d. He Built Better Than He Knew; 4 pp; **CPP.**

n.d. Avertin, the Basal Anesthetic Administered Rectally; 6 pp; foldout; **CPP.**

n.d. Distressful Disease; 4 pp; **CPP.**

n.d. Important Considerations in Administering Evipal Soluble, The New Anesthetic; 2 pp; **CPP.**

n.d. Salyragen Suppositories, Edema Treatment; 2 pp; **CPP.**

n.d. Theominal, The Essental Factor, High Blood Pressure; 2 pp; **CPP.**

n.d. The English Malady, Viosterol; 3 pp; **CPP.**

n.d. A Tragedy of Childhood, Viosterol; 4 pp; **CPP.**

n.d. Protargol, Efficient Organic Silver Derivative; 20 pp; **CPP.**

n.d. Novaldin, the Newest Agent for Subduing Pain, Analgesic; 2 pp; **CPP.**

WINTHROP-METZ
Winthrop Chemical Co., Inc.
H. A. Metz Laboratories, Inc.
170 Varick St. New York, New York.

1930 Catalogue, Materia Medica, with Therapeutic Index; 79 pp; **NYAM; MF/MAH.**

WIRTH, GEORG, INC.
Gerlgasse 16, Wien.
Est: 1894

1930 Inhalationsapparate und Inhalationseinrichtungen; 36 pp; **NLM** (W26 W799k).

WISEMAN BROTHERS SPECIALTY CO.
San Francisco, California.

1937 Interproximal Points, Victory Vibrator and Dentificator, Prophylactic Polishers and Mandrels; **MAH.**

WISSENSCHAFTLICH-TECHNISCHE MITTHEILLUNGEN AUS DEM MEDICINISCHEN WAARENHAUSE

Friedrichstrasse 108, Berlin N. 24, Germany.
   Apr. 1901   Catalogue; 64 pp; **NYAM; MF/MAH.**

WIZARD FOOT APPLIANCE CO.
St. Louis, Missouri.
   ca 1916   Orthopraxy of the Foot; 33 pp; **CPP.**

WOCHER, MAX, & SON
23 West Sixth Street, Cincinnati, Ohio.
 29-31 West Sixth Street, Cincinnati, Ohio.
Oldest House in the West
Est: 1837
   1896   Surgical Instruments Catalogue; 2nd ed.; 533 pp; **AFMM; BLEL; HDM.**
   1899   Apparatus for a Modern Office; Catalog of Dept. VI; 12 pp; **CPP.**
   1910   Surgical Instrument Catalogue; 322 pp; **HDM.**
   ca 1912   Book of Information of Orthopaedic Appliances Describing Their Use, Price and Application, Dept. 2; 20th ed.; **CS.**
   1924   Catalogue 37, Surgical Instruments, Hospital Furniture and Supplies; 475 pp; **CS; WOC.**

WOLF, GEORGE
   1910   Kystoskope; 47 pp; **URRR** (W-282).

WOLVERINE, THE OPTICAL
Grand Rapids and Battle Creek, MI.
   1896   Illustrated Catalogue & Price List of Surgical Instruments, Orthopedic Apparatus, Trusses, Elastic Hosiery, Electrical Batteries, Microscopes, Hospital & Laboratory Supplies, Office Furniture, Rubber Sundries, etc., Veterinary Instruments; 2nd ed.; 522 pp; **AFMM; BLEL.**
   1914   Modern Instruments and Sanitary Office Equipments, Sterilizers, etc.; **CPP** (Ed/46a).
   n.d.   Catalog C; 138 pp; **URRR** (W-38).
   n.d.   The List of Instruments Suggested by Charles Elton Blanchard, M.D., proctology; 4 pp; **CPP.**
   n.d.   Complete Instrument Kit for Ambulant Proctology; 7 pp; **CPP.**
 19, 21, 23 West Sixth Street, Cincinnati, Ohio.
   1917   Catalogue of Dept. V, Hospital Furniture and Appliances; 25th ed.; 200 pp; **NLM** (W26 W837c).
   1919   Catalogue of Dept. V, Hospital Furniture and Appliances; 28th ed.; 395 pp; **NLM** (W26 W837c).
   ca 1924   Catalog, The Cincinnati Automatic Pedestal Operating Tables with Benedict Nickel tops; 36th ed.; pp 305-857; **CUHSL** (RD 76 W81).
   ca 1930   Brochure, The Dr. Hugh H. Young and Young-McKim-Smith X-Ray Urological Tables with L-F Flat Bucky Diaphragms; 12 pp; **NYAM; MF/MAH.**
   1930   Catalogue of Surgical Instruments and Hospital Equipments; 44th ed., abridged; **MAH.**
   1930s?   Brochure, Complete Instrument Kit for Ambulant Proctology . . . suggested by Dr. Charles Elton Blanchard; 9 pp; **NYAM; MF/MAH.**

WONDER, CO., THE
180 North Michigan Avenue, Chicago, Illinois.
   n.d.   A New Way to Treat Gastric Hyperacidity; 8 pp; **CPP.**

WOODBURY-JELENKO
136 West 52nd Street, New York, New York.
    n.d.   Brochure, Electric Furnace; 10 pp; **NYAM; MF/MAH.**

WOODWARD, CLARKE & CO.
Portland, OR.
    1927   Optical Goods; 295 pp; **URRR** (W-40).
    n.d.   Home of the Genuine; 48 pp; **URRR** (W-39).

WOOLLEY, JAMES, SONS & CO., LTD.
Manchester, England.
    1890   Catalogue of Surgical Instruments and Medical Appliances,
           Electro-Therapeutic Apparatus, Sundries for the Surgery and
           Sick-Room; 94 pp; **BLEL.**
    1896   Catalogue of Surgeons Instruments and Medical Appliances,
           Electro-Therapeutic Apparatus; 3rd ed.; 408 pp; **YML** (R 856 896W).
    1905   Catalog of Chemical and Physical Apparatus, Scientific Instruments, etc.;
           430 pp, 16 pp on cameras; **URRR** (W-199).
  July 1928 Abridged List of Instruments, Dressing and Sundries for Surgeons and
           Hospitals, Surgical and Scientific Instruments; 72 pp; **SLSC.**

WORCESTER ELASTIC STOCKING AND TRUSS CO.
58 Front Street, Worcester, Mass.
    n.d.   Varicose Veins Best Relieved by the Worcester Improved Elastic Stockings,
           Catalogue and price List; 16 pp; **MAH** (8609).

WULFRING-LÜER, H.
6, rue Antoine-Dubois, Paris, France.
Gendre et successeur Maison A. Lüer
Est: 1837
    1894   Catalogue spécial des instruments pour les maladies des oreilles, du nez,
           de la bouche et de la gorge; 56 pp; **ZUR.**
    1904?   Catalogue général instruments de chirurgie; 328 pp; **NYAM.**

WUENCHE, MORITZ
Universitätsstrasse Nr. 5, Leipzig, Germany.
    L. 19 c   Chirurgische Instruments, Bandagen, Spritzen und Apparate zur
           Krankenpflege; 71 pp; **NLM.**

WYETH, JOHN, & BROTHER, INC.
1412 Walnut Street, Philadelphia, Pennsylvania.
1401 Walnut St., Philadelphia, Pennsylvania.
Est: 1860
Subsidiary of American Home Products Corp.; Mfg. Chemists
  See: CODMAN AND SHURTLEFF.
    1889   The Harmlessness of Saccharin to the Human System; 27 pp; **CPP.**
    1901   Therapy of the Glycero-Phosphates with Special Reference to Elixir
           Glycerophosphates or Soda and Lime; 7 pp; **CPP.**
    1903   Caprenalin, the Active Pressor Principles of the Suprarenal Capsule, as
           Suggested by John J. Abel; 6 pp; **CPP.**
 Jan. 1, 1904 Physicians' Pocket List; 286 pp; **NYAM.**
    1906   Clinical Excerpts, Sevetol; 10 pp; **CPP.**
  ca 1906 Petrogen, The Most Penetrating of All Vehicles; 14 pp; **CPP.**
    n.d.   Therapeutic Notes, Sevetol, Conserver of Tissues; 6 pp; **CPP.**

X-RAY TUBE CO., INC.
100 Fifth Avenue, New York, New York.
  1916 Catalogue of Standard X-Ray Tubes; 12 pp; ACR/MAH.

YARNALL, E. A., CO.
115 S. 10th Street, Philadelphia, Pennsylvania.
1020 Walnut Street, Philadelphia, Pennsylvania.
  post 1885 Catalogue of Surgical Instruments, Orthopedic Appliances, Trusses, etc., etc.; **MUM** (Ed31 pam12).
  1892 Catalogue of Surgical Instruments, Orthopedic Appliances, Trusses, etc., etc.; 320 pp, 16 pp advertisements, fragile; **MAH** (C 610.78085); **NYAM** (S 125); **CPP** (Ed/31a); **HML; WOC.**
  1894 Surgical Instruments, Orthopedic Appliances, etc.; 2nd ed.; 382 pp; **AFMM; CPP** (Ed/31a); **NLM** (W26 Y28).
  1897 Catalogue of Orthopedical Appliances and Invalid's Requirements; **MUM** (ED31 pam).
Yarnall Surgical Co., The
  1899 Surgical Instruments, Orthopedical Appliances, Trusses, etc.; **MUM** (Museum 1899 Ed 3).

YOUNG, ARCHIBALD
57 & 61 Forrest Road, Lauriston, Edinburgh, Scotland.
  n.d. Illustrated List of Surgical, Medical, and Sick-Room Appliances; 35 pp; **CPP; MUM** (Ed 52 pam7).
  n.d. Dr. Potain's Aspirator; 1 pp; **CPP; MUM** (pam 11).
  n.d. Portable Induction Apparatus; 1 pp; **CPP; MUM** (pam 12).
  n.d. Axis Traction-Forceps in the Low Operation; **CPP; MUM** (pam 13).

YOUNG, OTTO, AND CO.
Chicago, IL.
  1911 Illustrated and Descriptive Catalogue of Optical Goods; pp 637-693; **URRR** (Y-13).
  1921 Optical Catalogue; pp 861-938; **URRR** (Y-14).

YOUNG, RICHARD
Philadelphia.
  1925 Illustrated Catalogue of Surgical Instruments, Hospital Furniture, Physician's Equipment, Sickroom Supplies, Eclectic Therapeutic and Orthopedic Apparatus; 416 pp; **HML.**

ZEISS
See: E. ADNET & FILS, ca 1905; **NYAM.**

ZEISS, CARL
Jena, Germany.
Est: 1846
 See: BAUSCH & LOMB; E. ADNET, ca 1910 cat; **NYAM;** ZEISS-WINKEL, ARTHUR H. THOMAS CO.; **AFMM.**
  1878 Katalog ueber Mikroscope und Gegenapparate, Nr. 23; 25 pp; **NLM** (W26 Z47).
  ca 1882 Description of Abbe'schen Beleuchtungs-Apparat; 3 pp; **MUM** (AA60 pam13 [2]).
  1882 Price List of Object, Glasses made by Carl Zeiss, Optician at Jena; 4 pp; **MUM** (AA60 pam 16[5]).

1883 Katalog Nr. 26, der Optischen Werkstaette; 80 pp; **MUM** (AA60 pam 12 [1]).
1885 Microscopes and Microscopial Accessories; 98 pp; **CTY/B** (Uai Z 36).
1885 Mikroskope und mikroskopische Hilfsapparate, Nr. 27; 98 pp; **AFMM; CTY/B** (Uai 236).
1886 Catalogue Neue Mikroskop-Objective und Oculare aus Special-Glaesern des Glastechnischen Laboratoriums; 14 pp; **CTY/B** (Uai Z 36); **MUM** (AA60 pam 18 [6]).
1888 Beschreibung und Gebrauchsanweisung des neuen Apparates fuer Mikrophotographie; 52 pp, plates; **CTY/B** (Uai Z 36).
1889 Katalog über Mikroskope und Hilfsapparate, Nr. 28; 105 pp; **NLM** (W26 Z47); **AFMM; MAH** (C 681.4085 z247m); **HDM.**
1890 Nachtrag zu Katalog, Nr. 28; 20 pp; **AFMM.**
1891 Catalog of Microscopes and Microscopical Accessories, no. 29; 125 pp; **NLM** (W26 Z47); **AFMM; UBML** (W 26 Z47m).
1891 Catalog of Photographic Lenses; 23 pp; **AFMM.**
ca 1891 Directions for Using the Haemacytometer, agents: Charles Lentz & Sons, 18 N. 11th St., Philadelphia, Pa.; 4 pp; **CPP.**
1895 Katalog ueber Mikroskope und mikroskopische Hilfsapparate, Nr. 30; 119 pp; **NLM** (W26 Z47).
1898 Katalog über Mikroskope und mikroskopische Hilfsapparate; 31st ed.; 124 pp, index; **NLM** (W26 Z47); **MAH** (C 681.4085 z247m); **AFMM; HDM.**
1898 Catalogue of Instruments and Appliances for Photo-Micrography and Projection; 3rd ed.; 43 pp; **AFMM.**
1899 Catalog of Instruments and Appliances for Projection and Photo-Micrography; 4th ed.; 55 pp; **AFMM.**
1902 Catalog of Microscopes and Microscopical Accessories; 32nd ed.; 162 pp; **AFMM; MAH** (C 681.4085 z 247m); **NLM** (W26 Z47); **AFMM** (in French and German); **CPP.**
1902 Mikroskope und mikroskopische Hilfsapparate; 32 Ausg; 135 pp; **BLEL.**
1903 Catalogue of Photo-Micrographic Apparatus; 5th ed.; 61 pp; **AFMM; MAH** (578.08 and C 681.4085 z 247m).
1903 Mikrophotographische Apparate; 5th Ausg; 61 pp; **BLEL.**
1903? Brochure, Blutkörper-Zählapparate, Hamocytometer; 12 pp; **NYAM; MF/MAH.**
1904 Mikrophotographische Einrichtung fuer ultraviolettes Licht; 15 pp; **AFMM.**
1904 Auerbach, Felix: *The Zeiss Works and the Carl Zeiss Stiftung in Jena* trans. from the 2nd German ed. by Siegfried F. Paul and Frederic J. Cheschire, F.R.M.D. London; 1st ed.; Jena 1903; 146 pp; **AFMM; MAH.**
1906 Katalog über Mikroskope und mikroskopische Hilfsapparate; 110 pp; 33rd ed.; **HDM; AFMM.**
1906 Catalog of Microscopes and Microscopical Accessories; 110 pp; 33rd ed.; **MAH** (C 681.4085 z 247m).
ca 1906 Brochure, Prapariersysteme, Lupen, Praeparierstative, Lupenstative; 16 pp; **AFMM.**
1907? Brochure, Ultramicroscopie et éclairage a fond noir, no. 4; 4 pp; **NYAM; MF/MAH.**
1908? Brochure, Directions for Using the Haemocytometer; 4 pp; **NYAM; MF/MAH.**

1909   Brochure, Microscopes and Microscopical Accessories; 18 pp; **MAH** (C 681.4085 z 247m).

ca 1910   Brochure, P. Mayer's Large Dissecting Stand; 6 pp; **AFMM.**

1911   Brochure, Small Projection Apparatus for Lantern Slides; 4 pp; **AFMM.**

1913   Microscopes and Accessories for the Microscopes; 35th ed.; 123 pp; **MAH** (C 681.4085); **HDM.**

1913   Brochure, Microscopes and Microscope Accessories; 4th ed.; 28 pp; **MAH** (C 681.4085).

post 1919   Apparatus Equipped with 5-ampere Arc Lamp for the Projection of Microscopic Objects, Lantern Slides and for the Optical Demonstration of Physical Experiments; 14 pp; **MUM.**

1924   Microscopes and Accessories for the Microscopes; Preliminary Catalogue; **HDM.**

1926   Catalog of Photo-Micrographic Apparatus and Accessories; 107 pp; **AFMM.**

1926   Mikrophotographische Apparate und Zubehoer, Mikro 401; 107 pp; **CPP.**

1927   Catalog of Microscopes and Accessories for the Microscope, Ed Mikro 400 USA; 109 pp; **AFMM; HDM.**

1927   Catalogue of Microscopes and Accessories for the Microscope; 105 pp; **MAH** (C 681.4085).

1928   Catalogue of Stereoscopic Dissecting Microscopes; 3rd ed.; 20 pp; **MAH** (C 618.4085).

1928   Zeiss Objective and Eyepieces for the Microscopes; 5th ed.; 20 pp; **AFMM; MAH** (C681.4085 Z 247).

1929   Augenaerztliche Instrumente; **LACMA** (149 z 3a).

1930s   Catalog of Ophthalmological Instruments; 64 pp; **AFMM.**

1935   Brochure of Zeiss Microscopes; 12 pp; **AFMM.**

n.d.   Katalog, Specialfabrication von Mikrotomen mit Spitzenfuehrung, Nr. IV; 12 pp; **NYAM; MF/MAH.**

728 S. Hill St., Los Angeles, California.

n.d.   Booklet Med 128/II, Ophthalmological Instruments; 52 pp; **MAH.**

485 Fifth Avenue, New York, New York.

1927   Booklet Med 138/II, Ophthalmological Instruments; 52 pp; **MAH** (C 617.75085z).

n.d.   Catalogue, Special-Catalog ueber Apparate fuer Mikrophotographic; **CTY/B** (Uai Z36).

1938   Microscopes and Accessories; 23 pp; **AFMM.**

1938   Objectives and Eyepieces for Microscopes, Mikro 367c; 16 pp; **AFMM.**

n.d.   Projection Apparatus and Accessories; 1st ed.; **HDM.**

ZENTMAYER, JOSEPH

147 South Fourth Street, Philadelphia, Pennsylvania.
Est: 1853

1859?   Illustrated Price List of Microscopes, Microscopic Apparatus and Optical Instruments Manufactured by Joseph Zentmayer; 5th ed.; **MUM** (AA60 pam3).

ca 1880   Catalogue Microscopes, Microscopic Apparatus, Optical Instruments Manufactured by Joseph Zentmayer; 7th ed.; 36 pp; **MAH.**

209 South Eleventh Street, Philadelphia, Pennsylvania.

ca 1880   Catalogue Microscopes, Microscopic Apparatus and Optical Instruments; 9th ed.; 40 pp, fragile; **MAH.**

ca 1880   Catalogue of Microscopes, Microscopic Apparatus and Optical
          Instruments; 10th ed.; 41 pp; **MAH.**
1889   Illustrated Price List of Microscopes, Microscopic Apparatus and Optical
          Instruments; 40 pp; **URRR** (Z-2).
1891(7?) Illustrated Price List of Microscopes, Microscopic Apparatus and Optical
          Instruments; 13th ed.; 40 pp; **MUM** (AA60 Box 2); **MAH.**
n.d.   Illustrated Price List of Microscopes, Microscopic Apparatus and Optical
          Instruments; 14th ed.; **MUM** (AA60 Box 2).

228 South Fifteenth Street, Philadelphia, Pennsylvania.
n.d.   Illustrated Catalogue of Microscopes, Mechanical Accessories & Optical
          Apparatus; 16th ed.; 30 pp; **CPP.**

ZIEGLER, FRIEDRICH

Est: 1852
1893   Prospectus ueber embryologische Wachsmodelle, Atelier fuer
          wissenschaftliche Plastik in Freiburg in Baden; 37 pp; **CPP.**
post 1904 Prospectus ueber embryologische Wachsmodelle, Atelier fuer
          wissenschaftliche Plastik in Freiburg in Baden; 4 pp; **CPP.**
1906   Modelle zur Entwickelungsgeschichte und vergleichenden Morphologie des
          Schädels; 4 pp; **CPP.**
1908   Neue embryologische und vergl. anatomische Modelle; 4 pp; **CPP.**

ZIMMERMANN, E.

Emilien-Strasse 21, Leipzig, Germany.
Est: 1887
See: CENTRAL SCIENTIFIC CO.; May 1912; **MAH.**
1900   Spezial-Liste ueber automatische Mikrotome; 20 pp; **URRR** (Z-8).
Apr. 1905 Brochure, Psychologische und physiologische Apparate, Microtome; 4 pp;
          NYAM; MF/MAH.
1908   Mikrotomie, Mikroskopie, Mikrophotographie Mikroprojektion; 116 pp;
          URRR (Z-8A).
ca 1910   Brochure, Kehlton-Schreiber nach F. Krueger and W. Wirth; 4 pp;
          NYAM.
ca 1910   Brochure, Registrier-Apparat Kymographion fuer vertikale und horizontale
          Benutzung der Trommel; 4 pp; **NYAM.**

Chausseestr. 6, Berlin N. 4.
1912   Psychologische und Physiologische Apparate, Liste 25, Nr. 900; 252 pp;
          MAH.

Wasserturmstr. 33, Leipzig, Germany.
1921   Liste 42, ueber Registrier-Apparate und Zubehöre; 46 pp; **NYAM;
          MF/MAH.**
1922   Liste 40, Akustische und phonetische Instrumente; 28 pp; **NYAM;
          MF/MAH.**
1922   Liste 41, Über Unterbrecher, Zeitschreiber, Induktorien; 24 pp; **NYAM;
          MF/MAH.**
1922   Liste 43, Ueber Blutdruckapparate; 32 pp; **NYAM; MF/MAH.**
1925   Liste 47, Mikrotome und Zubehoer, Apparate fuer Psychologie,
          Psychotechnik, Paedagogik, Physiologie; 32 pp; **URRR** (Z-13).
1928   Liste 50, Psychologische und physiologische Apparate; 359 pp; **MAH.**

ZONTE PRODUCTS CO.

342 Madison Avenue, New York, New York.
n.d.   Feminine Hygiene, The Modern Personal Antiseptic; 14 pp; **CPP.**

ZYLITE OPTICAL CO.
12 East 22nd St., New York, New York.
    n.d.   The Frame Beautiful; 8 pp, 6 pp distributor's price list; **URRR** (Z-15).

T. A. WILLSON & CO., READING, PA., U.S.A.

Scenery Spectacles

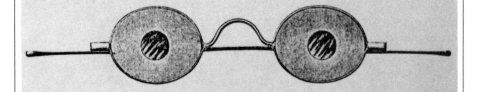

AN OPTICAL WONDER FOR YOUNG AND OLD.

Amber-colored lenses. A popular novelty, much used by tourists and sportsmen

"600" Grade

No. 601½ Nickel-plated Frame. Straight temples.

No. 617½ Nickel-plated Frame. Riding bow temples.

"400" Grade
(Better quality than "600" Grade).

No. 401½ Nickel-plated Frame. Straight temples.

No. 417½ Nickel-plated Frame. Riding bow temples.

ADDENDUM TO BIBLIOGRAPHY

ALLISON, W. D., CO.
133 E. South Street, Indianapolis, Indiana.

n.d.   The "Allison" Oto-Laryngological Cabinet and Sundries; 8 pp; **MAH** (C617.75085 A).

AMERICAN CABINET CO.
Two Rivers, Wisconsin.

May 1936   American Dental Manual; 39 pp, index, price list 8 pp; **MAH.**

AMERICAN METAL FURNITURE CO.
Indianapolis, Ind.

1925   American Aseptic-Steel Furniture for Hospitals, Physicians, Surgeons, Dentists and Optometrists; 120 pp, index, price list no. 21, 15 pp, additions and corrections to no. 21 (Nov. 1 1925); **MAH.**

ARGUS CO., THE
Jersey City, New Jersey.

1888   Our Eyes in Health and Disease, Spectacles, Their Use and Abuse; 18 pp; **MAH** (C681.411085 A694).

ASH, CLAUDIUS, & SONS
6,7,8,9 Broad Street, London, England.

1875   Catalog of Artificial Teeth, Dental Materials, Tools, Furniture, etc.; 302 pp, index; **MAH** (C617.6085 A).

1886   Artificial Teeth, Precious Metals, Stoppings, Furniture, Instruments, Laboratory Apparatus, Tools and Sundries; 488 pp, Appendix dated 1891, price lists, Jul 1, 1890–Sep 1891; **MAH** (C617.6085 A).

1891   Dental Engines and Appliances; 52 pp; **MAH** (C617.6085 A).

1891   Dental Forceps and Stump Elevators, etc.; 32 pp, pp 252-328; **MAH** (C617.6085 A).

Mar. 1891   Quarterly Circular; 88 pp; **MAH** (C617.6085 A).

Jun. 1891   Quarterly Circular; 168 pp; **MAH** (C617.6085 A).

1893   Catalog of Artificial Teeth, Precious Metals, Stoppings, Dental Rubbers, Furniture, Instruments, Nitrous Oxide Gas and Ether Apparatus, Laboratory Apparatus, Tools and Sundries; 656 pp; **MAH** (C617.6085 A).

1900   Dientes Artificiales, Metales preciosos, Materiales para Dentistas, Muebles, instrumentos, Aparatos de Laboratorio, Herramientas n Accesorios; 439 pp; **MAH** (C617.6085 A).

1904   Dental Catalog, List A-M; **MAH** (C617.6085 A).

5-12 Broad Street, Golden Square, London.

1908   Catalogue, General Index, Lists B-O; **MAH** (C617.6085 A).

Feb. 1912   Precious Metals and Filling Materials, List B; 64 pp; **MAH** (C617.6085 A).

1913   Forceps, Elevators, Lancets, Scissors, and Instruments, List D; 75 pp; **MAH** (C617.6085 A).

1916   Forceps, Elevators, Lancets, Scissors, Gags, Syringes, etc., List D; 64 pp; **MAH** (C617.6085 A).

C. ASH SONS & CO., LTD.
1913   Catalogue Dentaire, Lists A-O; **MAH** (C617.6085 A).

BARTLETT & CO.
New York.
pre–1900   Dental Cabinets, Cuspidors, Operating Stool, Custer Electric Oven, Electric Gold Annealer; 23 pp; **MAH.**

BAUSCH AND LOMB OPTICAL CO.
515-543 N. St. Paul Street, Rochester, New York.
1921   Magnifiers and Readers; 12 pp; **MAH**
1921   *LENS* Pamphlet, Deltar, New and Better Ophthalmic Lenses; foldout, 6 pp; **MAH.**
1921   *LENS* Pamphlet, Bitex, Popular Priced Solid Bifocals; foldout, 4 pp; **MAH.**
1922   Photomicrographic Equipment, Micro Projectors; 54 pp, index; **MAH** (C778.56085 BP).
1922   *LENS* Pamphlet, Deltar, Better Lenses for Better Vision; foldout, 6 pp; **MAH.**
1922   *LENS* Pamphlet, Important Lens Talk for Those Who Wear Glasses; foldout, 6 pp; **MAH.**
1923   *LENS* Pamphlet, Bitex, A New Improved B & L; foldout, 6 pp; **MAH.**
1923   *LENS* Pamphlet, Clear Vision, Both Near and Far, Kryptok, Invisible Bifocals; foldout, 4 pp; **MAH.**
May 1, 1924   Magnifiers and Readers; 3 pp; **MAH.**
1924   *LENS* Pamphlet, The Glare in Winter Sunlight, Crookes Lenses; foldout; **MAH.**
1924   *LENS* Pamphlet, The Light that Burns, Crookes Lenses; foldout; **MAH.**
1924   *LENS* Pamphlet, With Eyes of Youth; foldout; **MAH.**
1924   *LENS* Pamphlet, If You Need Glasses, Punktals; foldout; **MAH.**
1924   *LENS* Pamphlet, Come Out of the Sun, Crookes Glass Lenses; foldout; **MAH.**
1924   *LENS* Pamphlet, Why Torics, Advantages of Curved Lenses; foldout; **MAH.**
1924   *LENS* Pamphlet, Punktal Demonstrator; foldout; **MAH.**
1924   *LENS* Pamphlet, Supplement no. 2 Price List, Ophthalmic Products; foldout, 1 pp; **MAH.**
1925   Reading Glass Display Stand; **MAH.**
1926   Pamphlet, "Magnify It"; foldout; **MAH.**
1926   *LENS* Pamphlet, Value #1; foldout; **MAH.**
1926   *LENS* Pamphlet, The Nokrome; foldout; **MAH.**
1926   *LENS* Pamphlet, Surface Powers in Diopters, Lens Power in Vertex Refraction with Lens Measure; foldout; **MAH.**
1927   *LENS* Pamphlet, With Eyes of Youth, Kryptok Lenses; foldout; **MAH.**
1927   *LENS* Pamphlet, Glare, and How to Stop It, Crookes Lenses; foldout; **MAH.**
1927   *LENS* Pamphlet, Half of Them Blindfolded; foldout; **MAH.**
1927   *LENS* Pamphlet, Looking Young With Bifocals; foldout; **MAH.**
1928   Pamphlet, Nuway Floding Reading Glasses; foldout; **MAH.**

Nov. 1, 1928 Price List, Magnifiers and Readers; 10 pp, **MAH.**
1928 *LENS* Pamphlet, With Iris Eyes You're Smiling; foldout; **MAH.**
1928 *LENS* Pamphlet, Enjoy Youth, Beauty, Life with Nokrome; foldout; **MAH.**
1928 *LENS* Pamphlet, Half of Them Blindfolded; foldout; **MAH.**
1928 *LENS* Pamphlet, The Nokrome; foldout; **MAH.**
1928 *LENS* Pamphlet, The Light the Burns, Crookes; foldout; **MAH.**
1931 Optical Instruments for Examining and Analyzing Metals; 123 pp, index, additional foldout; **MAH** (C681.4085 B187 opc).
1935 Laboratory Microscopes and Accessories; 28 pp, index; **MAH** (C681.4085 B187 1a).
1937 Laboratory Microscopes and Accessories, Catalog D0185; 19 pp; **MAH** (C681.4085 B187 1a).
Jan. 16, 1939 Price List, Ray-Ban, Anti-Glare; 7 pp; **MAH.**
n.d. Manufacturers of Eyeglasses, lenses, Magnifiers, Readers, and other Optical Instruments; 6 pp, price list; **MAH.**
n.d. Manufacturers of Eyeglasses, Lenses, Magnifiers, Readers, and other Optical Instruments; 8 pp, price list; **MAH.**
n.d. Manufacturers of Eyeglasses, Lenses, Magnifiers, Readers, and other Optical Instruments; 17 pp, price list; **MAH.**
n.d. Adjustable Eye-Glass, no. 30, E. K. Josselyn's patent Jan 8, 1867 and J. J. Bausch's patent Jan 14, 1868 mentioned; 1 pp; **MAH.**

BECK, R. & J.
London, England.
L 19 C An Illustrated Catalogue of Microscopes and Apparatus, Specially Adapted for Physiological and Pathological Research; 18 pp; **MAH.**
1936 Beck Microscopes; 116 pp, index; **MAH** (C681.4085 Bb).

BETZ, FRANK S., CO.
Hammond Indiana.
Est: 1895
Aug. 1, 1922 Price List, Parts and Equipment for Invalid's Chairs, no. 205; **MAH.**
1925 Betzco Dental Supplies and Equipment, 30th year; 113 pp; **MAH.**
1923 Betzco Invalid Chairs, 40 pp; **MAH.**
1932 Betz Spring Clearance Sale, Sweeping Reductions on Dental Instruments, Equipment and Supplies; 32 pp; **MAH.**
Fall 1936 Betz Book for Physicians and Hospitals; 130 pp; **MAH.**
1936 Betz Book for Physicians and Hospitals; 118 pp; **MAH.**

BUSS, PAUL, DENTAL DEPOT
190 Fredrich-Strasse, Berlin.
1887 Operationsstühler, Schränken, Maschinen und Apparaten; 64 pp; **MAH** (617.6085 B).
1887 Zahnärzliche Maschinen, Apparate, Operationsstuhle, etc.; 62 pp; **MAH** (617.6085 B).

CAMP, S. H., & CO.
Jackson, Michigan.
1932 The Camp System of Physiological Supports, Their Scientific Application Analyzed and Illustrated for Women—Children—Men; 80 pp; **MAH.**

1934   Reference Book for Physicians and Surgeons, Camp Surgical Supports for Women- Children- Men, 9th ed.; 48 pp; **MAH.**

1938   Reference Book for Physicians and Surgeons, Camp Surgical Supports for Women- Children- Men, 10th ed.; 55 pp; **MAH.**

CLOW, JAMES B., & SONS
Chicago, Ill.

1908   The Clow Catalog of Sanitary Hospital Apparatus, Hydrotherapeutic Appartus, and Sanitary Plumbing Fixtures; 176 pp, index; **MAH** (9257).

CROWLEY & GARDNER
735 Boylston Street, Boston, Mass.

n.d.   Surgical Instruments, Hospital and Sickroom Supplies, 2nd ed.; 448 pp, index; **MAH** (3005).

DENTISTS' SUPPLY CO. OF NEW YORK
220 W. 42nd Street, New York.

1922   Trubyte Teeth for Vulcanite Plates; 75 pp; **MAH.**

EASTMAN KODAK CO.
Rochester, New York.

Apr. 1938   X-Rays in Dentistry, 6th ed.; 60 pp, price list supplement; **MAH.**

ELECTRO SURGICAL INSTRUMENT CO.
Rochester, New York.

1938   Electrically Lighted Diagnostic and Surgical Instruments, 11th ed.; 68 pp; **MAH.**

ERNEST, F. GUSTAV
"Orthopedic Mechanician to the National Orthopedic Hospital"

May 1906   Artificial Limbs for Use after Amputations and Congenital Deficiencies; 48 pp, 117 illustrations, photocopy; **MAH.**

FEICK BROTHERS CO.
809 Liberty Ave., Pittsburgh, Pa.

n.d.   Illustrated Catalogue of Veterinary Instruments (Kny-Scheerer mfd.), 3rd ed.; 112 pp; **MAH** (C636.0896 V586).

GEMRIG, J. H.
109 Eighth Street, Philadelphia, Penn.

ca 1870   Illustrated Catalogue of Surgical Instruments, Appliances, Bandages, Apparatus for Deformities, Dislocations, and Fractures, Trusses, etc.; 128 pp, photocopy; **MAH** (WLM '74 W26 H136).

GENEVA OPTICAL CO.
67 and 69 Washington Street, Chicago, Ill.

1893   Wholesale Priced and Illustrated Catalogue of Optical Goods; 157 pp, index; **MAH** (C617.75085).

HARVARD CO., THE
Canton, Ohio.

1905?   Dental Furniture, Catalog H; 88 pp; **MAH.**

JOHNSTON BROTHERS
1260 Broadway, New York.
    1881   Preliminary Illustrated Dental Catalogue of Materials; 219 pp; **MAH.**
    n.d.   Dental Catalog; 219 pp; **MAH.**

JOHNSTON BROTHERS DENTAL DEPOT
812 Broadway, New York.
    1876   Catalogue of Instruments for Dental Engines; 32 pp; **MAH** (C617.6085
          J).
1260 Broadway, and 340 Fulton Street, Brooklyn, New York.
    1880   New System Cone Sockett Instruments; 32 pp; **MAH.**

KENISTON AND ROOT
418 W. 6th Street, Los Angeles, California.
1010 10th Street, Sacramento, California.
See: KNY-SCHEERER.
    1915   Surgical Instruments; 20th ed.; 5216 pp, index 56 pp; **MAH** (C617.9 K).

KNY-SCHEERER
225-233 4th Ave., New York.
    1899   Illustrations of Surgical Instruments, Section 1: Dissecting Post-Mortum,
          Microscopical and Physiological Instruments, Diagnostic and
          Anthropometric Instruments, Apparatus for the Analysis of Urine and
          Blood, Cupping and Vaccinating Instruments, Syringes, Hypodermic
          and Injection, Temperature Regulators, Human Osteology; pp
          1001-1061; **MAH** (C610.78086 K).
    1899   Illustrations of Surgical Instruments, Section II: Anaesthetic, Amputating
          and Osteotomy Instruments, Bullet Extracting and Trepanning
          Instruments, Plaster of Paris Dressing Instruments, Aspirating, Pocket
          Case and Wound Dressing Instruments; pp 2001-2140; **MAH**
          (C610.78086 K).
119-125 7th Ave., New York, New York.
    1925   Surgical Instruments made of Stainless Steel; 7 pp; **MAH.**
    1924   Supplement to the 22nd ed., Surgical Instrument Catalogue; pp 3-5216;
          MAH.
    n.d.   Price List of Surgical Instruments, Section IV, 2nd ed.; 264 pp; **MAH**
          (C610.78085 K).
404-410 W. 27th Street, New York.
    n.d.   Electro-Pantostat; 4 pp; **MAH** (C615.84085 K).

LEITZ, E., INC.
    1929   Leitz Microscopes, Biological, Polarizing, Metallographic, Universal,
          Special Models, pamphlet no. 1138; 266 pp, price list dated Jun 15,
          1935; **MAH** (C681.4085 L247 b).
  Apr. 1931   Photo-Micrographic Apparatus, no. 50 G. en.; 42 pp, price list dated Oct
          8, 1936; **MAH** (C778.56085 L553).
  Jun. 1937   Panphot, Complete Combination of Polarizing and Ore Microscope resp.
          with Reflex Camera, Catalog no. 25, Supplementary ed.; 23 pp; **MAH.**
    1938   Microscopes; 129 pp, index; **MAH** (C681.4085 L247 le).

MARKS, A. A.
701 Broadway, New York City, New York.

pre–1904   A Few Who Wear Them, What They Do and Where They Live, (Artificial Limbs); 59 pp; **MAH** (C617.57085M).

MATTHAY HOSPITAL SUPPLY CO.
1321 W. 11th Street, Los Angeles, California.
1937?   Wholesale Distributors, Quality Matco Products (Kny-Scheerer Instruments); 479 pp, index: **MAH.**

McKESSON APPLIANCE CO.
Dec. 31, 1930   McKesson Nargraf for General Anesthesia, Recording and Indicating Types; 27 pp; **MAH** (C617.96085 M).

Sep. 1, 1932   Directions for Assembling and Care of the McKesson Indicating Nargraf; 36 pp; **MAH** (C617.96085 M).

1935   Directions for CO_2 Absorption to Assemble Absorber No. 941 with McKesson Nargrafs Now in use; 6 pp; **MAH** (C617.96085 M).

1938   McKesson Nargraf for General Anesthesia Recording and Indicating Types; 31 pp; **MAH** (C617.96085 M).

1939   McKesson Nargraf for Dental Anesthesia; 18 pp; **MAH** (C617.6085).

McKESSON & ROBBINS
91 & 93 Fulton Street, New York.
1883   Illustrated Catalogue of Druggist Sundries, Fancy Goods, Surgical Instruments, Sponges, Camois, etc.; 77 pp, photocopy; **MAH.**

MEYROWITZ, E. B.
104 E. 23rd Street, 125 W. 42nd Street, New York, New York.
1898   Illustrated Catalogue of Ophthalmological Apparatus and Eye, Ear, Nose and Throat Instruments, Part II, 4th ed.; 218 pp, index; **MAH** (C617.75085 M).

MODERN HOSPITAL SUPPLY CO., INC.
726 Nostrand Ave., Brooklyn, New York.
1923   Illustrated Catalogue of Surgical Instruments and Hospital Supplies, 1st ed.; 416 pp, index; **MAH.**
Jun. 1923   Price List; 33 pp; **MAH.**

MURRAY-BAUMGARTNER SURGICAL INSTRUMENT CO.
5 & 7 West Chase Street, Baltimore, MD.
1938   Fine Surgical Instruments, 5th ed.; 463 pp, index; **MAH** (C610.78085 M).

NATIONAL COLLEGE OF ELECTRIC-THERAPEUTICS
Lima, Ohio.
n.d.   Advertisement, 2 pp; **MAH** (C615.84085 N).

NEW HAVEN FOLDING CHAIR CO.
552 State Street, New Haven Conn.
1887   Price List of Invalid Rolling Chairs; 24 pp; **MAH** (C617.3078N532).

OHIO CHEMICAL AND MANUFACTURING CO.
1177 Marquette St., N.E., Cleveland, Ohio.
See: AMERICAN ATMOS. CORP.
1931?   Cecil-Plummer Oxygen Therapy Apparatus; 10 pp; **MAH.**

1939? Gas Anesthesia and Analgesia Apparatus, Dental Specialties; 16 pp; **MAH** (C617.96085 O).

PAINE FURNITURE COMPANY
48 Canal Street, Boston, Massachusetts.

1895–6 Makers and Dealers in Fine Furniture and Upholstery, also Manufacturers' Agents for Wheelchairs and Invalid Furniture; 48 pp; **MAH** (649.8 P2).

PENN SURGICAL MANUFACTURING CO.

1926 Illustrated Catalog of PSMCO Surgical Instruments for the Trade Exclusively; 360 pp, index; **MAH.**

QUEEN, JAMES W., & CO.

1887 Priced and Illustrated Catalogue of Microscopes and Accessories, Magnifying Glasses, Stereoscopes, Graphoscopes, etc., 66th ed.; 104 pp; **MAH.**

1888 Priced and Illustrated Catalogue of Microscopes and Accessories, Magnifying Glasses, Stereoscopes, Graphoscopes, etc., 68th ed.; 107 pp; **MAH.**

1889 Priced and Illustrated Catalogue of Microscopes and Accessories, Magnifying Glasses, Stereoscopes, Graphoscopes, etc., 71st ed.; 107 pp; **MAH.**

1889 Priced and Illustrated Catalogue of Ophthalmological Instruments, Spectacles and Eyeglasses, 72nd ed., Parts D and E; 175 pp, index; **MAH** (RE981 Q3p).

1893 Abridged Catalogue of Microscopes; 88 pp; **MAH** (175650 578.08).

QUEEN & CO.

1897 Priced and Illustrated Catalogue of Opthalmological Instruments, 79th ed., Part D; 90 pp; **MAH.**

1898 Trade Price List of Spectacles, Eye Glasses, Lenses, Cases and Materials; 90 pp; **MAH.**

1899 Priced and Illustrated Catalogue of Opera Glasses, Marine and Spy Glasses, Binocular and Astronomical Telescopes, 18th ed., Catalogue F; 57 pp; **MAH.**

1899? Queen Self-Regulating X-Ray Tube; 36 pp; **MAH** (C616.0757 Q).

1901 Priced and Illustrated Catalogue of Spectacles, Eye Glasses and Oculists' Prescription Lenses, 80th ed., Part E; 34 pp, photocopy; **MAH.**

1901 Astronomical Department; 14 pp; **MAH.**

1902 Catalogue of Engineering Instruments and Materials; 162 pp, index; **MAH.**

1902? Queen Self-Regulating X-Ray Tube; 36 pp; **MAH** (C616.0757 Q).

n.d. Queen Complete X-Ray Equipments and an Explanation; 15 pp; **MAH** (C616.0757 Q No. 1002).

RITTER DENTAL MANUFACTURING CO.
Est: 1887

1937 Fifty Years of Progress; 27 pp; **MAH.**

SILVERMAN, L.
1033 Chestnut Street, Philadelphia.

Oct. 1933 Silverman's Dental Supplies Catalog, 37th Year; 152 pp; **MAH.**

SKLAR, J., MANUFACTURING CO.
133-143 Floyd Street, Brooklyn, New York.
- 1923   Illustrated Catalogue of Domestic and Imported Surgical Instruments, 6th ed.; 368 pp, index; **MAH.**
- Jan. 1925   Supplement for 6th edition catalogue, 23 pp; **MAH.**
- July 1927   Wholesale Price List; 30 pp; **MAH.**

SPENCER LENS CO.
Buffalo, New York.
- 1934   New Spencer "Bright-Line" Haemacytometer; 3 pp; **MAH** (610.78085 S62).
- 1935   Inclinocular, Universal, Binocular Microscopes; 8 pp; **MAH** (C681.4085 S625 si).
- May 1935   Low Power Binocular Microscopes, Catalog M67; 15 pp, price list; **MAH** (C681.4085 S625 sp).
- 1939   Stereoscopic Microscopes; 17 pp; **MAH** (C681.4085 S 625 s).

STANDARD DENTAL PRODUCTS CO.
908 Chestnut Street, Philadelphia, PA.
- 1934   Standard General Catalog B of Dental Supplies; 31 pp; **MAH.**

SUNIC RECORD
- Mar. 1920   Diathermy Apparatus, Coolidge Tube, Progress in Radiometallography . . ., no. 10; pp 109-116; **MAH** (615.8 C).

VICTOR ELECTRIC CO.
- Jan. 1915   X-Ray Sundries, Bulletin no. 35-S; 16 pp; **MAH** (C616.0757 Q No. 35-S).

WAPPLER ELECTRIC CONTROLLER CO.
- 1898?   Galvanic, Farradic, Sinusoidal Cabinets, Switchboards and Accessories; 27 pp; **MAH** (C615.84085 W).

WAPPLER ELECTRIC MANUFACTURING CO., INC.
- n.d.   Manufacturers of Electro-Medical and Surgical Apparatus, Section 6; 34 pp; **MAH** (C615.84085 W).
- n.d.   The Wappler Interrupterless X-Ray and Treatment Apparatus, Catalog no. 4; 15 pp; **MAH** (C615.84085 W).

WATSON AND SONS
Parker Street, Kingsway, London.
- 1925   Catalog no. 68 of X-Ray Apparatus and Radium; 412 pp; **MAH.**
- 1929?   High Tension Transformers for the Production of X-Rays; 47 pp, index; **MAH** (C616.0757 W).

WATSON, W., & SONS, LTD.
- Jan. 1920   Prices for Microscopes and Accessories Contained in Catalogue 27th ed., Part 1, Student Instruments; **MAH.**
- 1920s   Catalogue of Watson Microscopes, part 2, Microscope Accessories for All the Biological Sciences, 34th ed.; **MAH** (C681.4085 W343).

WEISS, JOHN, & SON, LTD.
287 Oxford Street, London.

1934 Ophthalmic Instruments and Appliances; 296 pp, repair charges, index; **MAH** (C617.7085 W3).

WHITE, C. W., & CO.
99 Court Street, Boston, Mass.
1881 Illustrated Catalogue of Trusses, Supporters, Shoulder Braces, Elastic Stockings and Suspensory Bandages; 40 pp; **MAH.**

WHITE, SAMUEL S., DENTAL MANUFACTURING CO.
126 Great Portland Street, London.
n.d. Non-Filling Porcelain; 2 pp leaflet; **MAH.**
Chestnut and 12th Street, Philadelphia, PA.
Mar. 1893 Lathes and Equipment; 28 pp; **MAH** (C617.6085 W).
211-17 S. 12th Street, Philadelphia, PA.
Feb. 1900 Dental Office Furniture; **MAH.**
May 1901 Dental Office Furniture; **MAH.**
Nov. 1902 Dental Office Furniture; **MAH.**
1916 Amalgam, A Trilogy; 32 pp, revised price list, 1919; **MAH.**
1931 General Catalog of Dental Supplies; 308 pp; **MAH.**
1933 White Alloy Pin Teeth; 24 pp; **MAH** (C617.6085).
1935 General Catalog of Dental Supplies; 236 pp; **MAH.**
n.d. Non-Freezing Nitrous-Oxid, A Story of Nitrous Oxid Development with the Facts of an Important Advance, no. 2185; 14 pp; **MAH** (C617.96083 W).
n.d. Electrical and Compressed Air Instruments of the S. S. White Equipment Unit, no. 2615-A; 30 pp; **MAH.**

WIGMORE, WILLIAM H.
No. 7, South Eighth Street, Philadelphia, PA.
pre–1895 Wholesale Net Price List of Gold, Silver, Aluminum and Plated Surgical, Dental, and Veterinary Instruments, Poultry and Cattle Specialties; 168 pp; **MAH** (66629 610.78085 W435).

WILLIS, WM. V., & CO.
131 So. 11th Street, Philadelphia, PA.
n.d. Dr. Chevalier Jackson's Instrument for Peroral Endoscopy and Laryngeal Surgery; 16 pp; **MAH.**

WILMINGTON DENTAL MANUFACTURING CO., THE
No. 143 Filbert Street, Philadelphia, PA.
May 1893 Impression Trays, Pamphlet No. 2; 48 pp; **MAH** (C617.6085 W).

WILMOT-CASTLE CO.
Rochester, New York.
1928 Correct Sterilization with Full Automatic Heat Control, Catalog N, Section O; **MAH** (C610.78085 W).

WOCHER, MAX, & SON, CO.
29-31 West 6th Street, Cincinnati, Ohio.
pre–1891 Illustrated Catalogue and Price List, Surgical Instruments and Orthopedic Appliances; 318 pp, photocopy; **MAH.**
1930 Hospital and Physicians Equipment, Furniture, Instruments, Sundries, 44th Abridged ed.; 370 pp, index; **MAH.**

1938   A New Catalog, Surgical Instruments, Sanitary Furniture, Physicians and Hospital Supplies, 51st ed.; 240 pp; **MAH.**

ZEISS, CARL
Jena.

1898   Optische Werkstaette, Microscopes and Microscopal Accessories, 31st ed., 124 pp, in English; **MAH** (C681.4085 Z247m).

1912-3   Mikroskope and Mikroskopische Hilfsapparate, no. 35; 127 pp; **MAH** (681.4085 Z247m).

1927   Opthalmological Instruments; 52 pp; **MAH** (C617.75085 Z).

1934   Microscopes and Accessories, mikrol; 150 pp, index; **MAH** (578.1 z47).

1934   Microscopes, Accessories for Oblique Observation, mikro 478e; 11 pp; **MAH** (C681.4085 Z247 a).

1937   Photomicrographic Apparatus, mikro 414e; 50 pp; **MAH** (C778.56085 Z47).

INSTITUTIONS AND THEIR TRADE CATALOGUES*

ABD
Audrey B. Davis, Ph.D.
1214 Bolton St.
Baltimore, Maryland 21217

Claudius Ash and Sons
L. Bienaime
Bullock and Crenshaw
J. Condell & Son
J. Gardner and Son
W. R. Grossmith, Ltd.
Hausmann & Dunn Co.

Lord, Stoutenburgh & Co.
T. H. McAllister
George Maw
Mayer & Phelps, Ltd.
Ohio Chemical
  & Manufacturing Co.
Mario Padilla

ACR/MAH
American College of Radiology Collection of Literature,
  now located at The National Museum of American
  History Library
Room 5016
Smithsonian Institution
Washington, D.C. 20560
c/o Rhoda Ratner, Chief Librarian

American Vacuum Company
Anderson, Norden & Co.
The Baker Electrical Co.
Baker X-Ray Co.
Frank S. Betz & Co.
James G. Biddle
Geo. W. Brady & Co.
M. H. Bresette X-Ray
  & Radio Co.
Buck X-Ograph Co.
Burdick Research Laboratories

Campbell Bros.
Campbell Electric Co.
Clapp & Eastham Co.
Clapp, Otis and Son
Alfred E. Dean
The Dick X-Ray Co.
Eastman Kodak
Electro-Radiation Co.
Empire Electric Co.
Engeln Electric Co.
H. G. Fischer & Co.

*This list contains only the company's name. For specific information concerning which of the company's catalogs are available from each institution, please consult the manufacturers listing.

The Folmer & Schwing Mfg. Co.
Franklin X-Ray Corporation
R. Friedlander & Co., Inc.
Fuerstenau
General Electric Co.
General Electric X-Ray
  Corporation
Geneva Optical Co.
Graybar Electric Co.
Hanovia Chemical &
  Manufacturing Co.
Heinz-Wandner X-Ray Tube Co.
High Tension Co.
High Tension Transformer and
  Equipment Corp.
Hyfrex Coils
International X-Ray Corporation
The K & B Electric
  Equipment Co.
Keleket
Kelley-Koett Mfg. Co., Inc.
Kesslring X-Ray Tube Co.
Keystone Electric Co., Inc.
Kny-Scheerer Co.
Liebel-Flarsheim Co.
MacAlaster, Wiggin Co.
E. Machlett & Son
McIntosh Battery & Optical Co.
Marvex X-Ray Equipment
Metalix
William Meyer Co.
E. B. Meyrowitz
C. H. F. Mueller
Mueller X-Ray Tubes
Vincenz Mueller & Co.
Murley-Rolleston Corporation
Newton & Co.
Newton & Wright, Ltd.
Northern X-Ray Co.
Oliver Electric
  & Manufacturing Co.

Paragon
Patterson Screen Co.
Philips Metalix Corporation
James Picker Inc.
Picker International Corporation
Picker X-Ray Corporation
Precision
Precision Coronaless
The R-B Company
Rieber Laboratories
Roentgen Manufacturing Co.
Roentgen Appliance Corporation
Rogers Electric Laboratories Co.
Rotex
Schall & Son
Scheidel W. Coil Co.
Scheidel-Western X-Ray Coil Co.
C. L. Scheu
Siemens & Halske, A. -G.
Siemens-Reiniger-Veifa Co.
Smit Roentgen N. V.
W. B. Snook Mfg. Co., Inc.
Snook-Roentgen
  Manufacturing Co.
Standard Engeln Corporation
Standard X-Ray Company
Swett and Lewis Company
Synchronous Manufacturing Co.
T-E X-Ray Laboratory
Victor Electric Company
Victor X-Ray Corporation
R. V. Wagner & Co.
Waite & Bartlett X-Ray Mfg. Co.
Wander & Son X-Ray Tube Co.
Wappler Electric Co.
Williams, Brown & Earle
Willyoung & Co.
Elmer G. Willyoung
The Willyoung & Gibson Co.
The X-Ray Tube Co.

ACS
American College of Surgeons
55 East Erie Street

Chicago, Ill. 60611
c/o Ms. Jeri Ryan, Librarian

Allen & Hanburys, Ltd.
Ernesto Invernizze
Matthew Brothers
S. Maw, Son and Thompson
Sears, Roebuck and Co.

Sharp & Smith
Alb. Stille
George Tiemann & Co.
Charles Truax

ADA
American Dental Association
211 East Chicago Avenue
Chicago, Ill. 60611
c/o Aletha Kowitz, Director, Bureau of Library Services

Chicago Refining Co.
Codman & Shurtleff
Consolidated Dental Mfg. Co.
A. M. Leslie & Co.
John T. Nolde Dental Mfg. Co.

M. F. Paterson
Ransom & Randolph Co.
Ritter Dental Manufacturing Co.
Gustav Scharmann
Samuel S. White Dental Mfg. Co.

AFMM
Armed Forces Medical Museum
Armed Forces Institute of Pathology
Washington, D.C. 20306-6000
c/o Daniel W. Bennett, III, Archivist

Achili, Achille
E. Adnet et Fils
Aloe & Hernstein
William H. Armstrong & Co.
C. Baker
Bausch & Lomb Optical Co.
R & J Beck
Frank S. Betz & Co.
Wm. Boekel and Co.
C. W. Bolte, Nachf.
G. Boulitte
Cambridge Scientific
    Instrument Co.
A. Le Carpentier
L. P. Casella
Caswell, Hazard & Co.
The L. D. Caulk Co.
C. Cegielski
Charriere
Joseph Francois Bernard Charriere

Chicago Apparatus Co.
Chicago Refining Co.
Codman & Shurtleff
Collin
Collin & Cie
Collin, Maison Charriere
(Maison Charriere)
Columbia Dental Chairs
Consolidated Dental
    Manufacturing Co.
Cooke, Troughton & Siemens Ltd.
James Coxeter & Son
Samuel A. Crocker & Co.
Rudolf Detert
Diamond Brand
Les Fils d'Emile Deyrolle
James T. Dougherty
Down Bros.
William M. Eisen
Electro Surgical Instrument Co.

Elliotts and Australian Drug
  Prty., Ltd.
M. Esterlus
Evans & Wormull
Feick Brothers
F. L. Fischer
W. F. Ford
Franklin Educational Co.
Mfr. Belge de Gembloux, S.A.
J. H. Gemrig & Son
Geneva Optical Co.
The Graf-Apsco Co.
Fernand Guillot
Hagar & Meisinger
E. Hartneck
J. F. Hartz Co., Ltd.
Fred Haslam & Co.
Oskar Heimstadt
Heillige
William H. Horn & Bro.
International Equipment Co.
W. & S. Jones
Rudolf Jung
Kny-Scheerer Co.
D. W. Kolbe & Son
Freidrich Krupp
Leach & Greene
Ernst Leitz
Charles Lentz and Sons
LePlanquais
A. M. Leslie & Co.
Leune Etablissements
L. J. Loomis & Co., Inc.
Luer, Maison
J. F. Luhme & Co.
Mann Alfons, Sp. AKC
A. A. Marks
L. Mathieu
L. Mathieu, Maison
Raoul Mathieu
S. Maw and Son
S. Maw, Son and Sons
Ernst W. Mayer & Perry
  G. Meltzer
William Y. McAllister

McIntosh Battery & Optical Co.
McIntosh Galvanic & Faradic
  Battery Co.
A. Meisinger
Max Meyer
E. B. Meyrowitz
Miller & Brothers
Moock-Guillot
Vincenz Mueller & Co.
Gebruder Muenke
H. Mukerji & Co.
R. Nagashima Co.
J. Odelga
J. Oiso & Co.
Opplem Co.
Otto & Reynders
R. I. Pearson & Co.
Pfaltz & Bauer, Inc.
George P. Pilling & Son Company
Pittsburgh Electric Specialties Co.
Powell & Lealand
Jeremiah Quinlan Co.
Carl Reichert
John Reynders & Co.
Ritter Dental Manufacturing Co.
E. S. Ritchie and Sons
Robert & Collin
Dr. Hermann Rohrbeck
Sanitas
E. H. Sargent & Co.
Scientific Materials Co.
Shepard & Dudley
K. Yawata Shoten, Inc.
J. Sklar Mfg. Co., Inc.
Smith, Beck & Beck
Snowden & Brother
Spencer & Crocker
Spencer Lens Co.
Stainlessfrance
Alb. Stille
James Swift
Arthur H. Thomas Co.
George Tiemann & Co.
M. G. Trouve
Charles Truax, Greene & Co.

Voigtlander & Sohn, A. -G.
Charles Howell Ward
John M. Weiss
John Weiss and Sons, Ltd.
Western Electric Co., Ltd.
Samuel S. White Dental Mfg. Co.
Will Corporation

The Charles Willms Surgical
    Inst. Co.
Winkel
R. Winkel
Max Wocher and Son
E. A. Yarnall Co.
Carl Zeiss

AO

American Optical Co.
14 Mechanic Street
Southbridge, Massachusetts
c/o John M. Young, Director, Optical Heritage Museum

American Optical Company
B. B. W. Manufacturing Co., Inc.
Bausch & Lomb Optical Company
Bay State Optical Co.
A. C. Becken
Becton, Dickinson & Co.
N. P. Benson Optical Co.
Belgard Spero, Inc.
Frank S. Betz Co.
The Bishop Company
The Bourque Optical Co.
D. V. Brown
Brunswig Drug Company
The Buckeye State Optical, Inc.
Farrington Manufacture Company
The Faultless Rubber Co.
The Fibre-Metal Products Co.
Arthur Frank & Co., Inc.
The S. Galeski Optical Co.
Globe Optical Company
Gordon & Morrison
Gothom Optical Instrument &
    Machinery Corporation
Grout Manufacturing Company,
    B. T. Roberts
F. A. Hardy & Co.
J. M. & A. C. Johnston Co.
E. Kirstein Sons Company
F. A. Koch & Co.
Frank Krementz Co.
Leonard Krower

Kryptok Sales Company
Kryptok Company
Lancaster Optical Company
The Lion Optical Co.
L. Manasse Co.
Martin-Copeland Co.
May Manufacturing Co.
McIntire, Magee & Brown Co.
Michigan Optical Company
Midwest Optical Supply
Milwaukee Optical
    Manufacturing Co.
Mine Safety Appliances Co.
R. Mohr & Sons
Jno. L. Moore & Sons
The National Optical Company
New Orleans Optical Company
Newport Optical Mfg. Company
Omaha Optical Company
Onepiece Bifocal Lens Company
Onepiece Publishing Company
S.T. Nichols & Co.
The Oskamp Nolting Company
Johnston Optical Co.
Optical Products Corp.
J. Ouimetter, Jr. Co.
Pennsylvania Optical Co.
Rodney Pierce Optical
    Company, Inc.
James W. Queen & Co.
Riggs Optical Company

Shur-On Standard Optical
Co., Inc.
Standard Optical Company
Strauss Optical Co., Inc.
Leo Strauss
Street, Linder and Propert
Jas. Stuart & Sons
J. F. Sturdy's Sons Co.
Sussfeld, Lorsch & Co.
Sussfeld, Lorsch & Schimmel
E. & J. Swigart
The E. & J. Swigart Company

Taylor Instrument Companies
The Teller Optical Co.
Testrite Instrument Co.
Toric Optical Co., Inc.
Tortaline Mfg. Corporation
Trenkmann Bros.
Wappler Electric Company, Inc.
Charles Wilder Company
C. A. Wilkinson (&) Co.
T. A. Willson & Co.
Willson Goggles, Inc.

APS

American Philosophical Society
105 South Fifth Street
Philadelphia, Pa. 19106
c/o Mr Roy E. Goodman, Reference Librarian

Joseph Francois Bernard Charriere
Hebert
David & John Henshaw

Luke Howe
Amos Gerald Hull
Joseph Togno

BDA

British Dental Association
Robert and Lilian Lindsay Library
64 Wimpole Street
London, W1M 8AL
England
c/o Head Librarian

Allen & Handburys, Ltd.
Claudius Ash and Sons
Dental Manufacturing Co., Inc.
Down Bros.
George Maw
S. Maw, Son and Sons

Midland Dental Manufacturing
Co., Ltd.
C. J. Plucknett & Co.
W. M. Sharp Mfg. Co., Inc.
Smale Brothers
Samuel S. White Dental Mfg. Co.

BLEL

Bakken Library of Electricity in Life
3537 Zenith Avenue South
Minneapolis, Minnesota 55416
c/o Elizabeth Ihrig, Librarian

Adams-Morgan Co.
Allen & Hanburys, Ltd.

William H. Armstrong & Co.
Arnold & Sons

Claudius Ash and Sons
J. & L. Berge
Boericke and Tafel
G. Boulitte
Breguet
Breton, Freres
Butler Electro-Massage Co.
L. P. Casella
Central Scientific Co.
Charles Chardin
The Chloride of Silver Dry
   Battery Co.
Andrew Chrystal
Samuel A. Crocker & Co.
Gerrard Cuxson, & Co.
Daniel Davis, Jr.
Dental Manufacturing Co., Inc.
Down Bros.
Luis Drescher
J. J. Duck Co.
E. Ducretet et Cie
Eastern Laboratories, Inc.
Electro Surgical Instrument Co.
Fannin & Co.'s
Otto Flemming
A. Gaiffe
Galvano-Faradic
   Manufacturing Co.
General Electric Co.
General Electric X-Ray
   Corporation
German Electric Belt Agency
Good Health Publishing Co.
Sam J. Gorman Co.
Joseph Gray & Son
Hartmann und Braun, A.-G.
W. A. Hirschmann
Jeffrey-Fell Co.
Jetter & Scheerer
Kelley-Koett Manufacturing
   Co., Inc.
Keystone Electric Co., Inc.
Jerome Kidder
Kliegl Bros.
L. E. Knott Apparatus Co.

Kny-Scheerer Co.
Max Kohl
D. W. Kolbe & Son
Krohne & Sesemann
Josef Leiter
Liebel-Flarsheim Co.
Maison A. Luer
Maison Mathieu
Manhattan Electrical Supply Co.
S. Maw, Son and Sons
Mayer & Phelps, Ltd.
McIntosh Battery & Optical Co.
McIntosh Electrical Corporation
Curt W. Meyer
E. B. Meyrowitz
Meyrowitz Bros.
J. H. Montague
Vincenz Mueller & Co.
Nachet et Fils
Noyes Bros. & Cutler
J. Odelga
Ohio Electric Works
Edward Palmer
George P. Pilling & Son Company
Powers & Anderson Dental Co.
Pulvermacher Galvanic Co.
Queen & Company
Radiquet et Massiot
H. Reiner
Reiniger, Gebbert & Schall
John Reynders & Co.
Jules Richard
Rochester Surgical Appliance Co.
Rohrbeck and Goebeler
Rupalley & Cie
Sanborn Co.
William Edward Schall
Sears, Roebuck and Co.
Siemens & Halske, A. -G.
Singer Sewing Machine Co.
Swett and Lewis Company
The Thompson and Plaster Co.
George Tiemann & Co.
Chas. Truax, Greene & Co.
T. S. Brothers Co.

Charles Verdin
J. C. Vetter & Co.
Vibrator Instrument Co.
Victor Electric Co.
Voltaic Belt and Appliance Co.
R. V. Wagner & Co.
Waite & Bartlett X-Ray Mfg. Co.
Andre Walter Etablissements
Wappler Electric Co.
Ward, Montgomery and Co.
Watkins and Hill

John Weiss and Son
Western Dental
    Manufacturing Co.
Western Electric
    Manufacturing Co.
Samuel S. White Dental Mfg. Co.
H. A. Whiteside
H. Windler
Max Wocher and Son
James Woolley Sons & Co., Ltd.
Carl Zeiss

BRML

British Museum/Library
Great Russell St.
London WC1 3DG, England

Bath & Co.
J. Canzius

Lincoln Dental
    Manufacturing Co.

CDMC

Cresent Dental Manufacturing Co.
7750 W. 47th Street
Lyons, Illinois 60534
c/o Edward L. Chott

Frank S. Betz Company
Chicago Dental Mfg. Co.
Cleveland Dental Mfg. Co.
Crescent Dental Mfg. Co.
Detroit Dental Manufacturing
    Company
Electro-Dental Mfg. Co.
Goldsmith Bros. S. & R. Co.
Penn Surgical Mfg. Co.
George P. Pilling & Son Co.

Randall- Faichney Corp.
B. Rubinson
Gideon Sibley
J. Sklar Mfg. Co.
Snow Dental Co.
Specialty Manufacturing Company
Union Dental Instrument
    Mfg. Co.
Samuel S. White Dental Mfg. Co.

CHS

Connecticut Historical Society
1 Elizabeth Street
Hartford, Connecticut 06105
c/o Everett C. Wilkie, Librarian

Bull & Metcalfe
J. & W. Grunow & Co.

Hartford Dental Depot
McNeil & Washburn

CPP
Library of the College of Physicians of Philadelphia
Historical Collections
19 South 22nd Street
Philadelphia, Pa. 19103
c/o Tom Horrocks, Curator

Abbott Laboratories
Abbotts Aldernay Dairies, Inc.
Ahl
Dr. H. M. Alexander & Co., Inc.
The Alkalol Co.
Allen & Hanburys, Ltd.
A. S. Aloe Co.
The American and Continental
  Sanitas Co., Ltd.
American Apothecaries Co.
American Artificial Limb, Co.
American Ferment Co.
American Oxygen Association
American Peroxide and
  Chemical Co.
American Plasmon Syndicate Ltd.
The American Pharmacological
  Society
American Surgical Co.
Ammond Chemical Co.
Amsterdam Brothers
Angier Chemical Co.
Anglo-American
  Pharmaceutical Corp.
The Antikamnia Chemical Co.
George W. Archer
The Argol Co., Chemists
The Arlington Chemical Co.
Armour & Co.
Dr. John Aulde
L. A. Babcock
Emile Bachelet
A. C. Barnes Co.
Battle & Co.
The Battle Creek Sanitarium
  Food Co.
Baudin

Bauer & Black
Bausch and Lomb Optical Co.
Bayer Co.
R. & J. Beck
Becton, Dickinson & Co.
Prof. Dr. Wilhelm Beninghoven
Charles Peters and Robert Lee
  Benson
Charles Beseler
Frank S. Betz & Co.
James G. Biddle
The Biogen Co., Inc.
Bischoff
C. Bischoff & Co., Inc.
Douglas Bly
Boericke and Tafel
Bonshur & Holmes
Louis Book
John L. Borsch & Co.
Boulanger-Dausse et Cie
G. Boulitte
The Bovinine Co.
The J. P. Bush Mfg. Co.
Bradbury, Wilkinson & Co., Ltd.
Deane Bramhall Co.
Breitenbach, M. J. Co.
F. Bringhurst
Brin's Oxygen Co., Ltd.
Frederick W. Brown Co.
William and Earle Brown
The Brunswick Pharmacal Co.
Bullock & Crenshaw
Burnham Soluable Iodine Co.
Burroughs Wellcome & Co.
G. W. Carnrick, Co.
The Cellasin Co.
Chambers, Inskeep & Co.

Joseph Francois Bernard Charriere
Chicago Pharmacal Co.
The Chloride of Silver Dry Cell
  Battery Co.
Ciba Co., Inc.
A. C. Clark and Co.
Clark and Roberts
Clermont-Ferrand
Clin's Laboratories
Codman & Shurtleff
The Cold Electric Light Co.
C. M. Corbin
Cosby & McGovern
The Charles N. Crittenton Co.
Cystogen Chemical Co.
Dad Chemical Co.
John B. Daniel
S. A. Darrach
Davis and Geck, Inc.
Davis and Leyden
Denver Chemical
  Manufacturing Co.
The DeZeng Standard Co.
Direct Sales Co.
H. D. Dougherty & Co., Inc.
Dow Portable Electric Co.
L. Droll
The Drug Products Co.
J. Dubosco
Edison Manufacturing Co.
Eimer & Amend
Eisner & Mendelson Co.
Elberfeld Co.
Electric Ozone Co.
Electric Storage Battery Co.
Electro Surgical
  Manufacturing Co.
Electro Surgical Instruments
Electro Therapy Products Corp.
Energen Works
Engeln Electric Co.
Esocardio
Etna Chemical Co.
Eureka Rheostat
George B. Evans

Evans & Wormull
Fairchild Brothers & Foster
The Fairchild Chemical
  Laboratory
Farbenfabriken of Elberfeld Co.
Farbewerke-Hoechst Co.
Fellows Medical Manufacturing
  Co., Inc.
Joseph C. Ferguson, Jr.
The Ferment Co.
N. Finzelberg's
F. L. Fischer
G. W. Flavell & Bro., Inc.
The Fleischmann Co.
Otto Fleming
Flicoteaux & Co.
W. F. Ford
E. Fougera & Co., Inc.
Fowler's Pessaries
H. C. Fox & Sons
The Fraser Tablet, Triturate
  Mfg. Co.
Fries Bros., Manufacturing
  Chemists
George R. Fuller, Co.
C. Funk
William Gaertner and Co.
A. Gaiffe
Henri Galante et Fils
R. W. Gardner
J. H. Gemrig & Son
General Electric Co.
Geneva Optical Co.
Girard Co.
L. Giroux
Globe Manufacturing Co.
The B. F. Goodrich Co.
Frank W. Gorse Co.
A. Goubeaux
R. Graf & Co.
Emil Greiner
John Joseph Griffen and Sons
Charles F. Groshaly
Julius Grossman
Grosvenor and Richards

H. Gueride
Georg Haertel
Hahn's Trusses
G. W. Hall
W. D. Halsey & Co.
Theodore Hamblin, Ltd.
J. E. Hanger & Co., Ltd.
Hanovia Chemical &
  Manufacturing Co.
F. A. Hardy Co.
Harold Surgical Corp.
Harvard Fever Thermometers
Fred Haslam & Co.
Hazard, Hazard & Co.
Johann Georg Heine
P. Hermann
A. L. Hernstein
H. H. Hessler, Co.
E. W. Higbee
W. A. Hirschmann
Hoffman-LaRoche Chemical
  Works
Hollister, B. K.
The Hollister-Wilson Laboratories
The Home Vapor Bath
Hoos Albumin Milk
Edward H. Hoos
Hopkins-Weller Drug Co.
Horlick's Malted Milk
William H. Horn & Bro.
The Hospital Supply Co.
W. H. Hostelley & Co.
Hudson
Hudson Pharmacal Co.
Illinois Surgical Appliance Co.
Jenson-Salsbery Laboratories
H. W. Johns-Manville Co.
Johnson, Holloway & Co.
Johnson & Johnson
Rudolf Jung
Horatio G. Kern Co.
Kesslring X-Ray Tube Co.
Keystone Bedding Manufactory
Keystone Electric Co., Inc.
Keystone Surgical Instrument Co.

Jerome Kidder
P. J. Kipp & Zonen
E. Kirstein's Sons Co.
Klingelfuss & Co., Fr.
Kloman Instrument Co., Inc.
E. L. Kloss
Richard Kny and Co.
Kny-Scheerer Co.
C. A. F. Kohlbaum
D. W. Kolbe & Son
E. Krauss & Co.
Krohne & Sesemann
John F. Kuemerle & Kolbe
Kutnow Brothers Ltd.
Laboratoires Lancasme
Lambert Snyder Co.
La Motte Chemical Products
H. Landenberger
F. & M. Launtenschlaeger
J. Elwood Lee Co.
Charles Leedom
The Leeds & Northrup Co.
Thomas Leeming & Co.
Lehn & Fink
Josef Leiter
Ernst Leitz
Docteur F. G. Lemercier
Charles Lentz and Sons
M. Le Prince
Lenz & Lossau
A. M. Leslie & Co.
David B. Levy, Inc.
D. P. Levy
Lewis, Bailie & Co.
H. K. Lewis & Co.
Leyden
H. Lieber & Co.
S. Liebmann's & Sons
Life Saving Devices Co.
Eli Lilly & Co.
J. E. Limeburner & Co.
C. J. Lincoln Co.
Lindsay Laboratories
Lit Brothers
Lloyd Brothers

Adolph Long Co.
Loomis-Manning Filter Co.
Lord Electric Co.
A. Luer, Maison
J. F. Luhme & Co.
C. Lukens De Witt Co.
A. Lutter
Lynch & Co.
MacAllaster Wiggin Co.
J. C. MacLean
Major, Genisson & Co.
The Males' Method Company
Mallinckrodt Chemical Works
H. A. Malmsten
Manhattan Surgeons' Supply Co.
Dr. Marey
Alexander Martin, B. O. A.
Martin's Method Inc.
The Marvel Co.
William J. Matheson & Co., Ltd.
Mathews and Wilson Ltd.
L. Mathieu
Raoul Mathieu
Maussner Manufacturing
   Co., Inc.
William Y. McAllister
W. Mitchell McAllister
Prof. T. McIllroy
McIntosh Battery & Optical Co.
NcNeil Laboratories
Robert McNeil
Mead, Johnson & Co.
The Mears Ear Phone Co., Inc.
Medical Novelty Co.
Medical Supply Association
Meinecke & Co.
Mellin's Food Co.
G. Mennen
Edward A. Merkel
The Merz Capsule Co.
H. A. Metz Laboratories
Ferdinand F. Metzger
William Meyer Co.
E. B. Meyrowitz
Michigan Biological Supply Co.

O. E. Miller Hernia
   Treatment Co.
Miller Rubber Manufacturing Co.
John T. Milliken & Co.
John Milne
Josef Mion
P. Moria
Moritz Boehme
Morris & Schrader
Morse & Burt Co.
The Mu-Col Co.
Muelhens & Kropff
F. A. D. Mueller Sohn
Mueller & Co.
Vincenz Mueller & Co.
Nachet et Fils
Narrangansett Machine Co.
Nathan Anklet Support Co.
The National Drug Co.
The National Food Co.
The National Pathological Labs.
National Stain and Reagent Co.
The New England Vaccine Co.
New York Intravenous Laboratory
Nicolay & Co.
North Spanish Laboratories
Norwich Pharmacal Co.
Novocal Chemical
   Manufacturing Co.
Numotizine Inc.
C. Nyrop
A. J. Nystrom & Co.
Ostermoor & Co.
Ostertag & Walton
O'Sullivan Rubber Co.
F. G. Otto and Sons
Professeur Palasciane
Palisades Manufacturing Co.
B. Frank Palmer
Pan-Peptogen Co., Ltd.
Drs. Papp & Becker
L. Pardee
Samuel B. Parmelee
Partz Electric Battery Co.
Pathe-Cinema

Patho-Chemical Co.

L. Pautauberge

The Perfect Inhaler Co.

Perkins Bacon & Co., Ltd.

Petrolagar Laboratories, Inc.

H. Pfau, Inh.

Philadelphia Audio
Laboratory, Inc.

The Philadelphia Electric Storage
Battery Renting Co.

Philadelphia Pure Oxygen Co.

Philadelphia Surgeon's Bandage
Institute

The Philadelphia Truss Co.

Physician's Specialty Co.

Physician's Supply Co. of
Philadelphia

George P. Pilling & Son Company

The Pillow Inhaler Co.

Pittsburgh Electric Specialties Co.

The Pneumachemic Co.

The Pneumo-Chemic
Vaporizer Co.

Ponds Extract Co.

Ponds Sphygmograph Co.

Portable Hygienic Vapor &
Disinfector Co.

A. Prazmowski

Precision Thermometer &
Instrument Co.

Pulvermacher Galvanic Co.

The Radium Emanation
Corporation

Carl Reichert

The Relevaine Soluble Tablet
Mfg. Co.

Resinol Chemical Co.

John Reynders & Co.

Rio Chemical Co.

Ritter Dental Manufacturing Co.

Robert & Collin

Milton Josiah Roberts

Rochester Surgical Appliance Co.

The Roessler & Hasslacher
Chemical Co.

Dr. Hermann Rohrbeck

Edward Rowan

The Sanax Co., Inc.

Sanborn Co.

Sanitarium Health Food Company

The Sanitube Co.

E. H. Sargent & Co.

F. Sartorius

Savory & Moore, Ltd.

Scanlan-Morris Co.

J. W. Schermerhorn & Co.

The P. Schoonmaker Bronchoscope

Schimmel & Co. (Fritzsche
Brothers)

Schlotterbeck & Foss Co.

A. & B. Schmeink

Chr. Schmidt

F. Schwabe

Scientific Materials Co.

Seabury & Johnson

Sears, Roebuck and Co.

William Selpho

Philip Frank Shaffner

Sharp & Smith

Sharpless & Watts

G. H. Sherman, M.D.

Simplex Lamp Mfg. Co.

Herbert S. Smith

Lee S. Smith & Sons Dental Depot

Martin H. Smith Co.

(William) Snowden Company

Société D'Études Scientifiques

C. M. Sorensen Co., Inc.

Sorensen Scientific Corporation

William M. Speakman

Spencer Lens Co.

Thomas D. Spencer

The Spirella Co.

Sprague Apparatus Co.

The Sprague Institute

Spurlock Neal Co.

E. R. Squibb

The Standard Chemical Co., Inc.

Standard Optical Co.

A. J. Steele

Stevens Physician Supply Co.
Alb. Stille
Adam Storz
Walter F. Sykes & Co.
Table Rock Laboratories Inc.
W. A. Talbott, Micajad & Co.
Taylor Instrument Companies
The Terry Heater Co.
Wilhelm Jul. Teufel
J. Thamm
The Thermalite Co.
A. W. Thomas
The Thompson and Plaster Co.
L. L. Thurwachter & Sons
George Tiemann & Co.
Timken- Detroit Co.
Torbay Freres
The Triton Co.
Charles Truax
Chas. Truax, Greene & Co.
Trubner & Co.
Union Artificial Limb Co.
United Fruit Co.
Usona Biochemical Chemical
	Lab., Inc.
The Valley Chemical Co.
The Valzahn Co.
G. Van Abbott & Sons
Van Horn & Sawtell
Van Orden Corset Co.
Varoma Medical Co.
The Vass Chemical Co., Inc.
Charles Verdin
Veroform Hygienic Co.
The Vibrometer Co.
Victor Electric Company
George H. Wahmann Mfg. Co.
Wilhelm Walb
George Wale & Co.
George J. Wallau

Alfred Walton
John Wanamaker
Wappler Electric Co.
Wappler Electric
	Manufacturing Co.
Warmbrunn, Quilitz & Co.
W. R. Warner & Co.
Warrington and Pennypacker
Waterbury Chemical Co.
Watson and Sons
Watters Laboratories
H. Weinhagen
John M. Weiss
Paul Weiss
John Weiss & Sons, Ltd.
The Wellcome Chemical
	Research Labs.
Western Electrical Instrument Co.
Western Electrical Co., Ltd.
The Western Pasteur Filter Co.
Whitall, Tatum & Co.
Samuel S. White Dental Mfg. Co.
Williams, Brown & Earle
W. V. Willis & Co.
The Charles Willms Surgical
	Instrument Co.
The Wilson Laboratories
H. Windler
Winthrop Chemical Co.
Wizard Foot Appliance Co.
Max Wocher & Son
The Optical Wolverine
The Wonder Company
John Wyeth & Brother, Inc.
E. A. Yarnall Co.
Archibald Young
Carl Zeiss
Freidrich Ziegler
Joseph Zentmayer
Zonte Optical Co.

CS
Codman and Shurtleff, Inc.
Pasella Park Drive

Randolph, Massachusetts 02368
c/o Francis X. Herr, Manager of Professional Services

A. S. Aloe Co.
Claudius Ash and Sons, Ltd.
Frank S. Betz Co.
Carstens Manufacturing Co.
Codman & Shurtleff
Crocker-Fels Co.
Fuller and Fuller Co.
G. F. Harvey Co.
The Hospital Supply Co.
Holekamp-Moore Instrument Co.
Kny-Scheerer Co.
F. A. Koch & Co.
Leach & Greene
Charles Lentz and Sons

E. F. Mahady Co.
George F. Pilling & Son Co.
Powers & Anderson Surgical
    Instrument Co.
John Reynders & Co.
Scanlan-Morris Co.
Sears, Roebuck & Co.
Sharp & Smith
Theodore Tafel
Waite & Bartlett Mfg. Co.
John Weiss & Son, Ltd.
Winchester Surgical Supply Co.
Max Wocher & Son Co.

CTY-B
Yale Medical History Library
P. O. Box 3333
Yale University
New Haven, Connecticut 06510
c/o Mr. Ferenc Gyorgyey, Historical Librarian

Bausch & Lomb Optical Co.
R. & J. Beck
Felix Berguerand, Brévète
R. Boericke and Co.
Boyveau, Pelletier et Cie,
    Successeurs
Buffalo Dental Mfg. Co.
Cambridge Scientific
    Instrument Co.
J. Canzius
Central Scientific Co.
N. B. Chamberlain & Sons
Chicago Laboratory Supply and
    Scale Co.
Codman & Shurtleff
Warren E. Collins, Inc.
Continental Laboratory
    Specialties Co.
P. Desaga

Les Fils D'Emile Deyrolle
Emil & Vierth Dittmar
E. Ducretet
Dr. M. Th. Edelmann & Sohn
The Educational Supply Co.
Eimer & Amend
Electric Solar Co., Inc.
Electro Surgical Instrument Co.
The Fritz and Hawley, Co.
Galante, Henri et Fils
Goebeler, H., & Co.
Ernest Goldbacher
Peter Gray and Sons Inc.
Emil Greiner
Greiner & Fredrichs
Eduard Gressler
E. H. Griffith
Dr. Georg Gruebler
Gundlach's

Hall, Wilford Laboratories
Hanovia Chemical &
    Manufacturing Co.
F. A. Hardy Co.
Harold Surgical Corp.
The Heidbrink Co.
Henry
A. L. Hernstein
Samuel Highley
Holophane Co., Inc.
Horne & Thornthwaite
The Hospital Supply Co.
Dr. Jaeger's Sanitary Woolen
    System Co.
Jewell Models
Johnson & Johnson
Max Kaehler & Martini
Edward G. Kelley
Kelley-Koett Manufacturing
    Co., Inc.
J. E. Kennedy & Co.
Edward N. Kent
Charles B. Kleine
L. E. Knott Apparatus Co.
Kny, Richard and Co.
Kny-Scheerer Co.
Rudolph Koenig
Koenigliche Porzellan-Manufactur
Max Kohl
Fritz Koehler
E. Krauss & Co.
A. Kruess
The Laboratory and School Supply
    Co., Ltd.
William Ladd
La Motte Chemical Products
Leon Laurent
Thomas Laurie
Lehn & Fink
Ernst Leitz
G. A. Lenoir
Leppin & Masche
Lerebours et Secretan
J. F. Luhme & Co.
Edouard Lutz

Mariaud
Chez Marloye
Mathieu Fils
L. Mathieu
S. Maw and Son
T. H. McAllister
William Y. McAllister
McAllister & Brothers
W. Mitchell McAllister
Hulbert Merwin & Co.
E. B. Meyrowitz
Meyrowitz Brothers
Miller & Brothers
Charlers L. Mitchell
J. D. Moeller
George Morton & Co.
Mueller & Co.
Louis Mueller-Unkel
Muencke Gebrueder
Dr. Robert Muencke
Nachet et Fils
Nalder Brothers & Co.
The National College of
    Electro-Therapeutics
National School Furnishing Co.
New York Thermometer Co.
Charles Noe
W. F. Noellner
Christian Ludwig Oechsle
August Oertling
J. Orme & Co.
Palo Co.
Palo-Myers, Inc.
Benjamin Pike, Jr.
Pixii, Pere et Fils
Simon Ploessel
Prang Educational Co.
W. G. Pye & Co.
James W. Queen
H. M. Raynor
Carl Reichert
Rhenish Glass Works
Edward S. Ritchie
E. S. Ritchie & Sons
Ritter Dental Manufacturing Co.

Rohrbeck & Goebeler
Ross Ltd., Mfg. Opticians
George F. Sargent's
D. Fils Savalle, & Cie
Friedrich Wilhelm Schiek
Schlag & Berend
Schott & Genossen
Schott & Gen
J. Schroeder
Theodor Schroeter
Scientific Materials Co.
L. R. Sexton
John W. Sidle & Co.
Smith & Beck
Smith, Beck & Beck
Herbert S. Smith
Société Genevoise
H. Soleil
Spencer Lens Co.
Spencer Optical Co.
Spindler & Hoyer
Standard Scientific Company
C. A. Steinheil
August Stendicke
J. H. Steward
Charles Stodder
C. H. Stoelting Co.
Emil Jun. Stoehrer
M. Tauber

Taylor Instrument Companies
The Thermo Electric
  Instrument Co.
Sir William Thompson
Thum, Ed., Institut fuer
  Mikroskopie
R. B. Tolles
A. Treffurth
Troughton and Simms
Van Laer, J.-B.-P.
A. Verbeek & Peckholdt
Videx
Voight & Hochgesang
Voightlander & Son Optical Co.
George Wale & Co.
W. H. Walmsley & Co.
Warmbrunn, Quilitz & Co.
C. B. Warring
West Disinfecting Co., Inc.
Westinghouse
Edmund Wheeler
Whitall, Tatum & Co.
Samuel S. White Dental Mfg. Co.
Joseph M. Wightman
Wilford Laboratories
Williams, Brown & Earle
Elmer G. Willyoung
Wilmot Castle Company
Carl Zeiss

CUHSL
Health Sciences Library of Columbia University
701 West 168 Street
New York, New York 10032
c/o Mrs. Sharon Barns, Head, Reference Section

W. F. Ford
Manufacture Belge
  de Gembloux, S.A.
E. B. Meyrowitz
Palo-Myers, Inc.

John Reynders & Co.
Ritter Dental Manufacturing Co.
George Tiemann & Co.
U. S. Council of National Defense
The Optical Wolverine

HML
Hagley Museum and Library
P. O. Box 3630

Wilmington, Delaware 19807
c/o Mary Lou Neighbor, Reference Librarian

A. S. Aloe Co.
Frank S. Betz & Co.
Wm. Boekel and Co.
Bullock & Crenshaw
Canton Surgical and Dental
  Chair Co.
The L. D. Caulk Co.
Consolidated Dental
  Manufacturing Co.
The Dental Specialty Co.
The Dentists' Supply Co.
Edward P. Dolbey Co.
J. L. Dunkly Co.
E. I. DuPont de Nemours & Co.
F. Eissner & Co.
Evans Co.
Goldsmith Brothers Smelting and
  Refining Co.
Johnson & Lund
Keller Dental Co.
Charles Lentz and Sons
A. M. Leslie & Co.

Manhattan Dental Co.
J. G. Maynard & Co.
McKesson & Robbins
Moyer, The J. Bird Co., Inc.
G. F. Harvey Co.
Haynes Stellite Co.
A. Hewitt
The Hospital Supply Co.
Penn Surgical Manufacturing
  Co., Inc.
L. Silverman
Lee S. Smith & Sons Dental Depot
Terraplastica Manufacturing Co.
George Tiemann & Co.
John T. Toland
Samuel S. White Dental Mfg. Co.
W. V. Willis & Co.
The Wilmington Dental
  Manufacturing Co.
E. A. Yarnall Co.
Richard Young

FI
The Library at
The Franklin Institute Science Museum and Planetarium
20th and The Benjamin Franklin Parkway
Philadelphia, Pennsylvania 19103
c/o Mr. Charles Wilt, Librarian

H. D. Justi
S. Maw, Son and Thompson
Ritter Dental Manufacturing

Wappler Electric Co.
Samuel S. White Dental Mfg. Co.

HUBL
Baker Library
Harvard University School of Business
Archives and Manuscript Department
Boston, Massachusetts 02163

George C. Goodwin & Co.

HDM

Howard Dittrick Museum of Historical Medicine
The Cleveland Medical Library Association
11000 Euclid Avenue
Cleveland, Ohio 44106
c/o Dr. James Edmonson, Curator

A. S. Aloe Co.
W. H. Armstrong & Co.
Claudius Ash and Sons
Bausch and Lomb Optical Co.
Bullock and Crenshaw
Codman & Shurtleff
Eimer & Amend
Feick Brothers
Greiner & Fredrichs
Hausmann, C. Friedrich,
  Sanitatsgeshaft-Hechtapotheke
Johnson & Lund
Kny-Scheerer Co.
Ernst Leitz
A. A. Marks
S. Maw, Son and Thompson
Mayer & Phelps, Ltd.
McIntosh Battery & Optical Co.
Noyes Brothers & Cutler
H. Reiner

Reiniger, Gebbert & Schall
E. H. Sargent & Co.
Scanlan-Morris Co.
M. Scharrer, A. -G.
Schuemann-Jones Co.
Carl Reichert
Sharp & Smith
Spencer Lens Co.
George Tiemann & Co.
Charles Truax
Peter Van Schaak & Sons
Vereinigte Fabriken fuer
  Laboratoriumsbedarf
Watson & Sons
W. A. Weed & Co.
Samuel S. White Dental Mfg. Co.
The Wilmington Dental Mfg. Co.
Max Wocher & Son
Carl Zeiss

ISUM

Southern Illinois School of Medicine
Medical Library, Special Collection
801 North Rutledge Street
Springfield, Illinois 62708
c/o Rick Dilley, Head, Technical Services

C. L. Frame Dental Supply Co.
Physicians' Supply Co. of Phila.

Peter Van Schaak & Sons
Wappler Electric Co.

JHIHM

Johns Hopkins Institute for the History of Medicine
The Johns Hopkins University
1800 East Monument Street
Baltimore, Md. 21205
c/o Ms. Doris Thibodeau

A. S. Aloe Co.
American Cystoscope
  Makers, Inc.
Down Bros.
A. Gaiffe
Hynson Westcott & Co.
Charles Lentz and Sons
Luer, Maison
McKee Surgical Instrument Co.
Vincenz Mueller & Co.

C. F. Palmer, Ltd.
H. Pfau, Inh.
Fernand and Jules Porges
Sharp & Smith
Charles John Samuel Thompson
George Tiemann & Co.
John M. Weiss
The Charles Willms Surgical
  Instrument Co.
H. Windler

LACMA
Los Angeles County Medical Association
634 So. Westlake Avenue
Los Angeles, California 90057
c/o Mr. James J. Ochoa, Head, Technical Processes

Abbott Laboratories
William H. Armstrong & Co.
Bausch and Lomb Optical Co.
Frank S. Betz & Co.
Eimer & Amend
Evans & Wormull
Feick Brothers
William Hatteroth
Keniston and Root
Mayer & Phelps, Ltd.
Noyes Brothers & Cutler
Richards Manufacturing Co.
F. A. Ritter Co.

Scanlan-Morris Co.
R. L. Scherer Co.
Sears, Roebuck and Co.
Sharp & Smith
C. H. Stoelting
Arthur H. Thomas Co.
George Tiemann & Co.
Chas. Truax, Greene & Co.
Warner-Chilcott Laboratories
John Weiss & Sons, Ltd.
Western Wholesale Drug Co.
Carl Zeiss

The following companies are represented at **LACMA,** *but are*
not listed in the manufacturer's listing of this book.

A. S. Aloe Co.
American Cystoscope
  Makers, Inc.
Austenal Company
C. R. Bard, Inc.
Capintec, Inc.
Caswell-Massey, Ltd.
Center Laboratories, Inc.
Codman and Shurtleff, Inc.
Colorado Serum Co. Laboratories
Creative Playthings, Inc.
Dyna Med
The Ealing Corp.

Florida Brace Corp.
Gambale & Merrill Corp.
General Biochemicals
Girton Manufacturing Co.
Glendale Surgical Supply Co.
Ernst Grieshaber
Invalex Co.
K & K Laboratories, Inc.
Ernst Leitz, GMBH
Mann Research Laboratories, Inc.
Matthay Professional Syupply Co.
Microbiological Associates
Vincenz Mueller & Co.

Nuclear Associates, Inc.
Orthopedic Equipment Co.
Orthopedic Frame Co.
Pacific Bio-Marine Supply Co.
Permalab-Metalab Equipment
  Co., Inc.
George P. Pilling and Son Co.
Research Inorganic Chemical Co.
Research Plus Laboratories, Inc.

Singer Sewing Machine Co.
Storz Instrument Co.
The Upjohn Co.
Varimex
G. H. Wahman
  Manufacturing Co.
Walters Surgical Co.
Western Surgical Supply Co.
William V. Willis & Co.

LC
Library of Congress
1st and Independence Avenues, S.E.
Washington, D.C. 20450

Note: The Library of Congress is regarded as having everything printed in this country. Unfortunately, many catalogs, from natural deterioration and through neglect, do not last over time. Thus, it is not true that the LC has every catalog and, in addition to those lost naturally, they sometimes destroy duplicates of those found elsewhere in the country. These are a few of what is available.

A. S. Aloe, Co.
J. Canzius
Kny-Scheerer Co.

Samuel S. White Dental Mfg. Co.
Edmund P. Banning, M.D.
Charles Howell Ward

LON
McGoogan Library of Medicine
Rare Book and History of Medicine Room
University of Nebraska Medical Center
42nd and Dewey Ave.
Omaha, Nebraska 68105
c/o Helen Yam, Librarian

Noyes Brothers & Cutler
Hettenger Bros.
  Manufacturing Co.

Kny-Scheerer Co.
Seiler Surgical Co.

LLU
Loma Linda University
Vernier Radcliffe Memorial Library
Loma Linda, California 92350

A. S. Aloe Co.
Edmund P. Banning, Co.
Frank S. Betz, Co.
Down Brothers
Henry

Thomas Knaur
Jeffery Fell Co.
Claude A. Lombard
Horace Miller
Noyes Brothers & Cutler

Ambroise Pare
Reid Brothers
Sharp and Smith
Storz Instrument Co.
George Tiemann & Co.

Charles Truax
Philip S. Wales
John M. Weiss
Western Surgical Supply Co.
Samuel S. White Dental Mfg. Co.

MAH
The National Museum of American History
Library, Room 5016
Smithsonian Institution
Washington, D.C. 20560
c/o Mrs. Rhoda Ratner, Chief Librarian

The Abbott Alkaloidal Co.
Achilli, Achille
Acme X-Ray Co.
Acme-International X-Ray Co.
George Adams
Adams X-Ray Co.
Aderer Brothers
Julius Aderer, Inc.
E. Adnet et Fils
Akouphone Mfg. Co.
Albatross Steel Equipment Co.
W. D. Allison Co.
A. S. Aloe Co.
American Atomos Corp.
American Cabinet Co.
American Dental
    Manufacturing Co.
American Dentaphone Co.
American Hospital Appliance Co.
American Metal Furniture Co.
American Optical Co.
American Sterilizer Co.
American Surgical Instrument
    Co., Inc.
Anderson, Norden & Co.
The William Andrews Artificial
    Specialties
H. M. Anton
The Argus Co.
James Arnold
Artificial Limb
    Manufacturing Co.

Claudius Ash and Sons
James H. Ashmead & Sons
W. H. Bailey & Sons, Ltd.
Baker & Adamson Laboratory
    Agents
Baltimore Biological Laboratory
James Barker
Bartlett & Co.
Bausch and Lomb Optical Co.
C. Bruno Bayha
R. & J. Beck
Beck-Lee Corp.
Julian H. Becker
Becton, Dickinson & Co.
Julius Berbecker and Sons, Inc.
(J. & L.) Berge
Arlington U. Betts & Co.
Frank S. Betz Co.
P. Blackiston, Son & Co.
Boericke and Tafel
Boericke and Runyon
G. Boulitte
C. W. & R. M. Bowen Co.
British Thomson-Houston
    Co., Ltd.
W. R. Broughton
Buffalo Dental Mfg. Co.
W. H. Bulloch
Burdick Research Laboratories
Burroughs Wellcome & Co.
Paul Buss Dental Depot
Cameron-Miller

Cameron Surgical Specialty Co.
S. H. Camp & Co.
Campbell Electric Co.
The L. D. Caulk Co.
Celluloid Mfg. Co.
Central Scientific Co.
Arthur Chevalier
Charles Chevalier
Vincent Chevalier
The Chloride of Silver Dry Cell
   Battery Co.
Otis Clapp and Son
Clay-Adams
James B. Clow & Sons
Codman & Shurtleff
Chez Collin & Cie
Collin & Cie
The Colsen Co.
The Columbus Dental Mfg. Co.
J. Condell & Son
Consolidated Dental
   Manufacturing Co.
Continental Laboratory
   Specialties Co.
The Charles N. Crittenton Co.
James Coxeter & Son
Cresent Dental Mfg. Co.
Charles N. Crittenton Co.
Crodon
The Crosby Invalid Furniture Co.
Crowley & Gardner
Dr. A. C. Daniels, Inc.
Davis and Geck, Inc.
Demas, Barnes & Co.
Dental Manufacturing Co., Inc.
Dental Products Co.
The Dental Protective Supply Co.
The Dental Specialty Co.
The Dentists' Supply Co.
   of N.Y.C.
DePuy Manufacturing Co.
Detroit Dental Mfg., Co.
Devilbiss Manufacturing Co.
D. W. Dorrance
Down Bros.

Druggists Appliance Co.
Dunham-Reifel Co.
J. Durbin Surgical Supply Co.
Eastman Kodak Co.
The Educational Supply Co.
Jas. W. Edwards & Co.
Eimer and Amend
F. Eissner & Co., Inc.
Electro-Dental Manufacturing Co.
Electro Medical
   Manufacturing Co.
Electro Surgical Instrument Co.
Electro Surgical
   Manufacturing Co.
Engeln Electric Co.
E. H. Erikson Co.
F. Gustav Ernst
M. Esterlus
Feick Brothers
H. G. Fischer & Co.
Flatters & Garnet Ltd.
J. H. A. Folkers and Bros.
W. F. Ford
Aug. E. Fraas Co.
Franklin Educational Company
R. Friedlander & Co., Inc.
C. P. Fritz & Co.
Fuerstenau
Gall & Lembke
J. H. Gemrig & Son
General Electric Co.
Geneva Optical Co.
Goodyear Rubber Curler Co.
Gordon Manufacturing Co.
Grosvenor & Richards
J. & W. Grunow & Co.
Ernst F. Gustav
F. Hajek
Frank A. Hall & Sons
Thomas Hall
Le Docteur Adolphe Hannover
Hanovia Chemical &
   Manufacturing Co.
P. L. Hanscom & Co.
H. D. Hanway

E. Haran
R. A. Harding
F. A. Hardy Co.
Harleco
Harold Surgical Corp.
Hartford Dental Depot
The Harvard Co.
Fred Haslam & Co.
The Hastings and McIntosh
   Truss Co.
Hausmann & Dunn Co.
Hebbar Brothers, Ltd.
The Heidbrink Co.
Henry
John F. Henry
Dr. L. R. Herrick's
Hettinger Bros.
   Manufacturing Co.
Adam Hilger Co.
Hodgman & Co.
Hood and Reynolds
The Hospital Supply Co.
The Modern Hospital
   Publishing Co.
G. Huclin & Cie
Hudson Surgical Co., Inc.
Dr. Huertl
Hynson Westcott & Co.
Illinois Surgical Appliance Co.
International Distributing Co. for
   the Danish "LEO" Ltd.
Ernesto Invernizze
Dr. Jaeger's Sanitary Woolen
   System Co.
Jelco
J. F. Jelenko & Co., Inc.
Jepson Brothers
Johnson Brothers
Johnson & Johnson
Johnson & Lund
Johnston Brothers
Johnston Brothers Dental Depot
H. D. Justi
B. Kahn & Co.
Feliks Karolewski

Kelley-Koett Mfg. Co., Inc.
Keniston and Root
J. E. Kennedy & Co.
Horatio G. Kern Co.
Kimax
Kimble
Julius King, M.D., Optical Co.
P. J. Kipp & Zonen
Richard Kny and Co.
Kny-Scheerer Co.
F. A. Koch & Co.
Max Kohl
D. W. Kolbe & Son
Konrad Jarnuszkiewicz i Ska
Kromel Laboratories
Lawton Company, Inc.
Leach & Greene
Josef Leiter
Ernst Leitz
Lennox Chemical Co.
Charles Lentz and Sons
A. M. Leslie & Co.
Liebel-Flarsheim Co.
Life Saving Devices Co.
Lincoln & Luchesi
J. U. Lloyd
W. A. Lockwood
S. Louis
MacGregor Instrument Co.
E. F. Mahady Co.
Manesty Machines Ltd.
Manhattan Surgeons' Supply Co.
Manhattan Surgical
   Instrument Co.
Marietta Apparatus Co.
A. A. Marks
The Master Dental Co.
Matthay Hospital Supply Co.
McIntosh Battery & Optical Co.
McIntosh Galvanic & Faradic
   Battery Co.
McKesson Appliance Co.
McKesson & Robbins
McNeil Laboratories
Medicinisches Waarenhaus A.-G.

Meier Dental & Surgical
  Mfg. Co.
Meinecke & Co.
Meler
Merck & Co.
Merry Optical Co.
H. A. Metz Laboratories
William Meyer Co.
Dr. Theodore Meyer-Steineg
E. B. Meyrowitz
J(acob) and D(avid) Miller
Modern Hospital Supply Co., Inc.
Montgomery Ward & Co.
Vincenz Mueller & Co.
H. Mukerji & Co.
Murray-Baumgartner Surgical
  Instrument Company, Inc.
Myerson Tooth Corporation
Nachet et Fils
National College of
  Electric-Therapeutics
New Haven Folding Chair Co.
North Spanish Laboratories
Nurnberg Thermometer Co.
J. Odelga
Ohio Chemical and
  Manufacturing Co.
Paine Furniture Co.
Parke, Davis & Co.
Parker, Stearns & Sutton
E. L. Patch, Co.
The Paul-Bragg Pulsator Model II
R. I. Pearson & Co.
Pelton & Crane
Penn Surgical Manufacturing
  Co., Inc.
H. Pfau, Inh.
The Philadelphia Optical & Watch
  Co., Ltd.
Physician's Supply Co.
  of Philadelphia
George P. Pilling & Son Company
Moritz Pillischer
Pinches Dental
  Manufacturing Co.

Pittsburgh Electric Specialties Co.
Powers & Anderson Dental
  Co., Inc.
Precision
James W. Queen & Co.
Leon & Jules Raimal Frères
Ranson & Randolph Co.
The R-B Company
F. Alfred Reichardt & Co.
Carl Reichert
John Reynders & Co.
F. A. Ritter
Ritter Dental Manufacturing Co.
Roentgen Appliance Corporation
Rogers Electric Laboratories Co.
Edward Rowan
Rubencame & Barker
Sampson-Soch Co.
Sanitas
F. Sartorius
Sartorius-Werke, A. -G.
John H. Savigny
Schall & Son
C. L. Scheu
W. H. Schieffelin & Co.
Scully Steel & Iron Co.
Seabury & Johnson
Searle & Hereth Co.
I. B. Seeley's
Shafer-Pierce Co.
W. M. Sharp Mfg. Co., Inc.
Sharp & Smith
Shelton Electric Co.
Gideon Sibley
L. Silverman
J. Sklar Manufacturing Co.
Lee S. Smith & Son
Lee S. Smith & Sons Dental Depot
Prof. Dr. Spalteholz
Spencer & Crocker
Spencer Lens Co.
J. Staiman
Standard Dental Products Co.
The Standard Fountain Cuspidor
Standard Optical Co.

Standard X-Ray Company
Fred C. Steinman & Co.
Jonas Stelzig
Theo. E. Stemmle
Stevens & Co., Inc.
Alb. Stille
C. H. Stoelting Co.
F. J. Stokes Machine Co.
Stratford-Cookson Co.
Sunic Record
James Swift
Theo. Tafel Co.
Termax
Teter Mfg. Co.
Henry Thayer & Co.
Arthur H. Thomas Co.
Thompson & Capper
  Wholesale Ltd.
George Tiemann & Co.
Tokyo Ika-Kikai Dogyo Kumiai
John T. Toland
Toledo Technical Appliance Co.
Charles Truax
Edward Tucker
Ultek Corporation
Arthur S. Underwood
United Factories for Hospital
  Supplies
Unitron Instruments
Universal Ophthalmometer
Vereinigte Fabriken fuer
  Laboratoriumsbedarf
Victor Electric Company
Volta Belt Co.
R. V. Wagner & Co.
Waite & Bartlett X-Ray Mfg. Co.
D. N. Walford
Wall & Ochs
W. H. Walmsley & Co.

Wappler Electric Co.
Wappler Electric Controller Co.
Wappler Electric
  Manufacturing Co.
Watson and Sons
Weber Dental Manufacturing Co.
John M. Weiss
John Weiss & Sons, Ltd.
The West Gravitiser Corp.
William West
Western Surgical Instrument
  House
Westinghouse X-Ray
  Company, Inc.
Whitall, Tatum & Co.
C. W. White & Co.
Samuel S. White Dental Mfg. Co.
William H. Wigmore
Will Corporation
Wm. V. Willis & Co.
Williams, Brown & Earle
The Williams and Wilkins Co.
The Charles Willms Surgical
  Instrument Co.
T. A. Willson & Co.
The Wilmington Dental Mfg. Co.
Wilmot-Castle Co.
H. Windler
Winkley Artificial Limb Company
Wiseman Brothers Specialty Co.
Max Wocher & Son, Co.
The Optical Wolverine
Worcester Elastic Stocking and
  Truss Co.
E. A. Yarnall Co.
Carl Zeiss
Joseph Zentmayer
E. Zimmermann

MCFM
Medical and Chirurgical Faculty of the State of Maryland
1211 Cathedral Street
Baltimore, Md. 21201
c/o Mr. Joe Jensen or Deborah Woolverton

Frank S. Betz Co.
H. G. Fischer & Co., Inc.
Hynson Westcott & Co.
Kloman Instrument Co., Inc.
Kny-Scheerer Co.
E. B. Meyrowitz

Vincenz Mueller & Co.
Salt & Son, Ltd.
George Tiemann & Co.
Victor Electric Co.
John Weiss and Son

MF/MAH

Microfilmed Catalogs of the National Museum of American
*   History*
Library, Room 5016
Smithsonian Institution
Washington, D.C. 20560
c/o Mrs. Rhoda Ratner, Chief Librarian

Abbott Laboratories
Adlanco Industrial Products Corp.
Eugen Albrecht
J. Alexandre
A. S. Aloe Co.
American Agema Corp.
American X-Ray Equipment Co.
Annals of Surgery
Anon, Gillis & Geoghegan
Archer Manufacturing Co.
Claudius Ash and Sons
Baird & Tatlock
Baker and Co. (Baker Platinum
   Works)
Barton Manufacturing Co.
Battle & Co.
Bausch and Lomb Optical Co.
R & J Beck
P. Beiersdorf & Co.
Benas
Benas' Son
Prof. Dr. Wihl Benninghoven
Berstein Mfg. Co.
Frank S. Betz & Co.
James G. Biddle
Blue Island Specialty Co.
Boericke & Bunyon Co.
Boericke and Tafel
Bonschur & Holmes
J. & A. Bosch

Harry J. Bosworth
G. Boulette
Bradley-Collins Co.
Bramhill, Deane Co.
B. Braun
Breeding and Laboratory Institute
The Browning Mfg. Co.
Buffalo Dental Mfg. Co.
The Burkhardt Co., Inc.
Burns Dental Casting
   Machine Co.
Cambridge Scientific
   Instrument Co.
Carmen Projector
Carnes Artificial Limb Co.
Carpocapsa Laboratory
Calvin S. Case Co.
B. B. Cassel
Ludwig Castagna
Caswell, Hazard & Co.
The L. D. Caulk Co.
Central Scientific Co.
Chambers, Inskeep & Co.
Chappel Formula
Joseph Francois Bernard Charriere
Chicago Dietetic Supply
   House, Inc.
Chicago Flexible Shaft Co.
Chirurgie-Industrie G.M.B.H.
A. C. Clark and Co.

Clark and Roberts
Georges Clasen
The Clev-Dent Co.
  of New York City
Cleveland Dental
  Manufacturing Co.
James B. Clow & Sons
Cogit Etablissements
Collin, Charriere Maison
Columbia Dental Chairs
Columbia Dental & X-Ray Corp.
The Columbus Dental Mfg. Co.
Cooledge Dental X-Ray Unit
James Coxeter & Son
Crane Co.
Samuel A. Crocker & Co.
Josiah Crosby
Delamotte, Maison
Dental Manufacturing Co., Inc.
The Dental Specialty Co.
The Dentists' Supply Co.
  of N.Y.C.
Depuy Manufacturing Co.
Louis Derr
Detroit Dental Manufacturing Co.
Les Fils D'Emile Deyrolle
The DeZeng-Standard Co.
Dialoy
Henry C. Diamond & Co.
A. J. Ditman
Edward P. Dolbey, Co.
James T. Dougherty
Driver-Harris Wire Co.
Ch. DuBois
E. Ducretet
E. Ducretet et Cie
Dr. M. Th. Edelmann & Sohn
Edison Manufacturing Co.
Jas. W. Edwards & Co.
Eimer & Amend
William M. Eisen
Eisler Engineering Co., Inc.
Electro-Dental Manufacturing Co.
Electro Medical
  Manufacturing Co.

Electro-Therapeutic Co.
Elektrotechnisches Institut
  Frankfurt (am Main)
Engeln Electric Co.
C. Erbe
Ferdinand Ernecke
J. Eynard
Fettke & Co.
F. L. Fischer
H. G. Fischer & Co.
Flicoteaux & Co.
W. F. Ford
Fort Dodge Laboratories Inc.
Charles M. Frazier
R. Friedländer & Co., Inc.
Hugo Friedman
  Manufacturing Co.
Friedman Specialty Co.
R. Fuess
William Gaertner and Co.
A. Gaiffe
Henri Galante, et Fils
C. Gerhardt
J. Glaenzer and Co.
Green & Bauer Inc.
Greiner & Fredrichs
Griswold System
W. E. Griswold, D.D.S.
Gruber-Hollborn & Giemsa Stains
Hermann Haertel
Frank A. Hall & Sons
John F. Hammond
Hanovia Chemical &
  Manufacturing Co.
F. A. Hardy Co.
Harold Surgical Corp.
Hazard, Hazard & Co.
Hugo Heder
Hans Heele
C. G. Heynemann
Adam Hilger, Ltd.
The Holborn Surgical Instrument
  Co., Ltd.
Dr. Charles Hollborn
B. K. Hollister

The Hollister-Wilson Laboratories
John Hood Co.
The Hospital Supply Co.
Herbert B. Howard & Frederick
  A. Washburn
The R. Hyde Co.
The International Nickel Co.
J. W. Ivory
Chevalier Jackson Instruments
Jeffrey-Fell Co.
Max Kaehler & Martini
Hermann Katsch
Kayle Co., Inc.
Kellogg
C. F. Kingstone
Charles B. Kleine
Klewe & Co., Inc.
Knapp
Knauth Brothers
L. E. Knott Apparatus Co.
Richard Kny and Co.
Kny-Scheerer Co.
Koch & Sterzel
Max Kohl
Herman Kohlbusch
Fritz Koehler
Koken Companies
D. W. Kolbe & Son
Krohne & Sesemann
Rudolph Kueger
C. Kuechmann
Otto Kunz
Lambert Pharmacal Co.
La Motte Chemical Products
F. & M. Launtenschlaeger
T. LeClerc
J. Elwood Lee Co.
Lehn & Fink
Ernst Leitz
G. A. Lenoir
Lerebours et Secretan
Eli Lilly & Co.
Lindstaedt, Fr.
Lochhead Laboratories Inc.
Louis & H. Loewenstein

Loomis-Manning Filter Co.
H. S. Lowry, D. D. S.
A. Luer, Maison
C. Lukens De Witt Co.
Lunken Window Co.
Luxter Prism Co.
Lynch & Co.
The Magic Earphone
Major, Genisson & Co.
Manhattan Electrical Supply Co.
The Manning System
A. A. Marks
Carl Marshall
Mason Detachable Tooth Co.
L. Mathieu, Maison
Matthew Brothers
S. Maw, Son and Thompson
Ernst W. Mayer & Perry
  G. Meltzer
Mayer & Phelps, Ltd.
McIntosh Battery & Optical Co.
McKesson & Robbins
Medicinisches Waarenhaus A. -G.
Meier Dental & Surgical
  Mfg. Co.
William S. Merrell & Co.
Ed. Messter
Bernard Meyer
William Meyer Co.
E. B. Meyrowitz
Otto Moecke
A. Molteni
J. L. Mott Ironworks
Moyer, The J. Bird Co., Inc.
F. A. D. Mueller, Sohne
Vincenz Mueller & Co.
Nachet et Fils
Nakai Dental Supply Co.
National Scientific Corp.
Negretti & Zambra
New Era Optical Co.
New York Edison Co.
J. M. Ney Co.
Eduard Nowadowsky
G. Oberhauser & E. Hartnach

Obstetrical Society of London
Ohio Chemical &
  Manufacturing Co.
Optical Convention
Osteopathic Publishing
  Supply Co.
F. G. Otto & Sons
Ovington Manufacturing Co.
Palisades Manufacturing Co.
Paquelin-Cautery
Parke, Davis & Co.
Pederson Lubricator Co.
Pelton & Crane
W. L. Peterson
Peyer, Farvarger & Co.
H. Pfau, Inh.
James Picker Inc.
Picker X-Ray Corporation
The Pike Manufacturing Co.
George P. Pilling & Son Company
Pomeroy Co.
Fernand and Jules Porges
George Poulson
L. M. Prince
Pulvermacher Galvanic Co.
Radiquet & Massiot
Ranson & Randolph Co.
Camille Regnard
Carl Reichert
Reilly & Co.
H. Reiner
Reiniger, Gebbert & Schall
John Reynders & Co.
Ritter Dental Depot
Ritter Dental Manufacturing Co.
Robert & Collin
Roentgen X-Ray Apparatus
Dr. Hermann Rohrbeck
Rudolf Rothe
Albert Rueprecht
Russel Electric Co.
Sanitarium Equipment Co.
Schall & Son
Gustav Scharmann
Schering E. Glatz

Schmidt
F. O. Schoedinger
Hermann Schoenfeldt
Dr. M. Schwartz
Sears, Roebuck and Co.
E. J. Seibert
W. M. Sharp Mfg. Co., Inc.
Sharp & Dohme
Sharp & Smith
Shelton Electric Co.
Shepard & Dudley
Friedrich Siemens
Siemens-Reinige
Siemens-Reiniger-Veifa Co.
L. Silverman
Simmons Co.
John Simmons
Charles E. Simon, M.D.
Simonis
Heinrich Sittel
Alfred M. Slack
Lee S. Smith & Son
C. M. Sorensen Co., Inc.
Prof. Dr. Spalteholz
Spencer Lens Co.
Split Bar Co.
E. R. Squibb
Standard Comfort Window Corp.
Dr. Steeg and Reuter
Sterling Surgical Products
Stille-Scalan Company
G. S. Stoddard and Co., Inc.
Dr. Stohrer & Sohn
F. J. Stokes Machine Co.
C. & E. Streisguth
Samuel G. Supplee & Co.
Surgical Manufacturing Co., Ltd.
Surgical Products
Sutcliffe Keratometer
Syndicat des constructeurs en
  instruments d'optique
  & de précisions
Talrich
Taylor Bros Co.
Taylor Instrument Companies

A. T. Thompson & Co., Mfr.
George Tiemann & Co.
John T. Toland
Toril Mfg Co.
Trenaman Dental Co.
E. deTrey & Sons
Henry Troemner
Chas. Truax, Greene & Co.
O. B. Underwood & Co.
United Surgical Supplies Corp.
Universal Physiotherapy
  Equipment
Van Horn & Sawtell
Van Houten & Ten Broeck Co.
Charles Verdin
Vereinigte Fabriken fuer
  Laboratoriumsbedarf
M. Vergne
Victor Electric Company
Voightlander & Son Optical Co.
Volta Belt Co.
Waite & Bartlett X-Ray Mfg. Co.
Wappler Electric Co.

Wappler Electric Controller Co.
Wappler Electric
  Manufacturing Co.
Charles Howell Ward
Watters Laboratories
George A. Weichert & Co., Inc.
John Weiss & Sons, Ltd.
M. Weiss & Co.
Paul Weiss
Whitall, Tatum & Co.
Whitcomb Metallic Bedstead Co.
Samuel S. White Dental Mfg. Co.
The Wilmington Dental Mfg. Co.
H. Windler
R. Winkel
Winthrop-Metz
Wissenschaftlich-Technische
  Mittheimlungen aus dem
  Medicinischen Waarenhause
The Optical Wolverine
Woodbury-Jelenko
Carl Zeiss
E. Zimmermann

MRLB

Medical Research Library of Brooklyn
Downstate Medical Center
Dept. Anatomy, Box 5
State University of New York
450 Clarkson Avenue
Brooklyn, New York 11203
c/o Gordon Mestler, Emeritus Scientist

Abbott Laboratories
A. L. Hernstein
Hospital Supply Co.
Kny-Scheerer Co.

Ernst Leitz
E. B. Meyerowitz
George Tiemann & Co.

MSL

G. W. Blunt White Library
Mystic Seaport Museum
Mystic, Connecticut 06355
c/o Gerald Morris, Head

Hagerty Bros.

Whitall, Tatum & Co.

MUM

Mütter Museum
19 S. 22nd Street
Philadelphia, Pa. 19103
c/o Gretchen Worden, Curator

C. Baker
Bausch and Lomb Optical Co.
R. & J. Beck
Bonschur & Holmes
Maison Brequet
Bullock and Crenshaw
Charriere
Codman and Shurtleff
Arthur C. Cole and Son
Collin Maison Charriere
Davis and Leydon Surgical Depot
J. Doboscq
Otto Flemming
H. Galante & Fils
J. H. Gemrig
H. Gueride
W. D. Halsey & Co.
E. W. Higbee, M.D.
Jerome Kidder, M.D.
E. L. Kloss
Kny-Scheerer Co.
D. W. Kolbe & Son
Krohne & Sesemann
M. Kuermerle & Kolbe
Joseph Leiter
Ernst Leitz
Charles Lentz & Sons

Luer, Maison
A. Lutter
L. Mathieu
Mayer and Meltzer
McAllister
McIntire, Magee & Brown Co.
Dr. McIntosh's Natural Uterine
  Supporter Company
E. B. Meyrowitz Surgical
  Instruments Co.
Meyrowitz Brothers
Nachet et Fils
F. G. Otto & Sons
T. Morris Perot & Co.
George Pilling & Son Co.
James W. Queen & Co.
Carl Reichert
Ross & Co.
Sharp & Smith
William Snowden Co.
George Tiemann & Co.
H. Weinhagen
E. A. Yarnell Co.
Archibald Young
John Wyeth & Brother
Carl Zeiss
Joseph Zentmayer

NLM

National Library of Medicine
8600 Rockville Pike
Bethesda, Maryland 20209

Aesculap
Allen & Hanburys, ltd.
A. S. Aloe Co.
Arnold and Sons
C. Baker
R & J Beck
John Bell & Croyden

Frank S. Betz & Co.
Boston Optical Works
G. Boulitte
A. Boze, Firm
Breton
Bullock & Crenshaw
Burdick Corp.

S. H. Camp & Co.
L. P. Casella
Caswell, Hazard & Co.
The Clev-Dent Co.
  of New York City
Cleveland Dental
  Manufacturing Co.
Cleveland Electric Co. Ltd.
Codman & Shurtleff
Collin & Cie
Columbus Aseptic Furniture Co.
Henry Crouch
S. A. Darrach
Davidson Rubber Co.
De Puy Mfg. Co.
Deutsche Orthopadische Werke,
  G.M.B.H.
William Dixon, Inc.
Doniger & Co.
Down Bros.
Drapier et Fils
Electro Surgical Instrument Co.
Everill
Fabrique de Telegraphes et
  Appareils Electriques
Flicoteaux & Co.
W. F. Ford
Frosco
George C. Frye
J. H. Gemrig & Son
German Electric Belt Agency
S. Goldschmidt
Stephan Goodrich & Co.
Goodyear Rubber Curler Co.
Hermann Haertel
Harold Surgical Corp.
Hartford Woven Wire
  Mattress Co.
Fred Haslam & Co.
Chas. Hearson & Co., Ltd.
A. L. Hernstein
Adam Hilger, Ltd.
Dr. M. Hipp
The Hospital Supply Co. and the
  Watters Laboratories

Huston Bros. Co.
Hynson Westcott & Co.
Illinois Surgical Appliance Co.
Japan Medical Instrument Catalog
Jepson Brothers
J. Jungmann
Kingman and Hassam
Kny-Scheerer Co.
D. W. Kolbe & Son
John F. Kuemerle & Kolbe
William Ladd
Laundy & Son
Josef Leiter
Charles Lentz and Sons
Eduard Lipowsky
Heinrich Loewy
Lincoln and Luchesi
Manhattan Surgeons' Supply Co.
Mason
S. Maw and Son
S. Maw, Son and Sons
S. Maw, Son and Thompson
Ernst W. Mayer & Perry
  G. Meltzer
Mayer & Phelps, Ltd.
Medical Arts Supply Co.
Medicinisches Waarenhaus A.-G.
Miller Rubber Co.
Milvay
Moyer, The J. Bird Co., Inc.
Vincenz Mueller & Co.
Narrangansett Machine Co.
Noyes Brothers & Cutler
J. Odelga
Drs. Peters & Rost
George P. Pilling & Son Company
Simon Ploessel
Radium Company of Colorado,
  Inc.
John Reynders & Co.
Reynolds & Branson, Ltd.
Rizzoli Instituto de Bologna
Rowe Truss Company
Salem Leg Co.
John H. Savigny

Savory & Moore, Ltd.
Scalan-Morris Co.
Schall & Son
Adolf Schweichardt
Sears, Roebuck and Co.
A. W. H. Seerig
Sharp & Smith
Shaw Supply Co., Inc.
Shepard & Dudley
J. Sklar Mfg. Co., Inc.
Smith, Beck & Beck
Smith & Hodson
W. Sohngen & Co.
J. H. Steward
Charles Stodder
Surgical Manufacturing Co., Ltd.
James Swift
Arthur H. Thomas Co.
George Tiemann & Co.
R. B. Tolles
Charles Truax & Co.
U. S. Army Medical Department
U. S. Council of National Defense

Van Steenbrugghe
Charles Verdin
George H. Wahmann Mfg. Co.
Waite & Bartlett X-Ray Mfg. Co.
Martin Wallach, Nachfolger
W. H. Walmsley & Co.
Henry A. Ward
G. A. Watkins & Co.
John M. Weiss
John Weiss & Sons, Ltd.
Paul Weiss
Whitall, Tatum & Co.
Samuel S. White Dental Mfg. Co.
Will Corporation
T. A. Willson & Co.
Wilmot Castle Company
H. Windler
Winkley Artificial Limb Company
George Wirth, Inc.
The Optical Wolverine
Moritz Wuenche
Carl Zeiss

NLM *also has unspecified catalogs of the following companies in addition to those listed above that are not contained in this book.*

American Optical Co.
Chicago Apparatus Co.
Clay-Adams Co., Inc.
Davis and Geck, Inc.
E. I. DuPont de Nemours & Co.
Martin Gebruder
General Electric Co.
Liebel-Flarsheim Co.

Picker X-Ray Corp.
James W. Queen & Co.
Will Ross, Inc.
F. J. Stokes Machine Co.
Wincester Surgical Supply Co.
Max Wocher and Son
E. A. Yarnell Co.

NWUCML

The Archibald Church Medical Library
Northwestern University
303 East Chicago Avenue
Chicago, Ill. 60611
c/o James Shedlock, Head, Public Services

E. Guyot
A. L. Hernstein
Kny-Scheerer Co.

A. M. Leslie & Co.
Charles A. Schmidt
Sharp & Smith

Charles Truax
U. S. Council of National Defense

John M. Weiss
John Weiss & Sons, Ltd.

NYAM

New York Academy of Medicine Library
Reference Department
2 East 103rd Street
New York, New York 10029
c/o Ann Pascarelli, Assoc. Librarian

Abbott Laboratories
Aderer Brothers
Aderer, Julius Inc.
Adlanco Industrial Product Corp.
E. Adnet et Fils
Akers
Eugen Albrecht
James B. Alden
J. Alexandre
A. S. Aloe Co.
American Agena Corp.
The American Cabinet Co.
American Cystoscope
  Makers, Inc.
American Optical Co.
American X-Ray Equipment Co.
Annals of Surgery
Anon, Gillis & Geoghegan
Archer Manufacturing Co.
Claudius Ash and Sons
Baird & Tatlock
Baker and Co. (Baker Platinum
  Works)
Barton Manufacturing Co.
Battle & Co.
Battle Creek Health Builder
Bausch and Lomb Optical Co.
R. & J. Beck
P. Beiersdorf & Co.
Benas
Benas' Son
Prof. Dr. Wihl Benninghoven
(J. & L.) Berge
Berstein Mfg. Co.

Frank S. Betz & Co.
James G. Biddle
Blue Island Specialty Co.
Boericke & Bunyon Co.
Boricke and Tafel
Bonneels, Maison
Bonschur & Holmes
J. & A. Bosch
Harry J. Bosworth
G. Boulitte
Bradley-Collins Co.
Bramhill, Deanne Co.
B. Braun
Breeding and Laboratory Institute
Breton Frères
Brickerhoff & Penton
Britesun
The Browning Mfg. Co.
Buffalo Dental Mfg. Co.
The Burkhardt Co., Inc.
Burns Dental Casting
  Machine Co.
Burroughs Wellcome & Co.
W. J. Bush & Co.
Cambridge Scientific
  Instrument Co.
S. H. Camp & Co.
Carnes Artificial Limb Co.
Carpocapsa Laboratory
Calvin S. Case Co.
L. P. Casella
B. B. Cassel
Ludwig Castagna
Castle, Wilmot Co.

Caswell, Hazard & Co.
The L. D. Caulk Co. Central
Sci. Co.
Central Scientific Co.
Chambers, Inskeep & Co.
Joseph Francois Bernard Charriere
Chicago Dietetic Supply
House, Inc.
Chicago Flexible Shaft Co.
Chicago Pharmacal Co.
Chirurgie-Industrie G.M.B.H.
A. C. Clark and Co.
Clark and Roberts
Georges Clasen
Cleveland Dental
Manufacturing Co.
The Clev-Dent Co.
of New York City
James B. Clow & Sons
Codman & Shurtleff
Cogit Establissements
The Coleman & Bell Co., Inc.
Collin & Cie
Collin, Chariere Maison
Columbia Dental & X-Ray Corp.
Columbus Aseptic Furniture Co.
The Columbus Dental Mfg. Co.
Consolidated Dental
Manufacturing Co.
G. H. Cornelson
James Coxeter & Son
Crane Co.
Samuel A. Crocker & Co.
Crosby Invalid Furniture Co.
Josiah Crosby
Crown Surgical Instrument Co.
of N.Y.
Davis B. Levy Sterling
Delamotte, Maison
Dental Manufacturing Co., Inc.
The Dental Specialty Co.
The Dentists' Supply Co.
DePuy Mfg., Co.
Dermatological Research
Laboratories of Philadelphia

Louis Derr
Detroit Dental Manufacturing Co.
Les Fils D'Emile Deyrolle
The DeZeng-Standard Co.
Henry C. Diamond & Co.
A. J. Ditman
Edward P. Dolbey, Co.
James T. Dougherty
Driver-Harris Wire Co.
Ch. DuBois
E. Ducretet
E. Ducretet et Cie
Dr. M. Th. Edelmann & Sohn
Edison Manufacturing Co.
Jas. W. Edwards & Co.
J. Ehrlich & Sons
Eimer & Amend
William M. Eisen
Eisler Engineering Co., Inc.
F. Eissner & Co.
Elconap
Electric Heat Control
Apparatus Co.
Electro-Dental Manufacturing Co.
Electro Medical
Manufacturing Co.
Electro-Therapeutic Co.
Elektrotechnisches Institut
Frankfurt (am Main)
Endo-Form
Engeln Electric Co.
C. Erbe
Ferdinand Ernecke
J. Eynard
J. & E. Ferris
Fettke & Co.
F. L. Fischer
H. G. Fischer & Co.
Flicoteaux & Co.
W. F. Ford
Fort Dodge Laboratories Inc.
(Aug. E.) Fraas Co.
R. Friedlander & Co., Inc.
Hugo Friedman
Manufacturing Co.

Friedman Specialty Co.
R. Fuess
William Gaertner and Co.
A. Gaiffe
Henri Galante et Fils
Ga Nun & Parsons
Albert C. Gaudin
C. Gerhardt
J. Glaenzer and Co.
Globe Manufacturing Co.
Green & Bauer Inc.
Greiner & Fredrichs
W. E. Griswold, D.D.S.
GYSI Articulators
Hermann Haertel
Frank A. Hall & Sons
John F. Hammond
Hanovia Chemical &
 Manufacturing Co.
F. A. Hardy Co.
Harold Surgical Corp.
Hayem-Sahli Haemacytometer
Hazard, Hazard & Co.
Hugo Heder
Hans Heele
The Heidbrink Co.
C. G. Heynemann
Adam Hilger, Ltd.
The Holborn Surgical Instrument
 Co., Ltd.
Dr. Charles Hollborn
B. K. Hollister
The Hollister-Wilson Laboratories
John Hood Co.
Hoover Manufacturing Co.
The Hospital Supply Co.
Herbert B. Howard & Frederick
 A. Washburn
The R. Hyde Co.
L'industrie Française
The International Nickel Co.
J. W. Ivory
Jeffrey-Fell Co.
J. F. Jelenko & Co., Inc.
Johnson & Johnson

Max Kaehler & Martini
(Richard) Kallmeyer & Co.
Hermann Katsch
Kayle Co., Inc.
Kellogg
C. F. Kingstone
F. Kissner & Co.
Charles B. Kleine
Klewe & Co., Inc.
Knauth Brothers
L. E. Knott Apparatus Co.
Richard Kny and Co.
Kny-Scheerer Co.
Koch & Sterzel
Rudolph Koenig
Max Kohl
Herman Kohlbusch
Fritz Koehler
Koken Companies
D. W. Kolbe & Son
Krohne & Sesemann
Rudolph Krueger
C. Kuechmann
Lambert Pharmacal Co.
La Motte Chemical Products
F. & M. Lautenschlaeger
T. LeClerc
J. Elwood Lee Co.
Lehn & Fink
Ernst Leitz
G. A. Lenoir
Lerebours et Secretan
A. M. Leslie & Co.
Eli Lilly & Co.
Lindstaedt, Fr.
Lochhead Laboratories Inc.
Louis & H. Loewenstein
Loomis-Manning Filter Co.
P. C. Lorenz
H. S. Lowry, D.D.S.
A. Luer, Maison
C. Lukens De Witt Co.
Lunken Window Co.
Luxter Prism Co.
Lynch & Co.

Major, Genisson & Co.
Manhattan Electrical Supply Co.
A. A. Marks
Mason Detachable Tooth Co.
L. Mathieu, Maison
Matthew Brothers
S. Maw, Son and Sons
S. Maw, Son and Thompson
Ernst W. Mayer & Perry
G. Meltzer
Mayer & Phelps, Ltd.
McIntosh Battery & Optical Co.
McKesson & Robbins
Medicinisches Waarenhaus, A.-G.
Meier Dental & Surgical
  Mfg. Co.
Messter, Ed.
H. A. Metz Laboratories
Bernard Meyer
William Meyer Co.
Arthur Meyerstein
E. B. Meyrowitz
John T. Milliken & Co.
Otto Moecke
A. Molteni
A. Montaudon
J. L. Mott Ironworks
Moyer, The J. Bird Co., Inc.
F. A. D. Mueller, Sohne
Vincenz Mueller & Co.
Nachet et Fils
Nakai Dental Supply Co.
National Scientific Corp.
Negretti & Zambra
New Era Optical Co.
New York Edison Co.
J. M. Ney Co.
Eduard Nowakowsky
Noyes Brothers & Cutler
G. Oberhauser & E. Hartnach
Obstetrical Society of London
Ohio Chemical
  & Manufacturing Co.
Optical Convention

Osteopathic Publishing
  Supply Co.
F. G. Otto & Sons
Ovington Manufacturing Co.
Palisades Manufacturing Co.
Parke, Davis & Co.
Pederson Lubricator Co.
Pelton & Crane
Penton & Robinson
W. L. Peterson
Peyer, Favarger & Co.
H. Pfau, Inh.
James Picker Inc.
Picker X-Ray Corporation
The Pike Manufacturing Co.
George P. Pilling & Son Company
B. Platschick
Pomeroy Co.
Fernand and Jules Porges
George Poulson
Radiguet & Massiot
Ransom & Randolph Co.
Camille Regnard
Carl Reichert
Reilly & Co.
H. Reiner
Reiniger, Gebbert & Schall
John Reynders & Co.
Riker & Son Co.
Ritter Dental Depot
Ritter Dental Manufacturing Co.
Robert & Collin
C. M. Robinson
Dr. Hermann Rohrbeck
Rudolf Rothe
Albert Rueprecht
Russel Electric Co.
A. B. Sands & Co.
Sanitarium Equipment Co.
San-Methyl Capsule
Schall & Son
Gastav Scharmann
Schering E. Glatz
W. H. Schieffelin & Co.

Schmidt
F. O. Schoedinger
Hermann Schoenfeldt
Dr. M. Schwartz
Henry Schwindt
Sears, Roebuck and Co.
W. M. Sharp Mfg. Co., Inc.
Sharp & Dohme
Sharp & Smith
Shelton Electric Co.
Shepard & Dudley
Friedrich Siemens
Siemens-Reinige
Semens-Reiniger-Veifa Co.
L. Silverman
Simmons Co.
John Simmons
Charles E. Simon, M.D.
Heinrich Sittel
Alfred M. Slack
Lee S. Smith & Son
Smith & Damper
C. M. Sorensen Co., Inc.
Prof. Dr. Spalteholz
Spencer Lens Co.
Spencer Microtomes
Split Bar Co.
E. R. Squibb
Standard Comfort Window Corp.
Dr. Steeg and Reuter
Steele's
Sterling Surgical Products
Stille-Scalan Company
G. S. Stoddard and Co., Inc.
Dr. Stohrer & Sohn
F. J. Stokes Machine Co.
R. J. Strasenburgh Co.
C. & E. Streisguth
Sunbeam Ultra-Violite
Supplee & Co.
Samuel G. Supplee & Co.
Surgical Manufacturing Co., Ltd.
Surgical Products
Swan-Myers

Syndicat des constructeurs en
    instruments d'optique
    & de précisions
Talrich
Taylor Bros Co.
Taylor Instrument Companies
A. T. Thompson & Co., Mfr.
George Tiemann & Co.
Tillyer
Toril Mfg. Co.
Trenaman Dental Co.
E. deTrey & Sons
Henry Troemner
Charles Truax
Chas. Truax, Greene & Co.
O. B. Underwood & Co.
United Surgical Supplies Corp.
Univeral Physiotherapy Equipment
Van Horn & Sawtell
Van Houten & Ten Broeck
Peter Van Schaak & Sons
Charles Verdin
Vereinigte Fabriken fuer
    Laboratoriumsbedarf
M. Vergne
Victor Electric Company
Voightlander & Son Optical Co.
Waite & Bartlett X-Ray Mfg. Co.
Wappler Electric Co.
Wappler Electric Controller Co.
Wappler Electric
    Manufacturing Co.
Charles Howell Ward
Watters Laboratories
George A. Weichert & Co., Inc.
John M. Weiss
John Weiss & Sons, Ltd.
M. Weiss & Co.
Paul Weiss
Wellsworth
Whitall, Tatum & Co.
Whitcomb Metallic Bedstead Co.
Samuel S. White Dental Mfg. Co.
The Charles Willms Surgical

Instrument Co.
The Wilmington Dental Mfg. Co.
H. Windler
R. Winkel
Winthrop-Metz
Wissenschaftlich-Technische
  Mittheimlungen aus dem
  Medicinischen Waarenhause

The Optical Wolverine
Woodbury-Jelenko
H. Wulfring-Luer
John Wyeth & Brother, Inc.
E. A. Yarnall Co.
Zeiss
Carl Zeiss
E. Zimmermann

RCSL
Royal College of Surgeons Library
Hunterian Museum, Reading Room 3
Lincoln's Inn Field
London WC2 3PN, England

The names in this listing are from objects and a catalogue based upon research in Pagé and other sources by Raymond Russell.

A. S. Aloe Co.
Arnold and Sons
Claudius Ash and Sons
R. & J. Beck
William Boekel and Co.
Bogner
Brady & Martin (Co.)
John Browning
Burge, Warren & Ridgley
Burgoyne, Burbridges & Co.
Canali
A. Capron
Chandler
Arthur Chevalier
Georges Clasen
Cocker
Codman & Shurtleff
Dakin
Davis and Geck, Inc.
Davis and Lawrence Co., Ltd.
Denis
Dental Manufacturing Co., Inc.
Dewitt & Herz
Dingwall-Witham
Down Bros.
H. Druce
John Dungsworth
Ashford Elliott

Eppendorf Hamburg
F. G. Ernst
Fannin & Co.'s
Ferris & Co.
Fettke & Zeigler
Isabella Fischer
John Fischer
W. F. Ford
Thomas Fox
Henri Galante, et Fils
Gembloux, Manufacture Belge
  De, S. A.
J. H. Gemrig & Son
Genevoise, Société
Gennari
Gentile
Gerber
A. Glitschka
Goldenberg
S. Goldschmidt
A. Graiff
Ernst Greishaber
German Grible
A. Grunblatt
J. P. Hansen
Phillip Harris & Co.
A. L. Hernstein
Herzhause

Higden
Hilliard & Co.
W. B. Hilliard & Sons
The Holborn Rubber, Gutta
  Percha, and MacIntosh
  Waterproof Co.
Hunzinger
A. Hutchinson and Co.
W. & H. Hutchinson
James Jackson
Jetter & Scheerer
Johnson & Co.
Joyant
Richard Kullmeyer & Co.
A. Kunstehen
La Motte Chemical Products
Leon Laurant
Josef Leiter
LePlanquais
Lichtenberger
Lollini
Lufkin Rule Co.
A. Lutter
James E. Maddox
Mappin & Co.
Mariaud
Matsumioto
W. Matthews
Matthew Brothers
Ernst W. Mayer & Perry
  G. Meltzer
Medical Supply Association
Meyer & Kersting
Michault
Molinari
Morette
C. Muller
Nachet et Fils
Nestor
W. A. Norie
J. Nowell & Sons
C. Nyrop
Odoux
Oliver & Ogle
O'Neill & Thompson

J. Orme & Co.
Richard Paget
Palmer
Thomas Parr
Pastorelli & Rapkins
Henry Patton
A. Paul
Peacock
Peake, Allen & Co.
Pearce & Co.
Jonathan Perkins
Perret
Personne
Place & Thistlewaite
Plum
Hugh Powell
Joseph F. Pratt
T. Pratt
Preston
Price
Henry James Prockter
Thomas Pryor
Quiney
George Raeburn
Ratery
Rauschke
John Read
Thomas Read & Co.
Reay & Robinson
Reid and Read
John Reynolds
Reynolds & Branson, Ltd.
Rhodes, Champion & Son
Edwin Richardson
John Richardson
Thomas Richardson
Ridgeway, Sunderland
William Risley
Rizzoli Instituto de Bologna
John Robinson
Rodgers
Romelin
Rudford
John Walkin Ryley
Sabj, Neck

Richard Salt	Schmidt & Robinson
Samson	Scholl Mfg. Co.
Sawyer	Siber, Hagner & Co., Ltd.
A. Schaedel	Sinderie of Langres
Schaffer	Benjamin Smith
Schildknecht & Co.	George A. Tiemann & Co.
Schmidt	Chas. Truax, Greene & Co.

SBMC
Saint Bartholomew's Hospital
Medical College Library
West Smithfield
London, E.C. 1A7BE
c/o Mr. John L. Thornton, Librarian

Allen & Hanburys, Ltd.	Krohne & Sesemann
Brady & Martin Co.	John M. Weiss
Down Bros.	

SLSC
Saint Louis Science Center
Oak Knoll Park
St. Louis, Missouri 63105
c/o Mrs. Polly Coxe, Curator, Medical Technology

A. S. Aloe Co.	Kny-Scheerer Co.
Blees-Moore Instrument Co.	E. B. Meyrowitz
Buffalo Dental Manufacturing Co.	Vincenz Mueller & Co.
Consolidated Dental	O'Brien Worthen Co.
Manufacturing Co.	H. Pfau, Inh.
Dentist's Supply Co., of New York	St. Louis Dental Mfg. Co.
Henry Heil	Sharp & Smith
Hettenger Bros.	Chas. Truax, Greene & Co.
Manufacturing Co.	James Woolley, Sons & Co., Ltd.
H. D. Justi	

TMHM
The Museum of the History of Medicine
Academy of Medicine, Toronto
288 Bloor Street West
Toronto, Canade M5S 1V8
c/o Mrs. Filicity Nowell-Smith, Curator

Allen and Hanburys, Ltd.	Burroughs, Wellcome & Co.
Arnold and Sons	Down Bros.
Frank S. Betz Co.	Evans and Wormull

Fannin & Co., Ltd.
J. E. Hanger & Co., Ltd.
J. F. Hartz Co., Ltd.
A. L. Herstein
Ingram and Bell, Ltd.
Kny-Scheerer Corp.
A. Luer
Mayer & Meltzer
S. Maw and Son
S. Maw, Son and Sons

McIntosh Battery & Optical Co.
H. J. Milburn Co.
J. H. Montague
Pfau American Instrument Co.
Instituto Rizzoli
Schall and Son
Sharp and Smith
George Tiemann & Co.
John Weiss and Son

UBML
Health Sciences Library
State University of New York at Buffalo
Abbott Hall
Buffalo, New York 14214
c/o Sharon Keller, Head, Information Services Dept.

Claudius Ash and Sons
Albert L. Bernstein
Buffalo Dental Mfg. Co.
Consolidated Dental
  Manufacturing Co.
Jeffrey-Fell Co.

Kny-Scheerer Co.
Lee S. Smith & Sons Dental Depot
George Tiemann & Co.
Charles Truax
Samuel S. White Dental Mfg. Co.
Carl Zeiss

UCLABM
University of California, Biomedical Library
History and Special Collections Division
12-077 Center for Health Sciences
Los Angeles, California 90024
c/o Victoria Steele, Head

Bausch and Lomb Optical Co.
Dental Manufacturing Co., Inc.
Vincenz Mueller & Co.
R. L. Scherer, Co.

Sharp & Smith
Western Surgical Supply Co.
Samuel S. White Dental Mfg. Co.

UCSF
The Library, Special Collections
University of California at San Francisco
S 257 Medical Sciences Bldg.
San Francisco, California 94143
c/o Mrs. Nancy Zinn, Head

A. Aubry
Franks S. Betz Co.

Burroughs, Wellcome & Co.
Collins, Maison Charriere

Jas. W. Edwards & Co.
J. H. A. Folkers & Brother
Hospital Supply Co.
Langley and Michaels Co.
Ph. Lepine
A. Luer
S. Maw, Son and Thompson
National Scientific Corp.
Parke, Davis & Co.

Salt Lake Dental Depot
Sears, Roebuck & Co.
Sharp & Smith
Frederich Stearns & Co.
George Tiemann & Co.
Charles Truax & Co.
Western X-Ray & Coil Co.
Samuel S. White Dental Mfg. Co.
H. Windler

UNSW/A
University of New South Wales
School of Medicine
Prince Henry Hospital
P. O. Box 1
Kensington, N.S.W.
Australia 2033
c/o Professor Bryan Gandevia

L. Bruck

UPSDM
University of Pennsylvania
School of Dental Medicine Library
4001 Spruce Street
Philadelphia, Pa. 19104
c/o Mr. John M. Whittock, Jr., Head, Reference Librarian

Claudius Ash and Sons
Edward H. Angle
Arrow Supply & Importing Co.
Bausch and Lomb Optical Co.
Blue Island Specialty Co.
Dr. Bonwill
Boston Dental Mfg. Co.
Buffalo Dental Manufacturing Co.
Calvin S. Case Co.
The L. D. Caulk Co.
Chicago Dental Mfg. Co.
Cleveland Dental
   Manufacturing Co.
Codman & Shurtleff
Consolidated Dental
   Manufacturing Co.
The Dental Specialty Co.
The Dentists' Supply Co.

William Dixon, Inc.
John C. Fischer Mfg. Co.
Rudolf Funke
James Edmund Garretson
Charles Grafath
William P. Green
Hartford Dental Depot
John Hood Co.
Hood and Reynolds
Johnson Brothers
Johnson & Lund
H. D. Justi
Horatio G. Kern Co.
William King, Jr.
Friedrich Krupp
A. Meisinger
Moyer, The J. Bird Co., Inc.
Mynol Chemical Co.

Noyes Brothers & Cutler
Partrick & Carter
M. F. Paterson
George P. Phillips
George Poulson
Ransom & Randolph Co.
Ritter Dental Manufacturing Co.
Rochester Dental
  Manufacturing Co.
Edward Rowan

Rubencame & Barker
Wilhelm Schaper
Adolf Schweichardt
Lee S. Smith & Son
Lee S. Smith & Sons Dental Depot
George Tiemann & Co.
Samuel S. White Dental Mfg. Co.
The Wilmington Dental
  Manufacturing Co.

UPL

Health Sciences Library
Scaife Hall
University of Pittsburgh
Pittsburgh, Pennsylvania 15261
c/o Dr. John Erlen, Curator, History of Medicine

The library also has a special collection of dental catalogs, including C. Ash and Sons and S. S. White Dental Mfg. Co., called the David Archer Collection. None of this material has been catalogued.

Chicago Dental Mfg. Co.
The Dental Specialty Co.
Johnson Brothers

Johnson & Lund
L. J. Mason & Co., Inc.

UREGML

Edward G. Miner Library
University of Rochester
601 Elmwood Ave.
Box Libr.
Rochester, New York 14642

Bausch and Lomb Optical Co.
Boericke and Tafel
Giovanni Alessandro Brambilla
Jeffrey-Fell Co.
Kny-Scheerer Co.
Girindranath Mukhopadhyaya
The Paine Drug Company
C. F. Palmer, Ltd.

Ambroise Paré
Jean Jacques Perrett
Ippolito Rondinelli
John H. Savigny
George Tiemann & Co.
Charles Truax & Co.
The Charles Willms Surgical
  Instrument Co.

URRR

Rush Rhees Library
University of Rochester
River Campus

American Askania Corp.
American Optical Co.
American Spectacle Co.
Art-Craft Optical Co.
C. Baker
R. & J. Beck
Benson Optical Co.
C. L. Berger and Sons
Bickenbach Fabrikate & Co.
Bonschur and Holmes
John L. Borsch & Co.
Boston Optical Works
D. V. Brown
Emil Busch, A. -G., Rathenow
Cambridge Botanical Supply Co.
Cambridge Scientific
    Instrument Co.
Cameron Surgical Specialty Co.
Canada Optical Co.
Castle
Central Optical Co., Inc.
Chambers, Inskeep & Co.
Chicago Apparatus Co.
Clement Clarke Ltd.
Colonial Optical Co.
Commercial Optical Co.
Continental Optical Corp.
Cooke, Troughton & Siemens Ltd.
Cooper Hewitt
Cross Trifocal Lenses
C. V. Lens Co., Inc.
Darton & Co.
Davidson & Co.
Denoyer-Geppert Co.
Deraisme, Ad & Ed, Successeurs
DeZeng
The DeZeng-Standard Co.
Dockson Corp.
Charles E. Dressler & Bro.
Dumaurier Co.
Elliott Optical Co., Ltd.
Ellis Optical Co.

Charles Engelhard
Farrington Eye Glass Cases
Joseph C. Ferguson, Jr.
Flatters & Garnet Ltd.
J. & R. Fleming
Franklin Educational Co.
Frober-Faybor Co.
R. Fuess
J. Gambs
J. Gaspari & Co.
General Optical Co.
Geneva Optical Co.
Glarometer Co.
Globe Optical Co.
Gordon and Morrison Wholesale
    Opticians
William Gowlland, Ltd.
The Graf-Apsco Co.
Christian Hahn
Theodore Hamblin, Ltd.
Hanovia Chemical &
    Manufacturing Co.
F. A. Hardy Co.
E. Hartneck
Chas. Hearson & Co., Ltd.
Hellige & Co.
George S. Johnston Co.
Rudolf Jung
Hermann Katsch
Keeler
Kelley & Hueber
Ketcham & McDougall
Kimball Safety Products Co.
Julius King, M.D., Optical Co.
E. Kirstein's Sons Co.
Klett Manufactuirng Co.
Willy Koeppen
Max Kohl
F. Koristka
E. Krauss & Co.
Frank Krementz
A. Kruess

Kryptok Ltd.
H. L. Leibe Co.
Ernst Leitz
J. E. Limeburner & Co.
Max Lindemann
London Optical Co.
O. T. Louis Co.
Lowres Optical Mfg. Co.
Luer, Maison
Luneau et Coffignon
L. Manasse Co.
Alexander Martin, B. O. A.
Martin-Copeland Co.
S. Maw, Son and Sons
McIntire, Magee and Brown
McIntosh Battery & Optical Co.
Merry Optical Co.
Messter, Ed.
Dr. Robert Muencke
A. Meyer & Co.
E. B. Meyrowitz
Midwest Optical Supply
Gustav Miehe
Milwaukee Optical Mfg. Co.
R. Mohr and Sons
Jno. L. Moore and Sons
R. W. Munro Ltd.
Nachet et Fils
National Optical Co.
Negretti & Zambra
New Era Optical Co.
New Jersey Optical Co.
The Newport Novelty Mfg Co.
Newport Optical Mfg. Co.
Newton and Co.
Nitsche & Guenther
Norris, Alister-Ball Co.
Noyes Brothers & Cutler
Oculus Universal-
  Ophthalmoskop
Officina Costruzioni
Officine Galeleo
Ogilvy & Co.
Omaha Optical Co.
Onepiece Bifocal Lens Co.

Operay Multibean
Optical Import Co.
Optical Products Co.
Optical Specialty
  Manufacturing Co.
L'Optique Comerciale
Oskamp Nolting & Co.
Osterander-Seymour Co.
Palmer Slide Co.
Ph. & F. Pellin
Pennsylvania Optical Co.
Petitdidier Optical and
  Astronomical Instruments
Wilhelm Petzold
W. E. Phillips Co., Ltd.
Richard Pietzcsh
Pinkham & Smith Co.
Powell & Lealand
James Prentice and Son
Queen & Company
C. N. Quimby
Radu Surgical Instruments
Raphael's Optical
Rapsch Optical Co., Ltd.
Giuseppe Ratti, S.A.
Reid Instrument Co.
Reliable Optical Co.
E. W. Reynolds Co.
Reynolds & Branson, Ltd.
Riggs Optical Co.
Ritter Dental Manufacturing Co.
Josef Rodenstock
J. Rosenbaum
Ross Ltd., Mfg. Opticians
Saint Paul Optical Co.
Saniras Electrical Co., Ltd.
F. Sartorius
M. Schanze
John Scheidig & Co.
Franz Schmidt and Haensch
W. & H. Seibert
Sharland and Co., Ltd.
Simonds Machine Co., Inc.
Sioux City Optical Co.
Société Belge d'optique &

d'instruments de précision
Bruxelle
Société Française des instruments
d'optique
Société Genevoise
Société des Lunetiers
Soft-Lite Lens Co.
The Southeast Optical Co.
Southern Optical Co.
Specialty Optical Co.
M. A. Spencer Co.
Spencer Optical Co.
George Spiller, Ltd.
Spindler & Hoyer
J. H. Steward
Maurice Stiassnie
C. H. Stoelting Co.
Strass Optical Co.
Superior Optical Co.
Sussfeld, Lorsch & Co.
James Swift
E. J. Swigart Co.
Swigart Watch and Optical Co.
Emil Sydow
Symons, Bryant Co.
Paul Thate
Arthur H. Thomas Co.
Three Dimension Co.

T & P Optical Mfrg Co.
Chas. Truax, Greene & Co.
Twin City Optical Co.
Uhlmann Optical Co.
Uni-Bifocal Co., Ltd.
Univis Lens Co.
C. Verick
Voight & Hochgesang
Voightlander & Son Optical Co.
Paul Waechter
Wappler Electric Co.
W. M. Welch Mfg. Co.
W. B. White & Son
O. C. White-Haines
C. A. Wilkinson Co.
Williams, Brown & Earle
T. A. Willson & Co.
Winkel
R. Winkel
George Wolf
The Optical Wolverine Co.
Woodward, Clarke & Co.
James Woolley Sons & Co., Ltd.
Otto Young and Co.
Joseph Zentmayer
E. Zimmermann
Zylite Optical Co.

UTP
University of Toronto, Faculty of Pharmacy
Toronto, Ontario M5S 1A1
c/o Ernst W. Stieb, Assistant Dean
History of Pharmacy

Anon
William H. Armstrong & Co.
John Joseph Griffen and Sons
J. F. Hartz Co., Ltd.
Lawson & Jones, Ltd.
J. E. Livernors, Limitee
S. Maw, Sons and Sons

Meyer Brothers & Co.
Morrison & Plumber
Powers-Wrighman-
Rosengarten Co.
Henry Thayer & Co.
Samuel S. White Dental Mfg. Co.

UVHSL
The Claude Moore Health Sciences Library
Box 234
University of Virginia Medical Center

Charlottesville, Virginia 22908
c/o Joan Echtenkamp, Historical Collections Librarian

Artificial Limb
  Manufacturing Co.
Brady & Martin
Feick Brothers
Hynson, Westcott & Co.

Charles Lentz and Sons
Powers & Anderson Dental
  Co., Inc.
George Tiemann & Co.
Charles Truax

UWL

William S. Middleton Health Sciences Library
University of Wisconsin
1305 Linden Drive
Madison, Wisconsin 53706
c/o Dorothy Whitcomb, Historical Librarian

William H. Armstrong & Co.
J. Gardner
Physician's Supply Co.
  of Philadelphia

Scanlan-Morris Co.
K. Schall
Arthur H. Thomas Co.
George Tiemann & Co.

VM

V. Mueller
6600 Touhy Avenue
Chicago, Ill. 60648
c/o Mr. Howard W. Coates, Director of Advertising

W. R. Grady
F. A. Hardy Co.
Jetter & Scheerer
Charles Lentz and Sons
Vincenz Mueller & Co.

George P. Pilling & Son Company
Sharp & Smith
George Tiemann & Co.
Charles Truax

WMScM

Wellcome Museum at the Science Museum
Science Museum Library
London SW7 5NH, England
as listed in:

A Handlist of Trade Catalogues and Associated Literature in the Wellcome Museum of the History of Medicine, *compiled by Michael Jones and Jean Taylor, London, Science Museum, 1984.*
This publication contains more detail than we present, is revised every few years, contains more references than listed here, and microfilm copies of some of the most significant catalogs in their possession are available at the above address.

Aesculap

Allen & Hanburys, Ltd.

Antaos-Werke, G.M.B.H.
James Arnold
Arnold & Sons
W. H. Bailey & Sons, Ltd.
Baird & Tatlock
C. Baker
James Barker
Barker Vibrator
John Bell & Croyden
Bosch & Speidel
J. Boulitte
B. Braun
Brexton
The British Cystoscope Co.
S. H. Camp & Co.
Alfred Carter, Ltd.
L. P. Casella
Chiron-Werke G.M.B.H.
Express Equipment
Joseph Gray & Son
Ernst Greishaber
John Joseph Griffen and Sons
W. R. Grossmith, Ltd.
Theodore Hamblin, Ltd.
E. Hanford
George A. Henke
R. A. Harding
James L. Hatrick & Co., Ltd.
J. Hausmann, Sr.
T. Hawksley
Hawksley & Sons
Charles Hearson & Co., Ltd.
Samuel Highley
Hoffman-LaRoche Chemical
  Works
The Holburn Surgical Instrument
  Co., Ltd.
William H. Horn & Bro.
Hospital and General Contracts
  Co., Ltd.
J. G. Ingram & Son Ltd.

Injecta Ltd.
Jetter & Scheerer
Keeler
A. Kettner
A. Charles King Ltd.
Kirch & Wilhelm
Otto Kirschen
Krohne & Sesemann
Ernst Leitz
Louis & H. Loewinstein
F. Longdon & Co., Ltd.
Luer, Maison
McKesson
Qualitas Electric Co.
Raphael's Ltd.
F. W. Read & Sons, Ltd.
Rileyco, Ltd.
Rimmer Brothers
Roseberry Metal Works
RU-KA (Ratheman)
Charles Salmon and Son
Salt & Son, Ltd.
Sass, Wolf & Co.
K. Schall
Schall & Son
Adolf Schweichardt
Alfred Shrimpton & Sons, Ltd.
Silverdale Mfg. Co.
A. & J. Smith
John Smith & Son
Société des Lunetiers
Sparklets, Ltd.
Standard Surgical Manufacturing
  Co., Ltd.
Steinmetz & Knetsch
G. Albert Storz
Surgico
F. H. Taylor & Sons, Ltd.
Arthur von Terpitz & Co.
George Turton and Son

WOC
William O. Campbell, M.D.

201 Edney Bldg.
Chattanooga, Tennessee 37402

A. S. Aloe Co.
William H. Armstrong & Co.
Becton, Dickinson & Co.
W. T. Berry Surgical
  Instrument Co.
Frank S. Betz & Co.
Boericke and Tafel
George Clafin Co.
Clark and Roberts
Collin, Maison Charriere
H. D. Dougherty & Co., Inc.
A. Kettner
Kloman Instrument Co., Inc.
Knauth Brothers
Kny-Scheerer Co.
Charles Lentz and Sons

Manhattan Surgeons' Supply Co.
Mayer & Phelps, Ltd.
Meinecke & Co.
Nashville Surgical Supply
Penn Surgical Manufacturing
  Co., Inc.
George P. Pilling & Son Company
Sears, Roebuck and Co.
Sharp & Smith
Surgical Manufacturing Co., Ltd.
Theo Taefel Co.
George Tiemann & Co.
W. V. Willis & Co.
Max Wocher & Son
E. A. Yarnall Co.

YB

The Beinecke Rare Book and Manuscript Library
Yale University
121 Wall Street
New Haven, Connecticut 06520
c/o Mrs. Patricia Howell, Public Services Reference Librarian

*Note: These are not cataloged in the card catalog index, but were present in the library
when visited.*

Alvergniat Frères
American Optical Co.

Bausch and Lomb Optical Co.
Wellsworth Products

YML

Yale Medical Library
333 Cedar St.
P. O. Box 3333
New Haven, Connecticut 06510

Dr. David Ahl
Felix Berguerand, Brevété
Buffalo Dental Manufacturing Co.
J. Canzius
James Coxeter & Son
Rudolf Detert
Electro Surgical Instrument Co.

Thomas Fletcher, F.C.S.
Henri Galante et Fils
H. Gueride
B. B. J. Hagerty
A. L. Hernstein
J. E. Kennedy & Co.
Kny-Scheerer Co.

L. Mathieu Maison
Matthew Brothers
S. Maw & Sons
Vincenz Mueller & Co.
John Reynders & Co.
Sears, Roebuck and Co.
George Tiemann & Co.

Charles Truax
John M. Weiss
Benjamin Welch, M.D.
Samuel S. White Dental Mfg. Co.
H. Windler
James Woolley Sons & Co., Ltd.

ZUR

Institute of the History of Medicine
University of Zurich
CH-8006 Zurich
Ramistrasse 71, Switzerland
c/o Professor Huldrych M. Koelbing, M.D., Director

Dr. G. Beck
B. Braun
Cambridge Scientific
  Instrument Co.
Cezerac & Soux
Collin Maison Chariere
Date
Rudolf Detert
Down Bros.
F. L. Fischer
Hanhart & Zeigler
Hanhart & Co.
Hausmann, A. G.
Hausmann, C. Friedrich,
  Sanitätsgeshäft-Hechtapotheke
H. Heinecke
Krohne & Sesemann
Josef Leiter
Ernst Leitz

Charles Lentz and Sons
Maison Luer
J. F. Luhme & Co.
Carl Marshall
Maison L. Mathieu
Ernst W. Mayer & Perry
G. Meltzer
H. Pfau, Inh.
H. Reiner
Thomas F. Rumbold
A. Rusch & Cie
M. Scharrer, A.-G.
Chr. Schmidt
Alb. Stille
Chas. Truax, Greene & Co.
Waarenhaus Medicinisches
C. Walter-Biondetti
H. Windler
H. Wulfring-Luer

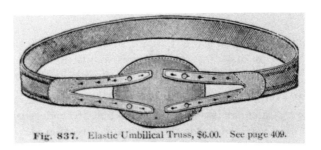

Fig. 837. Elastic Umbilical Truss, $6.00. See page 409.

ADDITIONAL SOURCES
AND LIBRARIES

COLLECTIONS:

University of Wisconsin, College of Pharmacy Library, especially the Kremers File, which contains trade catalogs, tear sheets and product information relating to American pharmaceutical companies.

Warshaw Collection of Business Americana, National Museum of American History, Smithsonian Institution, Washington, D.C. 20560.

The Geoffrey Kaye Museum for the Society of Anesthetists in Melbourne, Australia. In building that collection, Dr. Kaye canvassed hospitals and instrument manufacturers in Australia. He located nineteenth and twentieth century British, Australian, and American equipment and trade literature.

SELECTED HISTORICAL
REFERENCE PUBLICATIONS:

ALBUCASIS

1973   On Surgery and Instruments, a Definitive Edition of the Arabic text with English Translation and Commentary by N. S. Spink and G. L. Lewis; 850 pp, reprint; **UREGML.**

ANON

1893   The Chemists' & Druggists' Diary, London, England; ii pp diary insert to advertisements, to buyers guide, and to section on drugs and disease; iv, 454 pp; **UTP.**

1925   The Chemists' & Druggists' Diary, London, and Daily Calendar Insert between pp 368-369, advertising pages illustrated, trade directory and buyers guide; iv, 418 pp, index; **UTP.**

BEECHER, M. P.
New York

    1884   Beecher's Manual & Dental Directory of the U.S. edited and compiled by Beecher, M.P.; 163 pp; **NYAM.**

BRAMBILLA, GIOVANNI ALESSANDRO

    1782   Instrumentarium Chirurgicum Militare Austriacum; 160 pp; **UREGML.**

BRITISH MEDICAL ASSOC.

    1929   Official Catalog of the Exhibition of Surgical Instruments and Appliances, Drugs, Foods, Books, etc.; 162 pp; **NYAM; MF/MAH.**

July 22-26, 1929

    97th Annual Meeting in Manchester-Official Catalog of the Exhibition of Surgical Instruments and Appliances, Drugs, Foods, Books, etc.; The City Exhibition Hall. Deansgate, Manchester.; directory; 162 pp, index to exhibitors and advertisers, pp 9, 11 and 13; **NYAM.**

BROCKENHEIMER, DR. PH UND FROHSE, DR. FRITZ
Jena.
Gustav Fischer

    1905   Atlas typischer chirurgischer Operationen fuer Aerzte und Studierende, Nach Aquarellen von Maler Franz Frosche, Berlin, Mit erlaeuterndem Text und Abbildungen der gebraeuchlichsten Instrumente, Dritte Lieferung, Tafel XXV-XXXVI; 5 vol. excellent color plates, Virtually medical text in itself; (TM); **ZUR.**

BURROWS, HAROLD

    Nov. 1905   Surgical Instruments and Appliances Used in Operations, ". . . With Explanatory Notes;" 1st ed.; 103 pp; **WMScM.**

    1910   Surgical Instruments and Appliances Used in Operations. ". . . With Explanatory Notes;" 3rd ed.; 100 pp; **WMScM.**

CHASE, HEBER
Philadelphia, Pennsylvania.

    1837   The Final Report on the Committee of the Philadelphia Medical Society on the Construction of

Instruments, and Their Mode of Action in the Radical
Cure of Hernia . . . .; xvi, 243 pp; **LLU** (WI C487r
1837); **LC** (RD625. C48).

HOWE, LUKE
1787–1841

n.d. The Use and Application of an Improved Apparatus
for Particular Fractures and Dislocations of the
Extremities; 16 pp; illus; reprinted from the *Boston
Medical and Surgical Journal*; **APS** (610 Pam Bo. 90).

HULL, AMOS GERALD

1826 Practical Elucidation of the Nature of the Hernia,
together with some remarks of the unfit instruments
hitherto used for its confinement, with an explanation
of the experiences, utility, and effectual cures, of the
instrument now recommended; 3rd ed.; **APS** (610
Pam 191).

LEMERCIER, DOCTEUR F. G.
7 Rue Varin, Paris, France.

1882 Anatomie de structure chez l'homme; 10 pp; **CPP.**

LOMBARD, CLAUDE ANTOINE
Strasbourg, Trentel.

1786 Opuscules de chirurgie sur l'utilite et l'abus de la
compression; 395 pp; **LLU** (WZ 260 L841o 1786).

MUKHOPADHYAYA, GIRINDRANATH

1913–14 The Surgical Instruments of the Hindus: with a
Comparative Study of the Surgical Instruments of the
Greek, Roman, Arab and the Modern European
Surgeons; 2 Vol.; **UREGML.**

OBSTETRICAL SOCIETY OF LONDON

1867 Catalogue and Report of Obstetrical and Other
Instruments Exhibited at the Conversazione of the
Obstetrical Society of London, held by permission of
the Royal College of Physicians, March 28, 1866; 22
pp; **NYAM; MF/MAH.**

PARÉ, AMBROISE

1631 Three Hundred and Fifty Instruments of Chirurgery;
reprint Da Capo Press New York; 1969; **UREGML;
LLU** (WZ 250 P227t 1969).

RONDINELLI, IPPOLITO

    1766   Descrizione degl'instrumenti, delle macchine, e delle suppellettili, raccolte ad uso chirurgico e medico, dal p. don Ippolito Rondinelli Ferrarese, Faenza; 119 pp; **UREGML.**

ROYAL COLLEGE OF SURGEONS OF ENGLAND

    1850   Synopsis of the Contents of the Museum of the Royal College of Surgeons of England; 104 pp; **NLM** (W 28 R888).

    1865   Synopsis of the Contents of the Museum of the Royal College of Surgeons of England; 112 pp; **NLM** (W 28 R888).

ROYAL MICROSCOPICAL SOCIETY

    1928   Origin and Development of the Microscope, as illustrated by catalogues of the instruments and accessories, in the collections of the Royal Microscopical Society, together with bibliographies of original authorities, ed. Alfred N. Disney in collaboration with Cyril F. Hill and Wilfred E. Watson Baker; 303 pp; London; **APS** (578.1 R 81 o).

RUMBOLD, THOMAS F.
St. Louis, Missouri.

    1875   Description of New Instruments for Making Applications and Examinations to the Cavities of the Nose, Throat, Ear and Some Remarks about the Local and General Treatment of Affections in Which They are Applicable; 24 pp; **ZUR.**

SEERIG, A. W. H.

    1838   Armamentarium chirurgicum oder moglichst vollstandige Sammlung Von Abbildungen und Beschreibung chirurgischer Instrumente alterer und neuerer Zeit; Breslau; 2 vols; 145 tables; **NLM** (WO f s453a/MF 73-73).

STERN, WALTER G.

    Apr. 1907   Plaster-of-Paris, The Effects of Various Substances Upon its Rate of Setting and the Subsequent Strength and Durability of the Cost, Reprint *Am. J. of Orthopedic Surgery.*

1874   Le Bioscope by le Dr Collongues; Applications a la physique, a la botanique, l'etude des eaux minerales, a la physiologie; a la pathologie et la medecine legale; Paris; 32 pp; **CPP.**

THOMPSON, CHARLES JOHN SAMUEL
London, England.

1929   Catalog of the Museum, Royal College of Surgeons of England; **JHIHM** (RD 76.T46).

1942   The History of Evolution of Surgical Instruments; 113 pp; **LLU** (WO 162 T469h 1942).

TOGNO, JOSEPH

1839   An Account of a Solar and Gas Speculum and of an Obstinate Disease of the Ear Successfully Treated; 12 pp; *Eclectic J of Med*; **APS.**

REFERENCES RELATING TO INSTRUMENTS AND COLLECTIONS:

BENNION, ELIZABETH

1980   *Antique Medical Instruments*, Sotheby Parke Bernet/University of California Press. 355 pp, illustrated.

COLYER, SIR FRANK

1973   *Old Instruments Used for Extracting Teeth*, Boston: Milford House. 245 pp, illustrated.

CRELLIN, JOHN K.

1969   *Medical Ceramics.* A Catalog of the English and Dutch Collections in the Museum of the Wellcome Institute of the History of Medicine. Vol. 1, Museum Catalog 1. London: Wellcome Institute. 304 pp, illustrated.

DAVIS, AUDREY B.

1972   "Rudolf Schindler's Role in the Development of Gastroscopy," *Bulletin of the History of Medicine*, XLVI, pp. 150-170.

Jun. 1975   "Thomas Louis Jerome Auzoux and the Papier Mache Anatomical Model," *Proceedings of the First International*

Congress: Wax Modeling in Science and Art, Florence, Italy, v. 1, 1977, pp. 257-279.

1981 "Life Insurance and the Physical Examination: A Chapter in the Rise of American Medical Technology," *Bulletin of the History of Medicine*, v. 55, pp. 392-406.

1981 *Medicine and Its Technology: An Introduction to the History of Medical Instrumentation*, Westport: Greenwood Press. 185 pp, illustrated.

1982 "The Development of Anestehesia," *American Scientist*, v. 70, pp. 522-28. letter in response to article "Freud and Cocaine" from Frank Wesley and response, *American Scientist*, vol 71, 1983, p. 12. Article reprinted in *Virginia Dental Journal*, vol 60, Feb. 1983, pp. 12-24.

1985 "Dental Craftsmen in 19th Century America," in *Nineteenth-Century Scientific Instruments and their Makers*, Ed. Peter R. de Clerq, Leiden, Amsterdam, Communication 121 of the National Museum for the History of Science and Medicine Museum Boerhaase #17, The Netherlands, pp. 241-261.

DAVIS, AUDREY B., AND TOBY APPEL
    1979 *Bloodletting Instruments in the National Museum of History and Technology*, reprinted in 1983 by Arlington, Mass.: The Printers' Devil. 112 pp, illustrated.

DAVIS, AUDREY B., AND MERZBACH, UTA C.
    1975 *Early Auditory Studies in American University Psychology Laboratories*. Smithsonian Studies in History and Technology, No. 31. Smithsonian Institution, Reprinted and trans. into Italian in *Storia e critica della Psicologia*.

DILL, L. V.
    1953 *The Obstetrical Forceps*, Springfield: Thomas. 156 pp, illustrated.

DREYFUSS, MARK S.
    1985 *Medical Heritage*, Images column:
          "Trephined Skulls," Sep/Oct 85, Vol. 1, no. 5, Cover Notes.
          "Nurse's Saddlebag," Nov/Dec 85, Vol. 1, no. 6, pp 447.

1986   "The Anatomical Models of Dr. Auzoux," Jan/Feb 86,
Vol. 2, no. 1, pp 60-62.
"Yoruba Tribe Divination Bowl," Mar/Apr 86, Vol. 2,
no. 3, Cover Notes, pp 232.
"Social Necessaire," Mar/Apr 86, Vol. 2, no. 3, pp
168.
"Veterinary Surgery," Jul/Aug 86, Vol. 2, no. 4, pp
242.

FREDGANT, DON
1981   *Medical, Dental and Pharmaceutical Collectibles*, Florence,
Alabama: Books Americana. 171 pp, illustrated.

GLENNER, RICHARD A.
1984   *The Dental Office, A Pictorial History*, Missoula,
Montana. 152 pp, illustrated.

McKINSTRY, E. RICHARD
1984   *Trade Catalogues at Winterthur: A Guide to the Literature of
Merchandizing, 1750 to 1980*, New York: Garland
Publishing, Inc. pp 232-238. Microfishe available from
Clearwater Publishing Co., Inc., Medical entries
1332-1365.

ORR, HUGH
1985   *Illustrated History of Early Antique Spectacles*, Luton, Beds.,
England: Greenford Press. 112 pp, illustrated.

ROMAINE, LAWRENCE B.
1960   *A Guide to American Trade Catalogs, 1744-1900*, New
York: Bowker. 422 pp.

RUCKER, C. WILBUR
1971   *A History of the Ophthalmoscope*, Rochester: Whiting. 127
pp, illustrated.

GEOGRAPHICAL INDEX

NON-AMERICAN COMPANIES

SUBJECT INDEX*

---

* This index is based solely on the titles of the catalogs and publications. Most catalogs contain far more types of instruments, equipment, supplies, and goods than stated in the title. French and German entries were translated for use in this index.

336, 377

Extract, pharmaceutical, *45, 46, 84, 87, 260, 269, 274*

Extractor, dental, *348, 350, 351*

Eye, instruments, *39, 51, 68, 87, 90, 110, 112, 123, 131, 132, 156, 179, 186, 216, 217, 228-231, 237, 238, 251, 255, 257-259, 263, 270, 291, 330, 336, 373*

Eyeglasses (*see also* SPECTACLES), *40, 41, 54, 55, 58, 87, 90, 101, 114, 130, 141, 147, 156, 178, 181, 183, 184, 205, 208, 213, 220, 221, 226, 229-231, 234, 239, 240-243, 247, 254, 263-266, 271, 272, 321, 337, 369, 370, 374*

Fever, *41, 46, 61, 67, 103, 159, 182, 193, 245, 248, 325*

Field glasses, *46, 57, 138, 200, 201, 214, 221, 232, 234, 238, 248, 259, 308, 312, 316*

First aid, *127, 132, 245, 283*

Food, *52, 53, 75, 89, 114, 129, 133, 135, 204, 225, 226, 239, 250, 254, 281*

Foot, *43, 81, 151, 190, 347, 361*

Formula, *91, 137, 196, 223*

Fracture apparatus, *34, 109, 134, 143, 179, 187, 203, 221, 250, 311, 319, 333, 336, 337, 339, 371, 432*

Frames, spectacle, *48, 55-58, 62, 90, 100, 101, 142, 146, 148, 175, 176, 215, 221, 231, 232, 241-243, 247, 273, 280, 293, 295, 315, 321, 346, 347, 355*

Furniture, all types including office, dental, operating, hospital, etc., *35-37, 39, 46, 48, 49, 63-67, 79, 83, 88, 92-96, 100, 101, 103, 104, 107, 114-116, 120, 129, 130, 137, 139, 141, 153, 155, 158, 159, 161, 166, 167, 169, 171, 174, 186, 187, 189, 203, 207, 208, 218, 219, 226, 236-238, 252, 259, 275, 276, 281-283, 287, 289-291, 294, 297, 301, 322, 327, 339, 342-351, 356, 361, 363, 368, 371, 374, 376, 377*

Gangrene, *140*

Genito-urinary, *51, 179, 212*

Germicide, *31, 43, 51, 197, 250*

Glasses (*see also* EYEGLASSES), *50, 59, 60, 72, 87, 90, 103, 156, 157, 165, 200, 201, 221, 232, 234, 238, 241, 242, 247, 248, 254, 259, 261, 262,*

264-266, 273, 278, 287, 296, 297, 308, 310-312, 316, 323, 357, 363, 369, 374

Glucose, *37*

Goggles, *42, 134, 232, 234, 241, 254, 295, 310-312, 316, 357*

Gold
  dental, *33, 50, 100, 101, 108, 109, 173, 242, 279, 320, 347, 349, 354, 369, 376*
  optical, *41, 56-58, 182, 198, 215, 241, 243, 247, 355*

Gonorrhea, *51, 136, 196, 233*

Goods (*see also* ACCESSORIES, EQUIPMENT, SUPPLIES)
  dental, *46, 52, 134, 213, 344, 351*
  electro-medical, *211, 289*
  general, *163, 239*
  laboratory, *65*
  medical, *46*
  optical, *60, 72, 75, 78, 141, 144, 146, 157, 183, 184, 215, 220, 221, 228, 231, 241, 243, 244, 247, 248, 266, 272, 273, 293, 295, 300, 302, 303, 310, 313, 321, 355, 362, 363, 371*
  pharmacy, *224, 267, 373*
  physician's, *61, 224*
  rubber, *50, 62, 66, 106, 128, 133, 140, 156, 160, 166, 170, 171, 233, 261, 273, 320, 374*
  surgical, *66, 70, 130, 133, 170*
  veterinary, *160*

Gout, *303, 327*

Gynecology, *44, 47, 77, 95, 106, 109, 186, 215, 272, 274, 292, 314*

Hearing aid, *47, 113, 231, 238, 266*

Hernia (*see also* TRUSS), *96, 153, 168, 232, 432*

High frequency, *38, 42, 86, 94, 123, 124, 186, 189, 212, 222, 228, 229, 231, 242, 267, 272, 285, 312, 313, 328-330, 332, 334-336, 357*

Homeopathy, *70, 71*

Hospital, *36-38, 40, 42, 44, 46, 47, 49, 51, 57, 63-67, 69, 76, 83, 86, 89, 90, 94, 95, 100, 104, 109, 114-116, 118, 121, 123, 128-130, 137, 143, 147, 153, 157-162, 166-172, 177, 182, 184, 186, 187, 195, 202, 205, 206, 208, 210, 218, 219, 222, 225, 235-238, 247, 248, 256, 257, 259, 262, 281, 283, 287, 289, 291, 294, 298, 300, 309, 310, 320, 322-325, 327, 332, 335, 338, 339, 341, 342,*

351–353, 373